OPERATIONS MANAGEMENT

3RD EDITION

ALEX HILL & TERRY HILL

palgrave
macmillan

First edition 2000
Second edition 2005
This edition published 2012 by
PALGRAVE MACMILLAN

Palgrave Macmillan in the UK is an imprint of Macmillan Publishers Limited,
registered in England, company number 785998, of Houndmills, Basingstoke,
Hampshire RG21 6XS.

Palgrave Macmillan in the US is a division of St Martin's Press LLC,
175 Fifth Avenue, New York, NY 10010.

Palgrave Macmillan is the global academic imprint of the above companies
and has companies and representatives throughout the world.

Palgrave® and Macmillan® are registered trademarks in the United States,
the United Kingdom, Europe and other countries

ISBN-13: 978-0-230-36290-1

This book is printed on paper suitable for recycling and made from fully
managed and sustained forest sources. Logging, pulping and manufacturing
processes are expected to conform to the environmental regulations of the
country of origin.

A catalogue record for this book is available from the British Library.

A catalog record for this book is available from the Library of Congress.

10 9 8 7 6 5 4 3 2 1
20 19 18 17 16 15 14 13 12 11

Printed and bound in China

Brief contents

Contents

Case studies

About the authors

ALEX HILL is a Principal Lecturer at the University of Kingston (UK), an Associate Fellow at the University of Oxford (UK), a Visiting Professor at the University of Pretoria (South Africa) and a Visiting Professor at the University of Bordeaux (France). Prior to moving into university education, he worked extensively in industry and now researches and consults in a wide range of service and manufacturing organizations.

TERRY HILL is an Emeritus Fellow at the University of Oxford, (UK), an Affiliate Professor at the Milan Polytechnic (Italy) and at the Ohio State University (USA), and a Visiting Professor at the University of Pretoria (South Africa). He is a leading international figure in the field of operations management and operations strategy. Terry spent several years in operations management and continues to work as a consultant. He has held previous professorial appointments at London Business School (UK), and the University of Bath (UK).

Preface

The competitive nature of markets over the last 20 years has re-emphasized the key role of operations in bringing about the growth and profitability of organizations. Providing services and products fast, on-time, right first time and at a price that matches or betters competitors' are increasingly important factors in most markets. How well operations is managed to bring these about is a key corporate issue. However, not only does operations contribute much that enables a company to compete effectively, but it is also responsible for 60–70 per cent of costs, assets and people. The task of controlling costs and assets and the continuing need to reduce costs and release cash are equally critical and essential contributions to the welfare of an organization. Furthermore, the need to effectively manage and develop people adds yet more substance to the role of managing the operations function. From a historical bias towards techniques and systems, the emphasis of what is key in operations has swung to one that stresses and highlights the effective management of this large business function. This book is designed to contribute to this on-going focus. It is orientated towards a managerial perspective of operations and is set within the context of the function's significant contribution to the overall success of an organization. Operations has now rightly and appropriately returned to the top of the corporate agenda and this text has been designed to serve the needs of those who intend to take on the operations management role and also those whose roles will relate to this function in a range of businesses. In particular it can be used by:

- Postgraduate, MBA or Executive students, with explanations and further application through class discussion and the use of appropriate case studies.

- Managers who can apply the knowledge, concepts and ideas to their own business to increase their understanding of how to improve operations' contribution to an organization's overall performance.

Why choose this book?

This 3rd edition is a comprehensive and accessible guide to operations management. Here are just a few reasons why you should choose this book:

- It has been researched and written by a highly respected author team. Alex and Terry Hill both worked in operations management for a decade or more before switching careers and this experience and their continued research and consultancy within the field is the basis for the book's orientation towards the task of managing the operations function and the source of the numerous case studies that provide illustrations and teaching material throughout.

- The content is supported by a comprehensive pedagogy, and a modern and dynamic page design to draw in the reader.

- It reflects the mix of the service and manufacturing sectors that typify more developed economies.

- It contains excellent coverage of operations strategy – a key area that students find difficult to grasp.

- It is fully up-to-date both in terms of its content, data illustrations and case study material.

- It has an excellent supporting companion website which includes bonus chapters and cases for students and a comprehensive manual for lecturers which contains teaching notes for all the cases in the book, PowerPoint slides and much more. Visit **www. palgrave.com/business/hillom3e**

Alex Hill and Terry Hill

How to use each chapter

Learning objectives

- Show what you should have learned by the time you reach the end of the chapter
- Are linked to a central topic or issue in operations management

Chapter outline

- Highlights the key topics discussed in the chapter

Executive overview

Explains:

- How the ideas and concepts discussed in the chapter impact a business
- Why it is important to understand these ideas and concepts
- How these ideas can be used to improve business performance
- The key issues to consider when applying these ideas in practice

Introduction

Sets the scene for the chapter and explains the key topics that will be covered.

Text within the chapter

Explains the key ideas and concepts discussed within the chapter.

> **EXECUTIVE INSIGHT**
Highlights the key ideas and concepts being discussed and the issues to consider when applying them in practice.

Figures

Show data or concepts in a tabular or graphic format to provide a deeper illustration of the issues being discussed.

Key terms used within the chapter are explained in speech bubbles placed in the page margin.

CASES

Illustrate current business practices and show how the ideas and concepts discussed in the chapter can be applied in practice. Questions at the end of each case encourage critical reflection and web links are provided for further investigation.

Example answers to these questions can be found at www.palgrave.com/business/hillom3e

In practice

- Highlights the key issues to consider when applying the ideas and concepts to an organization

Driving business performance

Looks at how the ideas and concepts discussed within the chapter can be used to improve business performance by:

- Releasing cash
- Improving market support, and/or
- Reducing costs

Critical reflections

Discuss the issues addressed in the chapter and encourage critical evaluation and reflection on the key topics that have been discussed.

Summary

- Summarises the key points from the chapter as bullet points

Exploring further

Provides TED talks, journal articles, books, films and websites that allow you to explore further the ideas and concepts discussed within the chapter.

Study activities

Outlines discussion questions, assignments and groups exercises that can be used to debate and apply the chapter content.

END OF CHAPTER CASES

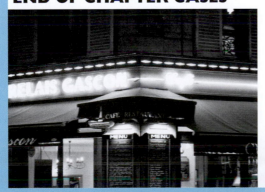

As well as the smaller cases within the chapter, there is also a longer case at the end of each chapter. This can be used for a tutorial, study group or class discussion based on the aspects covered within the chapter.

Extensive teaching notes for each of these cases can be obtained from www.palgrave.com/business/hillom3e

Publisher's acknowledgements

The authors and publishers are grateful to the following for permission to reproduce copyright material:

The American Marketing Association for Figure 11.17, 'The gap model for understanding the difference between customer expectations and perceptions', adapted from Parasuraman, A. et al (1985) 'A conceptual model of service quality and implications for future research', Journal of Marketing, 49 (Fall 1985), pp. 41–50.

The Baldrige National Quality Programme for permission to reproduce Figure 11.24.

Barclays Bank PLC for permission to reproduce the image used in Case 5.5.

The Benetton Group for permission to reproduce the image of the Regent Street Benetton Store (Oxford Circus) in Case 2.3.

Canon (UK) Ltd. for permission to reproduce the image of a Canon camera used in Case 12.9.

The Central Intelligence Agency for Figure 1.6, 'Percentage of GDP by sector for selected countries, 2001 and 2008'.

The Co-operative Financial Services for Figure 15.2, 'Percent of UK adults who undertake the following ethical behaviours at least once a year'; Figure 15.3, 'Ethical spending by the average UK household in 2009 compared with 1999'; and Figure 15.4, 'UK ethical consumerism (1999–2009)' from the Co-operative Ethical Consumerism Report 2009.

The EFQM for Figure 11.25, 'EFQM Excellence Model criteria and weights' © EFQM 2009.

Elsevier for permission to reprint Figures 12.4, 12.5 and 12.6 from R.H. Lowson, 'Offshore sourcing: and optimal operational strategy?', Business Horizons (Nov–Dec 2001), pp. 61–6.

Honda Manufacturing for permission to use the images in Figure 6.8.

Lloyds TSB for permission to use the image in Figure 5.12, from 2000.

Pearson Education Limited for Figure 11.17, 'The gap model for understanding the difference between customer expectations and perceptions', from Slack, N., Chambers, S. and Johnston, R. (2010) Operations Management, 6th edn), Essex. [Adapted from Parasuraman, A. et al. (1985) 'A conceptual model of service quality and implications for future research'. Reproduced by permission of the American Marketing Association.]

Upper Crust for permission to use the image in Figure 5.13.

The authors and publishers are also very grateful to the following for permission to use photographs in the book: Aldi, Asahi Breweries Inc., BMW Group, British Airways Plc., Dyson Ltd., Ernst & Young, Fotolia, Google, Herman Miller, HSBC and First Direct, Inditex, iStockphoto, Nissan Motor Ltd., Pret A Manger Ltd., Porsche Cars Ltd., Sainsbury's Supermarkets Ltd., TED Conferences, Threadless, Toyota, Veja, and Volvo Group. Special thanks are due to Jonathan Harris for permitting us to use a selection of his photographs in the short and long cases throughout the book.

Every effort has been made to trace all copyright holders, but if any have been inadvertently overlooked, the publishers would be pleased to make the necessary arrangements at the first opportunity.

The authors and publishers are particularly grateful to Judith Wilding at Delicious Industries for creating the page design for this textbook and typesetting the figures.

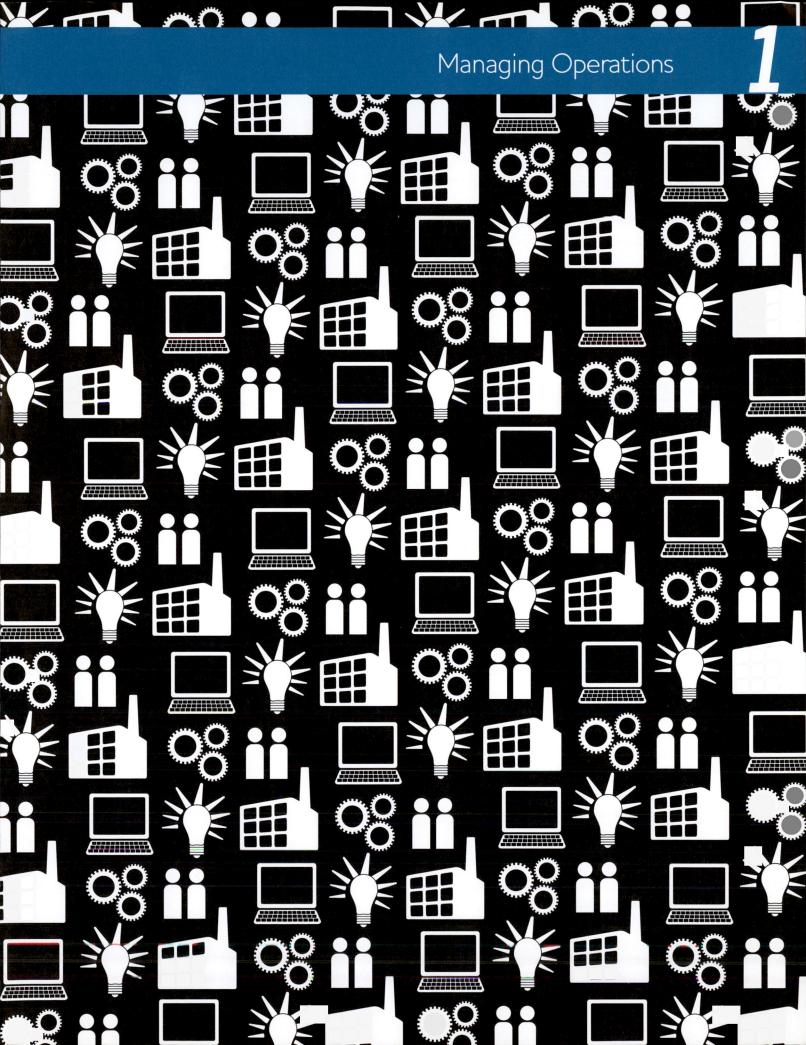

After completing this chapter, you should be able to:

- Explain the role of operations management in an organization and appreciate the dimensions that make up the operations task

- Be aware of the features that distinguish operations management in the service and manufacturing sectors

- Identify where the operations function fits into an organization

- Illustrate the crucial role of operations management in an organization's success

Chapter outline

Why is managing operations important?

- Organizations, whether commercial, public sector or non-profit making in nature, deliver services or make products that are purchased or provided for their users or customers. Operations completes these tasks

- Operations is central to an organization's activities in that it takes the inputs (such as people, data, materials and energy) and transforms them into the required outputs (such as services, products and information)

- Operations constitutes the essence of why an organization exists. How well this provisioning task is completed will directly impact customers' perceptions of an organization in terms of its reputation (and hence customers' willingness to recommend it to others) and repeat sales

How does operations impact on a business?

- The characteristic size of operations in terms of the assets used, cost budgets involved and people managed typically accounts for 60–70 per cent of the total

- Get it wrong and the economic wealth and welfare of the enterprise suffers

What are the key issues to consider in operations management?

- The strategic role of operations both in securing new and retaining existing customers is central to sustaining and growing the success of an organization

- Traditionally, operations executives have failed to appreciate this essential contribution and, as a consequence, have neither fully recognized nor fully fulfilled this key strategic role

- Given the size of its spend both in terms of cost budgets and asset investments, how well operations manages the conversion process of inputs into services or products, while meeting the increasingly competitive demands of today's markets, underpins the financial success of an organization

- The provision and delivery of services and products is made possible through the efforts and skills of the people within operations

- Harnessing and developing these key resources is a prerequisite for the continued and growing success of any organization

How does operations impact business performance?

- Retaining and growing market share owes much to the effective arrangement of the operations function

- Failings to meet customers' needs will, in the long-term, result in a loss of business

- The size of operations' budgets and investments underpins the day-to-day cost structures that have such a large and inherent impact on an organization's financial prosperity

Introduction

Let's first of all summarize what the **operations management** task comprises as this will give you an overall view of what is involved and what is covered by this book:

1. Companies sell **services** and goods to customers. To do this they purchase the **inputs** they need such as materials, services and energy. They then process these inputs through the skills of their people, the equipment/processes and systems/procedures into the required **outputs** (services and **products**) to be sold in their markets. How complicated the 'processing' phase is will vary. For example:
   - A retailer purchases products, unpacks and displays them and processes their subsequent resale
   - A hospital processes patients (its customers): the healthcare provided can range from relatively simple checks and procedures to complicated surgery necessitating lengthy aftercare
   - A restaurant buys in food and prepares this into a range of menus but buys in soft drinks, bottled water and wine, stores them and then serves them with relatively little additional processing
   - A garment manufacturer buys in a range of materials in terms of material types and colours, cotton threads, trims, buttons, zips and other accessories. The materials are then cut to meet different styles and sizes and sewn together, with relevant trim, buttons, zips and other accessories added during the operations process. After pressing and final inspection the finished garments are packed and despatched to different retail outlets.

2. The **operations function** concerns managing the inputs into the system (often referred to as the 'external phase of the supply chain') and also the systems and processes used for converting these into the outputs (services and products) sold to customers.

3. Operations is responsible for efficiently managing these tasks and seeking ways to make improvements throughout, in order to better meet the objectives and targets set by the business itself and the needs of its customers.

4. Underpinning these activities is the key task of managing the people within the operations function in such a way that meets agreed schedules, productivity levels and other business targets, while helping develop them in terms of broadening their skills base and facilitating personal development opportunities.

This book addresses the various aspects of these tasks and discusses and reviews the range of topics involved and the alternative approaches that may be followed under each heading.

Managing operations: an overview of the role

The contribution and value-adding role of operations management is at the heart of most organizations. Whether it is a pair of jeans, midday snack, live concert, haircut, a loaf of bread or hospital check-up, operations is central to its provision. To successfully manage operations within a business concerns two distinct but complementary aspects which, in turn, comprise a further two dimensions:

1. Content – what an operations manager does in terms of the tasks and responsibilities involved:
   - **The internal day-to-day or operational role** that involves managing the set of tasks and responsibilities within operations necessary to provide the services or products to be sold, for example, managing **capacity** and controlling costs

---

Operations management – the activities, responsibilities and decisions that make up the task of managing of the process of transforming inputs such as materials, people, energy and information into services and products.

Services – intangible items (i.e. you cannot touch them) that are consumed at the time of provision.

Inputs – the materials, staff, energy and other 'ingredients' necessary to provide a service or make a product.

Outputs – the services or products produced by a delivery system or manufacturing process.

Products (also known as goods) – tangible items (i.e. you can touch them) purchased by individuals or organizations for subsequent use.

Operations function – the function in an organization that is responsible for the resources necessary to deliver services and/or make products.

Capacity – comprises the staff, equipment and/or processes that make up the value-adding activities to meet a certain level of demand in a given period of time.

- **The external or strategic role** that concerns meeting the **order-winners** and **qualifiers** within a company's markets for which operations is responsible, for example, providing a service right first time and delivering a service on time.

2. Style – how an operations manager handles the people management task:
   - **The internal role** concerns managing the people within the operations function itself and also the people interface between operations and other functions within an organization, so as to meet people's own personal needs, the needs of the operations functions and also those of the overall business
   - **The external role** involves managing the people interface outside the organization at both the supplier and customer end of the supply chain.

Case 1.1 concerns a sandwich and coffee bar within London's finance centre and illustrates the characteristics of the operations management role.

> **EXECUTIVE INSIGHT**
> Day-to-day aspects of the operations role include managing within budgets, scheduling, serving customers, meeting output targets, and communicating and liaising with other functions in your organization.

As you will see from Case 1.1, the breadth of the tasks and range of management skills involved make the operations management area a demanding and, at the same time, fascinating role. It links strategy to action, requires coordination across functions and involves managing the largest part of an organization. To accomplish this, operations manages most of the assets, costs and resources necessary to produce the services and goods sold to consumers or other organizations. On the strategy dimension, the operations role is especially fulfilling as it supports many of the attributes that help sell the services and products involved, for example being on time, meeting the service or product specifications, fast delivery and low price.

The operations role is best described as exciting, rich in issues, full of challenges, central to the process of a business and about managing through and with people. The day-to-day role is full of interest and variety, while its strategic contribution is central to maintaining and growing sales and profits.

> **EXECUTIVE INSIGHT**
> Strategic aspects of the operations role involve providing those order-winners and qualifiers for which it is solely or jointly responsible in an effective manner in order to make the company competitive.

Origins of the name 'operations management'

The term 'production management' was predominantly used in the past with the early emergence of the manufacturing sector in a country's economy. Indeed, in many companies this title is still appropriately in use. However, the enlargement of the role to include responsibility for other tasks in the supply chain, such as purchasing and despatch, led to a change in title to that of 'operations management'. Furthermore, the growth of the service sector in industrially developed countries has reinforced this change to 'operations management' as a more appropriate, general title. The title of this book, therefore, reflects both this shift and the dual emphasis of the operations task in the service and manufacturing sectors.

The nature of organizations

To provide a service or product requires certain tasks to be completed. Essentially, they include design, buying materials and/or services from others, creating the services and

Opening at 7am to catch the early breakfast and coffee demands of nearby office staff, Portioli remains open throughout the day until 5.30pm when customer demand falls away.

CAPACITY MANAGEMENT

One of the core operations tasks is to meet the demands of customers in terms of, for example, providing the full range of products on offer, meeting the product specifications (for example the taste and freshness of the sandwiches and coffee) and matching **customer lead time** expectations. Using past experience to forecast demand in terms of the hour of the day, the day of the week and the week of the year will provide data in terms of the number of customers and the types and quantities of food and beverages involved. With these insights, operations can determine staff levels at different times of the day and week to ensure that queue lengths are in line with waiting time targets while staff costs are kept to a minimum.

SUPPLY CHAIN AND INVENTORY MANAGEMENT

Demand forecasts would also be used to manage the supply of beverages and food while taking into account existing inventory. This role would include ensuring that product specifications (for example taste, freshness and look of the different foods) were met by suppliers and maintained within the operations function by appropriate storage and refrigeration provision. To this end daily deliveries of a range of breads, pastries, food ingredients and salads are scheduled before 7am while other food and beverages (such as butter, coffee, tea and some sandwich fillings) are held in stock, with deliveries arranged once, twice or sometimes several times a week. Working with suppliers to guarantee that ingredients meet agreed

Customer lead time – the length of time a customer expects or is prepared to wait for a service or product from the point of making an order.

© elena moiseeva

specifications and that deliveries are on time are key features of all outlets in the Portioli Group.

SCHEDULING, DELIVERY SYSTEMS AND MANAGING QUALITY

Other aspects that directly affect the smooth running of the delivery system include layout, procedures and the movement of staff from the part of the service delivery system in which customers are served (known as the 'front office' to those parts of the delivery system that do not interface with the customer (known as the 'back office'), where activities such as the advance preparation of sandwich fillings take place.

As food preparation starts at 6am and staff typically work an eight-hour day, scheduling appropriate levels of staff in terms of the mix of skills needed is a key operations task, especially given the need for occasional overtime working to cover for holidays and absence. Scheduling staff to ensure that the necessary skills are available is an integral part of managing food and service quality levels at all times.

Front office – the area of a service delivery system in which contact with customers normally takes place.

Back office – the area of a service delivery system in which there is normally no contact with customers.

THE MARKET

Demand has increased year on year over the past decade. The competitive criteria that are considered as key features in Portioli's sales growth include the quality and freshness of the food and beverages sold, the range of products on sale, short waiting times, prices that are in line with nearby competitors and a no-quibble refund should customers feel dissatisfied. The outlet itself is well positioned in relation to underground and bus services and, while some seating is available, most customers prefer the takeaway service on offer.

Questions

Review Portioli's sandwich and coffee bar and identify, using the chapter outline at the beginning of this chapter:
- How the operations process works
- Which chapter topics in the book are reflected in the details provided.

Lecturers: visit www.palgrave.com/business/hillom3e for teaching guidelines for this case study

products to meet the needs of customers (for example by adding to them in some way, providing specialist diagnostic services, changing the shape of materials, assembling parts, giving advice, processing information or requests, arranging services or selling a product to customers), selling them and accounting for the cash or credit transactions involved. When an organization is small, several of these tasks are typically completed by one person. As a business grows, sets of tasks are separated off into departments or functions and managed by different people. While the tasks remain the same (albeit larger and more complex), the organizational structure to manage and provide them has altered.

To cope with the complexity that comes with size, organizations separate the tasks involved in managing the business into functions and these 'parts' of a business are then responsible for managing a range of tasks. Operations is one such function and, as explained earlier, its prime role is to provide the services or produce the products that are then sold to customers. Similarly, a sales and marketing function would be responsible for selling to and working with customers, while the accounting and finance function sends out the invoices for the services and goods sold and collects payment. In addition, these executive, or 'line functions' as they are called, will be supported by specialist departments (for example, IT) that provide advice and expertise within a given field to help better manage these executive functions and the organization overall (see Figure 1.1). As the function responsible for providing the services and products sold to customers, operations plays a key role in any organization, no matter what its size.

Figure 1.1 **Some typical functions within a business**			
Task	**Function responsible**		**Type of function**
• Generating new service and product ideas • Designing and developing new services and products	Services	Sales and marketing	Executive/line
	Products	Research and development	
• Promoting services and products • Selling services and products	Sales and marketing		
• Contracting with suppliers and managing the resulting external phase of the supply chain • Delivering the services and making the products sold to customers	Operations		
• Sending out invoices • Collecting payment • Preparing financial statements	Accounting and finance		
• Introducing new systems • Developing existing systems • Supporting the IT infrastructure	Information technology		Specialist support
• Recruiting staff • Employee relations	Human resources		

The operations manager's task

The operations function is that part of an organization responsible for providing the services or producing the goods that a company sells in its markets. Some organizations provide services such as medical care, the processing of information and requests, banking facilities and retail sales, while others produce physical items such as furniture, building materials and stationery.

The operations task, however, is common to all the diverse range of services and goods that make up a national economy. It concerns the transformation process that involves taking inputs and converting them into outputs, together with the various support functions closely associated with this basic task. Figure 1.2 provides a simplified overview of what is involved while Figure 1.3 gives examples from both the service and manufacturing sectors. The level of complexity within the operations function will vary depending upon several factors, including:

- The size of an organization and associated service/product volumes

- The nature of the services and products provided

- The technology levels embodied in both the services/products involved and the processes used within the operations function

- The extent to which the services and products are made in-house.

A final factor that impacts the design and management of the operations process or delivery system is the nature of what is processed. As Figure 1.4 illustrates, the presence of the customer in the system will impact its design and the operations management task involved, as explained more fully in Chapter 5. The examples given in Figure 1.4 have been chosen to illustrate these differences whereas often what constitutes the offering is a mix of these. For example, car servicing will comprise interfacing with the customer as well as processing the automobile (the **customer surrogate**) and invoice preparation and payment. Purchasing furniture will involve customer advice and the paperwork involved in the invoicing and guarantee phases of the purchase as well as the product itself.

> **Customer surrogates** – when what is processed represents the customer – for example, where clothes are being cleaned the clothes represent the customer within the service delivery system.

To sustain or improve corporate prosperity it is essential to achieve the level of effectiveness required to compete successfully in chosen markets. To do this, it is necessary for those activities responsible for the provision of services or goods to be well managed. These tasks are, therefore, critical to the success of an organization. Operations managers oversee these tasks. They control the inputs and processes that together provide the services or produce the goods that a business sells. But, as with other functional executives, operations managers have a strategic, as well as operational, dimension to their responsibilities. They have to develop a functional strategy as part of the corporate debate that identifies and agrees the strategic direction an organization should follow.

It is, therefore, the development and control of both these activities that constitute the role of the operations manager.

The operations manager within an organization

The operations manager is usually responsible for a whole range of tasks within an organization. These tasks will differ depending upon whether it is a service or manufacturing business, and the nature of the items provided. Figure 1.5 provides examples of typical core tasks within operations which are central to the provision of the service or product involved. In addition, and reporting into the operations function, will be a number of support departments, as shown for each example. Finally, there will also be a number of specialist functions that provide advice and expertise but report to elsewhere in the organization.

Figure 1.2 **Overview of operations process – transforming inputs into outputs**

ENVIRONMENT, NATIONAL/WORLD ECONOMY
INPUTS
People
Materials
Energy
Capital
Data
RESOURCES
OPERATIONS
PERFORMANCE MEASUREMENT

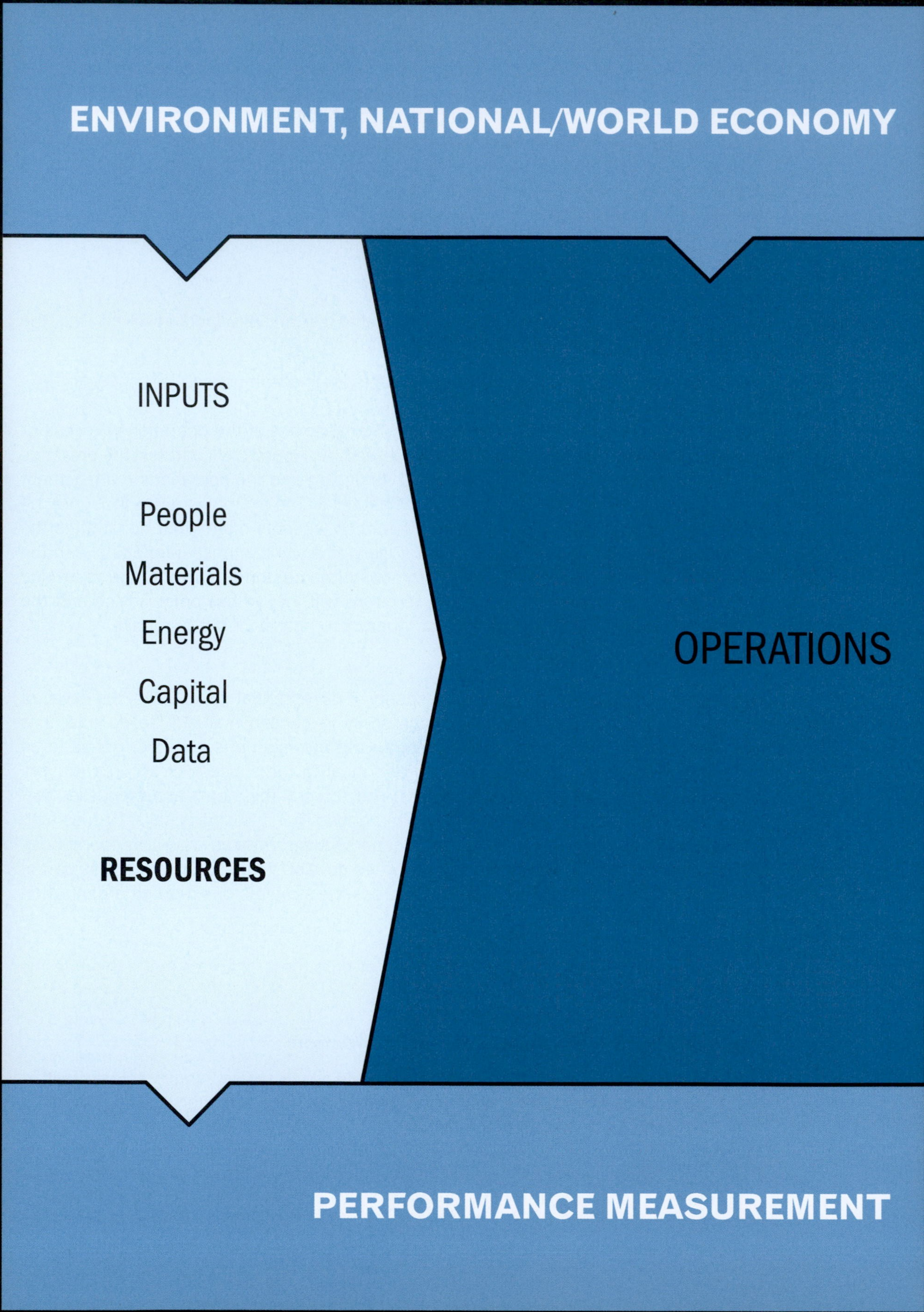

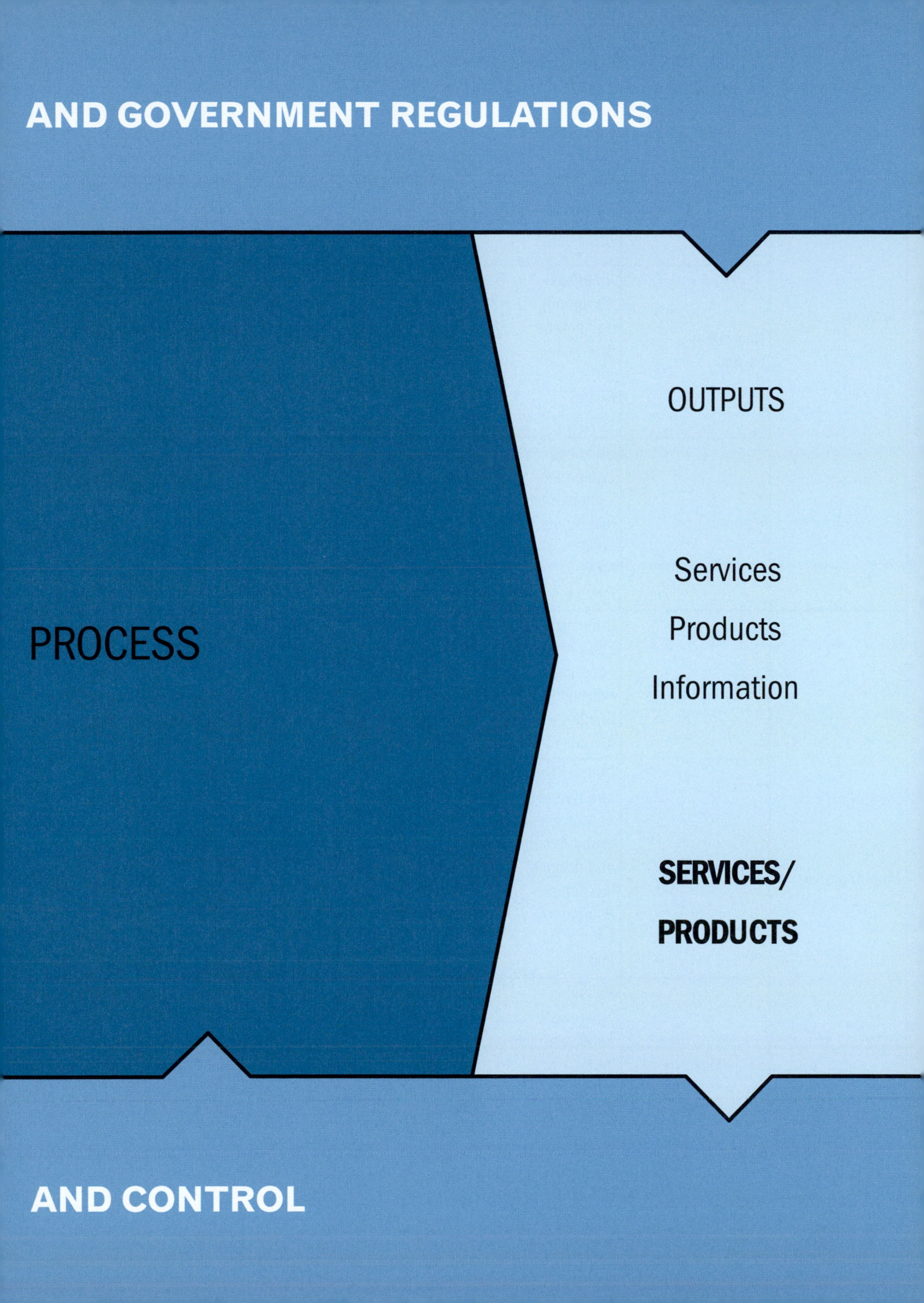

AND GOVERNMENT REGULATIONS

OUTPUTS

Services

Products

Information

PROCESS

SERVICES/

PRODUCTS

AND CONTROL

Figure 1.3 **An overview of the service and manufacturing sectors**

Sector	Organization	Inputs	Operations process	Outputs
Services	Air passenger transport	Airports Booking systems Aircraft Aircrews Ground staff Fuel Food	Passenger reservations Flight schedules Check-in Aircraft and equipment maintenance Aircraft cleaning and provisioning Meals and crew scheduling Boarding procedures In-flight procedures Baggage claim	Customers booked on appropriate flights in terms of timing and convenience Customers progressed through the pre-boarding phase of the service delivery system Customers transported safely and on time to chosen destinations
	Computing centre	Buildings Computing equipment Stationery Toner Energy People	Updating records Printing Enveloping Distribution	Information to internal and/or external customers using agreed distribution alternatives and in line with agreed schedules
	Restaurant	Buildings Equipment – kitchen and restaurant Food Energy People	Table setting Order taking Food preparation and cooking Table waiting Drinks provision Dishwashing General cleaning	Food, wine and other drinks provided in line with customers' selection and preferred timings Aim is repeat visits from satisfied customers
Manufacturing	Bakery	Buildings Equipment Food ingredients Packaging Energy People	Mixing Baking Packaging Equipment maintenance Distribution	Range of packed bakery items delivered to warehouses and retail outlets that are fresh and in line with consumer shopping patterns
	Garments	Range of cloths and threads Accessories (for example buttons and ribbons) Buildings Equipment Energy People	Cutting Garment making Packaging Equipment maintenance Warehousing Distribution	Range of garments Distribution to warehouses and retail outlets to meet seasonal demand patterns
	Packaging	Buildings Equipment Paper and film Inks Energy People	Cylinder and plate preparation Equipment maintenance Printing Slitting Packing Distribution	Packaging to meet customer specifications Distribution to customers' manufacturing plants in line with agreed schedules

Notes: 1. In services, customers (or their requests/enquiries), customer surrogates (a car being serviced in a garage is a customer surrogate) and/or information are processed.
2. In manufacturing, products are processed.
3. As you will see later, customers may provide capacity as part of the 'inputs', for example in fast-food restaurants.

Figure 1.4 Examples of service and product processing

Sector	What is processed	Examples	Customer involvement in the process or delivery system
Service	Customers	Beauty salons, hospitals, health farms, physiotherapists and restaurants	In the process or delivery system
	Customer surrogates	Garages, repair shops and dry cleaning outlets	Detached from the delivery system or process
	Information	Tax accountants, passport offices, lawyers, computing centres and insurance	
Manufacturing	Products	Chemicals, furniture, motor vehicles, personal computers, food and pharmaceuticals	

Figure 1.5 Operations jobs and specialist functions in three organizations

Type of business	Some typical jobs in operations		Typical specialist functions that report elsewhere in the organization
	Core tasks	Support functions	
Hospital	Hospital director Medical staff – Doctors – Ward sisters – Nurses	Reception Maintenance Cleaning Porters	Microbiology Pathology Pharmacy Physiotherapy Accounting
Print company	Operations director[a] Print manager Finishing manager Supervisors Team leaders Operators	Ink manager Plate production Scheduling	Design Pay office Accounts Quality assurance
Transport company	Operations director[a] Depot managers Drivers	Vehicle maintenance Scheduling	Building and equipment maintenance Pay office Accounting

Note: [a]Also entitled Vice-president (V-P) Operations.

The mix of sectors in different economies

National economies are made up of a mix of three key sectors:

• Primary sector: agricultural (producing food, feed and fibre)

• Secondary sector: industrial (production of products including fuels and fertilizers)

• Tertiary sector: services (economic activity not resulting in ownership).

As economies develop, the balance between these different sectors changes, as illustrated in Figure 1.6. The differences in the split across the three sectors reflect the general activities associated with the individual countries involved. For example, the relatively high percentage of gross domestic product (GDP) in the Chinese and Norwegian industrial sectors reflects a growth in manufacturing, and the North Sea oil and gas explorations, respectively. Similarly, the high percentage of GDP in the industrial

'**Operations transform materials** into products and **services** to meet customer needs'

sector for Singapore signals its role as a major manufacturing nation. On the other hand, the growing size of India's service sector GDP has been fuelled by the subcontracting of banking and other service activities from countries such as the USA and UK. However, the overall change from 2001 to 2010 shows a broad pattern: the service sector continues to grow as a percentage of GDP in most developed countries.

Figure 1.6 **Percentage of gross domestic product (GDP) by sector for selected countries, 2001 and 2010**

| Country | Percentage of gross domestic product by sector | | | | | |
| | 2001 | | | 2010 | | |
	Agriculture	Industrial	Service	Agriculture	Industrial	Service
Australia	3	26	71	4	26	70
Belgium	2	24	74	1	22	77
Canada	2	27	71	2	26	72
China	15	51	34	10	47	43
France[a]	3	26	71	2	19	79
Germany	1	31	68	1	28	71
India[a]	24	28	48	19	26	55
Italy	2	30	68	2	25	73
Japan	1	31	68	1	25	74
Norway[b]	2	31	67	2	40	58
Singapore	0	33	67	0	28	72
Spain[b]	4	31	65	3	26	71
UK[b]	1	25	74	1	22	78
USA[a]	2	18	80	1	22	77

Notes: [a] Data for these countries is for 2002.
[b] Data for these countries is for 2000.
Source: CIA – The World Factbook.

Although it is useful to separate activities into agriculture, industrial and service sectors in order to help identify trends, each sector is, in reality, dependent on and interacts with other sectors to form part of a 'total' economy. Each sector is an integral part of one economy in its own right, but its performance will often have an impact on other sectors. Arguments suggesting that developed nations can rely on the tertiary sector (services) as a way of sustaining standards of living or improving below-average trade performance are without foundation. For example, a large part of many service sales is made up of a product provided by activities in the primary and/or secondary sectors (for example, foodstuffs or IT equipment).

The operations management role, no matter what sector is involved, is similar in terms of its overall aim, the nature of the task and its central importance. Growing foodstuffs, extracting minerals, making products and providing services are parts of the basic task of relevant businesses and central to their continued success. Therefore, whether or not you are or intend to be involved in operations management, it is essential that you understand the concepts and approaches involved, the interfaces this function has within a business and its key role in helping to grow sales and meet an organization's short- and long-term financial goals.

The purchase – a mix of services and products

Goods are tangible items purchased by individuals or organizations for subsequent use. Services are intangible items that are consumed at the time of provision, with a customer taking away or retaining the benefits of that service. However, in many situations, what is provided or produced by an organization can be a mixture of both services and goods. In some instances there will be a heavy accent on service, and in others, the reverse. Figure 1.7 shows a range of items sold and the mix between the service and product content provided. The purchase mix represented here is intuitively derived, and others may consider the balance to differ from that shown. The purpose, however, is to illustrate that what we buy is a mix of both a service and a product and the mix will differ depending upon the offering. Take, for example, the difference between the purchase of 'regular maintenance' and 'breakdown maintenance' shown in Figure 1.7. Invariably, the technical aspect of the job content in a breakdown is less than for regular maintenance, whereas the service content is the reverse: if you break down, a skilled mechanic comes to you and your car thus constituting more service content in the offering mix than in regular service maintenance when you take your car to a garage. It is important, therefore, when considering Figure 1.7, to bear in mind that its purpose is to draw attention to the service/product mix that constitutes a business. Now take a look at Case 1.2 which provides a further example.

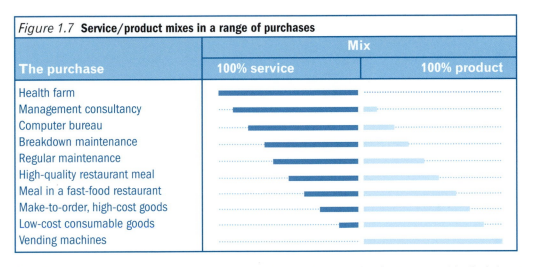

Figure 1.7 **Service/product mixes in a range of purchases**

The purchase	Mix	
	100% service	100% product
Health farm		
Management consultancy		
Computer bureau		
Breakdown maintenance		
Regular maintenance		
High-quality restaurant meal		
Meal in a fast-food restaurant		
Make-to-order, high-cost goods		
Low-cost consumable goods		
Vending machines		

Note: The purchase mix represented here is meant as a broad indication only; others may consider the balance to differ from that shown.

Size of the operations task

Operations management is concerned with handling the physical resources necessary to provide services or make products. To accomplish this, the available facilities need to be managed to meet the cost budgets laid down, while also readapting the resources as and when new services and products are introduced. In addition, this task is complicated by two factors. First, the dynamic nature of today's business environment, and the increasingly competitive nature of markets that require the effective management of these resources in times of economic uncertainty and social change.

Secondly, the size of the task compounds the problems associated with managing operations, as this function is unique in terms of its overall size. As explained below, in a typical organization the operations function employs most of the people, uses and manages most of the organization's assets and spends most of the money:

CASE 1.2 A CUP OF COFFEE – PRODUCT OR SERVICE?

Compare a cup of coffee provided by a vending machine with one provided in the lounge of a good hotel:

- The vending machine offers convenient, 24-hour, fast delivery of coffee. The product specification is controlled by the service delivery system, and hence the product range offered is limited; coffee is provided in a number of combinations (for example, regular or decaffeinated, with or without milk and sugar) and in a disposable cup. The price is likely to be low.

- On the other hand, coffee provided in the lounge of a good hotel involves significantly different service factors – better choice, superior coffee (in terms of higher-specification beans), better presentation, comfort and probably a slower, 'more leisurely' service, albeit delivered at a higher price.

In the former coffee provision, the ratio of product to service in the total package mix would be considerably higher than in the latter.

Questions

1. What operations factors might contribute to the fact that the hotel coffee is more expensive?

2. Now think about the last cup of tea or coffee you drank. How did it compare with the two scenarios outlined above?

Lecturers: visit www.palgrave.com/business/hillom3e for teaching guidelines for this case study

1. People – the operations task concerns the management of a large number of people. Most employees are usually involved in the mainline activities of a business (that is, those providing services or making products). A high percentage of the support staff will also come under an operations manager's control, as illustrated earlier in Figure 1.5. The result is that the total number of staff in this function usually accounts for 60–70 per cent of all those employed by an organization.

2. Assets – operations is responsible for the effective use of some 60–70 per cent of an organization's total assets. On the fixed assets side, it is usually accountable for land and buildings, together with plant and equipment, which make up a large percentage of the total fixed asset investment list. On the current assets side, it is responsible for the **inventory** holding which, as shown in Chapter 12, is a high percentage of the current asset investment. Since these together constitute a large part of the total investment made, the operations function takes on the responsibility for effectively managing the most significant proportion of an organization's use of funds.

3. Costs – the operations function accounts for the major portion of an organization's expenditure. As the majority of the direct costs, such as staff and materials, are incurred in this area, together with much of the **overhead costs** involved, it has by far the largest budget within a business.

These features mean that the sound management of the operations process is critical to an organization's short- and long-term success. The efficient use and control of the assets and costs involved are core to the cost structure and overall budget of a business. Similarly, as markets are changing quickly, understanding the business capability of operations is a key factor in successfully delivering business strategy. However, translating these tasks into the right combination of equipment, people, procedures and processes to meet the needs of customers and markets is a demanding and time-consuming job. These areas of activity are not only large in themselves but they are all interrelated parts of the whole task. Furthermore, decisions made in this area are difficult to change because of their complex nature and the high investment cost usually associated with past actions and future proposals.

The role of the operations manager

The last section highlighted the size of the operations management task. This section describes the key features that make up the role. Some of these features relate to successfully managing the internal or day-to-day tasks, some the external or strategic tasks, while others highlight the need to manage people. The features of the operations task, and their size and importance, create a demanding and absorbing management role. It is concerned with detail yet must address corporate issues of significant size and importance. The key aspects of the job are outlined below.

Managing a large cost centre

As explained in the previous section, operations accounts for a large part of the **asset investment** and typically has the largest budget within an organization. One consequence is that operations managers are responsible for a large **cost centre**. If operations budgets and output levels are met, then the cost structure of a business will be sustained.

Managing the short and long term

It is necessary that operations is managed efficiently in the short term. Providing services or producing goods is an ongoing, day-to-day task. A day's lost output will never be recovered without additional costs being incurred. Customers who go elsewhere are lost business, sometimes for ever. That is the nature of the short-term operations task. It is thus essential that the day-to-day activities are well controlled and coordinated, and meet

---

Inventory – inputs (materials) into the delivery system or manufacturing process, part-finished items (services or products) within the service delivery system or manufacturing process and outputs (finished items) to be sold or supplied to customers.

Overhead costs – those costs (for example, management salaries, building and equipment maintenance and interest on loans) incurred in the general running of a business or organization.

Asset investment – the investment in a range of valuable or useful items including land, buildings, equipment and inventory.

Cost centre – a group of costs controlled by a part of the business (such as a function).

budgeted output. To meet monthly targets requires that each day's target is met. Other departments, such as sales, work on a different time basis, with no one expecting the period sales target to be met pro rata each day. As a consequence, substantial pressure is, and has to be, exerted to meet short-term operations targets.

So, what are some of the consequences of needing to meet these short-term goals? They include:

- The job is problem-oriented and solution-driven. Operations managers need to react quickly to resolve problems at source. Handling the symptoms as they appear will only bring temporary respite. The causes need to be identified and handled.

- It is a job that requires practical outcomes, 'indeed in this sense its practicability is overwhelming'.[1]

- 'Pressure is also a distinctive feature'[2] of the job due to the tasks involved, the time constraints imposed and the dependency upon a whole range of activities, some of which are outside the direct control of the operations function either because of the organization's reporting system or because they are externally sourced.

The time pressures on operations managers often result in them having to make as good a decision as possible in any given situation. To think of a better decision at a later date is usually of little value as it would probably be too late and the consequences of the delay would normally outweigh the gains involved. It is essential, therefore, that operations managers use their experience to good effect.

However, it is equally important that the longer-term requirements do not take a secondary role. In a function controlling such a large portion of revenue expenditure, the longer-term developments of the operations function need to be given the necessary time and attention, because here small percentage improvements invariably lead to large actual savings.

> **EXECUTIVE INSIGHT**
 As an operations manager you need to think and work in terms of both the short and long-term timescales.

Managing the strategic contribution

Whereas operations' day-to-day task concerns essential activities such as managing within budgets, scheduling and communicating with other functions, its strategic task concerns providing those order-winners and qualifiers for which it is wholly or jointly responsible. For example, operations has a sizeable strategic role in retaining and growing market share – we will explore this in more detail in the next chapter. In brief, however, it is essential to the short- and long-term success of an organization that operations moves from being good in itself to being a front runner in meeting the needs of customers by creating competitive advantage. For example, in some markets, such as a fast-food chain, delivering products extremely fast (known as **delivery speed**) could lead to a competitive advantage over neighbouring outlets; in others, price might be the key factor in the market, and operations would be responsible for delivering products and services at a level of cost that allows them to be competitively priced. As Figure 1.8 illustrates, operations has a role both in gaining the first sale and securing the second. Whether or not customers return depends largely on how well their needs were met on their previous visit or how well their order was fulfilled, and this falls within the remit of operations. As you can see from this, it is the development and implementation of both the day-to-day and strategic tasks that characterize the key role of the operations manager.

Delivery speed – the customer's lead time (the length of time a customer expects or is prepared to wait) needs to be matched by the operations lead time. Short customer lead times create a delivery speed requirement.

Figure 1.8	Operations' role in gaining the first and securing the second sale	
Phase		**Principal contributor(s)**
Gaining	the first sale	Sales and marketing – customer relationships, advertising and selling Operations – creating a business's reputation through successfully meeting customer needs
Fulfilling		Operations – meets customer needs
Securing the second sale		Operations – meeting customer needs results in repeat orders

> **EXECUTIVE INSIGHT**
> Operations contributes to gaining the first sale, and procures the second sale.

Managing technology

The operations manager is a manager of technology, both service, product and process. However, the degree of technology will differ from sector to sector and one organization to the next. And, in many situations, the level of technology involved is quite low. In most instances, the operations manager needs not so much to understand the technology itself but more importantly the business trade-offs that can be delivered by the technology in place or being proposed. In this way, operations uses technology to provide services or make products for a company's markets, with technical expertise provided by support staff.

Coordinating the whole

Like managers of other departments, the operations manager breaks down the total task into subsystems as a way to control the whole. This is essential in order to cope. However, the operations manager's role is to control these subsystems while also controlling the total system. But, as the operations task is large, the subsystems will usually be numerous and interrelated, making this coordinating role all the more difficult.

In addition, the activities of many of the support and specialist functions that form part of an organization will be to help operations complete its tasks, as illustrated earlier in Figure 1.5. Therefore, it is equally important for operations managers to be involved with and contribute to the specialist's tasks and activities as far as they relate to their own area of responsibility. They need to set the agenda for these support activities and be proactive in establishing directives, agreeing the tasks and specification for the work in hand, and facilitate the essential relationship between and with them.

Using the common denominators of time and money

To help manage a business, the activities involved are expressed using the same common denominator. Many activities use money as the base as this is the most appropriate way to ensure that 'like is compared with like'. For example, in commercial businesses sales are expressed in terms of monetary value (£, € or $) and not in terms of the number of services or products sold. The reason is that for a restaurant to measure its level of activity by the number of meals provided would take no account of the number or type of courses selected and served.

Operations, on the other hand, uses time as a more appropriate common denominator by which to express and evaluate its activities. The reason is that the monetary value of the services and products provided does not adequately relate to the operations task involved. For example, it takes longer to produce a lasagne than prepare a fillet steak but the menu price for each would be the reverse. And as operations needs to assess, for example, the level of capacity it needs at different times of the day and week, it has to work out the number of hours involved to meet forecast sales and what this means in terms of different types of staff.

The use of time as a common denominator for the activities involved serves well the needs of operations. But these activities will also be translated into monetary terms to meet the needs of business reporting systems. How the one translates into the other has, therefore, to be well understood and managed by operations, although it will be the accounting and finance function in a business that will undertake the translation task. A distinctive part of the operations management role, therefore, concerns being able to work knowledgeably on both time and money fronts.

Managing the process through people

At the core of this role is the task of managing the operations process through people. The number of people within the operations function and the range of skills and responsibilities involved were highlighted earlier. Managing this key resource in order to meet both the short- and long-term dimensions of the task, while also addressing the wide range of development needs and career expectations of those involved, is central to the role of operations management. While the people issues are picked up throughout the book, they are also dealt with in detail in Chapter 3.

Linking the thinking and doing ends of a business

The operations function forms the interface between the thinking end (strategic direction) and the doing end (meeting the needs of customers) of a business. It provides the essential link between the business view and the operational task. On the strategy dimension, it links direction to action. Without action, strategic discussion and debate have little value. Thus, translating strategy into action is fundamental to the ongoing success of a business and operations has a key role in getting this done. In the same way, operations links business philosophies and values with the views of work held by those who complete the task. It is essential to link the top and bottom of businesses as this helps to forge the coherence and cooperation essential for the success of the enterprise.

Managing complexity

The perspective that best captures the essence of the tasks outlined here is that operations concerns the management of complexity. The size and diversity of the tasks involved and the implications of decisions in terms of investments, costs and people are significant in size and fundamental in nature. The challenge of the job comes not from the nature of the individual tasks and decisions for which the operations manager is responsible – in themselves they are often quite simple – but from the number of these that have to be completed or made at the same time and the complex interrelationships that exist. Also, as operations is part of the core activities of most organizations, the work of specialists will be largely concerned with giving support and advice to the operations function. They will be involved not only with improving this function per se but also with developing the interrelated activities of operations and other departments.

Taking this mix together results in a demanding and complex job that requires, on the one hand, the fast, day-to-day pace of the short term to be underpinned and delivered while, on the other hand, the long-term direction is secured, and all this within the context of providing appropriate interface and cooperation within the overall business. Add to this the essential need to manage the processes and interfaces through the key resource of people and the outcome is a job that is fascinating in its challenge and complex in its execution. Case 1.3 illustrates this complexity.

CASE 1.3 A KEY ROLE IN THE RETAIL CHAIN

Reproduced by kind permission of Sainsbury's Supermarkets Ltd.

Managers of large stores are crucial appointments with typically up to 700 staff and, in an average week, sales revenues of £1 million and 200,000 customers entering the door. While buyers can source products at competitive prices, and distribution can be fine-tuned to efficiently meet the varying patterns of demand, the key to customer retention is what happens inside the store. It is customers' experiences while shopping (layout, presentation, queue lengths, availability and, above all, service throughout the delivery system) that most influence a customer's decision of whether or not they come back.

According to many retailing experts, a 'good' store manager can increase the sales revenue of self-service outlets (such as supermarkets) by up to 5 per cent, while in stores heavily dependent on service (such as the electrical sector), the improvement can be as high as 15 per cent, and the best managers carry these increases down to the bottom line and vice versa. The essential contribution made by store managers in driving improvements through frontline operations and into higher retail performance is fundamental.

Retailers agree that managing operations (the stores themselves) has all the ingredients of what makes a complex job. Managing staff is a core skill, especially given the fast-moving environment, changing demand levels and long opening hours. The job concerns managing a sizeable budget and a large investment in the form of buildings, car parks and delivery areas, as well as the storage of products and their management in terms of waste and obsolescence. Knowing what goes on in both the store and the back office (including supply chain, logistics and inventory management) is essential to running the operation, as well as being good with customers and alert to actual and potential service issues.

Attracting the right calibre of person is difficult, as the long, unsocial hours and weekend working are unattractive. But, on the plus side, the job is people-centred, rich in content, full of energy and buzz, and addresses real problems, the solutions to which are fast and rewarding.

Questions

1. What makes the store manager of a retail company a classic example of an operations manager?

2. From the facts given here, assess the size of the operations task and its impact on business financial performance.

3. How is the store manager a key link in the supply chain?

Services versus manufacturing

This first chapter introduces the role of operations management and provides an introduction to some of the factors that impact the nature and characteristics of the operations task. As shown in Figure 1.7 earlier, organizations provide customers with a mixed offering of a service and product. In turn, this requires the provider to make a product, process information on behalf of a customer, provide a service for a customer, or some combination of these, as illustrated in Figure 1.4 earlier.

Embodied in these alternatives are different characteristics that either facilitate or restrict what operations can or can't do in the processing task. These differences are fundamental and, as such, are dealt with in more detail in subsequent chapters. What this section does is alert you to these differences so that you get a better feel for the types of issues that operations has to manage in one type of business compared to another. As you go through the different chapters these issues will be revisited and reaffirmed as part of learning about this subject area within the field of business studies.

Figure 1.9 summarizes some of those aspects that will be reviewed throughout the book and are now briefly explained.

Figure 1.9 **Aspects of product, information and customer processing**			
Aspects	**Processing**		
	Product	**Information**	**Customer**
Nature of the service/product	Tangible Durable Highly specified	⟶ ⟶ ⟶	Intangible Perishable Server discretion
Organizational arrangements	Back office	⟶	Front office
Level of customer involvement in the operations process	Low	⟶	High
Typical competitive environment	Traded	⟶	Sheltered

Note: The aspects when processing a customer surrogate (for example the maintenance of your car or suit/ dress to be dry-cleaned) are similar to those for processing information.

Nature of the service/product

The characteristics of product, information and customer processing vary in several ways. For example, services are consumed by the customer at the point of provision. This means that the capacity in the process (for example, an empty seat on a passenger airline, or an unbooked slot in a hairdressing salon) cannot be held over to another time. This inability to store capacity in the form of inventory results from the perishable nature of capacity in some **service delivery systems**. This contrasts sharply with a typical manufacturing company. Here, products can be made ahead of demand. For example, ice cream is made and stored in times of lower demand as a way of using operations ice cream-making capacity productively as well as helping to meet the higher demand levels of another period. For this reason, a manufacturing company typically finds it easier to handle the imbalances that occur between the levels of demand and capacity.

> **Service delivery systems** – the processes or systems used to deliver services to customers.

Information-processing and customer surrogate businesses also have some opportunity to determine when tasks are completed. For example, information-processing tasks can be cumulated and then held until the most suitable time for completion, thus enabling demand to be scheduled in line with available capacity or to cumulate volumes to help lower processing costs. Similarly, the timing of a vehicle or other repair can, to some extent, be managed to better meet the scheduling needs of the business. Even so, the length of time over which scheduling alterations can be made will normally be limited in scale compared to the manufacturer of products. With products, inventory can be made, if required, ahead of time and independent of demand profiles, whereas information processing will invariably be an integral part of a customer's own overall service or procedure. The processing task can only commence on receipt of relevant data and needs to be completed to fit in with a customer's own requirements. Take, for example, a data processing unit that updates the transactions of the customers of its own client, a large high street bank. The necessary data will be delivered at a given day each month, with agreed lead times for completing the updates and sending out the individual statements. Within this time frame, the unit is able to schedule the job to best fit its own total workload. Similarly, a garage can schedule the work within its repair shop on a given day around factors such as the skills available, spare part deliveries and the efficient use of staff.

The presence of customers in the system also brings the aspect of server interpretation into the delivery of a service – known as **'server discretion'**. In turn, this makes it more difficult to control **quality conformance** in terms of establishing service levels and measuring performance against these. In the provision of goods, the issues of quality control and measuring performance against specification are more easily managed, given the separation of the making and purchasing events and the control over what and how a product is made.

Organizational arrangements

When making products, the operations process is largely, and often totally, separated from the customer, whereas in the service sector customers are often involved in the provision. In a service company the delivery system, where possible, is split between the front office (where the customer is present) and back office (where the customer is not present). In the former the system interfaces with customers and, for example, handles requests or provides a given service. However, systems and procedures are designed so that certain tasks are undertaken in the back office and, in that way, processing can be delayed until a more convenient time and activities cumulated in order to gain **economies of scale**, so justifying investments as part of the way to reducing costs. Being separated from customers in the back office also allows procedures and tasks to be undertaken without making essential responses to customers' immediate requirements.

Competitive environment

The tangible nature of products enables the work and supporting technologies that go into making them to be easily transferred, in product form, from the place of manufacture to markets throughout the world. In this way, products are referred to as being **'traded'**. As a result, the manufacturing sector has been increasingly competitive from the latter half of the last century, highlighting the truly global nature of these markets. Many services, on the other hand, are classed as being **'sheltered'**, highlighting the fact that the extent of competition is restricted by the geographical boundaries of such markets – the 'you-do-not-go-to-Hong-Kong-for-a-Chinese-takeaway' syndrome. For example, retailers only compete with the high street outlets within their own town or city. In recent years, however, the format of competition for many service firms has changed. One source of this change has been the increasing use of technology. Online services for the purchase of items such as books, clothes, banking and airline tickets has increasingly moved many service sectors into the traded category. The role of operations in such instances has needed to reflect these new dynamics and business conditions, reinforcing its core contribution to the continued success of a business.

Server discretion – the extent to which a server may interpret their role in the delivery of a service and what the specification of that service comprises.

Quality conformance – providing a service or product to the design specification

Economies of scale – The decrease in cost per unit of a product or service as a result of processing high volumes within a large-scale operations facility that is geared up (including investment in processes and equipment) to handle such volume levels.

Traded – a product or service that can be transferred from the place of provision to be sold in markets throughout the world.

Sheltered – a product or service for which the extent of competition is restricted by the geographical boundaries of its markets.

Managing operations in practice

When managing operations in practice, it is important to consider the following aspects:

- **Operations is a large business function** – both in terms of its day-to-day role in managing costs, assets and people and its strategic role in retaining existing customers and attracting new ones.

- **Operations Directors play a key role in the success of a business** – given the large size of the function and its resultant impact on the business's day-to-day and strategic performance, it is critical to appoint an Operations Director with the appropriate technical knowledge, business knowledge and people-management capability.

- **Need to understand operations' strategic and day-to-day impact** – before determining how best to manage operations, it is important to first understand the market order-winners and qualifiers that need to be supported in current and future markets and the level of costs, assets and people that have to be managed on a day-to-day basis.

- **Link performance measures to market support, cost and cash targets** – given that the role of managing and improving operations is to better support markets, reduce costs and release cash, these business targets need to be clearly reflected in the performance measures used to manage operations.

- **Use only a limited number of key performance measures** – as many performance measures often conflict with each other, a decision needs to be made about which ones are 'key'. As stated above, these measures need to reflect the market support, cost and cash targets. However, it is also important to only focus on a small number of key measures (ideally less than seven). Otherwise, different parts of the business will consider different measures to be 'more key' than others and the functions will become misaligned with each other.

- **Use different performance measures to assess the support for different market segments** – markets should be segmented using the order-winners and qualifiers that need to be supported to both win and retain these customers. Operations performance should then be assessed using measures that reflect these different order-winners and qualifiers.

- **Consider splitting operations into different units to support different market segments** – given the different capabilities that are often required to support different market order-winners and qualifiers, it might make sense to split operations into a number of different units. Although this may result in an increase in overhead costs, this is often outweighed by the increased sales and profits generated through the improved market support.

- **Use internal benchmarks to identify improvement opportunities** – if you do manage a number of different operations units, then it is important that you benchmark performance between them and publish these results. This will start to highlight both strengths and weaknesses within your business and encourage your team to start investigating why they are performing better or worse than the other parts of the business.

- **If possible, also use external benchmarks to identify improvement opportunities** – it is often more difficult to access the data required to do this but, if you can, it is useful to benchmark your operations units against competitors and also those from other industries. Again, this will encourage the curiosity in your team to understand why they are performing differently.

Driving business performance

The operations management role is central to the successful performance of a business in the following ways.

Managing operations to release cash

As illustrated by Figure 1.10, operations provides a key role in managing both the work and cash flows within an organization. As the function responsible for the task of managing inventory, operations has the opportunity to improve the effective use of this sizeable resource hereby releasing cash to be used elsewhere in the business or help to ensure its essential liquidity.

Figure 1.10 **Work and cash flows**

Money flow Out	Money flow In	Current assets		Work and materials flow	Activity description
✓		Inventory	Raw materials and components	Materials/components	The necessary materials/components are bought from outside
✓		Inventory	Work in progress (WIP)	Staff and other materials/components added	The necessary tasks to provide the service or produce the product are completed
✓		Inventory	Finished goods	More staff and materials/components added	Service/product now complete and is or can be sold
	✓	Cash sales		Finished services/goods are sold	Cash sales
		Debtors		Finished services/goods are sold	Credit sales
	✓	Cash			Payment made for credit sales

Note: In some cases, payments are made when certain stages have been completed (for example stage payments may be made in the building/construction industry) or at the end of a time period (for example management consultations usually invoice on a weekly basis).

Managing operations to support markets

As emphasized throughout this chapter, the strategic role of operations is crucial both in gaining new business (in the form of increased market share or entering new markets) and retaining existing customers, both of which underpin sales revenues and future growth.

Managing operations to reduce costs

Typically having responsibility for 60–70 per cent of total costs points to a sizeable opportunity to reduce costs. Using the 80/20 rule to guide where best to look will invariably point to operations as the function that will offer the most opportunity to reduce costs. In turn, this will allow an organization to increase its profits or compete more effectively in price sensitive markets.

Critical reflections

Few operations managers would consider their role to be other than demanding, challenging, absorbing and satisfying. They would also tell of its frustrations and complexity: this is bound to be so where a function is required to handle a large number of variables and achieve many diverse and complicated short- and longer-term objectives. To manage such a task effectively requires a range of executive qualities as indicated earlier. To this list need to be added hard work, intellect and experience. To complete the day-to-day tasks requires much physical effort. However, to perceive the whole and instigate appropriate initiatives and developments through others also requires both intellect and experience; the former to appreciate the issues and perspectives involved and the latter to be alert to potential problem areas.

High levels of complexity involve the key role of efficiently managing most of an organization's assets and costs while providing support for the many different needs of customers. To do this is intellectually demanding. Unless operations managers are able to understand the whole, take it apart, fix the parts required and put it back together, they will not be able to efficiently and effectively manage the tasks involved. Figure 1.11 underlines this point. As you will see, management concerns the higher levels of learning, from application through to evaluation. The operations task is classic of these demands, a fact gaining increasing recognition not least because of the success of developing nations and the emphasis placed by the more successful upon the management of the operations function. By the early 1980s it was becoming clear that Japanese success was not based upon greater investment in processes but in management, particularly operations. Similarly, the successful growth of international retailers such as Walmart and IKEA has been built on world-class operations capability. Some believe that the managers needed to convert operations into 'a competitive resource may have to be the best rounded and most intellectually able of all corporate managers'.[3] The competences identified included: 'a knowledge of technology... as well as every business function... a thinking style that includes the ability to conceptualize as well as analyze complex tradeoffs... [and] managers who are architects of change not house-keepers'.[4]

Recognition of these operations management qualities is a prerequisite for both the service and manufacturing sectors. Those nations that have been unsuccessful in carrying out the operations tasks in manufacturing industries have stood by and watched this sector diminish dramatically in a few years. Next on the list are parts of the service sector. Passenger airlines, data processing, call centre provision, banking and other parts of the financial services sector have already experienced the full weight of global competition. This will not abate in these sectors and is already surfacing elsewhere. The sound management of operations in terms of its internal and external roles has a key contribution to make in the success of companies, sectors and hence nations.

The rest of this book reviews the essential tasks involved and some of the important perspectives that need to be understood by an operations manager. The book attempts to present the concepts underlying this function and show which approaches are the most useful to adopt in order to analyze and evaluate each major part of the whole operations task. The emphasis, therefore, is not on covering all existing techniques or mathematical approaches and explanations. As shown in Figure 1.11, the higher levels of learning are those concerned with application, analysis, synthesis and evaluation. Knowledge and understanding are the easier, lower levels of learning; the most difficult task is to do the job effectively. It is not an issue of knowing things but of knowing what to do. This requires the application of relevant knowledge, the analysis of the results of that application, the building back together of the results into an improved form (synthesis) and the evaluation of this in terms of what has to be done. Effective managers are those who are able to do this as a way of continuously developing their own set of responsibilities.

Thus, as well as describing the relevant concepts, approaches, tools and techniques within operations, the book also emphasizes the managerial dimension of the task. The book concerns operations management and the text, chapter questions, assignments and cases provide the opportunity to introduce materials to meet the requirements of all six learning levels.

Figure 1.11 **The levels of learning**

	Levels of learning	Descriptions
	Evaluation	Appraise, compare, conclude, contrast, interpret and explain
	Synthesis	Classify, compile, design, modify, reorganize, formulate, reconstruct and substitute
	Analysis	Select, discriminate, illustrate, separate and distinguish
	Application	Demonstrate, relate, use, complete and prepare
	Understanding	Explain, extend, generalize, infer, summarise and estimate
	Knowledge	Know, identify, list, name, outline and state

Increasingly higher levels of learning

The task of management

Source: Adapted from Benjamin S. Bloom et al. *Taxonomy of Educational Objectives*, Allyn & Bacon, Boston, MA. © Pearson Education 1984.
Adapted by permission of the publisher.

Summary

- The operations process transforms inputs into outputs that the organization then sells in its chosen markets. Figure 1.2 overviews this core task, while Figure 1.3 provides examples from both the service and manufacturing sectors.

- As operations typically accounts for 60–70 per cent of the people, assets and costs within an organization, its sheer size makes it a demanding management task. In addition to undertaking these activities, operations comprises a wide range of functions and support roles, examples of which are given in Figure 1.5.

- Most companies deliver a mix of both services and product, as illustrated in Figure 1.7. Where an organization chooses to position itself on this service–product mix continuum will influence its competitive position and the operations task involved.

- While most offerings are a combination of services and products, there are important distinctions in managing operations in the service and manufacturing sectors. These are outlined and overviewed in Figures 1.4 and 1.9.

- Most of the people within a typical organization work within the operations function and reflect a wide range of jobs, skills and personal needs. A critical part of the operations role is to manage the operations process through people in such a way as to meet the short- and long-term needs of the business, as well as the development needs and personal expectations of those involved.

- Operations has a significant strategic contribution to make in retaining and growing market share. It is responsible for meeting the requirements of the sale and this, in turn, affects whether customers purchase a second time (see Figure 1.8).

Discussion questions

1. Select two service and two manufacturing businesses of your own choice. From an operations perspective, what are the similarities and differences that exist?

2. What is operations management? What are the key elements of the operations task? Illustrate your answer with examples.

3. Based on Figure 1.2 and 1.3, select one manufacturing and one service business other than those used in Figure 1.3 itself. Then, complete a similar analysis to that given in Figure 1.3.

4. Select two other functions within a service or manufacturing business. For each, identify three links to operations and explain the key dimensions of the activities involved and how they would assist operations to complete its tasks and responsibilities.

5. Analyse the operations function in the university or college department in which you are registered or in the company in which you work in terms of:
   • The key operations responsibilities
   • The size of the operations task
   • The operations function in the context of the rest of the university/college department or organization
   • Four factors that illustrate the complexity of the operations task. Give reasons for your choice.

6. Identify an operations system in your own life. What are the inputs, operations process activities and outputs involved?

7. Consider the following processes that you frequently encounter:
   • Enrolling on a course
   • Taking lunch
   • Buying a ticket for a concert.

Identify the inputs, operations process and outputs involved.

Assignments

1. Look through McDonald's website (www.mcdonalds.com) and list the dimensions that concern operations. How many outlets are there throughout the world and how do you think the company ensures effective control over the operations task in order to maintain its desired standards within the service delivery system?

2. Make a list of the top ten companies in the Fortune 500 (http://money.cnn.com/magazines/fortune/fortune500/2011/full_list/) from 1962, 1982, 1992, 2002 and the current day. Compare these to the current list. Identify the fundamental differences and give reasons for these changes.

Exploring further

TED talks

Pink, D. (2009) *The surprising science of motivation*. Career analyst Dan Pink examines the puzzle of motivation, starting with a fact that social scientists know but most managers don't: traditional rewards aren't always as effective as we think. Listen for illuminating stories and maybe a way forward.
www.ted.com/talks/dan_pink_on_motivation.html

Schwartz, B. (2005) *The paradox of choice*. Psychologist Barry Schwartz takes aim at a central tenet of western societies: freedom of choice. In Schwartz's estimation, choice has made us not freer but more paralyzed, not happier but more dissatisfied.
www.ted.com/talks/barry_schwartz_on_the_paradox_of_choice.html

Sinek, S. (2009) *How great leaders inspire action*. Simon Sinek has a simple but powerful model for inspirational leadership all starting with a golden circle and the question 'Why?' His examples include Apple, Martin Luther King and the Wright brothers.
www.ted.com/talks/simon_sinek_how_great_leaders_inspire_action.html

Sivers, D. (2010) *How to start a movement*. With help from some surprising footage, Derek Sivers explains how movements really get started. (Hint: it takes two.)
www.ted.com/talks/derek_sivers_how_to_start_a_movement.html

Journal articles

Adler, P., Hecksher, C. and Prusak, L. (2011) 'Building a collaborative enterprise', *Harvard Business Review*, **89**(7/8): 94–101. Organizations must learn to: (1) Define a shared purpose (2) Cultivate an ethic of contribution (3) Develop scalable procedures (4) Create an infrastructure that values and rewards collaboration.

Gino, F. and Pisano, G.P. (2011) 'Why leaders don't learn from success', *Harvard Business Review*, **89**(4): 68–44. Companies should implement systematic after-action reviews to understand all the factors that led to a win, and test their theories by conducting experiments even if 'it ain't broke'.

Gouillart, F.J. and Sturdivant, F.D. (1994) 'Spend a day in the life of your customers', *Harvard Business Review*, **72**(1): 116–25. The article argues that a senior executive's instinctive capacity to empathize with and gain insight from customers is the single most important skill that can be used to direct a company's strategic posture approach. Yet most top managers retain only limited contact with consumers as their organizations grow, relying instead on subordinates' reports to define and feel out the market for them. To get a true sense of the market, senior executives should consider the wants and needs of every step in the distribution chain, right down to the end user of a finished product.

Grant, A.M. (2011) 'How customers can rally your troops', *Harvard Business Review*, **89**(6): 96–103. End users can inspire workers by demonstrating the impact of their efforts, showing appreciation for their work, and eliciting employees' empathy for them. To outsource inspiration effectively, leaders must identify end users (both past and present), collect their stories, introduce them to employees across the organization, and recognize workers' impact on customers' lives.

Books

Ford, H. (1988) *Today and Tomorrow*. Cambridge MA: Productivity Press. This is a reprint of Henry Ford's 1926 book, and its direct style and insights into business are well worth the effort of reading it. The approaches that Henry Ford developed have been acknowledged as the basis of Japanese approaches today. The text is fun to read, and you could benefit from looking at Chapters 1–4, which provide a general context for business as a whole and operations in particular.

Hill, A. and Hill, T. (2011) *Essential Operations Management*. Basingstoke: Palgrave Macmillan. The text provides a useful supplement to *Operations Management* by focusing on the essential aspects for managing operations within service and manufacturing organizations.

Hill, T. (1998) *The Strategy Quest: Releasing the Energy of Manufacturing Within a Market Driven Strategy: a Dynamic Business Story*. Available from AMD Publishing, 'Albedo', Dousland, Devon PL20 6NE, UK; email: amd@jm-abode.tiscali.co.uk; fax: +44 (0) 1822 882863. This book (written as a novel) describes how an art business and manufacturing organization restructure themselves to meet the changing demands of their customers.

Meredith, J.R. and Shafer, S.M. (2007) *Operations Management for MBAs*, 3rd edn. New York: John Wiley & Sons. This book includes a useful, easy-to-read opening chapter setting out the activities and dimensions of operations management as a function, within organizations and in an increasingly global economy.

Websites

Nuts About Southwest
Southwest Airlines have set up a blog to let its customers, employees and other stakeholders look inside its business and interact with it. Everyone is encouraged to join in without having to register to read, watch or comment. However, if someone wants to share photos or videos or rate a post, then they need to complete a profile. Even though the content presented on the website is moderated, it pledges to present opposing viewpoints and create discussion.
www.blogsouthwest.com

Notes and references

1. Lawrence, P.A. (1983) *Operations Management: Research and Priorities*, Report to the Social Services Research Council (April), p. 2.
2. Ibid., p. 14.
3. Meyer, R. (1987) 'Wanted: a new breed of manufacturing manager', in *Manufacturing Issues 1987*, New York: Booz Allen, pp. 26–9.
4. Ibid., p. 28.

Visit www.palgrave.com/business/hillom3e for self-test questions, guideline answers to some case study questions, useful weblinks and more to help you understand the topics in this chapter

SOUTHWEST AIRLINES

© Carlos Santa Maria

'Southwest Airlines hasn't put a foot wrong since its first flight in 1971', commented the analyst Paul Brown. 'Over the last 40 years it has risen from being the scrappy underdog to the second largest US domestic airline, flying over 100 million passengers last year (see Figure 1). When describing Southwest Airlines, it is difficult to avoid superlatives. It has the lowest costs, lowest fares, highest asset usage, best labour relations and highest wages in the industry. And it has achieved this through ignoring industry practice: there are no operations hubs, no service extras and little IT investment. Its success has come from being where its competitors aren't, by focusing on the markets they regard as unimportant.'

GUERRILLA WARFARE

In 1966, Herb Kelleher was practising law in California when a client named Rollin King proposed setting up a short-haul airline flying between Dallas, Houston

Figure 1 **Number of domestic passengers carried (1999–2009)**							
Airline	**Millions of domestic passengers carried**						
	1999	**2001**	**2003**	**2005**	**2007**	**2008**	**2009**
Alaska	14	14	15	17	17	16	16
American	82	78	89	98	98	86	86
America West	19	20	20	22	16	–	–
Continental	44	43	39	43	49	47	46
Delta	106	94	84	86	73	71	161
Northwest	55	52	52	57	54	49	–
Southwest	65	74	75	88	102	102	101
United	87	75	66	67	68	63	56
US Airways	56	56	41	42	42	55	51

Note: Delta merged with Northwest in 2008.

and San Antonio. By staying in Texas, they were able to avoid federal regulations and, after raising the necessary capital, they applied for regulatory approval from the Texas Aeronautics Commission in 1967. However, its competitors opposed the application by claiming the Texas market could not support another airline. Kelleher argued and won the case in the Texas Supreme Court and, after the US Supreme Court refused to hear an appeal, its first aircraft finally left the ground in 1971. After this confrontation, Southwest adopted a guerrilla warfare strategy and only attacked markets with low competition rather than fighting the enemy head on. It targeted routes badly served by other airlines and avoided large 'hub' airports. Instead, Southwest focused on mid-sized airports in mid-western cities like Little Rock, Las Vegas, Phoenix and Sacramento with less traffic and congestion.

Southwest soon realized there were two types of short-haul travellers: convenience, time-oriented business travellers and price-sensitive leisure travellers. It uses two-tier pricing to target these groups. After initially charging $20 for flights between Houston, Dallas, and San Antonio, $8 less than its competitors, it started to charge $26 for weekday seats before 7.00pm and $13 after 7.00pm and at weekends. Braniff Airlines reduced prices from $28 to $13 for all Dallas-Houston flights and Southwest launched its now famous advert announcing, 'Nobody's going to shoot Southwest out of the sky for a lousy $13.' It offered travellers a $13 flight or $26 with a free bottle of liquor and, after 75 per cent of the passengers chose the $26 fare, it became the largest distributor of Chivas Regal Scotch whiskey in Texas. Two years later, Braniff abandoned the Dallas-Houston route. Southwest also started competing with other forms of transport including trains, buses and private cars. By offering competitive fares and a fast, efficient service, it encouraged travellers to start flying. For example, when it entered the Los Angeles-San Francisco route, using the smaller and less crowded Oakland and Burbank airports, it grew from the 200th to the 21st busiest route in the US by the end of that same year.

Also key to Southwest's strategy is the lack of a central operation. Most airlines operate on a 'hub and spoke' system flying passengers between major hubs and then transferring them to smaller airports. This is, theoretically, the most efficient business model but, in reality, it requires significant hub resources. Any problems here also have severe knock-on effects and losing market share at the hub also reduces the number of transfer flights. Instead, Southwest uses a 'point to point' system with short flights and a route diagram looks like a spider web rather than wheel spokes. As there is no central operation, anyone wishing to challenge Southwest would have to attack a number of points at once.

Southwest's service is so popular that cities frequently ask them to begin operating from their airports. However, few of these offers are taken up (see Figure 2). Instead, Southwest only moves into markets where it has a clear advantage. Its margins are wafer-thin and new routes have to be

Figure 2	Southwest airlines market growth (1971–2009)		
Year	# new markets	Year	# new markets
1971	3	1994	7
1975	1	1995	1
1977	5	1996	4
1978	1	1997	2
1979	1	1998	1
1980	4	1999	3
1982	6	2000	1
1984	1	2001	2
1985	3	2002	–
1986	1	2003	–
1987	2	2004	1
1988	1	2005	2
1989	2	2006	2
1990	2	2007	1
1991	1	2008	–
1992	2	2009	–
1993	3		

Figure 3 Statistics for Southwest's ten most frequently used airports

City	Daily departures	# gates	Non-stop cities served	Year of first flight
Las Vegas	234	21	56	1982
Chicago	214	29	48	1985
Phoenix	187	24	42	1982
Baltimore	162	26	38	1993
Houston Hobby	135	17	29	1971
Dallas	134	15	15	1971
Los Angeles	120	11	18	1982
Oakland	118	13	19	1989
Denver	115	10	32	1996
Orlando	115	12	33	1982

profitable from day one. When it does go into a market, it goes in hard with a broad range of flights never more than an hour apart (see Figure 3) so passengers can turn up, buy a ticket from a dispenser in less than 20 seconds and jump on the next flight.

Low operating costs (see Figure 4) and large flight numbers mean Southwest can undercut competitors while still remaining profitable. It uses this to attack rivals and enter new markets with dramatic results. For example, it had 25 per cent market share in Little Rock after only five days of operation, and drove America West and Midway airlines into bankruptcy after attacking their Phoenix and Chicago hubs.

QUALITY WITHOUT FRILLS

Compared to its competitors, Southwest offers a no-frills service. There are no flight connections, no baggage transfers, no meals and no seat reservations. What it does offer is cheap, reliable and frequent flights with minimum fuss and excellent customer service. For example, a gate agent looked after a dog for two weeks when an Acapulco-bound passenger arrived without a dog crate; a pilot flew a passenger in his private plane after missing a connection to Houston where they were due to have a kidney transplant; and a ticket agent invited an elderly passenger into her home and escorted her around Phoenix for two weeks after discovering that she was flying there for cancer treatment and had no friends or family to look after her.

Figure 4 Operating expenses per available seat mile (1999–2009)

Airline	Operating expenses per available seat mile (in cents)						
	1999	2001	2003	2005	2007	2008	2009
Alaska	10.2	10.2	9.8	10.9	12.2	14.5	13.2
American	9.4	11.9	11.5	12.0	9.6	13.9	12.2
America West	7.3	9.3	7.9	11.5	12.9	–	–
Continental	9.0	10.3	9.8	13.1	10.2	17.1	15.2
Delta	9.0	10.1	12.9	13.1	10.6	18.7	12.7
Northwest	9.3	11.3	11.4	15.2	10.4	19.3	–
Southwest	6.6	7.5	7.9	8.3	9.1	10.2	10.3
United	9.7	12.4	12.4	12.9	13.8	15.7	11.1
US Airways	12.4	14.2	14.0	13.9	10.9	20.8	17.3

Figure 5 Passenger load factor (1999–2009)

Airline	Passenger load factor						
	1999	2001	2003	2005	2007	2008	2009
Alaska	69	68	69	76	76	77	76
American	70	69	74	79	82	82	81
America West	68	72	79	80	83	–	–
Continental	74	73	77	80	83	84	85
Delta	72	69	76	78	81	84	82
Northwest	75	74	76	78	81	85	–
Southwest	69	68	70	71	73	71	76
United	71	71	77	82	83	83	82
US Airways	70	69	75	75	80	83	83

Southwest calls this its 'Positively Outrageous Service' and when employees witness exceptional service, they are encouraged to fill out a 'LUV' report. There is then an annual 'Heroes of the Heart' award with the winning department having their name painted onto a plane for that year.

DOING MORE FOR LESS

Southwest works harder than its rivals to keep its operations simple, efficient and inexpensive. Planes are turned around faster and spend 11 hours flying each day, compared with an industry average of eight. They also on average fly 11 times per day from each airport gate, compared to an industry average of five. The frequent take-offs and landings increase fuel costs and landing fees, but Southwest still has the lowest cost per seat-mile of any major US airline (see Figure 4). Planes can, therefore, fly with fewer passengers (see Figure 5) and more flights can be scheduled.

It uses a limited range of fuel-efficient Boeing 737 aircraft to reduce spares and maintenance costs (see Figure 6) and operates with minimum staff and simple information technology. In fact, its ticket machines were designed in a bar one evening by employees who then built prototypes in their spare time using off-the-shelf components.

LEADING BY EXAMPLE

In 2001, Herb Kelleher stepped down as CEO at the age of 71, but remained Chairman until 2008. There is no doubt that his leadership was critical to Southwest's success. He could easily chair a board meeting or imitate Elvis Presley at a company party, and colleagues always talk about his mental brilliance, sense of humour and ability to gain his employees' respect. He led by example and spent a day every quarter in the front line serving drinks, handling baggage, selling tickets and getting to know passengers and staff. This type of tactic can backfire, but Kelleher's commitment was never questioned. At one point, he froze his salary for five years when the pilots agreed to freeze theirs and, during the Gulf War, staff set up a 'Fuel from the Heart' programme to reduce their pay and help offset increased fuel prices. In only a few months, they raised $130,000 without Kelleher's knowledge.

'Loyalty between a company and its employees may have vanished in many corporations, but it is stronger than ever at Southwest,' comments Paul Brown. 'Kelleher's personality and leadership style were key to this, but they seem to have lived on in the CEO, James Parker, and COO,

Figure 6 Southwest's airfleet (2009)

Boeing 737 aircraft type	# seats	# aircraft	Average age (years)
-300	137	184	13
-500	122	25	13
-700	137	331	7

Figure 7 Operating revenue (1999–2009)

Airline	Operating revenue ($bn)						
	1999	2001	2003	2005	2007	2008	2009
Alaska	1.8	1.8	2.0	2.4	3.1	3.2	3.4
American	16.1	15.6	17.4	20.7	17.2	23.8	19.9
America West	2.2	2.0	2.2	3.4	2.7	–	–
Continental	8.0	8.0	7.3	11.1	10.6	15.2	12.6
Delta	14.9	13.2	14.2	16.1	14.5	22.7	28.1
Northwest	9.9	9.6	9.2	12.3	9.5	13.6	–
Southwest	4.7	5.6	5.9	7.6	9.9	11.0	10.4
United	18.0	16.1	14.9	17.4	20.1	20.2	16.3
US Airways	8.5	8.2	6.8	7.2	6.5	12.5	10.5

Figure 8 Operating profit (1999–2009)

Airline	Operating profit ($m)						
	1999	2001	2003	2005	2007	2008	2009
Alaska	(12)	(65)	(11)	(8)	123	(22)	267
American	1,004	(2,558)	(1,444)	(351)	842	(2,054)	(1,004)
America West	198	(423)	24	(121)	(19)	–	–
Continental	480	(342)	30	(94)	552	(378)	(144)
Delta	1,730	(972)	(1,157)	(1,198)	1,040	(8,314)	(324)
Northwest	769	(797)	(277)	(895)	1,124	(541)	–
Southwest	782	631	298	548	791	449	262
United	1,358	(3,743)	(1,554)	(241)	360	(5,396)	(651)
US Airways	202	(1,181)	(421)	(213)	543	(1,800)	118

Figure 9 Fortune 10 most admired US companies (2001–11)

Company	Rank in 2000–11											
	0	1	2	3	4	5	6	7	8	9	10	11
Apple	–	–	–	–	–	–	–	7	1	1	1	1
Google	–	–	–	–	–	–	–	8	4	4	2	2
Berkshire Hathaway	7	7	5	3	2	10	7	4	2	2	3	3
Southwest Airlines	6	4	2	2	3	5	3	5	–	7	–	4
Procter & Gamble	–	–	–	10	–	6	4	10	8	6	6	5
Coca-Cola	–	–	–	–	–	–	–	–	–	–	10	6
Amazon.com	–	–	–	–	–	–	–	–	–	–	5	7
FedEx	–	–	8	8	9	8	2	6	7	7	–	8
Microsoft	2	5	4	7	6	4	10	–	–	10	–	9
McDonald's	–	–	–	–	–	–	–	–	–	–	–	10

Colleen Barrett, who voluntarily relinquished their salaries in the second half of 2001 to help the business survive the turbulent times after 9/11.'

A CULTURE OF COMMITMENT

When asked to summarize Southwest's culture, Kelleher commented that it is largely a lot of people taking pride in what they're doing and that people are the most important part of the business. How they are treated determines how they treat people outside of the company. People are given the licence to be themselves and motivate others – they don't have to fit in a constraining mould at work and they can have a good time.

Staff work hard and are committed to the company and its customers. It has the lowest staff turnover in the industry and one of the best labour relations records. In 1974, it became the first airline to introduce employee profit sharing and it still has the highest employee ownership of any major airline. Communication and camaraderie maintain the 'Southwest Spirit'. Employees are encouraged to have fun, sing and make jokes. In fact one flight attendant used to pop out of overhead luggage compartments until one day frightening an elderly passenger, who then had to have oxygen.

New staff are introduced to Southwest's culture through the Southwest Wheel of Fortune game show, scavenger hunts and the 'Southwest Airlines Shuffle' rap video in which each department introduces itself and Kelleher appears as Big Daddy-O. Further employee development occurs at their University of People in Dallas with programmes such as 'Leading with Integrity' for newly promoted supervisors and managers, 'Walk-a-Mile Day' to experience the day-to-day activities of other departments' and a 'Co-Hearts' mentoring programme for new recruits.

Like their employees, Southwest's customers are extraordinarily loyal. They are encouraged to tell the company what they think and over 5,000 letters are answered each month. Frequent flyers are often on first-name terms with employees and regularly form part of the interview panel for new staff.

THE FUTURE

'The US airline industry is notoriously competitive with over 100 bankruptcies in the last decade,' reflected Paul Brown. 'However, Southwest has consistently increased revenue and maintained profits by growing its market, taking share from competitors, cutting costs, promoting heroes and constantly innovating (see Figures 7 and 8).

Working within its own self-defined limits, it has become a major player in the US airline industry flying more passengers per employee, with the fewest employees per aircraft and lowest number of customer complaints. It continues to be recognized as one of the most admired US companies (see Figure 9) and received over 280,000 applications for 3,000 jobs last year.

No union strike has ever interrupted its service and no passenger has ever died from a safety incident. There is no doubt about its success, but what about the future? The airline industry is currently in turmoil and Delta and Northwest have emerged from bankruptcy with lower costs and more efficient operations. Can Southwest continue to be America's most prosperous airline? How and where should it look to expand next? Will the other major US airlines finally learn how to compete with them?

Questions

1. How does Southwest compete?

2. What makes it successful?

3. How can it continue to be successful in the future?

Lecturers: visit www.palgrave.com/business/ hillom3e for teaching guidelines for this case study

After completing this chapter, you should be able to:

- Appreciate how in large organizations strategy has evolved into three levels – corporate, business unit and functional

- Distinguish between an executive's day-to-day and strategic roles

- Identify how business unit and functional strategies interface with each other

- Appreciate why the critical first step in developing a functional strategy is agreeing the order-winners and qualifiers for the different markets in which a business competes

- Explain the role of operations' strategy within a business

- Identify when investments and developments are day-to-day or strategic in origin

- Understand the strategic mix within most organizations of being market-driven and market-driving

- Develop and implement an operations strategy

Chapter outline

Executive overview

Introduction

What is strategy?

Evolution of strategy within a business

Levels of strategy
Market-driven
Market-driving
The market-driven and market-driving strategic mix

A recap on functional strategy development

Operations strategy in action

Executive roles – day-to-day and strategic tasks
Use of resources

Business unit strategy

Reasons for current approaches to developing strategy
Statements on strategy developments stop at the interface
The pursuit of generic strategies
Strategy outcomes assume a similarity that does not exist
History of functional dominance
Markets versus marketing
The proactive role of marketing in strategy development
The reactive role of operations in strategy development

Reasons for reactive role of operations in strategy development
Operations managers' view of themselves
The company's view of the operations manager's role
Too late in the corporate debate
Lack of language

The need to recognize difference at the level of strategy formulation

Linking marketing and operations

Linking business objectives and functional strategies through markets
How the framework operates

Understanding markets – the reality

Understanding customer requirements

Understanding markets – the approach to follow
What is gained from understanding the market?

Implementing an operations strategy
Operations strategy – an illustration

Operations strategy in practice

Driving business performance

Critical reflections

Summary

What is the role of operations strategy?

- As the various functions in an organization make up that organization, together they are responsible for developing and then implementing its business strategy

- An operations executive is part of the group with this responsibility

- The strategy task requires this group to debate the company's markets and determine which customers to shed, win, retain or grow and the relevant order-winners and qualifiers involved now and in the future

- With the agenda agreed, operations' task (as with other relevant functions) is to analyze how well it currently provides those order-winner and qualifiers for which it is solely or jointly responsible, assess the gaps between current and required performance and then develop and implement an action plan to close the gaps

Why is operations strategy important?

- Operations is a major business player both in terms of gaining the first sale and retaining existing customers

- Once a sale has been made, operations handles the customer interface from there on in and, in so doing, establishes and develops the relationships and business reputation within a sector that are key to retaining customers and securing recommendations that lead to new customers and revenue growth

How does operations strategy impact business performance?

- Operations has a key role both in securing new and retaining existing customers that underpins sales revenue growth

- To bring this about operations needs to align its delivery systems and infrastructure to those order-winners and qualifiers for which it is solely or jointly responsible now and in the future

- This essential role in both market-driven and market-driving scenarios makes operations a key player in the profitable growth of businesses

What are the key issues to consider when developing an operations strategy?

- As one member of the management group responsible for developing a business strategy, an operations executive will be party to discussing and agreeing the way in which a company competes in its current and future markets

- This critical first step needs to involve all relevant functions and it is at this business level that differences are exposed and agreement on how the company competes are reached

- A key part of this 'understanding markets' phase is to agree customers that represent a segment and then check executive opinion on relevant order-winners and qualifiers and their respective weightings for these customers by analyzing orders that, in turn, represent these customers

Call-off – a call-off is the quantity that a customer asks to be delivered at one time. Consequently, a customer may order a certain quantity but later, or at the same time as the order is placed, request for parts of that order to be delivered at different times.

- Such analyses give detail on customer lead-times, margins, operations' performance in terms of on-time delivery and quality conformance, actual volumes ordered or **call-offs** requested, any changes by the customer to an order after placement and so on

- In this way customer voice (what a customer says or a company's perception of the key dimensions of a customer's business) is replaced by customer behaviour (the reality of a customer's business or requirements)

- When any gaps between current performance levels on key order-winners and qualifiers and what is required have been identified, operations (as with other functions) needs to alert the company to the size and realistic timescales of the investment necessary to close the performance gap(s)

- Operations needs to be proactive in securing regular discussions about markets and customers

- Bringing data to check opinion of what are relevant order-winners and qualifiers is essential and much of that information resides in operations

- Refining insight and understanding is a key factor in developing sound strategies and is essential for operations given the size and fixed nature of its investments

Introduction

Faced with the pressures of increasing competition, businesses need to coordinate the activities of their principal **functions** effectively in order to perform at their best in their chosen market(s). This involves developing a unified business strategy that embraces all parts of the organization. As a large function in most companies, and one that delivers the services and products sold to customers, operations has a key role in the development and implementation of strategy. This chapter will define strategy in relation to the organization and explore the levels within a business at which strategy must be developed and implemented, the relationship between strategic and **day-to-day tasks**, and the key step of understanding markets in the strategy development process. It will then go on to look at how operations can contribute to developing a successful strategy and the steps involved.

> **Functions** are the sub-divisions of an organization that together make up the total activities of a business unit, for example sales and marketing, operations and IT operational tasks.

> **Day-to-day tasks (or operational tasks)** involve managing and controlling the range of activities that fall within the function executive's area of responsibility as well as the crossovers between functions.

What is strategy?

Strategy embodies the aspects of both direction (what to do) and implementation (how to do it). The element of direction concerns the approaches a company can use to help it choose the markets (today and in the future) in which to compete, understand the competitive drivers in these markets while also assessing how it can influence its market position *vis-à-vis* its competitors. Implementation concerns how it can match or better meet the competitive drivers involved by prioritizing where and how to spend its time and money.

To help appreciate what this means it is useful to reflect on the meaning of the word itself. Derived from the Greek word *strategos* a general, from *stratos*, army and *aegin*, to lead, the origin of strategy concerned the art of planning and directing large military movements and operations of a campaign or war. The transfer of the word to business activities is understandable and appropriate, where the market becomes the theatre of competition.

The parallels don't stop there. The Greek general would also have divided his army into different units, for example archers, chariots and foot soldiers. As with functions in a business, this leads to specialist skills and capabilities being enhanced. But, the general also quickly found out that to win a battle it was much better if the different parts of his army faced the same direction and their roles and activities in battle were agreed and coordinated. The same parallels also transfer to business and the same need to interface the different aspects of strategy and ensure cooperation and coordination between the parts is one key to success.

Evolution of strategy within a business

As companies grow, they cope with the greater level of complexity that results by splitting the total business activity into parts that are called 'functions'. Similarly, further growth leads to companies separating the total, and increasingly diverse, activities that result into two or more **business units**, divisions or similar organizational arrangements to facilitate managing the increased diversity that comes with size. One outcome of these changes is that strategy development now takes place at three levels – corporate, business unit and functional (see Figure 2.1). The substance of this chapter concerns the development and implementation phases of one of the key functional strategies, that of operations. But first, let's look at the three levels of strategy.

Business units comprise the different parts of a whole organization, with each business unit serving a specific market or markets.

Levels of strategy

For most businesses, strategy needs to be developed at three levels (see Figure 2.1)

1. Corporate – concerns decisions by the business as a whole in terms of the sectors in which it wishes to compete. At this level, companies decide where to invest or **divest** in terms of the overall business mix they wish to develop today and in the future.

Divest – to sell all or part of a business.

2. Business unit – within each chosen sector, an organization will usually have, depending on the terminology used, one or more firms, companies or business units. Each will serve different segments within a sector, although there may be some overlap. Such overlaps could be for reasons of history, convenience, preference, to reflect customer wishes or failure to reach agreement within the overall business. Each business unit will need to develop a strategy in terms of its markets. Agreement on the current and future markets in which to compete is an essential strategic task and one in which all relevant functions must be involved. It is in these debates that functional differences need to be recognized and where resolution of strategic direction is taken. In that way, appropriate decisions on the markets in which to compete are taken at the business rather than functional level.

Figure 2.1 **Levels of strategy and their distinctive tasks**

Level of strategy	Distinctive tasks
Corporate	Strategic activity at the corporate level concerns the direction of the total business and addresses issues such as where to invest and/or divest, and priorities in terms of sales revenue growth. Implementation concerns the allocation of investment funds in line with these priorities.
Business unit	Business units comprise different parts of a total business. For example, corporate banking, retail banking, financial markets, mortgages, pensions and insurance would be separated into different business units within a bank. For each business unit, strategic direction concerns identifying the markets in which it competes, agreeing where it intends to grow (including new markets), the nature of competition and the relevant competitive criteria in its current and future markets, in terms of maintaining and growing share. Implementation concerns discussing and agreeing how and where to invest, in terms of functional tasks and alternative approaches.
Functional	Each business unit will comprise a number of functions such as sales and marketing, operations and IT that make up the total activities within a business unit. The strategic role of each function is to support those competitive dimensions within a market for which it is wholly or partly responsible. In this way, the market comprises the agenda for functional strategies and becomes the mechanism for determining development and investment priorities. Implementation concerns consistently meeting the competitive norms involved and selecting from alternative approaches to attain the improvement goals laid down.

3. **Functional** – functional strategies prioritize developments and investments in line with the needs of agreed current and future markets. Examples of those criteria relating to different functions are provided in Figure 2.2. The strategic task for a function is consistently to meet or improve its level of support for relevant performance criteria. These can either be the sole responsibility of a function (for example meeting the delivery speed requirements of customers is solely an operations management responsibility) or the joint responsibility of two or more functions (for example shortening service/ product development lead-times would be the joint responsibility of several functions such as design, marketing, engineering, IT and operations).

At this early stage in our discussion on operations strategy, it is useful also to distinguish between **market-driven** or **market-driving strategies**.

Figure 2.2 **Examples of functional strategic responsibilities**

Function	Examples of criteria for which it is solely responsible
Research and development	Product and service design[a]
IT	System developments
Marketing	Brand name, customer relationships and pricing
Operations	Delivery reliability, quality conformance, price (in terms of cost reduction) and delivery speed

Note: [a]In a service company the design function would typically form part of marketing's strategic responsibility.

Market-driven

Being market-driven concerns providing the competitive criteria in a market to the required levels, for example meeting the delivery lead-times that customers require or expect, such as keeping queue lengths in a bank to (say) three minutes or less.

Market-driving

On the other hand, market-driving concerns proactively seeking ways to change the competitive norms and hence create a situation where a company can influence its market position *vis-à-vis* its competitors. In this way, an organization can improve on current, required levels of a given driver to gain a competitive edge. The ways to do this can be either a market-based or a resource-based approach[1] as explained below and summarized in Figure 2.3.

- Market-based – here companies proactively identify where market advantage could be gained by outperforming the current norms on one or more relevant market drivers and then allocating resources to this end.

- Resource-based – continuing the theme of being more proactive in arriving at appropriate strategies has seen the emergence of resource-based competition. Again the emphasis is to be knowingly proactive in seeking ways to change the competitive norms for market advantage. The orientation here is to exploit the potential of existing resources and capabilities in order to outperform current norms on one or more competitive drivers. However, it is also essential to ensure that the competitive advantages that result by consciously looking to exploit existing resources or create **synergies** within the organization are, in fact, what customers need and are willing to pay for should additional costs be involved.

Market-driven strategies – aim to provide the criteria which enable it to compete in its chosen markets.

Market-driving strategies involve proactively seeking ways to change the competitive norms and hence create a situation where a company can influence its market position in relation to its competitors.

Synergies – the potential for actions or resources taken or used together to result in a greater outcome than the sum of the individual parts.

Figure 2.3 Market-driven and market-driving strategies

The strategic mix	Market-driven		Strategy based on understanding current and future markets and recognizing how the competitive drivers are time- and market-specific. Will differ depending on whether it concerns maintaining share, growing share or entering new markets
	Market-driving	market-based	Proactive approach to identify where advantage can be gained by outperforming current norms in one or more drivers and then investing in appropriate resources and capabilities
		resource-based	Exploit the potential of existing resources and capabilities to outperform current norms on one or more competitive drivers

The market-driven and market-driving strategic mix

For most companies their current and future markets will comprise a mix of both market-driven and market-driving strategies. Much of what a company sells, the customers it sells to, the markets in which it competes and how it competes within these today will be similar to yesterday and the same for tomorrow. But, being aware of the need to proactively seek ways to drive markets and exploit resource-based opportunities is an essential element of the strategic task in times when markets are increasingly different and competitive. For this reason, most companies will need to have a strategy that is a mix of the market-driven and market-driving approaches, as illustrated in Figure 2.3.

A recap on functional strategy development

At this point, let's pause and reflect. This chapter principally concerns the development of an operations strategy. As a key function within a business, one role of operations (as with other functions) is to contribute to meeting the objectives set by a business and, in so doing, needs to be party to their agreement in order to exploit available opportunities while recognizing the timescales and constraints involved. As Figure 2.6 shows, strategy development is an interactive process linking all parts of a business with one another and with the objectives set within a given period. And, core to this is the markets (recognizing the driven and driving dimensions referred to earlier) in which a company competes. Note that the separation of the operations strategy in Figure 2.6 from the other functional strategy elements is merely to reflect the orientation of this book. It is important to remember that what needs to dominate strategy development is the business itself and not one functional view. Similarly, the Walmart and Kmart illustrations in the next section are not intended to imply that emphasizing one functional strategy is better than emphasizing another but are provided to show the key roles of market understanding in giving direction and the implementation of functional strategies in bringing this about.

Operations strategy in action

To maintain profitable growth over time requires both sound direction and relevant functions providing support for the needs of agreed markets. Operations is increasingly and appropriately being recognized as a major, often dominant, player in determining and securing competitive advantage.

By comparing Walmart with its close rival Kmart in Case 2.1, we can show how a strategy may or may not work in practice.

The year 1962 saw the birth of two retailers in the highly competitive retail market in the USA. Both were discount stores that looked alike, sold the same products, sought the same customers and bore similar names – Kmart and Walmart. By the mid-1980s, Kmart was better positioned, with, twice the stores, three times the sales revenue and greater visibility through its advertising and large urban presence. In 1987, Joseph Antonini was brought in to head up Kmart and was heralded as having 'get up and go', and a sound plan for growth and profit improvement. Sam Walton, co-founder of Walmart and its CEO until his death in 1992, commented in his autobiography that in the mid-1980s so much about Kmart's stores was superior that at times it looked difficult to compete.

From 1962 to the late 1980s, Walmart had principally located outside small towns and was taking market share from ageing Mom & Pop outlets. Kmart, on the other hand, had competed against other large discount retailers in competitive and expensive urban locations. When Walmart decided to enter this arena, it did so on the back of its strategy to develop operations including extensive investments in sophisticated computer systems to help track

and replenish its merchandise quickly and efficiently. To prepare for the encounter, Antonini's strategic focus was on his own strengths marketing and merchandizing He invested heavily in nationwide television campaigns featuring glamorous television stars as presenters. Kmart's renewed emphasis on advertising and brand served to widen the gap between the two approaches. Kmart continued to be widely known through television, general advertising and its prime store locations. On the other hand, Sam Walton continued to concentrate investments and developments in operations. He invested tens of millions of dollars in a company-wide computer system linking cash registers to head office so enabling stores to quickly restock goods as they were sold. This, together with investments in trucks and distribution centres, not only increased control but also led to significant cost reduction. By the time Walmart's sales matched those of Kmart in 1991, its earnings before tax were more than double and since then the gap has widened (Figures 2.4 and 2.5).

So, Kmart relied heavily on a marketing-based strategy to improve its corporate image, reinforce the Kmart brand name and cultivate brand loyalty, while Walmart's strategy was oriented to operations as its source of advantage – cost reduction to effectively support a wide product range and an operations inventory, allocation and distribution system that kept the shelves filled with the right products. Before Walmart's 'invasion' of Kmart's urban-based territories, Kmart launched a five-year store refurbishmcnt and development initiative, with a budget of $3.5 billion – all part of a strategy to smarten the company's outward appearance. Although relatively few people had seen a Walmart advert let alone a store, the least visible parts of its operations-based strategy were, by the early 1990s, beginning to tell. Walmart's sophisticated scanner, distribution and inventory systems meant that shelves had the right stock and the price discount strategy could be supported by low-cost operations. Internal store procedures such as accurate price labelling meant that delays and customer concerns over the accuracy of the store systems and procedures were rare. Meanwhile, Kmart was filled with distribution horror stories. An internal company report highlighted major loopholes in its service delivery system; empty shelves, employees without the skills and training to plan and control inventory and an in-place replenishment system incapable of ensuring that the price on the shelf was the same as that stored in the cash registers – a problem which led to an out-of-court settlement of some $1 million relating to 72 instances of overcharging. Figures 2.4 and 2.5 show the results of the two strategies. Probably the most telling statistic is that whereas Kmart's share of the total market from 1982 to the mid-1990s fell from 34.5 to 22.7 per cent, Walmart's grew from 20.1 to 41.6 per cent in the same period. The ultimate statement of decline came in May 2003 when Kmart went into bankruptcy. Kmart's next president, Julian Day, then started to turn things around. Having led the company out of Chapter 11 Bankruptcy protection, he announced the first quarterly net profits in a long time – $276 million in the last quarter of 2003. In 2005, Kmart merged with Sears to form Sears Holdings.

Figure 2.4 **Sales revenue: Kmart and Walmart**

Year	Sales revenue ($bn)			
	Kmart		Walmart	
	$bn	Index	$bn	Index
1985	22.0	100	6.4	100
1988	27.3	124	16.0	250
1991	34.6	157	32.6	509
1995	32.5	148	82.5	1289
2000	37.0	168	165.0	2578
2002	30.3	137	217.8	3403
2006	53.0	241	308.9	4827
2008	43.3	197	373.8	5841
2010	46.8	213	405.0	6328
2011	n/a	n/a	421.8	6591

Notes: In 2005 Kmart was taken over by Sears Holdings.

n/a = not available

Figure 2.5 **Earnings before tax: Kmart and Walmart**

Year	Earnings before tax			
	Kmart		Walmart	
	$m	Index	$m	Index
1985	757	100	502	100
1988	1244	164	1069	213
1991	1301	172	2043	407
1992	1426	188	2554	509
1993	(306)	(40)	3166	631
1995	(313)	(41)	4262	849
1996	330	44	4346	866
1998	755	100	5641	1124
1999	959	127	7170	1428
2000	(370)	(49)	8715	1736
2001	(2725)	(460)	9957	1989
2002	(2900)	(483)	10568	2105
2008	184	24	22148	4412
2010	186	25	24052	4791

Note: Figures for 2006 onwards are for Sears Holdings, of which Kmart is now a part.

© Ermin Gutenberger

By giving careful thought to the processes of sourcing, logistics, pricing, inventory management and in-store presentation, profitability improved significantly.

Walmart's-sales now exceed the combined revenues of McDonald's, Coca-Cola and Walt Disney and it is the world's largest company by sales revenue. In the process, it has changed the face of global retailing. Sam Walton never claimed to be an original thinker but is quoted as saying:

People think we got big by putting big stores in small towns. Really we got big by replacing inventory with information.

By this he meant the retailing technology that Walmart pioneered: for example the company was first to share electronic point-of-sale (EPOS) information with its suppliers, thereby helping reduce inventory and cost.

In the early 1990s Walmart began its international expansion and by the new millennium was already the. biggest retailer in Canada and Mexico and had entered Brazil, Argentina, China, South Korea, Germany and the UK. By putting the customer as number 1 (for example the company's 'ten foot attitude' requires all employees coming within 10 feet of customers to look them in the eye, greet them and ask them if they need help), it has transformed the shopping experience for most customers. Couple this with its low-cost strategy based on highly efficient operations and distribution systems and it has developed the capability to dominate the retail market in several other parts of the world besides North America.

www.kmart.com
www.walmart.com

Questions

1. What is the key to Walmart's success to date?

2. Highlight the strategic role of operations in this success story.

Lecturers: visit www.palgrave.com/business/hillom3e for teaching guidelines for this case study

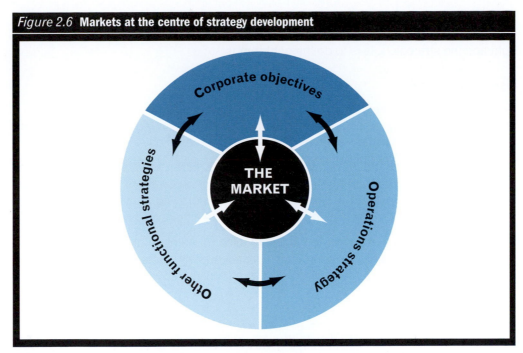

Figure 2.6 **Markets at the centre of strategy development**

Note: The phrase 'corporate objectives' here refers to the objectives set at the level of the business unit.

Executive roles – day-to-day and strategic tasks

As businesses grow, activities are separated out into clusters of similar tasks. These are then managed as functions, which provide a structure to handle the growing complexity that comes with larger organizations, including the opportunity for relevant staff to specialize in one part of the business.

Within each of these functions executives have two sets of tasks:

- Day-to-day – to manage and control the range of activities that fall within their area of responsibility as well as the crossovers between functions. Also known as the 'operational' task.

- **Strategic** – to develop a functional strategy in line with the needs of agreed markets.

The operational tasks that make up the day-to-day role within operations management are covered by the contents of the book. In simple terms this concerns managing and controlling those tasks necessary to provide services or make products and deliver them to customers. However, there is an equally essential role that concerns developing an operations strategy to support the needs of agreed markets and, although part of the same executive task, they are different in orientation. For operations management:

- The operational role is to manage and control the various, wide-ranging tasks involved in providing services and making products and to do this efficiently by bringing about developments and improvements.

- The strategic role is to contribute to the debate about and agreement on the markets in which to compete in terms of retaining customers, growing market share and entering new markets. This could involve a market-driven and market-driving perspective (see Figure 2.3). Operations then needs to develop and invest in the delivery systems and infrastructure to provide those competitive dimensions for which it is solely or jointly responsible, for example price and delivery speed. In this way, operational capabilities are guided by **strategic requirements** (the needs of agreed current and future markets) and so help provide competitive advantage.

Strategic tasks involve developing a functional strategy in line with those needs of the agreed markets for which that function is solely or jointly responsible.

Strategic requirements – refers to the order-winners and qualifiers of a market as a whole or customer(s) within a market.

Thus, while operational tasks are built on internal efficiency, strategic tasks need to be oriented to external effectiveness; or, put another way, the operational role is to do things right and the strategic role is to do the right things.

Use of resources

Undertaking either strategic or day-to-day tasks involves using key resources in terms of time (staff) and money (costs and investments). It is the reasoning behind decisions and the end goals that determine whether the use of resources is day-to-day or strategic:

- The use of resources is **day-to-day** if they are used to deliver services or make products, schedule customer requirements, record activities, monitor costs, supervise staff and manage the daily tasks of a business. Similarly, improving activities, procedures or systems to reduce costs by making these areas more efficient are also day-to-day tasks.

- The use of resources is **strategic** if they are used to maintain or improve a function's performance so that a service or product more adequately meets customer expectations or gives it an advantage over its competitors (and thereby influences a customer's decision to buy).

Let's look at an example of where the agenda involves using resources to reduce cost. The intent will be:

- **Day-to-day** if the benefits of the cost reduction are retained in the business and used to improve profits

- **Strategic** if the benefits of the cost reduction are passed on to customers in the form of a reduction in price.

Now we've looked at some of the issues that affect strategy on a functional level, let's move on to look at strategy across a business unit.

> ### EXECUTIVE INSIGHT
> The use of key resources can be either day-to-day or strategic in orientation depending on the:
> - Agenda – for which aspect of the day-to-day or strategic tasks are the resources to be used?
> - Intent – are the resources being used to maintain or improve efficiency (the day-to-day task) or to maintain or improve competitiveness (the strategic task)?

Business unit strategy

Functional strategies are an integral part of a business unit and, in that way, the two levels of strategy need to interface. While this chapter concerns developing an operations strategy, before addressing this let us first look at how a business unit strategy should be developed compared to how it often is in practice.

As discussed earlier, organizations use functions in order to facilitate the management task involved. However, businesses are not a number of different parts or functions, but are wholes. An essential task, therefore, is to rebuild the parts back into a whole and nowhere is this more critical than at the strategic level within a firm. Also, as Figure 2.7 illustrates, the heads of functions will appropriately form part of the strategy development group as these parts form the whole business.

Discussion and agreement about current and future markets have already been highlighted as an integral part of strategy development. This step requires functions to discuss their views on markets, address and resolve differences and agree on what is best for the business overall. Similarly, the outcomes of this debate would be major inputs into developing a strategy at the business unit level, with the desired process being in line with that outlined in Figure 2.8. Functions would debate current and future markets, and highlight constraints and opportunities as part of their input into developing a strategy for the firm while again providing both a market-driven and market-driving orientation. Similarly, opportunities and strategic initiatives would be signalled at the business unit level and form part of the essential debate and strategic outcome.

Figure 2.7 **Strategic group composition**

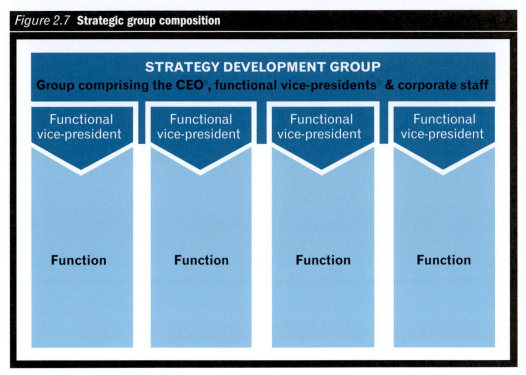

Notes: [a]CEO means corporate executive officer, also known as 'managing director'. [b] Vice-president is the term for the head of a function and is also known as 'director'.

Figure 2.8 **Ideal business unit strategy-making process**

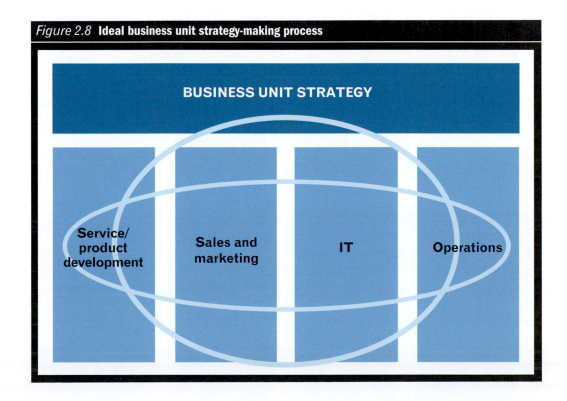

Reality is far from this. 'In many firms, business unit strategy is developed as a series of independent statements. Lacking essential integration, the result is a compilation of distinct, functional strategies that sit side by side, layer on layer in the same corporate binder. Integration is not provided if, in fact, it was ever intended.'[2] The outcome, rather than being similar to that represented by Figure 2.8 is more like that shown in Figure 2.9.

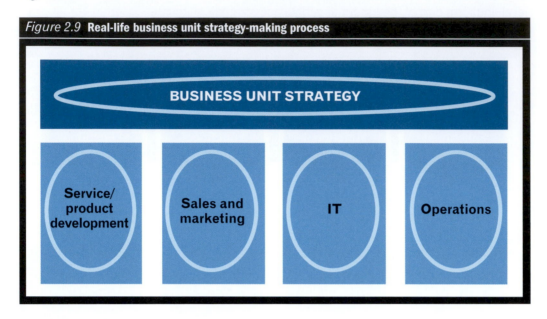

Figure 2.9 Real-life business unit strategy-making process

Reasons for current approaches to developing strategy

If the reality of strategy development is so divorced from the essential integrated nature of the task, the question which at once comes to mind is, why? There are several reasons and the key ones are summarized below.

Statements on strategy developments stop at the interface

Statements put forward by academics, consultants and other strategy specialists on how companies should go about developing a strategy allude to integration but in reality ignore this essential step. They stop at the interface. For example, a review of major textbooks and articles on both corporate strategy and marketing strategy would show that they fail to embrace the dimension of operations. Whether it would inhibit the approaches and arguments put forward, make it too complex to describe and explain or signal an implicit belief that delivering strategy is not an integral part of its development, the reality is that the essential interfacing central to Figure 2.8 is never aspired to, let alone delivered, in most approaches to corporate and marketing strategy development.

The pursuit of generic strategies

The problem outlined in the last point is made worse, however, when companies seek to resolve strategic approaches by reviewing business units as wholes, typically undertaken by overlaying corporate diversity with generic, strategic solutions. Niche, low-cost, core competence-type arguments are seductive in their apparent offerings.[3] The promise of uniformity is appealing to those with the task of developing strategies for businesses that are typified by difference and not similarity, as such approaches purport to identify a corporate similarity which, although desirable, is inherently not available.[4] What seems to drive the logic of this approach to strategy is, in part, similar to that which sparked the alchemist's dream of turning base metal into gold – that of finding the key that will unlock the strategic maze.

However, nothing could be further from the truth. Strategy problems are complex and the process of resolution is not provided by generalizations. Strategy development needs to be a process of distillation, with the task of identifying the very essence of what comprises a business. As competitive pressures grow, markets become increasingly different, not increasingly similar. Without adequate insight companies will be unable to decide the appropriate strategic direction. The overarching view of markets provided by generic strategies is typically reinforced by subsequent actions such as measuring actual sales in total and not by market and segment type. Such reaggregations reinforce the classic view of similarity that characterizes strategy by implying that one dollar of sales is the same as any other dollar of sales.

Strategy outcomes assume a similarity that does not exist

Markets are increasingly different not increasingly similar. However, when companies debate markets the outcomes assume a similarity that does not exist. The aim of the first phase in strategy is to reach agreement about the markets in which a business unit competes or wishes to compete. The key to this is to identify, test and reach agreement on the several markets in which a business unit competes or wishes to compete in the future.

The drift to generic strategies was highlighted in the last point. Side by side with this is the tendency for companies to assume a level of similarity within their business that, in fact, is not present. Business units are typically in more markets than they assume. This lack of insight exists because of an inadequate debate about markets, and a failure to seek to identify potential differences. In part this is due to executives allocating too little time to what should be an ongoing, in-depth, business-wide discussion. Furthermore, the role model followed in strategy discussion has not sought to clarify difference. The outcome is that this critical first step results in a lack of essential insights into the differences that increasingly make up a company's markets.

The extent of this corporate confusion was clearly illustrated by the outcomes of an extensive, case-based research programme that comprised in-depth reviews and data analyses within 54 of the 160 participating companies. These businesses were all part of a UK government initiative called the Manufacturing Planning and Implementation Scheme. The essence of the scheme was to help companies understand and apply the different phases in developing an operations strategy and then to use these outputs to set and implement priorities in terms of development and investment. To help provide resources to undertake this work, companies were given government grants of 50 per cent of the consultancy fees involved, up to a given maximum. To provide clarity on the context and purpose of the approach embodied in the scheme, guidelines on the intent and an in-depth statement on what to do was also given and further supplemented by forums, individual guidance and feedback on the initial results part way through the scheme.

To evaluate what happened in practice a team of researchers, led by the authors of this book, had access to all details within any application. Of the 54 in-depth reviews completed, in only one project was the market review sufficiently adequate to provide the insights necessary to develop an operations strategy. Typical of the outcomes was the following example.[5] The market review undertaken on a medium-sized food company failed to identify any differences within its markets and reported them to be homogeneous. Work by the research team with company executives and using customer data identified and agreed four segments with differing levels of price sensitivity and different delivery lead-time requirements, as shown in Figure 2.10. Research in the service sector has resulted in similar findings. The Cool2Serve programme also found that most companies do not reach agreement on the segments they serve and the competitive drivers involved.[6]

'Strategy concerns **direction** and **co-ordination**'

Figure 2.10 **Result of researchers' market review**

Note: The position of companies on these two continuums is intended to illustrate the degree of difference, one to the others.

Competitive factors – factors such as price, delivery speed, delivery reliability and specification which will influence the purchases customers make.

History of functional dominance

Approaches to developing corporate strategy have a history of being dominated by single functions. In many manufacturing companies, for example, the operations function dominated the corporate strategy process until about the mid-1960s. In a world where, up to that time, there was an undercapacity in relation to demand, selling what you could make was typically the dominant thrust of strategy. As the capacity/demand imbalance redressed itself, selling into markets became more difficult and heralded the birth of marketing's key role in the success of companies. This strategic role has, in many companies, been strengthened with the continued growth in competition, especially where markets are increasingly characterized by overcapacity as emerging nations develop or companies enter existing markets in which they currently do not compete. As with operations before, marketing has acquired the mantle of providing strategic direction not only in its own eyes but typically in the eyes of others and the firm as a whole. The outcome is that much of the time marketing's view goes undiscussed and unchallenged.

Markets versus marketing

Coupled with the last point is the fact that many firms fail to make the critical distinction between markets and marketing. Whereas markets comprise the business itself, marketing is a function. Thus, while marketing will play a necessary role in the debate and agreement about markets, it is critical that its views of market needs are countered, challenged and enlarged, or changed where necessary. For, while its insights are essential to the understanding of markets, they are limited in the perspective they offer on two counts:

1. The reality of delivering the needs of markets is only fully understood by those functions charged with undertaking those tasks. While marketing has the responsibility for meeting several of these criteria, there are many that are in the domain of others. In fact in some, if not many, instances, marketing's strategic role is limited, in that other functions are responsible for supporting most, if not all, of the needs of a company's chosen markets.

2. The constraints, timescales and investment implications involved in maintaining or improving support for those performance criteria that relate to market success can only be gauged and assessed by the function involved in that provision.

Not recognizing these essential differences and not incorporating all relevant perspectives within the strategy debate will only lead to inadequate and superficial outcomes.

The proactive role of marketing in strategy development

One consequence of the last two points is that marketing expects to, is expected to and does take a proactive role in strategy development. While this is the desired stance to be adopted by all relevant functions, many organizations, in acknowledging and supporting marketing's proactive role, fail to recognize the need to incorporate other perspectives essential to the discussion and agreement on markets and strategic direction. The proactive stance adopted by marketing is seen as an implicit (if not explicit) statement that markets and marketing are one and the same and that marketing has a singular role in these essential strategy decisions that are central to the business as a whole.

The reactive role of operations in strategy development

The fact that the operations function has an exacting and critical corporate role to play is never in dispute. Couple this with the high cost and fixed nature (changes take a long time to bring about) of its investments, then it is paramount for a company to understand the business trade-offs involved in operations decisions. As operations is a principal player in providing those criteria that maintain and improve market share and successfully allow the company to enter new markets, then not knowing how operations will ensure the provision of that support is risk-taking of the highest order, especially given the highly competitive and fast-changing nature of today's markets and the fixed and high-cost dimensions involved in development and investment.

Reasons for reactive role of operations in strategy development

Given this scenario, why is it that operations executives typically adopt a current reactive role in strategy development and why does the situation appear not to improve? There are several reasons, including those listed below.

Operations managers' view of themselves

A major contribution to this current position is that operations managers also see themselves holding a reactive business brief. They believe that their role concerns a requirement to react as well as possible to all that is asked of the operations delivery system. They see their role as the exercise of skill and experience in effectively coping with the exacting and varying demands placed on the system and to reconcile the trade-offs as best they can. But rarely do they explain or provide data to illustrate the relative size and impact of these trade-offs as part of the business strategy debate. As a result these decisions are consequently and inappropriately made at the level of the operations function rather than the level of the business.

The company's view of the operations manager's role

The view held by operations of its own role is reinforced by the company's view of its strategic contribution. Although chief executive officers (CEOs), managing directors or their equivalents are actively (and appropriately) engaged in discussions with marketing about decisions on markets and customers, the same level of time investment is typically not given to understanding key operations decisions and their impact on market support. A lack of recognition is thereby reflected in the typically low level of involvement that results.

Too late in the corporate debate

Very often operations executives are not involved in business unit strategy discussions until the decisions have started to take shape, so they have less opportunity to contribute to decisions on strategy alternatives. Consequently they may complain about the unrealistic demands made of them and the problems that invariably will ensue.

Lack of language

Underpinning these organizational barriers is the added difficulty that, on the whole, operations managers do not have a history of explaining their function clearly and effectively to others within the company. This is particularly so for any strategy issues that need to be considered and the operations consequences that will arise from the corporate decisions under discussion. Reasons for this failure, however, cannot wholly be placed at the operations executive's door. The knowledge base, concepts and language so essential to providing operations' perspectives and insights have not been developed in the same way. Surrogates for operations strategy in the form of panaceas have more often than not taken the place of strategic inputs, and the support given to these approaches by academics and consultants has reinforced this stance. For example, the regular heralding of just-in-time (JIT), lean operations and total quality management (TQM)-type initiatives (explained more fully in Chapters 10 and 11 respectively) have been seen, in part at least, as the strategic contribution of operations. In a similar way, calls to become flexible, for instance, point to an apparent state in operations that offers a capability to do most (if not all) things. Purposefully general, such overtures as these are without essential definition and direction and, more importantly, purport to offer the rest of the business an operations' capability to support any strategic alternative equally well and without involving any trade-offs. Furthermore, when the superficiality of this state is exposed, the pundits for such strategic alternatives merely switch the phrase (to become versatile and agile are two such), arguing that the subtle differences in definition remedy the serious misgivings inherent in the discarded phrase. The cycle then restarts.

For many businesses, strategy comprises the independent inputs of different functions. However, this invariably leads to functional conflicts that, without a way of being resolved, will result in inappropriate business decisions being taken. Where this concerns process and/or infrastructure investments, it involves two important characteristics. These investments are large in size and fixed in nature. Consequently, they typically take a long time to determine and install, and a long time to change. Thus, it is essential that companies understand the relevance of any proposed investments in terms of their current and future markets.

The need to recognize difference at the level of strategy formulation

Any executive being asked 'Are all your businesses the same?' or 'Are all parts of one business the same?' would answer 'no' to both questions. Strategy formulation must acknowledge that reality. To describe a company's strategy as having a uniform approach ignores the essential difference that characterizes today's markets.

In the same way, as markets are different, the strategic response by functions needs to recognize and reflect those differences, and none more so than in operations, with its large and fixed investments.

Developing a functional strategy involves deciding on development and investment priorities that are, in turn, determined by those market needs for which the function is solely or jointly responsible. The book addresses two sets of different but related issues:

1. How does operations management contribute to the business strategy debate in such a way that
   • its perspectives are understood
   • the needs of the different markets in which a company competes are exposed and agreed
   • the investments to develop and the performance criteria to measure those operations capabilities necessary to support the needs of current and future markets are clearly identified.

2. To illustrate the different implementation approaches at the operational (or day-to-day) level within operations so that appropriate consideration can be given to alternatives, both in terms of market support (doing the right things) and internal efficiency (doing things right).

This chapter outlines the approach to developing strategic direction within operations.[7] The rest of the book details the alternative implementation approaches that may be used at the operational level. Which ones are best for a company will depend upon the nature of the business itself, factors such as size and service/product complexity and the requirements of the markets in which a firm competes. It is necessary, therefore, to review the options detailed in each of the following chapters, both in terms of themselves and also within the context of the strategic trade-offs that have to be made.

Finally, most parts of a business have an impact on one another. Operations investments are substantial (typically 60–70 per cent of the business total) and embody a set of fixed trade-offs that will remain constant unless deliberately changed. The competitive dimensions that operations can support will be reflected in the trade-offs embodied in its investments. What operations can do well and less well needs to be clearly recognized as it will impair its level of support in different markets and will signal the desired changes in trade-offs that future investments must provide. Similarly, in its market-driving role, operations needs to clearly explain and communicate ways in which its resources and capabilities (either within the operations function or in conjunction with other functions) can provide competitive advantage and the investment and timescales involved to bring this about.

Similarly, marketing has an impact upon operations. Its decisions make demands upon delivery systems, processes and infrastructure provision. Incremental change, so often the way in which a company's markets move, often results in a gradual and increasing mismatch between the demands on the operations function and its ability to respond. While operations managers intuitively recognize the consequences of these changes, they typically do not have, as highlighted earlier, the concepts and language to argue their case and alert the company to such issues of strategic importance. The result is frustration and an ever-widening gap between the marketing and operations functions even though they are both essential contributors to the business, its strategy formulation and overall success.

This chapter addresses the need to close the gap by providing approaches to strategy building that bring together marketing and operations, facilitate open discussion about the business and enable sensible resolution of functional differences at the business level.

Linking marketing and operations

The importance of linking marketing and operations is as paramount as it is logical. They are, after all, two sides of the same coin. Together, they constitute the basic task in any business – the sale and delivery of services and products. On the surface it would seem simple to unite their efforts to meet the needs and expectations of customers. The reality is often far removed from what should be the desired goal of those involved.

Many current strategy approaches reinforce business misunderstanding and promote interfunctional differences and rivalry. Functional dominance in business strategy development is a typical source of such problems. The result is that key functions tend 'to treat one another as competitors for resources rather than coming together to serve the external customers'.[8] This is well illustrated by Figure 2.11 that lists the different, often opposing, views held by operations and marketing on a range of issues. In markets that are increasingly competitive, there is an urgent need to close the gap, increase business awareness of the differences and difficulties involved in the status quo and facilitate discussion based on an improved understanding of functional perspectives, business options and overall consequences. The way forward is to resolve interfunctional differences not at the level of the function, as is often the case now, but at the level of the business. These genuine conflicts need to be addressed and resolved in terms of what is best for the business as a whole. In that way the tensions, concerns and rivalries that typically characterize the marketing/operations relationship can be set to one side. The focus can then shift from competing functional views about what is best overall, to each function doing its part to implement the chosen strategy.

The question is how? Before addressing this issue, however, Cases 2.2–2.4 illustrate how the link has been established and the successful outcomes that result.

Figure 2.11 **Operations and marketing perspectives on key issues**			
Issues		**Perspectives and goals**	
		Operations	**Sales and marketing**
Services/ products	Range	Restricting range enhances volumes, helps reduce cost and simplifies control	Customers typically seek variety. Restricting range reduces segment coverage and sales revenues
	Standardization versus customization	Lack of change reduces uncertainty and room for error. Limiting server discretion (see Chapter 1) maintains cost and throughput targets	Customization is often important, particularly in mature markets. Server discretion personalizes service, often at little cost, and enhances customer retention
Costs and profit		Measured on meeting cost budgets. Resists orders that increase costs. Has no control over pricing	Sales revenue is the key performance measure. Profit implications are not part of the decision or evaluation. Higher costs are not part of its budget considerations
Productivity improvements		Reduce unit costs	May cause a decline in the provision of quality conformance
Location of facilities		Considerations relate to costs and the convenience for suppliers and staff	Customers may find it unattractive, undesirable and, for a service business, inaccessible
Managing capacity		High utilization of capacity has an effect on costs and assets. Pressure to manage capacity and thereby keep investment as low as possible	Service/product may be unavailable when needed. Quality compromised in high demand periods
Job design		Oriented to minimizing errors and waste. Simplify tasks and use technology where possible	Employees are oriented to operations task and not customer need. Restricts the ability to meet changing requirements as they occur
Queues		Optimize the use of available capacity by planning for average throughput	Increases customer lead-times. Customers facing long lead-times or queues may go elsewhere

The advent of the warehouse model for distributing food and dry goods provides a good example of companies competing on a **price leadership strategy**.

Aldi, the German-based food chain, provides an example of how this has been successful as the company has supported its chosen price leadership strategy with a clear integration of marketing and operations that co-operate rather than compete in providing this strategy. The basis of Aldi's retail offering is a no-fuss concept. The design is simple, making it easy to shop. Wide gangways, bare floors, inexpensive lighting (basic, bright and abundant), basic displays (often displayed in the manufacturer's original packaging), comprising warehouse-style racking and sturdy wire mesh cages, and limited support staff keep costs down. Of the product range on offer, Aldi keeps a limited (typically about 25 per cent of the range offered by traditional supermarket competitors), mainly an own-label range of goods.

IKEA, the Swedish firm that specializes in complete furnishings for the home from floor coverings and curtains to tables, chairs, bookcases and bedroom suites, provides a further example. In essence, IKEA is a chain of self-service warehouses with 2010 revenues of about $23 billion. Operations is clearly linked to the price leadership strategy of the business and delivers a no-fuss, broad and easy-to-take-away range of products. The provision of play areas and restaurant facilities as part of the service delivery system reflects and encourages the concept of the family-based shopping expedition that characterizes these outlets.

www.aldi.com
www.ikea.com

> **Price leadership strategy** – strategy employed by organizations to compete principally on the basis of offering the lowest price in the market.

Lecturers: visit www.palgrave.com/business/hillom3e for teaching guidelines for this case study

Photo: Benetton Group

Benetton is perhaps the most widely known brand in the world in the segment of Italian affordable fashion. After the death of his father at the end of the Second World War, Luciano Benetton first worked in a clothing store in Ponzano Veneto (a small town 30 km north of Venice) and then started a small business with his younger brothers Carlo and Gilberto and sister Giuliana, producing sweaters in bright, unconventional colours and selling them door to door. In 1965 they formed the Benetton Group. Three years later, the first innovative store (using the same room for displaying, selling and stocking the products, with a wide range of bright colours and affordable prices) was opened in Belluno, Italy, and soon the group opened its doors in other major European cities. Today, Benetton sales originate from 6,300 shops in over 120 countries.

INNOVATION AND OPERATIONS PROCESSES

Creativity and innovation are strongly emphasized with the help of 300 designers coming from several countries and travelling around the world in search of ideas and trends. In 2010 (as with most years) about 1.5 per cent of sales revenue went into researching and developing new materials (for example, very light cashmere at affordable prices), spinning, weaving and dyeing technologies and computer-aided design techniques, occasionally in partnership with multi-national companies and universities.

Up until the early 2000s, Benetton's retail was entirely based upon a licensor-licensee relationship channelled through more than 80 agents who were paid a commission of around 4 per cent of total sales in their region, supervised by seven area managers. The store owners entered agreements with agents, without any written contract with Benetton. No licence fee or royalty was paid by franchisees, but they were committed to stocking and selling only items supplied by Benetton, which operated on a no-return basis upon orders from agents about eight months in advance.

This system became increasingly unsuitable to manage the changing 'fast fashion' trend, very popular among young generations who were better served by competitors such as Zara and H&M, which owned their shops and offered up-to-date designs at affordable prices with up to 12 different collections a year (compared with the two collections offered by Benetton) at comparably higher prices. Franchisees became increasingly unhappy about their earnings, and Benetton felt a decline in margins and profitability. As a result, from the early 2000s, Benetton took a new market approach to the core wholesale business, introducing directly operated stores.

THE SUPPLY CHAIN
To further adapt to the fast-changing nature of its markets, Benetton moved in 2003 to a much more flexible 'dual supply chain', aimed at ensuring an almost continuous collection of new designs with fast adaptation to changing market trends. Key to their success is the short time to market for new styles and the quick delivery in response to high sales. One (sequential) chain from design, to research and development, to operations, to sales is matched by the other (integrated) chain, which

maximizes the speed of coordinated inter-connections between these basic stages of the production and distribution process.

Five kinds of collections stretch from an extreme of six to eight months before the season to the other extreme of one to two weeks before it. These fast feedback, short operations lead-times and quick deliveries better met market needs while cutting inventory and asset investments.

MANUFACTURING
The production of garments takes place in ten factories located in Italy and nine others across Europe and Asia. These operate both with vertically integrated processes and through outsourcing labour-intensive tasks (such as stitching, finishing and ironing), while more critical tasks (like cutting, weaving, dyeing, quality control and logistics) are kept within the company's own factories. Outsourcing includes many Central Eastern European suppliers and more recently directed to over 200 contracting and subcontracting Asian suppliers from China, India and East Asian countries such as Thailand and Laos. Today, about 50 per cent of production is carried out by third-party suppliers. Wool, cotton and other raw materials are purchased from some 180 suppliers worldwide.

MODERN OPERATIONS FACILITIES
Logistics has traditionally been a crucial function within Benetton's approach to production and distribution planning. A fully robotized logistics centre in Castrette (Italy), with an electromagnetic propulsion system for moving pallets, has been built on a 30,000 square metre site. The plant has a total capacity of 800,000 boxes (in which materials, part garments and completed garments are moved through the manufacturing process) and is able to handle 120,000 incoming and outgoing boxes a day, operated by just 28 staff. This centre works with two hubs in Shenzehn and Mexico City, for the Asian and American markets, respectively.
www.benetton.com

> **Operations lead-times** – the time taken by operations to provide a service or make a product.

Lecturers: visit www.palgrave.com/business/hillom3e for teaching guidelines for this case study

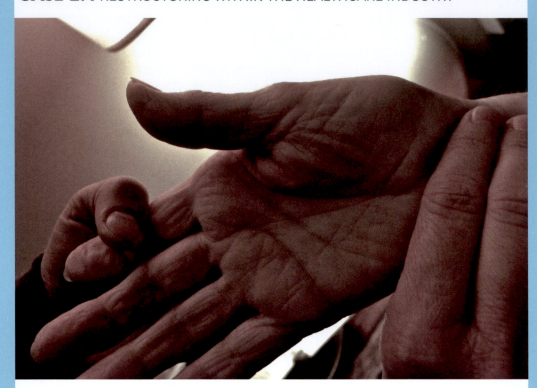

Restructuring within the healthcare industry grew apace in the 1990s, with worldwide annual mergers and acquisitions. However, delivering the potential is proving harder to bring about. Those that have are looking to change the delivery of care and the operations support involved.

Quantum Health Resources, an Indianapolis-based firm specializing in the treatment of haemophiliacs, reduced by over 20 per cent the typical annual patient bill of $100,000 by assigning 'personal care managers'. In this way drugs are now managed, hospitalization due to lack of personal care is cut and drug regimes are under constant review, improving fit and eliminating waste.

ParadigmHealth is a California-based company specializing in caring for people with catastrophic injuries such as brain damage and serious burns. Annual patient care costs can run as high as $2 million but this has been cut by half through specializing support for patients, treating more people at home and assigning support teams to sets of patients, thereby improving operational support and lowering costs.

The growing need to control and reduce the operational costs of delivering healthcare has led, in the USA, to a spurt of vertical integration by insurance companies moving into the management of hospitals and health clinics. In that way, they recognize that the essential need to link sales and operations can be made, enabling the business to grow, deliver a better service and become more profitable.

www.gentiva.com

Questions

Review the three cases above and consider the following questions:

1. Identify the key way in which operations supports each company's markets.

2. Now compare your three reviews and table the similarities and differences involved.

Lecturers: visit www.palgrave.com/business/hillom3e for teaching guidelines for this case study

Linking business objectives and functional strategies through markets

Functional strategies concern investing and developing in ways that support the needs of markets in terms of being both market-driven and market-driving. As Figure 2.6 showed earlier, the role of functional strategies is to contribute to meeting agreed business objectives. The form and size of contribution will vary from market to market but the strategic development process for all functions is similar:

- **Phase 1 – understand markets** and ensure both a market-driven and market-driving approach while maintaining an ongoing, rigorous review throughout this first critical step.

- **Phase 2 – translate** these reviews into strategic tasks. For example, if price is a competitive driver, then the task is to reduce costs; similarly if on-time delivery is a competitive factor, then improving the reliability of meeting customer due dates is the task.

- **Phase 3 – check** that what is currently provided matches what is required in a market-driven scenario or the new level in a market-driving scenario.

- **Phase 4 – develop a strategy** (the prioritizing of investments and developments) to close the gap where the level of provision falls short of the requirement or achieve the new level of performance in a market-driving scenario.

- **Phase 5 – implement** the necessary investment and development priorities.

In this way, companies are better able to coordinate functional contributions, with markets appropriately providing the common agenda for all. Invariably, two functions that are central to this task are operations and marketing, as the next section reflects.

The framework given in Figure 2.12 is intended to help explain what currently happens as well as what needs to take place so that the link between corporate marketing decisions and operations can be made. The figure shows that the framework has five columns, each representing a step.

> **EXECUTIVE INSIGHT**
> Sound strategy requires:
> - All functions to be involved
> - Frequent and regular discussion
> - Individual functional performance measures to be set in a business context.

Column 3 concerns analyzing and understanding the market and is at the centre of the framework. In Figure 2.13 the arrow going from left to right represents the need to link objectives and marketing strategy to the market, while the one going from right to left represents the need to link operations strategy to the market. In this way, how a company competes in its markets and how it may wish to drive the market is at the centre of the debate. This allows functions to discuss current and future markets, how competitors behave and their potential responses in the future, alternative ways of competing in these, the constraints, developments, investments and timescales involved and how they can coordinate their strategic efforts to meet the agreed objectives for the business as a whole. As Figure 2.13 illustrates, this is an interactive approach and reeds to be an ongoing process forming an integral part of the senior executives' role.

How the framework operates

The objective of using the framework in Figure 2.12 is to develop an operations strategy for a business. The steps involved are outlined below. Although presented here in a sequential form they will, in fact, constitute an ongoing set of discussions, with statements and

Figure 2.12 **Framework for reflecting operations strategy issues in corporate decisions**

CORPORATE OBJECTIVES	MARKETING STRATEGY	HOW DO YOU QUALIFY AND WIN ORDERS IN THE MARKETPLACE?	OPERATIONS STRATEGY	
			Delivery system choice	Infrastructure choice
Sales revenue growth	Product/service markets and segments	Price	Choice of various delivery systems	Function support
Survival	Range	Quality conformance	Trade-offs embodied in these choices	Operations planning and control systems
Profit	Mix	Delivery: speed reliability	Make-or-buy decisions	Quality assurance and control
Return on investment	Volumes	Demand increases	Capacity: size timing location	Systems engineering
Other financial measures	Standardization versus customization	Colour range	Role of inventory in the delivery system	Clerical procedures
Environmental targets	Level of innovation	Product/service range		Payment systems
	Leader versus follower alternatives	Design leadership		Work structuring
		Technical support		Organizational structure
		Brand name		
		New products and services – time to market		

Notes:
1. The bullet point entries in each column are to provide examples and are not intended to be a definitive list
2. Although the steps to be followed are given as finite points in a stated procedure, in reality the process will involve statement and restatement, for several of these aspects will impinge on each other.
3. Column 3 concerns identifying both the relevant order-winners and qualifiers.

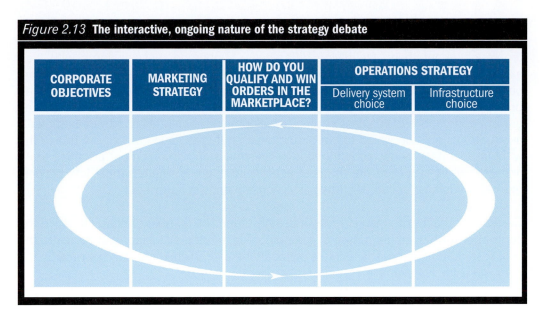

Figure 2.13 The interactive, ongoing nature of the strategy debate

CORPORATE OBJECTIVES	MARKETING STRATEGY	HOW DO YOU QUALIFY AND WIN ORDERS IN THE MARKETPLACE?	OPERATIONS STRATEGY	
			Delivery system choice	Infrastructure choice

restatements of corporate or business objectives and functional strategies comprising the outcome of the process.

1. **Corporate objectives** – these are set by the business as a whole and typically take the form of targets for sales revenue growth, profit, return on investment, social responsibility and other financial measures. They may well include non-financial objectives such as environmental targets.

2. **Marketing strategy** – developed by the marketing function to meet relevant corporate business objectives. It would typically be concerned with approaches to growing sales in existing markets and strategies to enter new markets.

3. **How do services and products qualify and win orders in the marketplace?** Addressing this question constitutes the core step in the development of functional strategies, where the executive group (see Figure 2.7) debates and agrees markets (to include both the market-driven and market-driving dimensions) and the qualifiers and order-winners involved. This step will be expanded on in the next sections.

4. **Operations strategy: choice of delivery system** – part of the strategic task of operations is to develop a delivery system to provide the services and products involved, as well as underpinning the qualifiers and order-winners (for example price, quality conformance and on-time delivery) that form part of the sale.

5. **Operations strategy: choice of infrastructure** – operations' other strategic task is to develop the relevant aspect of infrastructure (for example organizational structure, procedures and controls) that form part of the way it meets the qualifiers and order-winners for which it is responsible.

Understanding markets – the reality

Let us start by restating the important distinction made earlier in the chapter. Markets and marketing are not the same thing. Whereas markets constitute the business itself, marketing is a function. As there will typically be several markets served by a business, the relevant criteria to keep and grow existing market share, change the rules (become market-driving) and enter new markets will differ from market to market as well as from each other. The strategic role of functions (including marketing and operations) is to debate and agree the markets in which to compete, the qualifiers and order-winners involved and support those criteria for which they are solely or jointly responsible. In this way, the company becomes market- (as opposed to marketing-) driven.

The cornerstone in all of this is understanding markets. Markets are the essence of a business, the very reason for its existence and, consequently, you can never know too much about them. Identifying differences, supporting these insights with clear explanations and descriptions and verifying them with supporting data would, therefore, be reasonable to expect. The reality is, however, that the necessary clarity is usually not provided. The case examples given earlier are the exception rather than the rule. Instead, current approaches to business strategy development typically fail to provide sufficiently adequate insights on which to build functional strategies. One outcome of this is that without adequate clarity, each function's investment and development priorities are in line with what they think are the best aspects to improve. The essential link between market needs and functional strategies is consequently not provided.

Current approaches to market reviews usually embody a number of characteristics that contribute to the general nature of the outcomes and the provision of statements that lack essential meaning. The result is descriptions of markets that imply a similarity that does not exist. For example:

- Markets are usually only looked at and described from a marketing point of view. Segment descriptions are typically based on factors such as geographical regions (for example, Europe and North America) and sectors in which customers operate (for example, food and financial services) or service/product clusters. While this has a sound rationale from a sales and marketing viewpoint in terms, for instance, of arranging promotional and sales activities and the orientation of technical literature and support, the assumption is carried forward (as it is implied) that such segments are each coherent in terms of the way a company needs to compete. A pause for reflection will lead to a recognition that this is both an unreal and inaccurate inference to draw. Although from the viewpoint of marketing, Europe/North America or food/financial services, for example, are coherent segments, from an operations point of view there will be different sets of demands from groups of customers within these marketing segments and hence these will constitute different markets. Case 2.5 illustrates this point.

- Views of markets are positioned at too high a level in the strategy process. As emphasized throughout, with growing competition markets are becoming increasingly different rather than increasingly similar as competitors seek to gain customers by changing the offering. The only way to uncover this essential difference is to dig deep. Current approaches fail to do this and result in statements about markets that are broadbrush in nature and inadequate in terms of the insights they provide.

- The inadequacy of the outputs that result is further compounded by a use of general phrases to provide market descriptions. Words and phrases such as 'customer service' and 'quality' are examples of this. Each can be defined in more than one way, and once there is more than one meaning, misunderstanding and a failure to clarify will follow. The result is that general descriptions are used in analyzing markets that in themselves embody more than one segment. One dimension compounds the other, with the result that generalities mask critical and essential insights and necessary clarity is replaced by unhelpful ambiguity (see Case 2.5).

The result is that the key, first step of clarifying and agreeing markets, the basis on which to link business direction and relevant functional support, is not provided. As a consequence, the failure to coordinate strategic direction continues, interfunctional rivalries are reinforced and the approaches used to develop business strategy do not deliver the very essence of what is required or intended.

Given the increasingly dynamic, competitive and fast-changing nature of markets, it is of paramount importance that companies improve the way they develop business strategy and particularly the need to forge the link between marketing and operations.

CASE 2.5 CUSTOMER SEGMENTATION IN THE ELECTRICITY INDUSTRY

A major UK electricity distributor segmented its customers into large businesses, small and medium-sized enterprises (SMEs) and residential customers. The basis for the segmentation was the relative size of sales revenue per customer account. The initial marketing strategy was to grow sales revenue and, as a consequence, its efforts were directed towards increasing its large business customer portfolio as the best way of meeting this objective. However, a noticeable decline in profits as a percentage of sales followed and led to a review. Operations data revealed that profit margins in the large business segment were, on average, more than 40 per cent lower than for SME customers. Marketing's successful drive to increase sales revenue had also led to a

lack of effort to retain, let alone grow, SME customers. The outcome was an increase in overall sales revenue but a decrease in profit percentages. The marketing-led strategy had pursued below-average sales revenue growth.

Questions

1. List side by side the market dimensions used by marketing and operations above.

2. How would you use both perspectives to arrive at an operations strategy?

Lecturers: visit www.palgrave.com/business/hillom3e for teaching guidelines for this case study

In summary, what typically happens now is that:

- Market descriptions are limited to the views of marketing. While these views give essential insights from a marketing perspective, they fail to yield the key differences and provide essential insights into markets from the view of other functions, particularly that of operations.

- The words and phrases used to describe markets are not sufficiently precise to provide the clarity needed to yield essential insights.

- The procedures used are not sufficiently exacting to expose and challenge these critical deficiencies, and inadequate outcomes result.

Given the pivotal role of market understanding to strategy development, how does a company improve its approach in this key phase of the process? This question is answered in the following section.

> **EXECUTIVE INSIGHT**
  Understanding markets is difficult; identifying actions is easy; making it happen is difficult.

Understanding customer requirements

Before we explain the approach to follow in the process of understanding markets (the subject of the next section) let's first reflect on what customers buy when making a purchase.

When customers purchase a service or product, they buy a combination of:

1. The service/product itself (see Figure 1.7), which has a specification (what it comprises), and

2. A number of related criteria such as:
   - Price – it matches or betters an acceptable price, or the purchase price set by competitors
   - Delivery speed – it meets its customers' lead-time requirements
   - Quality conformance – the service/product is provided to the stated specification (see point 1 above)
   - Customer relationships – the company/staff have established relationships with customers
   - **Delivery reliability** – the service/product is delivered on time.

In some instances, the specification of the service/product may be the only or the dominant factor influencing a customer's decision to buy – for example, with a custom-made wedding dress, an expensive automobile or choice of restaurant. But, in most instances, the purchase is made on the basis of the specification together with a mix of related criteria such as those listed above, and is illustrated in Figure 2.14. The criteria and their relative importance in securing the sale will differ from one service/product to another and from customer to customer.

> **EXECUTIVE INSIGHT**
  Customer purchases are rarely made solely on the basis of the specification of a service or product, but are often also influenced by a mix of other related criteria, such as quality conformance, delivery speed and price.

Delivery reliability – providing a service or product by the agreed delivery date.

Figure 2.14 The purchase: the make-up of customer choice

The purchase	The service/ product specification	Examples of related criteria				
		Price	Delivery speed	Quality conformance	Customer relationship	Delivery reliability
The business task	Meet/better the design of competitors	Reduce costs	Shorten lead-times	Meet the specification	Develop customer relations	Deliver on time
Function responsible	Marketing for services, research and development for products	Operations	Operations	Operations	Sales and Marketing	Operations

Understanding markets – the approach to follow

Clarity about markets is essential. Companies are in multiple markets and the outcome of the debate on markets should identify, and provide a clear understanding of, the differences that exist.

The steps to secure these insights are as follow:

1. **Avoid general words and phrases** – as markets are at the core of a business, using general words and phrases needs to be consciously and rigorously avoided. Each dimension should be expressed on its own and a single definition needs to be associated with each word or phrase used. In this way, each competitive dimension put forward as being relevant can be discussed separately and its relevance assessed. One classic example of this is the phrase 'customer service'. While a desirable objective, the answer to the question 'what does it mean?' is not self-evident as it embodies a number of potential meanings. Using 'customer service' to describe the competitive nature of a market thus confuses rather than clarifies.

2. **Long lists denote poor strategy process** – the outcome of the discussion on how a company competes in its markets is typically a long list. The intention seems to be to leave nothing off the list, thereby covering all aspects. Nothing could be further from the truth. This phase of the strategy development process concerns distilling the very essence of how a company has to compete. In this way essential clarity is provided.

3. **Separate out order-winners and qualifiers** – a further step to improve a company's understanding of its markets is to separate relevant competitive criteria into:
   • **Qualifiers** – these criteria get a service or product into a marketplace or onto a customer's shortlist and keep it there. They do not in themselves win orders but provide the opportunity to compete. Conversely, the failure to provide qualifiers at appropriate levels will lead to a loss of orders. In this way, qualifiers are order losing in nature, as a failure to provide a qualifier results in not being on the list – the opportunity to compete is not in place. In such situations, competitors do not win orders from a rival, rather the rival loses orders to its competitors.
   • **Order-winners** – however, having gained entry to a market or onto a short list is only the first step. The task then is to know how to win orders against competitors who have also qualified to be in the same market. With qualifiers, you need to match customers' requirements (as do competitors), whereas with order-winners you need to provide them at a level better than your competitors.

Finally, when applying this concept there are some key points to remember:
   • Qualifiers are not less important than order-winners; they are different. Both are essential. With qualifiers, a company needs to qualify and requalify at all times to stay on a customer's shortlist. If you are not on the list, you cannot compete.

- Order-winners and qualifiers are time- and market-specific – they will be different from market to market and will change over time within a market.
- The relevance and importance of order-winners and qualifiers will typically be different to retain market share, grow share in existing markets and enter new markets.
- The relative importance of qualifiers and order-winners will change when moving from being market-driven to being market-driving.
- As highlighted earlier, not all criteria will be either a qualifier or an order-winner. Some criteria do not relate to some markets.

4. **Weight qualifiers and order-winners** – to improve clarity still further, it is necessary to weight qualifiers and order-winners in the following way:
   - **Qualifiers** – it is adequate and appropriate to limit the classification of qualifiers into two categories – qualifiers (denoted by a Q) and order-losing sensitive qualifiers (denoted by a QQ). The latter is intended to alert a company to the fact that failure to provide criteria which are considered to be 'order-losing sensitive' will lead to a rapid loss of business.
   - **Order-winners** – the appropriate step here is to allocate 100 points across all the order-winners within a market. This forces the different levels of relevance to be exposed and provides an essential step in distilling out importance. It is essential, therefore, to avoid procedures where stars (for example) are allocated as a way of indicating importance, as this approach avoids confronting and resolving the key step of determining the relative importance of one criteria with another. Such approaches bypass the need to discriminate between the relative importance of one criterion *vis-à-vis* another – as any level of importance can be attributed to any criterion.

> **EXECUTIVE INSIGHT**
> Market understanding is the critical first step in implementing an operations strategy:
> - Avoid general descriptions – only if you are clear can the appropriate direction be determined
> - Identify the qualifiers and order-winners
> - Weight the qualifiers and order-winners.

What is gained from understanding the market?

After gaining an understanding of market and customer needs, and identifying the relevant qualifiers and order-winners, the strategic task of functions can be developed. Clarity in terms of recognizing the market helps to identify the most appropriate direction (with which qualifiers and/or order-winners need to be provided), emphasis (the target) and resource allocation. For example, the greater the order-winner weighting, the more emphasis and importance it is given. Similarly, as qualifiers indicate a need to match competitors' norms, any gaps between a company's performance and the market norm need to be closed quickly, especially where a qualifier is order-losing sensitive in nature.

To illustrate this point, let's take the role of price in a particular market:

- When price is an order-winner, a company competes on price. The higher the weighting, the more emphasis is placed on reducing costs, which, in turn, allows a company to be more competitive on price while sustaining its profit margins.

- When price is a qualifier, a company needs to be price competitive (that is, by being at an acceptable level within market norms). For example, highly skilled specialists who win business primarily on the uniqueness of their skill sets will be able to pitch their fee rates at the top end of the acceptable range for their sector. In such instances, there will be limits on how high they can set their fees (because of the order-losing nature of failing to qualify by setting fees at an unacceptably high level) and this will, in turn, relate to the level of their skills compared with those of their competitors. Here, the key task regarding costs would be to control them within the agreed budget rather than seeking to lower them as a strategic objective. Acceptable profit margins would be created by the high level of price and not by cost reduction.

Having agreed the markets and relevant qualifier/order-winner mix and weightings, then, as mentioned earlier, the steps in developing functional strategies are to:

- Assess how well the relevant qualifiers and order-winners are being provided

- Identify the gap between the provision of a criterion, its relative importance and the level required to retain or grow a company's market share

- Work out how to close the gap – in terms of the level of investment and timescales

- Implement the plan.

In order to illustrate this, Figure 2.15 outlines some typical areas for review and the type of improvements to make against a list of possible operations-related qualifiers and order-winners.

Implementing an operations strategy

The reality of implementing a functional strategy is to translate the order-winners and qualifiers for which that function is solely or jointly responsible into relevant actions. The rest of this book addresses the key areas in operations and the detailed approaches to both managing the wide range of tasks that comprise the operations function and the approaches to improving operations, whether in terms of doing things right (the efficiency dimension integral to any management role) and doing the right things (the strategic role concerning support for those criteria in a market for which operations is solely or jointly responsible). Thus, support for markets is a mechanism for identifying those areas that need to be prioritized in terms of investments and developments.

As you will see from Figure 2.15 the translation from order-winners and qualifiers into actions is a straightforward step. Implementation, on the other hand, is typically far from easy. Knowing which approach to follow for the best results and then making the developments happen is the underlying management capability. What to do and how best to do it are addressed throughout the different topics covered by this book. The place to start in terms of operations strategy is linking the strategic tasks (that is, the relevant order-winners and qualifiers) to courses of action. Figure 2.15 gives an overview of what needs to be completed.

Operations strategy – an illustration

With an understanding of the approach to and outcomes of operations strategy developments, it is opportune to provide a short illustration of what is involved.

Figure 2.16 is the outcome of a company's full and extensive debate about its markets. The firm is a contract hire car company. Although it supplies vehicles to individual customers, the majority of its business is supplying fleets of vehicles to the public and private sectors. The review provided in Figure 2.16 covers the three segments that make up the majority of the company's sales. There are other smaller segments but these have been omitted in this illustration. The review here (as always it should form part of the market review) has included the forward look required to highlight any anticipated changes in the relevance of the order-winners and qualifiers and corresponding weightings. Where possible it should look two time periods forward so as to give a more extended look into the future.

Figure 2.15 Translating qualifiers and order-winners into actions

Relevant qualifiers and order-winners	Typical areas for review and improvement
Price	Reduce costs in all areas, particularly regarding materials and overheads, which can make up to 70–90 per cent of total costs
Quality conformance	Provide services or make products to specification. Build quality into the process and delivery system rather than checking conformance after the event. Improvements here also impact costs
Delivery reliability	Assess on-time delivery performance by service/product and customer. Review current approaches to meeting orders – involves discussions on the extent to which services and products can be or are made-to-order or made-to-stock and the role of activities and investments such as scheduling and inventory in meeting these requirements
Delivery speed	Review the elements of the operations process with the purpose of reducing the lead-time of the various steps making up the service delivery system or manufacturing process
Service/product range	Review the process capability and staff skill base in relation to current and future service/product range requirements. Identify and supplement capabilities in line with current and/or future needs
Demand spikes	Assess current capacity provision in terms of the ability to rapidly increase output in line with known or anticipated changes in demand. Approaches include short-term capacity and inventory-holding alternatives
New services/products – time to market	Identify the elements of lead-time within the new service/product development process for which operations is responsible. Assess the tasks involved and the opportunities to reduce the work content, bring forward the start times in relation to the overall procedures, and identify the possibility of completing part or all of the task in parallel (rather than in sequence) with other elements of the process
Meeting specific customer needs	Assess current approaches to identify how standard services and products can be modified in line with specific customer requirements and the impact on costs, lead-times, quality conformance and the overall schedule

Some key points highlighted by this review, and how they translate into an operations strategy, are now provided:

1. Markets – the review illustrates, from an operations strategy point of view, the multi-segmented nature of a company's markets. That the three segments highlighted are different is eminently clear.

2. Functional strategies – the criteria listed in Figure 2.17 are the sole or joint responsibilities of several functions. When developing each functional strategy, these qualifiers and order-winners would need to be reflected in each function's development and investment priorities. This review highlights ahead of time the growing emphasis on price as an order-winner in its three principal market segments and the need to prioritize cost-reducing initiatives throughout the business.

Figure 2.17 highlights those criteria that operations have to support. The remainder would form the strategic task of other functions. For example, service specifications would be a marketing task. Hence, marketing would need to review the current service specifications on offer and propose ways (if need be) to improve the overall specification. This would typically include the range of services provided and the extent to which the specific needs of large and small fleet users are being met and how any proposed changes would improve that provision. In turn, these marketing proposals would form part of a business strategy debate that would include an operations review of any proposals and highlighting any investment and development (together with timescales) that would need to be made to meet any proposed changes.

Figure 2.16 Order-winners and qualifiers in three markets of a contract hire car company

Criteria	Principal market segments								
	Public sector			**Private sector**					
				Large fleet users			**Small fleet users**		
	CY[1]	CY+1	CY+2	CY	CY+1	CY+2	CY	CY+1	CY+2
Price	60[3]	60	65	40	50	50	Q[4]	10	15
Quality conformance[2]	40	40	35	40	30	30	50	50	45
Financial stability of supplier	QQ	QQ	QQ	Q	Q	Q	–	–	–
ISO 9000 registration	Q	Q	Q	Q	Q	Q	–	–	–
Proximity of vehicle supplier	Q	Q	Q	–	–	–	–	–	–
Existing customer list	–	–	–	Q	Q	Q	–	–	–
Simplicity of documents and procedures	–	–	–	–	–	–	Q	Q	Q
One-stop-shop provision	–	–	–	–	–	–	20	15	15
Service specification[5]	–	–	–	20	20	20	30	35	25

Notes: 1. CY = current year; CY+1 = current year + 1 year; CY+2 = current year + 2 years.
2. Quality conformance concerns fulfilling the service specification within a contract. For new customers, access to existing customers' experience to verify the level of conformance quality achieved would be provided by the company.
3. Order-winners have a weighting, the total of which is 100.
4. Q = a qualifier and QQ = an order-losing sensitive qualifier.
5. For large fleet users this includes the ability to meet a customer's specific needs as well as the range of added-value products (for example fuel card provision) on offer.

Figure 2.17 Operations actions arising from Figure 2.16

Criteria	Some operations initiatives (that is, strategy) that may result
Price	Develop supplier relations and negotiate contracts for products (for example cars) and services (for example maintenance programmes and insurance) to reduce costs while meeting specifications. Streamline internal processes and procedures to reduce costs
Quality conformance	Meet the agreed service specification and improve its provision
ISO 9000 registration	Continue to meet the ISO provisions and requirements
Simplicity of documents and procedures	Continuously simplify documents and procedures to make them increasingly user-friendly
One-stop-shop provision	Develop the internal capability within operations to provide all aspects of the service offering

Figure 2.17 lists the criteria for which operations is partly or solely responsible and identifies some of the initiatives that operations may undertake to maintain or improve its provision of these: in other words, the operations strategy.

Operations strategy in practice

- Strategy development needs to be based on regular discussions (at least once a month) and involving all the functions within a business.

- Begin a review of a business strategy by selecting a segment. Then identify customers that represent that segment. Now seek executives' views on the order-winners and qualifiers that ensure you retain the business including the appropriate weightings. Reconcile any differences. Finally check the reality of the order-winners and qualifiers by analyzing a representative sample of orders from the chosen customers. From this you will be able to assess the following:
  - The role of price and its sensitivity by calculating the contribution made on each sales order
  - **Customer lead-times** and the role of delivery speed
  - Delivery reliability performance
  - Quality conformance performance
  - And so on.

- Be alert in market debates to the use of general phrases such as 'customer service' and 'delighting customers' as descriptions of competitive criteria. Such approaches provide little insight for a number of reasons:
  - Phrases such as 'customer service/delighting customers' are the desired outcomes of strategy and not the strategy itself for delivering or achieving such outcomes
  - Using general phrases such as 'quality' and 'delivery' blur essential insights.

- Opinions need to be checked by data as the way to establish what constitutes the real position.

- As typically a contributor to gaining the first sale and invariably the function that gets the second sale, operations executives need to take their place at the executive table and be proactive in formulating strategy.

- As operations executives move up the organization they need to develop into business contributors first and operations specialists second.

- Operations executives need to be increasingly proactive in their strategic role.

Customer lead-time – the length of time a customer expects or is prepared to wait for a service or product from the point of making an order.

Driving business performance

As we saw in the last chapter, operations is a business function of size and consequence. As such it typically has a major role in developing and implementing a business strategy and is characterized by a substantial day-to-day role involving the management of large cost budgets and sizeable investments. Its impact on business performance, therefore, will invariably be significant and critical to the short and long-term success of an organization.

Using operations strategy to release cash

As the function responsible for most fixed assets (such as offices and equipment) and current assets (such as part-processed services and materials at all stages in a process), operations needs to look for ways of releasing cash tied up in the business. Areas to review include:

- Eliminating inventory resulting from operational inefficiencies including delays

- Undertaking regular causal analyses of inventory to identify why inventory in the delivery system is there and to look for ways to change the rules and decisions that contribute to unnecessary inventory in the system

- Speed up work by deducing process lead-times and so converting work more quickly into saleable outputs and associated cash flows.

- Look at current make or buy decisions regarding the impact on cash including the size of the resulting pipeline inventory and operations lead-times.

Using operations strategy to improve market

As illustrated is Figure 2.14, much of what a customer purchases is provided by operations and, in turn, what influences a customer's choice is provided by operations. As typically a contributor to gaining the first sale and invariably the custodian of gaining the second sale, operations' strategic role cannot be overstated.

Using operations strategy to reduce costs

Being typically responsible for 60–70 per cent of both costs and investments brings with it not only a significant managerial role but also an ongoing mandate to control and reduce costs. This task embraces the internal phase of the supply chain (the in-house delivery systems and capabilities) and also the impact of make or buy decisions on cost and investment profiles including the task of managing the supply chain as an integral part of operations' strategic role to support customers' needs.

Critical reflections

Developing an operations strategy involves a number of phases and the first of these is the most critical but typically the one in which operations does not adequately partake. Being proactively part of and contributing to the ongoing debate about markets and where to shed, retain or grow share, agreeing the order-winners and qualifiers involved in current and future markets and being party to market-driving opportunities comprise the first critical step.

Market- or marketing-led?

Markets are the common denominator of functional strategies. With markets analyzed in depth and agreement reached on the current and future directions to follow, the strategic task in operations is to develop the capabilities to support relevant order-winners and qualifiers. However, as highlighted earlier, companies do not always keep in sharp focus the critical difference between being market-led and being marketing-led. To substitute the business (market) perspective by a functional (marketing) perspective will invariably lead to distorted strategies and eventually to corporate disadvantage. Unfortunately, in many businesses, marketing is increasingly characterized as having the perceived role of creating ideas, with the rigour of testing business fit left to others. This trend not only trivializes the important functional perspective of marketing, but detracts from its fundamental strategic contribution.

Moving to a business-level strategic debate

Markets are a business not a functional decision. Whatever the strategic mix between being market-driven and market-driving, they lie at the very centre of strategy development, interconnecting business objectives with their delivery and interfacing between functional strategies, as illustrated in Figure 2.18. In this way they form the agenda for the development of all functional strategies and help ensure that differences and alternatives are resolved at the level of the business and not the level of the function. Companies need to seek continuously to line up their functional strategies to the needs of

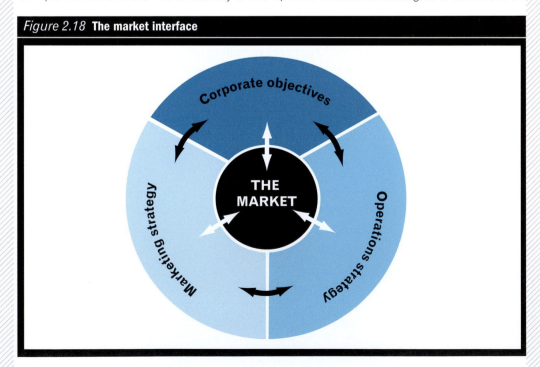

Figure 2.18 The market interface

Note: Although the marketing and operations functions are illustrated here, all functions with a strategic role would need to be involved in this interfacing procedure.

agreed markets. One of the major players in delivering strategy is operations. The critical nature of its role reflects the increasing importance of those order-winners and qualifiers for which it is jointly or solely responsible. As shown in the cases given throughout the chapter, getting it right in operations results in a sizeable and sustainable advantage. Although not the only strategic player, in most organizations its role will be important while in many it will be central to the continued success of the overall business.

Summary

- As companies grow, clusters of similar activities are separated out and managed as functions. Typical functions include accounting and finance, sales and marketing, human resources, IT, operations, and research and development. The principal reasons for this are to make it easier to manage the corporate complexity that follows growth, while also allowing for the development of specialist skills.

- Functions have a dual role: they must undertake the day-to-day management of the areas for which they are responsible while also developing strategies to support agreed markets. The latter role has been the subject of this chapter, and the former is addressed in the rest of the book.

- To cope with further growth and increasing complexity, organizations are split into different business units in which relevant functions are provided and developed. The outcome is strategy at three levels – corporate, business unit and functional.

- Operations, like other functions, contributes to the strategy debate about which markets to compete in, which customers to retain and with which to grow, and the order-winners and qualifiers that relate to these choices.

- Once markets have been agreed and the way to compete has been identified, the current level of support for relevant qualifiers and order-winners is assessed. Any gaps form the basis of a function's strategy, which specifies targets, investments and timescales.

- Operations needs to be proactive in encouraging discussion of the market, as changing operations is typically expensive and involves long lead-times.

- Throughout the chapter, examples of how organizations have successfully developed operations strategies in support of chosen markets have been provided. These examples illustrate how an operations strategy works, while the end of chapter questions cover issues raised throughout this chapter. Have a go at answering some of these as a way of checking your understanding.

Study activities

Discussion questions

1. Why would delivery reliability typically be designated an order-losing sensitive qualifier (QQ) for a carton company supplying packaging to a food company?

2. In the early 1970s, when the Japanese entered the European colour television market, they took market share partly on the basis of providing higher levels of quality conformance. Explain how the improvement of this factor worked in terms of gaining sales. In the period of the early 1970s was quality conformance an order-winner or qualifier in the European colour television market? What is this criterion in today's market – an order-winner or qualifier? Explain your reasoning.

Assignments

1. Identify the order-winners and qualifiers for the following enterprises:
   - A private medical company
   - A company hiring cars for business or leisure
   - A pharmaceutical company
   - A furniture removal company.

2. What would constitute the operations strategy for the four organizations reviewed in Assignment 1?

3. Search the internet to find a European company with operations in China. What is the stated rationale for this decision? Do you think any other factors are involved?

Exploring further

TED talks

Gladwell, M. (2004) *Spaghetti sauce. Tipping Point* author Malcolm Gladwell gets inside the food industry's pursuit of the perfect spaghetti sauce and makes a larger argument about the nature of choice and happiness.
www.ted.com/talks/malcolm_gladwell_on_spaghetti_sauce.html

Godin, S. (2003) *Standing out*. Seth Godin spells out why, when it comes to getting our attention, bad or bizarre ideas are more successful than boring ones.
www.ted.com/talks/seth_godin_on_sliced_bread.html

Jacques, M. (2010) *Understanding the rise of China*. Martin Jacques asks why the West often puzzles over the growing power of the Chinese economy, and offers three building blocks for understanding what China is and will become.
www.ted.com/talks/martin_jacques_understanding_the_rise_of_china.html

Pugh, L. (2010) *Mind-shifting Everest swim*. Lewis Pugh vowed never to take another cold-water dip after he swam the North Pole. Then he heard of Lake Pumori created by recent glacial melting at an altitude of 5,300 m on Everest, and so began a journey that would teach him a radical new way to approach swimming and think about climate change.
www.ted.com/talks/lewis_pugh_s_mind_shifting_mt_everest_swim.html

Schwartz, B. (2005) *The paradox of choice*. Psychologist Barry Schwartz takes aim at a central tenet of Western societies: freedom of choice. In Schwartz's estimation, choice has made us not freer but more paralyzed, not happier but more dissatisfied.
www.ted.com/talks/barry_schwartz_on_the_paradox_of_choice.html

Sinek, S. (2009) *How great leaders inspire action*. Simon Sinek has a simple but powerful model for inspirational leadership all starting with a golden circle and the question 'Why?' His examples include Apple, Martin Luther King, and the Wright brothers.
www.ted.com/talks/simon_sinek_how_great_leaders_inspire_action.html

Journal articles

Gavetti, G. (2011) 'The new psychology of strategic leadership', *Harvard Business Review*, **89**(7/8): 118–25. Leaders must use 'associational thinking' to learn from businesses in other industries.

Gino, F. and Pisano, G.P. (2011) 'Why leaders don't learn from success', *Harvard Business Review*, **89**(4): 68–74. Companies should implement systematic after-action reviews to understand all the factors that led to a win, and test their theories by conducting experiments even if 'it ain't broke'.

Gouillart, F.J. and Sturdivant, F.D. (1994) 'Spend a day in the life of your customers', *Harvard Business Review*, **72**(1): 116–25. The article argues that a senior executive's instinctive capacity to empathize with and gain insight from customers is the single most important skill that can be used to direct a company's strategic posture approach. Yet most top managers retain only limited contact with consumers as their organizations grow, relying instead on subordinates' reports to define and feel out the market for them. To get a true sense of the market, senior executives should consider the wants and needs of every step in the distribution chain, right down to the end user of a finished product.

Grant, A.M. (2011) 'How customers can rally your troops', *Harvard Business Review*, **89**(6): 96–103. End users can inspire workers by demonstrating the impact of their efforts, showing appreciation for their work, and eliciting employees' empathy for them. To outsource inspiration effectively, leaders must identify end users (both past and present), collect their stories, introduce them to employees across the organization, and recognize workers' impact on customers' lives.

Gulati, R. (2007) 'Silo busting: how to execute on the promise of customer focus', *Harvard Business Review*, **85**(5): 98–108. Shifting from selling products to selling solutions (packages of products and services) is a strategic alternative that many businesses need to consider. However, many companies are not structured to make that shift. Knowledge and expertise often reside in silos, and companies often have trouble effectively harnessing these resources. The article identifies four key sets of activities that need to be in place for this to successfully occur.

Heracleous, L. and Wirtz, J. (2010) 'Singapore Airlines' balancing act', *Harvard Business Review*, **88**(7): 145–9. Singapore Airlines (SIA) is widely regarded as an exemplar of excellence both in its service standards and as one of the civil aviation industry's cost leaders. SIA executes its dual strategy by managing four paradoxes: achieving service excellence cost-effectively, fostering centralized and decentralized innovation, being a technology leader and follower, and using standardization to achieve personalization. The results speak for themselves – SIA has delivered healthy financial returns, it has never had an annual loss and, except for the initial capitalization phase, the Asian airline has funded its growth itself while paying dividends every year.

Keiningham, T. L., Aksoy, L., Buoye, A. and Cooil, B. (2011) 'Customer loyalty isn't enough, grow your share of wallet', *Harvard Business Review*, **89**(10): 29–31. The article presents an algorithm for determining a brand's 'wallet share', which depends on both customer satisfaction with a brand relative to competing brands, and the number of competitors.

Khanna, T., Song, J. and Lee, K. (2011) 'The paradox of Samsung's rise', *Harvard Business Review*, **89**(7/8): 142–7. Twenty years ago, few people would have predicted that Samsung could become a world leader in R&D, marketing, and design. Fewer still would have predicted success given the path it has taken: grafting Western business practices onto its essentially Japanese model.

Kumar, N. (2006) 'Strategies to fight low-cost rivals', *Harvard Business Review*, **84**(12): 104–12. Successful price warriors, such as the German retailer Aldi, are changing the nature of competition by employing several tactics: focusing on just one or a few consumer segments, delivering the basic product or providing one benefit better than its rivals do, and backing low prices with superefficient operations. This article discusses the various approaches to competing against cut-price players.

Mittal, V., Sarkees, M. and Murshed, F. (2008) 'The right way to manage unprofitable customers', *Harvard Business Review*, **86**(4): 95–102. Customer divestment (whereby a company stops providing a product or service to an existing customer) was once considered an anomaly. However, it is fast becoming a viable strategic option for many organizations. The article reports its findings from interviews with 38 executives from 32 companies in a variety of industries, including IT, manufacturing, health care, finance and professional services. The research results identified four common reasons why businesses terminate relationships with end users.

Newstead, B. and Lanzerotti, L. (2010) 'Can you open-source your strategy?', *Harvard Business Review*, **88**(10): 32–6. This article discusses the open-source business strategy used by the Wikimedia Foundation and asks if you can effectively open-source your strategy.

Ramaswamy, V. and Gouillart, F. (2010) 'Building the co-creative enterprise', *Harvard Business Review*, **88**(10): 100–9. The article examines how a company can use its stakeholders including customers, employees and distributors to determine HR practices and design and market its services and products.

Simons, R. (2010) 'Stress-test your strategy', *Harvard Business Review*, **88**(11): 92–100. You must engage in ongoing, face-to-face dialogue with those around you concerning emerging data, unspoken assumptions, difficult choices, and, ultimately, action plans. You and they must be able to give clear, consistent answers to ensure that your strategy is firmly on track.

Washburn, N.T. and Hunsaker, B.T. (2011) 'Finding great ideas in emerging markets', *Harvard Business Review*, **89**(9): 115–20. A new kind of manager, a 'global bridger', can help companies take advantage of the innovative energy that permeates emerging markets.

Wilson, H.J., Guinan, P.J., Parise, S. and Weinberg, B.D. (2011) 'What's your social media strategy?', *Harvard Business Review*, **89**(7/8): 23–5. The article discusses four social-media strategies used by corporations.

Books

Cahill, M. (2010) *Making the right investment decisions*, 2nd edn, Harlow: Financial Times. This book examines how the stock market examines companies and values shares. It helps you understand the factors that drive long-term wealth creation as well as highlighting the key risks that lead to value being destroyed.

Fitzsimmons, J.A. and Fitzsimmons, M.J. (2000) *Service Management: Operations, Strategy and Information Technology*, New York: McGraw-Hill.

Hill, A. and Hill, T. (2009) *Manufacturing Operations Strategy: Text and Cases*, 3rd edn, Basingstoke: Palgrave Macmillan. The text provides a useful supplement to *Operations Management* by outlining an in-depth approach for developing and implementing operations strategy within manufacturing organizations.

Hill, A. and Hill, T. (2011) *Essential Operations Management*, Basingstoke: Palgrave Macmillan. The text provides a useful supplement to *Operations Management* by focusing on the essential aspects for managing operations within service and manufacturing organizations.

Hill, T. (1998) *The Strategy Quest. Releasing the Energy of Manufacturing Within a Market Driven Strategy: a Dynamic Business Story*. Available from AMD Publishing, 'Albedo',

Dousland, Devon PL20 6NE, UK; e-mail: amd@jm-abode.tiscali.co.uk; fax: +44 (0) 1822 882863. This book (written as a novel) describes how an art business and manufacturing organization restructure themselves to meet the changing demands of their customers.

Notes and references

1. See, for example, Gagnon, S. (1999) 'Resource-based competition and the new operations strategy', *International Journal of Operations and Production Management*, 19(2): 135–8; Grant, R. (1991) 'The resource-based theory of competitive advantage: implications for strategy formulation', *California Management Review*, 33: 114–22.
2. Terry Hill *The Strategy Quest*, AMD Publishing (1998) p. vii. Copies are available from the publisher whose address is 'Albedo', Dousland, Devon PL20 6NE, UK, or email amd@jm-abode.freeserve.co uk or fax 0044(0)1822 882863.
3. Illustrations of the generic approach to strategy formulation are found in the articles and books of several writers in the field of corporate strategy, of which two classic examples are provided by M.E. Porter and C.K. Prahalad and G. Hamel. Porter's early contributions include 'How competitive forces shape strategy', *Harvard Business Review*, March–April 1979: 86–93, *Competitive Strategy: Techniques for Analysing Industries and Competitors*, Free Press, New York (1980) and *Competitive Advantage: Creating and Sustaining Superior Performance*, Free Press, New York (1985). Prahalad and Hamel's contributions include 'The core competency of the corporation', *Harvard Business Review*, 68 (1990), pp. 79–91. Both approaches proposed overarching solutions to competitive strategy insights and resolutions – in this way they propose to resolve the increasing diversity that typifies today's corporations by overlaying it with generic solutions.
4. *The Strategy Quest*, op. cit, p. vii.
5. Manufacturing, Planning and Implementation Scheme – Analytical Coordination, Final Report (unpublished).
6. Hill, A. and Hill, T. 'Customer Service: Aligning Business to Markets', Executive Briefing, Templeton College, University of Oxford (2003).
7. These approaches and the issues involved are dealt with in greater depth in the following book by A. Hill and T. Hill *Manufacturing Operations Strategy*, 3rd edn, Palgrave Macmillan (2010) and T. Hill *The Strategy Quest*, op. cit.
8. Schneider, B. and Bowen, D.E. *Winning the Service Game*. Harvard Business School Press, Boston, MA (1995), p. 200.

Visit www.palgrave.com/business/hillom3e for self-test questions, guideline answers to some case study questions, useful weblinks and more to help you understand the topics in this chapter

'In 1985, Steve Jobs, CEO and co-founder of Apple Computers was fired for his highly opinionated and visionary approach to management and leadership only to return twelve years later and rescue it from dire straits', reflected the analyst Paul Keane. 'When he came back, he was still idealistic about design and technology, but his years in exile had made him more realistic and collaborative. As a result, he invited Microsoft to invest in Apple, developed iPod and iTunes products for Windows, fitted Macs with Intel chips, outsourced operations, developed supply chains and ventured into retailing. There is no doubt he has turned the business around, but the question is whether this is only a temporary up in the up-and-down story of Apple. Remember how sales suddenly slumped before he left last time, even though Macs were widely recognized as the best computers on the market.'

THE STORY

Steve Jobs and Steve Wozniak founded Apple Computer Inc in 1976 as a pair of 20-something college dropouts building Apple I computer circuit boards in Jobs' family garage. They soon started working with Mike Markkula, a millionaire who retired from Intel at the age of 33, to raise venture capital and bring out an easy-to-use personal computer (PC). It was a good team with Markkula as the businessman, Wozniak the technical genius and Jobs the visionary wanting to change the world through technology. In 1978, they started a computing revolution by launching Apple II, a relatively simple PC that could be used straight out of the box. Three years later, the PC industry was worth US$1 billion and Apple was the industry leader with 16 per cent market share, but things suddenly changed when IBM entered the market in 1982 (see Figure 1).

Figure 1 **Apple's worldwide PC share (1980–2010)**

IBM computers had a less secure operating system (Microsoft's DOS), slower processors (Intel) and looked grey and bland, but were easier to clone than the Apple machines. As a result, other manufacturers started making cheap IBM-compatible computers and Apple's market share fell to 6 per cent by 1982. To try to gain back share, Apple launched the Macintosh (Mac) computer in 1984. It was a breakthrough in ease of use, technical capability and industrial design, but the lack of compatible software limited sales. As a result, Apple's market share fell even further and in 1985 the company was in crisis. Jobs was moved out of an operational role and left later that year to set up another company called NeXT Software.

John Sculley who had been recruited two years earlier from Pepsi was appointed CEO. He focused Apple on desktop publishing and education customers by designing products from scratch with unique chips, disk drives, monitors, unusually shaped computer chassis, its own proprietary operating system and application software. Customers loved the simple, user-friendly and integrated desktop solution and sales exploded and by 1990 Apple had 8 per cent of the market. As Jamie Mayers, a senior analyst, commented, 'IBM-compatible users "put up" with their machines, but Apple customers "love" their Macs.'

Apple invested more in research and development (R&D) than its competitors and developed high-end, premium-priced products selling for as much as US$10,000. Sculley wanted to grow the business and move it back into the mass-market by becoming a low-cost producer launching new products every 6–12 months. As part of this strategy, he launched the Mac Classic in 1990 its first lower-end desktop and followed this with the PowerBook laptop later that year achieving rave reviews and significant product sales. However, other product and software developments didn't take off and although

Figure 2 **Gross margin and R&D as a per cent of sales for Apple, Dell and Hewlett-Packard (1997–2010)**

Performance	1997	2000	2003	2006	2007	2008	2009	2010
Gross margin (%)								
Apple	21	28	29	30	34	36	40	39
Dell	23	21	19	17	19	19	18	19
Hewlett-Packard	38	31	29	26	24	24	24	24
R&D/Sales (%)								
Apple	12	5	8	4	4	4	4	3
Dell	1	2	1	1	1	1	1	1
Hewlett-Packard	7	5	5	3	3	3	3	2

Sculley continued to outsource manufacturing and drive down costs, Apple's profits fell to 34 per cent of sales in 1993 after averaging 48 per cent in the previous decade. Apple's board asked him to step down and Michael Spindler took over as CEO later that year. In an attempt to restore profits he made 16 per cent of Apple's workforce redundant, slashed the R&D budget and licensed a handful of companies to make Mac clones. Despite this, Apple reported a US$69 million loss in 1996, announced further layoffs and two weeks later Gilbert Amelio replaced Spindler as CEO. Amelio refocused Apple on technically superior, premium-priced products looking to grow sales in high-margin segments such as servers, internet access devices and personal digital assistants. He cancelled the development of the much-delayed operating system, acquired NeXT Software to use a product they were already working on and appointed the founder of NeXT, Steve Jobs, as a part-time adviser. Despite these bold moves, Apple still lost US$1.6 billion in 1997 and its worldwide PC market share fell from 6 to 3 per cent. As a result, Steve Jobs replaced Amelio as CEO, 12 years after he had left.

Jobs quickly started to turn the business around. He immediately persuaded Microsoft to invest US$150 million in Apple and commit to develop core products such as Microsoft Office for the Mac. He ended the Mac cloning programme and consolidated its product range from 15 to 3 lines. The following year, the iMac was launched with a distinctive translucent case avail-

Figure 3 **Annual unit sales for Mac, iPod, iTunes, iPhone and iPad**

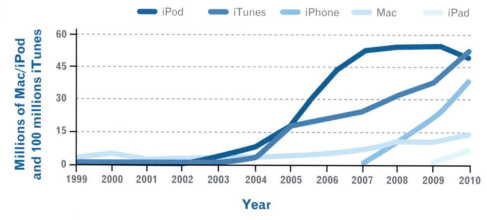

Figure 4 **Non-Mac product group development (2001–11)**

Product group	Development
iPod	Launched in Nov 2001 for Macs and then in Aug 2002 for Windows. It now offers a range of MP3 players from US$49 to US$399 including the shuffle, nano, classic and touch. Its sleek design and simple functionality made it a design icon. By Apr 2007, 100 million iPods had been sold and it owned 70% of the MP3 player market. Competitors are getting fewer and fewer as rivals leave the market. Research shows each iPod customer spends another 30% of the iPod value on accessories.
iTunes	Launched in Apr 2003 for Macs and then in Oct 2003 for Windows. Customers download songs for 99 cents. By Feb 2008, iTunes had sold 4 billion songs, owned 70% of the worldwide digital music market and was the third-largest US music retailer behind Walmart and Best Buy. Profits are low (about 9%), but iPod sales grew seven-fold when iTunes was launched in 2003. It also created specific standards in users' music libraries that locked them into using iPods.
Apple TV	Launched in 2005, it allowed customers to download TV shows (US$1.99 per episode) and movies (US$9.99 or more each) from iTunes and play them through their TV. In early 2008 movie rentals were introduced (US$2.99 to US$4.99 for 24 hours). In 2009, it updated the product to enable customers to access the internet directly.

Figure 4	(continued)
iPhone	Launched in Jun 2007, it combined the iPod touch with a mobile smartphone with a variety of software including: email, web access, text messaging, photos, video, camera, calendar, maps, visual voicemail, iTunes WiFi music store and address book. Instead of a keyboard, it has a multi-touch widescreen display. The entire system ran on a specially adapted version of Apple's OSX operating system. They cost between US$399 and US$499 to buy plus the cost of a contract with one of its mobile operator partners such as AT&T (US) or O2 (UK). By Jan 2008, just 200 days after its launch, Apple had sold 4 million iPhones.
iPad	Launched in Apr 2010, as a tablet computer for browsing the internet, watching media and gaming browsing, media. It runs a similar operating system to the iPod touch and iPhone, and costs between US$499 and US$829 to buy plus a mobile contract for the 3G version. By Jun 2010, just 60 days after its launch, it had sold 2 million iPads – an average of 1 every 3 seconds.

able in a variety of colours and supporting a wide range of 'plug and play' Windows-based peripherals. It was a success and sold 6 million units over the next three years. He continued to restructure the business by outsourcing the manufacture of Mac products to Taiwanese contractors and revamping distribution by eliminating relationships with smaller retailers and expanding its presence in national chains. Inventory reduced significantly and R&D investment grew (see Figure 2). In November 1997, the Apple website was launched to sell products directly to consumers and it began promoting itself as a hip alternative to the other computer brands on the market.

Apple finally introduced its new operating system called Mac OSX in 2001 offering customers a more stable, secure and user-friendly environment than Windows. The same year, it launched the iPod and although sales were slow for the first couple of years it now has 70 per cent of the portable media player market (see Figure 3).

A number of different models are now available and every year a new generation of each model is launched that is typically lighter, has more features and costs less than the previous version (see Figure 5). Since then, it has introduced other non-Mac products such as iTunes, Apple TV, iPhone and the iPad (see Figure 4).

In 2007, it began to use Intel chips in its Mac products to overcome problems with its existing chips that were blocking advances in laptop performance and preventing Macs from running Windows-based software. Alongside this product development it continued to invest in software applications such as iLife (iPhoto, iTunes, iWeb, iMovie), video editing (Final Cut Pro) and the Safari web browser now also available for Windows. Although in 2004 Microsoft had announced that it would no longer develop Internet Explorer for the Mac, it did agree to develop Office products for at least another five years. Meanwhile, Apple continued developing iWork (Pages, Numbers, Keynote) just to be safe.

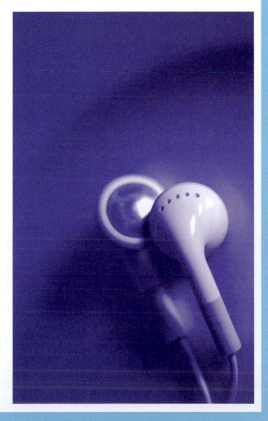

Figure 5	iPod model product development (2001–11)					
Model and generation		Storage (GB)	Price (US$)	Battery life (up to hrs)	Developments	Release date
Classic	1	5, 10	399, 499	10	New product with mechanical scroll wheel	Oct 01
	2	10, 20	399, 499	10	Touch sensitive scroll wheel and re-designed hold switch	Jul 02
	3	15, 30, 40	299, 399, 499	8	Touch sensitive buttons and USB connector port	Apr 03
	4	30, 60	349, 449	12	Photo viewer, buttons in 'Click wheel' and colour display	Jul 04
	5	30, 80	249, 349	20 audio, 3 video	Video player, slimmer, larger screen in white and black	Oct 05
	6	80, 160	249, 349	40 audio, 7 video	New software interface and silver or black front plate	Sep 07
		120	249	36 audio, 6 video	120GB replaced 80 and 160GB, new software interface	Sep 08
		160	249	36 audio, 6 video	160GB replaced 120GB	Sep 09
Nano	1	1, 2, 4	149, 199, 249	14	New product, slimmer design and colour screen	Sep 05
	2	2, 4, 8	149, 199, 249	24	6 colours, brighter screen and music search function	Sep 06
	3	4, 8	149, 199	24 audio, 5 video	New design, video player, larger screen and new software	Sep 07
	4	8, 16	149, 199	24 audio, 4 video	9 colours, new design, larger screen, built-in accelerometer and new software	Sep 08
	5	8, 16	149, 179	24 audio, 5 video	First iPod to include video camera, 9 colours, larger screen, FM radio and speaker	Sep 09
	6	8, 16	149, 179	24 audio	Multi-touch screen Video playback, speakers and camera removed	Sep 10
Shuffle	1	0.5, 1	99, 149	12	New product with no screen or 'click wheel'	Jan 05
	2	1	79	12	Smaller case and built-in clip available in 4 colours	Sep 06
	3	2, 4	59, 79	10	Smaller design and controls on earbud cable in 5 colours	Mar 09
	4	2	49	15	Controls return to body, 5 colours and voice controls	Sep 10

Figure 5 (continued)						
Touch	1	8, 16, 32	299, 399, 499	22 audio, 5 video	New product in one colour (silver) with multi-touch interface, built-in accelerometer and Wi-Fi connectivity Variety of software including: Safari web browser, Mail, Calendar, Contacts, Google Maps, iTunes web store, YouTube, Photos, Weather, iPod	Sep 07
	2	8, 16, 32	229, 299, 399	36 audio, 6 video	Modified product design: slimmer, contoured back, volume controls and built-in speaker Access to new third-party software applications through iTunes app store	Sep 08
	3	32, 64	199, 299	30 audio, 6 video	Faster processor and voice control	Sep 09
	4	8, 32, 64	229, 299, 399	40 audio, 7 video	Thinner design, two cameras for FaceTime and HD video recording, better display and faster processor	Sep 10

TODAY

Since Jobs' return in 1997 (he sadly died in 2011), the make up of the company has changed significantly. The company has refocused itself on developing cutting-edge, easy-to-use products that are updated every 12 to 18 months (see Figure 6).

As well as innovating products, it has also transformed its operations. 'Apple broke every rule of traditional retailing when it opened its first stores in 2001,' the analyst, Mark Jones commented. 'They were much larger than necessary and encouraged customers to linger by offering free internet browsing and provided extensive product training rather than just sales help.' These stores showcase Apple products and create a fun and enjoyable experience. Each store has a simple, intuitive and logical layout and is split into four sections: products, music, photos and accessories. They also offer a number of free services such as the 'Genius Bar' to solve customer technical problems and the 'Design Studio' to help customers create photos and design graphics. Regular workshops and presentations are held in theatre-like sections of the store to train customers on aspects such as the Mac operating system, editing home movies and recording music. In 2003, the stores became profitable and by 2007 Apple was the fastest growing retailer in the world with 197 stores drawing over 100 million visitors a year. This growth has continued and it now has 317 stores worldwide.

Four operations are used to supply products to the Apple retail stores, other resellers or customers who have ordered online. Two are located in the US serving the Americas, one in Ireland for Europe, Middle East and Africa and another in Singapore for the Asian market. All operations activities have been outsourced apart from the basic compiling of the products, peripherals, software, documentation and accessories necessary for each order. No products or materials are single sourced, but the number of suppliers has been significantly reduced in recent years and is now down to about 250. Long relationships are in place with key suppliers and Apple often accounts for 70 to 80 per cent of a supplier's total business. 60 per cent of components tend to be locally sourced by each of the four Apple operations while the other 40 per cent come from a number of global suppliers including Samsung, Wolfson Microelectronics, SigmaTel and Hotachi. Apple's global procurement function is split into product teams comprising buyers, engineers and designers who work

Product group	Model	Generation	Introduced	Discontinued
Desktops	iMac	G4 15"	Jan 02	Aug 04
		G4 20"	Nov 03	Aug 04
		G5 17"	Aug 04	Jan 06
		G5 20"	Aug 04	Mar 06
		iMac	Jan 06	Sep 06
		iMac	Sep 06	Aug 07
		iMac	Aug 07	Current
	Mini	Mini	Oct 05	Feb 06
		Core Solo	Feb 06	Sep 06
		Core Duo	Feb 06	Aug 07
		Core 2 Duo	Aug 07	Current
	Mac Pro	Mac Pro	Aug 06	Jan 08
		Harpertown	Jan 08	Current
Portables	PowerBook	Prismo	Feb 00	Jan 01
		G4 Titanium (15")	Jan 01	Sep 03
		G4 Titanium (12")	Jan 03	May 06
		G4 Titanium (17")	Jan 03	Apr 06
		G4 Aluminium (15")	Sep 03	Feb 06
	MacBook	14"	May 06	Feb 08
		14" (Penryn)	Feb 08	Oct 08
		13" (Unibody)	Oct 08	Oct 09
		13" (White)	Oct 09	Current
	MacBook Pro	13" and 15"	Sep 06	Feb 08
		17"	Apr 07	Feb 08
		13", 15" and 17" (Penryn)	Feb 08	Oct 08
		15" (Unibody)	Oct 08	Jun 09
		17" (Unibody)	Jan 09	Jun 09
		13", 15" and 17"	Jun 09	Apr 10
		13", 15" and 17"	Apr 10	Feb 11
		13", 15" and 17"	Feb 11	Current
	MacBook Air	15"	Jan 08	Jun 09
		15"	Jun 09	Oct 10
		11" and 13"	Oct 10	Current
Servers	Xserve	Xserve	May 02	Feb 03
		Slot loading	Feb 03	Jan 04
		Cluster node	Feb 03	Jan 04
		G5	Jun 04	Aug 06
		G5 Cluster node	Jun 04	Aug 06
		Xserve (Intel)	Aug 06	Jan 08
		Harpertown	Jan 08	Apr 09
		Nehalem	Apr 09	Current

Figure 6 **Mac product development for current models (2000–11)**

collaboratively with suppliers to plan capacity and meet delivery schedules. Suppliers deliver against daily requirements, are expected to reduce costs over time and are measured against price, delivery reliability, quality conformance and technical support (listed in order of importance).

As well as managing this physical supply chain, Apple has also developed a digital supply chain for its iTunes products. This has proved to be a huge success and AMR Research has identified it as the best supply chain within Fortune 500 companies for the last three years (see Figure 7). As the analyst Mark Jones commented, 'Apple have made significant supply chain developments and moved away from a 20th-century production efficiency mentality toward a new era of value, based on ideas, design, and content. In 2010, it delivered US$5 billion sales of zero-inventory iTunes

Figure 7 Top 10 supply chain management companies (2005–11)						
Company	Rank					
	2005	2007	2008	2009	2010	2011
Apple	–	2	1	1	1	1
Dell	1	–	3	2	5	2
Procter & Gamble	2	3	4	3	2	3
Research in Motion	–	–	–	–	9	4
Amazon.com	–	–	–	–	10	5
Cisco Systems	–	–	8	5	3	6
Walmart	8	6	6	7	4	7
McDonald's	–	–	–	–	–	8
PepsiCo	–	–	–	9	6	9
Samsung	7	10	9	8	7	10

Notes: 1. Based on data from AMR Research.
2. Rating is based on peer opinion (20%), research opinion (20%), return on assets (25%), inventory turns (25%) and revenue growth (10%).
3. Apple only became a Fortune 500 company in 2006.

Figure 8 Annual sales revenue by product group (2002–10)							
Product group	Annual sales (US$m)						
	2002	2004	2006	2007	2008	2009	2010
Desktops	2,828	2,373	3,319	4,023	5,622	4,324	6,201
Portables	1,706	2,550	4,056	6,313	8,732	9,535	11,278
Total Mac	**4,534**	**4,923**	**7,375**	**10,336**	**14,354**	**13,859**	**17,479**
iPhone	–	–	–	630	6,742	13,033	25,179
iPod	143	1,306	7,676	8,305	9,153	8,091	8,274
iTunes	4	278	1,885	2,496	3,340	4,036	4,948
iPad	–	–	–	–	–	–	4,958
Other hardware	527	951	1,100	1,303	1,694	1,475	1,814
Software, service and other	534	821	1,279	1,508	2,208	2,411	2,573
Total	**5,742**	**8,279**	**19,315**	**24,578**	**37,491**	**42,905**	**65,225**

products. Not only does this significantly improve cash flow, but it also creates a platform for selling its higher margin iPod, iPhone and iPad products. Rather than distributing through retailers, products such as music, movies, television shows, music videos, games and publications are delivered instantly and directly to customers through its online store. This has revolutionized not only the industries within which it competes, but also how we think about supply chains. The number and types of products being supplied through iTunes is increasing all the time and the possibilities seem endless.'

THE FUTURE

In early 2007, Apple changed its name from Apple Computer to Apple Inc to signify its growing focus on consumer electronics rather than computers (see Figure 8).

Some analysts feel its move into consumer electronics has made it more competitive as customers value its easy interface and simple design, but others feel it is losing its focus. 'Apple is still essentially only a small player in the PC industry (see Figure 9) and this diversification will only cause it problems,' Paul Keane concluded. 'iPod sales are starting to level off and both the iPhone and iPad have moved it into industries with fierce competition. Companies such as Nokia, Motorola, Samsung and LG are much bigger and more aggressive than Apple's iPod competitors and are not going to give up without a fight. Also, continually developing products and moving into new markets puts huge stress on all parts of its business. I'm not sure if its operations and supply chains can keep up with this.'

Questions

1. How does Apple compete in its major markets: Macs, iPhone, iPods, iPads and iTunes?

2. How does Apple support and drive these markets?

3. What must Apple do to maintain its competitive position in the future?

Figure 9 Comparison of market share for major PC vendors (1995–2010)

Vendor	Market share (% total)						
	1995	2001	2004	2006	2008	2009	2010
HP	4	7	16	17	18	19	18
Dell	3	13	18	18	15	12	13
Acer	–	–	4	5	11	13	12
Lenovo	–	–	2	6	7	8	10
Toshiba	3	3	3	4	5	5	5
Asus	–	–	–	–	-	3	5
Apple	8	3	2	2	3	3	4
Compaq	10	11	–	–	–	–	–
Fujitsu Siemens	5	5	6	–	–	–	–
IBM	6	6	6	–	–	–	–
Gateway	2	2	2	2	–	–	–
Other	59	50	41	46	41	40	33
Total (million units)	89	128	189	239	302	306	308

Notes: 1. Based on 'IDC: Quarterly PC Shipments'.
2. HP acquired Compaq in 2002.
3. IBM sold its PC business to Lenovo in 2005.
4. Acer acquired Gateway in 2007.

Lecturers: visit www.palgrave.com/business/hillom3e for teaching guidelines for this case study

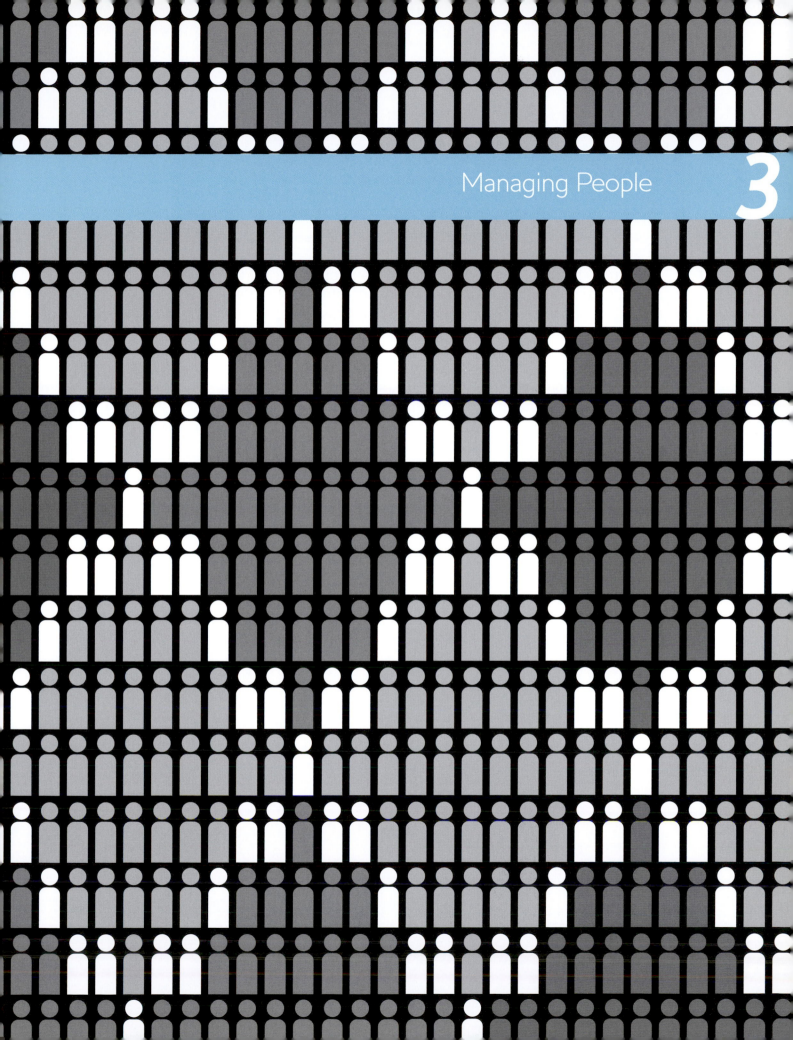

Managing People

3

After completing this chapter, you should be able to:

- Fully appreciate the essential role that motivated and engaged people have in the continued success of a business

- Understand the traditional ways used in work design as a prelude to reviewing alternatives that would better meet the needs of a business

- Recognize that reducing the technical content of jobs as part of the appropriate drive to reduce costs through investment brings with it the need to look for ways to build back interesting tasks as part of work

- Realize that though many people are self-motivated and find work challenging and interesting, there are many who need to be motivated to work well. Motivating people, therefore, needs to be high on the business agenda

- Identify the different approaches to employee involvement and empowerment and the steps from the 'involvement and collaboration' phase to 'self-managed teams'

- Recognize the growing range of people tasks involved in today's business environment such as the increased use of temporary and agent staff and the growing internationalization of large organizations that brings with it the task of managing overseas operations

Chapter outline

What comprises the task of managing people?

- People are central to the success of a business and progressive companies have long since recognized the need to safeguard and nurture their working capital

- Being responsible for the 60–70 per cent of staff who typically provide the services and products makes this a key element of operations management in the overall success of a business

- For operations the people element of the task stretches further. The relationship building that comes with cross-functional activities as well as interfacing with suppliers at one end and customers at the other end of the supply chain adds to the critical nature of this element of operations' task

Why is managing people important?

- As people within the operations functions are directly responsible for providing the services and making the products they are central to its activities and ongoing success

- While people complete the technical task embodied in delivering services and products, their essential contribution also needs to include using their inherent capability to self-manage their tasks and contribute to the continued improvement of operations so essential to the welfare of organizations in today's competitive environment

How does managing people impact business performance?

- Retaining and growing market share are key factors in the financial welfare of companies

- As people are at the heart of providing the services and products sold to customers their role is central to this core transaction

- Similarly, as the staff within operations and their associated costs are typically 60–70 per cent of the business total, then meeting output targets while maintaining staff budgets is a key factor in meeting the profit performance of the company

- Finally, and as highlighted in the last section, managing the capabilities of people as a source of continuously improving the systems and processes used within the organization brings sizeable and lasting benefits so essential in today's increasingly competitive markets

What are the key issues to consider when managing people?

- The ability to inspire the emotional and intellectual commitment of people needs to be high on the corporate agenda

- This is a critical skill that operations executives have to develop and apply

- Managing people is not only sizeable but also critical to the operations task and overall success of a business and so improving people's jobs, creating opportunities for them to influence, improve and control their working environment while linking their contributions to business outcomes must be provided and sustained

- Information-related technologies have changed work roles and organizational relationships

- Beepers, emails and mobile telephone systems empower people to interact with one another, including customers, outside the formal reporting structures of organizations

- Such innovations need to be accommodated within revised organizational structures and are challenging operations managers in the new millennium

- The pace of change is not easy to live with, but those companies that develop organizations that accept change as a way of life and progressively involve people in better serving their customers and in developing and improving their delivery systems are those that will succeed in the future

Introduction

How a manager manages people and relationships is one of the core tasks in managing operations, as it is with other functions. People are a key resource in a business and central to meeting both the operational (day-to-day) and strategic tasks and objectives. It is, therefore, appropriate that this chapter is positioned towards the start of this book as it signals the importance and universality of this dimension throughout the management role in a book on managing operations. Furthermore, as you proceed through the rest of the book, you will note frequent references to and detailed discussion about people and their roles within the successful tasks that make up the operations function. Operations managers have to meet the challenge of creating an environment that helps people develop their full potential, where people care sufficiently to want to do a good job and that the needs of both the people and the business are met within the workplace. Progressive companies have long since recognized the key role of people in the continued success of a business and, therefore, the need to safeguard and nurture their human capital.

Managing 60–70 per cent of those employed and the relationship building that comes with cross-functional activities, outsourcing work and interfacing with customers constitutes a significant 'managing people' task. While this challenging role competes for attention with all the other operations' priorities, the sound and responsive management of human resources (HR) in an organization is essential for its long-term success. Whereas companies are able to control materials, design business systems and processes and develop procedures to a level that will almost guarantee that the service or product specification is met, the role and contribution of people in the delivery system are essential to ensure this provision. To develop and maintain delivery systems that consistently meet customers' requirements and expectations, companies have to recognize the need for and embody the dimension of employee commitment into their design and delivery. Only in this way can processes be consistently maintained and developed to meet the increasingly competitive nature of today's markets.

Until the past two decades many organizations took the narrow view of the nature and extent of people's contribution in the delivery system – that of completing the physical tasks involved in service and product provision. The role of people in the planning, improvement and evaluation of processes was neither recognized nor required. Why this was so, the changes in managing people that are being adopted and the nature of their contribution in today's organizations are discussed in the rest of the chapter.

Changes in the workplace

As economies, societies and technologies develop, so attitudes, expectations and other dimensions that concern the workplace also change. Businesses need to recognize and anticipate how these developments will affect the nature of work, the changing roles of those involved and how best to manage the people within organizations as they evolve. This section sets out the principal changes that have and are taking place in the workplace so as to set the scene and provide context for the later sections that address approaches and developments to the ways of managing people.

Increasingly competitive nature of markets

The increasingly competitive nature of markets has been already highlighted and, as explained in the last chapter, the strategic role of operations concerns supporting the market-driven and market-driving order-winners and qualifiers for which it is solely or jointly responsible. In many markets, the order-winners and qualifiers that relate to operations are becoming more important in terms of retaining and growing market share and entering new markets. In such circumstances the ability of managers to organize resources to meet these needs is paramount. Central to this provision are the people that work in operations, and how they are managed and motivated is increasingly important to the eventual outputs. Managing an organization's human resources to meet the needs of a business while allowing and encouraging the people involved to attain their full potential is a critical role. As markets become increasingly competitive the contribution of everyone to help meet these new challenges is essential. Part of the way to bring this about lies in the structure of organizations, work design, how well people are motivated to do a good job and the involvement of people in managing and continuously improving all aspects of operations' task and work environment.

Outsourcing aspects of HRM and growing use of temporary staff

Two significant changes have entered the general style of running organizations in the past five years:

- Many people who work for organizations are no longer directly employed by those organizations, falling under the category of agency staff.

- More and more businesses have outsourced many of the tasks traditionally undertaken by the HR function.

The outcome is that often businesses no longer have a traditional relationship with their staff and no longer manage major aspects of this relationship with the people who are, in reality, their staff – a trend that is likely to grow in the future. While it's one thing to take advantage of the flexibility that comes with using temporary, or agency staff, or to outsource the more tedious aspects of HR management (HRM), it's quite another for companies to take their eye off developing their staff as an essential part of staying competitive and deriving strategic advantage.

If by outsourcing parts of the HR function organizations damp down the importance of, or even lose their capability to develop and retain, key people they will become seriously disadvantaged. While there is some rationale for outsourcing the more mundane aspects of people management to a third-party provider, organizations need to take great care that they don't damage or destroy their essential relationship with their people.[1]

Employee commitment

As economies develop, people's attitude to work and the inherent commitment they have to an organization's goals typically change. While organizations retain many people who are self-motivated, find their work challenging and wish to complete tasks as well as possible, there are many who need to be encouraged to work well. This is not really surprising. Many people go to work for reasons based on custom and necessity. Also, the job opportunities open to many rarely afford a wide choice and are, by and large, prescribed by education, experience, physical and mental abilities, personality and chance. Consequently, many take on jobs that, after a time, tend to become repetitious and dull, a situation that has been increased by the growing number of low-prestige jobs (often referred to as 'McJobs', for obvious reasons) in the retail and service sectors.

The ability to inspire the emotional and intellectual commitment of people needs to be high on the corporate agenda and a critical skill that operations executives have to develop and apply. Although the operations task is seen as being inextricably bound up with technology, processes, materials and other tangible dimensions of the job, managing people is not only sizeable (operations executives manage those directly involved in the delivery system as well as a range of support staff) but critical to the operations task and overall success of a business. Consequently, improving people's jobs, creating opportunities for them to influence and improve their working environment, and linking their contributions to business outcomes must be provided and sustained.

> **EXECUTIVE INSIGHT**
> Though many people are self-motivated, many are not. The need to develop the emotional and intellectual commitment of people, therefore, needs to be high on the corporate agenda.

Technical content of jobs

While the increasing use of technology developments in the workplace has increased the technical dimensions of some roles, for many jobs the technical content has declined. This trend will continue as it forms part of the base on which productivity improvement is built which, in turn, is so essential to becoming and remaining competitive in current and future markets. Where the technical content has grown, the associated higher levels of technology lead to improved processes, with fewer but better educated people for whom the motivational needs must be recognized and met. On the other hand, for those people where the technical content of work has declined, the inherently interesting nature of the task is diluted. To compensate for this loss, other ways to motivate people need to be sought and introduced.

Pace of change

Organizations also have to deal with the issues discussed so far in an environment where the rate of change is higher both in terms of frequency and extent. Furthermore, reducing service/product life cycles, the global nature of markets, the relative insecurity of employment and the worldwide sourcing of services and products all add to the dynamics of today's business environment.

Information-related technologies have changed work roles and organizational relationships. Beepers, emails and mobile telephone systems empower people to interact with others, including customers, outside the formal reporting structures of organizations. Teleworking requires different management skills and staff responses to work. The technology-based provision of services such as call centre arrangements is also changing the functional as well as individual roles.

Innovations such as these need to be accommodated within revised organizational structures and are challenging operations managers in the new millennium. The pace of change is not easy to live with, but those companies that develop organizations that accept change as a way of life and progressively involve people in better serving their customers and in developing and improving their delivery systems are those that will succeed in the future, as the San Diego Zoo development outlined in Case 3.1 illustrates.

Legislation

In more developed economies, legislation relating to the workplace has been on the increase over the past decade which, together with other government regulations, government-required paperwork and tax compliance, has added to the burden of employing people both in terms of time and cost.

However, it is not just the increased paperwork and procedures that managers need to understand, handle and follow but also the need to adhere to these in the context of the threat of legal action. Adding to the number of lawsuits are the growing incidents of sexual harassment cases. Between 2000 and 2008 the number of these cases filed with the Equal Employment Opportunity Commission in the USA increased almost six-fold from some 16,000 a year to over 95,000. And for every case filed, ten or more were being settled in-house, each requiring many hours of investigation and hearings. Operations managers are typically in the thick of this. One outcome is the time it takes away from the core tasks of meeting customer needs, improving performance and developing people. Managers no longer see people as the company's greatest asset but as its greatest liability![2]

General definitions

It will be helpful at this stage to check the definition of some general terms used when discussing work and jobs, such as job content, satisfaction and performance.

Job content

Job content establishes the scope and depth of work. Scope is the range of tasks that make up a job. Thus, a job with narrow scope means that it contains few tasks and will tend to be highly repetitive. A widening of **job scope** implies that the range of tasks involved is increased horizontally. This increases the variety of the work performed and reduces monotony, but does not increase the responsibilities within a job, or the depth of the work involved. Figure 3.1 illustrates how the content of job B is greater than job A on both the dimensions of scope and depth.

Job depth refers to the degree of authority people have to plan and organize the work for which they are responsible. It concerns the level of control that they have over their own working environment. Thus, if people have little or no influence over the planning of their work and have to carry out the plans of others, the job depth is low. Therefore, an assembly line worker whose rate of working is controlled by the pace of the line and who carries out the tasks planned by others has a low job content (both low scope and low depth).

Job satisfaction and motivation

Job satisfaction and **motivation** are not synonymous. Job satisfaction reflects a person's attitude to the job and the level of interest it holds, and increases organizational loyalty and commitment rather than performance. Motivation, on the other hand, concerns the desire to perform well which could lead to increased effort and a higher performance.

Job scope – refers to the range of tasks that make up a job. Widening the scope of work (also known as job enlargement) involves increasing the variety of tasks involved, but does not include additional responsibilities within a job or increasing the depth of work.

Job depth – refers to the degree of authority people have to plan and organize their work. Increasing depth is also referred to as job enrichment.

Job satisfaction – reflects a person's attitude to the job and the level of interest it holds. It increases organizational loyalty and commitment rather than increasing performance.

Motivation – concerns the desire to perform well, which could result in greater effort and higher performance.

Until recently, the wild animals were not the only ones plotting their escape from San Diego Zoo. Many employees felt as if they were in cages too. Although their cages were figurative, not literal, the effect was the same: the employees felt as if they were trapped in rigid, dead-end jobs, without the power to make a difference.

In an effort to raise the quality of life for both animals and employees, the managers of the zoo decided to radically restructure the way the zoo saw itself. Instead of a place that merely displayed wild animals, and it has over 4,000 animals and more than 800 species, San Diego Zoo transformed itself into an organization that could make each visit more interesting to its customers by creatively educating visitors about their animals and their habitats.

Zoo officials got rid of traditional cages and spent millions of dollars to create 'bio-climatic zones' throughout its 100 acres (40 hectares) where the animals could feel at home. These range from an African rain forest (featuring gorillas) to the Arctic taiga and tundra (featuring polar bears). The employees of each zone are organized into work teams to brainstorm ideas for making the zoo a better place to work in as well as for entertaining and educating visitors.

Throughout the zoo all the work teams now function, in effect, as separate organizations, with team members or immediate supervisors making most, if not all, the decisions on hiring, work rotas, holidays and budgets. 'It is like managing your own business here', one team member explained.

Not all employees were immediately enamoured with the new arrangement, however. Some cynically saw the work teams as a way for management to squeeze more work out of them. But even the sceptics have come round and now everybody agrees that the zoo is a better place to work in.

Employees are not the only ones to benefit from the restructuring. Many senior managers at the zoo are also top-notch curators, but the pressure of day-to-day decision-making had kept them too preoccupied to pursue their true vocations so providing a key contribution. With the work teams now handling most of these operating details, the curators can focus on their areas of expertise, such as in the zoo's Centre for the Reproduction of Endangered Species.

www.sandiegozoo.org

Questions

1. What aspects of the 'Changes in the workplace' section are illustrated here?

2. What were the key features that brought about these changes?

Lecturers: visit www.palgrave.com/business/hillom3e for teaching guidelines for this case study

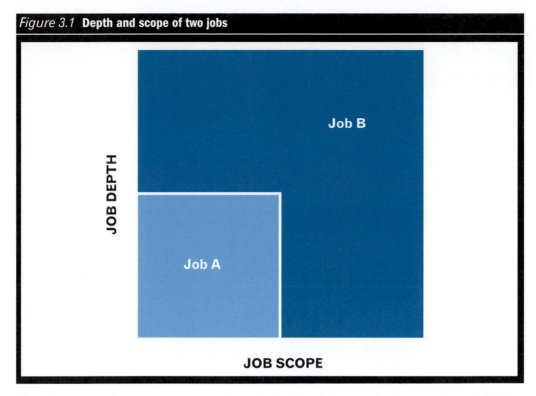

Figure 3.1 **Depth and scope of two jobs**

Job B

JOB DEPTH

Job A

JOB SCOPE

The distinction between aspects of work that lead to satisfaction or dissatisfaction and those that motivate people was well drawn by Hertzberg.[3] He emphasized the difference between those factors that led to dissatisfaction if not maintained (referred to as 'hygiene factors') and those that prompted motivation (referred to as 'motivators'). Factors such as physical conditions, security, pay and relationships were put forward as hygiene factors, while aspects of work such as personal growth, responsibility and achievement were classed as motivators. Motivation, therefore, plays an intermediate role between satisfaction and performance, for even a satisfied person will only tend to meet performance standards when adequately motivated.

Job performance

Job performance is dependent not only upon the level of motivation that exists but also upon a person's ability. For good job performance standards to be achieved and sustained, it is essential that both skill and attitude form the ingredients of the work situation. Unless both these aspects are reviewed and developed then the desired results and outcomes will neither be achieved nor retained.

Traditional approaches to work design

Some of the traditional philosophies of organizational design, role design and job design that have influenced business cultures are now reviewed. It is not intended that this is an exhaustive list. Its aim is to provide a basis for later discussion on some key features in work design that organizations are revisiting as a way to better harness the experience and capabilities of their staff. As the three topics are part of the same whole, you will note that there is some overlap between them.

Organizational design

As explained in Chapter 2, as organizations grow they cope with the resulting complexity that comes with size by breaking the business into parts that we call 'functions'. For most companies functions are used as the building blocks by which organizations are structured. While based initially on pragmatism, this approach brings with it a mix of advantages and disadvantages, some of which the following text highlights.

Control through specialists

Functions become responsible for parts of the total task. This design not only makes the total task more manageable but also enables staff to become proficient regarding the skills and capabilities that reflect the technical and behavioural dimensions of their part of the total task. In addition, organizations also introduce specialists whose brief is typically to improve relevant functions by developing and improving procedures, systems and activities within the broad area of their specialism. The result is that activities that were once all completed in one function (such as operations) are now under the control and auspices of one or more specialist functions. This takes place for several reasons:

- The traditional view often held by organizations is that all activities of a similar nature are best arranged and managed under one function.

- An executive function (one responsible for part of the principal activity of an organization such as operations and sales) was willing to shed some of its total task.

- A specialist function's inherent inclination is to grow the size of its area of responsibility.

These developments have, in turn, led to a number of problems:

- Developments in specialist fields often outpace the understanding of those managers responsible for the executive functions in which the specialist advice and developments will be applied. Hence, the eventual users and custodians of technology have difficulty in participating in discussions on the technology developments in question, both in terms of technical fit and appropriateness of application.

- Some tasks best performed by an executive function such as operations are now performed elsewhere.

- Ownership of the development and maintenance of the systems and procedures used in an organization are typically seen by that organization to be part of a specialist and not a user function's responsibilities. This view is compounded by the fact that the staff necessary to complete the development and maintenance tasks are available only in specialist departments. As a result, control over priorities and work orientation tends to reside outside the direct influence of user functions.

Hierarchical structures

The breaking down of work into executive and specialist functions is mirrored in the hierarchical structure that typifies most organizations. Staff groups are responsible to their own supervisors or team leaders and so on up the organization through different managerial reporting systems. The resulting structures are seen as being consistent with the functional approach to developing organizations and also serves to confirm this approach and style as being the best way to manage them.

Control from a distance

One further outcome is that the controls and procedures are often designed and installed from a distance. Where such an approach is adopted it brings with it a strong sense of analytical detachment from the reality of the function or business concerned, with the solution based upon some theoretical view of what should take place rather than developing the controls and procedures around what really happens. Classically these organizational developments reinforce the separation of the key specialist functions from essential aspects of the executive task. The outcome is an increased lack of ownership by those parts of a business that are responsible for meeting the needs of customers and markets.

Role design

The drive towards specialization and the hierarchical nature of organizations also impacts the roles within the different parts of a business as explained below.

Work patterns

The pattern of work that follows the executive/specialist elements of organizational design helps separate work into its constituent parts, so that the planning, doing and evaluating elements that make up work are undertaken by different groups of staff reporting in different functional structures, as shown in Figure 3.2. The resulting roles suffer from the inherent difficulty of having split tasks into parts and then trying to put them back together.

Specialization of staff

As volumes increase, the move towards higher volume systems and processes brought with it the design of jobs based on specialization. Higher investment in the delivery system, underpinned by higher volumes, often further reduces the technical content of jobs and presents a simple, repetitive task at each step in the process. These developments merely serve to reinforce the trend in work patterns.

> **EXECUTIVE INSIGHT**
> Approaches to work design result in staff whose tasks are limited to solely providing services or making products with all the 'planning' and 'evaluating' (often the more interesting) elements of work done by others.

This basic concept of specialization has been central to increasing the efficiency of delivery systems and has, without doubt, made a significant contribution to the growing prosperity of nations and the high standard of living now available to most industrialized communities. However, these potential gains in productivity are only maintained by the sound control of resources, continuous improvement and the effective management of people. Too often the role of staff is seen as serving a system which discourages participation and excludes the important contribution of most of an organization's people resource.

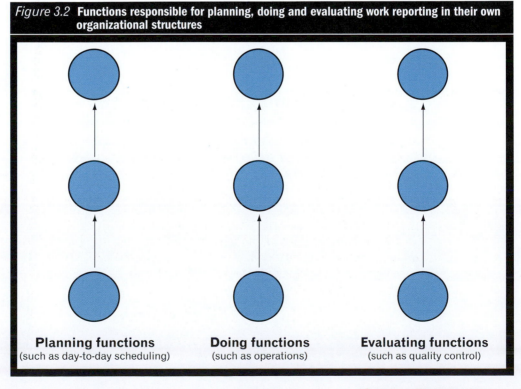

Figure 3.2 **Functions responsible for planning, doing and evaluating work reporting in their own organizational structures**

Planning functions
(such as day-to-day scheduling)

Doing functions
(such as operations)

Evaluating functions
(such as quality control)

'It's not what you say as a leader, but what you **do** that defines you'

Staff contribution

One result of the traditional organizational and job design approaches is that the overall contribution of staff is constrained. Invariably it constitutes the specific 'doing' element of the task (see Figure 3.2) and what is delivered is limited by the structures and expectations in place. Although some organizations may talk about a wider and fuller contribution, such statements can be at best ones of exhortation, with reality not matching expectation. These approaches are epitomized by the maxim that 'when staff come to work they leave their brains at the gate'.

Job design

How job design can be used to help overcome some of the downsides of traditional approaches to organizational and role design is now reviewed. This provides the context for the later sections on how to manage people more effectively in order to retain valuable staff while maximizing their contribution to the ongoing success of a business.

Job enlargement

Job enlargement increases the scope of a job by adding to the number of operations to be performed by a person. Such changes increase variety but may not include more demanding tasks or greater responsibility to control one's work. For this reason this type of increase is deemed to be horizontal in nature (see Figure 3.3). The advantages include increasing the variety of both the work to be completed and the skills to be used as well as providing an opportunity for a person to be responsible for a set of tasks that constitute, where possible, an identifiable programme of work.

> **Job enlargement** – refers to widening the scope of work by increasing the variety of tasks involved, but does not include greater responsibility within a job.

Job rotation

It is not always possible to enlarge jobs as a way of increasing their intrinsic interest. Also, in many service organizations certain jobs have to be performed throughout the normal day or over a 24-hour period, for example the checkout counter in a library or supermarket, and the night shift in fire, police and hospital services. In the first example, the task is monotonous but does not lend itself to enlargement. In the second example, although parts of the work often include areas of greater responsibility than tasks completed during other parts of the working day, the unsociable hours of the night shift make it undesirable to most people. In these circumstances, job or shift rotation is used periodically to change the job assignments or times of working.

Job enrichment

As with job enlargement, **job enrichment** widens the scope of the job while also increasing job depth, giving people a greater responsibility to organize and control the work that has to be done. The outcome is greater autonomy and personal development opportunities for the staff involved. For this reason such changes are deemed to be enriching in nature – see Figure 3.3.

> **Job enrichment** – widens the scope of a job while also increasing job depth by giving people more responsibility to organize and control their work.

For meaningful control to take place, the necessary information on which to base sensible decisions must be made available to those now responsible for making such decisions. In addition, the organizational climate necessary for a successful change of this kind must be provided by all concerned. In the early stages, at least, there will be some who will view job enrichment for other staff as including a measure of role reduction for themselves leading to an erosion of their own responsibilities.

Changes to working schedules

Where job designs are difficult to alter, organizations can introduce changes in the working week as a way to make work more interesting. For example, in more developed economies there is an ongoing call for a shorter working week. In response, changes have been introduced to achieve this end, such as the introduction of a working week comprising normal weekly hours but compressed into four days to allow a longer weekend. Another approach is the introduction of **flexitime**, which allows employees a certain amount of freedom in selecting their hours of working. In that way an opportunity to vary the pattern of hours worked in a day and/or week is achieved. The basis of a flexitime arrangement is that each person is required to be at work during certain 'core' hours, but at other times people can choose, within certain procedural agreements, the pattern of working for a particular day or week.

New approaches to work design

With the context set, this section looks at how approaches to organizational, role and job design have changed and the rationale that underpins these developments. Again, the topics in this section overlap and are interdependent, in that for developments to be completed in one topic area, developments would need to be made in another topic area. However, organizations can and do move forward at the organizational, role or job level even where there is overlap and, having done so, make these developments self-sustaining. Moving towards better ways of designing work often has to include an element of pragmatism – doing what the organization and people are ready for. This task is always a long haul and companies need to progress these developments as best they can.

Organizational redesign

Here we look at the ways that organizations are changing. These concepts and approaches form part of the way that progressive companies design their organizations and develop their people to help meet the demands of today's markets, while creating environments that provide those involved with the opportunity to contribute fully to the needs of the business.

The learning organization

The underlying argument and rationale for moving to an organization designed purposefully and continuously to improve and adapt to change is easy to recognize and overwhelming in its proposition. But designing and developing an organization that

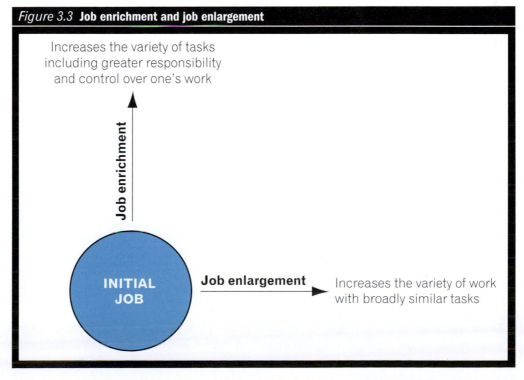

Figure 3.3 **Job enrichment and job enlargement**

Increases the variety of tasks including greater responsibility and control over one's work

Job enrichment

INITIAL JOB

Job enlargement

Increases the variety of work with broadly similar tasks

helps individuals, as well as the business as a whole, to embrace and adapt to change is as difficult as it is logical. Organizational commitment to such fundamental tasks is a prerequisite for success but often this is neither recognized nor forthcoming. Peter Senge puts forward the view that organizations, like individuals, can suffer from learning disorders. Learning disabilities are tragic in children but are no less tragic in organizations, he observes.[4] Because of these disorders, few organizations live even half as long as a person – most die before the age of 40. Senge's view of learning organizations includes a framework for understanding why some organizations are unable to develop team-based management styles that can adopt a proactive attitude towards, and an acceptance of, the necessity for change. He highlights the need for organizations to embrace change as an ongoing feature if they are to grow and prosper.

But these capabilities are not inherent in organizations. They need to be built into the structure and developed on an ongoing basis. Management teams do not start out great but learn how to produce extraordinary results. Teams and organizations that learn faster than competitors can gain a competitive advantage. Creating a learning organization is not only fundamental to long-term success but also cannot be purchased or created as the need arises. It can only be developed over time and those organizations that have embraced change and nurture and reinforce these attitudes and environments can create a sustainable advantage over their competitors.

To create an organization that can 'truly learn', Senge puts forward five essential dimensions:

1. **Systems thinking** highlights the need in a learning organization to understand and work at the 'big picture' level in order to evaluate developments and prioritize actions. The gestalt approach to learning emphasizes the need for organizations to understand the whole in order to better understand the parts, and firms need to develop a process for seeing the big picture in order to provide a context in which events, issues and developments are placed and evaluated.

2. **Personal mastery** involves a reciprocal relationship between individuals and an organization. Developing the emotional and intellectual needs of people and directing their energies towards achieving personal goals and development targets will enhance them as individuals as well as enhancing their contribution to the organization in which they work.

3. **Mental models** highlight one way in which individuals learn and carry forward experience and learning from the past into their current way of working. Deeply ingrained assumptions, generalizations and paradigms influence the way individuals see the world in general and the work environment in particular, and influence approaches to current ways of completing tasks and making changes. Mental models often form barriers to personal development and organizational change. People in learning organizations must have open minds that are receptive to the need for change, be willing and able to recognize and assess their own perceptions and address the underlying assumptions that underpin their own mental models in order to reduce or remove any inherent barriers to how they think about and review situations and opportunities.

4. **Building shared vision** involves developing common views of the future that foster genuine commitment and involvement rather than compliance. But developing a shared vision can only happen in an organizational structure where employees are truly empowered and learning takes place throughout. It's a long process underpinned by hard work.

5. **Team learning** requires people to set aside assumptions and stereotypes and instead address issues and problems in such a way that individuals, teams and the organization as a whole can learn and develop.

Developing a change-oriented organization

As competition increases, it is paramount that organizations anticipate the need for change. Companies have to be on the lookout not only for competitive threats but also opportunities to change proactively in order to keep ahead.

A change-accepting culture stimulates and reinforces awareness of development opportunities by creating an environment where experimentation is encouraged without recrimination. As Deming (a leading international figure in the field of quality management) listed as one of his 14 points for management, organizations need to drive out fear as a prerequisite for change.

Similarly, Senge[5] lists as one of the 'laws of the fifth discipline' that there should be a 'no blame' culture within organizations in order to encourage and stimulate a proactive response to change from inside companies. Too often managers create an environment that discourages individuals from proactively challenging current approaches and practices. The ensuing risk-averse culture is, at best, unproductive and, at worst, promotes political infighting to safeguard individual and functional boundaries. 'Turf protection', which refers to functions safeguarding the existing status, activities and responsibilities of staff in their part of a business, is the unproductive outcome.

Using external threats to prevent organizations becoming complacent can, however, be a constructive development. For example, Bill Gates, when he was CEO of Microsoft, frequently emailed staff to alert them to the ongoing threat of competition thereby helping to prevent complacency. In the same way, some organizations encourage staff to think 'outside the box' by making this activity an integral part of their work. For instance, 3M requires researchers to spend 10 per cent of their time on personal ideas that are not a part of the formal, corporate research and development agenda. Post-it notes are one example of the outcomes of this initiative.

The changing role of managers

As with executives who manage other functions, operations managers are responsible for two distinct sets of activities:

1. To organize, manage and control those areas of a business for which they are responsible – the internal day-to-day dimension

2. To develop and improve performance in operations with regard to the order-winners and qualifiers for which operations is solely or jointly responsible – the external, customer-facing, strategic dimension.

The first step is to separate the strategic directing tasks from those of managing and controlling the internal sets of responsibilities that concern making day-to-day, short-term events happen. With this separation in place, it is then necessary to recognize that managers do not manage people. On the contrary, people manage themselves. What executives manage and influence is the context and environment in which people work. The management task is to think through the structure and systems of an organization (that is, the way an organization works) in order to create the values, expectations and environment in which people can manage themselves more effectively.

The essential role of managers is to create conditions where people want responsibility, will learn and hence manage themselves in a way that maximizes their contribution to an organization as well as their own personal development. One result is that it makes the decision and action phases part of the same set of responsibilities. For this to happen, managers have to recognize that their role has to change from one of making decisions to one of communicating a vision and confirming business objectives while also getting people to recognize and appreciate their own behaviour, own their own problems and be responsible for putting things right.

To do this managers have to think through their own role and relationships as well as the roles of others. People interpret roles from their past experience of organizations and the sets of responsibilities, areas of decision-making and status associated with roles and titles.

What managers say, ask about or question signals interest and importance. Where they seek information or opinion and then take decisions, ownership of these areas of responsibility and the associated developments, solutions and decision-making roles consequently rest with them. Where managers call for decisions and explanations, then they reinforce the transfer of these responsibilities to others. For such changes to happen, managers need to recognize their key role in changing the status quo. Defining the areas of responsibility and boundaries for taking ownership of problems and solutions is part of the environment-setting task of managers, and a prerequisite for empowering people within an organization.

Flatter organizations

As mentioned earlier, in more developed economies most organizations make extensive use of specialists to run a business. The typical approach adopted has been to create specialist functions to supply expert advice, guidance and help in various areas to the main functions in a business (such as operations).

> **EXECUTIVE INSIGHT**
> The extensive use of specialists has contributed to organizations with too many layers making good communications and effective collaboration difficult to maintain.

The extensive use of specialists often results in organizations with too many layers (with the associated increased overhead costs) and makes good communications and

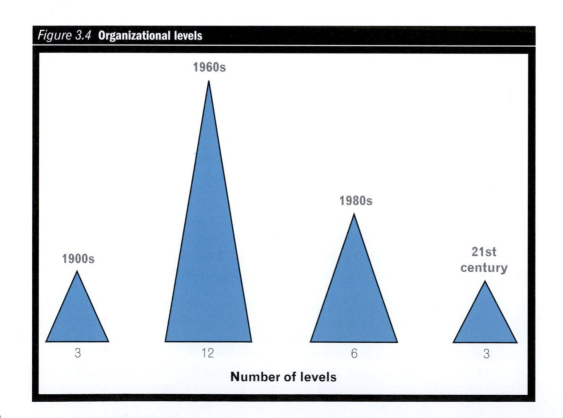

Figure 3.4 **Organizational levels**

effective collaboration all the more difficult to maintain. The results are reviewed in Figure 3.4, which illustrates the changes in number of layers of management through the twentieth century up to the present. The need to reduce the layers in most organizations is essential. But companies need to undertake this critical task with care. Avoiding across-the-board reductions is most important as this assumes that existing structures will be appropriate in a scaled-down form. Reshaping organizations is a job for a scalpel, not an axe. Reducing the size of organizations has to be carried out in line with business requirements, and must include top-down as well as bottom-up approaches. Reshaping an organization has to take into account the role of functions, establish the responsibility for decisions and boundaries of authority, and agree on which tasks are completed by specialists and which are best undertaken by the functions responsible for providing the services and making the products. This approach ensures that truly specialist activities are left to specialists, while all other activities are undertaken by those functions and people providing the services and making the products.

A business-related approach, therefore, enables a company to develop its organization in line with its needs and provides the opportunity to ensure that tasks are completed by the most appropriate function and at the most appropriate level in a firm. In this way, the role of managers, the need to empower people throughout an organization and where tasks are best undertaken can reflect the needs of the business in today's increasingly competitive markets.

Role redesign

Superior organizational performance is ultimately provided by people. Appropriate infrastructure in the form of procedures and systems is essential, but the capabilities that enable an organization to best support the order-winners and qualifiers of its markets are those that come from people. These capabilities include the skills, technical know-how, ability to solve problems and make decisions, capacity for learning and motivation to make things happen.

Also, what makes it difficult for one organization to match the people capability within another organization is the time and mind-set changes involved. Creating an environment in which people can manage themselves more effectively is difficult and involves long timescales. The purpose of this section is to introduce some of the important dimensions in role design and highlight some of the issues involved.

Employee involvement and empowerment

> **Employee involvement and empowerment –** the process of pushing information, knowledge and power down to appropriate levels in an organization.

Within the organizational changes described in the last section the need to change people's roles to ones that involve and empower them in relevant aspects of the organization was a common theme throughout.

Employee involvement and empowerment is the process of pushing information, knowledge and power down to appropriate levels in an organization. In that way it is a management initiative designed to increase employee information about, and commitment to, the organization. However, the idea of employee involvement is not new. Columella, a Roman agriculturalist, reflecting on the ways of managing his estate workers, wrote in AD 100: 'Nowadays I make a practice to call them [his estate workers] into consultation on any new work... I observe they are more willing to set about a piece of work on which their opinions have been asked and their advice followed.'[6] Clearly, Columella understood the impact on the level of worker commitment by involving them in the decision-making process from the start.

Over the past 30–40 years, companies have increasingly recognized that involving and empowering people in aspects of work other than the prime role of completing their principal tasks is essential if the abilities of all employees are to be harnessed to help improve the overall business. Suggestion schemes and quality circles (see later) are two ways of achieving this aim.

> **EXECUTIVE INSIGHT**
> Employee involvement and empowerment is the process of pushing information, knowledge and power down to appropriate levels in an organization.

Suggestion schemes

Such schemes encourage staff to come up with ideas that may lead to tangible savings or an improvement in the way something is done. In terms of the average annual number of suggestions per employee, results vary as does the success rate, but an organization can expect up to 20 ideas per year for each 100 staff employed and adoption rates of over 25 per cent. Some organizations do a lot better. Toyota, for example, records success rates far in excess of these norms, with 48 suggestions per employee per year and an adoption rate of over 90 per cent. To succeed, suggestion schemes need to meet the following criteria:

- They must be carefully planned and provided with the resources and management backing to sustain them over the long-term.

- They require constant promotion. Linking them to other regular events helps. For example, Richer Sounds, a UK-based hi-fi chain, funds a monthly brainstorming session for the teams working in each of the company's stores and the venue is each team's local pub.

- They should be fun, for example T-shirts and coffee mugs with appropriate logos for all who contribute. Schemes can also be enlivened with short-term campaigns based on themes such as customer care, energy saving or the environment.

- Suggestions must be handled quickly and efficiently. If staff have a good idea and get excited, they should not wait more than a day or two at most for a response, and a decision should be made within a week. Also 'not adopted' rather than 'rejected' reduces the demotivational aspect of a turndown.

- Suggestions should be rewarded. Although views vary on the extent and type of the reward, one-off payments tend to average about 20 per cent of the annual savings that result.

Quality circles

Quality circles are improvement groups that comprise structured, voluntary work groups of around six or eight people from a particular work area. Meeting for about one hour on a weekly or fortnightly basis, they address and resolve work-related problems that the groups themselves have selected. Those taking part are trained in new skills, such as problem analysis, as well as developing their all-round abilities such as working in groups, problem-solving and implementing change. Quality circles are a means of giving employees the opportunity to do something positive about the problems and issues they face, rather than just making suggestions for others in the organization to consider. They are based on the philosophy of making more effective use of an organization's most valuable asset, its people. The role of a group is to identify and select problems over which they have jurisdiction, while solutions that fall outside their remit are put forward as suggestions for change. Although generally having limited power, groups are able to fix certain problems that fall within their scope of activity.

The origins and development of quality circles have their roots in Japanese businesses. Many of the early problems facing Japanese companies concerned quality-related issues

Quality circles – improvement groups that comprise structured, voluntary work groups to address and resolve work-related problems that the groups themselves have selected.

and this led to the term 'quality circles', whereas, in fact, the problems addressed concern all aspects of work. Hence many organizations use the term 'improvement groups' to better reflect their purpose. Case 3.2 shows how these work at Unipart.

Self-managed teams

For many organizations employee involvement is the start of a long journey. As Figure 3.5 illustrates, there are four stages in the redesign of jobs, beginning with staff involvement and collaboration through to where jobs are designed around self-managed teams and the more extensive role that this comprises. Major redesigns at one level often require change at other levels and, in this instance, organizational design changes will need to reflect this fundamental job change within the management structure of a business. At Stage 4, the business becomes virtually an organization without rank.

Job redesign

Organizations are introducing extensive job redesigns so that employees use a variety of skills, often in teams. Under this development, staff have considerable freedom in deciding how to do the necessary tasks. Furthermore, work is designed to involve elements not directly associated with providing the services or products, such as aspects of planning, scheduling and evaluation. To bring this about requires organizations to rethink who does what. To illustrate let us see how the use of specialists has evolved.

Phase 1 of Figure 3.6 shows how activities that were originally undertaken by executive functions (such as operations see Figure 1.1) have been separated and housed under the auspices of a specialist function. For example, the tasks completed by a supply chain department may typically include supplier-related roles, contract negotiation, placing purchase orders and arranging for services and goods to be brought to site when needed. This is then reinforced by structures that create distinct reporting lines that separate the provision of an activity from the direct user, as shown in Phase 2, Figure 3.6.

The disadvantage of these arrangements is that whereas the first two tasks listed in the supply chain example above fall within that specialism, the other two tasks would be better undertaken by the function wanting the services and goods. In this instance, what services or products are required and when they are needed is best known and undertaken by the user. A central provision of these latter tasks results in additional procedures, additional communications and the potential for mistakes.

In most companies the decision concerning who does which task results in operations staff completing the doing task (that is, providing the service or product). But a job comprises the three separate elements of planning, doing and evaluating. As shown in Figure 3.7, these three parts of work have been separated and are now in different reporting systems within an organization – a byproduct of the use of specialists and the development of support functions within a business. Figure 3.7 is, therefore, an extension of Phase 2 in Figure 3.6. It illustrates a typical structure and shows the separation of important parts of the whole task into different sets of functional responsibilities that report in different systems and the gap that results between the reporting lines of these three intrinsic parts of work.

This has led to situations where the contribution from those responsible for providing the services and products to activities such as continuous improvement and the day-to-day scheduling of work has been lost, and the essential link between the responsibility for providing services and products and checking the quality conformance of the service or product involved has been severed.

STAGE 1

Involvement and collaboration

Traditional structure

Teams with supervisory control

Participate in problem resolution and improvement activities

Supervisor responsible for output and behaviour

External specialist support

STAGE 2

Shared responsibility

Traditional structure with overall control retained by management

Team-based – with appointed leader

Teams responsible for output of the process and participate in problem resolution and improvement activities

STAGE 3

Empowered ownership

Traditional structure with overall control retained by management

Self-directed teams with some integrated support and overviewed by operations manager

Teams responsible for all aspects of the process

STAGE 4

Self-managed teams

Teams responsible for all aspects of the process and site

Self-directed teams with integrated support from specialist groups

Site-based group for medium-to-long-term decisions

An organization without rank

Unipart, the employee-owned, Oxford (UK)-based company with 2010 sales of over £1.0 billion, channels some 250 million items a year from about 5,000 suppliers to about 30,000 individual customers including Vodafone, Hewlett-Packard, Virgin Trains, Jaguar and the UK's Ministry of Defence. Most of Unipart's 9,500 staff work on the distribution side of the business. It has five large warehouses which, together with 500 small distribution operations, handle some 6,500 different items a year.

Unipart's staff (whether in distribution or manufacturing) are grouped into 1,500 small teams that meet daily to discuss problems and opportunities for improvement. These 'improvement circles' include representatives of customers, suppliers and transport groups. In a circle, participants spend an hour or so a week discussing how to speed up deliveries or why part of an operation is not working properly and communicate their progress and end results to others in the company. Each work unit has a room fitted with IT systems linked to the intranet and the rest of the company. This keeps everyone in touch, allows anyone to contribute to a circle's project and enables circles to check previous discussions and outcomes so that people don't spend a lot of time going over old ground.

www.unipart.com

Questions

1. What are some of the ways that Unipart ensures that as many staff as possible contribute to the work of improvement circles, given the disparate nature of the group's structure?

2. Why do you think representatives from customers, suppliers and transport groups are sometimes included in an improvement circle?

Lecturers: visit www.palgrave.com/business/hillom3e for teaching guidelines for this case study

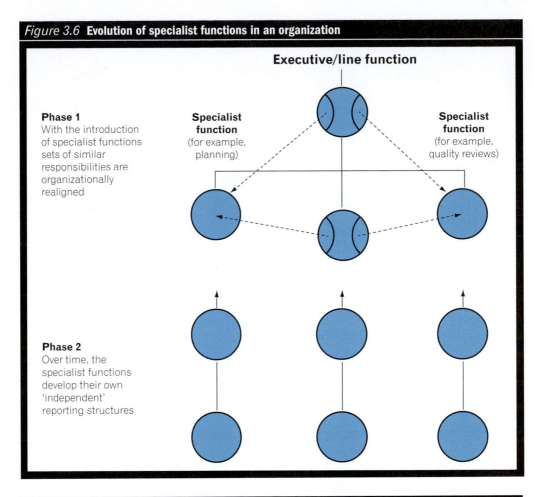

Figure 3.6 Evolution of specialist functions in an organization

Executive/line function

Phase 1
With the introduction of specialist functions sets of similar responsibilities are organizationally realigned

Specialist function
(for example, planning)

Specialist function
(for example, quality reviews)

Phase 2
Over time, the specialist functions develop their own 'independent' reporting structures

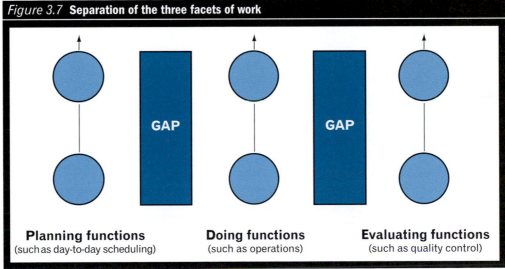

Figure 3.7 Separation of the three facets of work

GAP

GAP

Planning functions
(such as day-to-day scheduling)

Doing functions
(such as operations)

Evaluating functions
(such as quality control)

Figure 3.8 illustrates how appropriate planning and evaluating activities (presently completed by specialist support functions) should be reassigned to those currently responsible for providing the services or products (that is, operations). Such actions lend support to the arguments put forward earlier and also provide a tangible, common-sense illustration of the effect this can have. Such actions switch activities so that they now form part of the task undertaken by those responsible for completing the services and products, thus facilitating productivity improvements, the day-to-day scheduling of work and consistent conformance to specification, while at the same time creating greater job interest for all concerned. On the one hand it releases specialists from undertaking non-

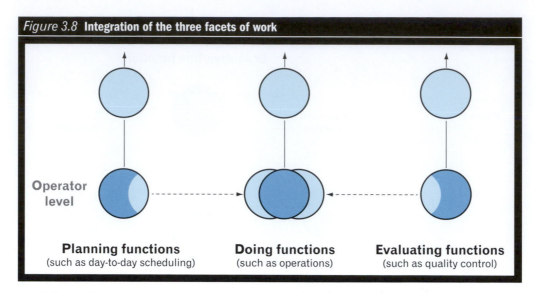

Figure 3.8 Integration of the three facets of work

Operator level

Planning functions
(such as day-to-day scheduling)

Doing functions
(such as operations)

Evaluating functions
(such as quality control)

specialist tasks, while on the other it gives those who provide services or products the responsibility for all three dimensions that make up meaningful tasks by broadening their activities and so allowing them to plan and evaluate the work they carry out.

> **EXECUTIVE INSIGHT**

If you reassign appropriate 'planning' and 'evaluating' tasks to those responsible for providing services or making products then this leads to gains all round.

Figure 3.9 includes the example of a supply chain as well as other functions to illustrate possible reallocations of activities from specialists to those who provide the services or make the products involved. Also, take a look back at Case 3.1, which provides an illustration of these points.

Figure 3.9 Examples of activities best undertaken by providers and those best completed by specialists

Aspect	Activities that are best undertaken by	
	Those providing services or products	Specialists
Purchasing	Placing orders or calling off deliveries of service or product against contracts	Supplier selection, supplier relations and contract negotiation
Operations planning and scheduling	Short-term operations control and day-to-day scheduling	Long-term planning and capacity planning
Quality assurance and control	Quality control including checking at all stages in the delivery system	Quality assurance including the development of sampling plans, customer reviews and material tests

In addition to the significant empowerment and involvement gains that come from increasing job scope by including indirect activities (that is, tasks that are not concerned directly with the provision of services or products) in the role of the providers, there are two further key advantages:

1. Decisions on day-to-day scheduling and the checking of services and products against specification are best completed at the point where the services or products are provided. It is here that the up-to-date position is known and the interval between finding faults and correcting the delivery system is shortest.

2. Where staff only undertake activities directly concerned with providing services or products, at times of low demand there are no alternative, indirect or non-providing

tasks for them to undertake. The available choice is to make inventory or incur non-value-adding costs.

Given these sets of gains, many companies are reallocating activities previously completed by overhead staff to the role of service and product providers. Now these latter staff have a mix of work that is more rewarding and reflects more appropriately the demand patterns and customer expectations in today's markets, the costs of which are met by reductions in overhead staff that follow.

Staff training and development

Naturally, these changes need to be underpinned by extensive training and staff development which would need to address three key areas:

1. Multiskilling – most job redesign initiatives need to be supported by the multiskilling of staff to facilitate team-based working and other organizational and role changes

2. The use of technology as well as new skills in the planning and evaluating activities that work would now comprise

3. Skills that concern the change in style and approach involved, such as group working, analysis, decision-making and implementation skills.

Flexitime and job sharing

To help create conditions that meet the needs of organizations and their staff, companies are turning to other work arrangements and packages that better fit the availability of their staff or provide people with more choice.

Flexitime offers staff an opportunity to adjust their working day to meet their domestic or social life patterns on a permanent or as-needed basis. The principal purpose is to help staff manage both their work and home commitments. In most schemes, the totalling and balancing of hours is made over a period of several weeks and allows for plus and minus balances to be carried forward within agreed limits.

Job sharing provides the opportunity for two people to meet the requirements of a job. These arrangements are usually on a 50/50 or 40/60 share basis.

Flexible benefit schemes

These schemes require staff to take part of their salary as cash but allow them to use the rest to buy extra benefits. For example, PricewaterhouseCoopers, a large UK accounting firm, gives staff a reward package comprising a notional salary and benefits entitlement. At least 80 per cent of salary must be taken as cash but the rest can be used to purchase benefits. In the PricewaterhouseCoopers' scheme, the range of benefits includes:

- Holidays – trade up or trade down by up to five days per year

- Childcare vouchers

- Sports and leisure club membership with discounts

- Group personal pension plan

- Luncheon vouchers useable at 30,000 outlets with 6 per cent discount

- Leased car scheme

- Substantial savings on group medical, dental and personal accident insurance.

Other people-related issues

This section provides an overview of several people-related issues and perspectives that form part of the task of managing people. While most are general in nature and application, some are specific to certain situations (for example, 'Managing operations overseas').

Recruitment and retention

Recruiting the right people is a major factor in helping ensure that the attitudes, values and work ethics required are met from the start. The need to allocate the time and attention to this task is self-evident. Analyzing recruitment and retention methods forms part of this investment, and for operations managers it is an essential part of their role at all levels in an organization. Although HR support is typically provided within a business, the ultimate responsibility for recruiting people rests with the function where they eventually work.

In his time as CEO of General Electric, Jack Welch personally interviewed candidates for the top 250 jobs in the organization. There is no better time to communicate expectations and requirements than at the start.

The use of short-term contracts is one way to help, as an organization can try people out and vice versa. One element of this development is the growing use of holiday work as a way to help pre-select employees. It needs to be used for what it is – a ten-week interviewing process. Selecting summer interns needs to have one eye on the long-term. The mutual opportunity to test skills and culture fit can reduce fall-out levels later. For example, Merrill Lynch, the investment banker, uses its summer programmes in this way. It takes up to 190 third-year students on its summer programme and typically offers up to 80 per cent a job on graduation.

How do organizations keep their skilled and experienced staff? The first thought that often comes to mind is pay! But this is only one element of a reward system. Reward refers to all the monetary payments and non-monetary and psychological benefits that an organization provides. The emphasis that staff place on each of these elements will differ by level in the organization and by individual at each level. What is sure is that paying more than the going rate rarely motivates for long and will not on its own retain staff. But, paying less will cause problems. The role of pay described here illustrates the insights provided by Hertzberg – the concept of hygiene factors and motivators. Pay too little and people are dissatisfied. Pay sufficiently well and the dissatisfaction factor is removed but will not in itself motivate. Other motivators need to be identified and provided, such as increasing the level of discretion in the job and more personal recognition.

Giving time and attention to people is at the root of understanding why they stay and why they leave and operations managers need to invest appropriately.

The growing use of temporary staff

Every working day, Adecco, a Swiss company and one of the world's biggest private employers, places nearly 700,000 temporary and full-time staff with businesses all over the world. Adecco is the 'temp industry' giant with 5,500 offices and sales revenues of €418.7 billion in 2010, but it only has a small share of the total market. In the USA alone there are thousands of such companies that together place some 2.5 million workers each day. The outsourcing of staff and the growing use of temporary staff is an international trend. For instance, Adecco's biggest market is France and its second largest is the USA. The task for operations managers is to recognize that much of its staff are either 'temps', employees of the outsourcer (for example, a call centre) or older part-time staff working on specific assignments. The underlying rationale for temporary staff is lower costs. But the productivity of people depends largely on how well they are managed and motivated. The fact that the organization doesn't own some staff does not discharge them from being responsible for motivating them. The challenge for operations in particular is managing all the people in the new regime.

Staff appraisals

The formal process of appraisals is still widely practised in many organizations. Although it varies by country and by sector, their use is still a characteristic part of the way managers manage people. Originally introduced as a way to help manage staff performance, in many organizations the annual appraisal round became the only time performance was discussed and resulted in a delay in addressing poor performance or praising good performance. Recognizing this, many organizations have now shifted ground on how best to use appraisals. Purposes range from making sure staff understand the aims of the business, identifying training needs, helping clarify roles and objectives and identifying ways to help improve performance and decisions on pay.

Where appraisal systems are in place, operations managers need to think through their role in the context of managing people and then discuss with and communicate to all concerned their purpose. Any help in managing people should be used and developed. With appraisals (as with much else) the key to getting the best out of the system includes keeping it simple with a clear purpose and ensuring that it is seen to be fair, so that expectation better matches reality.

Managing operations overseas

The growing internationalization of large organizations brings with it the task of managing overseas. While many organizations base their international expansion on their brand name, South African Breweries (since 2002 renamed SAB Miller following the acquisition of the US giant Miller Brewing) have based theirs on exporting people. South African Breweries (SAB) recognized that what made it initially successful (currently, it has a massive 98 per cent of the South African market) was its expertise and the experience of its people. As the company expanded overseas, it exported its home-grown technology, talent and management expertise to its operations around the world. But above all it exports its people – more than 200 South African expatriates work in the operations acquired abroad, with at least one (and sometimes as many as 20) in a business. SAB's initial focus was brewing beer in developing countries in Asia, Africa, Central and Eastern Europe and, most recently, Central America and India. Difficult emerging markets are where SAB honed its operations capabilities and business acumen. For example, it is now the second largest brewer in China but makes more profit than Tsingtao, the country's No.1 brewer.

The key here is that SAB transfers essential expertise in operations to elsewhere in the world. Often there will be a process technology mismatch but earlier experience of such situations resides in the capabilities of the company's existing operations managers. Getting the basics right and the foundations in place has been fundamental to SAB's successful development of these growth opportunities.

Ergonomics

Ergonomics is primarily concerned with how the human body fits with its environment. Reviewing and matching the physiological aspects of job design to the person doing a job contribute to greater productivity while reducing fatigue and avoiding conditions that may lead to physical strain and other types of health risks. It represents an important element of one of the key tasks in operations, that of managing people. Care for people makes sense all round and placing ergonomics in the managing people chapter, rather than in a later chapter addressing topics such as layout and improving operations, signals its integral role in the central dimension of operations management. Ergonomics addresses three key areas:

1. **Workplace factors** concerning the interface between the physical attributes of people and the workplace. The dimensions reviewed relate to features such as reach, relative heights of equipment to body positions such as seating to monitor dials or use of PC screens. The purpose is to design workplaces that reduce strain and fatigue over a working day while eliminating conditions that could lead to physical injury over time.

2. **Environmental factors** covering aspects of work that also impact job performance and could affect people's long-term health. Specified and supported by comprehensive occupational health and safety legislation, ergonomics lays down conditions concerning the temperature, lighting and noise levels for a variety of working environments.

3. **Behavioural factors** highlighting the role of these dimensions in effective workplace design. These factors link personal motivation and commitment to work design and build onto the change principles discussed earlier. Key factors include providing a meaningful set of activities that constitute a whole task, embodying aspects of planning, doing and evaluating within teams and establishing relationships, allowing staff to contact internal and external customers.

By combining these factors, companies are able to design workplaces that improve productivity, motivate people, encourage involvement and provide safe and stress-free environments.

Managing people in practice

- Ask yourself the question – if you see two 'workers' talking in the office or on the shop floor do you assume that they are not working? If so, it indicates that these staff are only engaged in 'doing' tasks.

- Starting with one function, review the indirect (overhead) functions in your organization and ask if there are any tasks that do not require specialist skills to complete. Then ask, would these be better completed by those staff responsible for providing the services or making the products you sell?

- Survey jobs to check on their content to identify any opportunities for increasing the depth and scope of work.

- Check out how improvement ideas are made and introduced in your organization and identify the channels you have in place for generating and using ideas from all your staff.

- Check the percentage of costs incurred by direct staff and indirect (overhead) staff. What does this reveal about how tasks are completed and where best to seek staff cost reductions?

- Check how many layers of staff there are in each department/function. Can the number of layers (and attendant costs) be reduced in part by changing the mix of work to not only reduce costs but also improve the job content and job interest for your staff?

Driving business performance

Managing the operations function through people and also the key interfaces with staff in other functions and the supply chain are essential to the successful performance of a business in the following ways.

Managing people to release cash

Reducing the response time to deliver services and products to customers is a key factor in accelerating the 'cash to work to cash' cycle outlined earlier in Figure 1.10. Partly–processed work, whether it be part-completed services or work-in-progress inventory, ties up cash that could be more productively used elsewhere in the organization while also delaying deliveries to customers.

Managing people to improve market support

As competition continues to increase, it is critical that organizations anticipate the need for change. Companies have to be on the lookout not only for competitive threats but also opportunities to change proactively to keep ahead. One key source to stay ahead in today's competitive markets is to tap into the capabilities of all the people in an organization. Operations need to link customers with the role of people in an organization to help ensure that customer retention is a key strategic objective.

Managing people to reduce costs

A business culture that accepts and embraces change stimulates and reinforces awareness of development opportunities by creating an environment where experimentation is encouraged without recrimination. A 'no blame' culture within organizations encourages and stimulates a proactive response to change from inside companies. In such environments the task of continuous improvement as part of the ongoing drive to reduce costs will more readily be taken on board by everyone in the organization.

Furthermore, redesigning jobs to incorporate indirect work into the roles of operations staff not only enriches their jobs but also taps into the capabilities of all staff in the continuous drive to reduce costs.

Critical reflections

The challenge to create a working environment that helps people to develop their full potential, want to do a good job and contribute fully to improving all aspects of work is central to the role of operations management. To bring this about will require businesses to fundamentally rethink their approach to organizational design and the structure of work.

One key to this is involving and empowering people. But this means more than employee participation. Even where companies delegate authority and resources, this does not, by right, lead to empowerment. Attempts to empower people from above will fail. The emphasis on empowerment needs to shift to one of providing the opportunity for staff at all levels to exercise increasing influence over their work and roles. But the giving of power itself without providing support in the form of training and direction will result in failure.

Where empowerment does exist it leads to power and control being exercised by individuals. Giving people more control over their own actions results in them accomplishing more and increasingly taking initiatives to get things done.

Creating the conditions where people are responsible for a meaningful set of activities is a key factor in these developments. This, however, can only be achieved with a fundamental reappraisal of work and organizational structures. Essential factors to making this happen include:

- **Self-managed teams** that are not only responsible for given tasks but are capable of making and implementing their decisions, are held accountable for results and influence the behavioural aspects of the job.

- **Sharing information** highlights the need for people to have full information about all elements of the job and ongoing performance. Without full information, teams cannot be held responsible for their performance as they do not know the full dimension of the company's problems. Aligning corporate and individual goals is a key factor here and is a two-way street.

- **Creating autonomy** is essential and needs to be developed. To help do this, structure needs to be built into these arrangements as it enables people to handle the uncertainty they feel when trying out new behaviours. As teams evolve, more autonomy can be created, which is essential for the sound and full working of teams.

However, these developments are dependent on how well people and, in particular, organizations learn. People, like businesses, need to be continually reinvented. But self-learning is not easy. 'It is no accident', Senge concludes, 'that most organizations learn poorly. The way they are designed and managed (and) the way people's jobs are defined... create fundamental disabilities.'[7] However, progressive companies have been addressing these issues of change as they recognize the key role that people play within the success of organizations. The outcome of such changes will help companies to capitalize on their key resource – the people within the business.

Summary

- Creating an environment in which people can fulfil their potential and one that meets both their needs and those of the business is a key operations management role. This is a difficult task, made more complex by the fast-changing nature of today's business in terms of market needs, level of employee commitment, the technical content of jobs, and the training and development needs this brings.

- General definitions concerning jobs set the scene while managerial philosophies of work and traditional approaches to managing people complete the introduction.

- We then discussed the need for companies to create change-oriented business environments that, in turn, bring implications for the current role of managers and the traditional shape of organizations.

- Then followed the core section of the chapter that introduced developments such as employee involvement and empowerment and a range of key dimensions from staff training and development through to issues such as flexitime, job sharing and ergonomics.

Study activities

Discussion questions

1. Name some factors that fall into hygiene and motivator categories. How may these differ for blue- (for example shop floor) and white-collar (for example administrative) staff?

2. Using Figure 3.1 and the accompanying narrative, give two illustrations of service and manufacturing jobs that illustrate the difference between job depth and job scope.

3. Why are companies increasingly building indirect tasks into the remit of those staff primarily responsible for providing services and making products?

4. How are job satisfaction and motivation different? Illustrate your answer with an example.

5. Why, in the past, did companies build organizations based on 'control through specialists' and 'the specialization of labour'?

6. Can all jobs be enriched successfully? Illustrate your answer with examples.

7. Why is it imperative that businesses turn themselves into learning organizations?

8. What are the advantages and disadvantages of job enlargement, job rotation and job enrichment? Give an example in operations where these would be beneficial and an example where it would be better not to employ these approaches.

Assignments

1. Review a wine bar, supermarket and take-away restaurant in line with the following:
   - How do these organizations each cope with the long opening hours involved?
   - Do they use flexitime? If so, give details. If not, could they and how would it work?

2. Together with two others, draw up a list of factors that affect people's attitude to work. Then review 12 staff from an organization of your choice in terms of how they would classify these chosen factors into hygiene and motivators. Analyze the results and explain your findings.

Exploring further

TED talks
Godin, S. (2009) *On the tribes we lead*. Seth Godin argues that the internet has ended mass marketing and revived a human social unit from the distant past: tribes. Founded on shared ideas and values, tribes give ordinary people the power to lead and make big change. He urges us to do so.
www.ted.com/talks/seth_godin_on_the_tribes_we_lead.html

Logan, D. (2009) *Tribal leadership*. David Logan talks about the five kinds of tribes that humans naturally form in schools, workplaces, even the driver's licence bureau. By understanding our shared tribal tendencies, we can help lead each other to become better individuals.
www.ted.com/talks/david_logan_on_tribal_leadership.html

Pink, D. (2009) *The surprising science of motivation*. Career analyst Dan Pink examines the puzzle of motivation, starting with a fact that social scientists know but most managers don't: traditional rewards aren't always as effective as we think. Listen for illuminating stories and, maybe, a way forward.
www.ted.com/talks/dan_pink_on_motivation.html

Sinek, S. (2009) *How great leaders inspire action*. Simon Sinek has a simple but powerful model for inspirational leadership all starting with a golden circle and the question 'Why?'. His examples include Apple, Martin Luther King, and the Wright brothers.
www.ted.com/talks/simon_sinek_how_great_leaders_inspire_action.html

Sivers, D. (2010) *How to start a movement*. With help from some surprising footage, Derek Sivers explains how movements really get started. (Hint: it takes two.)
www.ted.com/talks/derek_sivers_how_to_start_a_movement.html

Journal articles

Adler, P., Hecksher, C. and Prusak, L. (2011) 'Building a collaborative enterprise', *Harvard Business Review*, **89**(7/8): 94–101. Organizations must learn to: (1) Define a shared purpose (2) Cultivate an ethic of contribution (3) Develop scalable procedures (4) Create an infrastructure that values and rewards collaboration.

Amabile, T.M. and Kramer, S.J. (2011) 'The power of small wins', *Harvard Business Review*, **89**(5): 70–80. What is the best way to motivate employees to do creative work? Help them take a step forward every day. The key is to learn which actions support progress such as setting clear goals, providing sufficient time and resources, and offering recognition. On the flip side, small losses or setbacks can have an extremely negative effect.

Bernoff, J. and Schadler, T. (2010) 'Empowered', *Harvard Business Review*, **88**(7/8): 94–101. Companies can build a strategy around freeing employees to experiment with new technologies, make high-profile decisions on the fly, and effectively speak for the organization in public. It takes a while for corporate cultures to embrace this sort of innovation, but managers can move forward on their own by building internal communities, looking outside the company for creative strategies, reviewing their hiring practices, and reaching out to customer-facing departments.

Fernández-Aráoz, C., Groysberg, B. and Nohria, N. (2011) 'How to hang on to your high potentials', *Harvard Business Review*, **89**(10): 76–83. This article describes emerging best practices in executing 'high potential' development programmes, including the latest thinking on how to nominate and assess participants, design effective job rotations and stretch assignments, provide thoughtful rewards and incentives, and communicate about the programme with the rest of the organization.

Foote, N., Eisenstat, R. and Fredberg, T. (2011) 'The higher ambition leader', *Harvard Business Review*, **89**(9): 94–102. This article discusses how 'high ambition leaders' create long-term value for their companies while also benefiting the communities in which they operate.

Gavetti, G. (2011) 'The new psychology of strategic leadership', *Harvard Business Review*, **89**(7/8): 118–25. Leaders must use 'associational thinking' to learn from businesses in other industries.

Gino, F. and Pisano, G.P. (2011) 'Why leaders don't learn from success', *Harvard Business Review*, **89**(4): 68–74. Companies should implement systematic after-action reviews to understand all the factors that led to a win, and test their theories by conducting experiments even if 'it ain't broke'.

Grant, A.M. (2011) 'How customers can rally your troops', *Harvard Business Review*, **89**(6): 96–103. End users can inspire workers by demonstrating the impact of their efforts, showing appreciation for their work, and eliciting employees' empathy for them. To outsource inspiration effectively, leaders must identify end users (both past and present), collect their stories, introduce them to employees across the organization and recognize workers' impact on customers' lives.

Hewlett, S.A., Marshall, M. and Sherbin, L. (2011) 'The relationship you need to get right', *Harvard Business Review*, **89**(10): 131–4. Effective sponsors can help catapult junior talent into top management, and good protégés can expand the reach and impact of senior leaders. But the relationship works only when both parties see it as a mutually beneficial alliance.

Ibarra, H. and Hansen, M.T. (2011) 'Are you a collaborative leader?', *Harvard Business Review*, **89**(7/8): 68–74. This article describes tactics used by executives from Akamai, GE, Reckitt Benckiser, and other firms to foster high-performance collaborative cultures in their organizations.

Kahneman, D., Lovallo, D. and Sibony, O. (2011) 'Before you make that big decision', *Harvard Business Review*, **89**(6): 50–60. This article proposes a 12-question checklist to help leaders examine whether a team has explored appropriate alternatives, gathered all the right information and used well-grounded numbers to support their case.

Ramaswamy, V. and Gouillart, F. (2010) 'Building the co-creative enterprise', *Harvard Business Review*, **88**(10): 100–9. The article examines how companies can use its stakeholders including customers, employees and distributors to determine HR practices and design and market its services and products.

Tushman, M.L., Smith, W.K. and Binns, A. (2011) 'The ambidextrous CEO', *Harvard Business Review*, **89**(6): 74–80. This article suggests firms only thrive when senior teams foster a state of constant creative conflict between the old and the new.

Vlachoutsicos, C.A. (2011) 'How to cultivate engaged employees', *Harvard Business Review*, **89**(9): 123–6. Managers can engage employees by: (1) Being modest (2) Listening seriously (3) Inviting disagreement (4) Focusing the agenda (5) Not trying to have all the answers (6) Not insisting that a decision must be made.

Washburn, N.T. and Hunsaker, B.T. (2011) 'Finding great ideas in emerging markets', *Harvard Business Review*, **89**(9): 115–20. A new kind of manager, a 'global bridger', can help companies take advantage of the innovative energy that permeates emerging markets.

Books

Binney, G., Wilke, G. and Williams, C. (2009) *Living leadership: A practical guide for ordinary heroes*, Harlow: Financial Times. By observing business leaders in top companies on a day-to-day basis, the authors found out how these top managers really spent their time and how they really made an impact. They saw how leaders hold key discussions with their teams; formulate strategies, plans and visions; and observed their behaviours, ambitions and frustrations. What emerged was a powerful set of principles for managers who want to develop their leadership skills.

Goffee, R. and Jones, G. (2006) *Why should anyone be led by you?*, Harvard: Harvard Business School Press. Copy-cat leadership will never result in another Jack Welch, Richard Branson or Meg Whitman. What organizations need, and what followers want, are authentic leaders who know who they are, where the organization needs to go, and how to convince followers to help them take it there.

Hersey, P., Blanchard, K. and Johnson, D.E. (2008) *Management of organizational behaviour: Leading human resources*, 9th edn, Harlow: Prentice Hall. This book provides a comprehensive review of motivation and behaviour, situational leadership, building effective relationships, planning and implementing change, leadership strategies, the organizational cone and integrating situational leadership with the Classics.

Kouzes, J.M. and Posner, B.Z. (2008) *The leadership challenge*, 4th edn, San Francisco: Jossey Bass. The authors' central theme is that 'Leadership is Everyone's Business' offering 'five practices' and 'ten commitments' to help achieve this and continues to be a best seller after four editions and 20 years in print.

Lundin, S.C., Paul, H. and Christensen, J. (2002) *Fish!: A remarkable way to boost morale and improve results*, London: Hodder Paperbacks. Imagine a workplace where everyone chooses to bring energy, passion and a positive attitude to the job every day. In this engrossing parable, a fictional manager has the responsibility of turning a chronically unenthusiastic and unhelpful department into an effective team.

Notes and references

1. Drucker, P.F. (2002) 'They're not employees, they're people', *Harvard Business Review*, February, pp. 71–7.
2. Drucker, op. cit., p. 73.
3. Hertzberg, F. (1996) *Work and Nature of Man*, Cleveland: World Publishing; and Hertzberg, F. (1987) 'One more time: how do you motivate employees?' (with retrospective comment), *Harvard Business Review*, 65(5).
4. Senge, P.M. (1990) *The Fifth Discipline*, New York: Doubleday, p. 18.
5. Ibid.
6. Columella as quoted in Saskin, M. (1976) 'Changing toward participative management approaches: a model and methods', *The Academy Review*, pp. 75–86.
7. Senge, op. cit., p. 18.

In the early 1980s, the Lloyds Banking Group was struggling to meet its financial targets and the promises that it had made to its shareholders. It was a difficult situation needing radical change. The turning point seemed to come in 1986, when Brian Pitman (the CEO at the time) decided to sell their retail banking operation in California. In 1974, this acquisition had been hailed as a healthy diversification away from their UK home market, and many executives still viewed Lloyds Bank California as a crucial foothold in a state with one of the world's largest, most affluent and fast-growing economies. The problem was that, however appealing the market, they didn't seem to have any competitive advantage there. Their market share was negligible and they didn't seem to be in a position to compete with giants like the Bank of America.

This was the first of a number of activities over the next couple of decades that resulted in turning the business around, increasing its market capitalization 40-fold and delivering an average annual shareholder return of 26 per cent, a rate that not only outpaced its UK banking rivals but also put it in a league with market stars such as Coca-Cola, GE and Gillette.

To many people the decision to sell off the California operation may have been seen as short sighted. But, in reality, it was not earning back its cost of equity and thus not contributing to the value of the overall business. In fact, as the outcome showed, it proved a sound decision. A Japanese bank paid over the odds for it and the Lloyds TSB share price rose overnight. For Pitman and his team, this experience was a defining one. It showed them that managing a business involves making some difficult and often testing decisions. But, at the same time, it also showed the benefit of setting a course and sticking to it, a belief that grew stronger over the following years as they changed the business direction from sales growth to profitability.

Pitman was presumably pleased with how well this decision went as it seemed to prove that Lloyds TSB were starting off down the right track. However, it soon became apparent that creating change in a business is not simply about putting in place some new performance metric or a new accounting method. Lloyds TSB had to work hard to get people to change their beliefs and put in place the appropriate infrastructure and delivery systems necessary for the new way of working. Only then could they create a significant and sustainable improvement.

SETTING THE OBJECTIVE OF THE BUSINESS

When Pitman arrived at Lloyds in 1983, his initial task was to get the whole company to agree on a definition of 'success'. Initially, he had to get the consensus of the board members and then later the management team that would implement the change and transform the business. Pitman emphasized that he didn't have a hidden agenda and didn't know what the right answer was. But, he wanted to come up with a single definition of success and a single means of measuring it. Without this clarity, he feared the efforts of the business would be diluted by the pursuit of multiple goals.

The objective of the discussions with other board members was to create a single, well-defined performance measure that would replace the existing array of implicit objectives currently being used to manage the business. He believed that with a single objective, you are much more likely to get coordinated and concentrated action. Their current, woolly business goals were getting them nowhere as they weren't specific enough to really focus people's performance.

The board set about this task during two long, hard meetings. Finally, and somewhat reluctantly, they agreed on a single governing objective of improving shareholder value with return on equity (ROE) as a means of measuring this. They decided to use ROE as their key measure because it is not only a key indicator of profitability, but also one that investors use to measure how well a company is using its money. The target for this measure was that each

business in the group must deliver an ROE that exceeds the cost of equity, which at the time was about 17–19 per cent.

To ensure that the corporate objective of improving shareholder value was consistent throughout the organization, it was linked into how executives were measured and rewarded. Previously, managers' salary increases had been linked to inflation, now they were linked to the ROE of their part of the business and the business as a whole. Before long, the cry 'improve ROE' could be heard all around the organization. However, it wasn't just top executives who benefited from this change in policy. High performance standards were set for people throughout the organization and they were rewarded when these standards were met. The metrics varied of course. They didn't tell someone in cheque processing to improve his operation's return on equity; they measured him on something over which he had control, such as productivity and quality conformance levels. But, whatever the measure, they made sure it represented at least a part of the shareholder value puzzle.

On top of this, they set up stock incentive plans enabling people to accumulate a level of capital that would have been impossible through their own savings. This meant that within only a few years, nearly everyone in the company had stock options in Lloyds, not only at senior management level but also throughout the business.

SELECTING THE RIGHT MARKETS

Once people started to accept that profitability was more important than sales growth, Pitman and his team analyzed their markets to determine which were creating value and which were not. They were astonished to find that only a small proportion of the total business generated most of the value, while more than half the business was earning less than the cost of capital.

As a result, they decided to exit the Californian business with an ROE of 8 per cent, which was less than half the cost of capital. The decision to move out of the merchant banking business came next, because they knew they couldn't compete effectively against the big US investment banks, even in the UK markets. Closing down the merchant banking operation, although a highly unpopular decision in the business, resulted in a significant improvement in overall company results.

However, not everyone in the business saw the light so quickly! At one point Pitman got so exasperated that he told his people to start their business plan for the year with a list of the businesses they were going to get out of. He didn't want to know what they were going to get into. Getting out of the underperforming businesses then freed up resources to invest in business activities that would guarantee a profitable future.

But, slowly the change started to come with the outcome that the business became more focused on the UK financial services market providing retail banking, mortgages, insurance and investment services as shown in Figure 1. Although the traditional retail banking activities that Lloyds had were not that profitable, they provided both a distribution channel and customer relationships that allowed it to move into the more lucrative mortgage, insurance and investment segments.

Initially, Lloyds started selling insurance products purely as a broker. However, this proved so successful that the decision was made to acquire Abbey Life in 1988. Shortly after this, it acquired Cheltenham & Gloucester, a building society specializing in home mortgages. In both instances, the companies retained their brands but sold their products through the existing Lloyds branch network. The subsequent merger with TSB in 1995 then further expanded its distribution capabilities.

They then decided to concentrate on UK financial services, completing extensive customer research to understand what their drivers were and what they wanted from a bank. They realized that trust in their brand name and their existing relationships with customers meant they could sell more products in this market. Part of the bank's strategy was then to acquire and retain higher value customers by expanding their customer relationship management capabilities and develop tailored offerings for key market segments. It introduced a number of new products and services such as the Premier credit card and the Lloyds TSB branded gas, electricity and home telephone products. Another success was its wealth management facility that provided a tailored service to their most affluent customers. Given the increasingly competitive nature of the UK financial services market, it has been important that Lloyds TSB has continued to find new and innovative products that add value for its customers.

An outline of the products that the bank currently sells in each of its markets is shown in Figure 2.

CREATING THE RIGHT CULTURE

At the heart of all the improvements made was a change in the business culture. Pitman realized that for people to become truly committed to a strategy, they had to believe in it. In its case, the bank's staff had to believe that profitability was more important than sales growth. They also had to believe in the importance of concentrating on businesses with profit potential and selling off the others. If they adopted such convictions, and didn't simply pay lip service to them, then they could completely change the way the business operated.

However, the reshaping didn't occur without huge resistance. Individuals' beliefs are hard to change and the adoption of a management philosophy imposed a tough discipline on the whole business. People had to accept that it was right for the company to become smaller, stay closer to home and concentrate on unglamorous products like mortgages and insurance, while exiting more prestigious services such as investment banking and currency trading. This proved difficult. There was great resistance to shedding unprofitable customers and products, getting out of unprofitable markets and closing unprofitable facilities.

Getting people to change by simply imposing a mindset didn't work. Instead, refocusing the business emerged from a learning process in which the people working there became persuaded that the new objective was worthwhile and then they decided to focus their talents on achieving it. This process often involved heated debate; indeed, they found that disagreement was the key to getting agreement. Without disagreement, people simply fell into line with no real commitment to the change programme. Instead, it was important to get people to arrive at a meeting of minds around a small number of central beliefs, which could then determine their behaviour and ultimately the company's performance. Pitman couldn't do this by being a dictator. He had to do this by leading people on a journey of learning where everyone discovered how to create value for their shareholders.

MAKING THE CHANGE

Once the direction of the business had been set, the markets selected and the product portfolio defined, the next stage was to make the change happen. The first step was to convince people that the change was right, but then the operational changes in the business had to be made.

They knew they wanted to concentrate on the UK financial services and increase the number of services sold into this market. But, they didn't know how to deliver these services and structure their operations. Customer research showed that its branch network gave them a significant advantage over many competitors, but they also needed to develop other service delivery systems. The first step was to set up telephone banking and their internet banking service followed shortly after. Both proved to be highly popular with retail customers.

As well as setting up the new delivery systems, significant changes had to be made to their organizational infrastructure. The sale of the business in California meant that certain facilities and operations had to be closed down. At the same time, significant work was done developing new areas, such as the call centres for telephone and internet banking, and merging the business with the activities gained through the acquisition of Abbey Life and

C&G. In addition, they started looking for ways to further improve efficiency in the rest of the business. As a result, they set up an operational centre in India and explored the possibility of moving more processes offshore.

THE FUTURE

Although Brian Pitman retired in 2001, the values he created are still present in the business. The bank has developed a reputation for being a conservatively run, low-risk and steady performing bank. Then, in 2008 the financial credit crisis hit and HBOS, one of its major competitors who owned Halifax and the Royal Bank of Scotland, collapsed and the UK government asked Lloyds TSB to acquire it. Even though Lloyds was the UK's strongest bank, it still had to borrow £260 billion from the UK government with 83 per cent of this covering HBOS bad debt. As a result, the UK government now owns 75 per cent of the Lloyds Banking Group. Since then, it has started to turn things around and moved back into profit as a group last year (see Figure 3). However, the previous poor management of HBOS's wholesale markets means that this part of the business is still underperforming.

The acquisition of HBOS has undoubtedly improved the strategic positioning of the Lloyds Banking Group and helped position the Group for future growth. It is now the largest UK retail bank with well recognized brands and a large customer base. However, it also acquired quite a number of problems, which it is now having to clear up. The recent sale of its Bank of Scotland and Halifax operations in Ireland has helped improve the performance of its Wealth business and it is starting to shed some of the underperforming HBOS assets in its Wholesale business. However, it can be argued that to really turn the business around, it needs to go back to Pitman's principles of prudent and sustainable revenue growth from the creation of value for customers, tight management of its cost base and strong credit risk management.

Lecturers: visit www.palgrave.com/business/hillom3e for teaching guidelines for this case study

Figure 1 Key dates and developments (1983–2010)

Year	Development
1983	Brian Pitman appointed CEO
1984	Unsuccessful attempt to acquire Royal Bank of Scotland
1986	Sold California (US) operation. Sold Merchant banking operation. Unsuccessful attempt to acquire Standard Chartered Bank
1988	Merged with Abbey Life to create Lloyds Abbey Life. Sold Portugal operation
1991	Sold Far East (China, Singapore, Korea, Taiwan) operations
1992	Changed to performance-related employee pay structure. Attempted to acquire Midland Bank, but then withdrew
1994	Acquired Cheltenham & Gloucester building society
1995	Merged with TSB bank
1996	Peter Ellwood appointed CEO. Brian Pitman appointed Chairman. Closed New York Treasury operation
1997	Sold Corporate Banking Paris (France) operation. Sold SMH (Germany) operation
2000	Acquired Scottish Widows (a UK pension specialist). Acquired Chartered Trust (the UK consumer finance arm of Standard Chartered Bank)
2001	Brian Pitman retires. Maarten van den Bergh appointed as Chairman
2002	Eric Daniels appointed CEO. UK Competition Commission rules out merger with Abbey National
2004	Acquired Goldfish (UK credit card and personal loans specialist). Sold Guatemala, Honduras and Panama operations
2006	Sir Victor Blank appointed Chairman. Sold Argentina and Paraguay operations
2007	Failed attempt to acquire Northern Rock (UK mortgage specialist)
2009	Sir Winfried Bischoff appointed as Chairman. Acquired HBOS (Halifax and Royal Bank of Scotland)
2010	Closed Bank of Scotland (Ireland) small business and retail operations. Closed Halifax (Ireland) retail operation

Figure 2 Lloyds TSB services and products within its different markets

Services and products in retail	
Services and products	**Detail**
Key operating brands	Lloyds TSB, Halifax, Bank of Scotland, Cheltenham & Gloucester, Birmingham Midshires and Intelligent Finance
Current, savings and investment accounts; and consumer lending	The retail branches offer a broad range of branded products and investments through its branch network and a postal investment centre
Card services	Provides a range of card-based products and services, including credit and debit cards and card transaction processing services for retailers
Cash machines	Customers withdraw cash, check balances and obtain mini statements
Telephone banking	Provides one of the largest telephony services in Europe
Internet banking	Provides online banking facilities for personal and business customers
Business banking	Dedicated small business managers provide a range of tailored business services from traditional banking products through to non-financial business solutions

Figure 2 (continued)

Wealth management	Provides a range of tailor-made wealth management services to individuals including asset management, tax and estate planning, executor and trustee services, deposit taking and lending, insurance, and personal equity plan and ISA products
Stockbrokers	Provide retail stockbroking through Sharedeal Direct telephone service
Mortgages	Sold to customers through retail branches, telephone, internet and postal service

Services and products within wholesale	
Services and products	**Detail**
Key operating brands	Lloyds TSB, Corporate Markets, Bank of Scotland, Black Horse and Lex Autolease
Corporate Markets	Provide relationship-based banking, risk management and advisory services to business customers, principally in the UK
Treasury and Trading	Provides access to financial markets to meet the Group's balance sheet requirements, and support execution of customer-driven risk management transactions
Asset finance	Consists of a number of leasing and speciality lending businesses including Contract Hire and Consumer Finance

Services and products within wealth and international banking	
Services and products	**Detail**
Key operating brands	Private Banking Lloyds TSB, Look at Things Differently Bank of Scotland, Scottish Widows Investment Partnership, Lloyds TSB International
Wealth	Comprises private banking, wealth management and asset management for Lloyds Banking Group customers as well as pension funds, charities, local authorities, discretionary managers and financial advisers
International	Comprises the Group's international banking businesses outside the UK. Clients include corporate, commercial and asset finance business in Australia, Ireland and Continental Europe and retail businesses in Germany and the Netherlands

Services and products in insurance	
Services and products	**Detail**
Key operating brands	Scottish Widows, Clerical Medical, Lloyds TSB, Halifax, Bank of Scotland
Life, Pensions and Investments	Provides long-term savings, protection and investment products distributed through the bancassurance, intermediary and direct channels in the UK and Germany
General insurance	Distributes home insurance UK products through the branch network, direct channels and strategic corporate partners

Figure 3 Financial performance 1998–2010

Summary of financial performance

Measure	Annual financial performance							
	1998	2000	2002	2004	2006	2008	2009	2010
Total income (£m)	7,442	8,776	8,878	19,283	19,263	8,230	12,726	13,822
Operating expenses (£m)	3,876	4,279	4,915	5,297	5,301	5,651	11,609	10,928
Profit before tax (£m)	2,948	3,785	2,607	3,320	3,841	2,426	(6,300)	2,212
Earnings per share	22.2	30.6	34.2	42.8	49.9	14.3	7.5	-0.5

Income by business area

Business area	Income (£m)							
	1998	2000	2002	2004	2006	2008	2009	2010
Retail	3,606	4,105	4,232	4,924	5,263	11,193	9,774	10,985
Wholesale	1,379	1,521	1,949	2,138	3,374	5,450	8,909	8,562
Wealth and international	1,086	1,139	931	1,426	838	2,505	2,345	2,336
Insurance	1,371	2,011	1,766	11,157	1,796	3,148	2,020	2,009
Other items	–	–	–	(362)	7,992	(460)	1,553	94
Total	**7,442**	**8,776**	**8,878**	**19,283**	**19,263**	**21,836**	**24,601**	**23,986**

Profit by business area

Business area	Profit before tax (£m)							
	1998	2000	2002	2004	2006	2008	2009	2010
Retail	1,424	1,682	1,172	1,639	1,549	2,542	1,382	4,716
Wholesale	948	1,447	1,231	1,133	1,541	(10,479)	(4,703)	3,257
Wealth and international	729	749	626	120	99	277	(2,356)	(4,824)
Insurance	434	501	379	778	950	1,540	975	1,102
Other items	(587)	(594)	(801)	(350)	(298)	(593)	(1,598)	(2,039)
Total	**2,948**	**3,785**	**2,607**	**3,320**	**3,841**	**(6,713)**	**(6,300)**	**2,212**

Note: 'Other items' includes aspects such as: central group items, pension provision, (loss) profit on sale and closure of businesses, write-down of finance leases and restructuring provision.

Questions

1. What are Lloyds TSB's corporate, marketing and operations strategies?

2. How did it use people to develop and change its business in the 1980s and 1990s?

3. Could a similar approach help it turn around the business again?

After completing this chapter, you should be able to:

- Appreciate the key role of new services and products as the lifeblood of an organization

- Identify the alternative approaches in service and product innovation

- Differentiate between long-term and tactical research and development programmes

- List the steps involved in designing and developing services and products

- Recognize and use the insights that can be gained by placing services and products into the correct positions on the respective life cycles and into the portfolio analysis grid

- Select from and use a range of techniques and approaches related to design

Chapter outline

Executive overview

Introduction

Designing and developing services and products

The research and development process
Long-term programmes
Tactical programmes

The design and development process for services and products
1. Generating ideas
2. Screening ideas
3. Feasibility study
4. Preliminary design and development
5. Testing prototypes
6. Market sensing and testing target markets
7. Final design

The decision

Reviewing the service and product mix
Service/product life cycles
Service/product portfolio analysis

Designing services and products to meet the needs of different market segments

Developing a specification
The inherent nature of services and products
Developing a specification to reflect the service/product mix
The implications of the non-repeat or repeat nature of a service or product

Techniques for improving design
Standardization
Modular design
Mass customization
Taguchi methods
Quality function deployment and the house of quality
Value engineering and value analysis
Simultaneous engineering
Variety reduction

Designing services and products in practice

Driving business performance

Critical reflections

Summary

What is the role of designing services and products?

- Introducing new and developing existing services and products is the lifeblood of organizations

- Creating and maintaining an innovation culture is a prerequisite to support this core task

- This needs to be done while looking to external as well as internal sources as a key part of maintaining the flow of ideas essential to remaining competitive in today's markets

Why is service/product design important?

- The extent and rate of new service and product introductions will have a significant impact on both the short- and long-term success of a business

- Market pressures require that designs never remain static

- As service/product life cycles reflect the phases through which offerings go as they move into and out of their markets, then introducing new ones to replace those already in the cycle is necessary to maintain sales revenue levels let alone grow market share

- Rigorously and systematically seeking ways to gain the potential advantages of experience must form an integral part of the design and development activities of an organization

How does operations impact service/product design?

- As the function responsible for delivering the services and making the products sold to customers, operations managers have key insights into how customers respond to designs and how easy it is to provide current services and products in terms of quality conformance, margins and lead times

- Operations' responsibility for providing existing services/products brings with it in-sights into possible opportunities to reduce the costs of design and provision as organizations seek to gain the advantages that accrue from experience

What are the key issues to consider when designing new and developing existing services and products?

- The introduction of new and development of existing services and products is the lifeblood of organizations

- For this to become an integral part of the way in which companies grow and prosper, they need a way to generate ideas and then translate them into reality

- While breakthroughs will always gain the spotlight, most companies will typically sell today what they sold yesterday and the same for tomorrow

- This does not imply that thinking outside the box is not required; on the contrary, nothing could be further from the truth

- The key is more to do with where to focus attention, which for many companies concerns thinking differently about what they currently provide and the markets in which they currently compete

- With ideas being the spark that ignites development, companies are realizing that they need also to seek perspectives from less traditional sources

- Key areas among these alternatives are the staff who provide the service or make the product and customers who buy the offerings

- Breaking the mould of past approaches is difficult but in today's competitive world it is essential

- While the first step is essential, getting from idea to market reality is critical

- For much of the time this part of the process changes from being one of inspiration to one based on hard work

- Systematically checking and rechecking needs time and effort

- While new services and products create tomorrow's success, a company needs to get the most out of today's offerings

- On the scale of being inherently interesting, generating ideas is at the top, with developing existing services and products much lower down

- However, on the scale of what impacts business success and prosperity, the order is often the reverse

- The attraction of stars and the mundane nature of cash cows often results in an imbalance of time, attention and recognition

- Keeping all the corporate balls in the air is an essential element of successfully managing the process for the design and development of services and products

- The research and development (R&D) process involves procedures to develop new knowledge and ideas, or using existing knowledge or ideas, on which service, product, process and system designs are based

- Growth and success are to a large extent based on an organization's ability to introduce new services or products and develop existing ones

- Although a natural market may exist for some essential needs (for example, food and clothing), for others a market has to be created

- In either case, most organizations have changed from the ad hoc approach to the planning of new services/products that they used in the past, to one that is an organized activity involving a process from generating ideas through to market launch

Introduction

This chapter will first outline the phases of the **research and development (R&D) process** from generating ideas through to the final design. It will then address key issues and considerations in service/product design, including life cycles, portfolio analyses and design contributions to help support different service/product market segments. Finally. it will cover the role of operations techniques and approaches to improving design, including standardization, modular design, Taguchi methods, **quality function deployment (QFD)**, value analysis, **simultaneous engineering** and variety reduction.

Designing and developing services and products

Introducing new and developing existing services and products is the lifeblood of organizations. However, the task involves more than initiating new ideas, although that is where it typically all begins. The procedure is one of checking ideas and alternatives and verifying that what is proposed can be done within the context of the market, the organization's own objectives, the company's capabilities and the impact on other parts of the business, including operations. It concerns generating ideas, setting financial targets, providing detailed **specifications** and checking and assessing what will be involved in providing them prior to the marketing and provision of the services or products in question. Ideas come from internal or external sources depending upon an organization's allocation of resources (for example, research spend), its approach to stimulating and processing contributions and its attitude towards the degree of risk it is prepared to take, for example whether to be a leader or follower in its chosen markets.

Some of the issues are now overviewed as a way of outlining what is involved. The sections that follow then look at the various aspects in more detail and address some of the key points to be considered throughout this core task. One thing is for certain, however: in many markets service and product design can have a telling impact on the success of an organization, as Case 4.1 illustrates.

The research and development process

The objective of research and development (R&D) activity is to bring about technological change and innovation within both the services and products to be sold and the delivery systems and processes by which these will be produced. The total cycle of events to achieve this embraces programmes classified as being either long-term or tactical.

Long-term programmes

Long-term programmes concern research activities that are both fundamental and applied in nature. Although it is convenient to highlight this split when defining what is involved, in reality the distinction between fundamental and applied research is often blurred:

- **Fundamental research** studies the basic relationship between cause and effect, with the aim of increasing knowledge, making discoveries and establishing new applications that may eventually be used on a commercial basis.

Research and development (R&D) process – the procedures used to develop new knowledge and ideas or how to use existing knowledge or ideas on which service, product, process and system designs are based.

Quality function deployment (QFD) – a formal system to ensure that the eventual service or product design meets the needs of customers while eliminating wasteful features and activities that do not add value or contribute to meeting these needs.

Simultaneous engineering – when the stages in the design process are overlapped (that is, partly or wholly undertaken in parallel with other stages) in order to reduce the time taken to introduce services/ products into the market and cut costs.

Specification – a detailed statement of the required features and elements (such as materials, parts or information) that make up the service or product design.

Long-term programmes – a plan or schedule of tasks to be completed that are considered to need a long time to undertake. The meaning of the phrase 'long-term' will vary from one business to another but will usually exceed one year.

Asahi Breweries, Japan's biggest beer company with $8.7 billion sales in 2010, is still revered as the company that transformed the Japanese beer industry by launching its 'Super Dry' beer towards the end of the 1980s. Developed in 1987, the country's first *karakuchi* (dry) beer became an overnight success. In 2008, the company held in excess of 50 per cent of the Japanese lager market. One of the secrets of Asahi's success was that its taste had been developed to suit the Japanese market. As such, it was a new type of beer and the first new beer for over 40 years. Furthermore, Asahi Breweries was the first company in Japan to offer beer in cans, and the first to sell beer in 3-litre containers.

In the 1990s, Asahi Breweries began exporting, first to China, which consumes over 25 billion litres of beer a year, then to the UK and later to the rest of Europe.
www.asahibeer.co.jp/english/

Questions

1. Is the role of design an order-winner or qualifier in the Asahi Super Dry example?

2. Explain the reasons for your view.

Lecturers: visit www.palgrave.com/business/ hillom3e for teaching guidelines for this case study

- **Applied research** is concerned principally with practical applications and solutions to practical problems. Its function concerns classifying and interpreting basic knowledge from fundamental research activities to facilitate problem solving. The return on this research investment is quicker and more assured than for fundamental research. Since applied research is directed towards solving particular problems in the later stages of service and product planning (for example, advanced development work), the practical usefulness of the results is inherent in the activity. However, an organization may well subcontract some or all of this task until its own research demands can justify employing its own staff.

The level of commitment to strategic programmes is an important corporate decision. Organizations may decide to adopt either an offensive or a defensive design strategy, while others fall in between, making a moderate R&D commitment by, for instance, contracting out research or licensing other organizations' existing service and product designs.[1]

The offensive strategy brings with it a relatively large research spending commitment, with the objective of being a leader in service and product innovation within a given market. The defensive strategy usually limits the amount of research spending to a minimum and will be largely directed towards the development of existing knowledge to enhance service and product position in a market or in response to customer requirements.

To help to explain these alternative strategies, the following categories are often used.[2]

- A 'first-to-market' posture focuses on cutting-edge research that leads to the introduction of new technologies ahead of competitors.

- A 'fast-follower' posture requires a quick response to technical innovation by industry pioneers and may include modifying the technologies involved.

- A 'me-too' approach, on the other hand, is aimed at imitating widely available technologies by the introduction of close substitutes.

- A 'late-entrant' approach is concerned with making incremental changes to existing technologies for limited applications.

Case 4.2 illustrates one approach.

Other strategic approaches also exist, such as manufacturing under licence or providing a service under a franchise. In the former, services provided and products manufactured successfully elsewhere are produced under licence agreements. Here, invariably the methods of working and environment are highly specified and materials and other supplies are from prescribed sources (for example fast-food restaurants). In that way, a tight control on service and product specifications and their provision is maintained by the franchiser.

Returning to what companies need to do in their R&D process, one further essential step is to ensure that the research outcomes lead into new, or the development of, existing services and products. Much investment is wasted if the fruits of the research are not adopted. Without this there is no commercial payback so essential to justify past and future R&D spend. But this transfer will not happen by itself. Companies need to create the organizational conditions, attitudes and expectations in order to facilitate this essential conversion, as Case 4.3 illustrates.

CASE 4.2 R&D EXPENDITURE AT MICROSOFT

© paxi – Fotolia.com

In 2011, Microsoft the world's largest software company announced that, while most of its rivals were cutting back on costs, it was going to spend $9.6 billion on R&D. That is not only big but is, in fact, more than the rest of the software industry's R&D budgets combined. This commitment to R&D has been a significant feature in Microsoft's strategy throughout.

Microsoft set up its R&D division in the early 1990s and has consistently increased its annual spending on this area – in fact, it more than tripled its budget between 1998 and 2010. Bill Gates stressed the worthwhile and essential nature of Microsoft's continued commitment to high levels of research expenditure, explaining that customers underestimate the software's potential and outlining his belief that the industry and the market 'are going to be stunned at the advances we make'. Clearly, Microsoft intends to maintain its position in cutting-edge technology as it supports its belief in the significance of software in the future.

www.microsoft.com

Questions

1. In which category of strategy would you place Microsoft?

2. Explain your choice.

Lecturers: visit www.palgrave.com/business/hillom3e for teaching guidelines for this case study

Microsoft's awareness of the need to transfer research into product development is clear. Bill Gates reflected on Xerox's failure to do just this. 'In our industry the most famous story of all is that of Xerox's Palo Alto Research Centre (PARC)', he explained. '[It] managed to do amazing research but the company did not ... get the benefit of it. In fact, the few things they did from that research, like the Xerox Star (the first computer with windows, icons and a mouse), well, most of them lost money.'[3] To try to ensure that it would not suffer the same fate as Xerox's PARC, Microsoft has developed structures and approaches aimed to increase the transfer of research outputs into product development. Partly, its approach concerns organizational structure. Almost without exception, all parts of Microsoft's research organization are actively engaged in at least one product group. Specific approaches to improve the transfer of research activities include:

- The research organization has dedicated programme managers. Their job is to spot technology that might transfer and show it to the product side at the right time. Too early and it won't have relevance, too late and it can't be incorporated. In fact, the research group measures its success by assessing the level of awareness of various technologies within the business and their take-up within product development.

- Off-site meetings (known as 'mindswaps') are set up between research and product teams to discuss selected topics. Being located off site also means less distractions and a more relaxed atmosphere.

- Researchers organize annual fairs on site, known as 'tech-fests'. Attracting upwards of 20,000 staff, the research teams monitor the level of interest by staff in different ideas and developments. Also, visits to these fairs by top executives within the company signal the level of corporate importance and commitment to the broadcasting of ideas.

www.microsoft.com

Questions

1. What are the key factors that Microsoft uses to aid the transfer of research ideas into product development?

2. From your list select the most important and give reasons for your choice.

Lecturers: visit www.palgrave.com/business/hillom3e for teaching guidelines for this case study

Tactical programmes

Tactical programmes – a plan or schedule of tasks to be completed in the short-term. The meaning of the phrase 'short-term' will vary from one business to another but will usually be less than one year.

Following these long-term activities come the tactical steps to develop services or products. Although excellent and innovative services and products are conceived and designed by a whole range of businesses, a feature frequently experienced by many organizations is that the requirements of subsequent steps in the procedure are not adequately taken into account at the design stage. The result leads to higher than necessary costs. The typical view held is that design determines 70 per cent of costs.[4] While others may disagree with the percentage,[5] what is not contested is the significant impact on costs at this stage in the process. A good way to illustrate this relationship is provided by the design costs 'effectiveness lever', which illustrates the impact upon effectiveness that can be achieved at each of the principal stages in the procedure from design through to operations (Figure 4.1).

Tactical programmes cover all stages throughout the development of a service or product including its launch. They are concerned with the functional aspects of design and address basic questions covering:

- What will it do?
- How will it do it?
- How will it be made or provided?
- What is the maintenance and repair requirement?
- How will it be distributed?

The link between market need, technology, development, design and the operations delivery system is essential to the profitable provision of a service or production of a product and all the steps have to be addressed.

The approach to development involves defining a service or product using a procedure that checks successive designs until the required specifications are met as economically as possible. This usually involves testing several designs to evaluate their feasibility in terms of functionality and cost. The following section looks at these steps in detail.

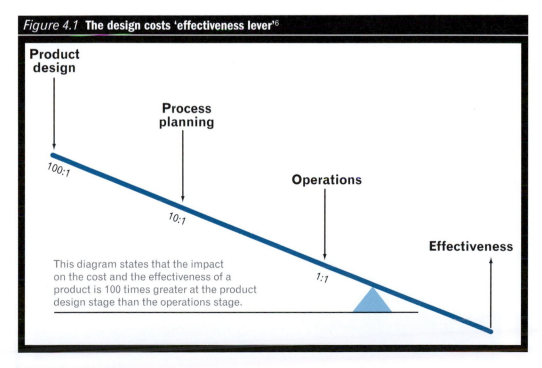

Figure 4.1 The design costs 'effectiveness lever'[6]

Product design

Process planning

100:1

10:1

Operations

1:1

Effectiveness

This diagram states that the impact on the cost and the effectiveness of a product is 100 times greater at the product design stage than the operations stage.

The design and development process for services and products

The first step in designing and developing a new or modifying an existing service or product is generating ideas. But a good idea does not necessarily indicate a successful outcome. A significant amount of development work is required before a service can be provided or a product produced and made available to customers. These steps are described as the service and product design and development process and are outlined in Figure 4.2. However, before discussing these in some detail, it is important to make two observations about Figure 4.2.

1. **Sequential** – the process outline shows the steps as being sequential, whereas in fact parts of several stages will be completed in parallel with one another. This allows for a reduction in development lead times so enabling the earlier introduction of final designs.

2. **Reiteration** – although shown as being principally sequential, the steps actually involve much reiteration throughout. Questions are posed at each stage and these often take the proposal back one or more steps in order to clarify and resolve the fresh issues raised.

1. Generating ideas

The need to generate ideas is a key step in this process especially as the ratio between ideas and successful service and product introductions is often as low as 1 or 2 per cent. Ideas for new services and products can arise from a variety of sources within and outside a firm.

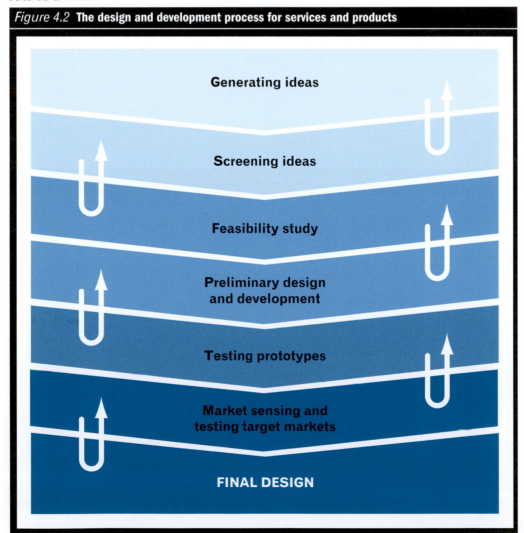

Figure 4.2 **The design and development process for services and products**

Generating ideas

Screening ideas

Feasibility study

Preliminary design and development

Testing prototypes

Market sensing and testing target markets

FINAL DESIGN

Internal sources

An important source of ideas comes from within the company. Some of these include:

- **Employees** – companies stimulate ideas from this key source in several ways. For example, suggestion schemes (where prizes of various values are awarded for useable ideas) or including the generation of ideas as part of employee evaluations have long been effective ways of getting ideas on the table.

- **Research and development** – investing in resources solely committed to generating ideas as discussed earlier.

- **Market research** – the systematic process of discussing with or using customers to identify needs and ideas. For example, part of the procedure used by Asahi Breweries when launching its Super Dry beer (see Case 4.1) was to visit pubs, restaurants and parks asking drinkers what they wanted from a beer. As well as confirming that people mainly wanted something to drink with food, the company also received a resounding message: people wanted a beer that was 'nodogoshi' (easy to drink) with a somewhat dry bite. So, Asahi Super Dry was launched to meet these characteristics. A new taste was developed and a success story was born.

- **Sales force** – by remaining alert to potential customer needs and systematically recording and evaluating customer comments and discussions, sales staff can consistently add to the stream of ideas at this stage in the design and development process.

- **Reverse engineering** – this involves taking existing services and products (competitors' as well as the company's own) and systematically analyzing them to check the design concepts and principles being used. In this way existing thinking and current approaches are challenged, and the transfer of concepts used in one application to another helps to create a source of new ideas.

> **Reverse engineering** – the process of analyzing an existing service or product (often made by a competitor) to understand what it is made of, how it has been made and how it works, with the purpose of improving existing designs or designing new services or products.

The need to rethink approaches at this stage in the design and development process has been recognized by many organizations, as Case 4.4 illustrates.

External sources

Equally important, and sometimes more important than ideas from internal sources, are those ideas generated outside the firm. These sources include customers, legislative requirements, environmental pressures and technology advances.

Customers[7]

There has been a marked change in the past 30 years regarding the source and approach to new service and product design. Gone are the days when the role of researchers was to come up with ideas that then went into the services and products that customers were encouraged to buy. Although this still happens (see, for example, the section on technology below), there has been a recognition that customers can be involved and, through focus groups, be given the opportunity to express preferences and ideas and interface with the design process for services and products such as vehicles, retailing, financial services and housing, to bring consumer-led ideas into the design arena. For example:

- Having closed their doors on a Saturday for over 30 years, UK banks, recognizing the changing lifestyles of many customers, asked how they could better meet their needs. One outcome was that selected high street branches reopen on a Saturday morning and stay open later on at least one day per week. In this way they provide services at times that best suit many customers. The service provision has now increased to a point where in all UK banks an almost full service is on offer when many customers are best able to use it.

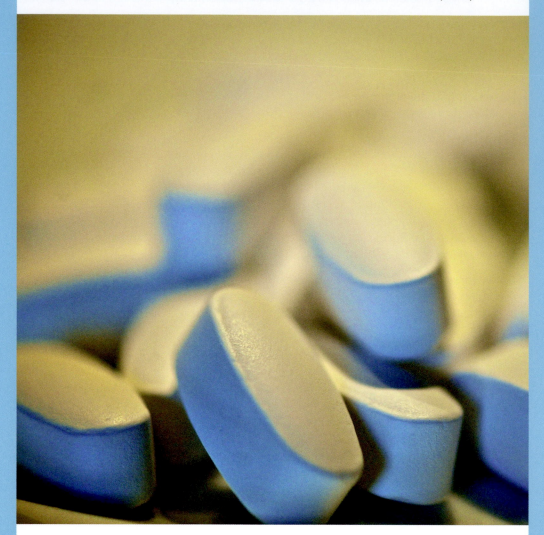

During the 1990s, the pharmaceutical industry, where new product introduction is a key factor for success, saw 'a quantum leap in the mechanics of drug research' that promised 'to revolutionize pharmaceuticals in the way PCs reinvented the computer industry'. During this period, GSK (a leading health care company) started to use 'combinatorial chemistry', which creates tens of thousands of new molecules – the building blocks of new medicines – within a few hours, compared with conventional chemistry that results in an average of some 40 new molecules a year. Linked to this was a robotized screening station that evaluates a compound's effectiveness against specific disease-causing genes at the rate of 50,000 a week and, in the process, allows new compounds to be developed in a cost- and time-effective way on an industrial scale. However, in more recent years, GSK has overhauled its R&D system. Andrew Witty took over as CEO of GSK in May 2008, promising to move away from the industrial-scale drug discovery processes of the 1990s. The upheaval was radical, but there have been qualitative and quantitative benefits. The focus has been on developing smaller scientific teams that take a more lateral approach to problem solving.

www.gsk.com

Question

What is the fundamental change in approach adopted by GSK?

- Over the past decade the number of US business trips involving children has grown to 15 per cent. Several factors are fuelling this trend (including two-career families and more single-parent households) and many working parents see business trips as a way of squeezing in precious time with their families. When the travel industry monitored these trends and also sought customer opinion on what changes would improve overall travel provision, the answer was to develop service delivery systems to meet these changing requirements. Hotels and airlines are now tailoring services to do just that – licensed babysitter bookings, children's menus and sightseeing programmes for children illustrate some of the service development responses in many hotels.

- In more developed economies, the growing awareness of consumers to eat healthily has resulted in changes to the range of food being offered. Vegetarian options are now typically included while many fast-food restaurants now include non-beef main courses together with a wide range of fruit and salad options.

- Companies are realizing that new social media such as Facebook and Twitter can be an asset in the development of new services and products and can help reshape the way companies create new ideas and bring them to market.

Such social network sites (Facebook has more than 750 million active users) are a first source of up-to-the-minute news including comments on the products and services the users buy and consume. In the same way, blog writers comment on many offerings in today's marketplace. Progressive companies have recognized that these social networks offer valuable insights into all the steps in the new service and product development process as they offer firms the opportunity to tap into consumer comment on a real time, continuous basis. In addition, certain types of buyers are willing to be involved in the new service and product development process and, when carefully selected, bring high levels of skill and knowledge to the process including providing a comparative judgement about new or proposed developments.[8]

Legislative requirements

Government legislation invariably requires organizations to adapt and change, often necessitating new services and products to meet new requirements. For example:

- The European Commission's year-on-year higher targets for waste management continue to have an impact on packaging design and stimulate change to meet future requirements.

- Citizens' Charters introduced by many governments will increasingly have an impact on service design within several industries.

- Legislation concerning issues such as noise and pollution has required product design changes to meet the new requirements. The increasing use of active noise cancellation in turboprop aircraft to reduce noise levels, the pressure on emission levels in vehicles and the research work on battery-driven vehicles illustrate the impact of legislation on design.

Environmental pressures

Concerns and pressures from the 'green lobby' are forcing change often independent of government action. For example:

- Over 400 German companies have set up the Duales System Deutschland (DSD) to establish the infrastructure needed to recover and reuse packaging waste. At an estimated set-up cost of £3.5 billion and annual running costs of £0.7 billion, DSD is in response to growing consumer awareness about waste. These recycling targets are influencing European standards and the impact on packaging and waste collection services is already widespread. One such example is the Green Dot Scheme for recycling packaging. Originally introduced by DSD, the scheme has now been rolled out to some 25 European countries involving 130,000 companies and encompassing 460 billion packages.

'**Good design** involves identifying what is **critical** and taking everything else away'

- The sales growth in rechargeable batteries (a nickel-cadmium battery can be recharged 1,000 times) reflects concerns not just about price but also the environment.

Technology advances

Technology shifts have far-reaching effects on service and product design. In some instances the changes revolutionize design and in others provide a plethora of new offerings. Dupont's invention of nylon and the impact of plastics, semiconductors, integrated circuits and computing on new service and product opportunities have been significant. The examples of the new services and products spawned from these new technologies are numerous – telephone and internet banking, internet shopping and the purchase of air tickets, theatre tickets, books, films, music and holidays online.

Enhancing services and products by incorporating new technologies is also widespread. For example, Federal Express interlinks stages in the service system by using computers to monitor and track deliveries throughout its whole delivery system. On receipt of a customer call a Federal Express operator enters details onto a computer. This information is then radioed to a courier and displayed on a hand-held computer terminal. After pick-up, the package is logged into the company's central computer in Memphis. With the use of industrial bar codes, packages can be tracked in the system and customers can access these details at any time on request.

> **EXECUTIVE INSIGHT**
  During the design and development process, organizations need to use both internal and external sources to generate ideas.

2. Screening ideas

The purpose of screening ideas is to eliminate those that do not appear to have high potential and so avoid the costs incurred at subsequent stages. Proposals, supported by graphics, models and an outline specification, are then judged against a set of criteria to enable each design to be evaluated overall. The criteria used in such assessments include the potential impact of the idea on a firm's future success or survival, its role in filling out an existing service or product range, the degree of overlap with existing services and products, the utilization of existing delivery systems, processes and capabilities, a reflection of the firm's core interests and expertise and the overall impact on estimated sales and profits.

To provide greater insight, organizations often score each dimension of each idea on a 0–10 scale and then apply weights to each of these dimensions. The resulting aggregate score helps when deciding which ideas to progress and which to terminate.

3. Feasibility study

The next step is to complete a more detailed check on the ideas still being considered. This part of the process will look at a whole series of dimensions that relate to a service or product idea and its intended markets, for example:

Service and product development

- Development lead time – how long to develop a service or product from idea to provision?

- Uniqueness or design

- Previous experience

- Anticipated length of its life cycle – how long will the sales levels of a service or product be sufficient to justify keeping it on the sales list?

Market(s)

- Relevant order-winners and qualifiers
- Selling price
- Sales volumes over time
- Fit with the company's corporate strategy
- Level of existing and future competition
- Stable or seasonal nature of forecast patterns of demand
- Advertising required
- Technical demands on support staff in both the selling and after-sales stages.

Operations

- Degree of match with existing capabilities
- Quality conformance requirements – what is needed to provide the service or product specification
- Ability to support the relevant order-winners and qualifiers
- Capacity needs
- Potential process investments.

Financial

- Capital outlays
- Return on investment
- Cash flows.

Whereas the scoring model adopted in the initial screening stage provides a rough, quantitative measure, the purpose of the analysis at this stage in the design process is to determine more specific qualitative measures on all important dimensions. This is necessary in helping to decide whether or not to commit further resources to the development of an idea. From this stage forward development costs tend to increase significantly.

4. Preliminary design and development

This stage of the process involves developing the best design for a new idea. Here the outline of the new service or product will need to be specified in much greater detail. Many trade-offs will have to be made concerning features, costs and producibility. Reconciling these, often conflicting, demands is a difficult task and one that needs to be resolved at this stage.

5. Testing prototypes

The physical embodiment of the functional and aesthetic requirements of a service or product is known as the **'prototype'**. Using this step in the process serves many ends. In addition to illustrating the aesthetic dimension, it serves to check the functionality of the idea, its robustness and the operations implications of its provision. In this way it tests the specification of the service or product, its physical or other dimensional properties or use under actual operating conditions. Part of this involves questions about the need for specific capabilities, material requirements, use of standard components, process steps, layouts, packaging and despatch implications. Typically there will be several, if not many, prototypes. It is a way of checking reality beforehand and enables savings in both time and costs to be secured.

Prototype – an initial design of a service or product to help evaluate a design option.

6. Market sensing and testing target markets

Above we explained the need to test the functionality of an idea and undertake the continuous and critical task of checking prototypes. At the same time assessing potential demand needs to continue. That the idea works and can be reproduced is one side of the coin and whether customers will buy it is the other. As with prototype testing, this step is an ongoing task.

For example, a prototype may constitute the introduction of a new or revised service in one or more test sites where the concept can be evaluated and modified as necessary. Once a new service and its delivery system have been tried and proved to be successful it can be introduced into other outlets. This would typically be the approach adopted in national retail and fast-food restaurant chains. Here, a new range of clothing or a new line of meals would be trialled in selected outlets and, if successful, then launched throughout the rest of the business.

In the same way, product prototype testing is a way of verifying the technical performance and sales potential of a new idea. Test marketing in a selected geographical area is a similar approach to that outlined above for services. Throughout, screening and testing is a continuous activity aimed at checking and rechecking in order to reduce uncertainty before large capital investments are committed.

7. Final design

Prototype testing often identifies necessary changes to the initial design and these will be incorporated during the final design phase. At this stage, specifications will be completed and the essential tasks of marketing plans, material supply, operations tasks and associated investments will be confirmed.

The decision

As mentioned earlier, the design process is characterized by reiteration and a non-sequential nature. Steps into the unknown embody uncertainty and the rigours of the design and development process are intended to flush out questions essential to arriving at a viable design. The final decision as to whether or not to go ahead rests with top management, and the levels of investment, corporate profile and reputation, and the strategic direction of the firm are invariably central to these decisions. Rejection stems from a combination of experience, judgement and placing a decision in the context of other investment opportunities. Approval commits a firm's efforts and resources one way and to a course of action whose success may not be measurable for months, even years later and yet may harm a company's success or even jeopardize its very survival.

The design of services or products and the design of the service delivery systems or manufacturing processes to provide them are interlinked. However, the separation of these aspects by addressing them in different chapters has been deliberate. Providing detail on both is essential, but incorporating them in a single set of statements can often be confusing. Separating the two aspects adds clarity without significant disadvantages. In the discussions on service delivery system and manufacturing process design in Chapters 5 and 6, links to service and product design will be recognized throughout.

Reviewing the service and product mix

All organizations have a range of services or products at a given time. To be competitive, it is necessary to have a set that is complementary, relates to the organization's strategic decisions on issues such as growth and market share, and takes account of tactical considerations such as completeness of range, system/process capability and distribution costs. Furthermore, the mix is always undergoing change as services or products are necessary for survival and growth. It is essential, therefore, for an organization to review its service and product mix as a whole. When undertaking this review, there are three important factors to be considered:

1. The development and introduction of new services and products is both risky and costly.

2. Services and products tend to follow a life cycle.

3. Some services and products are or have the potential to be more successful than others – so service/product portfolio analysis is necessary.

The issues around the first point have been addressed earlier. Here we look at **service/ product life cycles**, service/product portfolios and designing services and products to meet the needs of different market segments

Service/product life cycle – the process of introduction, initial growth, maturity and eventual decline in sales that a service product typically undertakes as it moves into and then out of its market.

Service/product life cycles

The extent and rate of new service and product introductions can make a significant impact on a business. However, of equal concern in these decisions is the life cycle pattern anticipated or experienced once the service or product has been introduced. Market pressures require that designs never remain static and continuous endeavours are made to increase the fit with customer needs while scrutinizing the relationships between cost of provision and the service/product specification that has to be provided. Despite the attention that most organizations give to this, many services and products enter the market and are then quickly phased out due to a lack of sales.

The process of introduction, initial growth, maturity and eventual decline in sales is referred to as the 'service/product life cycle' (see Figure 4.3). It outlines the phases through which a service or product may go as it moves into and out of its market. New services and products are required to replace those already in the cycle, no matter how extended the timescale may be. The phases detailed in Figure 4.3 are now explained.

> **EXECUTIVE INSIGHT**
> Assessing where services and products are on their respective life cycles helps when forecasting sales revenues.

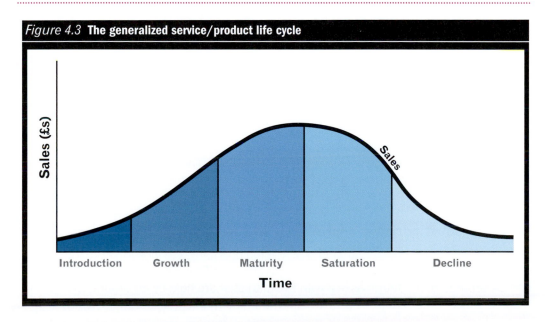

Figure 4.3 **The generalized service/product life cycle**

Introduction

Initially, the sales pattern of many services and products shows a slow rate of growth. Market awareness is low and the service product has not yet been accepted. The concept is often new, and initial teething troubles are usually experienced. This makes for low sales with slow growth.

Growth

In the growth phase, the market has now been conditioned to the service or product. With acceptance comes a rapid growth in sales resulting from promotion, increased dependability, past sales and often lower selling price.

Maturity

At the maturity stage there is increased overall demand as a service/product becomes well known, accepted and established within its market segment. However, the rate of sales for a company begins to slow due to competitors entering the market. It is also here that companies often use increased levels of customization as a way to help stimulate demand.

Saturation

In the saturation stage, most of those who want the service or product have typically now bought it. Market demand is, therefore, restricted to the need for replacements plus a small quantity of new sales. Service and product promotion is often used more extensively here, not to publicize the item but to differentiate it from its competitors.

In service firms, this phenomenon is often not as marked. For example, restaurant chains still keep selling but often the sales levels plateau because of overcapacity in their sector or the reasons stated earlier. Also, some decline may take place as alternatives enter and prosper. For example, KFC sales have declined in the last decade even though overall sales in the fast-food sector have grown. This is due to the success of fast-food alternatives.

Decline

In the decline phase of a life cycle, sales continue to fall off, invariably at a rapid rate. The introduction of competing services and products, either as improvements or substitutes, accelerates the decline to the point where it becomes obsolete, or is phased out. For example, the traditional telephone had been in the mature/saturation stage for a long time but over the past 20 years has been replaced by, first, the cordless and then mobile phones.

Reporting current and forecast sales of services and products in terms of the stage in their life cycle provides an insight into the spread of sales by phase, future patterns and the levels of new services and products that need to be targeted in the future. Also, different strategies are more relevant to one cycle stage than another. For example, an applications-oriented strategy is appropriate in the mature stage by offering modifications to existing services and products in order to serve particular market segments, whereas the emphasis on reducing costs and keeping designs fixed is most appropriate in the saturation phase of a typical cycle.

Service/product portfolio analysis

Portfolio analysis provides another way of helping companies to look forward and decide on the allocation of development resources. As shown in Figure 4.4, services and products can be separated into four classes, with the market share held by an organization being measured horizontally and the growth rate within the market measured vertically.

Services and products are then placed throughout or across two or more of the four segments to illustrate their relative positions against these two dimensions. The resulting 'portfolio' of services and products serves as part of the basis by which an organization can determine the appropriate allocation or concentration of resources and particularly R&D funding. These quadrants are explained below.

An organization that has analyzed its services and products in this way is then able to look at its current or proposed mix in terms of cash and profits. This will help it to ensure continuity of a suitable service or product mix by determining a series of business issues. These include which markets to aim for and the degree of support required, particularly with regard to decisions on research and operations investment.

Dilemmas
Dilemmas are services/products with a small percentage of a high growth market. In order to maintain or improve its position, an organization will have to allocate more cash than the services and products generate. Although the environment is favourable, current performance is questionable, thus requiring close examination and often remedial action. Consequently, it will be uncertain as to whether a service or product in the future will become a star or a pet.

Stars
Stars are services/products with a high market share (typically a market leader) in a high growth market but often in a position where the cash generated is, at best, equal to (and often less than) the cash needed. Stars will eventually become cash cows if they hold their market share; if they do not they will become pets.

Cash cows
Cash cows are services/products with a high percentage of a low growth market and in the latter half of their life cycles. These are the principal generators of funds. Cash cows can and should be 'milked' to generate more cash than can be profitably reinvested. However, they can in no way be forgotten: they have to be managed efficiently, new developments within a service or product range have to be made and customers have to be carefully tended, with the emphasis on cash flow rather than building market share.

Pets
Also known as cash traps, pets describe services/products where individual market share is low, market growth is low and they are cash absorbers, with little or no hope of changing the situation. For many organizations the majority of their services/products fall into this category. They may show an accounting profit but the profit must be reinvested to maintain market share. They leave no cash surplus for investment elsewhere and often absorb cash surpluses created by other services and products. As a rule, they should be deleted from the range.

> **EXECUTIVE INSIGHT**
> Service/product portfolio analysis helps pinpoint these services or products with the greatest potential in terms of revenue and cash generation while also highlighting these services and products that should be candidates for deleting from the range.

A service/product portfolio analysis is essentially static but is a useful selection technique to help organizations to both understand more fully their current position and reposition their service/product portfolio in the future. Its primary functions are to aid resource allocation and cash management by pinpointing those services and products with greatest potential and maintain a balance within the current mix. On the other hand, the service/product life cycle is a dynamic model with associated market-related strategies built in. Thus, combining the two analyses allows companies to assess their service or

Figure 4.4 **Service/portfolio analysis**

SERVICE/PRODUCT MARKET

High

GROWTH RATE OF THE MARKET (CASH USED)

High

STARS

Cash generated is equal to
or less than the cash used

£€$

CASH COWS

Cash generated is greater
than the cash used

Low

?

DILEMMAS

Cash generated is less
than the cash used

PETS

Cash generated is less
than the cash used

product mix on both dimensions. This, in turn, gives further insights to help determine decisions such as investment priorities and where best to harvest existing services and products.

So far, we have looked at the introduction of new services/products, the design process and the need for organizations to review what they currently offer. Now we turn our attention to the key task of developing a specification and the role that operations has in this part of the design process.

Designing services and products to meet the needs of different market segments

Firms invariably compete in more than one market segment, and recognizing and addressing the differences involved in terms of service or product development, as well as marketing, operations and other functional tasks, is essential. To illustrate how companies have developed different services and products to meet the needs of different market segments, take a look at Cases 4.5 and 4.6.

Developing a specification

As we learned earlier in the chapter, developing a specification is an important part of the process of service/product design and development. It is self-evident that services/products need to be defined in terms of what they comprise. What is equally important, however, is to identify within the development process those aspects of the design that will later affect other functions tasked with selling and providing the service or product. As highlighted in Chapter 2, the need to link decisions made within functions to one another is essential and because of this, the development of a specification (what a service/product comprises) has to be detailed from several perspectives. For example, the design of services/products and the design of the service delivery system or manufacturing process to provide them are interlinked. The following sections will explore the factors that must be considered when developing a specification.

The inherent nature of services and products

The physical nature of products brings with it an inherent need to specify what a product comprises when it is being developed. Services, on the other hand, are less tangible and consequently the task of defining what a service comprises needs to be a more specific undertaking. Without this recognition, the rigour necessary to define a service may not be applied and the required detail may not be provided.

In manufacturing, products and customers are invariably decoupled in the system, for example through inventory or the wholesale and/or retail stages in the total supply chain. In services, however, the provider and customer are invariably linked at the point of provision. The result is that the opportunity to interpret what is meant by 'service' is also at the point of provision. It is necessary, therefore, for organizations to determine the level of discretion to be allowed in the service delivery system. This concerns what a service comprises and what a server can provide as part of a service offering.

Developing a specification to reflect the service/product mix

Most offerings comprise a mix of service and product and Figure 1.7 provided some examples of this. When detailing a specification, it is useful to identify the nature of the service and the nature of the product within the mix. One way to highlight the corresponding roles of the service and product elements in the mix is to ask whether this is a service within which there is a facilitating product (that is, the offering is

CASE 4.5 PRODUCT DESIGN FOR DIFFERENT MARKET SEGMENTS AT HANDELS BANK NW

Handels Bank NW (Zurich) provides a different service offering for the following market segments:

- Institutional investors
- Portfolio management clients
- Large investors
- Standard investors
- Medium investors
- Small investors.

These segments reflect the needs of its investors, the appropriate investment tools to be used and the differential costs the bank applies in providing its different services. In this way, the bank more clearly identifies the type and level of service to be provided and the operations support required in that provision.

In the same way, UK banks have been segmenting their market and developing services to meet the needs of 'high earners'. Tailoring products and allocating more management time are high on the agenda and linked to different segments. Natwest, for example, divides its customers by age, family status and income, and addresses each segment differently.

www.lhb.de

Questions

1. For the six market segments above, identify two elements of service where the level or type of provision would not be the same for each segment.

2. For two of the six segments above, suggest how the two elements you selected could differ.

Lecturers: visit www.palgrave.com/business/ hillom3e for teaching guidelines for this case study

Hotels continue to emphasize segments within their offering and support these with appropriate service developments. In the 1970s it was in-room mini-bars, while health clubs were all the rage in the 1990s. Now executive floors have emerged in the top business hotels in North America and Europe. Billed as a hotel within a hotel, the premium floors have their own check-in and check-out facilities, an executive lounge and sometimes a dedicated, express-elevator service. For five-star hotels, executive floors are a way of differentiating themselves at a time of intense competition in downtown and airport sites. For example, the Hilton Hotel in the Boulevard des Waterloo, Brussels offers for a $60 supplement, an executive floor room which includes a complimentary breakfast (normally $30), free drinks in the lounge until 22.00 hours, butler service, a library of CDs and videos for guests to play in their room and a mobile phone loaned free, for which they can obtain their individual phone number three days in advance.

Finally, with the growing number of guests who are businesswomen travelling alone, hotels are providing services to reflect this. The Meridien Hotel, Piccadilly, London offers a female executive traveller package including female room service attendants and increased awareness of security at all stages in the hotel process. The Thistle Hotel chain includes special features in its rooms allocated to women and some of its hotels offer women-only wings. A recent survey showed that some 40 per cent of all business travellers are women, with the number expected to rise rapidly.

Questions

1. What are the three most significant ways in which hotels have addressed the 'executive' and 'female guest' segments described above?

2. Explain your choice.

Lecturers: visit www.palgrave.com/business/hillom3e for teaching guidelines for this case study

predominantly a service but includes a product that contributes to influencing customer choice) or this is a product that also involves a facilitating service (that is, the offering is predominantly a product but includes a service that contributes to influencing customer choice). This helps to clarify the mix issue and identify which elements are an integral part of the specification and which elements will enhance the offering in the eyes of a customer.

Figure 1.7 reminds us that what is purchased is a combination of services and goods and the mix will vary, for example purchasing a television set compared with tailored kitchen units requiring installation, or a meal provided by a high-class restaurant compared with a fast-food outlet.

The explicit and implicit benefits of the offering

When developing a specification, it is useful to separate the elements of the specification into explicit and implicit dimensions. For example, a bank provides the explicit service of money transactions; a hotel provides food and accommodation; and a hairdresser, the styling of hair. Customers may choose from a range of quality levels related to the provision of a service and this will typically influence their selection of which organization will provide it for them.

In addition, the offering may also include a range of implicit dimensions: for example, security and privacy within a banking system; level of attention, promptness and recognition of a regular customer by hotel staff; and the magazine and hot/soft drink provision and levels of cleanliness within a hairdressing salon. In fact, in some markets the implicit services may well be a more important factor in influencing a customer's selection as the explicit service that lies at the core of the purchase. However, no matter what comprises the relative importance of the explicit and implicit dimensions involved, recognizing these differences helps in developing a specification and in signalling in detail what the offering should involve.

The supporting structural facilities

Developing a specification also involves determining the support facilities that are required. These reflect the nature of the service or product provided and customers' perceptions of what is entailed. Typical examples are the quality of buildings, reception areas, meeting rooms, furniture, fittings and equipment, appropriate decor, level of maintenance and general upkeep, delivery vehicles, appearance and technical know-how of after-sales support staff.

The implications of the non-repeat or repeat nature of a service or product

The design of a service or product must also reflect the characteristics of the market in which it is to be sold. At one extreme a service or product may comprise an offering that is not repeated, that is, it is designed specifically for one customer. This is termed a 'special' service or product, referring to its unique, non-repeat nature. Examples include in-depth financial advice regarding a multinational takeover, the interior design for corporate offices, the logo for a blue-chip company, the public relations campaign for a political party, the garden design for a large country house and an ocean-going yacht designed to compete in the Melbourne to Hobart race or America's Cup. As you will see from these examples, markets characterized by non-repeat offerings are unusual and not the norm.

Most services and products are of a repeat nature (provided more than once and to more than one customer) and at the extreme will be high volume. Examples of repeat offerings include post office services, petrol or gas stations, supermarkets, sandwich bars, fast-food outlets and cash machines in the service sector, with computers, mobile phones

ASPECTS		NON-REPEAT	REPEAT — Low volume	REPEAT — High volume
Service or product	type	Special	→	Standard
Service or product	range	Wide	→	Narrow
Number of customer orders		Low	→	High
Level of service/product change required in the process		High	→	Low
Design predominantly determined by		Customer	→	Provider
Orientation of innovation – process or service/product		Service or product	→	Process
What does the company sell?		Capability or skill	→	Standard offering
How does the company win orders?	order-winners	Unique skills, repeat business or recommendations	→	Price
How does the company win orders?	qualifiers	Price, delivery on time, quality conformance	Delivery on time, quality conformance	Delivery on time, quality conformance

and T-shirts providing examples in the manufacturing sector. With this fundamental change, dimensions of the service and product such as volumes, order size, level of change required and typical order-winners and qualifiers will also differ, as shown in Figure 4.5.

Figure 4.5 illustrates some of the aspects that relate to service and product design issues that, in turn, will have implications for operations. The special (non-repeat) or standard (repeat) nature of the service or product is reflected in the width of the range offered. As a capability or skill seller, companies in non-repeat design markets typically offer a wide range, the width of which is only limited by the skill base available. On the other hand, companies selling high volume, repeat services or products will typically restrict the range. The higher the volume, the less the choice. And the dimension of range is not service- or product-related but reflects the volumes involved. For example, the options available on a Honda Civic are significantly less than those available on a Rolls-Royce. Although both products are cars, they represent very different markets, differences which are duly reflected in the design-related features highlighted in Figure 4.5. Hence, in non-repeat markets, service and product designs are predominantly determined by the customer, while with repeat service/product offerings designs (including the options available) are determined by the provider – a customer's choice is limited to what is on the option list. Finally, the way a company wins orders will similarly reflect these non-repeat/repeat and volume dimensions and the role of design is to contribute to these strategic requirements. Innovation of the offering and the potential order winning role of unique skill or capability will progressively be replaced by the design task of taking out cost and contributing to the need for a simple-to-provide offering that helps reduce costs while making repeatability an easy-to-achieve characteristic.

Techniques for improving design

This final section outlines some of the operations techniques and approaches used to help improve the design process in the overall context of a business:

- Standardization
- Modular design
- Mass customization
- Taguchi methods
- Quality function deployment and the house of quality
- Value engineering and value analysis
- Simultaneous engineering
- Variety reduction.

Standardization

As shown in Figure 4.5, the service/product continuum ranges from specials, where each item is unique, to offerings where there is little, if any, choice: the Model T Ford 'any colour as long as it is black' syndrome. For the most part, today's markets lie between these extremes. To help enhance volumes, designers, where possible, use the same components, ingredients or materials to provide a range of offerings. For example, designers use the same chassis in more than one car and, similarly, the same engines in more than one model. In the same way, suppliers of prepacked food use much the same packaging from one item to another, while fast-food restaurants use the same containers, food items and disposable packaging wherever possible. In doing so, the volumes of these standard items are enhanced which helps to reduce costs.

Thus, the concept of standardization helps provide a range of options, while enhancing the volumes of parts from which end services and products are built. The concept can be applied to components, materials, processes and delivery systems to great effect, as Case 4.7 illustrates.

Modular design

The use of modules as standard building blocks in designing and providing services and products is an extension of the concept of interchangeable parts. Using common sets of parts enhances volumes, lowers costs and reduces inventory levels, as Case 4.7 illustrates.

Mass customization

The increasingly competitive nature of today's markets has increased the need to provide customers' requirements without imposing prohibitive prices and lead times. While process investment is at the core of this provision, the decision to customize products as the way to run a business will mean substantial changes throughout an organization. Ever since General Motors (GM), by offering choice and alternatives, took over the world leadership mantle from Ford and its 'no choice' strategy in the 1920s, the automobile industry has offered a wide choice on many dimensions. The result is that the potential number of different automobile configurations (engine types and size × colours × options) for most models runs into six figures and they are all assembled using the same process. This approach to broadening the options on offer continues to spread into other markets.

© istockphoto.com/Dale Taylor

OIL AND GAS

Oil and gas production platforms, historically custom-built to a bespoke specification, are moving towards standard designs built on a modular basis as part of a cost-cutting orientation to ensure the future profitability of big oil companies.

TOYOTA

Toyota launched its smaller, recreational vehicle RAV4 at around half the price of most vehicles in this segment in part by using existing components and sub-assemblies from other cars – for example, the engine and steering wheel from Celica, a sports car, and door mirrors from Carina, a four-door sedan.

www.toyota.com

SONOCO

Offering modular services in support of products enabled the Industrial Products Division of Sonoco (a large US packaging company with sales in 2010 of $4.1 billion) to customize its packaging of support services 'to meet more precisely the requirements of its spectrum of customers'. The concept of offering only essential services as part of the **sales package** and then offering modular services at set prices enables companies such as Sonoco Products, Baxter Healthcare International, Asea Brown Boveri (ABB) and AZKO to tailor packages to customer needs and keep prices lower.

www.sonoco.com

> **Sales package** – the mix of services and/ or products that make up a sale.

Questions

1. Why were oil and gas platforms originally custom-built, non-repeat products?

2. Compare the use of standardization in the oil companies and Toyota. What similarities do you find?

3. How is modular design used by Sonoco and others?

Lecturers: visit www.palgrave.com/business/ hillom3e for teaching guidelines for this case study

The proliferation of faster, smarter and more affordable computers, software and telecommunications equipment allows more choice or customization on a mass (that is, high volume) scale. Aspects of modular designs and interchangeable parts offer choice to the customer and, with the necessary process investment required in place and an organization geared to meet these offerings, the ability to customize a standard product is a viable option. Whereas mass customization is not in itself new (the GM strategy was launched in the late 1920s), its application to a wider range of product offerings is, and the phrase 'mass customization' is intended to herald this growing phenomenon.[9]

Taguchi methods

The approach to design developed by Japan's Genichi Taguchi[10] received considerable attention in the early 1990s and now forms an integral part of the approach to design. His principle is simple. Instead of constantly directing effort to control a process so as to assure consistent quality conformance, it is better to design the service or product to achieve desired levels of quality conformance in the first place despite the variations that will occur in the service delivery system or production process. Based on his work in manufacturing, Taguchi's approach uses statistically designed experiments to optimize design and operations costs. This approach requires a service or product to perform to its specification in extreme conditions. For example:

- **Above-average demand** – ability of operations to increase capacity quickly

- **Absenteeism** – staffing plans to provide short-term cover

- **Dietary needs** – range of options to provide alternative menus

- **Weather shifts** – alternative activities to meet changeable weather patterns

- **Unexpected demand** – plans to meet early arrivals

- **Working conditions** – developing products to withstand harsh climates or extreme patterns of use.

This approach brings the service delivery system/manufacturing process and service/product design together and agrees the parameters to meet a range of conditions and then builds these into the specification. In so doing, it moves to a more proactive approach that emphasizes the prevention of defects and enables organizations to meet design specifications more consistently and achieve higher levels of quality conformance, a key factor in many of today's markets.

Quality function deployment and the house of quality

Two dimensions that affect the success of the design effort are the extent to which a service or product design meets customers' needs and how well an organization can produce or deliver the design. Quality function deployment (QFD) is a way to evaluate how well the service/product design and the operations process meet or exceed customers' needs. Using competitors' offerings as an additional part of the assessment helps organizations to identify both where they need to improve and also the service and product features and activities that are non-value adding.

QFD had its origins in US tyre manufacturer Bridgestone Corporation and Mitsubishi's Kone (Japan) shipyards in the late 1960s. Professor Yoji Akao (Tamagawa University) and Shigeru Mizuno gave QFD its name in the late 1970s and popularized the concept of formalizing customer inputs into service and product design procedures. The complete QFD approach involves a sequential set of matrices (see Figure 4.6) through which the links between customer needs and the technical, component/material and operations requirements are identified and maintained.

Figure 4.6 How quality function deployment links customer needs to operations requirements

House of quality

Customer needs and wants | **Technical requirements** | *Competitive review*

Components, procedures and systems requirements

Technical requirements | **Components, procedures and systems requirements** | *Competitive review*

Operations requirements

Components, procedures and systems requirements | **Operations requirements** | *Competitive review*

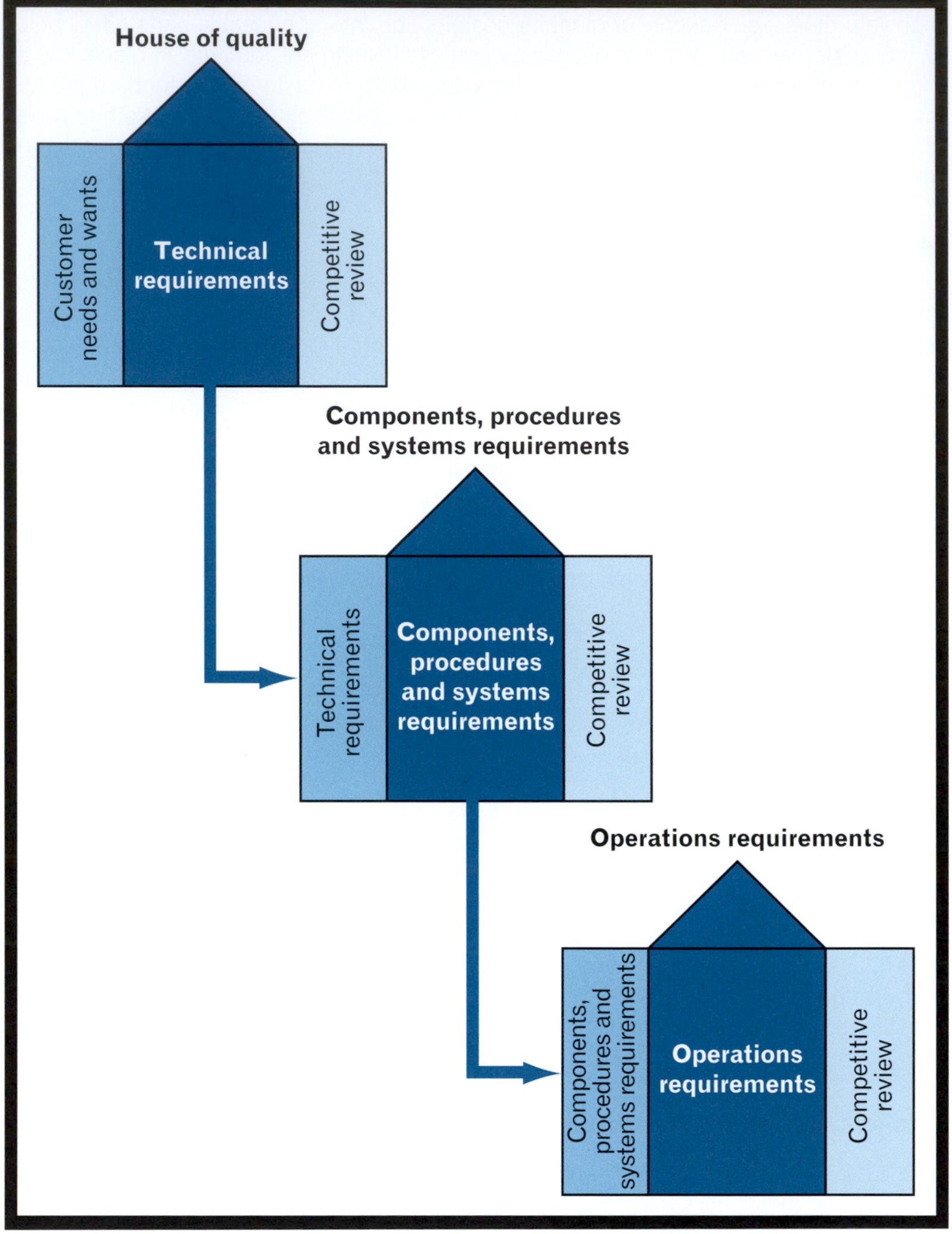

The most commonly used phase of QFD is the stage 1 matrix, often called the 'house of quality'. Figure 4.7 illustrates the general steps involved and will be used to show how the approach is applied, in this instance to a fast-food restaurant.

1. **Establish customers' needs and wants** as well as the characteristics and attributes of the services and products involved. Furthermore, the relative importance of these must then be established and weights agreed as a percentage, as shown in Figure 4.7.

2. **Establish the customers' view of competition** – how well does this facility satisfy customers' needs compared with competitors' outlets? In Figure 4.7, three competing restaurants are compared, with OP (own performance) representing this outlet and A, B and C representing the competitors' facilities. Where 1 is the best and 5 the worst, category comparisons can be made which will reveal areas that potentially need improving.

3. **Identify the technical requirements necessary to provide for customers' wants and needs.** For example, fast service may be achieved, in part, by making food ahead of time or reducing the process lead time involved. Measuring the factors that affect these and other dimensions would then be completed as an input into step 5 below.

4. **Look for links between technical requirements and their effect on different customers' needs and wants** – these are recorded in the body of the house of quality with a + or – sign indicating the extent to which it would potentially improve or harm relevant service or product attributes. For example, let us consider the technical requirement 'Decrease average time food is stored' in Figure 4.7. While decreasing the average storage time of food is potentially harmful to service speed (the chance of being out of stock increases and customers will have to wait; therefore, both are given a [–] sign) it potentially helps the attributes 'food tastes good' and 'food served warm' (and, therefore, both are given a [+] sign). Obviously, if we changed this technical requirement from 'decrease' to 'increase average time food is stored', the + and – signs would be reversed.

5. **Complete technical comparisons** – check the extent of your technical provision with that of your competitors. The actual figures involved (as in Figure 4.7) or using a scale of 1–5 will help comparisons and assessments. For example, related to the technical requirement 'Decrease process steps – main meal', the number of steps currently undertaken in 'Own performance' is 8, whereas for 'Competitors' A, B and C, it is 6, 6 and 5 respectively.

6. **Evaluate the trade-offs for different design features** – in the 'roof' section of the house of quality, information is recorded relating to the trade-offs of different design features, using + or – signs. This highlights the effect of changing the extent of one requirement on the other technical dimensions in the process. In Figure 4.7 you will see a + sign recorded between the first and fourth technical requirements. This highlights the need for both these requirements in order to increase menu variety and improve delivery speed. However, there is a – sign between the first and fifth and the first and sixth technical requirements – whereas increasing the grill area will help to improve service speed, decreasing storage times will have the reverse effect.

Value engineering and value analysis

In most industries, the ratio of purchases to employment costs is typically around 3:1. It makes sense, therefore, for companies to give time and attention to reducing material costs so as to secure the significantly higher potential benefits and savings.

The purchasing bill is made up of two elements – the price of the materials, components and services purchased and the amount of materials, components and services used. Whereas the former is the concern of the supply chain function (which to some extent will be influenced by world markets, competition and usage volumes), the latter is influenced by service/product design (the specification itself) and how well these purchased items are utilized. There are several approaches to checking the amount of materials, components and services used which we will now review.

An important, but often underused technique to help provide a systematic approach to reducing the cost of a service or product without impairing its function is *value analysis*. Each product, component or service is methodically examined with the purpose of minimizing its cost without reducing its functional value.[11] The process can be successfully applied to services, products and overhead costs. The term *value engineering* is often used synonymously with value analysis but, strictly speaking, it refers to the use of this technique in the initial stages of service or product design.

Customer needs & wants		Weights %	Increase grill area	Increase server staff at peak times	Increase server stations	Increase kitchen staff at peak times	Decrease average time food is stored	Decrease maximum time food is stored	Decrease process steps - main meal	1 (Best)	2	3	4	5 (Worst)
Decor & layout		5									OP&B	A&C		
Menu variety	Child	5	+			+					OP&C	A&B		
	Adult	10	+			+				C		B	OP&A	
Service speed		30	+	+	+	+	-	-	+	C		OP&A	B	
Food	Tastes good	15	+	+	+	+	+	+	+		OP&C	A&B		
	Served warm	10	+	+	+	+	+	+	+	C	A	B	OP	
	Ingredients	5									OP&C	B	A	
Low price		20	-	-		-	-	-			OP	A&B		C

Technical evaluation of competitors		m²	#	#	#	mins	mins	#	Comments
Own performance (OP)		2.5	5	5	7	6	9	8	
Competitors	A	2.4	5	5	7	6	8	6	
	B	2.7	5	5	8	6	7	6	
	C	3.0	6	7	8	4	7	5	
Target technical specifications		2.9	6	7	8	4	7	5	

Value analysis, like other methods of continuous improvement, aims to reduce costs. However, its orientation is different. Continuous improvement methods (discussed in detail in Chapter 13) tend to accept the service or product as a given and instead concentrate on the way it is provided or made. The principal aim of these methods, therefore, is to reduce aspects such as staff costs, rejects, wastage and lead times. Value analysis, however, considers the functions that the components, services/products or overhead activities are intended to perform. It then reviews the present design in order to provide these functions at a lower cost without reducing the value, that is, the specification of a service or product to meet a given customer requirement or support provided by an overhead activity will be maintained and will continue to be met by any proposed changes.

The need for value analysis to be introduced and maintained throughout an organization is an essential part of any approach to systematically reduce costs. As Lawrence Mills, who developed these concepts in the early 1960s, said: 'On average, one fourth of (processing) cost is unnecessary. The extra cost continues because of patterns and habits of thought, because of personal limitations, because of difficulties in promptly disseminating ideas and because today's thinking is based on yesterday's knowledge.'[12]

Value can be classified under two headings:[13]

1. **Use value** – the properties and qualities that accomplish the function of a service or product

2. **Esteem value** – the properties, features or attractiveness that cause people to want to own or use it.

Value, therefore, consists of a combination of use and esteem properties related to the cost of providing them.

The analysis of value

When analyzing value, three aspects need to be taken into account:

1. Design of the service/product or overhead activity

2. Purchase of materials or services

3. Service delivery system/manufacturing processing methods/overhead activity provision.

Design
Too often design decisions are made without due consideration of the effects on service or product costs. There are a number of reasons, including:

- Designers are often preoccupied with the initial task of designing to fully determine and meet the functional requirements involved.

- Traditional designs are often concerned with reliability and meeting the specification and do not ask value-for-money questions.

- Designers often adopt a safety-first policy and thereby overspecify.

- A lack of current information results in designs based too much on yesterday's principles and information sources.

- Functional specialisms help create barriers between design and other functions.

- Too often service specifications are not clearly determined.

Supply chain
In many organizations too little attention is given to the need to obtain services and materials that meet design requirements at lowest cost. This is because:

- The resources allocated and importance attributed to this critical role are insufficient, and so the cost-reduction and value-oriented approaches are overlooked.

- It is too easy to: (a) rely on previous or known suppliers, or allow other functions to specify the source for items; (b) avoid investigation and questioning as an integral part of the purchasing procedure; and (c) be reactive in this role.

- As in other areas, managing the supply chain also suffers from the barriers created by functional specialisms.

Operations

Many firms are increasingly looking to improve all aspects of their organization. This has long been so in the operations function. But in the past, reviews of working procedures have been limited:

• Investigations have been based on an operation or department rather than the service or product through all its stages including design.

• Reviews undertaken usually concentrate on the process, the way the work is completed. Thus, essential questions regarding design and materials are not addressed.

> **EXECUTIVE INSIGHT**
Value analysis is a systematic approach to lowering costs without reducing the services/product specification.

Value analysis procedure

Value analysis comprises two parts: (1) selecting those responsible for completing the analysis, and (2) the procedure to be followed.

The make-up of those responsible for completing the analysis work is quite wide-ranging. The classic structure is to have a group made up of a full-time specialist (the value analyst) and representatives from design, supply chain, costing and operations. However, other forms have proved equally successful and, in the case of many Japanese companies, include groups constituted under the title of 'quality circles'. In each instance, prerequisites for applying value analysis successfully are that those concerned must be trained in the procedures involved and that corporate goodwill is demonstrated at all points throughout, including adequate time to complete the tasks, access to cost and other data and liaison with outside suppliers. Eight steps are involved:

1. Select the service or product.

2. Gather information about it.

3. Analyze its function and its value for money.

4. Speculation/brainstorming generate alternative ways to provide the same function.

5. Assess the worth of these ideas.

6. Decide what is to be done.

7. Implement the decisions.

8. Evaluate the results.

In step 4, it is essential to use someone with experience (the value analyst) and carefully select the group involved. The selection should avoid the potential problems of seniority and provide a wide range of disciplines within the group. This stage is key to applying the technique successfully and needs to be handled with care.

The items selected are usually known to be of high cost and the use of the 80/20 rule (that 20 per cent the items or parts will constitute 80 per cent of the total cost of a service or product – see Chapters 10 and 11 for a fuller explanation of this rule) – will help in the procedure.[14] However, it is important not to select a service/product that is nearing the end of its life cycle. Value analysis is not a prop to help non-viable services or products become viable although it can form a legitimate part of extending the life cycle of existing services/products.

When introducing value analysis, the procedure should in no way bring with it an air of recrimination. Those concerned need to contribute to the process in an objective way without implying criticism of any department's or person's previous work. The following questions will help when applying value analysis to each item or part of the service, product or overhead activity:

- How does it contribute to the esteem or use value of the service, product or activity?

- Does the cost of each part or feature appear to be in proportion to its function?

- Are all the features essential? Which ones are questionable?

- If it is necessary, what else could provide the same function:
  (a) Standard part?
  (b) Alternative part?
  (c) Alternative approach?

- Is the way in which the service/product is currently provided or made in line with current volumes? Often volumes change, but the delivery system or process does not.

- Has anyone asked the supplier if an alternative is available to provide the same function?

- Have alternative suppliers been sought recently re current volumes and prices?

Value analysis consists of taking each part of a service or product and looking in detail at its function. Every feature, tolerance, hole, degree of finish, piece of material, part of the service or activity is vetted to ensure that none of these is adding to the total cost without providing a useful function.

The application of value analysis principles to products can be readily visualized. However, these principles are increasingly, and appropriately, being applied within service companies and to review overhead activities in all sectors. One example is provided in a review of the Paul Revere Life Insurance Company's application of value analysis as part of achieving its strategic objective of improved levels of quality conformance. Management groups formed value analysis workshops to address the question, 'Are we doing the right thing?', which resulted in recommendations to improve basic work functions and processes. The responsibility for implementing these organizational and work process changes was delegated to those running the individual sections, with department managers themselves eventually taking part in the value analysis workshops. Having identified the more important departments and the functions within a department, standard value analysis procedures were applied. Annual savings in the first six months were $6 million.

The sources of savings from value analysis come principally from reducing activities, steps in the system or process and material costs. They include:

- Eliminate parts (for example components, transactions or steps in a service system) without reducing the functional qualities involved.

- Combine the functions of two or more components or services by redesign.

- Reduce tolerances that are unnecessarily tight and make for higher operations costs.

- Extend the concept of standardization.

- Simplify the service delivery system or manufacturing process and consequently reduce staff costs.

Simultaneous engineering

The speed with which services and products can be designed and introduced into a market directly affects sales revenue and profit. Simultaneous engineering is an approach to reduce design lead times. It involves all relevant functions within a business (for example design, marketing, IT and operations) as well as suppliers. Its purpose is to undertake tasks, partly or wholly in parallel rather than sequentially. Receiving ideas and contributions from functions early in the process reduces time-consuming redesigns and delays and teamwork encourages co-ownership of the design and a greater commitment to making a service/product succeed. Jobs are also enriched and creativity is stimulated. Because everyone is communicating with everyone else throughout the design process, the specification of the service/product is improved, service/product lead times are dramatically shortened and service/product costs are cut. The principles underlying what happens are shown in Figure 4.8.

To achieve reductions similar to these, companies use a number of approaches:

- **Contracting out activities** – using external resources for one or more of the stages increases the available capacity and reduces delays. Possible tasks range from design, marketing and IT through to prototypes, initial launch and public relations.

- **Increased use of suppliers** – as explained later in Chapter 12, suppliers are increasingly being asked to take on several phases during the design and introduction of a service or product as part of the supplier package. This reduces the overall demands on a company's own design team and shortens the total time involved.

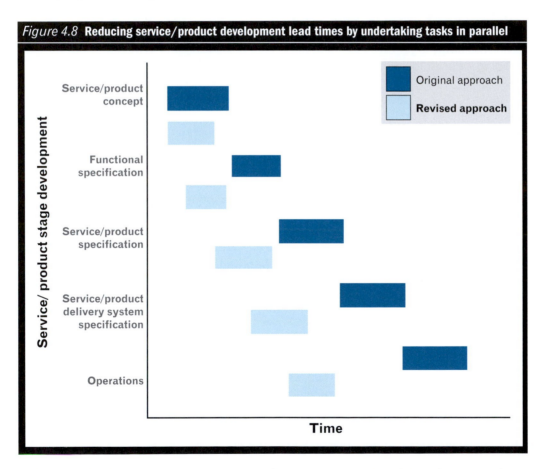

Figure 4.8 Reducing service/product development lead times by undertaking tasks in parallel

- **Teamwork** – forming service, product and process teams stimulates ideas, speeds up the process and eliminates problems.

- **Combining or eliminating stages** – combining or eliminating stages by re-examining existing procedures rigorously tests current practices and reduces lead-times throughout.

- **Overlapping stages** – as illustrated in Figure 4.8 identifying opportunities to begin the next phase before the current stage is complete moves the overall procedure away from a sequential process to one in which some activities (in part or in total) take place in parallel. The result is that overall lead times are dramatically reduced.

- **Incremental versus breakthrough innovations** – in the past breakthrough innovations have often been the desired goal of designers. These are harder to come up with, involve longer lead times in all phases of the design process and experience a higher failure rate. Switching the emphasis to incremental improvements and introducing clusters of these at the same time still gives rise to significant improvements but reduces the lead times to bring them about.

- **Using standard parts and modular designs** – earlier we looked at the principles and benefits of using standard parts and components and modular approaches to designs. A further design lead time advantage is also made available where 'common' parts are introduced into new designs with corresponding benefits.

- **Using new technologies** – employing technologies such as computer-aided design (CAD) and computer-aided engineering (CAE) reduces lead times within the overall process as well as eliminating stages. For example, CAE takes CAD designs and subjects them to stress, load and vibration tests to assess their strength and reliability, thus eliminating later elements of the design and prototype process.

Variety reduction

The approaches and techniques listed so far have addressed issues around the design itself. Variety reduction, on the other hand, is a quantitative appraisal of the current range of services and products. The process questions whether or not retaining all the services and products currently on offer is best for the business as a whole.

In any service/product range some items will generate more sales, more profit or contribute more to fixed costs than others. Consequently, checking the contribution (selling price less variable costs = contribution) that they make can reduce the items that are uneconomical and provide some control over future variety.

Using the Pareto principle, the first step in the process it to arrange all the services or products in a list with highest total value of sales at the top and lowest at the bottom. This often reveals that about 20 per cent of items account for about 80 per cent of the total sales revenue – the 80/20 rule described earlier (see Chapters 10 and 11 for a further explanation). As you can see in the example in Figure 4.9, the top six of the 24 products account for about 74 per cent of total sales (see note 3 to the figure), whereas the bottom 15 products account for only 17 per cent. In addition, these top six account for some 76 per cent of the total contribution (see the note with the figure), whereas the bottom 15 (or 62 per cent) contribute only £375,000, about 13 per cent.

The next step is to check the relative performances of the items with a low percentage of the sales revenue over the last three or four years in order to determine whether the individual trend is going up, staying the same or going down. Further checks are then made on the level and downward trend items to see if their contribution can be improved by reducing variable costs and/or increasing the selling price. If this action does not bring about the required changes in terms of percentage contribution to selling price, the company should consider phasing out the service or product.

The advantages of variety reduction include:

- Longer operations runs, with less downtime through fewer changeovers

- Potential savings in plant/equipment requirements

- Lower inventory, resulting in less capital, reduced inventory management requirements and lower space costs

Product reference number	Sales revenue (£000)	Percentage of total sales	Total variable costs (£000)	Total contribution (£000)	Percentage of total contribution
054-19	2480	19.5	2128	352	12.7
303-07	2134	16.8	1684	650	23.4
691-30	1720	13.5	1372	348	12.5
016-10	1440	11.3	1028	412	14.8
418-50	980	7.7	676	304	10.9
402-50	620	4.9	580	40	1.4
155-29	428	3.8	390	92	3.4
900-01	360	2.8	240	120	4.3
308-31	308	2.4	220	88	3.2
341-17	280	2.2	212	68	2.4
540-80	260	2.0	200	60	2.2
701-91	232	1.8	160	72	2.6
650-27	220	1.7	202	18	0.6
712-22	192	1.5	140	52	1.9
137-29	180	1.4	152	28	1.0
003-54	172	1.4	168	4	0.1
541-21	140	1.1	122	18	0.6
543-61	136	1.1	112	24	0.9
305-04	96	0.8	86	10	0.4
097-54	88	0.7	86	2	0.1
323-34	72	0.6	68	4	0.1
542-93	68	0.5	62	6	0.2
386-07	44	0.3	36	8	0.3
440-18	20	0.2	19	1	–
Total	**12,724**	**100.0**	**7463**	**2781**	**100.0**

Figure 4.9 **Product analysis by annual sales revenue**

Notes: 1. Contribution = selling price – variable costs.

2. Further analysis could be enhanced by grouping like products together and showing the product group totals for columns 'Percentage of total sales' to 'Percentage of total contribution' inclusive.

3. The '80/20' relationship implied in the rule is only an indication of the size of the actual figures involved. Thus, in the example here, 25 per cent of the products account for 74 per cent of sales, illustrating clearly the concept of a relatively small number of products accounting for a high percentage of the sales revenue.

- Less sales effort and less need for after-sales service

- Easier operations planning and day-to-day scheduling of tasks

- Appropriate reallocation of capacity (particularly scarce resources) to the overall benefit of the business.

Loss leader – a service or product offered at below cost to attract customers.

The disadvantages of this approach are a reduced service/product range and the danger of cutting out services/products that serve as **loss leaders**. Thus it is the net business effect that needs to be considered and on which such decisions should be based. Case 4.8 highlights some of the issues.

Few products have resisted standardization as much as the common door lock. In Europe alone, several hundred thousand types are sold – a product range diversity that reflects the doors and buildings that have evolved in different countries over several centuries.

Today, demand for security is growing and prospects are good. Assa Abloy (the Swedish lock maker with worldwide sales of more than SEK36 billion) is now No. 1 worldwide with 6 per cent of total global sales. Its growth (in 2012 it was over ten times larger than in 1994) has been partly generic and partly by taking over other businesses: in recent years Assa Abloy has bought out more than 20 lock companies worldwide. Its current sales profile is 50 per cent in Europe, 35 per cent in the USA, 10 per cent in the Pacific Rim and the remaining 5 per cent in the rest of the world. Despite this international breadth, products sold in more than one country account for only 25 per cent of sales.

Where possible, Assa Abloy tries to capitalize on the potential high volumes involved, for instance all exit bars for its fire and emergency doors are made in one plant in France. But this is more the exception than the rule. The outcome is over 40 manufacturing plants around the world, each mainly supplying its domestic market.
www.assaabloy.com/en/com

Questions

1. Why are some product ranges less open to variety reduction than others?

2. Choose a product suitable for standardization and variety reduction. Compare and contrast this with the example above on locks.

Designing services and products in practice

- Check the extent to which new services or products are impacting your business by analyzing the trend of new services/products as a percentage of total sales revenues both annually and for different periods where your sales experience seasonal fluctuations. If any sales are seasonal then use this insight to direct your search for new services/products.

- Identify in the past (say) five years the sources of any new services/products to ascertain where to spend more/less of your R&D budget that would fit the low sales period(s).

- Assess the timescales from initial concept to saleable service/product to highlight opportunities to reduce service/product development lead times and subsequently improve your time to market performance.

- Analyze your existing services/products in terms of their position on their life cycles to identify any 'gaps' as sales of some of your existing services/products decline.

- Systematically identify services/products that could be candidates for deleting from your existing ranges. Be aware that there will typically be resistance from the sales and marketing function to shed any potential sales opportunity now matter how small.

- Ensure techniques for improving design are regularly and systematically used in your organization and that data are provided to underpin those analyses.

Driving business performance

Designing services and products is core to the successful performance of a business in the following ways.

Designing services and products to release cash

Reducing the design and development time delivers services and products faster to market, impacts sales revenue and shortens the initial cash flow cycle. Only when launched do services and products begin to plough back cash.

Designing services and products to improve market support

Sustaining and growing sales are keys to success and introducing new and extending the life of/developing existing services and products are fundamental to this task. Systematically reviewing existing service/product mixes ensures that key resources are best used, highlighting gaps in sales mix profiles ahead of time.

Designing services and products to reduce costs

Materials can account for more than 50 per cent of total costs. Using value engineering approaches as part of new service/product design procedures helps reduce unnecessary costs from being designed in. Overhead activities also account for a large portion of costs, so using value analysis checks will allow these to be monitored and reduced.

Critical reflections

All organizations have a range of services or products at a given time. To be competitive, it is necessary to have a set that is complementary, that relates to the organization's strategic objectives (such as growth and market share) and takes account of tactical considerations (such as completeness of range, process capability and distribution costs). Furthermore, the mix is always undergoing change, as organizations continuously introduce new services and products in a never-ending bid to meet customers' requirements and grow sales. On the one hand, developing and introducing new items is typically expensive and risky and involves long timescales while, on the other hand, it is the very lifeblood of businesses, as new services and products are necessary for survival and growth.

> ## EXECUTIVE INSIGHT
> New services and products are the lifeblood of a business.

Attitudes and norms concerning the level of innovation and the introduction of new services and products are affected by internal and external forces. Decisions to invest in R&D or to seek to exploit developments in technology will vary from industry to industry and company to company, often markedly so. In product-based companies, the tradition of investing in R&D and actively seeking to introduce new products has noticeably increased over the past few decades. This varies from superficial modifications (for example, in markets such as customer durables, there is a traditional 'facelift' to existing models/products on a regular basis) to major product changes.

A review of service industries also highlights changes over the past decade in what is on offer. Protected for a long time by geographical distance, commercial legacies and legal constraints, many service industries remained conservative and insensitive to the needs of their customers. They competed in what are known as 'sheltered markets'. However, the impact of deregulation, advances in data processing and increased global competition in many areas of the service industry have moved many sectors into what are known as 'traded markets'. For instance, deregulation and advances in data processing have had an enormous impact in the travel industry. Whereas 20 years ago high street travel agents commanded a prime position (as a sheltered market), the advent of online selling has moved much of the industry into a traded market, bypassing high street outlets and, in some instances such as airlines, bypassing the travel agent altogether. In the same way the limited competition that banks enjoyed from the very beginning changed with the alterations to trading rules, the opening up of financial markets, investments in data-processing and the entry of non-finance organizations (for example, supermarket chains, other retailers and a wide range of other businesses) into banking, credit sales, personal loans and the like. One outcome has been a dramatic alteration to the basis and form of competition in the finance sector.

A tough business lesson that top managers need to draw from the history of progress is that most services, products and technologies will be replaced and most efforts to replace them will fail. This is somewhat a game of Russian roulette in which companies need to participate if they wish to grow and prosper with high stakes and high uncertainty. The stakes, however, will vary with the nature of the service and product and the level of change involved. But it is easy to be misled. Changes to existing, well-established markets of a non-dramatic nature can result in major shifts in success as Case 4.9 illustrates.

While cost-cutting, rationalization and restructuring are key components on any business agenda, companies need to recognize the key role of innovation in the quest for growth. In part, this stems from a recognition that improved efficiency is no substitute for

CASE 4.9 SMALL CHANGES WITH DRAMATIC EFFECTS

INCREASE THE FRESHNESS OF BREAD IN SUPERMARKET BAKERIES

A small change in existing specifications is enough to make a significant impact. For example, increasing the freshness of food provision has enabled supermarkets not only to match local high street outlets but outperform them. Bread technologies now enable doughs to be held for several days without deterioration. This enables in-store, supermarket bakeries to produce bread several times each day, thereby increasing product freshness. In addition, part-baked breads to be oven-finished at home have opened up a new dimension to fresh bread provision.

PRODUCT DESIGN CHANGES AT ALTRACK

Traditional markets are as vulnerable to the impact of design changes as any other. For example, alternatives to pneumatic tyres for off-road vehicles in order to reduce punctures and the costs involved have long been needed. Traditional solutions of solid and foam-filled wheels have the drawbacks of lack of comfort for the driver and wear on vehicle suspension due to increased rigidity. Altrack, an Australian tyre company, introduced a puncture-free wheel for construction equipment where

punctures are up to ten times more likely than on other vehicles. The new tyre design comprises a number of hollow-moulded, rubber segments that bolt on to a special wheel rim. A damaged rubber section takes only 15 minutes to replace with the vehicle (and its load) still in place.

Questions

1. List what you think is the most significant aspect of the design changes for these two examples and explain your reasons.

2. What aspects in these two examples are similar to one another? How do they link to the issues, concepts and approaches discussed in the chapter?

Lecturers: visit www.palgrave.com/business/hillom3e for teaching guidelines for this case study

growth. Organizations that have for some time pursued activities to reduce costs often experience anxious times as they have difficulty in moving back towards an innovative culture. Many businesses are stressing innovation as a corporate goal, while others (for example BP Chemicals, 3M, Elf Aquitaine, Siemens and British Airways) are introducing innovation schemes as a way to further stimulate these essential activities. But the area of innovation is as difficult to embrace as it is essential for continued success. Some pointers to these issues and ways forward include the following:

- Encouraging more creativity only addresses part of the problem. Much of the difficulty lies in establishing a clear link between innovation and business success.

- One common mistake is to believe that innovation can compensate for competitive disadvantages elsewhere.

- It is a misconception to think that innovation is a technical issue. Akio Morita (the founder of Sony) dismissed descriptions of the Walkman as an innovation marvel. 'Frankly,' he observed, 'it did not contain any breakthrough technology. Its success was built on product planning and marketing.'

- There is a need to move away from a preoccupation with R&D to the totality of innovation, in terms of scope (the Sony Walkman syndrome) and organizational style. Innovation is potentially in everyone and everywhere.

- Using customers is essential. One-third of the toy company Hasbro's annual sales come from new products. To ensure this trend continues, Hasbro goes to great lengths to keep its designers in touch with children. To this end it has built a crèche (known as the 'fun lab') for 25 children next to its R&D department. Recognizing the growth in social media (such as Facebook and Twitter) as a way to tap into customers' ideas, observations and reflections is a recent example of looking outside the more traditional sources of creativity.

- The task is to generate good services and products on a continuous basis. A culture of innovation is essential for this to happen. Ways of encouraging and incorporating the need to spend time on creating ideas has to become part of the corporate culture. 3M allows designers to spend up to 15 per cent of their time on any research project they wish – the Post-it note pad had bottom-up origins. Other organizations need to break down the status quo dimension that traditionally goes with innovation – they need to create a culture that encourages and develops innovation in order to bring everyone and their ideas on board.

Summary

- The introduction of new services/products and the development of existing ones is the lifeblood of organizations. For this to become an integral part of how companies grow and prosper, they need a way to generate ideas and then translate them into reality.

- Although breakthroughs will always gain the spotlight, most companies will typically sell today what they sold yesterday, and will do the same tomorrow. This does not imply, however, that they do not need to 'think outside the box'. On the contrary, nothing could be further from the truth. The key is more to do with where to focus attention, and for many companies this means thinking differently about what they currently provide and the markets in which they currently compete.

- With ideas being the spark that ignites developments, companies are realizing that they also need to seek views from less traditional sources. Key among these are the staff who provide the service or make the product, and the customers who buy it. Breaking the mould of past approaches is difficult, but in today's competitive world it is essential.

- While the first step of the process is vital, getting an idea to a market reality is critical. For much of the time, this part of the process changes from being one of inspiration to one based on hard work. Systematic checking and rechecking involves much time and effort.

- Finally, although new services/products create tomorrow's success, a company needs to get the most out of today's offerings. On the scale of being inherently interesting, generating ideas is at the top, with developing existing services/products much lower down. However, on the scale of what affects corporate success and prosperity, the order is often the reverse. The attraction of stars and the mundane nature of cash cows often results in an imbalance of time, attention and recognition. Keeping all the corporate balls in the air is an essential element of successfully managing the process for the design and development of services and products.

Study activities

Discussion questions

1. The section 'The service/product mix' explained that a service or product can be expressed as a combination of dimensions (that is 'a service within which there is a facilitating good', 'the explicit and implicit dimensions of an offering' and 'the supporting structural facilities'). Analyze the following businesses in line with these dimensions:
   - A supermarket
   - A high street post office
   - An upmarket restaurant.

2. Select a service and a product that are at different points of their life cycles. Explain their progress to date, where they are now and what you expect will happen in the future.

3. In what types of organization might new ideas have:
   - A low mortality rate (that is, they last for a long time)
   - A high mortality rate (that is, they last for a short time)?

   Explain your choice with supporting arguments and details.

4. Since markets for services typically have lower entry barriers than product markets, why do overseas companies not start with services when they first begin to compete in foreign markets?

5. A major German shoe company launched a new range of tennis shoes. There were two styles, one for men and one for women. Within each of these two styles there were six colour combinations and the shoe sizes ranged from size 7 and 14 for men and 4 to 9 for women. How many shoes would a store have to stock to have one pair of each shoe within both ranges?

6. Give two examples (with supporting details) for each of a service and manufacturing firm of the impact of technology in service and product design.

7. Give one example of the use of standardization and modular design for both a service and product of your choice.

Assignments

1. Apply the value analysis principles to a service or product and see if you can identify opportunities for cost reduction without reducing value.

2. Complete a review of two fast-food restaurants of your choice using the quality functional development approach. In this task, use the outline in Figure 4.7 but check, where possible, the detail for:
   - Customers' needs and wants, and weight the resulting percentages, as in Figure 4.7
   - Technical requirements
   - Customers' ratings for each restaurant.

3. In what types of organization might new ideas have:
   - A low mortality rate (that is, they last for a long time)?
   - A high mortality rate (that is, they last for a short time)?

   Explain your choice with supporting arguments and details.

4. Give two examples (with supporting details) of the impact of technology on:
   - A service
   - A product design.

5. Since markets for services typically have lower entry barriers than product markets, why do overseas companies not start with services when they first begin to compete in foreign markets?

Exploring further

TED talks

Brown, T. (2008) *Creativity and play*. At the 2008 Serious Play conference, designer Tim Brown talks about the powerful relationship between creative thinking and play, with many examples you can try at home (and one that maybe you shouldn't).
www.ted.com/talks/tim_brown_on_creativity_and_play.html

Iyengar, S. (2010) *The art of choosing*. Sheena Iyengar studies how we make choices and how we feel about the choices we make. She talks about both trivial choices (Coke v. Pepsi) and profound ones, and shares her groundbreaking research that has uncovered some surprising attitudes about our decisions.
www.ted.com/talks/sheena_iyengar_on_the_art_of_choosing.html

Johnson, S. (2010) *Where good ideas come from*. People often credit their ideas to individual 'Eureka!' moments. But Steven Johnson shows how history tells a different story. His fascinating tour takes us from the 'liquid networks' of London's coffee houses to Charles Darwin's long, slow hunch to today's high-velocity web.
www.ted.com/talks/steven_johnson_where_good_ideas_come_from.html

Leadbeater, C. (2005) *Innovation*. In this deceptively casual talk, Charles Leadbeater weaves a tight argument that innovation isn't just for professionals anymore. Passionate amateurs, using new tools, are creating products and paradigms that companies can't.
www.ted.com/talks/charles_leadbeater_on_innovation.html

Mitra, S. (2010) *The child-driven education*. Education scientist Sugata Mitra tackles one of the greatest problems of education: the best teachers and schools don't exist where they're needed most. In a series of real-life experiments from New Delhi to South Africa to Italy, he gave kids self-supervised access to the web and saw results that could revolutionize how we think about teaching.
www.ted.com/talks/sugata_mitra_the_child_driven_education.html

Journal articles

Amabile, T.M. and Kramer, S.J. (2011) 'The power of small wins', *Harvard Business Review*, **89**(5): 70–80. What is the best way to motivate employees to do creative work? Help them take a step forward every day. The key is to learn which actions support progress such as setting clear goals, providing sufficient time and resources, and offering recognition. On the flip side, small losses or setbacks can have an extremely negative effect.

Bettencourt, L.A. and Bettencourt, S.L. (2011) 'Innovating on the cheap', *Harvard Business Review*, **89**(6): 88–94. This article suggests that almost every company has previous discoveries with overlooked market potential. For example: (1) Products that failed to launch (2) Extras that could be spun out as stand-alone offerings (3) Components that could be combined into an enhanced offering, and (4) Over-designed products that could be simplified to reach new markets.

Brown, B. and Anthony, S.D. (2011) 'How P&G tripled its innovation success rate', *Harvard Business Review*, **89**(6): 64–72. In the early 2000s, Procter & Gamble created a 'new-growth factory' to rapidly shepherd new products and even business models from inception to market.

Dougherty, D. and Murthy, A. (2009) 'What service customers really want', *Harvard Business Review*, **87**(9): 22. This article argues that while superior customer service is a key to future growth, managers need to understand the extent to which consumers' expectations have shifted.

Hansen, M.T. and Birkinshaw, J. (2007) 'The innovation value chain', *Harvard Business Review*, **85**(6): 121–30. The challenges of coming up with fresh ideas and realizing profits from them are different for every company. This article provides a framework for evaluating innovation performance entitled 'the innovation value chain'. The article illustrates how smart companies (such as Intuit, P&G, Sara Lee, Shell and Siemens) modify the best innovation practices.

Keiningham, T. L., Aksoy, L., Buoye, A. and Cooil, B. (2011) 'Customer loyalty isn't enough, grow your share of wallet', *Harvard Business Review*, **89**(10): 29–31. The article presents an algorithm for determining a brand's 'wallet share', which depends on both customer satisfaction with a brand relative to competing brands, and the number of competitors.

Martin, R. L. (2011) 'The innovation catalysts', *Harvard Business Review*, **89**(6): 82–7. This article discusses how Intuit, a software development company, created a team of nine design thinking coaches called 'innovation catalysts' to help its employees learn from customers, run experiments and create prototypes. The process they use includes: (1) a 'painstorm' to determine the customer's greatest pain point (2) a 'soljam' to generate and then winnow possible solutions, and (3) a 'codejam' to write code good enough to take to customers within two weeks.

Ramaswamy, V. and Gouillart, F. (2010) 'Building the co-creative enterprise', *Harvard Business Review*, **88**(10): 100–9. The article examines how companies can use its stakeholders including customers, employees and distributors to determine HR practices and design and market its services and products.

Shankar, V., Berry, L. and Dotzel, T. (2009) 'A practical guide to combining products and services', *Harvard Business Review*, **87**(11): 94–9. Many firms are trying to combine products and services into innovative offerings to boost revenue and profit by attracting new customers and by increasing demand among existing ones as a result of offering them superior value. The findings are based on an analysis of more than 100 winning hybrid solutions from a variety of business-to-business (B2B) and business-to-customer (B2C) companies.

Verganti, R. (2011) 'Designing breakthrough products', *Harvard Business Review*, **89**(10): 114–20. Ideas and solutions are now easier to access through open innovation and collaboration. Companies need to work out how to take advantage of these new opportunities.

Books

Akao, Y. (ed.) (2005) *Quality Function Deployment: Integrating Customer Requirements into Product Design*. Cambridge, MA: Productivity Press. Using a wide variety of case studies, charts and diagrams, this book looks at how quality function deployment can be used to design services and products to meet customer demands.

Gladwell, M. (2001) *The tipping point: How little things can make a big difference*, Ilford: Abacus. This book tries to analyze why some products, ideas and ways of behaving cross a threshold or 'tip' and take off and, conversely, why so many more fail.

Hill, A. and Hill, T. (2011) *Essential Operations Management*. Basingstoke: Palgrave Macmillan. The text provides a useful supplement to *Operations Management* by focusing on the essential aspects for managing operations within service and manufacturing organizations.

Kelley, T. (2001) *The art of innovation: Lessons in creativity from IDEO, America's leading design firm*, London: Profile Books. Tom Kelley, general manager of the Silicon Valley-based firm IDEO, developer of hundreds of innovative products including the Palm hand-held, takes readers behind the scenes of this wildly imaginative company to reveal the strategies and secrets it uses to turn out hit after hit.

Websites

Inside Dyson There is a wide range of videos on the website showing how the company works and the technology behind the products that it has developed.
www.dyson.co.uk/insidedyson/default.asp

Notes and references

1. This explanation of design strategies was first put forward by Schonberger, R.J. in *Operations Management*, Plane Business Publications, Texas (1981).
2. Zahara, S.A., Sisodia, R.S. and Das, S.R. (1994) 'Technological choices within competitive strategy types: a conceptual integration', *International Journal of Technology Management*, 9(2): 172–95.
3. Abrahams, P. (2003) 'A meeting of Microsoft's minds', *Financial Times*, 5 February, p. 11.
4. For example, Daetz, D. (1987) 'The effect of product design on product quality and product cost', *Quality Progress*, 20: 63–7; Sheldon, D.F., Perks, R., Jackson, M., Miles, B.L. and Holland, J. (1990) 'Designing for whole life costs at the concept stage', *Journal of Engineering Design*, 1: 131–45; Suh, N.F. (1990) *The Principles of Design*, Oxford University Press, Oxford.
5. Barton, J.A., Love, D.M. and Taylor, G.D. (2001) 'Design determines 70 per cent of costs? A review of implications for design evaluation', *Journal of Engineering Design*, 12(1): 47–58.
6. See, for example, 'Combinatorial and Artificial Intelligence Methods in material Science', MRS Proceedings, VG 1024E, Fall 2004 and J.N. Cause (ed.) (2002) *Experimental Design for Combinatorial and High Throughput Materials Development*, John Wiley & Sons, Chichester.

7. For example, see Thomke, S. and von Hippen, E. (2002) 'Customers as innovators; a new way create value', *Harvard Business Review*, April: 74–81.

8. Such ideas are discussed in Chander, R. (2010) 'Consumer Co-creation in New Product Development', *Journal of Service Research*, 13(3).

9. Articles giving different perspectives on mass customization include Berman, B. (2002) 'Should your firm adopt a mass customization strategy?', *Business Horizons*, July–August: 51–60; Feitzinger, E. and Hau, L.L. (1997) 'Mass customization at Hewlett-Packard: the power of postponement', *Harvard Business Review*, 75(1): 116–21; Gilmore, J.H. and Pine, II, B.J. (1997) 'The four faces of mass customization', *Harvard Business Review*, 75(1): 91–101; Kasanoff, B. (1997) 'Mass customization and customer intimacy pay off for Dell' at www.1to1.com/articles/il-4-10-97; Salvador, F., Forza, C. and Rungtusanathan, M. (2002) 'How to mass customize: product architectures, sourcing and configurations', *Business Horizons*, July–August: 61–9; Zipkin, P. (2001) 'The limits of mass customization', *Sloan Management Review*, 42(3): 81–7.

10. References include Noori, H. (1989) 'The Taguchi methods: achieving design and output quality', *Academy of Management Executive*, November: 322–6; Taguchi, G. and Clausing, D. (1990) 'Robust quality', *Harvard Business Review*, January–February: 65–75.

11. Value analysis is defined in BS 3138 as: 'a systematic interdisciplinary examination of factors affecting the cost of a service or product, in order to devise means of achieving the specified purpose most economically at the required standard of quality and reliability'.

12. Miles, L.D. (1961) *Techniques of Value Analysis and Engineering*, McGraw-Hill, Maidenhead.

13. In Chapter 4 of *The Four Kinds of Economic Value*, Harvard Business Press (1926), Walsh, C.M. describes four kinds of value: 'Use-value is a thing's power to serve our ends. Esteem-value is its power to make us desire to possess it. Cost-value is its power to impose upon us effort to acquire it. Exchange-value is its power to procure other things in its place'.

14. This refers to the principle put forward by Vilfredo Pareto (1848–1923) that a few items in any group contribute the significant proportion of the entire group. Pareto was an Italian sociologist and economist who used this law to express the frequency distribution of incomes in society. Chapter 12 provides another example of its application.

Visit www.palgrave.com/business/hillom3e for self-test questions, guideline answers to some case study questions, useful weblinks and more to help you understand the topics in this chapter

DYSON

Since launching the first bagless vacuum cleaner in 1994, Dyson has grown to a point where it had sales of £74 million in 2009 with 32 per cent of the US market and 46 per cent of the UK market (see Figure 1). It has achieved its market leadership through focusing on engineering and innovation, but how did it get this to happen? According to Sir James Dyson it is all about having 'the ability to first grasp that creative moment and then having the scientific aptitude to bring that idea forward'. In 2010, it decided to focus on a number of more profitable core businesses and sell off the rest. It now plans to grow these over the coming years.

CREATE THE RIGHT ENVIRONMENT

By creating an innovative environment, Dyson aimed to encourage its employees to think creatively. The inside of the offices of its UK factory in Wiltshire are painted bright colours such as lilac, purple and lavender, and its employees all sit on £400 Vitra chairs. The shop floor is also bright, airy, air conditioned and spotless. Staff are well paid, recruited straight from university and encouraged to wear casual clothes. James Dyson believes that a suit is like a biker's leathers or a fireman's protective kit – it is merely protection – whereas he would rather that the qualities of his employees shone through in what they did, rather than what they wore. To encourage creativity in its workforce, the company employs young graduates, recruited straight from university, with no experience at all. 'They haven't learnt it all by heart', Dyson says. 'They're not institutionalized. Engineering requires free-thinkers.'

COMMUNICATE EFFECTIVELY

The business is managed using a flat, informal structure and an open plan office. A daily meeting with employees is held to discuss how well the business is performing and what its competitors are up to. There are also 'feedback sessions' twice a week to highlight problems and identify solutions, and a suggestion box is provided for employees uncomfortable talking in front of a large group.

Figure 1 Dyson performance (1996–2010)									
£m	1996	1998	2000	2002	2004	2006	2008	2009	2010
Sales revenue	56	63	56	71	60	59	64	74	48
Gross profit	3	3	3	7	8	5	8	7	16
R&D	0	0	1	2	4	4	2	2	2

Source: Dyson, *Annual Reports* (1996–2010).

Gross profit = sales revenue – direct costs

MAKE TINY STEP-BY-STEP CHANGES

Although the company is known for vacuums, digital motors and hand dryers, it is also working on plenty of other inventions. The company approach to innovation is to seek out items that do not function or perform properly and to think about how they could be improved. Engineers are encouraged to follow Edison's design approach. Instead of spending ages planning and sketching, they build prototype after prototype making tiny, step-by-step changes until they get it right.

THINK ILLOGICALLY AND NUTURE IDEAS

Employees are encouraged to think differently, as Dyson believes most people in the world think in straight lines because they've been taught to think logically. He also believes that ideas are often fragile and ephemeral when they have just been generated; and have to be nurtured to help them grow strong.

MAKE MISTAKES

The term 'innovation' is often associated with a 'Eureka' moment, but to Dyson it involves constant experimentation and making mistakes. Error and failure are acknowledged as an important and positive part of the design process, leading to new and exciting developments. In fact, along with the usual appraisal methods, employees are also assessed on their ability to take risks and their willingness to make mistakes.

WORK AS A TEAM

Teamwork and collaboration are vital to the design process at Dyson, as individuals must bring together their different areas of skill to solve problems and create an integrated product. The graphic designers and engineers are located in the centre of the factory and team members rotate between projects to share expertise and cross-fertilize ideas. Ideas can come from anyone. For example, someone in customer service came up with the idea of putting Dyson's helpline number on the handle of their vacuum cleaner. Dyson sees himself as part of the team, and for him a vital part of his job is communicating with his employees in their working environment, and making sure that all staff, not just engineers, are working creatively. 'I don't mean go around like a policeman,' he says, 'more just encouraging creativity.'

Questions

1. How does Dyson encourage innovation and creativity within its business?

2. What are the lessons from this for other businesses?

Sources: Dyson, J. (2005) 'James Dyson on Innovation', *Ingenia*, 24: 31–4; 'Sir James Dyson: Britain needs to copy the French and love its engineers', *Telegraph*, 27 July 2010. Available at: www.telegraph.co.uk (retrieved 3 August 2010); 'James Dyson at the Design and Technology with Science Show', *Journal of Design and Technology Education*, 5(1): 16–19; Wallis, I. 'James Dyson', *Growing Business*, 1 April 2004. Available at: www.growingbusiness.co.uk/james-dyson.html (retrieved 3 August 2010).

Lecturers: visit www.palgrave.com/business/hillom3e for teaching guidelines for this case study

After completing this chapter, you should be able to:

- Recognize the technical and business requirements that need to be met when delivering services

- Identify the distinctive characteristics of service operations

- Identify the difference between categories of service and types of service delivery system

- Explain the approach of the overall design of service delivery systems

- List the key phases in the detailed design of service delivery systems

- Give examples of the impact of IT on the design of service delivery systems

- Identify opportunities to enhance service provision such as making intangible aspects of service into a tangible form

- Recognize opportunities for customer participation in service delivery systems

- Undertake a service profiting exercise to check alignment between market needs and delivery system provision

Chapter outline

Executive overview

Introduction

Factors affecting service delivery system design

Characteristics of service operations
Service/product mix
Intangible nature of services
Simultaneous provision and consumption of services
Time-dependent capacity
Customers as participants in the service delivery system
Customer management
People skills
Effective services are reproducible
Site selection: proximity to the customer and multi-site management
Lack of patents on services

Factors involved in delivering services
The roles of technology and people in service provision
The nature of the services to be delivered
Categorizing services
Complexity of the service
Volumes
Order-winners and qualifiers

Service delivery system – overall design

Service delivery system – detailed design
Phase 1: the point of customer interface: back office or front office?
Phase 2: the delivery system

Single-step or multi-step process

IT-based service delivery system designs
E-commerce
Further aspects of service delivery
Customer participation in service delivery
Maximizing the use of skilled staff
Determining the level of server discretion within the delivery system

Service profiling
Procedure

Delivering services in practice

Driving business performance

Critical reflections

Summary

What is the role of operations in delivering services?

• The core task in a service business is delivering services to customer needs

• To undertake this task, operations transforms inputs (such as staff and data) into outputs (such as services and information) as overviewed earlier in Figure 1.2

• In the service sector, organizations process either
  – customers – for example, as in beauty salons and hospitals
  – customer surrogates – for example, in a garage and dry cleaning outlet this is the customer's car and dress/jacket respectively
  – information – for example, as in tax accountants and passport offices
  – some combinations of those

Why is delivering services important?

• The raison d'être of organizations is to sell services and provide them. As explained earlier in Figure 2.14 a customer purchase comprises
  – the service specification (what the service comprises) **plus**
  – a number of related criteria such as quality conformance (delivering the service specification), delivery speed (meeting customer lead-times), price (matches or betters an acceptable or competitor's prices) and delivery reliability (delivery on time)

• As you will see from the above, consistently providing a customer's purchase is principally the remit of operations, and consequently central to the success of any business

Delivering services to customers' expectations impacts performance

• As highlighted above, to gain a sale operations needs to deliver both the specified service and the relevant criteria that together comprise the basis of customer choice

• Do it well and customers will probably return; fail to meet customers' expectations and they will go elsewhere and tell others

What are the key issues to consider in the task of delivering services?

The service delivery system will involve different designs depending on the type of service that is being provided. Factors that impact the design include:

• Service complexity – impacts the number of steps it takes to deliver the service

• The market – a delivery system has to provide the following:
  – the technical dimension – what a service comprises
  – the business dimension – the order-winners and qualifiers that make up the sale

Designing the detail of a service delivery system comprises two principal phases:

• Phase 1 – Customers at some point interface with the delivery system. When and for how long a customer is involved are important factors when designing the system. The phase where customers are present is referred to as the 'front office' and the phase where they are not is known as the 'back office'

• Phase 2 – as services differ, so will their delivery system designs. The key characteristics that underpin these differences are the non-repeat or repeat nature of a service, the range of volumes involved in the latter and whether the delivery system is designed as a single or multi-step process.

Introduction

As explained in Chapter 1, transforming inputs into outputs is central to the task of managing operations and the system used for delivering services or products is a vital part of this transformation process. In this chapter, we will look at how the characteristics of services affect the design of service delivery systems, the different methods available to an organization for delivering services to customers, the task of choosing and designing a service delivery system, and the development of IT-based designs. In the next chapter, we'll go on, in a similar way, to look at the process of making and delivering products.

Factors affecting service delivery system design

> **EXECUTIVE INSIGHT**
   As services differ, so will the designs of their delivery systems.

The service delivery system will (as you might imagine) often involve different designs, depending on the type of service that is being delivered. We'll explore how particular aspects of services affect service delivery system design in a moment but, as an introduction, let's look at how two more general aspects of services impact the design – the complexity of the offering itself and the characteristics of the market in which the service is sold:

- **Service complexity** – this will directly impact the number of steps it takes to complete the delivery of the service. In many organizations the provision of a service is completed as a single step (for example returning books to a library or paying cash into your account at a local bank), whereas the processes involved to meet the needs of different patients in a hospital will be made up of several steps and combinations of steps. The design of the service delivery system will, therefore, reflect this complexity factor.

- **The market** – a delivery system has to provide the following dimensions to meet market needs:
  - **the technical dimension** – what the service comprises. For example, bread needs to be baked and credit card payments need to be processed. Completing these tasks requires appropriate technology (in the form of skills and equipment) within the delivery system, in these instances a baker and ovens, and skilled staff and processing equipment, respectively
  - **the business dimension** – how operations decides to provide a service will reflect the volumes involved and the order-winners and qualifiers to be supported.

In order to gain an idea of how market requirements might affect a business in practice, consider how the approach to service delivery might differ between a small town bakery and a large bakery company that bakes and delivers bread throughout a city and its suburbs, with several sites around the country. Both businesses must consider:

- The **technical requirements** that comprise the specifications (recipes) of the bread to be made. These will include the types and quantities of ingredients, and the processing

> **Technical requirements** – the tangible and/or intangible features that make up the technical dimension of a service/product sale.

and baking cycles for the range of breads in order to provide the desired taste and texture of the products.

- The **business requirements** that comprise the order-winners and qualifiers that, along with the technical dimension, make up the sale. These will include quality conformance (making bread to specification), price and the availability of the products on the shelf.

Business requirements – the order-winners and qualifiers that make up the business dimension of a service/product sale.

All these requirements are dealt with by operations. In addition, factors such as location, which will be decided by another function in the business, must be taken into account.

In order to deliver the product/service, operations needs the support of technical experts such as systems and IT specialists. For example, the large bakery would have engineering specialists to maintain the equipment and be on hand to respond to technical problems. Similarly, operations managers in call centres would not themselves meet the technical requirements of the systems used by their staff but would look to specialists to fix any technical problems and undertake technical developments.

Operations managers use the necessary system technologies together with other inputs, particularly staff capabilities, to meet a market's needs and the cost profiles and profit targets of the business. Working hand-in-hand with technical specialists, a key role of operations managers is to choose and develop the service delivery systems that best meet customers' needs. Each delivery system has trade-offs (things it can do well and less well), and these need to be understood by a business and form part of making these key investment decisions.

Characteristics of service operations

Before discussing alternatives, let's look at the characteristics of services that have to be taken into account when designing delivery systems. These include the service/product mix, the intangible nature of services, the simultaneous provision and consumption of services, the time-dependent nature of service capacity (that is, the fact that service capacity cannot be held over for use at a later time), the role of customers in the delivery system and managing services across a range of sites. The extent to which these characteristics will affect the design will, as you would expect, differ from one service offering to another.

Service/product mix

Earlier in the book we highlighted two important dimensions of services and it is important to bear these in mind when discussing delivery system design:

- Customer purchases are a mix of both services and products. As Figure 1.7 illustrated, the ratio between these two elements within the mix will vary. In some instances there can be a heavy accent on services, while in others, the reverse.

- The service component of the mix is a package of explicit and implicit benefits performed within a supporting facility. The need to identify these three elements was highlighted in Chapter 4, where these terms and concepts were explained.

Customers receive impressions about an organization through their experience of the way a service is delivered. These impressions will affect repeat business and will be created by how well the specification (the technical dimension) and its delivery fit with a customer's expectations together with the experience a customer has within the service delivery system itself.

Intangible nature of services

While products are tangible (a customer is able to see, feel, inspect and even test a product before purchase), services are not. This presents a problem for both providers and customers. While customers rely on a firm's reputation, recommendations or 'pot luck', the provider needs to develop a service delivery system for the service dimension of the package such that existing customers purchase again and new customers are attracted by factors such as reputation and recommendation. In this way the delivery system creates the intangible customer experience that constitutes the service element of the purchase, so becoming a critical element of the sale.

Simultaneous provision and consumption of services

The simultaneous provision and consumption of most services precludes the use of **inventory** as one way to help absorb fluctuations in demand. Whereas manufacturing companies may use inventory as a way of transferring capacity from one time period to be sold in a later time period, most service companies cannot do this. In a manufacturing firm, inventory also serves as a convenient boundary line, separating the management of the internal process from the external environment of the market. The result is that inventory can be used to cushion the process at both ends: it **decouples** the system from suppliers by holding materials and parts at the beginning of the process and from fluctuations in customer demand by holding finished products at the end. The manufacturing process can thus operate as a 'closed system' and, as a consequence, at a level of output that is deemed most efficient for the overall business. Services, on the other hand, operate as 'open systems' and are thus exposed to the full impact of variations in market demand.

For service delivery systems, the decoupling role of inventory is typically less available. In some situations, inventory of the product element of the offering is used in various forms. For example, a sandwich bar holds ingredients, pre-makes a range of fillings for sandwiches and makes and packages some sandwiches ahead of demand. But the most universal way to cushion a delivery system in a service firm is by using a combination of capacity and customer queues. For example, the number of beds in a hospital or teller windows in a bank are designed to exceed average demand. In so doing, above-average demand levels, when they occur, can be met. In such situations, operations managers need to balance excess capacity provision and queue lengths, while meeting the needs of customers.

The simultaneous provision and consumption of services also reduces (and often eliminates) the opportunities for controlling the quality of the service provision in terms of meeting the service/product specification. Unlike manufacturing where a product can be checked before delivery, services must build other ways into the system to ensure that the specification is met as it is delivered.

Time-dependent capacity

Linked to the last point is the fact that capacity in a service firm is time-dependent. If a hotel room, passenger airline seat, space on a container ship, goods train or truck is not used at the time it is available, that sale is lost forever. Likewise, if a restaurant cannot seat you for dinner, the sale of that capacity is lost forever. Therefore, a service firm has to find ways to handle the fact that unused capacity is perishable (and thereby expensive) while insufficient capacity will lose sales.

Capacity also involves a complex set of issues, as decisions on how much is needed have to be made in the different phases of a delivery system. These design issues include not only how much capacity there needs to be in terms of structural facilities (for example, teller windows in a bank) and staff, but also the shape of the capacity, for example the

---

Inventory – also known as stock, comprises the inputs (materials) into the delivery system or manufacturing process, part-finished items (services or products) within the service delivery system or manufacturing process and outputs (finished items) to be sold or supplied to customers.

Decouple – one role that inventory provides is to separate two consecutive elements of a delivery system from each other, a role known as decoupling. This allows the two parts of the delivery system involved to work independently of one another.

hours worked and mix of part- and full-time staff and which aircraft sizes are needed to best meet the demand profiles of a bank and a passenger airline's routes respectively.

Customers as participants in the service delivery system

In most service firms, the customer forms part of the delivery system and is often actively engaged in the system itself. The popularity of supermarkets, self-service stores, internet purchasing and online banking are illustrations of this phenomenon.

From the firm's point of view the customer provides capacity within the system that helps lower costs and also helps some aspects of the operations management task. For example, where customers undertake part of the role of a server, staff costs and the need to plan staff capacity in this phase of the delivery system are both reduced.

Customer management

Relating to the last point, the design of the delivery system is such that customers and staff are linked. Customers are not just onlookers; their presence creates a dynamic that needs to be managed. For example:

- The supporting structural facilities (such as decor, furnishings and cleanliness) need to meet customer expectations.

- Staff need to be conscious of their roles, how they affect a customer's experience and sense of participation and the lasting impression that is made (see Case 5.1).

- The level of server discretion (the extent to which staff are permitted to customize the offering) within the service specification needs to be identified, agreed and managed.

- The social dynamics of the customer experience, from entering to leaving the delivery system, need to be accommodated by and accounted for within the system itself. The approach to meeting these dimensions also needs to form part of the system design, part of the people skills development and part of the operations management task.

People skills

In service organizations, some staff deal directly with customers and the customer/server interface often combines both selling and serving. As a result the range of people skills that staff need to develop as part of the delivery system often has a significant effect on a customer's perceived value of the service.

Part of the skill set essential to staff that serve customers is the effective use of the levels of discretion they are allowed to exercise. Ensuring that the systems reflect the varying needs of customers as and when necessary is a critical feature of a responsive system in which agreed degrees of customization can be provided.

Effective services are reproducible

One of the reasons for the emergence of large service companies in some sectors lies in the improved method of reproducing service delivery systems. Franchise companies (for example, fast-food chains) are classic examples of this. Here, there is control over key elements of the offering and delivery system such as the physical layout, internal and external decor, range of offerings, purchasing of inputs (for example food ingredients), service delivery system design, training and equipment – and these are routinely checked

CASE 5.1 TIPPING AS A MEASURE OF CUSTOMER SERVICE

Tipping is not a trivial business. For staff it often represents a substantial portion of their income while for the organization it provides a tangible measure of the customer's satisfaction with the service provided. Research on what makes customers tip at the end of a service encounter (such as a meal in a restaurant) highlights certain aspects of customer management that can have general application elsewhere. Some of the key findings include:

1. Interacting with a customer throughout the delivery of a service. For example:
   - Making initial eye contact and then reinforcing this contact throughout the service encounter
   - Personalizing the service – introducing oneself by name works better than a badge, while even gestures such as writing 'thank you' or drawing a cartoon on a bill together with one's name help personalize the service
   - Smiling warmly and genuinely when greeting a customer and being pleasant throughout
   - Making additional, discreet, non-task visits to check all is well and ensuring that nothing extra is required.

2. Speed of service – there are four occasions when speed of response is important:
   - Delivery of the menu and pre-dinner drinks
   - Taking the food order
   - Delivery of the food
   - The payment process from presenting the bill to conclusion.

But the key is to gauge the optimum speed rather than the maximum speed, and this concerns trying to understand the level of speed a customer wants. Getting the timing right is an essential part of the overall service specification and the clues are not hard to find.

3. Goodwill gestures. Providing symbols of goodwill such as a complimentary aperitif, bite-size nibbles, pre-meal nibbles, a truffle with the bill, or an overtly generous measure of pre- and post-dinner drinks all help to create an impression of goodwill and good value.

To an extent, tips reflect fulfilling customers' expectations about the quality (both in terms of the specification and conformance to specification) of the food and the service provided. Getting these right not only leads to satisfied staff but also satisfied customers, repeat business and recommendations.

Questions

1. What makes up the total service offering for a customer during an evening meal at a restaurant?

2. How would the examples here translate into customer management in a boutique clothes shop or hairdressing salon?

Lecturers: visit www.palgrave.com/business/hillom3e for teaching guidelines for this case study

by the franchiser. This approach allows companies to expand using the same model and a tried and tested approach.

Site selection: proximity to the customer and multi-site management

Whereas products are shipped to the customer, in many service companies the provider and customer must physically meet for a service to be performed. As a consequence, such service organizations are typically made up of small units of capacity sited close to prospective customers. Either the customer comes to the facility (as in a restaurant, retail store, hairdresser or hospital) or the service provider goes to the customer (as in a mobile library or ambulance service). Of course, there are exceptions (such as distance learning) and especially with the growing use of IT systems (for example, telephone and internet banking, online shopping and passenger airline, holiday and theatre ticket sales).

Travel time and costs are thus reflected in the economics underpinning the selection of sites, with many small units of capacity bringing the added task of multi-site management. The resulting challenges for an organization include the fact that services are performed in the field, so to speak, and not in a controlled factory environment. To achieve and maintain consistency across multiple locations requires a combination of standardization within the service delivery system, extensive training, licensing and third-party or peer reviews.

Lack of patents on services

Firms that design their own products have the advantage of patents and licensing agreements to protect them, but the intangible nature of services makes them more difficult to protect using these legal formats. Although some protection of a service may be afforded by copyright and trademarks, the most effective way to guard the service idea or concept is through designing robust delivery systems that meet the needs of customers and that respond to and proactively lead change and development. Reproducing a comparable delivery system often constitutes an effective barrier against competition.

Factors involved in delivering services

Understanding how services differ is an important prerequisite when designing delivery systems, especially in organizations that offer a range of services that typically require different delivery systems. Here, we will highlight several key differences between services.

The roles of technology and people in service provision

A company needs to select the delivery systems that it will use to provide the services it sells. In part, this concerns the technical dimensions of the items involved, for example:

- A restaurant would need to prepare food in line with the menus on offer and customers' requirements. It would, therefore, need the equipment and skilled staff to undertake the food preparation involved.

- A computer services bureau would need the hardware and skilled staff to enable it to process the information requirements of customers.

While the need for appropriate equipment and levels of skilled staff is obvious, a suitable mix and suitable levels further depend on the volumes of sales involved. As we saw in the earlier example of a small town baker and a large company bakery, the lower the sales levels, the less justification there is for investing in equipment and processes to complete the task and this will need to be reflected in the technology/people mix selection. Figure 5.1 illustrates this point while also giving examples of the mix of equipment and staff in a range of service businesses.

Figure 5.1 Range of operations requirements within the service delivery system		
Predominant base	**Level of automation and people skills**	**Examples**
Technology	Automated	Cash dispensing
		Ticket machines
		Vending machines
		Mechanized car washing
	Monitored by unskilled/semi-skilled people	Photocopying
		Dry cleaning
		Gardening
		Tree surgery
		Taxi firm
	Operated by skilled people	Air traffic control
		Computer time-sharing
		Data-processing
People	Unskilled	Cleaning services
		Security guards
	Skilled	Catering
		Vehicle maintenance
		Appliance repairs
	Professional	Lawyers
		Management consultants
		Accountants

The nature of the services to be delivered

The services to be processed by the operations system are different not only in themselves (for example, fast-food and high-quality restaurants provide a different service and product mix, as illustrated earlier in Figure 1.7) but also by the nature of what is involved. Figure 5.2 highlights these differences. The key dimensions that make up these differences are listed below and illustrated in Figure 5.2:

- the complexity of the service to be provided (that is, the number of steps to complete)

- what is processed in the delivery system – customers, customer surrogates, products, information or some combination of these.

Understanding how services differ is, therefore, an important prerequisite when designing the delivery systems to be used. Organizations typically design and develop a number of delivery systems to meet what they sell. Additional ways of categorizing services will help explain this still further and these are provided in the next section.

Figure 5.2 The nature of service processing	
Nature of the service	**Examples**
Customers	Hairdressing, passenger airlines and health care
Customer surrogates	Car maintenance and repair, dry cleaning and furniture restoration
Products	Retail outlets and vehicle purchases
Information	Mortgage applications, insurance claims and tax advice

Categorizing services

The key dimensions that help to classify services are provided in Figure 5.3. This shows that the system design to deliver a professional service needs to be different from that used in a retail bank or supermarket. Such differences, therefore, need to be taken into account when designing the service delivery system. For example, volumes, levels of service variety and the degree of customization will differ significantly and will need to be catered for within the delivery system design.

Complexity of the service

Many customer-based services are relatively simple in terms of the operations process involved and can be delivered as a single-step transaction, for example the front-office process in a retail bank and a takeaway food restaurant. Other services, however, need multi-step process provision. For example, whereas a 'dry cut' in a hairdressing salon is a single transaction, a cut and blow-dry would require two or more processes depending upon what is involved. Similarly, the delivery system to provide dinner at the Ritz in London would involve many more stages than having dinner at McDonald's.

Volumes

We've already introduced the idea of the impact of volumes on service delivery systems. Figure 5.3 shows the relationship between different categories of services, levels of volume and service variety. The key factors concern the non-repeat or repeat nature of the service offering and the volumes involved. The design of the delivery system will then need to reflect these fundamental dimensions.

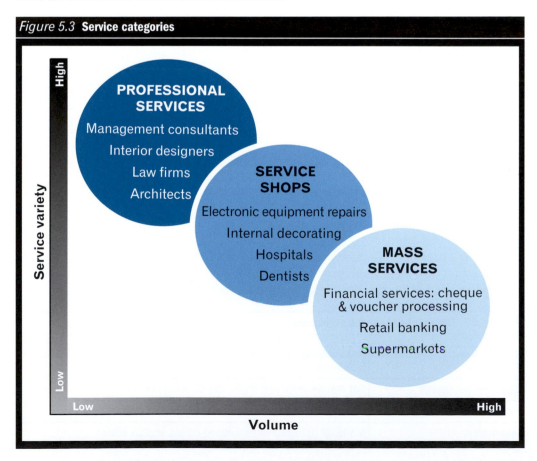

Figure 5.3 **Service categories**

Order-winners and qualifiers

Service delivery system design needs to reflect the order-winners and qualifiers for which operations is solely or jointly responsible. These comprise the business dimension of the offering and the system design needs to be built around this as well as the technical aspect of the service specification.

Service delivery system – overall design

Now we've got an idea of the features that characterize services, let's take a closer look at service delivery system design. We'll first deal with aspects of the overall design and then go on to look at the phases involved in the more detailed design of service delivery systems. Figure 5.4 provides a way of analyzing and developing the overall design of a service delivery system and the principal phases are now discussed:[1]

- **The market** – the market provides the external context in which the service delivery system needs to be set and where the process of design and development starts. Identifying volumes and the relevant order-winners and qualifiers to retain and grow the company's share in chosen markets, together with the service mix and design specifications, are the requirements to be met when designing the system.

- **The service encounter and experience** – the service encounter (where and what is delivered) and the service experience (the reality of the service delivered) are the essence of the delivery system. But, as shown in Figure 5.4, each dimension needs to take into account both customers' expectations and what the service delivery system has been designed to provide. For example, the service encounter needs to ascertain customers' expectations of what will be provided which, in turn, need to be set against what the delivery system has been designed to provide (the operations standards that the organization has set). Similarly, the reality of the service delivered (the service experience) needs to match customers' perceptions with operations performance. In this way, customers' needs and the reality of provision (what the company sets out to do and how well it does it) will be in line with one another.

Where customers' expectations exceed what the delivery system has been designed to provide, organizations need to work to adjust customers' expectations. Unless this happens, even though the delivery system meets the specification set, it will fall short of what is expected, and customers will be dissatisfied.

- **Retention** – one aim of the service delivery system is to help retain and grow market share. The delivery system design, therefore, needs to monitor its level of success while determining what to do to recover failure situations.[2] As Figures 5.5, 5.6, 5.7 and 5.8 show, although failure impacts retention rates, service recovery by satisfying customers' complaints can help to counteract the loss of repeat business that follows. On the other hand, getting it wrong and leaving customers dissatisfied with the outcome or being too slow or too involved spells trouble![2]

Service delivery system – detailed design

Designing the detail of a service delivery system comprises two principal phases:

- Phase 1 – addressing the issue of the delivery as a whole. This includes decisions about how and where a system will deliver the service and the point of customer interface.

- Phase 2 – the design of the delivery system itself.

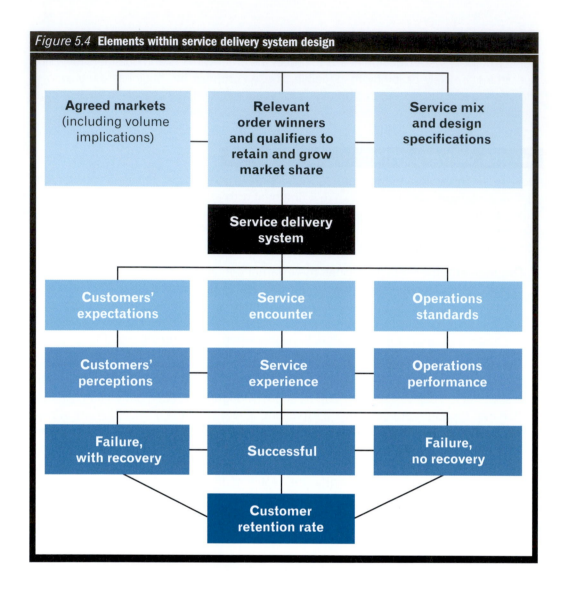

Figure 5.4 Elements within service delivery system design

Figure 5.5 **Customer problems and retention rates**

Sector	Percentage total of customers experiencing problems	Retention rates (percentage total) for customers having	
		no problem	problem
Consumer goods	22	83	54
Appliance repairs	44	73	40
Car rentals	47	92	75
Branch banking	49	86	76
High-tech (business customers)	60	91	81
Air travel	69	91	77

Figure 5.6 Repurchase intentions of dissatisfied customers

Level of service recovery	Percentage of customers who will buy again by level of complaint	
	Major	Minor
Complaint not resolved	19	46
Complaint resolved	54	70
Complaint resolved quickly	82	95

Figure 5.7 Customer satisfaction: response time

Response time	
# days	% Customers satisfied
1–7	52
8–21	42
22–28	38
29+	23

Figure 5.8 Customer satisfaction: number of contacts

Contacts to handle complaints	
#	% Customers satisfied
1	58
2	37
3	32
4	29
5+	11

Phase 1: the point of customer interface: back office or front office?

In many businesses, for a service to occur the customer will at some point interface with the delivery system. But at which point and for how long a customer is involved are important factors when designing the service delivery system. The phase of a delivery system where customers are present is referred to as the 'front office' (or sometimes, 'front of house') and the phase where they are not is known as the 'back office' (or sometimes, 'back of house').

In some instances (for example a hairdresser and restaurant) a customer's involvement is not the subject of a decision. Here, the service can only be provided with the customer present. In other instances, how long a customer is involved in the delivery system's front office is, to some extent, a matter of choice. In some circumstances, a company may decide to limit the front-office service provision to what is essential and complete as much of the service as possible in the back office. For example, paying a bill at the local high street branch of your bank has both front- and back-office elements. In the front office, the bill and payment are presented and checked by the teller, processed and set aside. The remainder of the transaction is completed in the back office. Similarly, taking garments to be dry-cleaned involves the front-office tasks of the customer explaining what is required, payment and the issue of a receipt. The cleaning takes place in the back office with the garment being later collected from the front office.

What, then, are the characteristics of the back office and front office that influence the design of the service delivery system?

Back office

As we've just mentioned the key distinction between back office and front office is that in the former the activities take place without the customer being present or involved. For this reason, the separation of front and back office is sometimes referred to as the **'line of visibility'**, highlighting what of the delivery system a customer can and cannot see. Some of the advantages of completing work in the back office include:

- **Easier scheduling** – undertaking tasks in the back office means that the system does not need to respond immediately to customer demands and this allows completion of the work to be planned for when it best suits the system itself. For example, choosing to delay completing work means that scheduling what to do and when to do it can occur in line with staff availability, when it best fits in with other work priorities and so on.

- **Higher processing volumes** – similarly, delaying completion allows the back-office system to accumulate volumes of work so that tasks can be undertaken more efficiently as all the work can be done at the same time. Furthermore, in a bank, for example, back-office tasks such as bank statement preparation can be accumulated still further by bringing together the demands of many high street bank branches. Using regional or even national centres for these tasks creates even higher volumes that justify more investment leading to lower overall processing costs.

> **Line of visibility** – marks the separation between the front and back offices. The 'line' is often, but not always, physical in nature (for example a wall or partition).

Front office

On the other side of the 'line of visibility' is the front-office portion of the system in which customer contact occurs. The characteristics inherent in this part of the system include:

- **Structural facilities** – as the customer is present in this part of the system, the structural facilities need to reflect the standards of the organization and meet the needs of customers. Ambience, decor, staff presentation and speed of response need to reflect the organization's desired image and its customers' expectations.

- **Lead times** – as customer contact occurs here, the system needs to be able to meet the service specification involved while ensuring sufficient capacity to meet the service targets related to queuing (the time a customer waits) as well as the length of time it takes to deliver the service and the costs of having too much capacity.

- **Ease of customer use** – the design must make it easy for customers to interface with the system as customers will then be encouraged to use the organization's preferred method of delivering the service, for example getting cash from an ATM instead of inside the bank branch.

- **Staff roles** – the skills and roles of staff are essential to the task of providing the delivery system effectively. This involves the need for staff to be trained in the delivery of the service specifications to be provided as well as the level of multiskilling desired, the role of staff in the task of cross-selling other services or products and the extent to which a server can customize an offering (referred to as the level of server discretion).

Back office, middle office or front office

To help give more insight into delivery system design, some organizations recognize that in their businesses there is a middle-office phase, as illustrated in Figure 5.9. Whereas in the back office there is no customer contact and in the front office the customer is involved, the middle office recognizes the indirect impact that certain tasks in this phase have on customers.

The purpose of identifying a middle-office phase is to help in designing delivery systems. Without this recognition, for the examples provided in Figure 5.9 the activities listed under this phase would have been allocated to the back-office function. One outcome is that the customer-facing dimensions of these tasks may not have been adequately recognized by or incorporated into the system design itself.

Figure 5.9 **Examples of front-, middle- and back-office activities in selected service organizations**			
Part of the delivery system	**Illustrations**		
	Passenger airline	**Hotel**	**Fund management**
Front office – direct customer contact	· Reservation and booking changes · Check-in · Departures and arrivals lounges · In-flight attendance · Flight transfers · Airport information desk · Ticket pricing	· Sales agents · Reservations · Reception · Concierge · Restaurant and bar staff · Switchboard	· Pre-trade compliance and and decisions · Trade order management · Client reporting · Client extranets
Middle office – indirect customer contact	· Flight schedules · Self-check-in system development · Frequent flier programme · Holiday and flight · Refund offers	· Marketing · Pricing – rooms and banqueting · Menu fulfillment · Wine selection · Housekeeping · Maintenance	· Transaction reconciliation · Compliance checks · Trade support · Risk management
Back office – no customer contact	· Aircraft maintenance · Flight preparation · Accounts · Refunds · Administration · Self-check-in system maintenance	· Administration · Accounts · Human resources · Kitchen	· Custody of assets and documents · Fund accounting · Fund administration · Transfer agency

Determining the customer interface within the delivery system

Some services do not allow the server to be separated from the customer (for example, hairdressing and passenger transport). However, other service businesses do allow for a measure of server/customer decoupling. Where this is so some parts of a service, if desired, can be completed without the customer being present. This not only allows them to be completed using different methods and at different times (thus, as explained earlier, enabling low-cost opportunities to be exploited by cumulating demand and thereby increasing volumes prior to processing) but also allows firms to improve customer perceptions of the service itself, as illustrated in Case 5.2.

However, there are times when interfacing the back office and the customer brings significant benefits. One such example where coupling the front office and back office together is provided in Case 5.3.

Phase 2: The delivery system

Earlier, Figure 5.3 provided a useful starting point by introducing the principal ways to categorize services as 'professional services', 'service shops' and 'mass services', But, in reality, many organizations provide a range of services that fall into more than one of these three categories. For example, within a law firm, house conveyancing (the

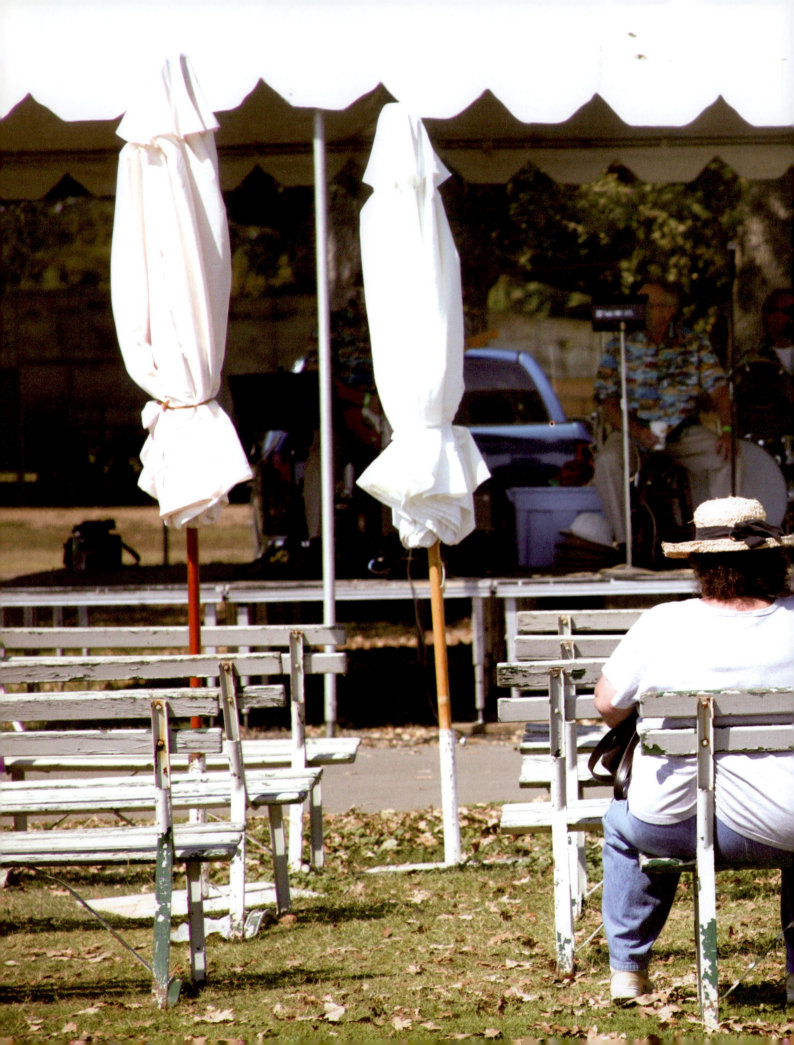

'**Organizations** must clearly understand **customer** needs to **deliver** services effectively'

CASE 5.2 INFLUENCING CUSTOMER PERCEPTIONS AT THE ROYAL BANK OF CANADA

The Royal Bank of Canada believes that customers' perceptions are a critical factor in service provision. The bank considers that when queues form, customers' attitudes to waiting are affected by both the server's attitude when they are eventually attended to, and the fact that when waiting, customers judge service by the level of staff attendance shown in the front office. Thus, if bank staff are doing jobs other than attending to customers, and the queues are long, customers' attitudes to the bank's overall regard for service provision are affected. Thus, the bank's aim is to transfer as much paperwork as possible to head office or a branch's back office.

www.royalbank.com

Lecturers: visit www.palgrave.com/business/ hillom3e for teaching guidelines for this case study

An electrical repair shop recently changed the customer interface point in the delivery system. Whereas previously the customer explained the repair needs to those in the front office, the customer now takes the repair to the back office and discusses the problem with the person who will complete the repair. Everyone gains. The repair person can now ensure that all pertinent questions are covered and the customer is able to discuss the repair both before and after the service is completed. This, of course, has long been the arrangement in many good quality dressmakers and tailors.

Questions

1. How do the examples in Cases 5.2 and 5.3 differ?

2. What are the benefits and disadvantages of the alternative approaches in these two examples?

Lecturers: visit www.palgrave.com/business/hillom3e for teaching guidelines for this case study

steps to transfer the legal ownership of a property from the seller to the buyer) involves a set of standard procedures typically completed by junior staff. The process is known; there are well-documented steps to be followed, with clear guidelines and pre-printed forms containing questions that need to be answered by third parties as well as internal staff themselves. At the other end of the spectrum, there will be one-off, non-repeat, complicated cases requiring technical and legal advice in a specialist field. Clearly these two tasks do not fall within the same service category. Similarly, the services in a hospital range from refreshment facilities through reception to surgery, postoperative care and rehabilitation. There will be outpatient clinics, accident and emergency provision and ambulance services that range from paramedic tasks at the scene of an accident to routine collection services for disabled or elderly patients. Although categorized as a service shop, the full scope of services provided by a hospital will need to be allocated to all three broad categories.

> **EXECUTIVE INSIGHT**
Although service firms can be placed in one of three service categories (professional services, service shops and mass services) they often provide a range of services, some of which fall into two or more of these categories.

It therefore follows that as services differ, so will their delivery system designs. Below we describe the different systems that are used and the types of service they are used to support. The key characteristics that underpin these differences are the non-repeat or repeat nature of a service, the range of volumes involved in the latter, and whether the delivery system is designed as a single-step or multi-step process.

Non-repeat services

As the name implies, services in this category are unique (known also as 'specials') and will not be provided in the same format a second time. Examples include interior design, legal advice for a business merger or takeover, financial advice for a stock exchange placement, executive development by one-to-one coaching, board-level consultancy advice regarding future corporate strategy decisions and the design and installation of a tailor-made IT system.

Providers of **non-repeat services** sell their skills and capabilities to meet the specific needs of a customer. In this way, the service specification is determined by the customer, with changes to what is required being made throughout its delivery. Order-winners such as having a unique set of skills (being the best), referrals and repeat business are characteristic of the way this type of market works. Although customer orders will not be price-sensitive, the price for a service will need to be competitive (that is, in an acceptable price band) but one that yields high margins. For non-repeat services, price is a qualifier (prices have to be competitive by being in the acceptable price band) and not an order-winner. The more unique the set of skills that a company possesses, the higher the point in the acceptable price band it can command. On the other hand, where price is an order-winner, a company will compete on price, with services and products typically yielding lower margins.

The delivery system used for non-repeat services involves one person or a small group of skilled people providing all the service. The provider's role will include helping to identity what is required, determining the best process to follow and undertaking all the other steps involved through to and including the implementation of the service. As the service will not be repeated, the opportunity to invest in the delivery system is not available and could not be justified, given the volumes involved. What is transferred from one service provision to the next is the provider's capability and skill base, and the experience gained from providing other one-off services in the past.

Non-repeat services – unique services that are not provided in the same format more than once; the term also applies to services where the gap between one provision and the next is too long for the gains of repetition to be realized.

Repeat services

Most organizations provide services that are deemed standard or **repeat** (that is, they have been provided before) rather than special or non-repeat. The repeat and higher volume nature of standard services signals a need to consider a different delivery system designed to take advantage of these characteristics. The volumes involved, however, can range from low to very high and this factor will be reflected in the design of the service delivery system used.

Repeat services
– services that are provided more than once. The level of repetition may range from low volume (which makes delivery system design more like that for non-repeat services) through to very high volume.

To illustrate, let's take a transcontinental air flight. At the extremes there will be first-class and economy cabins. Although all passengers are travelling to the same destination and both classes of seat are repeat service offerings, the delivery system will show marked differences. Check-in arrangements, pre-boarding lounge and dining facilities, carry-on luggage allowances, cabin staff to passenger ratios, the range of food, drinks and beverages, the level of customization provided, choices of in-flight entertainment, and disembarkation and luggage collection priorities will all differ, and the design of the service delivery system will reflect these differences.

Earlier, Figure 5.3 provided other examples of repeat services and illustrated the different volume levels associated with these offerings. Where volumes are higher, factors such as service variety, level of price sensitivity and degree of customization will change as shown in Figure 5.10. Higher volumes justify the higher levels of process investment necessary to support the associated order winning nature of price. Where possible, work is deskilled, with the process investment completing more of the task: this in turn, will result in lower staff costs in terms of both skill levels and work content. Figure 5.10 summarizes some of the principal factors in delivery system design that reflect the non-repeat/repeat nature of the service offering and the level of volumes involved.

Now take a look at Case 5.4, which gives an example of an unusual service delivery system design in the field of eye surgery.

Single-step or multi-step process

A key decision in the design of a system concerns the number of steps to be taken in delivering the service. A single-step design implies that the complete service is delivered as a single transaction – for example, getting cash from an ATM and purchasing a newspaper from a shop. In a **multi-step delivery system**, the service is delivered in two or more steps. The first task when designing a multi-step process, therefore, is to break down the service into the required steps. How many steps there are will depend on the complexity of the service involved. The activities in each step that make up the total service will then be determined. These will be done separately, often by different staff and normally in different parts of the system. Splitting the task into a number of smaller steps is a form of investment in itself, and is one way to help undertake the task more efficiently by accumulating similar activities from a range of services and completing these in the same part of the delivery system (for example, the pharmacy and X-ray functions in a hospital). This also provides the potential for staff specialization and process investment. Consider for example, customers entering a service delivery system such as a hospital. The patients (that is, the customers) would initially go to reception and the staff would process them, such as recording relevant details. Patients will then go to the next step in the process (for example, to see a specialist consultant) and, having waited, would go through that stage of the treatment. They will then go through the next steps in the same way until the total service was completed. A similar example is provided in Figure 5.11 which outlines the steps in two delivery systems in a dental surgery.

Multi-step delivery system – when a service is completed in two or more steps.

With information processing, the procedure is again broken down into a number of steps, the total of which completes the whole process. As in the hospital example, the

FACTORS REFLECTED IN SERVICE DELIVERY SYSTEM DESIGN	
Service variety	
Level of customization	
How orders are won?	typical order winners
	typical qualifiers
Volumes	
Delivery system	design
	level of flexibility
Ability of delivery system to cope with	service change
	new services
Dominant factor of utilization	
Prior knowledge of the operations task	
Level of process investment	
Staff skill levels	

NON-REPEAT SERVICES	REPEAT SERVICES	
	Low volume	High volume
Wide	→	Narrow
High	→	Low
Unique expertise, recommendations	→	Price
Price, on-time delivery & quality conformance	On-time delivery & quality conformance	
Low	→	High
General & unspecified	→	Specified & dedicated
High	→	Low
High	→	Low
High	→	Low
Staff	→	Process
Not well-defined	→	Well-defined
Low	→	High
High	→	Low

CASE 5.4 SERVICE DELIVERY AT THE MOSCOW SCIENTIFIC INSTITUTE FOR EYE MICROSURGERY

For most of us, our perception of hospital surgery is one of delicate and sensitive operations. In reality, though, many surgical approaches are routine and comprise a series of standard steps and procedures. One surgeon who took this dimension to an extreme was the prominent Russian eye surgeon, Dr Svyatoslav Fyodorov. In his Institute for Eye Microsurgery (which has continued to operate in his name since his tragic death in an accident in 2000), the surgical treatment for myopia (short-sightedness) is a procedure called radical keratotomy. During this, patients lie on moving theatre tables, six surgeons perform their part of the operation, and then each patient moves on to the next stage. Surgeons check the previous step(s) in the surgical process, perform their own step, and then the process continues onwards. TV screens, microphones and headsets enable visual and voice contact to be maintained throughout and between the surgeons.

http://eng.mntk.ru

Question

What advantages and disadvantages does this approach bring compared with alternative approaches?

Lecturers: visit www.palgrave.com/business/hillom3e for teaching guidelines for this case study

documents go from step to step, with each step typically involving waiting time, a single set-up or preparation stage and processing all the documents at the one time. This waiting between stages allows processes to work independently of one another (known as decoupling) and hence more efficiently, while processing all documents at one stage reduces the number of set-ups involved and increases the volume processed for any one step at any one time.

You will see from these examples that similar steps for all customers are undertaken in the same function, hence increasing overall volumes at each stage and providing the opportunity to reduce costs to complete this step by, for example, process investment.

Now let's address the question of why organizations choose a multi-step rather than a **single-step delivery system** design. The factors to be taken into account include the following:

Single-step delivery system – when a service is delivered using a single step.

- **Delivering the service involves a range of staff skill levels** – when delivering a service that comprises a range of skill levels, organizations seek to keep costs low by allocating the activities and tasks involved to staff with the relevant skill sets. If a hospital was set up as a single-step system, the health care specialist would, for example, record a patient's details, undertake the consultation, complete the X-ray, check to confirm the nature of the broken limb, apply the plaster and make the next appointment. But the delivery of such a service is much more suited to a multi-step design where these various tasks are performed by different staff who specialize in different areas to deliver different parts of a service. Thus, health care specialists restrict their involvement to their area of specialism, with other tasks being completed in a more cost-effective way in terms of staff skill and corresponding salary grade and with each step of the process being provided by specialized and more effective procedures and approaches to completing the tasks involved. By processing customers step by step, the capacity at each stage in the process is used and reused to meet the different requirements of different customers, with volumes justifying process investment leading to a more overall cost-effective provision.

- **The service specification is complex** – where services are relatively simple they lend themselves to being delivered by a single-step system. Where services are more complex companies typically provide them in a multi-step format. One reason is that matching the task requirement to the appropriate skill set is easier to schedule.

- **Volumes can be enhanced** – using a multi-step design to provide a number of services brings together similar steps from two or more services to be completed in the same function or area. The higher volumes that result provide scope for cost reduction by creating the opportunity to invest in the process, develop specialist skill sets and match each step in the service to the required skill levels and salary grades that go with these. As a result, work content is reduced, staff become better in specialist skill areas and aspects of the service are delivered by the appropriate level of skilled person.

Now look at Case 5.5 to reflect on the choices that need to be considered.

IT-based service delivery system designs

When designing delivery systems, many organizations have used developments in information technology (IT) to rethink approaches. Such developments have not only reduced costs and lead times within systems and procedures but also enabled organizations to redesign many of these delivery systems as the following cases illustrate.

If you go into the local high street branch of your bank and want to collect foreign currency, pay cash into your account and discuss your account details, you will have to use three different, single-step delivery systems to meet your needs. Each of these will only deal with a limited number of the total range of services the bank provides. On the other hand, if you go into a post office, you will stand in one queue, and all the services you require will be delivered by the one teller.

Question

What is the fundamental difference in service delivery design between these two examples?

Lecturers: visit www.palgrave.com/business/ hillom3e for teaching guidelines for this case study

Figure 5.11 Patients visiting a dental surgery – an example of a multistep delivery system

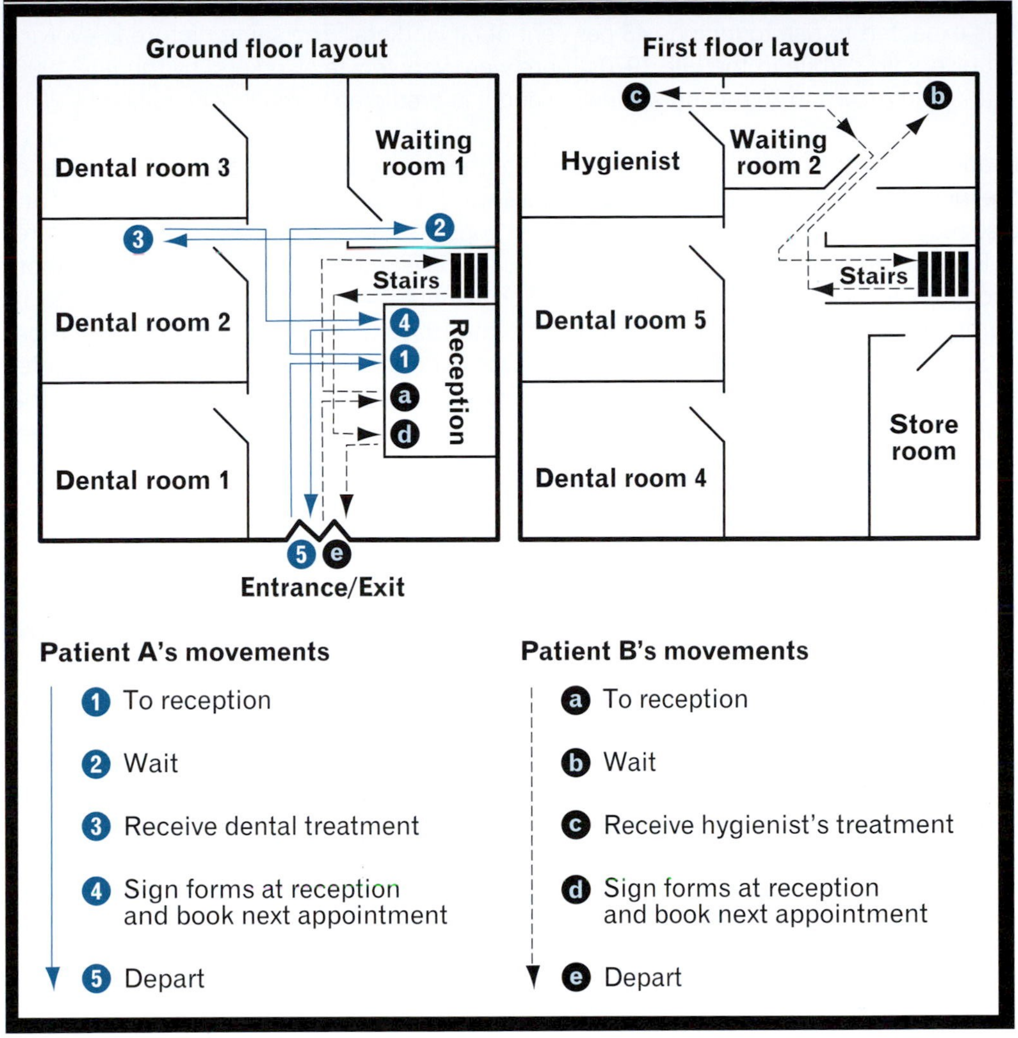

Ground floor layout

Dental room 3

Waiting room 1

③ ◄——— **②**

Stairs

Dental room 2

④

①

Reception

a

d

Dental room 1

⑤ **e**

Entrance/Exit

First floor layout

c ◄——— **b**

Hygienist

Waiting room 2

Stairs

Dental room 5

Store room

Dental room 4

Patient A's movements

① To reception

② Wait

③ Receive dental treatment

④ Sign forms at reception and book next appointment

⑤ Depart

Patient B's movements

a To reception

b Wait

c Receive hygienist's treatment

d Sign forms at reception and book next appointment

e Depart

- **Automated banking** – banks are continuing to cut costs by automating more of their services. For example ATMs are now the principal way to get cash from your bank account. Increasingly banks are adding video displays selling insurance and providing details on loans as well as screens offering share quotations. In parts of Europe and the USA fully automated bank branches are replacing traditional set-ups, offering all the usual range of services but without bank tellers and in Europe and the US automated machines for depositing cash and cheques have become commonplace.

- **Teleworking** – since the early 1980s, companies have been extending the practice of using computers and telephone links so that their staff can work away from the office. Home offices are part of this growing trend while companies are making increasingly heavy use of telecommuting, a policy that allows employees to work in the office one or two days a week and spend the rest of the time with clients and working from home. Jack Nilles, the 'father of teleworking', coined the phrases 'teleworking' and 'telecommuting' in 1973 while leading a research project at the University of Southern California into the impact of IT at work.[3]

Teleworking brings benefits including productivity increases of 20 per cent or more, reduced office space requirements and lower staff turnover levels.[4] In addition, benefits to a nation's economy are significant. It is estimated that traffic congestion costs the UK economy more than $100 billion in lost productivity annually while London commuters waste more than ten hours per week going to work. In the USA, clean air legislation is obliging large firms to reduce their commuter workforce. By 2009, there were 34 million US workers who at least occasionally worked at home and by 2016 this is expected to rise to include 43 per cent of all workers.[5] The same picture is evolving universally. While in the late 1970s there were very few teleworkers, by the late 1990s this had grown to 20 million worldwide and it is predicted to reach 200 million by 2016.

In addition, automated or 'predictive' dialling (that connects agents to customers just as the incoming call rings out) is being increasingly installed to cut the time to answer and also reduce the number of times a customer rings off. Favoured locations for call centres in Europe are Ireland and Scotland due in part to wage rates in a service where labour accounts for 45 per cent of total costs. For example, American Airlines relocated its European reservation centre to Dublin in the late 1990s where staff costs were half those in Switzerland. In fact, in the late 1990s it was estimated that Ireland alone accounted for 30 per cent of all pan-European call centres in the EU. The problem, however, that Dublin, Edinburgh, Glasgow and their immediate hinterlands now face is how to keep staff. The concern is not so much one of losing staff to competitors but to other job opportunities.

E-commerce

The internet offers the capability to personalize a service as it can be tailored to every one of its millions of users. Furthermore, the internet crosses borders, which means that pressure on prices is going to increase almost overnight. For example, European companies are finding it tough competing with US competitors in many retail markets – books in the UK and CDs in Europe and Japan are both about 30 per cent more expensive than in the USA.

The benefits on the retail end of the spectrum have also increasingly been realized through company inter-trading. But e-commerce is not just shopping by another name. It encompasses companies' relationships with their suppliers as well as their customers. Corporate intranets can be linked so as to provide a safe, secure, manageable, business-to-business environment, with e-commerce becoming an integrated part of the customer/supplier partnership. Dealing with customers and suppliers through e-commerce has profound implications for the way companies operate and, as more customers use the internet, the need for organizations to embrace relevant technologies into the design of their delivery systems is crucial. Below are some examples of online service developments.

Travel booking

Since its early days, online travel booking has grown rapidly. The European online market is forecast to continue to grow by 20–30 per cent a year compared with single-digit growth for the travel industry as a whole. Part of this growth has been boosted by the no-frills passenger airline phenomenon and the pressure from companies such as Ryanair and easyJet to force customers to book online.

Call centres

Whether the vendor is a PC manufacturer providing a help desk for users, a gas or electric distribution company answering queries or a financial services company handling account and general enquiries through to mortgage and personal loan applications, a call centre has become the preferred provider.

Advances in computer telephony integration have enabled call centres to replace traditional service departments by linking the telephone to a computer that routes calls to the most appropriate agent, prompts the agent with caller data (known as 'screen popping') and leads the agent through a script to produce answers to thousands of different questions. Call centres cut staff costs compared with multi-site arrangements,

© Neustockimages

Thomas Cook Group has been providing travel services since 1808 and operates the world's largest network, with over 3,000 travel agencies and 31,000 staff worldwide. It serves 12 million customers each year, with sales in 2011 of $3.4 billion.

Thomas Cook has now added Global Services to provide value-added travel emergency assistance services. This entails providing detailed assistance at the end of a telephone line with the use of computer telephony integration that identifies a caller's number and places that call in the queue for a call centre agent with appropriate skills. Further developments link a caller in Shanghai (say) with a map showing the location of the caller and the closest medical services displayed so the agent can tell the caller how to get there. Details of all incidents are also stored, allowing an agent to pull up a full history of a customer's problems on future occasions. The main site in Peterborough (UK) can handle queries in 60 languages. This £20 million investment is attracting a new group of corporate customers and is now being offered to third parties such as airlines and government agencies.

www.thomascook.com

Questions

1. Why would corporate customers be attracted to this service?

2. How is a call centre uniquely appropriate for providing these services?

Lecturers: visit www.palgrave.com/business/hillom3e for teaching guidelines for this case study

First Direct (HSBC's telephone banking business) was the first to challenge the traditional branch-based provision that characterized the banking industry in the last century. Based on call centre provision (it now provides both telephone and internet banking options), First Direct presents itself as a gateway through which customers pass to access their money, obtain advice and control their financial affairs. Compared to conventional banks, which tend to focus on margins and returns, the staff at First Direct are taught that the customer is key. When the bank was launched on 1 October 1989, the strategy amounted to a blank piece of paper with the word 'customer' in the middle and the business has encouraged its people to hold this simple concept at the centre of everything they do ever since. A basic tenet is to offer customers an equal relationship with their bank manager. To inculcate this into their behaviour and values, staff are themselves treated with equality in the workplace. First, very few of their customer service reps have ever worked in banking before; they're hired for their customer service skill and telephone manner then taught the financial skills required. Second, the 24-hour banking service is run on flexible shift patterns where staff choose their own patterns (anything from 16 to 32 hours) while recognizing the peaks and troughs in demand. Staff also decided themselves how they should dress for work and opted for a smart dress code to better reflect the way they needed to carry out their jobs. Creche facilities at the Leeds (UK) centre have always been available, allowing staff to mix family and work commitments. Basic pay relates to an employee's skills which are heavily weighted towards the behavioural (communicating, handling stress, influencing, assessing information, judgement and decision-making) end of the skill continuum. Staff are also required to match certain standards covering call duration, availability and signed on times.

www.firstdirect.com

Questions

1. Why are call centres attracting customers away from conventional bank branch provision of services?

2. What aspects of First Direct have helped make its call centre a success?

Lecturers: visit www.palgrave.com/business/hillom3e for teaching guidelines for this case study

in terms of both the number of staff required and the opportunity to locate centres in lower wage rate areas. With call centres, customers are offered free or low-rate telephone calls to encourage their use, and international centres allow customers to call a local number while the system then transfers them to an overseas agent who speaks their own language.

In addition, some companies (for example, Dell) transfer calls from one region to another (for example, mainland Europe to the UK or Ireland and then to the eastern seaboard of the USA and so on) as a way of efficiently handling the times during a 24-hour period when the number of calls in a particular region are low. For example, bookings and enquiries for Radisson Hotels in Europe and the Middle East are handled by the group's call centre in Dublin from 7am to 7pm. The operation handles more than 1,000 calls daily, with 22 incoming telephone lines (all free phones) operated by 25 staff speaking 11 different languages. From 7pm the service switches to operations in the USA. The range of services suited to call centre provision is well illustrated in Cases 5.6 and 5.7.

Grocery shopping

After its first tentative steps, online grocery shopping is gaining ground. Competitors in the field have, however, chosen different ways to provide this service. Ocado, the UK's first e-grocer, has taken a warehouse-based approach. Its dedicated picking and delivery system is based at its depot in Hatfield, north of London, which is the size of seven soccer pitches or about 20 average supermarkets. Others using the warehouse model include Simon Delivers in Minneapolis, Greengrocer.com in Australia and Carrefour, Europe's biggest retailer, based in France.

Tesco (the UK's largest supermarket), among others, has taken a different approach. It developed its own technology to enable it to use store-based picking – a low-investment route to this new type of shopping. This approach is now gaining ground in the USA, with Safeway, California's biggest supermarket group, being one of the early adopters. In 2010 Tesco's internet sales had risen to close on £800 million, with profits exceeding £20 million. With 350,000 customers, Tesco processes 150,000 orders per week and has 65 per cent of the UK market. Using this model, Tesco estimates that it can service £2–3 billion of sales through its existing stores. On the other hand, Sainsbury's (a large UK supermarket) has chosen a hybrid model, with a warehouse in north London but most sales done through store-based picking. Now take a look at Case 5.8 for a further illustration.

Further aspects of service delivery

Here we introduce some additional issues that organizations may consider when developing the overall design of their service delivery systems.

Enhancing services: making the intangible tangible

Companies basing their approach on service differentiation employ several strategies to enhance the service they are providing. One way is to bring the intangible aspects of a service to the attention of a customer by making them tangible. By doing this, parts of a service package that may go unnoticed by the customer now become a visible part of the provision. For example:

- Maid service in a hotel bedroom to include collars placed on toilets with words similar to 'sanitized for your personal use', end-folding toilet roll paper, folding down the bed in the evening, with a personalized note and guest room checklist duly completed.

Customers use the online nursery Garden Escape not just because the website offers unusual plants, but also because Garden Escape creates a 'personal store' just for each individual customer. Greeted by name on their personal page each time they visit, customers can make notes on a private online notepad, tinker with garden plans using the site's interactive design programme, and get answers from the Garden Doctor. With such support many customers don't plan to shop elsewhere.

www.burpee.com

Questions

What are the advantages of shopping on the internet? Do you see any problems?

Lecturers: visit www.palgrave.com/business/hillom3e for teaching guidelines for this case study

Figure 5.12 **Informing customers about standards**

Lloyds TSB

3 MINUTE WARNING

We at SOLIHULL Branch feel
that you shouldn't be waiting
any longer than 3 minutes
in this queue.

If you feel that you have been
waiting longer than this, please
complete your details below and
hand to a member of staff.

Thank you

Name...

Account Number...

Time............................... Date......................................

Enquiries or Cashiers Queue....................................

Source: Courtesy of Lloyds TSB (2000).

- Fast, attentive service is signalled by prominent positioning of the '3-minute warning' notice in some high street branches of the UK bank Lloyds TSB (see Figure 5.12). Supported by the prompt opening of additional tellers when queues start to form, this draws customers' attention to this dimension of service provision.

- Hotels are increasingly making in-room, hot drink provision a feature. Moreover, many also provide the highest quality amenities such as French-milled and smooth facial soaps, shampoo, conditioner, bath foam, hand lotion and shower caps; aftershave for male travellers, and make-up remover and styling preparations for their female counterparts. All designed, in part, to give a tangible feel to the quality of service provided elsewhere by the hotel.

- In a similar vein, some hotels now display notices in the en-suite bathrooms informing guests that should they have forgotten any essential toiletry item, to telephone reception for complimentary provision.

- Prompt service is also made tangible in one of several ways – many hotels guarantee an in-room breakfast that will be delivered within ten minutes of the requested period or it will be provided free of charge. Domino's Pizza's promise to deliver an order to your home within 30 minutes (normal times) or 40 minutes (peak demand times) or it will be replaced or money refunded. In practice, this means that if a delivery is late, customers would be asked to pay for the pizza(s) but not (say) the soft drink(s) or dessert(s). Furthermore, if a delivery is considered very late (20 plus minutes), the whole order is offered free of charge. Domino's Pizza's replace or refund policy also applies to its quality guarantee.

- In maintenance work, cleaning up after completion provides a 'reverse' example of this same perspective. Similarly, a car wash given free with a routine service or paper covers left inside the vehicle demonstrate to the customer the level of care taken by the company when providing the core element of the service.

- Guarantees on quality are now standard for most products where reimbursement of price and postage is prompt and is encouraged by companies where a customer has any concerns whatsoever. With food, the time of preparation also signals freshness, as demonstrated in Figure 5.13.

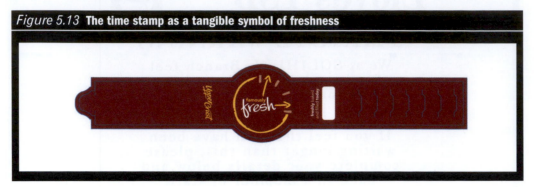

Figure 5.13 The time stamp as a tangible symbol of freshness

Source: Courtesy of Upper Crust.

Customer participation in service delivery

When designing the delivery system, organizations need to decide the extent to which customers will or will not participate in the creation of the service. The degree of customer involvement in the system affects many factors including the provision and management of capacity, service levels, staff training requirements and costs.

Higher levels of customer participation in a delivery system make capacity management easier and reduce the cost of its provision, while decreasing the degree of customer contact and the opportunities to personalize the service and encourage customer loyalty. The trade-offs involved need to be understood and the operations implications for supporting alternative service delivery system designs need to be fully assessed. For example, while banks in Europe are increasingly standardizing procedures for bank loan applications, in Japan the procedure has already progressed to the use of a score sheet. Answers to several questions are graded and if the customer's score is above a certain level, the loan application is handled quickly. The impact upon operations provision is significant.

However, for do-it-yourself approaches to be successful, companies must assess the whole requirement of the service delivery system and carefully complement the customer inputs by providing well-trained staff, reliable equipment and appropriate and well-maintained systems and procedures.

Employing the do-it-yourself concept in service delivery systems has been gaining ground over the past few decades. Various examples can be given of service sectors increasingly using this approach:

- **Supermarkets** control over 80 per cent of the gross retail market and sell principally on a self-service basis.

- **Fast-food** outlets form a growing part of overall restaurant provision.

- **Telephone services** are principally based on subscriber dialling, with most telephone calls now being made by customers.

- **Petrol stations** use self-service as the basis for providing fuel, screen washing, and oil, water and tyre pressure checks.

- **Online shopping** is a major provider in the retail industry. It requires a customer to complete the selection, application and payment parts of the procedure, with the business providing fast delivery once the transaction is fed into the service system.

- **Financial services** provide a growing range of products through self-service delivery systems such as ATMs, general banking, insurance, mortgages and personal loans.

The reasons for the growth in these sectors vary. Figure 5.14 summarizes some factors that relate to their success, while Cases 5.9 and 5.10 provide illustrations.

Figure 5.14 **Success factors of self-service approaches**						
Success factors	**Selected service sectors**					
	Super-markets	**Fast-food outlets**	**Telephone services**	**Petrol stations**	**Online shopping**	**Financial services**
Faster service	✓	✓	✓	✓	✓	✓
Lower price	✓	✓	✓	✓	✓	✓
Improved product quality	✓	✓				
Increased product variety	✓				✓	
More convenient	✓	✓			✓	✓
More customer control within the delivery system	✓	✓	✓	✓	✓	✓

Maximizing the use of skilled staff

Businesses that offer a wide range of services will typically employ a wide range of skilled staff. As higher skilled people are more difficult to find and command higher salaries, ensuring that there is a match between the level of difficulty of the task and the level of staff skill needed to deliver it is an important factor in delivery system design. The approach is referred to as 'maximizing the leverage of scarce resources', with scarce resources here referring to the skill and experience level of staff. This concept is designed to highlight the need to ensure that staff do not undertake tasks for which their skills are too high.

For example, the auditing divisions of big accounting firms employ large numbers of juniors or associate staff on relatively low salaries and these junior staff make up the majority of the audit teams. In this way, the less difficult tasks are completed by less experienced staff, with more senior staff leading the team and business partners responsible for more than one team. One result is that the sales and profit per partner are enhanced. Furthermore, with little opportunity for advancement, the staff turnover at the lower skilled levels is high and so junior and associate staff are continuously being replaced by new entrants so helping to maintain the sales and profit levels per partner.

Determining the level of server discretion within the delivery system

The system–customer interface allows for servers to exercise discretion. It is important, therefore, for organizations to establish the appropriate level of discretion to be exercised within each service category and delivery system (that is, the extent to which it is desired or appropriate that a server is allowed to interpret what should constitute the service specification actually provided to a customer). Earlier issues concerning aspects such as customer participation, service enhancement, the non-repeat or repeat nature of a service and the extent of customer interface within the system will impact the lever of server discretion. Firms need to recognize that these factors are ways of reducing or increasing customization and then use them to develop a service delivery system that supports the desired level of customization.

The downside of supermarket shopping is queuing to pay. To speed up this part of the delivery system, retailers are looking for ways to involve customers in this last step of the process. For some time now, the facility has been available for self-scanning your purchases as you go and then paying at a designated checkout. Similarly, self-checkouts are gaining popularity and are now well established throughout major supermarket stores. With these, the system uses visual and voice commands to talk customers through the process. Bar codes are swiped in the normal way, while for loose items such as vegetables and fruit, price by weight details are stored on a database. If an item does not register properly, the voice system asks the customer to scan it again.

Lack of pre-registering and ease of use appeal to those who simply wish to shop and go. With the average person in the UK spending two hours in queues every week (even with internet banking and shopping), user-friendly forms of self-service are gaining ground.

www.ncr.com; www.safeway.com
www.sainsbury.co.uk
www.optimalgrp.com
www.marksandspencer.com
www.waitrose.com

Questions

1. Why are supermarkets introducing self-checkout systems?

2. Consumers recently ranked self-checkout technology as second only to cash machines in terms of the self-service they were most likely to use. Why?

Lecturers: visit www.palgrave.com/business/hillom3e for teaching guidelines for this case study

There are over 20 million private motorists in the UK and car ownership continues to grow. As a result, motor insurance is big business, with an £8 billion annual premium spend. Launched in 1985, Direct Line was the first insurance company to use the telephone as its primary medium for sales and other transactions. Cutting out the middleman and commissions enabled it to speed up the application process and reduce premiums. Now, it the UK's largest private motor insurer, with over ten million policyholders. Direct Line has also successfully expanded its product range and the Direct Line Group now offers the following:

- Direct Line Insurance plc – motor, rescue, home, travel and pet insurance and a 24-hour home emergency call-out service
- Direct Line Financial Services Ltd – mortgages, savings, personal loans and credit cards
- Direct Line Life Holdings Ltd – personal pensions, life insurance and ISAs.

In 1995 Direct Line opened its first industrial-scale Accident Management Centre. By 2010, it operated seven throughout the UK together with some further 300 approved garages in its network that contribute to the quality and efficiency of the service within its overall claims business.

A strong feature of the early years was Direct Line's speed of growth. By year 3 it was profitable even though it offered premiums that were typically 20 per cent lower than competitors. The concept of the telephone as its primary tool enabled Direct Line to deal directly with the public and use the advantages afforded by its technological efficiency and underwriting precision to cut costs. Less than a decade after its entry, Direct Line became the UK's largest private motor insurer.

Direct Line's entry set new service standards for the insurance industry. It offers extended hours, with lines open from 8am to 8pm on weekdays and 9am to 5pm on Saturdays. It enables customers to register and complete their claims by telephone and provides 24-hour emergency helplines. The idea brings greater simplicity, improves the level of customer support through the process and results in better value for money.

Where Direct Line extends its range, it adopts the same tactics of low prices, straightforward products and telephone-based service delivery systems. As the company transacts the vast majority of its business by telephone, operations is at the core of the Direct Line service proposition. To ensure standards are maintained, the company provides extensive customer care training and re-engineers processes to cut out complicated forms and jargon. One of its first revolutionary moves was to eliminate cover notes (that were traditionally sent to customers as confirmation of insurance cover but were not the official documents) by laser printing and mailing policies, insurance certificates and other documents the same day.

Innovative technology helps Direct Line keep down costs. For example, most products are paid for by credit card or direct debit, allowing payments to be processed electronically and so reducing staff and overheads. Similarly, automated call handling systems ensure that the 15 million calls received each year are quickly and effortlessly rerouted between Direct Line's different call centres to minimize customer waiting time.

Today, Direct Line continues to improve its operations so as to offer additional customer benefits and better customer support. These range from the use of daily interest calculations for mortgages to a 'pet bereavement' helpline for pet insurance customers. Staff development is also a key activity, with initiatives such as cross-training sales and claims staff so that the same people can handle both sets of tasks. The result is that work interest increases while customers are served more quickly.
www.directline.com

Questions

1. Why is Direct Line so successful and how has operations supported the business growth?

2. How do (if at all) the products offered by Direct Line differ from its competitors?

3. Analyze Direct Line in terms of the 'factors for success' introduced in Figure 5.14.

Lecturers: visit www.palgrave.com/business/hillom3e for teaching guidelines for this case study

Service profiling

Organizations need to understand the business trade-offs of alternative delivery systems and build these into their decisions. Similarly, as markets change or as companies enter new markets with different competitive needs, they must check whether the changing or different needs of their markets can be adequately supported by the operations investments already in place. These critical checks stem from the fact that whereas markets are characterized by change, investments in operations are characterized by their large size and fixed nature. As a result, making changes in operations typically takes a long time and a lot of money. Thus, where market needs and operations capabilities are not matched then a company can be strategically disadvantaged.

Now, place these considerations in the context of the characteristics of today's competitive environment. Markets are changing faster and are becoming increasingly different rather than increasingly similar. For operations to align its capabilities to the needs of the company's markets today and tomorrow, it needs a way of assessing the level of alignment between today's market needs and what operations is set up to support and also a way of being alerted to future changes that may reduce the current level of alignment.

The concept for undertaking this check is called service profiling.[6] It offers an organization the opportunity to test the current or anticipated degree of fit between the needs of its market(s) and what the existing or proposed system process and infrastructure investments in operations can provide. The principal purpose of this assessment is to provide a way to evaluate and, where necessary, improve the degree of fit between the way in which a company qualifies and wins orders in its markets and operations ability to support these criteria.

The ideal is to achieve this fit to the required level. In many instances though, companies will be unable or unwilling to provide the desired degree of fit due to the level of investment, executive energy or timescales involved to make the necessary changes. Sound strategy improves the level of consciousness an organization brings to bear on its business decisions. In such circumstances service profiling increases business awareness allowing conscious choices between alternatives.

Inconsistency between the competitive factors in markets and an organization's capability to support them can be induced by changes in either market needs or delivery system investments, or a combination of the two. Mismatches are due to the fact that while investments within operations are large and fixed, market changes are brought about by competition and the fact that corporate marketing decisions can sometimes be changed quickly and significantly. While the latter decisions allow for change and repositioning, operations decisions can bind a business for years ahead. Thus, linkage between these two parts of an organization is not just a felt need but an essential requirement.

> **EXECUTIVE INSIGHT**
> As market needs differ, so does the choice of service delivery system. However, as markets change or companies enter new markets with different competitive needs, checks need to be made to ensure that market needs and delivery system support are aligned.

Procedure

Alignment involves checking how well market needs are matched by the characteristics of the operations systems used to provide them. Such checks assess the level of business fit that exists and also serve to alert companies to alignment issues in the future as a result of current strategies in a business.

Completing a check links aspects of the chapters on 'operations strategy' and 'designing services and products' respectively to aspects of this chapter to do with service delivery system design. The procedure for developing a service profile involves the following steps and analyses:

1. Select aspects of the business (some of which are given in Figure 5.10) that are relevant to the business under review. The key here is to keep the number of chosen dimensions small thereby keeping insights sharp, remembering that this approach is designed as a mechanism for communicating strategic issues within a business. Keeping to the point highlights the message, avoids digression and concentrates discussion on the strategic issues under review.

2. Next, put down the characteristics associated with each chosen dimension in the same way as they are displayed in Figure 5.10. Figure 5.15 is an example of the outcome of service profiling and a glance at this will show you how to proceed.

3. Now profile the service(s) by positioning them on each of the characteristics selected. Where the circle is drawn indicates the relative position of a service on a dimension.

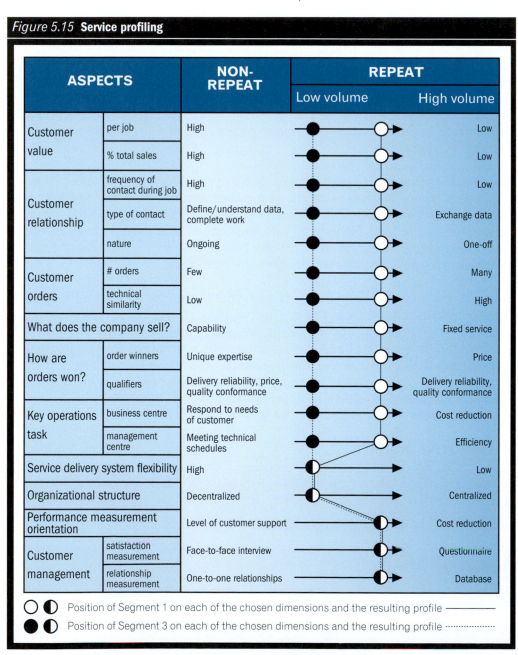

Figure 5.15 **Service profiling**

Figure 5.16 The nature of work, customer relationships and key management tasks within each market segment

Market segment	Nature of work completed	Customer relationships to be managed	Key management task
1	Short duration High volume Repeat tasks	One-off Non-repeat	Cost reduction
2	Long duration Medium volume Repeat tasks	Ongoing High contact during project	Project management
3	Long duration Low volume Non-repeat tasks	Ongoing High contact during project	Product development

Figure 5.17 Service profiling

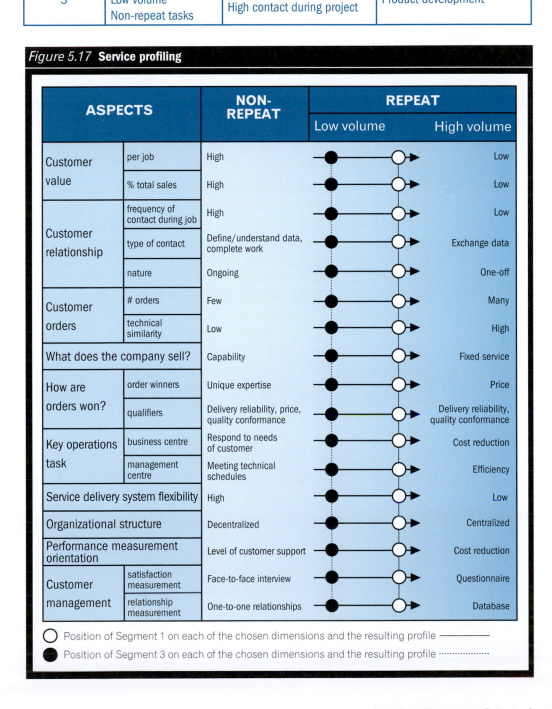

ASPECTS		NON-REPEAT	REPEAT	
			Low volume	High volume
Customer value	per job	High		Low
	% total sales	High		Low
Customer relationship	frequency of contact during job	High		Low
	type of contact	Define/understand data, complete work		Exchange data
	nature	Ongoing		One-off
Customer orders	# orders	Few		Many
	technical similarity	Low		High
What does the company sell?		Capability		Fixed service
How are orders won?	order winners	Unique expertise		Price
	qualifiers	Delivery reliability, price, quality conformance		Delivery reliability, quality conformance
Key operations task	business centre	Respond to needs of customer		Cost reduction
	management centre	Meeting technical schedules		Efficiency
Service delivery system flexibility		High		Low
Organizational structure		Decentralized		Centralized
Performance measurement orientation		Level of customer support		Cost reduction
Customer management	satisfaction measurement	Face-to-face interview		Questionnaire
	relationship measurement	One-to-one relationships		Database

○ Position of Segment 1 on each of the chosen dimensions and the resulting profile ————
● Position of Segment 3 on each of the chosen dimensions and the resulting profile ········

The example in Figure 5.15 shows the resulting profiles for two of the three segments within a part of a large utilities company. The dogleg nature of both profiles provides a way to identify the lack of fit between some key activities and dimensions of the total business with the different market needs of these two market segments. Note that to simplify this example only two of the three segments of the company have been profiled.

The story behind Figure 5.15

To better meet the needs of its markets in the face of growing competition, this company was set up as a stand-alone business. With some 3,000 staff, it meets the requirements of over 0.25 million new customers each year and is split into the three segments shown in Figure 5.16:

- **Segment 1** – with 110,000 domestic and small business customers, service provision is of a once-and-for-all nature, typically completed in less than a day and differs little from customer to customer. The principal order-winner is price and the key task is to take advantage of the high volume, repeat nature of the business to reduce costs.

- **Segment 2** – involves larger projects in the course of which the company needs to respond to short lead times and to meet customers' schedules. These larger business customers are typically developing several sites at any one time with the result that there is an opportunity to undertake repeat contracts.

- **Segment 3** – comprises a small number of very complex jobs of a highly technical nature. Meeting customer specifications and schedule deadlines is essential and may lead to additional large contracts.

To meet the needs of its markets the company had developed a single organizational approach. The rapid growth in sales revenue during the past few years had put increasing strain on the company's ability to support these diverse needs. Profiling these businesses as shown in Figure 5.7 highlighted the fact that the company was currently managing the three different segments using the same approach. Having identified this, the company changed aspects of its operations and the resulting profiles are shown in Figure 5.17.

Delivering services in practice

When designing and managing service delivery systems in new business, it is important to consider the following aspects:

- Complete frequent and in-depth market reviews to identify any volume or order-winner/qualifier changes and ensure the delivery system design meets these requirements.

- As your business grows, you will tend to offer a wider range of services. It is, therefore, critical to continually review the design of delivery systems used to ensure they are appropriate for the services they deliver.

- Look for opportunities to use IT in the delivery system to help reduce costs and lead times.

- Identify where customers can be involved in delivering services. This not only reduces costs, but also gives customers 'ownership' of appropriate parts of the system and allows them to customize it to their needs.

- Remember that the decision to create a front and back office is a strategic one. Having more steps in the back office will help reduce costs, whereas more steps in the front office will increase the level of customization.

Driving business performance

The operations task to deliver the services it sells to customers is central to the successful performance of a business in the following ways.

Delivering services to release cash

Transforming inputs into saleable outputs is at the root of the cash cycle. Decisions affecting the design of the service delivery system need to include the impact on cash flow throughout the business, as a feature essential for its well-being and growth.

Delivering services to improve market support

Operations' role in terms of designing and managing service delivery systems to meet the needs of customers is central to retaining customers and growing sales. As such it impacts market share, underpins sales revenue and the prosperity of a business.

Delivering services to reduce costs

Service delivery systems need to be designed to meet the characteristics and requirements of the markets in which a company competes. Built into their designs are the cost structures that underpin pricing decisions and profit expectations. However, markets often change due to the competitive activity that characterizes them and operations needs to regularly review the level of fit between customer needs and delivery.

Critical reflections

Although how a company chooses to meet the technical specification of its service offerings will affect the design of its delivery systems, operations managers must also ensure that their design decisions:

- Are aligned to the order-winners and qualifiers of its chosen markets

- Reflect the internal requirements of the organization, such as capacity utilization, control of costs, queue lengths and the interface with customers

- Incorporate IT and other development opportunities to help keep the business competitive and improve its ability to meet customers' requirements.

Figure 5.18 **Factors in reactive and proactive service delivery system design**

Factors		Service delivery system design	
		Reactive	**Proactive**
Delivery system design	objective	Streamlined and efficient	Customer-focused
	structure	Rigid	Responsive
	design premise	Events are consistent and unchanging	Change acknowledged and built into the design
	approach to service failure	Prevention	Recovery
	response to service failure	Not designed in the system	Integral part of system design
	role of server in quality conformance provision	Procedures specify server behaviour	Proactive response expected
Achieving quality conformance	systems design	Built into the system	Built into the staff
	error handling	Refer to another level	Dealt with on the spot
	level of recovery	Low and slow	High and immediate
	response to failure	Back-office management	Frontline staff
	quality objective	System has zero defects	Customer-centric
Staff	attitude	Lack of involvement	Part of provision and solution
	level of discretion	Low and not encouraged	High and encouraged
	attitude to failure	Part of failure	Part of recovery solution and then part of success
	level of motivation	Frustration leading to lack of interest	Part of service provision leading to becoming involved and motivated

This chapter has emphasized how businesses must recognize the key differences that exist between services and then incorporate these differences into the design of their delivery systems. As part of this, organizations need to decide how reactive or proactive the service delivery system design should be, recognize the fundamental differences in approach that result (see Figure 5.18), check the desired position on relevant factors and then incorporate these approaches into their delivery system designs.

What underpins the drive to develop delivery systems that meet the needs of customers is the impact they have on market share, customer retention and growth. Online retailers estimate that there is no overall profit on transactions until a customer has returned three or even four times. Similarly, as Figure 5.19 shows, keeping customers grows profit. Aligning delivery systems to markets is a key task, therefore, and requires sound business understanding about what is needed and how systems are to be developed.

Figure 5.19 Trends in annual profit per customer

Sector	Annual profit/customer				
	1	2	3	4	5
Car servicing	100	140	280	350	350
Credit cards	100	250	283	290	309
Distribution	100	220	270	320	373

Note: Figures indexed on Year 1.

Summary

- A key decision for any company is how to deliver its services in order to meet both the needs of its customers and the objectives of the business.

- Factors that must be taken into account are divided into the technical requirement (what the service specification comprises) and the business requirement (the order-winners and qualifiers for the chosen market). Together, these requirements form the service offering, which is experienced by the customer.

- Decisions about service delivery system design are influenced by the distinctive characteristics of the service and the features of the overall and detailed service delivery system design.

- The impact of IT and other developments on design alternatives has been described in this chapter, and examples have been provided to illustrate the continued impact on service delivery.

- Finally, the other issues to be considered in delivering services were explained, with examples.

Study activities

Discussion questions

1. Choose a service company that uses at least two of the delivery systems detailed in this chapter. Explain why a company would have made such choices.

2. Give an example where you consider that an operations delivery system is not aligned to an organization's market(s). Explain key aspects that illustrate this. What steps would you take to improve the level of fit between market needs and operations capabilities?

3. Select a single-step and multi-step service delivery system in a service organization of your choice. Explain how they work and why you think that the design was the one chosen.

4. Why is queuing often an integral part of a service delivery system design?

5. For a service company of your choice explain:
   - The service delivery system design
   - How the company could reduce queues within the system.

6. Review the data in Figures 5.5, 5.6, 5.7 and 5.8. Why do the results seem to make sense?

Assignments

1. Envisage going to the emergency unit of your local hospital with a suspected broken wrist. List the key steps in the delivery system in which you would be involved. What type of system is used at each step?

2. Select a company (other than the examples provided in the chapter) to illustrate a:
   • Non-repeat business
   • Repeat business – low volume
   • Repeat business – high volume.

For each, outline the service delivery used.

Exploring further

TED talks

Brown, T. (2008) *Creativity and play*. At the 2008 Serious Play conference, designer Tim Brown talks about the powerful relationship between creative thinking and play, with many examples you can try at home (and one that maybe you shouldn't).
www.ted.com/talks/tim_brown_on_creativity_and_play.html

Leadbeater, C. (2005) *Innovation*. In this deceptively casual talk, Charles Leadbeater weaves a tight argument that innovation isn't just for professionals anymore. Passionate amateurs, using new tools, are creating products and paradigms that companies can't.
www.ted.com/talks/charles_leadbeater_on_innovation.html

Mitra, S. (2010) *The child-driven education*. Education scientist Sugata Mitra tackles one of the greatest problems of education: the best teachers and schools don't exist where they're needed most. In a series of real-life experiments from New Delhi to South Africa to Italy, he gave kids self-supervised access to the web and saw results that could revolutionize how we think about teaching.
www.ted.com/talks/sugata_mitra_the_child_driven_education.html

Journal articles

Dixon, M., Freeman, K. and Toman, N. (2010) 'Stop trying to delight your customers', *Harvard Business Review*, **88**(7): 116–22. The notion that companies must go above and beyond in their customer service activities is so entrenched that managers rarely examine it. The article studied more than 75,000 people interacting with call centre representatives or using self-service methods and found that over-the-top efforts made little difference: all customers really wanted was a simple, quick solution to their problem.

Ramaswamy, V. and Gouillart, F. (2010) 'Building the co-creative enterprise', *Harvard Business Review*, **88**(10): 100–9. The article examines how companies can use their stake-holders including customers, employees and distributors to determine HR practices and design and market their services and products.

Books

Hill, T. (1998) *The Strategy Quest. Releasing the Energy of Manufacturing Within a Market Driven Strategy: a Dynamic Business Story*. Available from AMD Publishing, Dousland. This book (written as a novel) describes how an art business and manufacturing organization restructure themselves to meet the changing demands of their customers.

Rowley, J. (2002) *E-business: Principles and Practice*. Basingstoke: Palgrave Macmillan. This provides a comprehensive review of e-business, including the choice of technologies, website design, serving customers and e-business strategies.

Teboul, J. (2006) *Service is Front Stage*. Basingstoke: INSEAD Business Press/Palgrave Macmillan. This provides a classification of services and identifies the quality gaps that occur while emphasizing the need to meet customer requirements.

Notes and references

1. Also refer to the approach to service delivery system design in Heskett, J.L., Jones, T.O., Loveman, G.W., Sasser Jr, W.E. and Schlesinger, L.A. (1994) 'Putting the service-profit chain to work', *Harvard Business Review*, March–April: 164–74.
2. Also refer to Hart, C.W.L., Heskett, J.L. and Sasser Jr, W.E. (1990) 'The profitable art of service recovery', *Harvard Business Review*, July-August: 148–56; and Reinartz, W. and Kumar, V. (2000) 'The mismanagement of customer loyalty', *Harvard Business Review*, July: 4–12.
3. J. Nilles' books include *Managing Telework*, John Wiley, New York (1998).
4. Mam, G. (1997) 'The Future of Work', *Financial Times Information Technology Review*, 8 January, p. x.
5. Schadler, T. (2009) 'Telecommuting will rise to include 43 percent of US workers by 2016', Forrester Research, 13 March, p.1; Paino, M. (2011) 'The slow, but promising, rise of telecommuting,' *Chief Learning Officer*, 4 March, p.1.
6. Based on Hill, A. and Hill, T. (2003) 'Customer service: aligning business to markets', Templeton Executive Briefing, University of Oxford.

Visit www.palgrave.com/business/hillom3e for self-test questions, guideline answers to some case study questions, useful weblinks and more to help you understand the topics in this chapter

The past three years have been somewhat of a rollercoaster for British Airways. In 2008, they achieved 10 per cent gross profit for the first time ever (see Figures 1 and 2) and significantly improved their operational performance (see Figure 3), but then the financial crisis hit and they made a 2 per cent loss the following year while announcing a merger with Iberia to try to spread overhead costs and recover the situation. Things seem to be working and they only made a 1 per cent loss in 2010. They have finally reached an agreement with their employees so there shouldn't be any more strikes, but fuel prices are back on the rise and the response to their last Club World service upgrade was mixed. Their loyal customers love what they've done, but others feel they're still lagging behind the competition. Singapore Airlines recently spent $310 million upgrading its fleet and its new business class flat bed now has memory stick ports allowing passengers to fly without a laptop. The question is, how can BA maintain sales and profits within such a competitive and constantly changing market?

HISTORY

BA's origins go back to the birth of civil aviation following World War I when in 1919 it offered the world's first daily international scheduled air service between London and Paris. Since then it has been through some turbulent times. It lost $1 billion in 1986, was privatized in 1987, was voted the world's best airline in 1989, but then started losing customers to low-cost airlines in 1992.

To fight back, BA asked passengers and cabin crews how it could improve its service. The feedback showed that as an airline it was acceptable, but predictable. To rectify this, it redesigned cabins and services based on the idea that 'if you don't do it on the ground, why do it in the air?' A cradle seat was introduced giving full-body adjustable support, a much wider footplate, a cushion support behind the knees, an adjustable leg rest extension and an adjustable headrest that included wings to support the head while a passenger slept. The pitch (the distance between one seat and that of the seat in front) increased from 40 to 50 inches and the recline level from 100° to 140°. Hand baggage allowance, wardrobe and other storage space were increased, white china, coloured glass wear and full-sized knives and forks were introduced with simpler and higher-quality food such as pastas and salads. Passengers were encouraged to design their own service, for example they could sleep as long as they wanted on overnight flights without being woken for breakfast and were encouraged to 'raid the larder' that offered a range of snacks. The aim was to create a comfortable atmosphere in which passengers could design their own service.

Customers responded well, but BA didn't stand still. In 1999, it launched its Putting People First Again programme where all 62,000 employees underwent intensive customer service training to improve the level of service given and make passengers' end-to-end journeys as smooth as possible. The number of executive lounges was increased and redesigned with 'zones' to suit customer needs or moods including a combiz centre (business centre), world wine bar, library, larder, cappuccino and juice bar, sanctuary and terrace. Passengers flying from the US east coast to Europe could also have dinner before take-off. Arrivals lounges were introduced at Heathrow, Gatwick and Johannesburg where customers can shower, breakfast, have their clothes pressed and make telephone calls before starting their day. These were all significant improvements, but the revolution came with the introduction of

Figure 1 **Financial performance (2000-10)**

Financial performance (US$M)	British Airways				Emirates			
	2000	2004	2008	2010	2000	2004	2008	2010
Revenue								
Passenger	13,877	13,193	14,019	12,976	1,277	2,594	7,708	9,044
Other	2,742	861	2,253	1,885	407	930	2,281	2,867
Total	16,619	14,054	16,272	14,861	1,684	3,524	9,989	11,912
Costs								
Employee	4,612	4,053	4,027	3,714	311	618	1,512	1,739
Fuel and oil	1,495	1,714	3,820	4,410	210	448	2,817	3,264
Operating	2,469	1,736	1,816	1,853	201	333	483	598
Other	7,888	5,798	4,982	5,313	838	1,717	4,406	5,333
Total	16,463	13,301	14,645	15290	1,561	3,116	9,218	10,934
Gross profit	156	753	1,627	(987)	123	408	771	977

Financial performance (US$M)	Singapore				Virgin Atlantic			
	2000	2004	2008	2010	2000	2004	2008	2010
Revenue								
Passenger	5,957	5,988	8,573	7,318	–	–	–	–
Other	2,245	1,200	2,771	5,389	–	–	–	–
Total	8,202	7,188	11,344	12,707	2,355	2,365	3,980	4,382
Costs								
Employee	1,222	1,227	1,685	2,159	–	–	–	–
Fuel and oil	1,210	1,416	3,881	4,195	–	–	–	–
Operating	1,357	1,081	1,354	1,589	–	–	–	–
Other	3,596	3,313	3,397	4,701	–	–	–	–
Total	7,385	7,037	10,317	12,644	2,348	2,326	3,893	4,627
Gross profit	817	150	1,027	63	7	39	87	(245)

beds into business class in March 2000. Customers could now turn their seat into a flat 1.83m bed at a click of a button and the number of seats in each cabin reduced to give 30 per cent more personal space. It seemed that BA had the business traveller market all wrapped up, but the competition had other ideas.

BATTLE FOR THE SKIES

Competition for business class customers increased significantly in the early 2000s, but its intensity varied depending on the regulatory environment, route, number of competitors and whether they were state-owned or state-supported. At one extreme, some international routes had regulated fares and BA only competed with state-owned competitors. At the other end, on internal European flights any European airline could operate on any route and set whatever fares they wished. Strong competition in this European market led to consolidation between airlines trying to

---

Figure 2 **Sales revenue by region (2000–10)**

Financial performance (US$M)	British Airways				Emirates			
	2000	2004	2008	2010	2000	2004	2008	2010
Europe	10,964	9,183	10,366	9,092	–	–	2,953	3,183
The Americas	3,077	2,504	3,155	3,069	–	–	643	1,097
Africa, Middle East & India	1,277	1,333	1,526	1,359	–	–	3,396	4,385
Far East & Australasia	1,301	1,034	1,225	1,340	–	–	2,997	3,246
Total	**16,619**	**14,054**	**16,272**	**14,861**	**1,684**	**3,524**	**9,989**	**11,912**

Financial performance (US$M)	Singapore				Virgin Atlantic			
	2000	2004	2008	2010	2000	2004	2008	2010
Europe	1,674	1,708	1,957	1,793	–	–	–	–
The Americas	1,903	649	1,017	1,319	–	–	1,552	1,709
Africa, Middle East & India	829	668	875	871	–	–	677	745
Far East & Australasia	3,706	5,550	7,514	8,724	–	–	1,751	1,928
Total	**8,112**	**8,575**	**11,363**	**11,363**	**2,355**	**2,365**	**3,980**	**4,382**

Figure 3 **Operational performance (2000–10)**

Operational performance		British Airways				Emirates			
		2000	2004	2008	2010	2000	2004	2008	2010
Number of	Aircraft	283	291	245	238	32	61	109	142
	Passengers (M)	47	36	33	32	5	10	21	27
	Destinations	566	570	302	324	50	73	89	104
	Flights (000s)	538	391	281	257	32	59	102	131
Passenger load factor (% seats)		73	76	79	72	73	80	78	75

Operational performance		Singapore				Virgin			
		2000	2004	2008	2010	2000	2004	2008	2010
Number of	Aircraft	92	85	73	108	32	30	38	39
	Passengers (M)	14	13	18	16	4	4	6	5
	Destinations	118	56	64	68	25	28	32	32
	Flights (000s)	32	30	40	50	28	27	35	34
Passenger load factor (% seats)		73	79	78	–	–	–	–	–

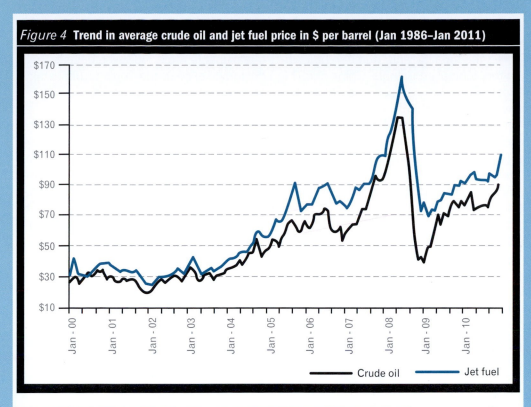

Figure 4 Trend in average crude oil and jet fuel price in $ per barrel (Jan 1986–Jan 2011)

—— Crude oil —— Jet fuel

Figure 5 British Airways lounges by type and region

Region	# lounges		Arrivals
	Departures		
	First	**Club**	
UK and Ireland	5	30	3
US and Canada	13	40	–
Europe	–	70	–
Africa	–	14	1
Middle East	1	13	–
South Asia	2	6	–
Asia Pacific	2	8	–
Australasia	–	5	–
South America and Caribbean	2	11	–

Figure 6 Business traveller awards (2005–10)

Award (Best)		Year			
		2005	**2006**	**2008**	**2010**
Frequent flyer programme Cabin staff		BA	BA	BA	BA
		Virgin	Virgin	Singapore	Singapore
Class	First	BA	BA	Singapore	Emirates
	Business	BA	Virgin	BA	Singapore
	Premium economy	Virgin	Virgin	Virgin	Virgin
	Economy	BA	BA	Singapore	Singapore
Airline	Short haul	BA	BA	BA	BA
	Long haul	BA	BA	Singapore	Singapore
	Overall	BA	BA	Singapore	Singapore

reduce costs. Air France merged with KLM, and Lufthansa with Swiss Air. Meanwhile, the quality and number of competitors increased in India, China and The Middle East. Airlines such as Etihad Airways, Emirates, Cathay Pacific, Singapore Airlines and Malaysia Airlines all significantly increased the number of routes out of their respective hubs. They also invested heavily in their in-flight entertainment systems and introduced new seat technologies, additional services and, in some cases, dedicated premium terminals. For example, Emirates offered business-class customers a pre-flight five-course dinner at the Ritz-Carlton hotel, Etihad boasted the largest legroom and Singapore the most extensive in-flight entertainment system. Despite these developments, it was actually BA's old UK rival, Virgin Atlantic, who took away its coveted 'Best Business Class' Business Traveller Award in 2006 (see Figure 6) after a $312 million investment in cabin seat configuration, flat beds, four limousine journeys per return flight and number of in-flight services such as a bar, a massage and a place to sit and have a meal with one's partner. Not only were these airlines offering a superior service to BA, they were also often less expensive.

Private charter airlines were also increasing with their fast and flexible, but very expensive, premium service. In 2007, a change in legislation created more competition with the advent of the business-class only-carriers EOS, MAXjet and Silverjet. They focused on the London to US market, typically from Stansted or Luton to New York. Carrying only 100 passengers at a time, they offered a 30-minute check-

in time, gourmet meals ordered pre-flight and access to exclusive airport lounges at a reasonable price. However, despite their customer appeal, they proved unsustainable and all three folded in 2008

BACK TO THE DRAWING BOARD

To workout how to improve its service, BA again surveyed business class passengers who had flown with them in the last five years. It found that space, comfort, privacy, control and storage were of utmost importance. Using this feedback, it launched its new Club World service in 2007 by investing $184 million in new seats with disappearing arm rests to make the bed 25 per cent wider, audiovisual on demand with 50 films, 60 hours of TV and 50 hours of music, 10-inch touch screen TV screens, noise-cancelling headphones, larger privacy screens, a laptop plug socket and storage drawer. A more extensive and flexible food menu was also introduced with a greater range of hot and cold snacks and drinks in the Club Kitchen that replaced the 'raid the larder' concept.

Major IT investments were also made to improve customer service and lower costs. All employees were moved onto email and an Employee Self Service (ESS) extranet site was created allowing administration tasks to be completed online from either work or home. The 'ba.com website' was also updated to improve its look, feel and functionality enabling customers to compare products, buy tickets, reserve hotels, hire cars, book tours, manage bookings, check in and print boarding passes before arriving at the airport. By 2008, 80 per cent of customers booked tickets using ba.com

Figure 7 **Airline alliances**				
Members and network		**Alliance**		
		Oneworld	**Star Alliance**	**Skyteam**
Members	Founding	4	5	4
	Additional	6	12	6
	Associate	15	3	-
Network	Countries	129	139	133
	Destinations	588	795	684
	Daily departures	8,160	15,000	15,207
	Passengers (M)	245	344	384
	Fleet	1,998	2,554	2,069

Figure 8 **Emirates: business class**

On 25 October 1985, Emirates flew its first routes from Dubai using just two leased aircraft. Its goal has always been quality rather than quantity, but an average 20 per cent year-on-year sales growth since then meant it had over 21 million passengers in 2007. Wholly government owned, but run as an independent business, Emirates has grown on the back of the economic expansion in the region. The continued success of Dubai as a financial and international transport hub is critical for Emirates and 85 per cent of its population are expatriates from regions such as the UK, India, Bangladesh and the Philippines. The Dubai International Airport needs to keep expanding and Dubai's reputation as both a business and tourist destination has been enhanced through events and developments such as the annual Shopping Festival and the Dubailand theme park.

Increasing competition

Over the past ten years, the Middle Eastern business-class airline passenger market has grown by an average of 20 per cent each year despite total business-class traffic remaining static across the world as a whole. Emirates has grown with this market, but so have the number and strength of its competitors. It is unlikely to lose any significant share while the market continues to grow, but things may start to change when it slows down. As well as competing against the more traditional business class airlines such as British Airways, Singapore Airlines, Cathay Pacific and Virgin Atlantlic on routes between Dubai and their own hubs, Emirates is also up against an increasing number of Middle Eastern airlines.

Qatar Airways was relaunched in 1997 as part of a US$20 billion investment by the Qatar government to increase tourism in the region. Since then, sales revenues have grown by an average of 40 per cent year-on-year. In 2006, it opened the world's first dedicated premium terminal in Doha International Airport (Qatar) with a spa, jacuzzi, fine dining, meeting rooms and duty-free shopping. It entered the North American market in 2007 and has developed relationships with nine other airlines allowing its loyalty programme members to redeem their airmiles with Lufthansa, Middle East Airlines, All Nippon Airways, Kingfisher Airlines, US Airways, Asiana Airlines, United Airlines, bmi and Virgin Atlantic. In 2008, it had 62 aircraft, with a further 183 on order, and served 83 destinations across Europe, Middle East, Africa, India and Asia. It competes with Emirates by offering discount fares and attractive packages on routes all over the world, but in particular between UAE and South Africa.

Another emerging competitor is Etihad Airways owned by the Abu Dhabi government based in the UAE. It started in 2003 offering direct flights from Abu Dhabi to Bangkok and has since become the fastest growing airline in the history of commercial aviation flying to 45 destinations in the Middle East, Europe, North America, Africa, Asia and Australia. In 2008, it opened its 855 square metre business-class lounge at Abu Dhabi airport and upgraded its service to include a limousine to and from the airport, in-flight massages and 'on demand' à la carte dining either before or during a flight. It plans to grow the number of large aircraft it owns from 29 to 37 in the next three years. At the same time it plans to triple its number of smaller aircraft seating only 140 passengers to 12, thus allowing it focus on growing premium sales to destinations in the Gulf and Indian subcontinent.

The future

Emirates has managed to increase sales year-on-year by introducing new routes or increasing the number of flights and the size of aircraft to existing destinations.

Figure 8 **(continued)**

American perceptions of Dubai are now of a safe Middle Eastern city and it has raised its profile by sponsoring a variety of sports like golf and horse racing, and exclusive sports teams such as Chelsea, Arsenal, Milan and Saint Germain. High investment in new aircraft fitted with special interiors has allowed it to offer the fastest flights from the Middle East to New York with high levels of service and grand introductory offers. It has chosen to ignore the growth possibilities of takeovers, mergers or alliances believing that these only create problems. Instead its strategy is to keep inventing itself and make Dubai one of the world's largest hubs for scheduled flights. Emirates is now responsible for 40 per cent of all flights in and out of Dubai International Airport and wishes to increase this to 70 per cent by 2010. The question is can it keep growing without compromising its reputation for quality?

and 70 per cent managed their bookings before flying. Almost 250 self-service check-in desks are also now available across 43 airports and agreements are in place with the airlines in its alliance (see Figure 7) to move to 100 per cent eTicket in 2009.

Significant improvements were being made and customers were starting to respond well, but then Heathrow Terminal 5 opened. This new terminal was meant to be the jewel in BA's crown offering smoother check ins, fewer queues, less waiting around, a huge range of eating, drinking and relaxing options and the world's largest complex of premium passenger lounges.

Despite three years planning and more than $600 million investment, during the first few months of opening passengers experienced long delays and baggage often didn't arrive at its destination. What was meant to be a great success turned out to be a huge disaster and tarnished BA's reputation. Even loyal customers were forced to look to their competitors for alternatives.

THE FUTURE

British Airways has worked hard to improve the operational performance and customer experience at Heathrow Terminal 5. They have started introducing their first new long haul aircraft since 2001, which are substantially quieter, greener and more efficient than before. They have set their sights on becoming the world's leading global premium airline, which

seems like a risky strategy when premium industry sales fell by 19 per cent last year. In line with this strategy, they are starting to roll out their new First Cabin along with lounge upgrades in line with those at Terminal 5. Heathrow is still their most critical hub where they own over 40 per cent of its available landing slots. However, the decision by the new UK government not to build a third runway means they need to keep looking elsewhere. As a result, they launched a 100-seat business-class-only flight in October 2009 from London City airport to New York, but many analysts have argued that it is still too soon to know if this will be a success and that controlling and reducing costs will also be critical given the global economic slowdown, high competition and increasing oil prices.

Questions

1. How has British Airways responded to increasing competitive pressure in the business class market?

2. Outline BA's service delivery system for business class passengers.

3. How well does this meet the needs of business class customers?

4. How is Ryanair's (as a low cost airline) approach to carrying passengers different to BA's approach?

Lecturers: visit www.palgrave.com/business/ hillom3e for teaching guidelines for this case study

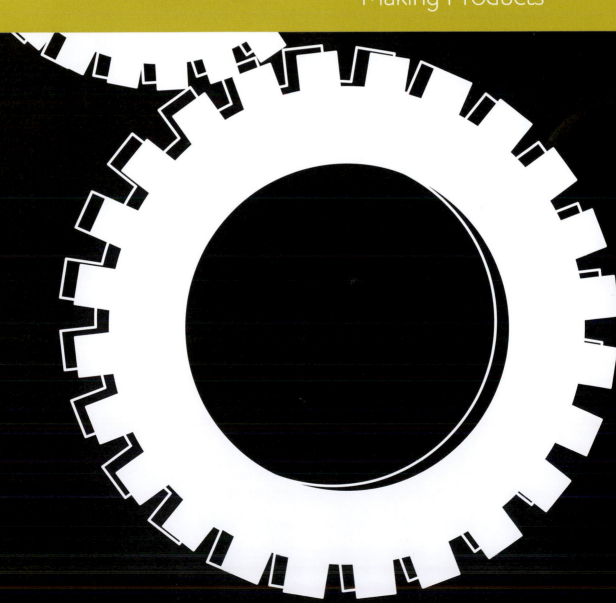

After completing this chapter, you should be able to:

- Recognize both the technical and business requirements when making products

- Describe the choice of manufacturing process decision and how it is influenced by the volume of demand

- Define the different manufacturing processes – project, jobbing, batch, line and continuous processing

- Identify the difference between categories of product and types of manufacturing process

- Appreciate the key business implications of the types of manufacturing processes

- Explain why hybrids, such as cells, may be introduced

- Recognize the use of product profiling, be able to identify its purpose as part of an operation's strategy development and know how to draw a profile to illustrate different business situations

What is the role of designing manufacturing processes?

- Operations is responsible for making the products companies sell

- Matching manufacturing process design to both the product characteristics (the technical fit) and the market characteristics (the business fit) is a key task

- This includes the volumes and the order-winners and qualifiers of the market(s) into which it is sold

Why are manufacturing process design decisions important?

- The fundamental task in a manufacturing company is to sell products and then to make them in line with agreed profit margins and the needs of customers

- However, as markets change and products go through their respective life cycles, the mix and relative importance of the relevant order-winners and qualifiers will change

- Monitoring such changes and realigning the process design accordingly is essential to meet profit targets while retaining and growing market share

How does manufacturing process design impact business performance?

- Operations has a key strategic role in that it needs to support a company's markets in terms of a range of competitive factors such as low cost where price is an order-winner, on-time delivery, quality conformance (making products to specification) and short operation lead-times

- Different choices of process bring with them different trade-offs such as process costs, inventory levels and speed of response

- Matching these trade-offs to market needs will impact business performance

What are the key issues to consider when designing manufacturing processes?

- Processes need to meet both the technical requirements and market characteristics of the products a company sells

- The different sets of trade-offs associated with alternative processes need to be explained and taken into account when making these key investment decisions.

- Companies typically wish to invest in a manufacturing process just the once

- However, as a manufacturing process has to support a product through the changing characteristics (such as volumes and order-winners and qualifiers of its life cycle), operations needs to recognize and then manage the trade-offs that result

- The use of words such as flexible and agile need to be made with care as they embrace a range of meanings and, therefore, can be misleading

- To improve the level of fit between the characteristics of their existing processes and the needs of their markets, companies turn to hybrid alternatives (such as cells) to better align the revised characteristics that hybrids bring and the market requirements that need to be provided

Introduction

The last chapter looked at the operations management tasks when delivering services, and this chapter does the same for making products. First, we'll look at the factors involved in this task, including product categories (from special to mass products), the complexity of a product and the volumes involved. We'll then go on to define the different types of process (from project through to continuous processing) before looking at a number of hybrids that mix two of the other process types.

Factors affecting the design of the manufacturing process

Manufacturing companies sell products, and operations is responsible for making them. A key decision for the operations function in executing this task is selecting the appropriate manufacturing process for the product (the technical fit) while at the same time meeting the order-winners and qualifiers of the market into which it is sold (the business fit). These two factors are interlinked as the choice of manufacturing process will directly influence how well order-winners and qualifiers such as quality conformance, price, delivery speed and on-time delivery are provided.

The manufacturing process is the method of transformation or conversion (refer back to Figure 1.2) of inputs (materials, people skills, processes, and so on) into outputs (the products). As highlighted above, the design of this process will need to cover two related but distinct dimensions.

1. The *technical requirement* comprises the technical steps that need to take place in order to transform the inputs into products. For example, packaging for food products will need to be produced by taking card or paper and printing this on flexographic machines and then cut to size using slitting machines. Plastic containers, on the other hand, need to be produced by loading the appropriate tooling (a mould designed to provide the shape and detail of the product) onto a machine and then injecting material under pressure to fill the cavity within the mould – a process known as injection moulding.

2. The *business requirement* involves deciding on the appropriate manufacturing process to meet the requirements of both customers and the market, for example which printing and slitting machines and which injection moulding machines would best suit the volumes, order-winners and qualifiers for food packaging and plastic containers sold to customers, respectively.

> **EXECUTIVE INSIGHT**
>
> Designing the manufacturing process to make products needs to meet both the technical requirement and the business requirement of those products.

Categories of product

When manufacturing a product, the starting point is to determine the steps involved in making the product and the order these steps should follow. However, the type of product to be made will itself affect the design of the manufacturing process. For example, the process of making a Formula One racing car will differ from the process of making a high-volume line of cars such as the Ford Focus. Although both are cars, the associated volumes, range of colours and options and other market factors require a different response in terms of the manufacturing process. Figure 6.1 divides products into three categories, which reflect some of the key differences to be taken into account. Let's look at how some of these factors affect the manufacturing process.

Product complexity

As you might imagine, the complexity of a product can vary dramatically. A plastic screw top for a soft drinks bottle is much simpler to make than a decorated coffee mug, and a jet engine is a much more complex product to make than a coffee mug. In fact, the number of steps to make the Rolls-Royce Trent 700 and 1000 engines for the Airbus 330 and Boeing 787 passenger aircraft respectively, runs into hundreds in each case. As the product complexity increases, the number of steps and different processes involved will also increase, and this will have an impact on the process design.

Volumes

Figure 6.1 shows the important relationship between the three categories of product and the volume of items to be produced. As you will see from the list of process types below, this factor is central to the choice of process design.

Types of manufacturing process

There are five classic manufacturing process designs (project, jobbing, batch, line and continuous processing), together with a number of hybrids (processes that are a mixture of two of the classic process types). This section explains these classic processes and provides examples to illustrate the differences between them.

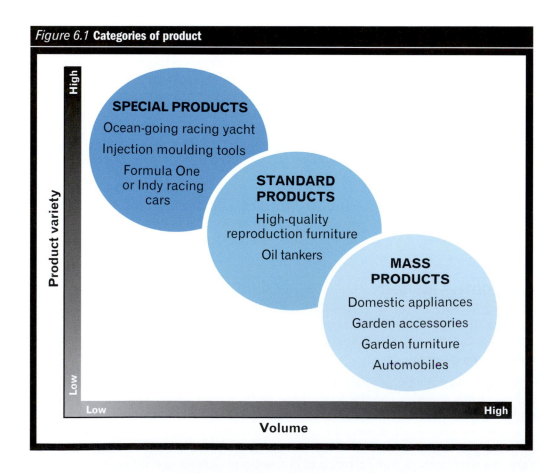

Figure 6.1 Categories of product

SPECIAL PRODUCTS
Ocean-going racing yacht
Injection moulding tools
Formula One or Indy racing cars

STANDARD PRODUCTS
High-quality reproduction furniture
Oil tankers

MASS PRODUCTS
Domestic appliances
Garden accessories
Garden furniture
Automobiles

Product variety — High / Low

Volume — Low / High

Project process

Organizations selling large-scale, complex products that cannot be physically moved once completed will normally provide them using a **project process**. Examples include civil engineering contracts to build reservoir dams, housing, roads, tunnels and bridges. It can involve the provision of a unique product (for example, the Sydney Opera House or the Gotthard Base Tunnel, a 57 km rail tunnel in Switzerland due to be opened in 2016), or a standard product such as estate housing. The former examples are made to unique, specific requirements, while the latter are of a standard design with limited options. But, in each instance, the resource inputs will be taken to the place where the product is to be built.

If you reflect on these examples, you will probably be able to envisage what the process looks like. All the activities, including support functions, will normally be controlled by a total system for the duration of the project and under the direction of a coordinating team. Similarly, resources will be allocated for the duration of the project and these, like the supporting functions, will be reallocated once their part of the task is completed or at the end of the project. The operations manager's challenge, then, is one of coordinating a large number of interrelated activities and resources so as to achieve the customer's requirements while minimizing costs throughout the process.

When a product has to be made on site, the choice of using a project process is forced upon an organization. This process incurs costs and, as resources need to be moved to and from the job as it progresses, is, therefore, not an efficient way of working. Because of this, companies try to produce as much as possible of the product off site and then transport these parts to the site. For example, concrete sections and timber framing for buildings will be made off site and assembled or arranged on site as required. Overall, the improved process efficiency of making components off site outweighs the additional transportation costs of getting the parts to the site. Figure 6.2 summarizes the main points here.

> **Project process –** resources to make the product are brought to the site, allocated for the duration of the project and then reallocated once their part of the task is complete or at the end of the job.

Figure 6.2 **Project process – key characteristics**	
Products	Made or provided on site as they are too large or too difficult to move after completion. Examples include building reservoir dams, tunnels, roads, bridges and houses
Process	Resources to make the product are brought to the site, allocated for the duration of the project and then reallocated once their part of the task is complete or at the end of the job

Jobbing process

If products are transportable, it is more efficient for companies to use another process to make them. The **jobbing process** is designed to meet the one-off (that is, unique) requirements of customers where the product involved is of an individual nature and tends to be of a smaller size (and, therefore, transportable) than that provided by a project process. Product examples include a purpose-built piece of equipment (for example, injection moulding tools), handmade, built-in furniture to meet specified customer requirements, a customer-designed and specified control unit, and hand-crafted shoes and clothing. A jobbing process is where the person making the product interprets the design and specification of the job, applying high-level skills in the conversion process.

> **Jobbing process –** one person or a small group of skilled people do everything, including interpreting the product specification, clarifying issues with the customer and ensuring that what is made meets the specification.

Although some elements of these products may be provided on site, usually they are completed in-house and transported to the customers. The producer then typically installs and commissions the product before it is accepted by a customer.

Figure 6.3 **Jobbing process – key characteristics**	
Products	Special (that is, will not be repeated) products. Examples include the design and installation of a control system, a purpose-built piece of equipment, handmade, built-in furniture and hand-crafted shoes and clothing
Process	One person or a small group of skilled people do everything, including interpreting the product specification, clarifying issues with the customer and ensuring that what is made meets the specification

Normally, one person or a small group of skilled people will be responsible for completing all or most of the product. It is a one-off provision, which means that the product will not usually be required again in its identical form or, if it is, the demand will be very low, with either irregular or long periods between one sale and the next. Figure 6.3 summarizes the main points of this type of process.

Batch

Most organizations provide products that are deemed standard (that is, they have been provided before) rather than special (that is, unique). The repeat and higher volume nature associated with standard products signals the need to consider a different process designed to take advantage of these characteristics. A **batch process** is one alternative.

As the product has been provided before or will be provided again in the future, it makes sense to invest in the process in order to simplify and reduce costs. The level of investment that can be justified will relate to the repeat nature and total volumes involved. This investment can range from recording and establishing the best way to complete a job through to substantial investment in equipment to reduce costs.

When using a batch process, the first task is to break the job down into a number of steps. How many steps will depend, in part, on the complexity of the product involved. When a product is simple, it might be completed in one step. A more complex product will be made using several steps (known as a multi-step process), as with the example given in Figure 6.4. In a batch process, each step or operation (that together make up the whole product) is completed separately, by different people/equipment and normally in a different part of the process. The purpose of splitting the task into smaller operations is a form of investment in itself, and is one way to help undertake the task more efficiently and to introduce the potential for specialization.

The following explains how a batch process works. A product would first be split into an appropriate number of steps or operations and the decision taken on how best to complete each of these. The order quantity to be produced (which may reflect the size of a customer's order, operations rules concerning the quantity to be produced at any time or forecast sales projections) would then go to the process where the first operation is to be completed. The appropriate process is set up to undertake the first step or operation and the whole order quantity is completed. In this way, each process is only set up once per order quantity. This minimizes the amount of lost capacity due to set-ups/changeovers. With step 1 completed, the whole order quantity then moves on to the next process in which step 2 will be completed. The order quantity would often wait for this process to become available, as typically there are other products being, or waiting to be, completed. When available, this process is set up to complete step 2 of the given product

Batch process – having broken down the products into different operations, the quantity to be produced is taken to process where the first operation is to be undertaken. The process is made ready/set up and the whole order quantity is completed. The part-made product(s) typically goes into work-in-progress inventory, awaiting the next step in the process.

and the whole order quantity is processed. Meanwhile, the process needed to complete step 1 is now available to be reset to complete a given operation on another product. Thus, a product goes from process to process until all the steps or operations necessary to complete the job have been undertaken.

The key features that distinguish batch processes are:

- The volumes for a particular product are not sufficient to justify dedicating processes to this product. If they were sufficient, another process (such as line) would be the appropriate choice. As a result, batch processes are designed to be used and reused by different products.

- To use and reuse a process it will need to be reset each time in line with the requirements of each product.

- Having set up a process, the whole of the agreed quantity is produced. The process is then available to be reset for the next product.

- As different products use some of the same processes as other products, products will often have to wait in a queue until the process is available. The outcome is part-processed products throughout the total production system (known as **work-in-progress inventory**) waiting to be processed.

Now take a look at the example given in Figure 6.4. Here, a repeat customer order is received for a particular label (say), and the details are passed to operations. The order will be scheduled to be made in line with the customer's delivery requirements. The details on the order will specify the label and the quantity required. The cylinder and existing plates for printing this label and the type and quantity of paper (in our example a large roll) will be issued to the printing area. The order will then be in a queue and, in line with the production schedule, the cylinder and plates for the job and the roll of paper will be loaded onto the designated printing machine (in our example in Figure 6.4, P2). The printing stage will be completed, and the printed roll of paper will go into an area awaiting the next stage. The part-completed material is now classed as **work-in-progress inventory**.

Work-in-progress inventory – part-finished items (services or products) in a process.

The next stage (slitting and collation) will have its own schedule of work, and the order in our example will be loaded, in line with this schedule, onto an appropriate slitting and collating machine. Here, the roll of paper will be cut or slit (depending on what is required by the customer). Again, the order will go into a work-in-progress area awaiting the packaging stage. You will have noticed from this description of a batch process that a product goes into and out of work-in-progress inventory between steps. The role of inventory here is to decouple the various processes one from the other. This allows processes to work independently of one another (that is, a process is not waiting for another process to complete its stage on a product). There will typically be one or more part-processed products from which a process can draw.

All batch processes are designed to be used and reused by a range of products, and this cumulative volume enables a company to invest in equipment in order to reduce costs. The downside of a process being used by a range of different products is that each change requires the process to be reset, known as a 'changeover', and these changeovers are costly. First, because of the skilled staff time to make the change and second, because there is a loss of output during each changeover as no products can be made on the machine in question. Figure 6.5 summarizes the main points of this type of process.

Line process

If volumes are sufficiently high, the company can justify investing in a process dedicated to the needs of a given range of products. As with batch processing, the product is split into a number of steps and the process is arranged to complete these, step after step

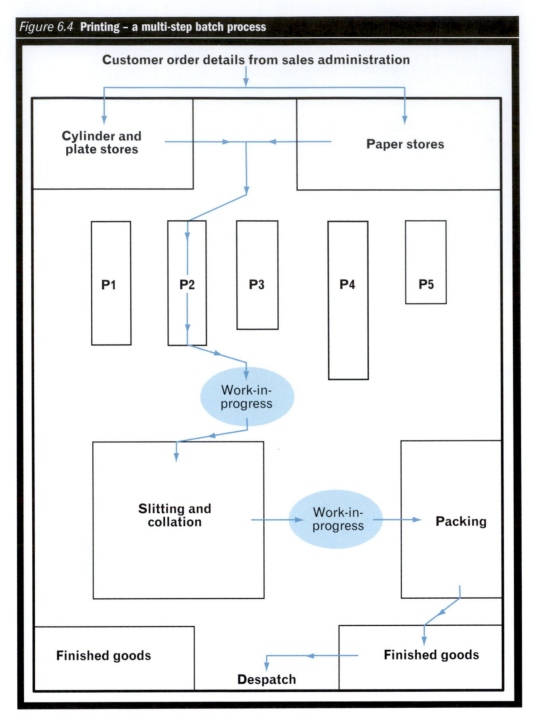

Figure 6.4 Printing – a multi-step batch process

Customer order details from sales administration

Cylinder and plate stores

Paper stores

P1   P2   P3   P4   P5

Work-in-progress

Slitting and collation

Work-in-progress

Packing

Finished goods

Despatch

Finished goods

Note: 1. The 'P' in P1 to P5 is an abbreviation for printing machine.
2. (⟶) Movement of a typical order.

and in a **line**, hence the name. Products are then processed, with each product passing through the same sequence of operations. The result is that operation 1 is completed on the first product, which goes immediately to operation 2. Meanwhile, operation 1 is being completed on the next product and so on. The line has also been designed to cope with any item within a given range and, therefore, an essential characteristic of line is that, in order to produce another product within the given range, the process does not have to be stopped and reset; that is, there are no set-ups. Examples include the production of domestic appliances and motor vehicles. Figure 6.6 provides a summary of the key characteristics of a line process, while Figure 6.8 shows some of the steps on the Honda Civic assembly line.

Line process – the making of products is separated into steps. The line process is then designed around a series of sequential processes through which all items pass.

Continuous
processing –
materials are
processed through
successive stages,
with automatic
transfer of the
products from
stage to stage. The
costs of stopping
and restarting are
typically so high that
the process is not
stopped – hence the
name continuous
processing

Figure 6.5	**Batch process – key characteristics**
Products	Standard, repeat products, the volume demand for which justifies the process investment. Examples include machined parts, injection moulding and printing
Process	Having broken down the products into different steps, the order quantity to be made is taken to the process where the first operation is to be undertaken. The process is made ready/set up, and the whole order quantity is completed. The part-made product typically goes into work-in-progress inventory awaiting the next process, which will complete the second step. When available, that process is made ready, the order quantity is processed and so on until the whole product is completed

Figure 6.6	**Line process – key characteristics**
Products	Standard, repeat, high-volume (mass) products. Examples include motor vehicles and domestic appliances. It is not found in many manufacturing sectors today as the volumes required to justify the investment are not typical of current markets
Process	Products are separated into different steps. These are met by a series of sequential processes through which all items in a selected range pass. As far as the process is concerned, all the products are the same and, therefore, the line does not have to be stopped and reset between one product and the next. However, the line can only cope with the predetermined range for which the process has been designed. Widening the existing range would require additional (often substantial) investment

Continuous processing

With **continuous processing**, one or several basic materials are processed through successive stages and refined into one or more products (for example, petrochemicals). Unlike a line process, the costs of stopping and starting up at the end of a working day are very high (often prohibitive) so the process will have been designed to run all day every day with minimum shutdowns for tasks such as major maintenance work. Materials are transferred automatically from one part of the process to the next, with the staff tasks being predominantly ones of system monitoring. Closing down and restarting such a plant would take several days, due to the complex process and safety requirements involved. Figure 6.7 provides a summary of the key characteristics.

Figure 6.7	**Continuous processing – key characteristics**
Products	Standard, very high-volume (mass) products. Examples include oil refining and some petrochemicals
Process	Materials are processed through successive steps, with automatic transfer of the product from step to step. The costs of stopping and restarting are typically so high that the process is not stopped, hence the name – continuous processing

Designing the manufacturing process

Figure 6.9 summarizes the different types of manufacturing process, including the category of product to which they are most suited (look back at Figure 6.1 for an overview of product categories). You will see that the transition from special through to mass products given in Figure 6.1 corresponds, in general, to the type of process used. We'll now explore how the manufacturing process is designed and tailored to the type and volume of the product to be produced.

Figure 6.8 Different stages on the Honda Civic assembly line

Source: © 2009 Honda of The UK Manufacturing Limited.

1. *Project for special and standard products* As shown in Figure 6.9, both special and standard products can be made using a project process. For example, a new estate of 120 houses comprising six designs would, for the builder, be a standard product – that is, the house specifications would be known, the method of build would be decided ahead of time, and any possible options for the six basic designs would be fixed. However, the houses would need to be built on site as they could not be moved. On the other hand, a large country house built to a unique design would, for the builder, be a special product, and it would again need to be built on site.

2. *Project and continuous processing are specific to certain product types* Typically, a project process would be used only when a product has to be built on site. Setting up and dismantling a site, and moving equipment and people to and from a site, increases costs and makes the management task more difficult compared with making a product in-house. As a consequence, a project process is typically used only where there is no other option as the product has to be made on site.

   Similarly, the use of continuous processing is limited. The products best suited to this process would be high volume, with the physical characteristics that would allow them to be moved from step to step in the process using pipework, such as in the refining of oil and the production of petrochemicals.

   So, the appropriate use of a project process and continuous processing is restricted (as shown in Figure 6.10), and most organizations choose from jobbing, batch and line processes for their business needs.

3. *Combinations of processes* Companies often use more than one process type to meet the overall needs of their business. The reason is that different processes best meet the different needs of a particular product or part of a product. For example, building the 120 new houses we discussed earlier would use a combination of processes:
   * *Project* to meet the overall requirements of bringing resources to and from the site, with one person having the overall management responsibility for undertaking this task to ensure the effective use of resources and to meet the cost budgets involved.
   * *Batch* would typically be used to meet several phases of the work. For example, once the footings had been completed on a number of houses, the concreting of the ground floor areas for these homes would be completed one after the other. Other phases in the building of several houses would similarly be completed one after another (for example, roofing, glazing, electrics, plastering, bathroom fitting and kitchen installation). In this way, a builder would take advantage of the increased volume associated with completing the same phase on several houses one after the other, thus looking to reduce costs and make the management task easier. So all roofing tiles for several houses would be delivered to the site at the same time, as would the materials for the glazing, electrics and other phases. In addition, contractors to complete each phase would be less costly as they would have several consecutive days (even weeks) of work, which would, in turn, reduce their costs.
   * *Jobbing* Where specific alterations or additions to a standard design are requested and agreed, they will be completed using jobbing as the appropriate process. Here, skilled staff such as bricklayers and joiners would receive drawings, interpret these and be fully responsible for fulfilling the specification(s) and checking the results.

4. *Jobbing, batch and line* These are the processes from which most companies choose, and again they often select more than one to best meet their needs, as illustrated in Figure 6.11.

   This shows that companies typically make components or parts in batch processes, while using a line process to assemble products. For example, the body panels for a Honda Civic will be made on a press. This will be set to make the left body panel, stopped and reset to make the right body panel, and so on. However, Honda uses a line process to assemble and test cars.

'**Organizations** must clearly understand **customer** needs to **make** products effectively'

Figure 6.9 **Manufacturing processes and their relationship to product categories**			
Process type	**Product**		**Process description**
	Category	**Examples**	
Project	Special	• Sydney Opera House • Øresund bridge connecting Denmark and Sweden • Gotthard Base Tunnel in the Alps	Products that cannot be physically moved once completed use a project process. Here resources (materials, equipment and people) are brought to the site where the product is to be built. These resources are allocated for the duration of the job and will be reallocated once their part of the task is completed or at the end of the job.
	Standard	• Estate housing • Prefabricated industrial and warehouse units	
Jobbing	Special	• Ocean-going racing yacht • Injection moulding tools • Formula One and Indy racing cars • The design and installation of a process control system	Once a product can be moved, companies will choose to make it in-house and then despatch it to the customer. Jobbing is the name of the process that is used for special (that is, unique) products that will typically not be repeated. Here, one person or a small group of skilled people will complete all of the product. Often the provider is required to install and commission the product as part of the order.
Batch	Standard ↓ Mass	• Business cards • Golf tees • Wheel rims • Packaging • Plastic bottles	The repeat and higher volume nature of standard and mass products requires a process designed to take advantage of these characteristics. Batch, line and continuous processing are the alternatives, but which one to use depends on the volumes involved. Batch can be appropriately used for low through to high (mass) volumes. As how to make the product is known, the steps involved are also known and products move from step to step until completed. Batch is chosen for standard products with volumes insufficient to dedicate processes. Thus, different products share the same processes by setting and resetting each time. Consequences of this include waiting between steps and the prioritizing of jobs using the same process.
Line	Mass	• Domestic appliances • Cans of Coca-Cola • Automobiles • Pet food • Mobile phones	Higher volumes mean that processes can be dedicated to the needs of a given range of products. Whereas in batch a process has to be reset each time a new product is to be made, in line the process does not have to stop as it has been designed to make the range of products required without being reset. The steps to make them are sequentially laid out in a line, and a product goes from step to step until completed. Although the range of products will vary, in terms of the process they can be made without stopping and resetting the line. Unlike with continuous processing below, stopping a process at the end and restarting it at the beginning of a shift, day or week is not expensive.
Continuous processing	Mass	• Petrochemicals • Oil refineries • Some chemical plants	For some products, the high volumes involved are best handled by continuous processing. In addition to high volumes, the nature of these products will need to be of a type that is transferable through piping or in liquid form. Continuous processing is similar to line in that it handles mass products without being stopped and reset. Its distinguishing feature is, however, that stopping and restarting the process is lengthy and expensive, and consequently it is designed to be run continuously, hence its name.

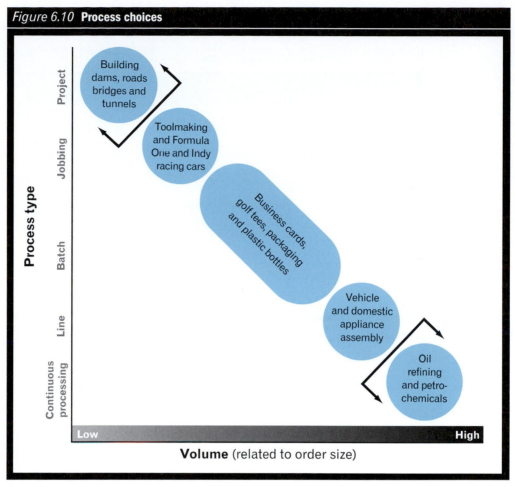

Figure 6.10 Process choices

Process type (y-axis, bottom to top): Continuous processing, Line, Batch, Jobbing, Project

Volume (x-axis): Low → High

- Building dams, roads bridges and tunnels
- Toolmaking and Formula One and Indy racing cars
- Business cards, golf tees, packaging and plastic bottles
- Vehicle and domestic appliance assembly
- Oil refining and petro-chemicals

Volume (related to order size)

Note: The elongated shape of batch reflects the range of volumes (from standard to mass) that this process covers[1].

5. *What comprises volume?* – as volume is a fundamental factor in choosing appropriate processes, it is important to clarify its meaning. When choosing an appropriate process, the following dimensions of volume are involved:

- Order quantity, that is, how many products will be made at one time on the process before it is reset. As jobbing typically involves making an order quantity of one then order quantity volumes are low. With a line process, on the other hand, the order quantity volume is high as it comprises, in effect, the total volume made during the life of the process. That is, a line process is designed and installed to make a given range of products and is not changed during the life of those products. The order quantity, in reality, is the combined volumes over that period and it is these volumes that justify the process investment. The use of batch processes involves making standard (repeat) products where the order-quantities do not justify allocating an entire process to their production, as in a line process. Batch processes, therefore, are intended to be used to make order quantities of a number of different products. To do this, the process has to be reset (changed over) between an order quantity (batch) for one product and an order quantity (batch) for another product.
- Volume is a combination of order quantity × unit time. The time taken to make the left body panel of the automobile is far less than to assemble the automobile itself, and so although the quantity of panels and cars is the same the panel is lower volume than the automobile and hence more suited to a batch process.

6. *Widening product ranges to increase volumes* – several factors in today's markets have eroded demand for individual products and with it the volume to be processed by operations. Foremost among these factors is the trend to offer greater variety as one way to increase sales. As a result companies have had to rethink process configurations,

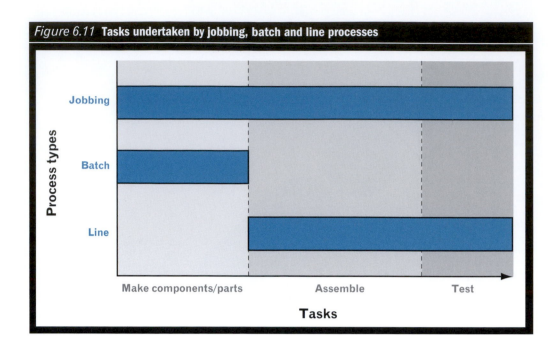

Figure 6.11 Tasks undertaken by jobbing, batch and line processes

both in terms of the overall capacity (how many products in total a facility can produce) and the range of products that a process can make (the produce range dimension of flexibility). A classic example of the impact of this need to rethink process capability is automobile assembly, as shown in Case 6.1.

7. *Process flexibility* One recent trend is to access and seek to improve the 'flexibility' and 'agility' of a manufacturing process. Although these terms can be useful, they are often employed in too general a way, without taking into account their many different meanings. It is important to understand that a manufacturing process can be flexible in a variety of different ways. Each type of flexibility has its own strategic relevance (that is, provides a different market advantage) and will determine where investment is focused. When using these words it is most important to identify which aspect of flexibility or agility is being put forward. In that way, the discussion will have the level of clarity essential to agreed outcomes. Achieving an improvement in any of the following areas will result in more investment, so knowing the costs and benefits of each needs to form part of the decision of where and how to improve flexibility.

- *Introduction of new products* The flexibility of the operations process in terms of handling the introduction of new products is vital to the long-term success of any business, as operations is one of the functions that plays a key role in this task.
- *Handling a range of products* Most, if not all, companies produce a range of products and product options. Even Ford with its Model T car and 'any colour as long as it's black' approach of the 1920s was soon replaced by General Motors and its willingness to provide choice. The process flexibility to handle variety is, in most markets, a key factor in the successful growth of a business as it reflects the nature of today's demand.
- *Handling a range of volumes* As explained earlier, the level of volume is typically not high enough to justify dedicating processes to a given range of products. For this reason, batch is the most commonly used process as it is designed to be used and reused by a range of products. One key feature that results is the ease (that is, how long it takes to change a process from making one product to making another product) with which a process can cope with different levels of volume. The volume requirements of products will differ not only from one to the next, but also over time. How quickly a process can be changed from making one product to another will directly affect the loss of potential output while the process change is taking place. Hence, the shorter the changeovers, the more flexible the process is regarding this dimension.

- *Meeting demand peaks* If the demand for a product is seasonal, having the flexibility to ramp up the manufacturing process in order to cope with sudden increases in demand is vital to the success of such a business.

The key factors then in managing the need for flexibility are to:
- Specify what type of flexibility is required – this brings clarity to an analysis and prevents confusion in communicating within a business
- Identify where the investment needs to be made – this helps to ensure that the investment is appropriate to what is needed and that unnecessary investment is kept to a minimum.

8. *The use of batch to best meet the requirements of most companies* As explained in points 2 and 4, for most companies the choice is between jobbing, batch and line and, of the three, batch is the most commonly used process. The reason is the nature of today's markets. Special products (using jobbing) and mass products (using line) are not commonplace. Demand for specials is limited, while the increasing level of difference required in today's markets has eroded volumes. For these reasons a batch process is the most suitable as invariably companies do not make standard products with the levels of volume that would justify investing in a line process. Instead, companies invest in batch processes that can be used and reused by a range of products. In this way, companies are able to make a range of products whose volumes vary.

Finally, it is useful here to explain that as the process is stopped and reset for each different product, the use of the process capacity is categorized in three ways:
- *Unproductive time* – when the utilization of process capacity is unproductive. A classic example of this category is a machine breakdown.
- *Non-saleable productive time* – while process capacity is being used in a productive way, the outcome is non-saleable. Examples here include making samples and resetting the process for the next product (change orders). The time spent on samples is a productive use of the resource but the output cannot be sold. Similarly, setting up a process for another product is productive (it has to be done) but again the outcome does not result in saleable output.
- *Saleable productive time* – when a process makes completed products that will be sold to customers.

The non-saleable productive time element of this mix of outputs is a characteristic of batch as the process will need to be reset for each different product. Keeping the ratio between nonsaleable and saleable productive time in balance is most important for a business. If the nonsaleable percentage increases, saleable output goes down which will have an adverse effect on sales and profits. Now take a look at Case 6.2 which illustrates several of these issues.

Implications of process design

Investing in the means to make products takes many forms. It can range from investment in process equipment through to the task of determining how best to make a product and preparing the necessary process details, procedures to follow and supporting information. But no matter what form the investment takes, switching the making of a product from one type of process to another will invariably be costly. For this reason, when a product is introduced companies choose the process they judge best, with the intention of not changing their decision and thus avoiding future additional investment.

No one is ever likely to build another car plant like Volkswagen's Wolfsburg plant in Lower Saxony, Germany (which is capable of producing 750,000 vehicles a year) or another Toyota city, near Nagoya in Japan. Most new factories are now built to make around 200,000 cars a year, and some believe that many future plants could be a quarter of this current size.

To create the volume required to justify these new plants, the process is designed to handle a wider product range. For example, Ford's truck assembly plant at Rouge in Dearborn, Detroit (which was opened in 2004) makes light trucks and sport utility vehicles and can handle three basic platforms (the chassis and underpinnings of a vehicle) and nine different model varia-tions built on these. The mix scheduled to be made will depend on which models are most in demand.

www.volkswagen.de
www.toyota.com
www.ford.com

Questions

1. The process type used at Ford's assembly plant at Rouge is line. Why?

2. Why would you classify the Rouge plant as inflexible (see Figure 6.12)?

Lecturers: visit www.palgrave.com/business/hillom3e for teaching guidelines for this case study

CASE 6.2 MANUFACTURING PROCESSES AT MEINDORF GMBH

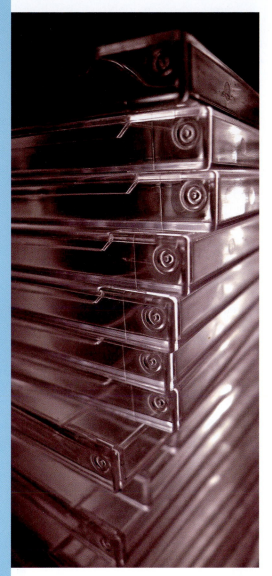

Meindorf GmbH is part of a large German cable company that manufactures compounds (the material used to cover the copper or aluminum conduit) to meet inter-group and external demand. It has four process units that heat and mix the various fillers and oils that make up a range of standard product specifications. Order sizes from customers range from 1 to 40 tonnes. To meet a customer order typically requires several mixings and the four process units are scheduled as follows:

- **Process Unit 1** produces natural and coloured elastomers

- **Process Unit 2** manufactures the whole range of thermoplastics

- **Process Unit 3** makes black elastomers

- **Process Unit 4** produces small order quantities of thermoplastics and experimental compounds for the R&D department. This unit is not fully utilized.

On leaving these process units, the compounds move on to the next stage that involves shaping, cutting and packaging.

The mixing stage lasts 8–14 minutes and the number of mixes required to meet a customer order are completed one after the other. At the end of a run the process units are changed to make the next product.

Colour and compound changeovers take 40–120 minutes. The most difficult colour changes involve moving from a dark to a lighter colour. In order to minimize changeovers, similar colours and similar compounds are run together wherever possible and in line with customer schedules. Typically, changeovers for Process Unit 2 account for 20 per cent of available time and those for Process Units 1 and 3 each account about 10 per cent of available time.

Delivery reliability is an order-losing sensitive qualifier for most customers and the trend towards smaller customer orders is giving concern to operations in terms of meeting schedules.

Questions

1. Which process type (project, jobbing, batch, line or continuous processing) is used to heat and mix compounds in this plant?

2. Give reasons for the different changeover levels (10, 20 and 10 per cent respectively of available time) for Process Units 1, 2 and 3.

3. Why are the reducing size of order quantities of concern to operations?

Lecturers: visit www.palgrave.com/business/hillom3e for teaching guidelines for this case study

Figure 6.12 illustrates and reinforces the point that there is not typically a transition from one process to another. Organizations do not, for instance, choose project and later replace it with jobbing; similarly, companies rarely move from jobbing to batch and then line. However, as Figure 6.12 illustrates, some marginal transitions may take place between jobbing and low-volume batch, low-volume batch and higher volume batch, and high-volume batch and line, but these are unusual and not the norm. You will notice in Figure 6.12 (as earlier in Figure 6.10) that batch is depicted as an elongated shape, highlighting the fact that batch covers a wide range of volumes and other factors, as the next section explains.

As implied throughout the chapter, each process is associated with different characteristics and alternative sets of trade-offs (things a process can do well or less well). To illustrate these, Figure 6.13 provides an overview of some of the factors involved, and recognizing and understanding these forms part of the decision on which process to buy. You will note in Figure 6.13 that the format used to reflect the elongated shape depicting batch in Figure 6.12 is that of an arrow. In this way, the wide range of volumes and other characteristics that the batch process covers is again appropriately depicted. Finally, the format of Figure 6.13 also reflects the specific nature of the type of businesses in which project and continuous processing would be used.

Some comments on Figure 6.13 will help to explain the trade-off alternatives and different characteristics that go hand-in-hand with each type of manufacturing process. The first part of the table illustrates the fact that as the choice moves to the right, high volumes justify more dedicated processes which, by their nature, are less flexible and less able to cope with the introduction of new products or changes to existing products. In essence, it is the process that makes the product here which, in turn, requires a high level of prior

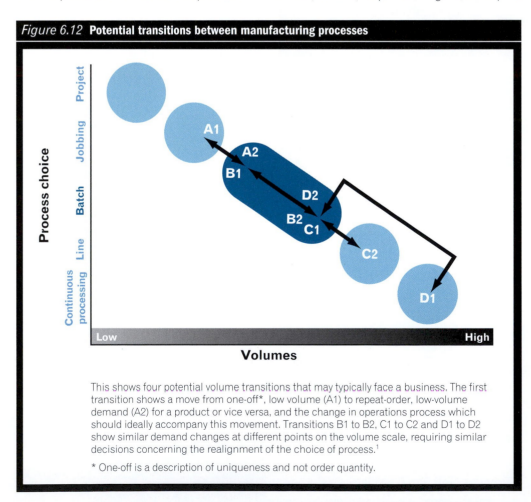

Figure 6.12 Potential transitions between manufacturing processes

This shows four potential volume transitions that may typically face a business. The first transition shows a move from one-off*, low volume (A1) to repeat-order, low-volume demand (A2) for a product or vice versa, and the change in operations process which should ideally accompany this movement. Transitions B1 to B2, C1 to C2 and D1 to D2 show similar demand changes at different points on the volume scale, requiring similar decisions concerning the realignment of the choice of process.[1]

* One-off is a description of uniqueness and not order quantity.

knowledge in order to design and develop it. One outcome is that process utilization becomes more important than the utilization of staff as the process is, in fact, the key resource.

You will note that three of the last four dimensions in Figure 6.13 do not conform to the arrow principle. Regarding waiting time, there can be some occasions in the project process when one group of skilled people has to wait for another aspect of the job to be completed. But in all other processes, except for batch, the waiting time between one part of the system and the next tends to be low. In jobbing, the skilled person is always moving the job forward, whereas with line and continuous processing, the product moves automatically from one part of the system to the next. In batch, on the other hand, because products use the same processes, priorities need to be determined and, as a consequence, some products will have to wait.

This need to prioritize means that day-to-day scheduling is most complex in batch. Once materials are brought to a line or continuous process, on the other hand, the scheduling of products through the system is straightforward. With jobbing, the person making the product schedules the work, but the unknown (as all products are new) brings with it a level of complexity. In project, the building of a product on site, the uncertainty of resource and material supply, together with potential problems of weather, leads to scheduling difficulties.

Finally, process layout is functionally based in both jobbing and batch processes, and is product-based in line and continuous processing.

Now test your understanding of these insights and issues by analyzing Case 6.3.

Hybrid processes

In many markets, manufacturing capacity is growing faster than demand. The excess capacity that has resulted will continue as newer industrial nations such as China and India keep growing. One outcome is that the emerging competition is driving product offerings to become more different, and companies have responded by developing processes to reflect these changing demands. For example, line processes are now often developed to produce a relatively wide range of products, with a marked increase in the level of investment necessary to make this increased variety. In addition to investing directly in the process itself, companies may also choose to rearrange or use existing processes in a different way in order to provide the required set of trade-offs. Processes that are redesigned or created by mixing original processes are known as **hybrid processes**.

Cells

Figure 6.13 illustrated how the trade-offs on a range of dimensions changed depending on the process chosen. Companies may seek to alter some of these trade-offs by rearranging existing processes. One such example is changing from a batch process to **cells or cellular manufacturing**.

As a company choosing batch processes will be providing standard products, the only practical alternative to a batch process is line. Companies tend to choose batch rather than line on the basis of volume: where products do not have sufficient volumes to justify dedicating processes, as in a line process, a batch process is used. As explained earlier, these processes are designed to allow products to share processes and thus make more sense of the utilization/investment equation. However, batch processes embody trade-offs, and companies may look to change some of these. Cells are a hybrid process that, although still batch in origin (as the process will still have to be stopped and reset to

FACTORS		TYPICAL
		Project
Process	nature	General purpose
	flexibility	Flexible
Level of process investment		Variable
Ability of the process to cope with	product changes	High
	new products	High
How are orders won?	typical order winners	Capability
	typical qualifiers	Price, delivery on time, quality conformance
Operations volumes		Low
Set-ups or changeovers	number	Many
	expense per	Variable
Dominant utilization		Predominantly people
Pre-knowledge of the	operations task	Variable
	material requirements	Known at tendering stage
Level of waiting time in the process		Varies
Difficulty of the day-to-day scheduling task		Complex
Process layout		Fixed position
Operations key strategic task		Respond to product & scheduling changes

CHARACTERISTICS OF MANUFACTURING PROCESS ALTERNATIVES

Jobbing	Batch	Line	Continuous processing
General purpose	→	Dedicated	Dedicated
Flexible	→	Inflexible	Inflexible
Low	→	High	Very high
High	→	Low	Nil
High	→	Low	None
Unique capability	→	Price	Price
Delivery on-time, quality conformance			Delivery on time, quality conformance
Low	→	High	Very high
Many	→	None in life-time of process	None in life-time of process
Inexpensive	→	Prohibitive	Prohibitive
People	→	Process	Process
Known but often not well-defined	→	Well-defined	Well defined
Some uncertainty	→	Well-defined	Well defined
Low	High	Low	Low
Complex	Very complex	Easy	Easy
Function	Function	Product	Product
Respond to product and schedule changes	→	Low cost	Low cost

© Radu Razvan – Fotolia.com

In Toshiba's manufacturing facility in China, workers assemble nine different word processors on the same line while on an adjacent one, 20 varieties of laptop computers are assembled. Usually they make 20 of one product and then change. Workers on the line have been trained to make each model and they are further supported by a computer display at every workstation that shows a drawing and provides detailed instructions. When the model changes, so does the display. Product life cycles of some models are measured in months, so making in small order quantities helps guard against being unable to support sales peaks and overproducing when sales fall off.

www.toshiba.com

Questions

1. What type of process does Toshiba use to manufacture its word processors and laptop computers?

2. What key operations developments have enabled the company to match process capability to its market needs?

Lecturers: visit www.palgrave.com/business/hillom3e for teaching guidelines for this case study

Figure 6.14 **Batch layout**

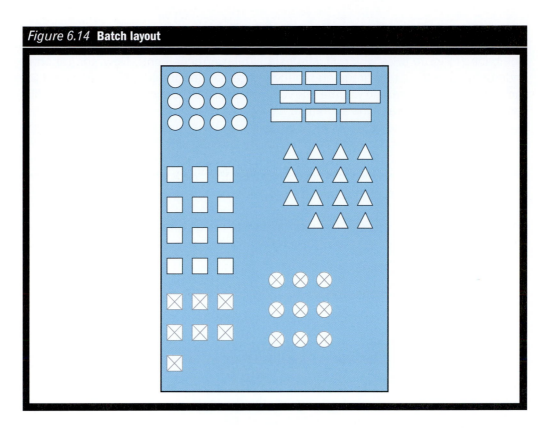

Figure 6.15 **Cellular layout**

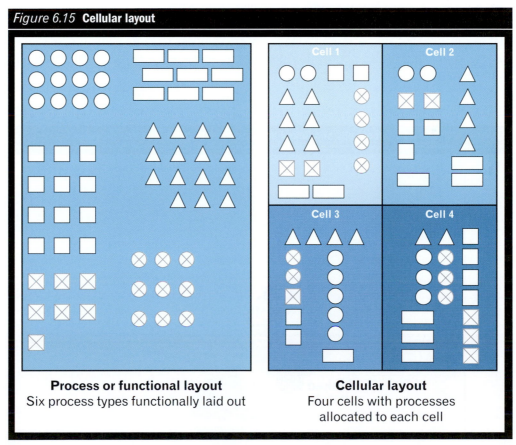

Process or functional layout
Six process types functionally laid out

Cellular layout
Four cells with processes
allocated to each cell

handle a product change), are, in fact, a mix of batch and line, and so offer changes in terms of some key variables. First let's discuss what cells are, and then we'll review the key trade-off changes that result.

Figure 6.14 shows the functional layout of a batch process (similar processes are grouped together in the same geographical area; it might also be helpful to take a look back at Figure 6.11, which illustrates a similar arrangement). Now, the rationale underpinning cells is that grouping products together and treating them as being the same leads to an increase in volume (the volumes of all the products under consideration can be added together and the aggregate viewed as a whole). This then allows processes to be allocated to these products for their sole use. What happens in cells is that the necessary processes, in terms of both capability and capacity (that is, they are able to provide the product requirements in terms of both its technical and demand dimensions) are allocated to the sole use of these products; this 'dedication' is justified by the enhanced level of volume that results (Figure 6.15).

Compared with a batch process, this rearrangement brings with it changes in certain key dimensions, for example:

• Process waiting time is reduced.

• Work-in-progress inventories are lower.

• The day-to-day scheduling of operations is made easier.

These positive changes result from the hybrid process shifting towards a line process (although still being on the batch process dimension), as shown in Figure 6.16. The production process will be laid out within a smaller physical area and handle a reduced range of products. This will, in turn, simplify the day-to-day scheduling task and enable lead-times and work-in-progress inventory to be reduced, as the waiting time between processes is more easily managed.

Just as these 'gains' come from moving the hybrid process towards a line process, cells, compared with batch, also incur certain disadvantages associated with their repositioning on the process continuum. Compared with batch, cells:

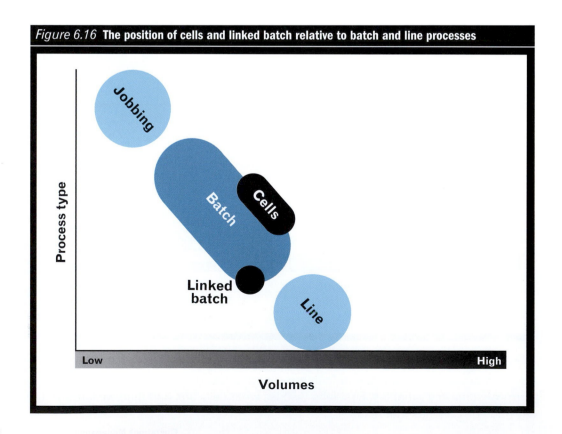

Figure 6.16 The position of cells and linked batch relative to batch and line processes

- Are less flexible

- Result in a lower utilization of equipment, which may lead to additional process capacity having to be purchased.[2]

Both these are characteristic of a line rather than a batch process.

Linked batch

Companies investing in line processes often find that, over time, the demand for the products made on a line process may decline. With spare capacity resulting from this reduced demand, companies seek to reuse the available process capacity by making other products. The outcome of this decision is that whereas originally the process would not have to be stopped and reset to accommodate a product change, now it would, as the added products fall outside the original process arrangement. The result is that the process, although it still looks like a line (with processes set out sequentially) is, in fact, a batch hybrid known as linked batch (see Figure 6.16). The key change resulting from this move from line to a hybrid batch process is the impact of set-up or changeover times now incurred to provide the revised range of products. As the stages in a linked batch process are coupled (as it was originally configured as a line process), a changeover will involve resetting all the parts of the total process before the process can begin to make the next product. In addition, the total set-up time in linked batch is often further increased as not only do all parts of the process need to be reset at the same time but there will sometimes be an interference factor during the overall changeover between parts of the process one with and another, which adds to the total changeover time.

Nagare production system

The Nagare production system was developed within the disc brake division of Sumitomo Electric. The layout is a derivation of cells and, in the same way, provides an alternative to the process layout used in batch, as illustrated in Figure 6.17. The key differences between this system and cells are:

- The sequence of steps reflects the flow of materials in making the product.

- Operators move the part from step to step and hence complete a whole product.

- Operators typically produce to a JIT system using a kanban-type arrangement (this and JIT systems are explained fully in Chapter 9).

- The quantity of products produced at any one time is relatively small.

- The Nagare production system is ideally suited to making products that are similar to one another. This helps keep the level of change involved low and hence set-up times are reduced.

Transfer lines

Where the volume demand for products is very high, further investment is justified. Transfer lines are a hybrid between line and continuous processing. The high demand leads to investments designed to reduce the manual inputs associated with a line process and move more towards a process that automatically transfers a part from one station to the next, positions it, completes the task and checks the conformance quality. Furthermore, deviations from specified tolerance levels will be registered within a process and automatic tooling adjustments will often be part of the process capability.

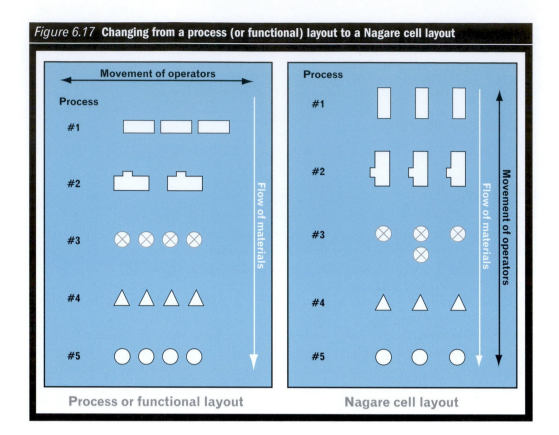

Figure 6.17 Changing from a process (or functional) layout to a Nagare cell layout

Movement of operators

Process

#1

#2

#3

#4

#5

Flow of materials

Process or functional layout

Process

#1

#2

#3

#4

#5

Movement of operators

Flow of materials

Nagare cell layout

Product profiling[3]

When companies invest in manufacturing processes, recognizing the implications for their business has to be part of the evaluation and decision. Similarly, as markets change or companies enter new markets with different competitive needs, checking whether existing processes can meet the business dimensions of these changes is part of the strategic task.

As emphasized earlier, investments in operations are large and fixed, whereas today's markets are fast-changing and becoming increasingly different rather than increasingly similar. For operations to align its capabilities to the needs of a company's markets today and tomorrow, it needs a way of assessing the current level of alignment and being alert to future changes that may weaken this essential support. Similarly, in its market-driving role, operations needs to agree with the business ahead of time those order-winners and qualifiers it has to improve in order to maintain or grow share in existing markets or enable it to successfully enter new markets.

As explained earlier, on the one hand, investments enable operations to meet the technical dimensions of the products to be provided, while on the other hand, they enable operations to meet the business dimensions (that is, the order-winners and qualifiers for which operations is solely or jointly responsible, for example delivery speed, on-time delivery and price) that comprise the other part of the market requirements. This section explains how organizations can check alignment, that is, how well market needs are matched by what operations is set up to provide.

The concept of undertaking this check is called 'product profiling'. It offers an organization the opportunity to test the current or anticipated degree of fit between the characteristics of its markets and the characteristics of its existing or proposed process and infrastructure investments. The principal purpose of this assessment is to provide a method to evaluate and, where necessary, improve the degree of fit between the way in which a company qualifies and wins orders in its markets and the ability of operations to support these criteria.

The ideal is to achieve fit. In many instances, though, companies will be unable or unwilling to provide the desired degree of fit, due to the level of investment, executive energy or timescales involved to make the necessary changes. Sound strategy concerns improving the level of consciousness an organization brings to bear on its corporate decisions. Knowing what needs to be done and implementing the necessary changes is the aim, but knowing what needs to be done while being unable to justify the change still constitutes sound strategy. Product profiling increases corporate awareness of what strategic changes need to be made and allows a conscious choice between alternatives.

> **EXECUTIVE INSIGHT**

Aligning manufacturing processes to the needs of the market is a key requirement in developing an operations strategy. Product profiling is an effective way to check the level of fit both initially and as a way to assess the impact of market changes overtime.

Procedure

Alignment involves checking how well the requirements of markets are matched by the characteristics of the operations process used to provide them. The purpose of the check is to assess the level of business fit that exists. It also serves to alert companies to future potential alignment issues that could arise as a result of current strategies in a business. Completing a check links aspects of Chapter 2 on operations strategy and Chapter 4 on product design and development to aspects of this chapter that address the design of the manufacturing process. The procedure for developing a product profile involves the following steps:

1. Select aspects (some are given in Figure 6.13) that are relevant to the business situation under review. The key here is to keep dimensions small in number so as to keep the insights sharp. Remember, this approach is a mechanism for communicating strategic issues to other parts of the business and so keeping to the point highlights the message and avoids digression.

2. Next, put down the characteristics associated with each chosen dimension (see Figure 6.13 for some illustrations). Figure 6.18 is an example of the outcome of product profiling and a glance at this will show you how to proceed.

3. Now profile the product(s) by positioning them on each of the characteristics selected. Where the circle is drawn indicates the position. The example in Figure 6.18 profiles two plants to illustrate why one was successful and the other was not. Different circles represent the two different plants as shown in the footnotes to Figure 6.18. Profiling the product and market characteristics served by both plants and also profiling the operations and investment characteristics involved is the procedure used to check alignment. Thus, these profiles show the needs of the markets under review and the capability of operations to provide these requirements. In this way it tests the fit (current or future) between market requirements and operations characteristics.

4. The resulting profiles illustrate the degree of consistency between the requirements of the market and the operations strategy to support these needs. The higher the level of consistency, the straighter the profile. Inconsistencies will result in a dogleg profile.

Product profiling, therefore, is a way of illustrating the level of fit between a company's markets and operations capabilities, in terms of current or future requirements. The lack of alignment can be caused by a strategy that moves the company in part or in total to

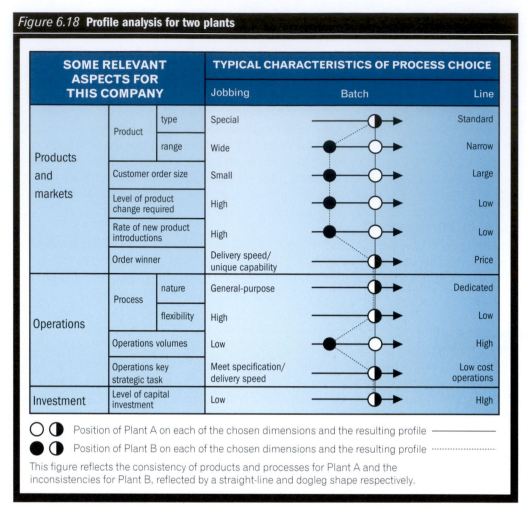

Figure 6.18 Profile analysis for two plants

SOME RELEVANT ASPECTS FOR THIS COMPANY			TYPICAL CHARACTERISTICS OF PROCESS CHOICE		
			Jobbing	Batch	Line
Products and markets	Product	type	Special		Standard
		range	Wide		Narrow
	Customer order size		Small		Large
	Level of product change required		High		Low
	Rate of new product introductions		High		Low
	Order winner		Delivery speed/ unique capability		Price
Operations	Process	nature	General-purpose		Dedicated
		flexibility	High		Low
	Operations volumes		Low		High
	Operations key strategic task		Meet specification/ delivery speed		Low cost operations
Investment	Level of capital investment		Low		High

○ ◐ Position of Plant A on each of the chosen dimensions and the resulting profile ────────

● ◐ Position of Plant B on each of the chosen dimensions and the resulting profile ┄┄┄┄┄┄┄

This figure reflects the consistency of products and processes for Plant A and the inconsistencies for Plant B, reflected by a straight-line and dogleg shape respectively.

Source: Alex Hill and Terry Hill *Manufacturing Operations Strategy*, 3rd Edition, Palgrave Macmillan, Basingstoke (2009) p. 196.

new markets and new requirements or an operations strategy that is not in line with the needs of current and/or future markets.

The story behind Figure 6.18

Faced with a decline in sales and profits, the company illustrated here undertook a major internal review of its two manufacturing plants. To provide orientation to its business, it decided to manufacture different products at its two sites. Two or three years later the number of product types handled by Plant B was eight times as many as Plant A and, as one would expect, product volume and order size differences resulted from this decision. While in Plant A, average volumes for individual products rose by 60 per cent, in Plant B they decreased by 40 per cent. To further help redress the overall decline in profits, the company also embarked on major operations developments at each plant, involving identical process investments and infrastructure changes. Figure 6.18 illustrates how these changes fitted Plant A's markets while they led to a significant mismatch for Plant B.

The procedure followed to complete Figure 6.18 is the one given in the previous section. Again, the first step is to choose the characteristics of markets and operations pertinent to the business. Next, the characteristics that reflect the change between jobbing, batch and line are described. On the one hand, the product range associated with jobbing is wide and becomes increasingly narrow as it moves through to line. On the other hand, customer order size is small in jobbing and becomes increasingly large as it moves through to line and so on. These dimensions represent the classic characteristics of the trade-offs embodied in choosing a process, as illustrated in Figure 6.13. Plant A's profile shows a straight-line relationship between the markets and the process and infrastructure provision. That is, the requirements of Plant A's markets are matched by the characteristics of its operations investments and capabilities (its operations strategy). However, Plant B has a dogleg profile because the process and infrastructure investments, although similar to those in Plant A, did not relate to the requirements of Plant B's market and hence a mismatch occurred. That is, the needs and characteristics of Plant B's markets are not matched by the characteristics of its operations investments and capabilities (its operations strategy).

When using product profiling it is important to note the following:

- As companies are often in more than one market, profiles will need to be drawn on a market-by-market basis.

- Another cause of non-alignment may be that market changes are not matched by the developments in operations necessary to support these new requirements. As changes in markets are often incremental, the impact of the aggregate change over time often goes undetected and an increasing lack of alignment is the result. Whereas in Figure 6.18 the comparison made was between two plants in the same time frame, a review of one business over time compares one time period to another. If, during this period, the strategic position of operations continues unaltered whereas market needs had changed, alignment problems would result. These reviews should form part of a forward look by organizations to detect potential mismatches, and hence avoid them.

- Product profiling is an important and constructive way to illustrate current or future alignment problems. The picture format is the key to providing this insight and must, therefore, be kept focused on the underlying issues within a business. Keeping the number of dimensions small and relevant is an essential part of ensuring clarity of presentation.

- One fundamental reason why alignment problems develop is that companies typically and understandably, wish to invest in processes just once. Propositions that companies link process investment to stages in the life cycle of products[4] are not borne out in reality.[5] Although theoretically attractive, this proposition is not followed because of associated investment costs. To invest and reinvest as volume grows would involve very high overall investment. Although companies use different processes at the R&D phase, once a product enters operations to be provided commercially, investment decisions are made on the basis of forecast volumes, with the aim of minimizing associated costs. That is, they intend and plan to invest only once unless, of course, sales grow to the point where extra capacity is needed. Any transitions, therefore, will tend to be restricted, as explained in Figure 6.12.

Making products in practice

- Operations uses process technologies to meet the needs of a company's markets.

- Operations' role is not one of being a process technology expert but one of assessing how well a process can meet current markets' requirements and as these change in the future such as:
  - The capability of a process to meet quality conformance levels
  - The ease and speed of changeovers/set-ups (the non-saleable productive elements of capacity) in relation to handling different order qualities (the saleable productive element of capacity)
  - The scope, timescales and costs of reducing changeovers/set-ups
  - The extent to which investment can shorten process lead-times.

- When deciding how best to make a product, it is essential for operations to evaluate:
  - The robustness of sales forecasts (including product life cycle projections) and the feasibility of selecting appropriate processes to meet the different, anticipated levels of demand now and in the future
  - To ascertain whether the manufacture of a product can be switched to an alternative process as it goes through its life cycle and, if not, the business consequences of a product not being aligned at a certain point in its life cycle.

- Alert the executive group to the business trade-offs associated with the choices of process that are being considered or are in place.

- Look for opportunities to rearrange process configurations (for example, cells) to better meet business requirements.

Driving business performance

The operations task to make the products it sells to customers is central to the successful performance of a business in the following ways.

Making products to release cash

Inventory in all its forms absorbs significant levels of cash. How much inventory is a decision that reflects rules within the business and the manufacturing process used in making products such as:

- Make-to-order vs make-to-stock takes into account the capability of the manufacturing process to meet short lead-times.
- Volume flexibility – how well a process can meet the varying levels of demand will directly influence the level of inventory it needs to carry both in terms of the decoupling and capacity-related roles (see Chapter 10).
- The levels of work-in-progress inventory reflect the characteristics of the manufacturing processes and the decoupling and cycle roles provided by inventory (see Chapter 10) necessary to meet the demands of a company's markets, the capacity in place and the costs inherent in the manufacturing process.

Making products to improve market support

Operations makes the products a company sells. Whereas the technical fit of a process (that is, the process can make the products sold) is recognized and built into the decision of which equipment to purchase, the choice of process also needs to reflect the volumes and order-winners and qualifiers that characterize the market and, furthermore, through their life cycles.

Making products to reduce costs

The choice of process needs to reflect product volumes and the opportunity to reduce costs such as:

- Labour costs reflected in throughput speeds

- Material costs in terms of reject levels and process losses

- Indirect costs associated with process support such as set-up times and process monitoring and refining

- Overhead costs such as maintenance and spare parts

- Volume flexibility and associated levels of inventory.

Operations makes the products that a company sells. To be competitive, products need to meet customers' needs (the design must be right) and must be made to that design (known as quality conformance, and a prime task of operations). But when customers choose to buy a product in the first place (and make a repeat purchase where that would take place), they are influenced by aspects such as variety, price and availability.

As operations fulfils most of the wide-ranging set of factors that affects sales, how it chooses to make products will have a significant impact on sales revenues and profits. The different sets of trade-offs that result from the alternative ways of making products need to be explained to the business and need to be a key factor in the decision-making procedure. However, given that demand changes over time but manufacturing processes will only change with further investment, which process is chosen needs also to reflect the life cycle of a product.

Operations, therefore, needs to provide these key business insights in the debate about markets and customers. As the provider of the products, how it makes them is a key factor in the short- and long-term success of a business.

Markets are different and they change over time. The main issue in this chapter concerns understanding markets in terms of volumes and requirements, and processes in terms of what, in relation to market support, they can do well and less well. Thus, as markets are different so will be the nature of operations support. The reality in most businesses is that this essential link between operations and market needs is not adequately provided. One source of this problem comes from the structure of organizations themselves.

When most organizations start to grow, the initial functional division that usually takes place separates operations from other functions. With further growth, procedures and systems

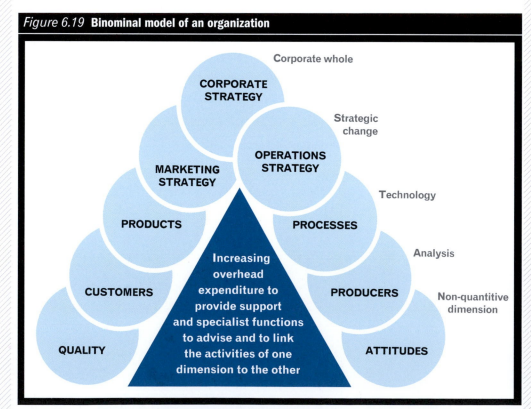

Figure 6.19 **Binominal model of an organization**

Source: Developed from N.K. Powell, 'Steps towards a definition of operations management', *Management Education and Development*, 9(3), (1979), pp.162–7.

are developed, and support and specialist functions are introduced to link the marketing dimension with the operations dimension. Figure 6.19 illustrates this development.

The task facing operations is to ensure, through its joint ownership of the links between products and processes, between customers and producers, and between quality and attitudes, that it makes its essential contribution towards the improvement of these within an organization. In many instances, operations managers have shed this major responsibility to the detriment of the operations function, their own managerial role and the business as a whole. Given the important strategic role to be provided by operations and the essential task within this of supporting agreed markets, understanding and explaining to the rest of a business the trade-offs being faced is a prerequisite in the strategy debate and its outcomes.

With organizations typically being developed on the basis of functions and specialists, the key links between products and processes and between customers and producers have been separated in their essential task of providing and selling products to customers. The task of any business is to provide products and sell them in chosen markets, but using functions and specialisms as the basic building blocks of organizations has separated the provision from the sale. The key links between products and processes and between customers and producers have been severed. As highlighted in Chapter 2, operations (as with other functions) needs to proactively close this gap. Providing the necessary insights to do this is a key role of all functions.

Summary

- A key role in operations is to determine how best to make the products an organization sells to its customers. In the context of the business, 'how best' means selecting manufacturing processes that can meet both the technical dimensions and the market needs (the order-winners and qualifiers) of its customers.

- Meeting the technical characteristics leads to certain, often predetermined, choices – commercial bread-making requires ovens of a given size, plastic mouldings need injection moulding machines and so on. While this is a key issue, alternative process technologies normally form part of the role of engineering and other technical functions. Operations must use these technologies to make products in line with the needs of a company's chosen markets.

- Operations has to choose the type(s) of manufacturing process to best meet customers' demands. This chapter has described the process choices and their associated trade-offs.

Study activities

Discussion questions
1. Select one simple (involving one or two steps) and one more complicated (three or more steps) batch process in manufacturing companies of your choice. Explain how they work.

2. What are the essential differences between the following processes:
   - Project and jobbing
   - Jobbing and batch
   - Batch and line
   - Line and continuous processing?

3. When assembling a car, there will be five tyres (four plus a spare) for each vehicle. Why is it that tyre-making uses a batch process, whereas the car itself is typically assembled using a line process?

4. Why is waiting time an integral part of a batch process design? Illustrate with two examples.

Assignments

1. Visit the website of a major petrochemical company. Find information on one of its oil refineries and explain:
   - How it handles the product range that is processed in the particular plant
   - How often the plant is shut down and why.

2. Select a business/organization (other than the examples given in this chapter) to illustrate the five types of process – project, jobbing, batch, line and continuous.

Exploring further

TED talks

Brown, T. (2008) *Creativity and play*. At the 2008 Serious Play conference, designer Tim Brown talks about the powerful relationship between creative thinking and play, with many examples you can try at home (and one that maybe you shouldn't).
www.ted.com/talks/tim_brown_on_creativity_and_play.html

Leadbeater, C. (2005) *Innovation*. In this deceptively casual talk, Charles Leadbeater weaves a tight argument that innovation isn't just for professionals anymore. Passionate amateurs, using new tools, are creating products and paradigms that companies can't.
www.ted.com/talks/charles_leadbeater_on_innovation.html

Journal articles

Holweg, M. and Pil, F.K. (2001) 'Successful build-to-order strategies start with the customer', *MIT Sloan Management Review*, **43**(1): 74–84. The article outlines a true build-to-order strategy in which managers systematically improve the value chain's flexibility in three areas: process, product and volume.

Takeuchi, H., Osono, E. and Shimizu, N. (2008) 'The contradictions that drive Toyota's success', *Harvard Business Review*, **86**(6): 96–104. Toyota Motor Corporation's unorthodox manufacturing system – the Toyota Production System (TPS) – enables it to make the best automobiles at the lowest cost and to develop new products quickly. As described in the article, TPS is a 'hard' innovation that allows the company to keep improving. But Toyota has also mastered a 'soft' innovation that relates to corporate culture: Toyota believes that efficiency alone cannot guarantee success. Some key contradictions that Toyota fosters and how other companies can learn to thrive on contradictions are discussed in this text.

Books

Ford, H. (1988) *Today and Tomorrow*. Cambridge, MA: Productivity Press. Originally published in 1926, this book outlines Henry Ford's ideas on manufacturing and the impact that these still have. Even influential Japanese ideas such as just-in-time have been influenced by Ford's ideas. Similarly, using low-cost, high-quality manufacturing to win markets inspired many Japanese companies to do the same.

Hill, A. and Hill, T. (2009) *Manufacturing Operations Strategy: Text and Cases*, 3rd edn. Basingstoke: Palgrave Macmillan. The text provides a most useful supplement to the current book by outlining an in-depth approach for developing and implementing operations strategy within manufacturing organizations.

Hill, A. and Hill, T. (2011) *Essential Operations Management*. Basingstoke: Palgrave Macmillan. The text provides a useful supplement to *Operations Management* by focusing on the essential aspects for managing operations within service and manufacturing organizations.

Hill, T. (1988) *The Strategy Quest. Releasing the Energy of Manufacturing Within a Market Driven Strategy: A Dynamic Business Story*. Available from AMD Publishing, 'Albedo', Dousland, Devon PL20 6NE, UK; email: amd@jm-abode.tiscali.co.uk; fax: +44(0) 1822 882863. This book (written as a novel) describes how an art business and manufacturing organization restructure themselves to meet the changing demands of their customers.

Notes and references

1. Steve Brown (2012) 'An interview with Terry Hill, Emeritus Fellow at the University of Oxford, UK', *International Journal of Operations and Production Management*, **32**(3): 375–384.
2. If you compare the batch layout in Figure 6.14 to the cellular layout in Figure 6.15, you will notice that additions to some process types have been made. This is because when similar processes or capabilities are brought together and managed as a single group, utilization and reutilization will be facilitated, and this is what happens in process layouts. Process design in cells, on the other hand, moves away from the principle that underpins batch processes of grouping all similar processes together and one outcome is that process utilization levels fall. At one extreme, if a company has a single process or capability and moves from a process-based arrangement to (say) two cell-based arrangements that both require this capability, a company would have to buy another process to have a source of capacity in each cell.
3. The concept of product profiling is more fully explained in Terry Hill's book *Manufacturing Strategy: Text and Cases*, 3rd edn, McGraw-Hill/Irwin, Burr Ridge, IL (2000), Chapter 6, and Alex Hill's and Terry Hill's book *Manufacturing Operations Strategy*, 3rd edn, Palgrave Macmillan (2010), Chapter 6.
4. The proposition of linking process life cycles and product life cycles was most noticeably argued by Hayes, R.H. and Wheelwright, S.C. in 'Link manufacturing process and product life cycles', *Harvard Business Review*, January/February (1979), pp. 133–40.
5. A comparison between how useful the insights in note 3 are in evaluating the source of alignment problems between markets and operations strategy, compared with those of product profiling, was reported in an article by Hill, T., Menda, R. and Dilts, D.H. 'Using product profiling to illustrate manufacturing–marketing misalignment', *Interfaces*, **28**(4) (1998), pp. 47–63.

Visit www.palgrave.com/business/hillom3e for self-test questions, guideline answers to some case study questions, useful weblinks and more to help you understand the topics in this chapter

It is a cold December afternoon in Eastborough, a small town in southern England. Some of the hardy shoppers are busily making day-to-day purchases, with others getting organized for Christmas. The main shopping area is pedestrianized and at the end of the street, shining through the gloomy light, is a bright yellow M indicating the site of one of the town's two McDonald's restaurants. As you enter the restaurant, the interior is warm and well lit, with a hubbub of activity around the counter area.

Asking a few customers why they use McDonald's produces few surprises. An energetic six-year-old nudges his younger sister and declares 'we like the chicken nuggets'. As their mother explains, 'It's convenient at the end of our shopping, right in the town centre. It's not too expensive and the children like the food.'

But, it's not only the food that appeals to the younger generation. The two youngsters dash over to select from a tree laden with balloons and flags to add to the toy they received earlier. The restaurant encourages this idea of the 'McDonald's Experience', with a strong focus on what

appeals to children. Children's parties for special occasions (such as birthdays) are regularly catered for and special events (like face painting) are frequently organized. On the previous Mother's Day, daffodils were available for children to give to their mothers. On Father's Day phone cards were distributed, so that children could ring the lucky parent.

But the age range using the Eastborough restaurant is wide. As an older couple explain, 'The service is quick and you know what to expect. The quality of the food on this visit will be as good as when we came in last week and the week before.'

The expectations of product quality and speed of service at a reasonable price, in clean and bright surroundings, are reiterated by other customers. Richard and Maurice McDonald laid down the original philosophy shortly after World War II as: Everything prepared in advance, everything uniform. All geared to heavy volume in a short amount of time.

The success of the McDonald's approach led to dramatic growth. In 1954 the McDonald brothers first appointed Ray Kroc, the driving force in the expansion of the McDonald's chain, as a franchisee in California. Then in 1961, Kroc bought the rights to the McDonald's concept for $63 million and opened 500 restaurants in the US over the next two years. In 1967, the first restaurants were then opened in Canada and Puerto Rica and by 1996 McDonald's had 21,000 restaurants in 101 countries with sales of $11 billion.

RESTAURANT LAYOUT

The Eastborough restaurant layout comprises a seating area, spread across two floors, and a working area (see Figure 1). In quiet periods, sections of seating are closed off for cleaning and the seating area is regularly patrolled by dining area hosts who keep the area clean and tidy. The main sections in the working area are shown in Figure 2, comprising:

- Counter – this restaurant has ten tills

- Production area – where food is prepared and held in bins waiting to be served to customers

- Grill area – where the meat, chicken and fish products are cooked.

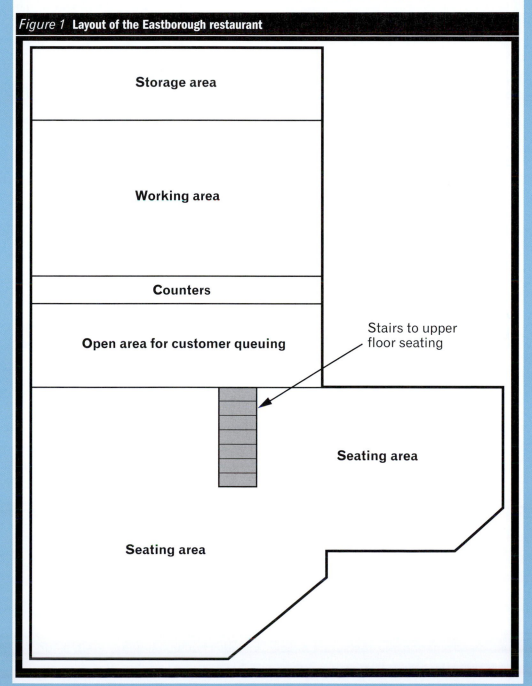

Figure 1 **Layout of the Eastborough restaurant**

Storage area

Working area

Counters

Open area for customer queuing

Stairs to upper floor seating

Seating area

Seating area

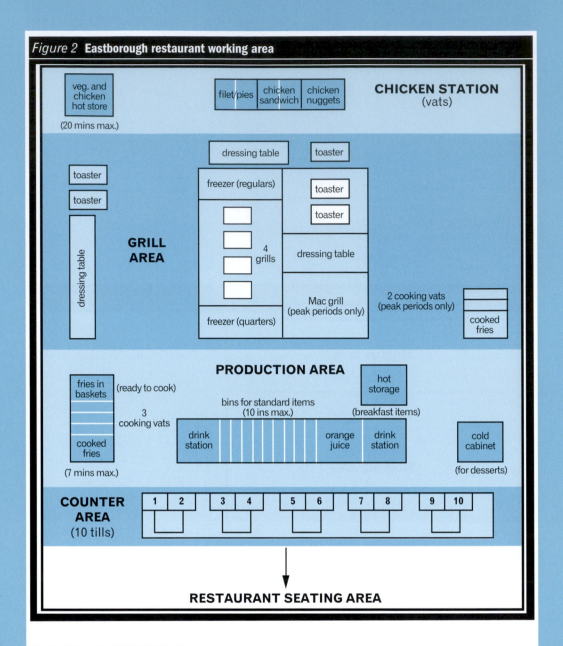

Figure 2 **Eastborough restaurant working area**

veg. and chicken hot store
(20 mins max.)

filet/pies | chicken sandwich | chicken nuggets

CHICKEN STATION
(vats)

toaster
toaster

dressing table

dressing table

toaster

GRILL AREA

freezer (regulars)

toaster
toaster

4 grills

dressing table

Mac grill
(peak periods only)

freezer (quarters)

2 cooking vats
(peak periods only)

cooked fries

PRODUCTION AREA

fries in baskets   (ready to cook)

hot storage

(breakfast items)

3 cooking vats

bins for standard items
(10 ins max.)

cooked fries

(7 mins max.)

drink station

orange juice

drink station

cold cabinet

(for desserts)

COUNTER AREA
(10 tills)

1 | 2 | 3 | 4 | 5 | 6 | 7 | 8 | 9 | 10

RESTAURANT SEATING AREA

SERVING CUSTOMERS

As a result of competition in the fast-food industry and increasing consumer preference for healthier food, McDonald's has steadily expanded its original offering of burgers, drinks and fries to include breakfast, salads and deli options (see Figure 3). Many of the products are also packaged as Extra Value Meals for adults or Happy Meals for children. For example, the Big Mac Meal consists of a Big Mac, a drink and a portion of fries. Special promotional items are also added from time to time such as ribs or Mexican chicken.

Customers entering the restaurant typically divide into those who know exactly what they want, and immediately join the shortest queue, and those who stand and study the menu panels. When the customer reaches the front of the queue and asks for his food, the counter person employs two selling techniques. The first is known as 'selling up', which involves either suggesting a larger portion or an additional item, such as a drink. For example when a customer requests 'hamburger and fries', the counter person responds 'Would you like large fries'? The second is called 'suggestive selling' where an order for a 'Big Mac and medium fries' would be greeted by a suggestion of an Extra Value Meal (for example a Big Mac Meal) that includes additional items, such as drinks or fries.

Figure 3 Menu development

Original

BEEF

Hamburger - beef patty, onions, pickles, mustard and tomato ketchup in a sesame seed bun

Cheeseburger - beef patty, cheese, onions, pickles, mustard and tomato ketchup in a sesame seed bun

Double Cheeseburger - two beef patties, cheese, onions, pickles, mustard and tomato ketchup in a sesame seed bun

Big Mac - Two beef patties with lettuce, onions, pickles, cheese with Big Mac sauce in a sesame seed bun

Quarter Pounder with Cheese - quarter pound beef patty, two slices of cheese, onions, pickles, mustard and tomato ketchup in a sesame seed bun

DESERTS

Hot apple pie - crispy pie filled with hot apple chunks

FISH

Filet-O-Fish - Alaskan Pollock or Hoki, half a cheese slice and tartare sauce in a crisp breadcrumb coating.

CHICKEN

Chicken sandwich - chicken breast meat in a roll

Chicken premiere - coated chicken patty, salsa sauce, sour cream and chive sauce in a focaccia bun

Chicken McNuggets - chicken breast in batter

Chicken Selects - crispy costed chicken breast strips

SIDES

Fries - French fries

DRINKS

Soft drinks - coca-cola, Fanta, Diet Coke, Sprite

Coffee & tea - black or white

Milkshakes - banana, chocolate, strawberry or vanilla

Breakfast

Sausage & egg McMuffin - pork sausage patty, egg, butter and cheese slice in an English muffin

Double sausage & egg McMuffin - two pork sausage patties, egg, butter and cheese slice in an English muffin

Bacon & egg McMuffin - streaky bacon, egg, butter and cheddar cheese slice in an English muffin

Big breakfast - scrambled eggs, pork sausage patty, hash brown, butter and English muffin

Hashbrown - crispy hashbrowns

Bacon roll - streaky bacon, brown sauce and butter in a roll

Pancakes with sausage - pancakes with pork patty

Pancakes with syrup - pancakes, butter and syrup

Toasted bagel - with cream cheese or jam

Sausage, egg & cheese bagel - pork sausage patty, egg, butter and cheese slice in a bagel

Bacon, egg & cheese bagel - streaky bacon, egg, butter and cheese slice in a bagel

Double chocolate muffin - with chunks of plain and milk chocolate pieces

Low fat blueberry muffin - with blueberries scattered throughout

Fruit bag - slices of fresh apple and grapes

Oatso simple porridge - with jam or syrup

Donut - sweet sugar coated donut

Coffee & tea - black, white, latte or cappuccino

Orange juice - pure orange juice

The counter person punches the order into the till and picks the food in a set sequence:

1. Cold drinks

2 Hot drinks

3 Fries

4 Boxed burgers/sandwiches

5. Wrapped burgers/sandwiches.

Standard items such as a Big Mac or a Quarter Pounder with Cheese are usually available in the bins in the production area. The drinks machines have buttons that automatically dispense the appropriate amount of liquid and standard containers are used to serve regular, medium and large portions of fries. The sequence for a typical order for a Big Mac, coffee and fries, to eat in the restaurant, is as follows:

1. Punch order into the till, as the customer details the items

2. Place tray on counter

3. Pour coffee and place on tray

4. Walk over to fries and fill container

Figure 3 **(continued)**

Salads, deli, sides and extended deserts

SALADS

Grilled chicken salad - grilled or crispy chicken, mixed salad and tomatoes with caesar or balsamic dressing

Grilled chicken & bacon salad - grilled chicken, bacon, mixed salad, tomatoes and caesar or balsamic dressing

Garden side salad - mixed salad, carrot and cherry tomatoes with balsamic dressing.

Carrot sticks - ready to eat carrot sticks

Fruit bag - ready to eat slices of apple and grapes

SIDES

Savoury cheese bites - melted cheese in breadcrumbs with dip

DESERTS

McFlurry - soft dairy ice cream with various toppings

Hot apple pie - crispy pie filled with hot apple chunks

Brownie - made from real Belgian chocolate

Sundae - soft dairy ice cream with toffee or strawberry sauce.

Donut - sweet sugar coated donut

Double chocolate muffin - with plain and milk chocolate pieces

Low fat blueberry muffin - with blueberries scattered throughout

DELI

Grilled chicken salad wrap - grilled chicken, tomato, cucumber, lettuce, onion, smoky sauce and tomato salsa in a soft tortilla

Sweet chilli crispy chicken wrap - chicken, cucumber, iceberg lettuce, mayo and sweet chilli sauce in a soft tortilla

Spicy vegetable wrap - veggie patty (chickpeas, coriander and cumin), lettuce, sweet chilli and ranch sauce in a soft tortilla

Crispy chicken & bacon wrap - crispy chicken with smoky bacon, tomato, lettuce and mayo in a soft tortilla

Sweet chilli crispy chicken sandwich - chicken, cucumber, lettuce, mayo and sweet chilli sauce in a roll

Grilled chicken salad sandwich - grilled chicken, tomato, cucumber, lettuce, onion, smoky sauce and tomato salsa

Spicy vegetable sandwich - veggie patty (made from chickpeas, coriander and cumin), lettuce, sweet chilli and ranch sauce in a roll

LITTLE TASTERS

Chicken & spiced onion snack wrap - chicken, lettuce, mayo and spiced onion chutney in a soft tortilla

Chicken & cheese bacon snack wrap - chicken, bacon lettuce and mayo in a soft tortilla

5. On way back to counter, take Big Mac from bin

6. Place items on tray

7. Take the money.

If an item of food is not available in the production area, the counter person calls the order to the production person who then calls the grill area. This item is then prepared as a priority. In slack periods, certain standard items with low demand are only cooked to order. In the Eastborough restaurant, the salad and deli options fall into this category. When an order is not immediately available, the counter person takes the money for the order (as a till can only deal with one order at a time), asks the customer to stand aside and wait, and starts to deal with the next person in the line. At the server's discretion, the customer is requested to take a seat and the order is brought over by the staff. This might apply to an elderly customer or a parent struggling with children.

If a customer requests a non-standard item (for example, a Big Mac with no cheese) a 'grill slip' is automatically printed in the grill area after the order has been punched into the till. When the item of food is prepared, the grill slip travels with it to the production area who then let the counter person know that it is available. A customer should wait in line for no more than two minutes to be served and receive their order in less than a minute after the order has been placed. Actual performance against these targets is periodically checked with a stopwatch.

PRODUCTION PLANNING

The schedule manager, who can be either the restaurant manager or the first assistant manager, prepares a daily chart of projected sales by hour throughout the day based on sales of the previous three weeks and sales for the same period the previous year. From the sales forecast, a computer package proposes the bin levels to be held in the production area for each product. The resulting chart is then put on the wall to help guide the production person in charge of maintaining the bin levels. This is only a guide and, in practice, the production person can often spot more precisely a surge or fall in demand, for example when schoolchildren call in at the restaurant before catching their buses home.

The required crewing levels for the different areas of the restaurant are also estimated from the weekly sales forecast. The volume and type of demand varies substantially during the week. In the Eastborough restaurant, the periods of high demand are lunchtimes, Friday evening after 5pm, and all day on Saturdays and Sundays. Some typical manning levels for different days and times are shown in Figure 4.

The Eastborough restaurant employs a total of 100 staff, of whom only 12 are full time and 70 per cent are between 16 and 20 years old. Having the right number of staff at the right time is key to the restaurant running smoothly. If there is excess staff, the manager will ask if anyone wishes to go home and if demand is unexpectedly high, staff not scheduled to work are contacted. But there is no guarantee they will be available or willing to come in at short notice. When they are short staffed, the manager asks for 'aces in their places', where all employees perform the jobs they know best with everyone in the restaurant focused on serving customers, including the restaurant manager.

PRODUCTION CONTROL

All food and drink is prepared in a defined McDonald's approach. At the start of the day, the production person fills up the bins in the production area to the required levels by requesting sufficient products from the grill area and chicken station. In periods of high demand, a person is allocated to 'the bin', which involves acting as the interface between the staff preparing food and the counter staff who serve the customers by managing the flow of products, calling for production as needed and keeping the bin stock organized and fresh. During slow periods, counter staff simply call orders from the back as required to maintain minimum inventory levels. To guarantee that customers are only served hot and fresh products, food is only held for seven minutes after wrapping before it is either sold or discarded.

Sue Kemp, who often runs the bin during busy times, described her job, 'Having worked here for some time, I have a good sense of when our peaks occur and how demand levels vary. But, there are still times when I get caught out. I'll build up the bin before the peak starts and then try to run production smoothly through the busy times. Demand variability at busy times puts us under pressure and can cause some tension between the different areas. There are charts showing how much stock to hold at different levels of demand, but I need to watch what is selling, gauge customer flows and take into account the level of experience of the production staff to judge how much we should hold in each bin. I'd rather have too much stock than keep a customer waiting.'

Figure 4 **Example manning levels for the Eastborough restaurant**						
Type of period	**Example**	**# staff within each area**				
		Supervision	**Dining area**	**Counter area**	**Grill area**	**Total**
Quiet	Weekday afternoon	1	1	2	3	7
Medium activity	Mon to Thurs lunchtime	1	2	4	5	12
Busy	Sat lunchtime	3	8	13	24	48

PREPARING PRODUCTS

The main products use several common ingredients as shown in Figure 3. All food preparation is carried out according to carefully detailed procedures. For example, fries must be left for a minimum of 45 minutes to defrost before they can be cooked. Once they are in the vat, a duty timer sounds after 30 seconds as a reminder that the fry basket must be lifted and shaken. They are then cooked for a further three minutes and can only be held for seven minutes before they are either sold or discarded. During busy periods, an operator works full time on cooking fries, while in slack periods counter staff cover this task.

To ensure employees are familiar with all these procedures, an Observation Check List (OCL) is prepared for each product. A typical sequence for preparing food is described below:

1. A call comes from the production person for 'Four Big Macs, please'.

2. The Big Mac bun has three sections: a heel, a club and a crown. The operator on the dressing table loads the four heels and clubs of the buns into a toaster. After 35 seconds a timer sounds and the operator transfers the heels and clubs onto the dressing table.

3. The operator loads the crowns into the toaster.

4. At the same time, the grill operator, prompted by the timer alarm, lays eight pieces of meat onto the grill for exactly 42 seconds to grill both sides of the meat.

5. While they are cooking, the operator puts a preset amount of Mac sauce, onions, lettuce and cheese onto the heels and clubs at the dressing table.

6. Two pickled gherkins, which must not be touching, are then placed on the club.

7. The grill operator then puts a piece of meat onto each dressed heel and club.

8. The dressing table operator assembles the buns, adds the toasted crowns, stacks the buns and takes them to the production area.

9. The production person then wraps the product and places it in the rack, with the appropriate time card. The whole process takes about two minutes.

STAFF TRAINING

Good teamwork and familiarity with the set procedures for serving customers, storing food and preparing meals are critical in running any McDonald's restaurant. After joining McDonald's, staff are expected to reach a set level of expertise, designated by five stars, within five months, or ten months if working part-time. An employee's performance is assessed by the restaurant manager or area manager using the appropriate OCL. To gain five-star status, employees must undertake two satisfactory OCLs for each area of operation.

To help maintain the corporate motto QSC&V (Quality, Service, Cleanliness and Value), an external audit is carried out each quarter by a manager from another McDonald's restaurant. Fifteen employee files are selected and the restaurant is graded, based on the OCL scores achieved. There is also a more intensive annual audit, known as the 'Full field,' where a group of supervisors from other restaurants complete OCLs on all operations during one day shift and one night shift.

GROWING PRESSURE

When the first McDonald's restaurant opened in 1940, it was a breath of fresh air for the American population. Since then it has expanded at a dramatic rate and has now reached 122 countries on six continents (see Figure 5). However, this high profile international presence means it has been the target of pressure from a growing number of competitors and increasingly health-conscious consumers.

In response to the increased competition from Burger King and Wendy's, who many believed offered hotter and tastier food, McDonald's introduced its 'made for you' delivery system in 1998 where products were made-to-order instead of being stocked in bins. To make this happen, it installed computers, 'rapid toasters', and temperature-controlled 'launching zones' in each of its stores. It seemed like a step change but, in reality, it was simply catching up with its competitors.

McDonald's also started to diversify its portfolio of businesses by purchasing stakes in Donatos Pizza, Boston Market, Chipotle Mexican Grill and Pret A Manger. But, these changes seemed to be too little too late. Its share price started falling (see Figure 6) and it announced its first ever loss of $344 million in the last quarter of 2002.

Figure 5 **International expansion (1940–2011)**

Year	Country	Year	Country	Year	Country
1940	US	1985 (cont)	Italy	1995 (cont)	South Africa
1967	Canada		Mexico		Qatar
	Puerto Rico	1986	Cuba		Honduras
1970	US Virgin Islands		Turkey		Saint Martin
	Costa Rica		Argentina		Croatia
1971	Guam		Macau		Western Samoa
	Japan	1987	Scotland		Fiji Islands
	Netherlands	1988	Serbia		Liechtenstein
	Panama		South Korea		Cyprus
	West Germany		Hungary	1996	India
	Australia	1990	Russia		Peru
1972	France		China		Jordan
	El Salvador		Chile		Paraguay
1973	Sweden		Indonesia		Dominican Republic
1974	Guatemala		Portugal		French Poynesia
	Curacao		Northern Ireland		Belarus
	UK	1991	Greece		Ukraine
1975	Hong Kong		Uruguay		Yemen
	Bahamas		Martinique		Republic of Macedonia
1976	New Zealand		Czech Republic		Ecuador
	Switzerland		Guadeloupe		Renunion
1977	Ireland	1992	Poland		Isle of Man
	Austria		Monaco		Suriname
1978	Belgium		Brunei		Moldova
1979	Brazil		Morocco		Nicaragua
	Singapore		Northern Marianas		Lebanon
1981	Spain	1993	Israel	1998	Pakistan
	Denmark		Slovenia		Sri Lanka
	Phillipines		Saudi Arabia	1999	Georgia
1982	Malaysia	1994	Kuwait		San Marino
	Norway		New Caledonia		Gibraltar
1984	Taiwan		Oman		Azerbaijan
	Andorra		Egypt	2000	French Guiana
	Wales		Bulgaria		American Samoa
	Finland		Bahrain	2001	Mauritius
1985	Thailand		UAE	2003	Mayotte
	Aruba	1995	Estonia		Kazakhstan
	Luxembourg		Romania	2004	Montenegro
	Venezula		Malta	2006	Iraq
			Colombia	2008	Algeria
			Slovakia	2011	Bosnia

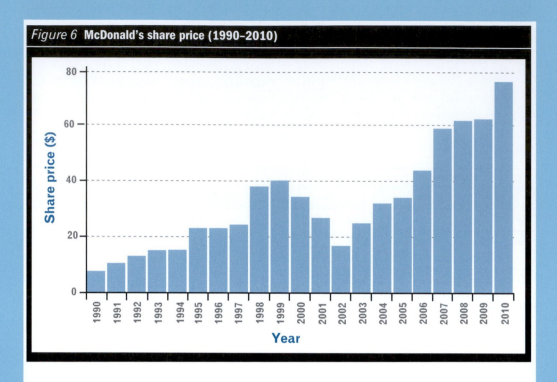

Figure 6 McDonald's share price (1990–2010)

As McDonald's started closing restaurants, analysts asked:

- Has the McDonald's way failed to adapt quickly enough to match changing consumer tastes?

- Is the company lacking in strategic direction and focus?

- As sales slump, restaurants close and customers vote with their feet, what does McDonald's plan to do to stop the rot?

THE 'PLAN TO WIN' STRATEGY

In 2003, it introduced its 'I'm lovin' it' advertising campaign and a 'Plan to Win' strategy to try to turn the situation around. The strategy focused on five Ps: product (menu), people (service), place (dining experience), price (value) and promotion (connection with customers). It introduced healthier options such as salads, sandwiches, wraps and fruit (see Figure 3) and started providing nutritional information for all its products. It then launched its 'It's what I eat and what I do' advertising campaign to help younger customers understand the importance of diet and exercise for a healthy lifestyle. These initiatives managed to stop its share price from falling, but it was still a long way from recovering its former glories.

BACK TO BASICS

In 2004, Jim Cantalupo (the newly appointed CEO) announced that McDonald's needed to get 'back to basics' and focus on serving burgers not salads. The healthier options accounted for only 10 per cent of their sales and he saw no reason to continue with them. Instead, he thought they should simply introduce healthier burgers and healthier cooking oils. He also felt that while people talk about wanting a healthier lifestyle, they don't necessarily do anything about it. However, this seemed to be a very US centric point of view and his team persuaded him that there should be regional differences. As a result, they started pushing local offerings such as McWraps in Europe, Angus Burgers in Australia and McCafe speciality coffees and smoothies in the USA.

In keeping with its 'back to basics' philosophy, it then sold its share in Donatos Pizza, Chipotle Mexican Grill, Boston Market and Pret A Manger in 2004, 2006, 2007 and 2008 respectively. Globally, sales and profits were improving (see Figure 7), but it was still struggling in the UK where it faced stiff competition from not only the big fast food chains such as Burger King, Subway, Nando's, Wimpy, Wagamama and KFC, but also coffee shops, sandwich bars and even supermarkets. As a result, in 2006 it closed 25 of its 1,225 restaurants, relocated

Figure 7 Business performance (1990–2010)

Sales revenue, operating income, size and share performance

Measure	1990	1994	1998	2000	2002
Sales revenue ($m)					
Company-operated	5,019	5,793	8,895	10,018	10,622
Franchised	1,621	2,528	3,526	3,776	3,905
Total	**6,640**	**8,321**	**12,421**	**13,794**	**14,527**
Operating income ($m)					
Company-operated	1,104	1,159	1,633	1,643	1,471
Franchised	1,345	2,098	2,848	3,054	3,065
Selling, general & admin expenses	(854)	(1,016)	(1,719)	(1,353)	(2,420)
Total	**1,596**	**2,241**	**2,762**	**3,344**	**2,116**
Size (No. of restaurants)					
Company-operated	2,643	3,216	5,433	6,841	8,115
Franchised	9,160	12,683	19,080	21,055	22,099
Total	**11,803**	**15,899**	**24,513**	**27,896**	**30,214**
Shares ($)					
Market price year end	7.25	14.63	38.41	34.00	16.08
Dividends declared	0.09	0.12	0.18	0.22	0.24

Sales revenue by region

Region	1990	1994	1998	2000	2002
USA	2,656	3,328	4,868	5,259	5,423
Europe	2,125	2,663	4,467	4,754	5,136
APMEA	1,062	1,331	1,633	1,987	2,368
Other countries	797	999	1,453	1,794	1,600
Total	**6,640**	**8,321**	**12,421**	**13,794**	**14,527**

Operating income by region

Region	1990	1994	1998	2000	2002
USA	850	1,098	1,202	1,773	1,673
Europe	552	746	1,167	1,180	1,022
APMEA	234	306	360	442	64
Other countries & corporate	(40)	91	33	(51)	(643)
Total	**1,596**	**2,241**	**2,762**	**3,344**	**2,116**

76 and turned 50 into franchises. To help change its image, it then started refurbishing its restaurants by introducing designer furnishings, low level lighting and muted green and yellow interiors. At the same time, it launched a free Wi-Fi service and installed espresso machines serving cappuccinos and lattes. As a result, it sold ten million more cups of coffee in 2008 than 2007.

In 2008, McDonald's launched a website called www.makeupyourownmind.co.uk to help improve the public perception of its business. On the site, consumers are encouraged to ask questions, go behind the scenes at McDonald's, check the quality of its raw materials and report their findings. It also started taking its environmental responsibilities seriously and has redesigned its packaging and cutlery to make them recyclable and introduced sustainable energy sources such as solar panels and wind turbines in some outlets.

THE FUTURE

'McDonald's can be accused of many things, but sitting on its laurels is not one of them', comments Alex Hardy (retail ana-

Figure 7 **(continued)**

Sales revenue, operating income, size and share performance					
Measure	**2004**	**2006**	**2008**	**2009**	**2010**
Sales revenue ($m)					
Company-operated	13,055	15,402	16,561	15,459	16,233
Franchised	4,834	5,493	6,961	7,286	7,842
Total	**17,889**	**20,895**	**23,522**	**22,745**	**24,075**
Operating income ($m)					
Company-operated	1,949	2,497	2,908	2,807	3,173
Franchised	3,838	4,435	5,731	5,985	6,464
Selling, general & admin expenses	(2,233)	(2,499)	(2,196)	(1,951)	(2,164)
Total	**3,554**	**4,433**	**6,443**	**6,841**	**7,473**
Size (No. of restaurants)					
Company-operated	8,179	8,166	6,502	6,262	6,399
Franchised	22,317	22,880	25,465	26,216	26,338
Total	**30,496**	**31,046**	**31,967**	**32,478**	**32,737**
Shares ($)					
Market price year end	32.06	44.33	62.19	62.44	76.76
Dividends declared	0.55	1.00	1.60	2.10	2.30

Sales revenue by region					
Region	**2004**	**2006**	**2087**	**2009**	**2010**
USA	6,525	7,464	8,078	7,944	8,112
Europe	6,737	7,638	9,923	9,274	9,569
APMEA	2,721	3,053	4,231	4,337	5,066
Other countries	1,906	2,740	1,290	1,190	1,328
Total	**17,889**	**20,895**	**23,522**	**22,745**	**24,075**

Operating income by region					
Region	**1990**	**1994**	**1998**	**2000**	**2002**
USA	2,182	2,657	3,060	3,232	3,446
Europe	1,471	1,610	2,608	2,588	2,797
APMEA	200	364	819	989	1,200
Other countries	(299)	(198)	(44)	32	30
Total	**3,554**	**4,433**	**6,443**	**6,841**	**7,473**

Notes:
1. Corporate includes general and administrative expenses.
2. The UK, France and Germany collectively account for over 50% of Europe's revenues.
3. China, Australia and Japan collectively account for over 50% of APMEA's revenues.

lyst). 'It has performed well in the economic downturn compared with many of its competitors. However, its move to serving salads, wraps and lattes means that it's now competing with everyone from Burger King to Starbucks, Subway and the local cafe. It seems to have become very unfocused and I'm not sure if that is a good long-term strategy.'

Questions

1. How does McDonald's delivery system meet its business needs?

2. What has been the impact of the recent changes made in the business?

Lecturers: visit www.palgrave.com/business/hillom3e for teaching guidelines for this case study

After completing this chapter, you should be able to:

- Appreciate the significance of location decisions regarding their size (£s), fixed nature and uncertainty of choice going forward

- Understand the background issues that affect the choice of location for a facility or outlet

- Recognize the levels at which location decisions need to be made

- Appreciate the factors affecting both the choice of region, country and area/city and also those affecting the choice of the site itself

- Describe the different techniques for choosing a location and explain how they work

- Explain the factors that influence layout design decisions

- Recognize the three basic types of layout and how they meet specific business requirements

- Describe hybrid delivery system layouts in terms of their origin and business fit

- Explain the process of layout design

Chapter outline

Executive overview

Introduction

Choosing a location
Levels of decision
Choosing the continent or region
Choosing the country
Choosing the area or city
Choosing the site

Background factors influencing location decisions
Factors affecting the choice of continent/region, country and area/city
Factors affecting the choice of site
Impact of site location on potential demand

Site location techniques
Weighted factor method
Centre of gravity method

Choosing a layout
Factors influencing layout
The nature of the core task
Available space
Making space for future expansion and layout changes
Health and safety
Aesthetics

Basic types of layout
Fixed position layout
Process or functional layout
Service or product layout

Hybrid delivery system layouts
Cellular layout
Nagare cellular layout
Transfer line layout

Other layout formats
Flexing process layouts to reflect varying levels of demand
Flexible office layouts

Impact of IT on delivery systems and layouts

Detailed layout design
The features of good layouts
Designing fixed position layouts
Designing process or functional layouts
Load, movement or trip frequency charts
Relationship charts
Designing service or product layouts
Hybrid layouts
Queuing and waiting line analysis

Location and layout in practice

Driving business performance

Critical reflections

Summary

What is the role of location and layout decisions?

- Locating facilities needs to reflect the potential impact on customers in terms of the distance to travel and ease of access, and the costs of bringing both goods and materials to the site and the distribution of goods and services to customers

- Layout needs to take into account ease of customer movement within a facility or the movement of materials throughout the internal phase of a supply chain

- As you can see, both location and layout affect the day-to-day task in operations of serving customers and making products

Why are location and layout decisions important?

- In many instances, location decisions once made are difficult to change

- Even where constraints, such as new investment, do not exist the disruption to the on-going business and customers alike make relocation undesirable

- Choosing a location, therefore, needs to be carefully considered and embraces a whole range of issues from accommodating future expansion to the effect on costs

- Layouts form the basis for the day-to-day running of a business

- How and how easily customers move within a facility is an integral part of the service delivery system design and the customer experience

- Similarly, the layout in a manufacturing plant will have an impact on the efficiency of the process both in terms of costs and lead times

How do location and layout decisions impact business performance?

- Choosing the best position of a facility or outlet and how best to layout the systems, processes, equipment and staff used in providing services or making products will have a direct impact on business performance

- The factors affected by these decisions include ease of serving customers, costs of delivery to and from the site, speed of service provision and level of customer support

- While the impact of location and layout decisions on performance will vary from business to business, the aspects that these decisions influence are wide-ranging and significant to overall business performance:
  - Location and customers – proximity to customers, level of customer support, costs of delivery and ease of customer access (including available parking and public transport) will typically affect demand
  - Location and costs – in addition to site costs, location will also affect staff costs and the costs of moving materials and goods to and from the facility
  - Layout and customers – the ease with which customers can move through the delivery system and how easy it is to shop (from width of aisles to the number of check-out counters) will affect repeat business and overall sales
  - Layout and costs – moving materials and goods through delivery systems and manufacturing processes has a direct bearing on the day-to-day costs

What are the key issues to consider when making location and layout decisions?

- Location – the decision where to locate is significant in terms of three factors:
  - The size of the investment
  - The fixed nature of the choice – the organization will have to live with the choice for a long time or prematurely incur the costs of relocation
  - The uncertainty of the future – the reasons for choosing a site may become less valid in the future

- In order to secure the best net gains an organization needs to take into account the following factors:
  - Investments and cost – the investments (now and in the future) and trading costs (including supply and distribution) that will be incurred
  - Sales recurrences – the impact on new and repeat business

- Finally, when choosing a site, the decisions made will often have to be on some or all of the following levels:
  - Continent/region
  - Country
  - Area/city
  - The site itself

- Layout – decisions on how best to lay out facilities involve several factors including:
  - The nature of the business itself will determine some of the parameters involved in a facility layout
  - The amount of available space brings a mix of constraints
  - Making space for future expansion and layout changes
  - Accommodating health and safety requirements
  - Incorporating the desired aesthetics into the layout decisions

Introduction

This chapter addresses the two issues of location and layout – where best to position a facility or outlet, and how best to lay out the processes, equipment and staff used in providing the services or making the products. Choosing the best location and layout is crucial, as both will have a direct impact on the sales and profit margins of a business. The factors that will be affected by location and layout include ease of serving customers, speed of service provision, level of customer support and costs of delivery, all of which influence both sales and profits.

In the first part of the chapter, we'll look at the process of choosing a location, including the levels at which the decision needs to be made, general factors (such as the origin of existing decisions, political constraints and need for market access) and specific factors influencing location decisions (including existing infrastructure, proximity to markets and suppliers, staff availability, costs and government policies). Finally, some of the techniques used in making these decisions (weighted factor and centre of gravity method) are described.

The second part of the chapter addresses layout – the task of how best to arrange the processes, systems and staff used. First, background factors such as existing space, health, safety and aesthetics are discussed. Second, the basic types of layout (fixed position, process or function, and service or product) are described, together with those for hybrid delivery systems. The final section looks at detailed layout design, the approaches used for each of the basic types of layout and how to analyze queues and waiting times.

Choosing a location

The location of any business or organization must be chosen carefully in order to secure the best net gains both now and in the long term. Choice of location can affect initial as well as future development costs, the resulting trading costs when providing services or products to customers, sales revenues and the extent to which a facility is able to provide agreed levels of customer service.

No matter what the facility, whether it be a hospital, an office, a retail outlet, a warehouse or a manufacturing plant, the decision of where to locate is significant in terms of three factors:

1. The size of the investment

2. The fixed nature of the choice – the organization will have to live with the choice for a long time or prematurely incur the costs of relocation

3. The uncertainty of the future – the pros and cons on which the site selection was made may well be less relevant in the future.

Much time and effort needs to be put into identifying and assessing the key variables on which these decisions are based as the size and binding nature of the investments involved mean that relocation is hard to justify. In fact, many organizations are, in reality, committed indefinitely to a location once it has been chosen.

In order to secure the best net gains for an organization, the following factors need to be taken into account when deciding upon a suitable location:

- Investments and costs – the initial investment and any later site or facility investments, and the trading costs (including supply and distribution) that will be incurred when providing services or products to customers

- Sales revenues – the impact on sales revenue includes whether customers can easily see, recognize and access the site, factors that will influence both initial and repeat sales, particularly in the service sector.

Levels of decision

The location of an outlet or facility might involve decisions concerning which continent or region, which country, area or city, and finally which office block, business park, shopping centre or street to choose. Depending on the type of outlet, the number of decision levels and the importance attached to the factors determining choice at each level will change. For example, the factors that Disney's management considered when deciding where to locate a new theme park in Europe would have been at all levels and embraced more parameters than (say) Burger King's decision on where to locate its next outlet in Stockholm. While Disney would place great importance on factors such as staff availability, transport infrastructure, proximity to potential customers, climate and level of government support, for Burger King's local management factors such as immediate customer density, location of competitors, zoning and building regulations, space availability and ease of access would have been more important.

Not only do the number of levels involved differ, but the factors to be taken into account will also change for each decision to be made. Let's first look briefly at each possible decision level and afterwards review the factors that organizations may have to take into account when deciding where to go.

> **EXECUTIVE INSIGHT**
The number of levels and factors involved in selecting a location differs decision by decision.

Choosing the continent or region

For many larger organizations, there is an increasingly regional dimension to deciding where to locate a facility. In more recent times, many service companies have also been locating in different regions. For some companies (for example, hotel chains such as Marriott and Holiday Inn, coffee outlets such as Starbucks and Costa Coffee, accountancy firms such as PricewaterhouseCoopers and retailers such as Walmart and IKEA), the prime reason is access to new markets. For others, the main reason is to lower costs – for example in 2011, an estimated 3.3 million call centre jobs in the financial services industry were relocated from the USA to India, Malaysia, China and other Asian countries, as were over 2 million jobs from Western Europe. And for some organizations (for example, management consultancy companies such as Accenture and McKinsey & Company), the reason is a combination of market access (via a local presence) and a less-expensive service provision, with local consultants commanding lower salaries and requiring lower living costs than expatriate staff brought in from the country where the company is based.

Choosing the country

In many instances, the choice of country is an integral part of the regional decision. For example, where the prime aim is to access markets, the regional and country choices are typically part of the same decision. In other instances, however, they will be a separate issue. Disney's decision to build a theme park in Europe was only the first step. While choosing Europe may have involved selecting from only a very few options, deciding on the best country in Europe would have involved considering a whole range of alternatives before choosing from several viable alternatives to arrive at a shortlist of two (France and Spain being the two alternatives in question). Similarly, choosing France ahead of Spain would have meant carefully judging the relative importance of a number of variables, while weighting the relevant criteria over the timescales involved.

Choosing the area or city

For Disney, the decision to choose France rather than Spain still left a long way to go. Similarly, choosing northern France still left the decision of which area or city would best meet corporate objectives. Again, trade-offs between factors such as climate, availability of staff and density of potential customer catchment areas would have come into play. Analyses would have then been made, and models used to provide options and identify one or more possible optimal locations. A whole range of parameters, as discussed in the next section, would have been used to assess alternatives, and different scenarios would have been considered to test the impact of changes in key variables at alternative sites. For companies whose locations comprise smaller sized outlets, this level of decision is often more straightforward, with the 'which site?' decision becoming the one that needs greater care and being the more difficult to make.

Choosing the site

Selecting the actual site takes into account other considerations. This is the domain of the micro-scale decision that deals with the precise location within a city centre, regional centre, business or industrial park, or the site in relation to major roads, rail links, airports or seaports. At this level of detail, a whole range of factors come into play, as discussed in the following sections.

Background factors influencing location decisions

Before looking at the specific factors to be considered when deciding on a location, we will begin by recognizing that although the choice of where best to locate should, as with other management decisions, be set against objective criteria, reality is often a major factor in determining what is and is not feasible. This section now looks at six factors. Of these, 1 and 2 below are of a general nature, 3 and 4 result from recent technology changes and globalization trends, while 5 and 6 are of an economic nature:

1. *The origin of existing locations* Many organizations are located where they are now as a result of decisions made in the past, with the cost of changing to a more suitable location not being justifiable. Over time, as organizations grow and the investment to meet that expansion also grows, the cost of relocation can often become prohibitive compared with extending an existing site. As a result, organizations stay where they are.

2. *Politically based constraints* Countries wish to develop their own industrial and service sectors in order to create the wealth essential for national prosperity. To this end, one step being taken by governments is to require **multi-national corporations** (MNCs) to build facilities locally in order to reduce imports and create value-adding activities. Joint ventures are an increasingly common way of meeting these requirements. Such arrangements dictate the location and often the size of facilities as MNCs seek to

A **multinational corporation** (MNC) – manages operations or delivers services or products in more than one country.

increase their global presence. These pressures relate not only to developing nations as marked balance of payment deficits can result in governments of more developed economies putting pressure on foreign competitors to locate their facilities locally. This is one reason why Japanese car makers have located plants in the USA and Europe and are continuing to increase the capacity of these over time.

3. *Technology developments* Technology is not specific to a location and, in that way, is redefining what makes a location feasible. Advances in technology and electronic communications are undermining the emphasis once placed on key factors such as proximity to customers. The opportunities that these technologies provide have already changed the pattern of location in several industries.

4. *New countries are opening up* Areas of the world that had for decades been closed to outside investments due to political dogma and/or social or economic instability have now opened up. Notable examples were parts of South East Asia in the 1980s and China and Eastern Europe in the past 20 years. Being close to new markets, low labour costs and the opportunity for companies to take over existing, often not well-managed, facilities have driven many recent location decisions.

5. *Market access/local presence in large consumer markets* There is no more clear-cut example of how large markets are attractive locations for businesses than the recent and continuing investments in North America and Europe. This is primarily because of market access. The USA is a very large market in its own right, and the North American Free Trade Agreement (NAFTA) set up in 1994 with the aim of removing barriers to trade and investment between the USA, Canada and Mexico had a consumer base of some 460 million in 2011. The opportunity to become direct participants in this highly competitive and innovative market was one reason why Honda and Toyota built plants and established joint venture agreements in the 1980s and have continued to expand these facilities through to the present day. This was also part of the rationale for BMW and Mercedes-Benz in building their first manufacturing plants outside Germany, locating them in South Carolina and Alabama, respectively. Similar patterns are also present in Europe, where the total market continues to grow as membership of the European Union increases. One outcome reflecting the growing importance of this combined market is the level of foreign direct investment within Europe. Since the mid-1990s, this has consistently been more than 40 per cent of the world total, although the continent was hit by the global recession in 2008, when the figure fell to 39 per cent as investors sought other locations in which to invest.

6. *Currency value fluctuations* As the relative values of currencies change, the impact on costs may force a company to rethink the location of its manufacturing plants, particularly those serving local markets. The most marked example of this is Japan. In order to enable them to remain competitive, particularly in export markets, a whole range of Japanese companies have moved the location of their manufacturing plants to the regions to which they export. The motor industry examples above were also influenced by this factor. Other examples include electronics and consumer products companies.

The specific factors influencing the choice of where to locate can be broadly separated into those which relate to the higher level decisions of continent/region, country and area/city, and those which relate to the choice of the site itself. Let's first look at the factors affecting higher level decisions and then consider the factors affecting choice of site. The various techniques that can be used to select a site will then be discussed.

Factors affecting the choice of continent/region, country and area/city

When making the decision of which continent or region, country and area or city to locate in, the following factors need to be considered:

1. *A well-developed infrastructure* Ease of access to road and rail systems and sea and air links will often be high on a company's list of requirements, particularly where the inputs and outputs of the transformation process are high volume and bulky. Similarly, other aspects of infrastructure such as communication and power systems will be important factors in deciding where, in general, to locate. In addition, the availability of appropriate support services is an increasingly important factor. For example, the growing technology base, particularly the role of IT, that characterizes many businesses today, places great emphasis on the need for local technical support.

2. *Proximity to markets* It makes sense for services and goods to be produced as close to their markets as possible. The benefits include lower distribution and provisioning costs and shorter distances, especially where aspects such as product freshness are involved.

3. *Proximity to suppliers* As well as the obvious cost implications of distance, being a long way from suppliers also incurs longer lead-times, introduces a higher level of uncertainty and reduces a supplier's ability to respond quickly.

4. *Hospitable business climate* The long-term nature of location decisions places the business climate high on the agenda. The combination of an environment of free trade, free thought and the opportunity to create wealth is key in attracting investors. For this reason, Europe and North America continue to attract a high percentage of global foreign investment.

5. *Availability of staff* Recent surveys of the factors cited by executives when making location decisions all point to a pool of suitable and sufficient staff as one of the most important. Concerns about the skill levels and flexibility of staff are high on the location agenda, while MNCs will also take into account the traditional attitudes to work (the work ethic) within different regions.

6. *Quality of life for employees* It is not enough that sufficient skilled staff are to be found in the region or area: a prospective employer must also be satisfied that facilities are or will be made available at a level that will help retain staff. Schools, accommodation and social infrastructure all affect the quality of life for employees, particularly expatriates, whose skills and experience may be particularly critical in the earlier phases of a project.

7. *Variable cost structures* These remain a critical factor in location decisions and concern several dimensions that make up total variable costs:
   - *Staff costs* Locating in lower staff cost areas of the world such as Mexico, Eastern Europe, China and parts of the Asia Pacific region is often fundamental in the decision process. In the past, these decisions were often made by businesses using less skilled staff, but developments in IT and communications systems have extended this location alternative to businesses using more highly skilled people.
   - *Energy costs* Where the energy costs of processing are high, companies often choose to locate near to a less expensive source of power, such as hydroelectricity.
   - *Transportation costs* Incoming materials and the distribution of finished goods involve not only the actual costs of haulage, but also excise duties and tariffs, which may vary depending on the country of origin.

8. *Fixed costs and investments* These are the costs of getting started and also the fixed costs of doing business in a country or region:
   - *Investment factors* Governments can offer sizeable incentives to encourage companies to locate in a particular country or area, including financial assistance in the form of special grants, low-interest loans and tax allowances on building and material imports. For example, AMD, the US computer chip maker, confirmed that it would build a second chip plant in Dresden, Germany only after it had won $1.5 billion in German government-backed funding. The $2.4 billion plant began

production in 2006 and by 2010 was employing about 1,700 people. It is one of the biggest investment projects in the former East Germany since reunification in 1990.
- *Fixed costs* These can include inducements in the form of low local rates bills, low rents and low employment taxes.

9. *Favourable government policies* – in addition to investment and cost inducements, national and local government departments can facilitate the siting of a new business by how easy or difficult it makes the process the company has to go through. This includes the political stance towards:
   - Environmental concerns: the extent to which building and planning regulations embody stringent regulations regarding all forms of pollution including noise, toxic emissions, odour and the types and levels of effluent
   - Political attitudes towards inward investment
   - Barriers and licences: individual countries and trading blocs may impose restrictions in the form of quotas or increased tariff levels for different importers. The task of overcoming or circumventing such restrictions often leads MNCs in particular to choose locations that reduce or even eliminate such disadvantages
   - Easing capital movement restrictions to allow companies to transfer money in and out of the country
   - Government planning assistance – including simplifying planning procedures and shortening the time taken for planning applications to be approved
   - Making suitable land available – an important constraint on relocation activity in certain areas of the world is the availability of suitable land. In densely populated regions such as Europe, the failure of some governments to identify and account for this factor has curtailed opportunities and hence attracted less relocation investments. While Eire, France and the Netherlands, for example, can supply land to suit most requirements, Denmark, Greece and Italy are seen to be short of suitable relocation sites and consequently are considered less attractive areas.

10. *Being near to other company facilities* – the level of integration with other parts of the same organization may influence the general area for a new location. The ease of giving support to one another, switching staff to meet short-term needs or integrating the work across associated business units can be a significant factor for companies where the gains of managing the whole company as one entity may outweigh other considerations.

11. *Being close to resources* – the cost of transporting raw materials often influences where to locate. Similarly, being close to less expensive, renewable sources of energy can be a major factor in deciding where to build a facility.

12. *Being near to the customer* – customers, especially those requiring deliveries of materials in a just-in-time (JIT) context, increasingly require suppliers to build plants close by. In this way frequent deliveries can be made, sometimes several times a day, thus keeping inventories low. Also, being close to your customer signals commitment and provides reassurance, as Case 7.1 illustrates.

13. *Individual preferences* – senior executives within an organization may prefer a new site to be in one region, country or city for their own convenience or preferences and this can have a substantial bearing on the eventual choice.

Factors affecting the choice of site

The final step is to decide the precise location within the chosen city centre, regional shopping centre, business park, industrial complex or street. At this micro-level, an array of factors specific to this particular decision come into play. To help review these, the different factors have been grouped under two headings: the site (addressed here), and the impact of site location on potential demand (discussed in the next sub-section).

In 1947, Pierre Burelle, founder of Plastic Omnium, a parts supplier, published his strategic blueprint. It was a drawing of an automobile showing all the components then made of metal that he thought could be replaced by ones made of plastic. More than half a century on and guided by Burelle's earlier strategic vision, Paris-based Plastic Omnium is, through joint ventures, the world's biggest maker of plastic fuel tanks and the second largest supplier of bumpers for automobiles.

In 1987 the company had just four factories, three of them in France, but by 2011 the company had 96 plants (74 outside France) in 27 countries and employing 18,000 staff. The key to this growth has principally been the company's willingness to build plants next to its customers' premises. It all began in 1990 when Plastic Omnium agreed to build a plant near to BMW's Munich assembly plant and, in that way, gain second-supplier status.

Since then, it has adopted the same location strategy many times over, for example with VW in Slovakia, and with General Motors, VW and others in Mexico. More recently, the focus has been on emerging markets in Asia, especially China. Of Plastic Omnium's 3.0 billion sales in the automotive sector in 2011, revenue from China doubled to over 100 million, which represented 5 per cent of the company's total automotive revenue, and this is set to increase in the coming years as two new plants were opened in China in 2010.

www.plasticomnium.fr

Question

How has plant location been central to Plastic Omnium's rapid growth in the past 25 years?

Lecturers: visit www.palgrave.com/business/hillom3e for teaching guidelines for this case study

The factors affecting the choice of site comprise a whole range of issues, including:

- Adequate, off-street parking for both staff and customers

- The building's design related to both its external impact and the internal arrangements in terms of the basic tasks involved and the front-office space where customers are to interface with delivery systems

- Attractive rental costs and local taxes

- The appropriateness of the existing space to the business's specific needs, including the amount of time and investment to bring it up to the required level

- Proximity to support services

- Room for future expansion and associated development costs

- High traffic volumes, which may be beneficial in terms of demand but may be an unwelcome factor in terms of customer access

- Being visible from the street or highway, which is particularly relevant where call-in trade is an important factor

- Convenience of site entries and exits to major road systems

- Closeness of the site to public transport for customers and employees

- A fully developed site increases overall convenience – accesses are fully developed, site facilities (for example, roads and street lighting) are in place and disruption from on-site development work is at a minimum.

Impact of site location on potential demand

The factors here include the following:

- *High levels of customer traffic* in the area as this influences demand for a whole range of businesses such as hotels, restaurants and retailing.

- *Proximity to competitors* When shopping for services such as banking, hotel accommodation, clothes, shoes, accessories and restaurants, customers prefer to be able to choose from a range of options – the concept of **competitive clustering**. For example, research[1] has shown that hotels located in areas with many competitors nearby experience higher occupancy rates than those in isolated locations. Furthermore, many budget hotels are located by motorways or major highway intersections to reflect the fact that their market is not the local population but business people and others on the move.

- *Market saturation strategy* In Europe and North America, this unconventional strategy is gaining ground. Examples include Benetton, the Italian clothing company, and Au Bon Pain cafés in the USA. The idea is to locate the same outlets close to one another in the same area. For example, Au Bon Pain's US cafés are concentrated in Boston, Cambridge (Massachusetts), New York, Philadelphia, Miami, Pittsburg and Washington DC. As Figure 7.1 illustrates, the company's deliberate policy is to locate several cafés, all selling a wide range of gourmet sandwiches, salads, muffins, croissants, bread and soups, in the same area. As you can see, the pursuit of this strategy is a key factor in the company's location decisions.

Competitive clustering – the tendency of similar and/or competing organizations to site facilities in the same geographical area in order to increase the overall productivity with which they work.

Market saturation strategy – where an organization groups multiple outlets closely together in urban and other high traffic areas.

> **EXECUTIVE INSIGHT**
> Site location can have a sizeable impact on potential demand (sales) in service companies.

Before moving on to the next section, take a look at Case 7.2, which illustrates a growing phenomenon in call centre location, and review the case questions.

HSBC, the world's largest banking and financial services corporation, cut 4,000 UK staff when it relocated work to India, Malaysia and China. The decision by the bank follows similar moves by other companies including BT, Goldman Sachs and Prudential. The jobs involved were principally processing work and telephone enquiries.

The number of offshore operations belonging to UK financial service companies grew from 200 employees in 1996 to about 250,000 by 2011. HSBC was already running a number of global processing hubs in Hyderabad and Bangalore in India, and also in Malaysia, and much of the UK work was relocated to these sites. India, in particular, has emerged in the past decade as a new location for call centre operations, given its large number of well-educated, English-speaking young people and lower staff costs. By 2011, some 10,000 (15 per cent) of HSBC's staff were in service centres in Asia.

www.hsbc.com

Questions

1. HSBC's chief executive is quoted as saying that such moves are essential to the bank's continued success and to help ensure job security for the bank's staff worldwide. Why?

2. Why does HSBC relocate work to its existing hubs in India and Malaysia?

Figure 7.1 The location of most of Au Bon Pain's outlets (2011)	
Locations	**Outlets**
New York City	25
Boston	22
Washington DC	18
Miami	18
Chicago	17
Philadelphia	11
Cambridge (Massachusetts)	8
Pittsburg	8
Airports — Dallas Forth Worth	8
Airports — JFK	6
Airports — La Guardia	5
Airports — Logan International	4

Site location techniques[2]

Although site selection is often based on opportunistic factors such as site availability and cost benefits (such as government grants and favourable tax rates), undertaking a quantitative analysis brings an important perspective to the decision and helps to identify the optimal location based on the key benefits an organization is seeking. A number of approaches have been developed to help companies make location decisions. This section introduces the more commonly used techniques, but first let's look at the basic ideas on which they are built.

The objective underlying the optimal choice of location is to maximize the desired benefits, but which aspect(s) of benefits an organization wishes to maximize will differ. In the private sector, the driver will typically be either maximizing sales revenue, in the case of retail outlets or restaurants, or minimizing costs, as with a distribution centre or courier service company. In the public sector, on the other hand, the drivers will reflect the needs of the community that a facility serves. For example, a hospital may be located to offer the easiest access to local people in terms of distance and availability of public transport.

Each facility will approach the problem of where best to locate by assessing the various factors involved. For example, a company building a distribution centre will focus on the trade-offs between the building costs and operating costs of the centre and the transportation costs to its various sites. For a retail outlet, the trade-offs will include building and operating costs versus the attractiveness of different sites to potential customers and its potential impact on sales revenue. In the public sector, location decisions are often more difficult to assess as the factors involved are not as easily defined. However, two of the factors more commonly used to maximize the location benefits for a community are:

1. Distance per visit – to minimize the average per-visit distance to a facility (for example, a hospital or health centre) for potential users

2. The utilization level of the facility – to maximize the total number of visits to a facility by choosing a location that will make visiting it easier if the use of the facility is optional as, for example, in the case of a library.

The first task in location analysis is an accurate assessment of the spatial demand for a service, that is, the demand by geographical area. To establish this, the target population needs to be defined. For a distribution centre, the sites that the centre is intended to serve will be known. For a community health centre, on the other hand, the target population could be the total number of people it is intended to serve, broken down by groups to reflect the level and type of service to be provided (for example, family units and age groups). The area being served will then be split into smaller geographical units for which demand will be assessed, and from these a complete picture can be established of the spatial demand requirements for the whole community to be served by the health centre in question.

The second task is then to use one or more of the following techniques to evaluate how best to meet the demand requirements in terms of selected criteria. Of the various techniques and models that exist for locating facilities, the appropriate one to use will reflect the nature of the location problem on hand. Here, two more commonly used techniques are reviewed – the **weighted factor** and **centre of gravity** methods.

Weighted factor method

Consider the example of a chain of coffee and sandwich bars choosing between three potential sites in Copenhagen. The company's experience of what makes a good location has highlighted the factors that influence sales and the importance of these relative to each other. To assess each site, these factors are then scored on a scale of 0–10, and a weighted average score for each site is then calculated, as shown in Figure 7.2. The individual scores are multiplied by the weight (%) given to each factor, and the one with the highest total is the best potential site based on this measure. For example, Site 1 in Figure 7.2 gets a score of 630, as shown below:

Site 1 = (40×6)+(20×7)+(15×5)+(10×8)+(10×6)+(5×7) = 630

Figure 7.2 Weighted factor method of choosing a coffee/sandwich bar site							
Factor	**Weight**	**Site 1**		**Site 2**		**Site 3**	
Closeness to office customers	40	6	240	8	320	7	280
Visibility from street	20	7	140	7	140	6	120
Nearness to metro station/bus stops	15	5	75	8	120	8	120
Closeness to tourist attraction(s)	10	8	80	5	50	5	50
Ease of access/width of sidewalk	10	6	60	8	80	6	60
Ease of parking for suppliers	5	7	35	7	35	7	35
Totals	100	–	630	–	745	–	665

In the example given in Figure 7.2, Site 2 is clearly the best potential location for the proposed coffee and sandwich bar as it has the highest score.

Centre of gravity method

Where the choice of site needs to be made in relation to a number of existing locations, the centre of gravity method provides a way to address the factors involved. As the name implies, the outcome will be the location point that strikes the optimum balance between all the variables involved.

The best way to explain this approach is to provide a worked example of the steps to follow. A German supermarket chain is planning to build a distribution centre to serve the Bavarian region where, over the past five years, it has built seven outlets. Until this

Weighted factor method – a method of determining the optimum location for a facility which involves allotting points to each site on the basis of how well it meets the various criteria for location, with more points given proportionally for meeting the more important criteria.

Centre of gravity method – a method for determining the best site for a facility where the outcome will be the location point which strikes the optimum balance between the set of variables involved.

time, it has supported these with a combination of approaches including direct supply and deliveries from its existing distribution centres located further north. Several ranges of product will continue to be delivered directly from producers, but the company's past experience has shown that a combination of direct supply and distribution centre supply works best. The location of the seven supermarkets is shown in Figure 7.3.

You will see from the figure that a reference grid has been superimposed on the map. The centre of gravity method identifies the lowest distribution cost location for the new centre by calculating the mean of X and Y. To add to this, Figure 7.4 shows the number of weekly van deliveries to each supermarket.

The information in Figures 7.3 and 7.4 is then combined in the following way in order to identify the optimum position for the new supermarket:

Mean of X $= \dfrac{\sum X_i A_i}{\sum A_i}$ where X_i = site locations on the X axis
A_i = # weekly van deliveries to each supermarket

Mean of Y $= \dfrac{\sum Y_i A_i}{\sum A_i}$ where Y_i = site locations on the Y axis
A_i = # weekly van deliveries to each supermarket

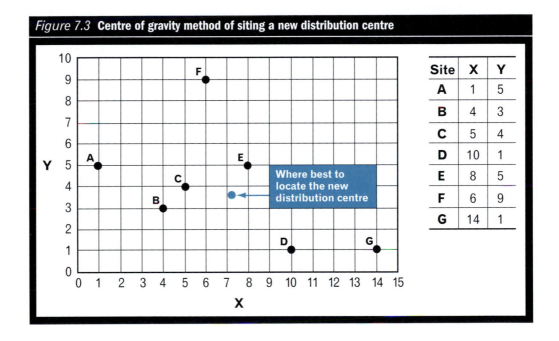

Figure 7.3 **Centre of gravity method of siting a new distribution centre**

Site	X	Y
A	1	5
B	4	3
C	5	4
D	10	1
E	8	5
F	6	9
G	14	1

Figure 7.4 **Number of weekly van deliveries to each supermarket**

Supermarket	# weekly deliveries
A	6
B	14
C	14
D	10
E	8
F	12
G	14
TOTAL	**78**

'Many
organizations
never change
location'

So, in this example:

$$\text{Mean of X} = \frac{(1\times6)+(4\times14)+(5\times14)+(10\times10)+(8\times8)+(6\times12)+(14\times14)}{78}$$

$$= 7.23$$

$$\text{Mean of Y} = \frac{(5\times6)+(3\times14)+(4\times14)+(1\times10)+(5\times8)+(9\times12)+(1\times14)}{78}$$

$$= 3.85$$

Now that we've identified the factors that influence the choice of location, and the methods for identifying the optimal site, let's move on to look at the process for deciding on a layout.

Choosing a layout

The following addresses the task of how best to arrange the delivery systems, processes and staff used in providing services or making products. First, we will review the general background factors to be taken into account in layout design. This will be followed by an overview of the basic types of layout and where and how each is used, together with an explanation of a hybrid layout (a mix between one basic type of layout and another) and a review of the techniques and approaches used in layout design.

Factors influencing layout

There are several background factors that will dictate some design parameters when laying out facilities. These include the nature of the organization's task, the available space, the need for flexibility in the future and health and safety. The relative importance of these will differ from one organization to another, but they will need to be incorporated into an organization's layout design.

The nature of the core task

The nature of an organization's core task will dictate some of the parameters involved in a facility layout. For instance, a supermarket will need to incorporate sufficient customer parking as well as adequate access for the delivery of goods. Similarly, it will have a stockholding area that needs to include cold storage facilities for fresh dairy, meat and fish products. The branch of a bank will need to incorporate an area for ATMs that can be accessed by the public when the branch is closed, cashier facilities inside the bank that afford sensible levels of security and areas that will provide privacy when customers are seeking advice on personal finances from banking staff. And so on.

Available space

The space available for a facility often comes with a mix of constraints including ease of access, building regulations, land costs and the actual area itself, and the facility design will need to accommodate all these. As an example, where land is at a premium (in terms of either availability or cost), a facility incorporating several floors will be a design prerequisite. For instance, while the classic McDonald's outlet is a single-storey, free-standing facility, in cities such as Stockholm, Copenhagen and Madrid, the outlets are designed with several floors and are not free-standing.

Making space for future expansion and layout changes

Organizations are dynamic and need to adapt to future changes in terms of space requirements and the layout of facilities. It is important, therefore, during the design phase of a facility to take account of the possible need for change. The dimensions of such future changes may include:

- *Activity volumes* – for example, how many passengers could be handled by an airport in the future, or how many customers could be served in a retail outlet or accommodated in an upmarket restaurant if the businesses were a success

- *The range of services and products* to be provided

- *The nature of the services or products* on offer, for example whether a bank or a fast-food outlet will incorporate a 'self-service' or 'drive-thru' option in the future.

Health and safety

The increasing and appropriate emphasis on health and safety in the workplace has to be incorporated into the design of facilities, in terms of both staff and customers. Factors range from chemical and other pollution hazards and fire risks through to eliminating possible accidents in terms of flat walking surfaces, the width and depth of stairwells, the provision of handrails and adequate entrances and exits.

Aesthetics

Decisions may be required about staff areas of work (the back office) and areas where customers interface with the delivery system (the front office) or general business areas such as the main reception. In the staff work areas decisions on a range of features need to be made such as the size and number of windows, lighting, height of partitions, floor coverings, floor surfaces, the size and number of break or refreshment areas as well as decisions about open plan versus half-height dividers versus private office arrangements. In the front-office phase of the delivery system, decisions would need to be made on several factors including lighting, decoration, wall coverings, space and formal versus informal layouts. The response by customers and staff to these aspects of layout are split into three categories:

1. *Cognitive response* refers to the affect on customer and staff perceptions and expectations of the organization. Dimensions such as decor, fittings and fixtures and staff dress codes will communicate a sense of the level of service or product to be provided. For example, smart/casual and matching clothes in a hairdressers will give a feeling of uniformly high quality.

2. *Emotional response* comprises the characteristics of pleasantness and excitement generated by the aesthetics of a facility. The immediate surroundings on entering a restaurant will help create an appropriate emotional response that will set the mood for customers while helping to motivate staff to meet their expectations.

3. *Physiological response* – characteristics such as decor, space, furniture and level of privacy will affect customers' responses to the service experience that is, in turn, reflected in their behaviour. For example, how relaxed a customer feels and the length of stay over dinner in a restaurant.

Now take a look at Case 7.3 to reflect on some of the background factors we have just covered.

Basic types of layout

The objective of a layout is to arrange the delivery systems, processes and related equipment, work areas, storage areas and staff needed to provide a service or make a product such that these resources operate at peak effectiveness and efficiency. This section looks at the three basic types of layout: fixed position, process or functional, and service or product. Some organizations seek to improve the level of effectiveness and efficiency of these basic types by mixing elements of each together. Such hybrids,

When push comes to shove, more than 50 per cent of airline passengers cite elbow room as their first choice when it comes to extra space (having an empty seat next to them being the ideal). Economy seats are about 17 inches, or 42 cm, wide, the same as they have been for years. Making aisles dangerously narrow and putting fewer seats in a row and sacrificing revenue are difficult calls to make. But more elbow room is starting to influence an airline's choice of which aircraft to buy. Denver-based Frontier Airlines has cited the 7 inch (17 cm) wider interior as 'a big selling point' in ordering 20 Airbus 318s and 319s over the principal alternative, Boeing 737s.

As most airlines report, one of the biggest drivers for satisfaction is whether the seat next to a person is empty. When the number of seats filled crosses the 60 per cent line, customer satisfaction plummets, while at a 70 per cent load factor, only 25 per cent of passengers view a flight as being satisfactory. The consideration of seat layouts on today's passenger jets has taken these issues on board – Continental Airlines specifically designed the coach-class seating layout in its new Boeing 777s in a way that increased the chance that passengers would have an empty seat next to them.

Questions

1. Why is elbow room on passenger airlines an increasingly important factor in the new millennium?

2. Why is legroom often easier to provide than elbow room in passenger jet design?

Lecturers: visit www.palgrave.com/business/hillom3e for teaching guidelines for this case study

as these new types are known, are discussed in the next section. The appropriate basic layout type reflects the service and product characteristics involved, as will now be explained.

Fixed position layout

Some services and products have to be provided or made where they are to be consumed or used because there is no other way for customers to access them or they are too large to move. Where the service needs to be undertaken on a customer's site (for example, a management consultancy assignment, or the regular or breakdown maintenance of a computer system or a large piece of manufacturing equipment) or the completed product cannot be moved as this is not feasible (for example, with a roadway) or the product is too large (for example, a bridge or office block), the layout arrangement used is known as fixed position (see Figure 7.5). This requires staff, equipment, materials and other resources to come to or be brought to the place or site where the service is to be provided or the product is to be made.

As a consequence of the fixed position nature of this provision, the layout design requires the scheduling of materials, equipment, skilled staff and other resources at a site and the rescheduling of these to other jobs when their phase of the work has been completed or the job is finished. The consequence is that the capabilities and resources needed to complete a service or product are brought to and arranged on site, are managed on site and are then dismantled or redistributed during or at the end of a task. The layout, therefore, needs to:

- Reflect the space requirements of each part of the task while recognizing that the levels of activity will vary over the duration of the project

- Provide for the delivery and storage of materials

- Accommodate staff and equipment needs over the time it takes to provide the service or make the product

- Facilitate the movement of staff and equipment on site

- Minimize the total movement of resources on site.

However, fixed position layouts are complicated by a number of factors, including:

- Typically, there is limited space. When building an office block, the total site is limited in area and has to accommodate the various construction as well as support activities that are part of the building process. Similarly, when completing the maintenance programme on a large piece of equipment, the space available for accommodating the tasks restricts the optimum layout.

- The tasks that make up the service or product will vary in nature and volume during the provision, so the layout needs to accommodate these often sizeable differences.

- The steps involved are often uncertain, and plans change due to delays. Consequently, the schedule has to be rearranged, and the layout needs to be able to cope with changes such as these.

Fixed position layout – a layout where the tools, staff and equipment are brought to the product or service, which remains fixed in one location. This layout is necessary if, for example, the product is too large to be moved.

Process or functional layout – a layout that involves operations of a similar nature or function being grouped together in one area.

Service or product layout – when the layout is designed sequentially around the steps taken to deliver a service or make a product, with each step of the process being completed at a particular workstation.

Process or functional layout

The term **process or functional layout** reflects the fact that the layout is arranged by putting similar processes or functions together in one area. The customers, information or products then move to the various process or functional groups in a given sequence. So whereas, in a fixed position layout, the resources (for example, staff and equipment) move to the point where the service or product is to be provided, with process or functional layouts the reverse happens – the resources stay still and the customers, information or products move to them in a given sequence. Once the service or product does not have to be provided or made on site, companies typically prefer to use a process or functional layout as it usually is a lower-cost way to provide a service or make a product.

There are several advantages to this delivery system layout, including:

- Similar skills are located together, which allows for skill levels to be enhanced and experience to be transferred within the group.

- The utilization of processes, skilled staff and equipment improves as it is easier to access these total resources because they are grouped in the same area.

- A wide range of services and products can be accommodated.

- The delivery system can handle many customer requirements at the same time.

As indicated in Figure 7.5, a process or functional layout is used for both non-repeat (special) and repeat (standard) services and products: the examples that follow illustrate how the delivery system and layout would work for these types of service and product.

Non-repeat (special) services and products

As these services and products are unique and will not typically be repeated, the skilled person or team undertaking the job will determine and then follow the best sequence of steps to complete the job, accessing the relevant processes, functions or other resources as appropriate.

For example, a management consultancy assignment would be completed by a small team of specialists. The consultants would access or compile the relevant data and complete the appropriate analyses to meet each phase of the assignment. When discussions with executives and staff were necessary, a consultant would typically meet with them in their own office, area or location. Similarly, analyses of the data, procedures, systems and facilities would be undertake in the various functional or area locations involved. In this way, the tasks necessary to undertake each phase of the consultancy assignment would be completed (sometimes in parallel) until the job was finished.

A further illustration of a company using a process layout to complete a non-repeat job is given in Figure 7.6. This figure represents a toolmaking company that builds unique tools, moulds and dies for customers. Having reviewed and discussed the details of a customer's drawing, a skilled toolmaker will complete the whole task of machining and building the tool to the required design. To do this, the toolmaker completes the machining requirements by taking the part-finished die from workbench to machine, from machine to machine and so on to undertake each appropriate step until it is completed. Here, just as with the management consultancy assignment described earlier, both product and skilled person move from process to process until the work is finished.

Now you understand what happens, why does a process or functional layout best suit these requirements? The principal reason is that this layout design enables a skilled person to access the resources (processes or people in a function) in any chosen sequence to complete the whole of a task. In the toolmaking example above, there will

Figure 7.5 **Types of layout used by different types of service delivery system and manufacturing process**

TYPES OF			
Service delivery system		Layout	Manufacturing process
Non-repeat		Fixed position	Project
Repeat	low volume	Process or functional	Jobbing Batch
	↓ high volume	Service or product	Line Continuous processing

be several skilled toolmakers machining and building customer-specific tools, moulds or dies. With this layout, each can access a specific resource in the order that best meets the task on hand and, as the sequence of steps will differ for any particular product, the layout must facilitate the use of the various machines and other pieces of equipment to meet these various work patterns.

Repeat (standard) services and products

As explained in Chapters 5 and 6, when services and products are completed more than once, the higher volumes and repeat nature mean that a different delivery system is more appropriate. What is processed (that is, customers, information or products) will determine the people skills and equipment required, but the layout of the delivery system will be designed on a process or functional basis (see Figure 7.6).

Examples of process layouts for delivering standard services and products include:

- *Hospitals* The functions in a hospital (for example, operating theatres, pharmacy, consulting rooms, reception area, X-ray facilities, wards and laboratories) are laid out functionally. That is, the facilities and staff who run the pharmacy services will be put together in one department, all operating theatres will similarly be located in the same area, and so on.

- *Printing companies* The activities in a printing company that comprise design, plate preparation, ink laboratory and stores, printing and post-printing tasks such as cutting and creasing, slitting, collation and packing will be brought together each in their own area, such that all designers and the relevant equipment are in the same department, similarly with plate preparation, and so on, as shown earlier in Figure 6.4.

- *Supermarkets* The layout in a supermarket is based on the principle that similar merchandize (for example, bakery items, soft drinks, wines, cheese, cooked meats, fresh vegetables and cereals) are located in the same aisles, and similar activities (for example, checkouts) are positioned in the same area. Where merchandize and activities are positioned will also reflect the levels of demand, traffic flows, nature of the purchase and similar factors. But the reason for locating similar merchandize and activities in the same area is twofold: it is easier for customers to shop and it is easier for staff to replenish the shelves.

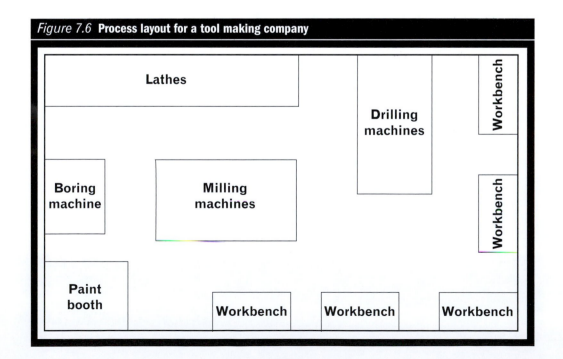

Figure 7.6 **Process layout for a tool making company**

Facilitating delivery

Now let's look at how the process or functional layout facilitates the delivery of the required services and products. First, with this type of layout, facilities are laid out with like kinds (functions, processes or merchandize) grouped together, which brings with it economies of scale and other gains, such as improving the utilization of the resources as all services or products can access and use them, keeping skill groups together, reducing operating costs and lowering investment (due to higher utilization and a minimization of unnecessary process, equipment and space duplication).

Second, the total service or product is often provided in two or more steps. In such instances, the task is broken down into the required number of steps, and each step is completed at a different process. This is achieved by the customer, information or product going to each function or process group in the appropriate order and the required step then being completed. In some service delivery systems, for example fast-food restaurants, the total requirement is provided as a single step. But the principle is the same as in a multi-step provision. The food preparation processes and counter service operation are laid out in their own area. The customer then goes to a server at the counter and is 'processed' (that is, orders, pays and is given the food).

To illustrate a multi-step process, let's imagine you need to go to hospital as you have injured your arm. You will typically be 'processed' by the hospital in the following way, with potential delays (queues) between steps, as shown in Figure 7.7:

1. Go to the hospital reception, queue and then provide your details.

2. Go to the orthopaedic consultant and wait for your turn. The consultant assesses that you may have a broken arm and asks you to go for an X-ray to confirm and provide details of the suspected break.

3. You queue, and then your arm is X-rayed.

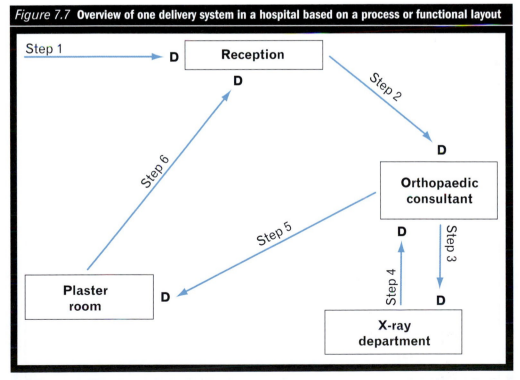

Figure 7.7 Overview of one delivery system in a hospital based on a process or functional layout

Notes: 1. Explanation of steps 1 to 6 is given in the accompanying text.
2. **D** indicates a delay (in this instance, a queue).
3. The hospital layout (not to scale) comprises corridors, rooms and waiting areas. Patients (the customers being processed) will move between departments using corridors, lifts and chairs.

4. You return to the consultant with the X-ray pictures and wait. The consultant reviews the X-rays and instructs the plaster room on how the arm is to be bound and supported.

5. You then go to the plaster room, where first you wait and then your arm is treated.

6. Then it's back to reception to arrange your follow-up appointment.

As you will see from this, the processes or functions (in this instance, skilled staff and equipment) remain in place, and the patients (that is, the hospital's customers) move from function to function to be processed. This movement by customers, information or products is an underlying characteristic of this type of layout design. Furthermore, they will typically wait between steps for a process to become available. In this way, several of the advantages of this type of layout that were highlighted earlier will be provided. For example, utilization of skilled staff is enhanced as the layout design requires that patients wait (queue) to see them. As a result, these key resources do not have to wait for patients, and utilization is thereby increased. Also, this type of layout allows the hospital's delivery system to treat a wide range of requirements at the same time, with patients going through their own sets of steps. The system can therefore handle different customer needs requiring different combinations of skilled staff and equipment, with the amount of any resource required at each step being variable and unknown. These characteristics are those associated with low to relatively high volume, repeat (standard) services and

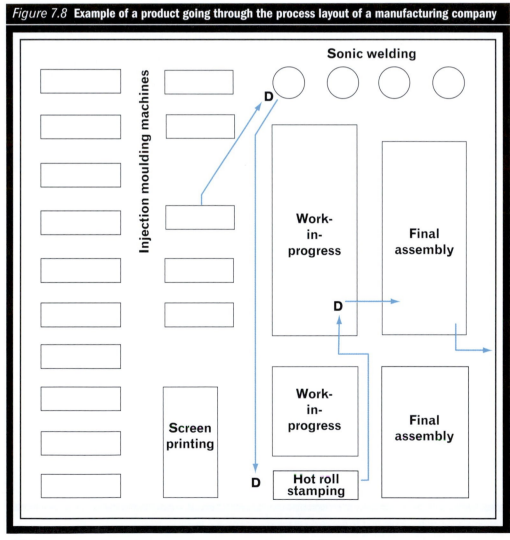

Figure 7.8 Example of a product going through the process layout of a manufacturing company

Notes: 1. **D** indicates a delay: a product here is waiting its turn to be processed.
2. ⟶ provides an example of one product's movements from injection moulding to sonic welding to hot roll stamping to work-in-progress to final assembly.

products. Similarly, in our supermarket example, customers move from aisle to aisle selecting the food items they wish to purchase. This functional layout means that many customers can be served at the same time.

In manufacturing, the process layout and the way in which a product is completed follows the same format as in the previous examples. Similar processes are grouped together in the same geographical area (Figure 7.8). Products are broken down into a number of steps, and a product moves from process group to process group to be completed. So, looking at Figure 7.8, a product that requires moulding, sonic welding, hot roll stamping and final assembly would go through the necessary series of steps with periods of waiting between one step and the next.

Finally, with functional layouts, the position of processes in the overall layout may reflect the flow of the services or products through the different steps or stages, but this will only be the case where the services or products involved all follow (at least in part) the same sequence. Hence, for the examples provided so far:

- For the printing company example given earlier in Figure 6.4, you will see, when you glance back at this figure, that the functional layout reflects the sequence involved. That is, all the products will start with cylinders/plates and paper stores, through printing and then to slitting and collation (if required), before going on to packing and finally to finished goods.

- Figure 7.8 is similar to Figure 6.4.

- Figure 7.6 on the other hand, does not reflect service/product flow as here the products will all take different routes and may, in fact, go back to earlier processes at some stage. This lack of similarity in process sequence is also well illustrated in the hospital example shown in Figure 7.7. As you can imagine, the sequence of steps for one patient's treatment will differ greatly from that for another patient, and consequently patients' routes will differ.

Service or product layout

Like the last type of layout, this type is oriented around similar services or products, but the volumes will be higher, demand patterns will be more stable, and the services or products will again be standardized. Line and continuous processing use product layout in their manufacturing processes. As explained in Chapter 5, examples in the service sector are infrequent, with Dr Svyatoslav Fyodorov's eye microsurgery unit (see Case 5.4) being one of the exceptions.

Here the facilities are oriented in relation to the service or product. The first task is to determine the steps involved in providing a service or making a product, and then the process is designed to complete each step at a different workstation. For example, an assembly line is designed with several workstations, and at each of these the parts making up the product are put together in a given order. To design a continuous processing system, for example to refine oil, the steps to complete this task are determined and the process is then designed to complete these in sequence. Both these examples illustrate the high volume and standard nature of the products involved (they all go through the same steps in the same sequence). As highlighted earlier, high volumes justify the dedicated investment, and the standard nature of the products means that the process design involves the same sequence of steps. Finally, this leads to the fact that both line and continuous processing need to be balanced. That is, the work performed at each workstation must be balanced (that is, take the same amount of time to complete) with the work at all the other stations. While assembly lines tend to be paced (in terms of how long it takes to complete the work at a station) by people, continuous processing systems will be paced by the processing equipment.

Going back now to Dr Fyodorov's eye clinic. The radial keratotomy treatment for myopia (short-sightedness) described in Case 5.4 illustrates all the features of a service-oriented layout. The patients to be treated fit the medical specification for this treatment procedure; the eye operation performed is the same for each patient; the surgeons each complete their designated step in the total procedure; the patients, who lie on operating tables, are all then moved one step further; and so the process continues. At each step, the work involved takes a similar time to all the other steps, with the activities monitored on TV screens and the surgeons linked to each other through an audio system.

Other examples include:

- Automobile assembly – the steps to assemble a car form the basis for the process design of an automobile assembly line, with each vehicle passing along the same track where it is systematically built in line with the colour, type, engine size and other options from which customers can select.

- Fast-food restaurant – burger preparation in the back stage of a fast-food restaurant is often designed as a line process. The preparation is separated into a number of steps and each burger is completed by going through each step at a time.

- Self-service restaurant – customers entering a self-service restaurant will walk through the service line and select the food they wish to purchase and pay the bill at the end.

- Petrochemicals – the steps to process oil into a range of chemicals provide the blueprint for the design of a petrochemical plant. The refining process diverts part-processed products into different routes, with each going through its own required set of steps to complete the range of end-products.

Hybrid delivery system layouts

Given the increasing difference in markets, companies have responded by developing alternative delivery systems to reflect these changing demands. One outcome is that companies often choose to rearrange the layout of their facilities to create a better fit between the modified delivery system and the needs and characteristics of the markets served by these systems. Some of the more common examples of these layout redesigns are now discussed. This section reflects on the nature and rationale of the layout changes that go hand in hand with the delivery systems developments.

Cellular layout

As explained earlier, process or functional layouts are based on grouping similar processes or functions together in the same geographical area. Without sufficient volumes to justify dedicating facilities (staff and/or equipment) as with a service- or product-oriented layout such as line, process or functionally based layouts allow a range of services and products to share skilled staff and equipment thus improving the utilization/investment equation. What cells do is mix the process or functional and service or product layouts to create a hybrid as was illustrated earlier in Figure 6.15 and that has been reproduced here as Figure 7.9. A look at this figure shows that the **cellular layout** comprises processes allocated to one of four cells based on the skills and equipment required to make the products within a cell (thus reflecting the service or product layout principle) and with like skills and equipment in a cell positioned in the same geographical area (thus reflecting the process or functional layout principle). Hence it is termed a hybrid.

The same use of the cellular layout is now gaining ground in the service sector, as Case 7.4 illustrates.

Cellular layout – a mix of functional and service/product layouts where the necessary staff/equipment to provide a service or make a product are positioned in the same area. The work stations are grouped together according to the process requirements for a set of similar items that require similar processing and the relevant services and products are then processed in the 'cell'.

CASE 7.4 FUNCTIONS AT A TELECOMMUNICATIONS COMPANY CALL CENTRE

A large US telecommunications company used to organize its call centre on a functional basis. Using three tiers of staff, customers' correspondence (including payment collections), requests and queries by phone were initially handled at the Tier 1 level. Any issues that could not be resolved here would be passed to Tier 2 technicians who worked in the same call centre but in another function and reported to their own Tier 3 supervisor. There were frequently delays in transfers between Tier 1 and Tier 2 staff, and when Tier 2 technicians could not resolve issues, these would be passed back to the Tier 1 originators to give to their own Tier 3 supervisor, who would further investigate it and then give it back to the relevant Tier 1 staff to advise the customer. The passing back and forth between Tier 1 and Tier 2 staff could often happen two or more times. The result was that an issue requiring (say) half an hour to resolve could involve two or more days before a reply was given to the customer.

So the company decided to reconfigure its call centres. Now, cells have been formed to handle specified groups of customers, with both Tier 1 and Tier 2 staff contained within each cell, this being headed by a Tier 3 cell team leader. Hand-offs between Tier 1 and Tier 2 staff now occur within a cell, with the result that over 90 per cent of customer queries are resolved quickly and fall within a single team leader's span of control. Tier 3 cell team leaders are ultimately responsible for ensuring that every customer query is followed through to a satisfactory conclusion.

Questions

1. How did the original call centre structure result in delays?

2. How did the cell-based redesign reduce delays?

3. What other advantages or opportunities would a cell-based structure offer this company?

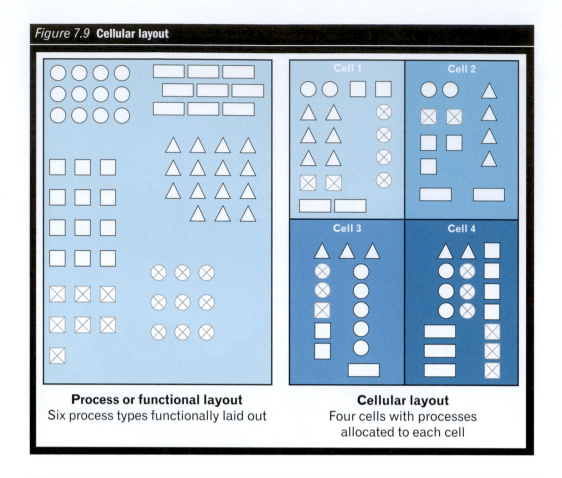

Figure 7.9 **Cellular layout**

Process or functional layout
Six process types functionally laid out

Cellular layout
Four cells with processes
allocated to each cell

Nagare cellular layout

As explained in Chapter 6, the Nagare production system is a derivation of cellular manufacturing. You will see the similarity to a cellular layout when you look back at Figure 6.17. This illustrates the change from a process or functional layout to a product-oriented layout. It is designed to facilitate a skilled person to take a product through all its process steps. The products in question are of a repeat and low volume nature and are typically produced on a make-to-order basis.

Transfer line layout

For high volume products the hybrid process known as a transfer line is sometimes developed. The process layout is product-oriented, with the basic line process enhanced by the inclusion of systems that automatically complete process steps and are typically self-adjusting for any deviation from the specification. The resulting layout is thus a hybrid between line and continuous processing and has been designed to reflect the high volume, standard nature of the products involved.

Other layout formats

The previous sections have addressed the concepts and issues that relate to the general approach to layout design. This section highlights other dimensions and formats that, while relating to more specific delivery system layouts, provide additional approaches and insights to meet the needs of particular markets and organizational requirements.

Flexing process layouts to reflect varying levels of demand

In many companies, sales demand can vary significantly. To meet these changes in activity levels, companies incorporate these requirements, where possible, into their layout design. For example:

- Car assembly plants are often able to increase the number of positions on an assembly line layout thus decreasing the work content per station and thereby allowing operations to increase the speed of the process and raise output levels.

- Bank and post office branch layouts have several more teller positions than are normally required so enabling them to 'flex' capacity in line with queue lengths.

- Some fast-food restaurants have developed a process layout that can be altered to meet the requirements of peak and non-peak sales periods, as shown in Figure 7.10.

Flexible office layouts

For jobs such as consultants, service engineers and sales staff, the need for an office layout with dedicated desks occupying expensive floor space is often unnecessary. Companies now provide an office where the layout comprises a number of desks that can be used by staff on an as-needed basis. The combination of variable space to work and somewhere to hang a coat provides the alternative layout described as the 'virtual office', 'hot offices' or 'hot desks'.

Examples of other dimensions of the concept of flexible office layouts are mobile desk base units that can be put out of the way when the owner is out and computer screens that descend from the ceiling on demand. Add to these changes the growing trend towards flexitime, working from home and the increasing use of part-time staff, then the need for a more flexible office layout to accommodate fewer permanent staff is a growing phenomenon of the new millennium. Arriving at the office, picking up their personalized mobile phone from the recharging rack and then finding a place to work is the layout design that many staff will be using in the future.

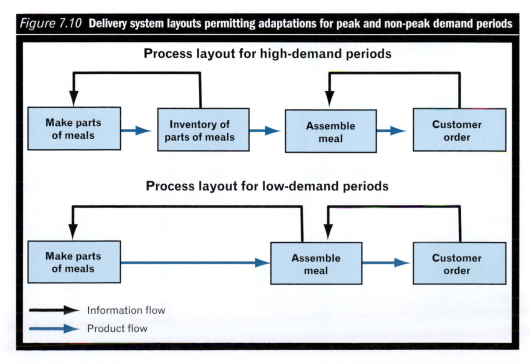

Figure 7.10 **Delivery system layouts permitting adaptations for peak and non-peak demand periods**

Process layout for high-demand periods

| Make parts of meals | → | Inventory of parts of meals | → | Assemble meal | → | Customer order |

Process layout for low-demand periods

| Make parts of meals | → | Assemble meal | → | Customer order |

→ Information flow
→ Product flow

Impact of IT on delivery systems and layouts

IT developments have not only reduced costs and lead times within systems and procedures but have also enabled companies to redesign many of these delivery systems. These changes also bring layout changes, as the following examples illustrate:

- Automated banking – high street banks are continuing to cut costs by automating more of their services. In parts of Europe and the USA, fully automated branches are replacing existing arrangements. These offer all the usual customer services but no tellers. Such changes necessitate layouts that accommodate these new delivery systems. The space needs to provide for varying numbers of customers, informal queries, areas to complete paying-in slips and the like, sufficient space to allow secure transactions to take place and a layout that allows access when the branch is closed.

- Call centres – telephone access has had a significant impact on the delivery of several services over the past 20 years. Sectors such as financial services, utilities, hotels and travel have made extensive use of telephone-based provision through call centre operations. The principle on which these are built is that customers telephone the centre (usually free or local rate charges) and either call centre staff or computer systems handle queries and requests in a fast and customized manner. Call centre staff are linked to sophisticated telephone and computer systems, with the latter providing up-to-date information on the current position and past transactions of customer accounts and dealings so that requests can be handled promptly and accurately. Telephone calls handled by a computerized system use either voice or key pad responses to questions or to complete a transaction.

Extended opening hours facilitate the use of these services particularly for customers who are unable to visit the high street branches or offices of the service provider. Figure 7.11 illustrates the layout features that typify a call centre. With the service delivery system now front-office based and opening hours up to 24 hours a day, layouts need to be able to meet peak demands and the several staff changeovers and staff combinations that will occur.

Figure 7.11 **Layout of a typical call centre**

© WavebreakmediaMicro – Fotolia.com

At this point take some time out by looking at Case 7.5 and review the case questions.

Detailed layout design

Having selected the appropriate basic layout, the next step is to design a detailed layout. The objectives of this phase are to decide:

- where to position the staff, processes, equipment and other facilities involved in providing the services and products

- the position, size and number of the other facilities that are not part of the delivery system such as meeting areas, rest rooms and cafeterias

- the number and dimension of other aspects such as entrances, exits, emergency routes, walkways, corridors, stairways and elevators

- the space to be allocated to each of the above.

In parallel with the detailed design phase, the steps involved in providing the services or making the products, the sequence to be followed and where these steps are ideally positioned will need to be determined. As space restrictions or layout advantages may influence the preferred sequence and position of the steps involved, the process routes will need to be considered at the same time as finalizing the layout and then be integrated into the detailed design.

The features of good layouts

Before discussing the techniques and approaches we can use to help in detailed layout design, let's first look at the aspects and features to be taken into account when developing a detailed layout. A comprehensive review of what needs to be addressed is given below but the relative importance of these will change depending on the type of organization involved:

- *System flow charting* – system flow charting is a visual aid to help determine and clarify the sequence of steps involved in providing services and products as part of the detailed design. With service delivery system design, the flow chart (also known as a 'service blueprint') would also establish what is known as 'the line of visibility' that separates front-office and back-office activities.

- *Use of space* – identifying space requirements is a prerequisite to developing a good layout. It helps ensure the effective use of the office, building or warehouse space available while accommodating any future long-term flexibility as needs change.

- *Use of equipment* – decisions about the equipment to be used including elevators, conveyors and automatic carts.

- *Cost of movement* – in many delivery systems an overriding objective of the detailed layout is to minimize the distance travelled and hence the overall cost of movement. In others, the overriding objective would be to maximize sales revenue by, for example, routing customers through a retail store in such a way as to increase exposure to the products on offer.

- *Health and safety* – a good layout design needs to incorporate essential health and safety features (for example, emergency exits and access points) while also designing in other dimensions that will contribute to the overall health and safety considerations for both staff and customers. For example, adequate lighting and ventilation, width of aisles, corridors and walkways and the number and size of entrances and exits.

CASE 7.5 BUILDING COMMUNAL LEARNING SPACES AT VARIOUS NORTH AMERICAN UNIVERSITIES

North American universities are constructing a whole series of new buildings to house their existing business schools, with the underlying design aimed at encouraging creative, open, flexible, informal and interactive learning. To do so, these new building layouts include 'forums', 'marketplaces' and other communal areas. Current learning approaches mean that students spend much more time working together on campus and the new layout designs reflect this. Here are a few examples:

- **University of Chicago, Graduate School of Business** built at a cost of £78 million; the layout of the new school allocates just over 30 per cent of the 415,000 square feet facility to space for students, with lounges, a dining area, 34 group study rooms, 18 classrooms for MBAs and PhDs and 36 interview rooms where corporate recruiters can meet students.

- **York University's Schulich School of Business in Toronto** covers about 350,000 square feet. The basic layout is designed to increase the level of interaction between faculty and students by, for example, making it impossible to get into or out of the school without passing through the main space known as the marketplace. In addition, the marketplace is packed with everything from high-tech information screens around the lobby to a cluster of internet cafés and shops.

- **Wharton's Jon M Huntsman Hall** cost £90m to build and comprises 324,000 square feet. Here, lecture halls, study areas and classrooms brim over with technological connections including high speed networking and video conferencing that links the Philadelphia campus with Wharton West in San Francisco. Classroom podiums all have a microphone, computer keyboard, audiovisual control system and laptop computer link-up. Multi-screen systems facilitate video projection and teleconferencing, with all video and audio equipment linked to the internet. The 57 group study rooms are equally geared up.

- **At the Ohio State University's Max Fisher Business School**, the final phase of a six-building development project is the residence for the college's executive education programme and includes a 151 bedroom hotel, an executive education centre and an upmarket restaurant.

Questions

1. How does the space created by the new designs challenge business schools to consider alternative ways of doing things?

2. Building layouts can have a big impact on human behaviour. How?

Lecturers: visit www.palgrave.com/business/hillom3e for teaching guidelines for this case study

- *Aesthetics and the quality of the working environment* – linked to the last point are decisions that will affect the quality of the staff's working environment, including the levels of natural light, wall colours, use of planters, height of partitions and ways to increase airflow, reduce noise and provide privacy.

- *Communications* – a good layout needs to facilitate essential verbal and visual communication between the parts of an organization and different steps in a delivery system or process. Proximity of staff, and open plan versus enclosed offices are typical of the features to be considered.

- *Image and brand* – some organizations use the detailed layout of their outlets as one way to reinforce the image and brand of the business. Fast-food companies such as McDonald's and Burger King and hotel chains such as Budget Inns and Holiday Inn Express are examples of this feature. Having the same entrances, reception areas, room layouts and front-office arrangements from decor to carpets and fittings to furniture provides familiarity for the customer, maintains standards (including franchisees) while reinforcing the company's image and brand.

Designing fixed position layouts

The techniques and approaches for designing fixed position layouts are not well developed and often the layout issues are addressed on a somewhat ad hoc basis due to the level of uncertainty inherent in this type of service or product provision.

Even where the task has been completed before (for example, building set house designs on an estate), many variables are liable to change. Delays in material shipments, design alterations and adverse weather conditions are some of the dimensions that can create uncertainty. Add to this the limited space on site, the changing availability of this space as work progresses (for example, an area may be available for material storage at one stage but has been designated as a roadway or site for a building at a later stage), the varying volumes of materials and storage areas required and the changing priorities as a job progresses, all of which create uncertainty within layout decisions. Similarly, in a management consultancy assignment, the availability of suitable on-site office space at a client's premises and the changing need for and availability of consultancy staff throughout an assignment, particularly where the orientation of the assignment changes, make what ought to be relatively simple layout decisions more complex.

These uncertainties seldom yield an optimum solution, as the decisions are often more expedient than analytical and are handled on an ad hoc basis that reflects the position, progress and current dynamics of the task and situation.

Designing process or functional layouts

The objective of these layout designs is to arrange these processes or functions in line with the aspects and features of a detailed layout design listed at the start of this section. This procedure involves the following steps:

- Clarify the total space on hand and the costs of any possible extensions.

- Identify any constraints that exist, the possibility of reducing or eliminating these and the costs that would be involved.

- Determine the area required by the different facilities, processes and functions.

- Determine the size of other facilities that are not part of the delivery system such as meeting areas, rest rooms and cafeterias.

- Assess the number, size and position of the entrances, exits, corridors, gangways and walkways required.

- Assess the direction and flow of staff, information and materials through the processes and functions.

The detailed design of these layouts is made more difficult by the large number of different services or products typically handled by the same set of processes or functions. As one of the fundamental tasks in designing these layouts is often to minimize the cost of movement, determining where the different processes or functions are best positioned relative to one another is essential. The common approaches to help resolve this step in the procedure are described below.

Load, movement or trip frequency charts

To help evaluate alternative process or functional layouts, load, movement or trip frequency charts are often used to analyze the number of movements or trips between the processes or functions involved. In the example in Figure 7.12, this is entitled Step 1. So the number of movements or trips from Department 1 to 2 was 12, the number from Department 2 to 1 was 20 and so on.

The next step is to select the dimension that the detailed layout design seeks to minimize, for example the total distance travelled or the total cost of the movements. In Figure 7.12, it was decided to minimize the distance travelled, and Step 2 provides these data for the existing layout. In most instances, it can be seen that the distance travelled between two departments in one direction was the same as the distance travelled going in the

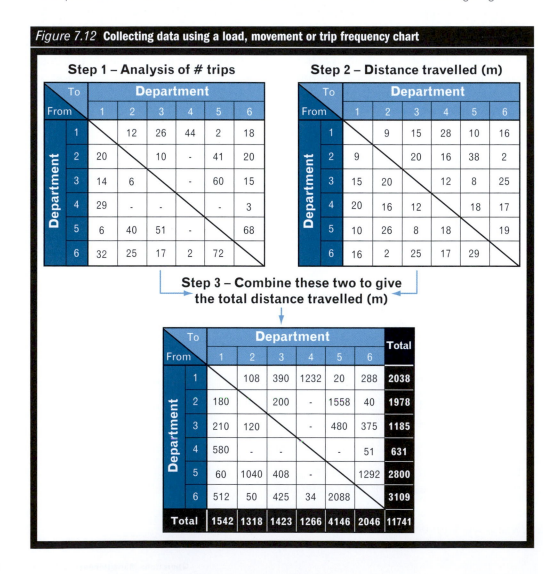

Figure 7.12 Collecting data using a load, movement or trip frequency chart

Step 1 – Analysis of # trips

From \ To	1	2	3	4	5	6
1		12	26	44	2	18
2	20		10	-	41	20
3	14	6		-	60	15
4	29	-	-		-	3
5	6	40	51	-		68
6	32	25	17	2	72	

Step 2 – Distance travelled (m)

From \ To	1	2	3	4	5	6
1		9	15	28	10	16
2	9		20	16	38	2
3	15	20		12	8	25
4	20	16	12		18	17
5	10	26	8	18		19
6	16	2	25	17	29	

Step 3 – Combine these two to give the total distance travelled (m)

From \ To	1	2	3	4	5	6	Total
1		108	390	1232	20	288	2038
2	180		200	-	1558	40	1978
3	210	120		-	480	375	1185
4	580	-	-		-	51	631
5	60	1040	408	-		1292	2800
6	512	50	425	34	2088		3109
Total	1542	1318	1423	1266	4146	2046	11741

opposite direction. However, there were three instances where this was not the case due to a one-way system introduced for reasons of safety:

From/To	1 to 4	2 to 5	5 to 6
Distance (m)	28	38	19

From/To	4 to 1	5 to 2	6 to 5
Distance (m)	20	26	29

If the distance travelled both ways between all departments was the same, the procedure could be simplified by combining the number of trips between Departments 1 and 2 and Departments 2 and 1 and so on, and then using the total trips in subsequent calculations. However, it is always best to first complete the analysis given in Steps 1 and 2 of Figure 7.12 as subsequent layout options may need to use this data split.

The outcome of this analysis is given in Step 3 of Figure 7.12. The 633 trips involved a total distance travelled of 11,741 metres. This would then be used as a benchmark against which to measure alternative layouts and the gains to be made in terms of reducing travel distances. When considering possible changes, this factor as well as aspects such as the cost of changing an existing layout would then help to evaluate alternatives.

Relationship charts

A second approach to detailed layout design that also uses a matrix format is the relationship chart. This helps to identify the relative closeness between departments. As the example in Figure 7.13 illustrates, this approach uses a priority code to show the preferred proximity of two departments (shown as the 'degree of closeness') and a justification code specifying the 'reason' for the desired proximity.

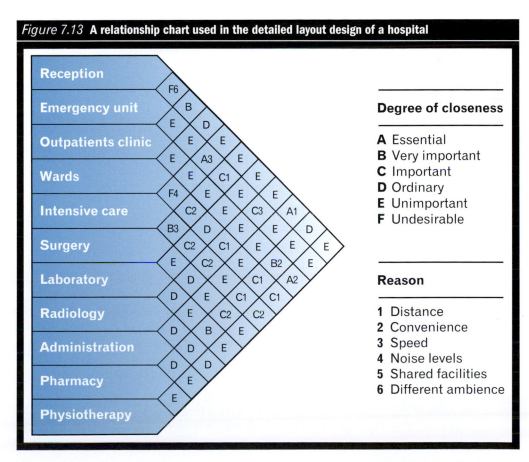

Figure 7.13 **A relationship chart used in the detailed layout design of a hospital**

Degree of closeness

A Essential
B Very important
C Important
D Ordinary
E Unimportant
F Undesirable

Reason

1 Distance
2 Convenience
3 Speed
4 Noise levels
5 Shared facilities
6 Different ambience

As the complexity of the detailed layout design task increases, these approaches to detailed layout solutions are unable to cope with the number of multiple flow patterns and constraints involved. Several computerized methods are available to overcome these limitations, which use logical rules to list alternatives and then evaluate them against relevant criteria. The link to a computerized system allows more variables to be included, refinements to alternatives to be assessed and more layout alternatives to be considered.

Designing service or product layouts

As explained earlier, this type of layout is based around similar services or products, and its degree of appropriateness reflects the following assumptions:

- The services or products are standardized and involve the same sequence of activities.

- The volumes involved are sufficient to give rise to adequate levels of staff or process utilization to justify a dedicated investment.

- Demand is stable and predictable.

The services or products using this type of layout invariably involve a multi-step process and two design outcomes of this result:

- The layout design will mirror the sequence of steps in the process.

- The work content at each step will be similar in length – the concept of **line balancing**.

Some high-volume, repeat service delivery systems and both line and continuous processes in manufacturing use this type of layout. In assembly lines where parts of products are put together, and in service delivery systems where people provide the services, the work content at one step will be designed to match the work content at the next step, and so on – which is known as line balancing.[3] If the work content at each step is not similar, delays and waiting will occur. Figures 7.14, 7.15 and 7.16 illustrate this.

Line balancing is the assignment of tasks so as to ensure that the work content (time taken to complete each step) is equal (or closely similar) at each step of the process.

Figure 7.14 **Cafeteria process times**				
Step	**Activity**	**Served by**		**Average time in seconds**
		Self	**Staff**	
1	Collect tray/take water	✓		15
2	Select cold drink	✓		15
3	Select salad	✓		10
4	Select dessert	✓		10
5	Serve main course		✓	30
6	Serve vegetables		✓	20
7	Pour hot drink		✓	15
8	Pay cashier		✓	55

The cafeteria staff in this example were concerned about the long queues that formed both at lunch times and in the early evening. The team found that the work was unevenly divided between the four staff. A flow diagram (see Figure 7.15) clearly illustrates this. The hourly flow rates for the staff providing Steps 5 to 8 shows the imbalance of these current arrangements. The **bottleneck** is at Step 8. Here, a member staff can only serve a maximum of 65 students per hour, almost half that of the next lowest rate. Bottlenecks arise because of an imbalance in capacity in relation to the amount of time taken to complete the task at one stage in a process. Here it is staff capacity at Step 8 in relation to the time to complete the 'pay cashier' task, compared with the equivalent ratio at other steps.

Bottleneck – in business terms, a bottleneck refers to the capacity-constraining stage in a service delivery system or manufacturing process that governs the output of the whole system or set of processes.

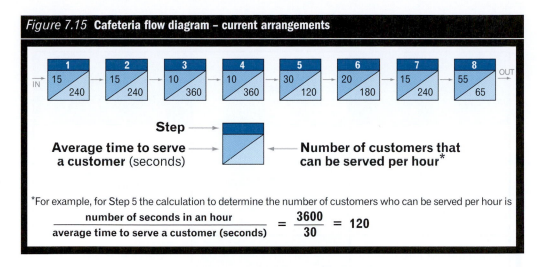

Figure 7.15 Cafeteria flow diagram – current arrangements

Step

Average time to serve a customer (seconds)

Number of customers that can be served per hour*

*For example, for Step 5 the calculation to determine the number of customers who can be served per hour is

$$\frac{\text{number of seconds in an hour}}{\text{average time to serve a customer (seconds)}} = \frac{3600}{30} = 120$$

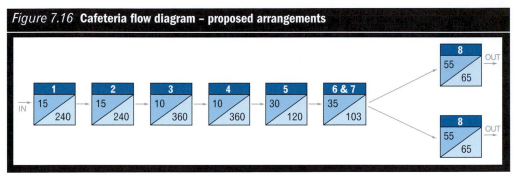

Figure 7.16 Cafeteria flow diagram – proposed arrangements

The team recognized that an additional cashier would need to be added in order to increase the flow rate. If Steps 6 and 7 were combined and undertaken by one member of staff, this would release someone as an additional cashier. As the diagram in Figure 7.16 shows, the flow rates at the four staffed positions were now more in balance, and the hourly flow rate increased from 65 (the bottleneck or limiting factor at Step 8 in the current arrangements) to 103, with the bottleneck or limiting factor now lying at Steps 6 and 7. The two staff now at Step 8 can together handle 130 students per hour.

The above example illustrates, in principle, how line balancing works. As you would imagine, the line balancing requirements of the processes in high-volume manufacturing or chemical plants would be more finely tuned than in this cafeteria example. This would involve small adjustments and readjustments to the process layout until the optimum balance had been achieved, and the line or continuous process would then be designed and built in order to maximize daily output, and hence improve productivity and reduce the unit cost of the product. But the principles involved would be the same.

Hybrid layouts

As explained in Chapters 5 and 6, hybrid systems will have their origins in one of the basic types of process. Of the four hybrids illustrated in the last chapter, three have their origins in a batch process and the fourth in a line process, as shown in Figure 7.17. In horticulture, when grafting one tree onto the rootstock of another tree to produce a hybrid, it is the latter tree type that is the dominant factor in the resulting mix. This is also the case with process hybrids. Thus, the techniques and approaches used to help develop a detailed design for process or functional and service or product layouts will also be used for the hybrids which have a similar process origin.

Figure 7.17 Hybrids and their process origins

Type of hybrid	Process origin	Approach to layout design
Cells Linked batch Nagare production system	Batch	Process or functional
Transfer line	Line	Service or product

Queueing and waiting line analysis

Even where line balancing is part of the delivery system design, queues will invariably occur as customers rarely, if ever, arrive at a steady and predictable rate. Consequently, several factors need to be taken into account when designing delivery systems:

- *Arrival rate* Arrival rates need to be assessed in terms of probability distributions: at times there may be no customers to serve, while at others there may be too many all at once.

- *Variability of service times* The length of time to serve a customer may vary, particularly where a wide range of services can be provided by each server.

- *Rejecting customer access to a queue* Where customers are already waiting, the system can be designed to refuse to let further customers enter the queue and thus ensure some control over waiting-to-be-served times. For example, some telephone-based services and websites are designed to prevent additional customers entering the existing queue until the queue length has reduced. Customers may feel equally dissatisfied but recognize that the cost benefits of not making a call are a plus factor.

- *Balking* On entering the system, customers may decide not to join the queue but to go elsewhere or, at best, return later.

- *Change of mind* Where queues reduce slowly, customers may decide after a while to leave.

- *Queueing time equality* Queue design should aim to ensure that waiting times are similar. A single queue feeding into two or more server positions, as opposed to customers entering the system and joining one of several queues of their choice, is such an example.

- *Psychology of queues* The design of systems should take into account customers' perceptions of waiting. The psychology of queues can be used to influence customers' responses and attitudes:

  - Unoccupied time feels longer than occupied time. The system may, therefore, request customers to complete part of the service process, or it may provide some activity to distract customers.
  - Pre-process waits feel longer than in-process waits, so engaging with customers as quickly as possible (such as handing out menus and taking pre-dinner drink orders as soon as customers arrive) ensures customers know that the service has started.
  - Queueing time equality – seeing noticeably different waiting times can raise anxiety levels, and uncertain and unexplained waiting times drag more than finite waits. Designing systems that advise customers of the approximate waiting time returns the choice of waiting to the customer and reduces the unknown factor.

Location and layout in practice

- Give that, in reality, many organizations are committed indefinitely to a location, then choosing where to site a business needs careful consideration of how well future business requirements will be met by that choice.

- Companies need to choose sites using objective criteria and be sensitive to the fact that while personal preferences can often unduly influence these decisions, executives move on to other jobs but the site remains put.

- Companies should always include quantitative data and analyses when making location decisions. In that way, qualitative factors can be checked to ensure that such critical decisions are made using sound business criteria

- While short-term decisions (both in terms of location and layout) may delay major investment and postpone the trauma of change, the size of the eventual move is not reduced and being in the wrong place or continuing to cope with an inappropriate layout continues to increase costs and work loads.

- Existing layouts need to be checked regularly to ensure that they continue to meet business objectives and the changing needs of markets.

Driving business performance

Decisions on where best to locate and how best to lay out facilities are ones that typically are infrequently reviewed. As a consequence, ensuring that anticipated future requirements as well as current needs form part of these decisions is critical as they underpin business performance in the following ways.

Using location and layout decisions to release cash

Shortening operations lead times from customers order to delivery can not only win orders but will also improve cash flow within a business as materials and part-finished goods and services are reduced.

- Materials – locating close to sources of materials reduces the need to hold inventory.

- Work-in-progress – shorter lead times reduce the amount of part-finished goods and services within operations. Cutting out waste is a key factor here and well-designed layouts facilitate movement and reduce delays.

- Finished items – once complete, moving goods to the customer completes operations process and signals the final phase of the cash-to-cash cycle described earlier in Figure 1.11.

Using location and layout decisions to improve market support

Attracting new and retaining existing customers are key factors in the financial welfare and growth of business. In many service companies, choosing a location close to customers or one that provides easy access either by car or public transport will directly influence customer choice. Once inside the premises, the ease of moving around, the feeling of space and the provision of appropriate facilities will help create a customer experience that will influence future choice.

Using location and layout decisions to reduce costs

Where moving goods to and from a facility is a feature of the business, then choosing where to locate will be a significant factor in the overall cost of running such organizations. Similarly, the layout of facilities will directly affect the costs of providing the services or making the products sold to the customers. And, as such costs are an inherent by-product of the current layout, then only a redesign of the facility can significantly reduce such costs.

Critical reflections

Where best to locate and how best to arrange the people, systems and processes, both within a facility and throughout the delivery system, impact both sales and costs. Consequently, it is essential to reflect both the external (customer/market) and the internal (operational) dimensions in these key decisions. As with many operations investments, their large and fixed nature involves high costs and long timescales where changes are to be made, so getting it right needs care and analysis.

Although convenience often plays a part in location and layout choices, organizations need to be aware of any less than favourable aspects of their decisions and factor these into their expectations and the day-to-day running of the business. Expectations will then be grounded in reality, and performance will be measured against attainable targets. In this way, control will be exercised and developments set in the context of both the short- and long-term objectives of the business.

Summary

- The two tasks of deciding location and layout are distinct yet related. They are distinct in that location concerns where best to site a facility, whereas layout concerns how best to arrange the staff, processes and equipment within that facility. And they are related in that they form two parts of a key decision – how best to position facilities in order to perform the operations task and meet the needs of the business.

- Decisions about where to locate may need to be taken at several levels, from deciding on a continent or region down to the choice of the site itself.

- Within these choices, the factors to be taken in account can be categorized into those of a general nature (broad-based issues that could influence or even override other factors, such as the origin of existing sites and politically based constraints) and those which have economic implications (such as market access).

- A number of specific factors, such as infrastructure and proximity to markets and suppliers, also affect the location decision at each level.

- Weighted factor and centre of gravity methods are two analytical techniques that help companies when making these key decisions.

- Layout decisions are affected by background factors such as the availability of space and meeting the potential need for future flexibility.

- The basic types of layout are fixed position, process or functional, and service or product. The choice of which to use will depend on the type of service delivery system and manufacturing process involved.

- Cells are a hybrid delivery system, developed from a mix of functional and service/ product layouts.

- Having decided on the appropriate basic layout, the next step is to design a detailed layout. Frequency charts and relationship charts are used to analyze and design process or functional layouts, while line balancing and waiting line analysis are important aspects of service and product layout design.

Discussion questions

1. Select a service outlet and identify the good and bad points of its chosen location.

2. Review the layout of a high street branch of three different banks. List the principal similarities and differences of each layout. Why do you think these similarities and differences exist?

3. Lord Sieff, when CEO of Marks & Spencer, the UK-based retailer is reputed to have said: 'There are three important factors in retailing – location, location and location.' Why would such a comment be made?

4. What are the advantages and disadvantages of a qualitative (as opposed to a quantitative) approach in location choices?

5. One location adage is: 'Manufacturers locate near their resources while retailers locate near their customers.' Discuss.

6. Contrast the location of a food distributor with one of the supermarkets to which it delivers products. Which important factors are similar and which are dissimilar in their respective choice of location?

7. Review the layout of a service organization of your own choice and identify examples of 'the features of good layouts' given in this chapter.

8. What are the advantages and disadvantages of hot desking?

9. Complete a similar exercise to that given in Figures 7.15 and 7.16. How well balanced is your cafeteria service delivery system? What improvements could you suggest?

Assignments

1. As a team of three, select two supermarkets and individually assess them against the criteria listed in the section 'Factors affecting the choice of site'. Then review each of your individual ratings against each other's, discuss and list the key areas of agreement and disagreement.

2. As a team of three, individually select one of the following facilities to review: a large retail pharmacy, a large bookstore and a multiplex cinema.
   a. In your team, agree for each location the factors to be used to review each site.
   b. As individuals assess one of the three locations using the agreed factors.
   c. Discuss the three sets of findings and then identify the two most important factors that each facility shares and the two most important factors that are facility-specific.

3. Complete a similar exercise to the last assignment, but this time analyze the layout of each location with particular reference to customer flows and the type of layout used. Compare and contrast your results. What were the key determinants on layout design for each outlet?

4. A US-based engineering firm has been awarded a contract to build the assembly and fabricating facilities for a new automobile plant in Mexico. The need to complete the project on time is critical, given the proposed vehicle launch, and, as with all such assignments, staying within budget is essential. For these reasons the project manager needs to be continuously kept up to date. The client has assigned its own on-site staff to handle issues as they arise. The desired relationships for the specialist areas involved in completing the project are given below. The space allocated to the project team comprises an office for each of the seven sections (see below), plus an office for the client's own staff.
   a. Using a relationship chart complete a suggested layout.
   b. Give reasons for your layout proposal.

c. Why do the reasons above differ to the reasons used in the chapter example, Figure 7.13?

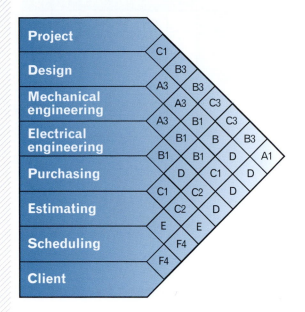

Degree of closeness

A Essential
B Very important
C Important
D Ordinary
E Unimportant
F Undesirable

Reason

1 Convenience
2 Shared facilities
3 Day-to-day working
4 Potential interference
5 Different ambience

The eight offices are of similar size and comprise four offices on both sides of the same corridor and facing each other

5. Electronic Controls International (ECI), a US-based technology group, has narrowed down its location choices to four possible sites in Europe. ECI will need to train relevant staff, and the key factors, their weights and ratings for each location are shown in the table opposite. High scores represent favourable values.
   a. Calculate the weighted-factor score for each of the four sites.
   b. Which site would you choose?
   c. Would you reach the same conclusion if the weightings for operating costs and labour costs were reversed?

Factor	Weighting	Location			
		A	B	C	D
Staff availability	15	7	8	7	8
Operating costs	25	8	6	8	6
Government incentives	15	8	8	7	6
Land, construction and other set-up costs	15	7	6	7	7
Labour costs	10	8	8	6	6
Local technical infrastructure	10	4	7	8	7
Transport	10	4	8	8	7

6. The accountancy firm Thomas and Mason comprises six main sections. Due to the growth of the business over the last five years, the partnership is planning to move into new premises. These comprise six offices of equal size on each side of a corridor. The distance between the six offices is shown below, as are the number of trips between each sector. From this information, assign each of the six sections to an office in a way that minimizes the total distance travelled.

Distance between offices (metres)

Office	1	2	3	4	5	6
1	–	8	16	24	16	8
2		–	8	16	24	16
3			–	8	16	24
4				–	8	16
5					–	8
6						–

 # trips between offices

Office	1	2	3	4	5	6
1	–	26	31	82	64	14
2		–	45	29	40	101
3			–	20	39	27
4				–	30	46
5					–	56
6						–

Exploring further

TED talks

Johnson, S. (2010) *Where good ideas come from*. People often credit their ideas to individual 'Eureka!' moments. But Steven Johnson shows how history tells a different story. His fascinating tour takes us from the 'liquid networks' of London's coffee houses to Charles Darwin's long, slow hunch to today's high-velocity web.
www.ted.com/talks/steven_johnson_where_good_ideas_come_from.html

Steffen, A. (2011) *The shareable future of cities*. How can cities help save the future? Alex Steffen shows some cool neighborhood-based green projects that expand our access to things we want and need while reducing the time we spend in cars.
www.ted.com/talks/alex_steffen.html

Journal articles

Aron, R. and Singh, J.V. (2005) 'Getting offshoring right', *Harvard Business Review*, **83**(12): 135–43. In the past five years, a rising number of companies in North America and Europe have experimented with offshoring and outsourcing business processes, hoping to reduce costs and gain strategic advantage. According to several studies, half the organizations that have shifted processes offshore have failed to generate the expected financial benefits. The article discusses a rethink on current offshoring strategies.

Elsbach, K.D. and Bechky, B.A. (2007) 'It's more than a desk: working smarter through leveraged office design', *California Management Review*, **49**(2): 80–101. Current trends in telecommuting and non-territorial office design (where the desks or workspaces are used by several staff, thereby increasing the utilization of existing office areas and reducing the need to increase space on the one hand, or being able to reduce the space needed on the other) have changed what it means to work in an on-site office and, subsequently, have increased the number of functions that office design is expected to meet. This article offers a framework for office design that illustrates how managers can make design choices that both capitalize on the newest innovations in office design and serve the emerging needs of workers across a company.

Farrell, D. (2006) 'Smarter offshoring', *Harvard Business Review*, **84**(6): 84–92. The article looks at new offshoring locations including Morocco, Tunisia and Vietnam as alternatives to the most popular current locations, such as India and Eastern Europe.

Fayard, A-L. and Weeks, J. (2011) 'Who moved my cube?', *Harvard Business Review*, **89**(7–8): 103–10. The article discusses how companies have devised open floor plans and common areas within their offices to promote trust, cooperation and innovation by increasing causal interactions between employees. However, it suggests that these spaces must effectively balance three things: proximity, privacy and permission.

Huang, J. (2001) 'Future space: a new blueprint for business architecture', *Harvard Business Review*, **79**(4): 149–58. The article offers guidelines to help managers and entrepreneurs think creatively about the structures within which their businesses operate in order to reflect the needs of people when designing stores, offices and factories.

Laing, A., Craig, D. and White, A. (2011) 'High-performance office space', *Harvard Business Review*, **89**(9): 32–3. This article discusses how drug company Lilly created a more open office layout that stimulated creativity.

West, A.P., Jr., and Wind, Y. (2007) 'Putting the organization on wheels: workplace design at SEI', *California Management Review*, **49**(2): 138–53. To create an environment that would embody a culture of flexibility, egalitarianism, teamwork and entrepreneurship, SEI Investments built a distinctive headquarters. The article discusses how the offices are open and the desks are on wheels, making it easy for teams to interact and quickly reorganize themselves.

Wieckowski, A. (2010) 'Back to the city', *Harvard Business Review*, **88**(5): 23–5. Several companies are relocating away from suburban sprawls and back to cities. Many workers prefer to live in cities or revitalized outskirts, where homes, shops, schools, parks and other amenities are close together. The impact for many types of business is discussed.

Books

Hill, A. and Hill, T. (2011) *Essential Operations Management*. Basingstoke: Palgrave Macmillan. The text provides a useful supplement to *Operations Management* by focusing on the essential aspects for managing operations within service and manufacturing organizations.

Oshri, I., Kotlarsky, J., Willcocks, L.P. (2008) *Outsourcing Global Services*. Basingstoke: Palgrave Macmillan.

Salvaneschi, L. (ed.) (2002) *Location, Location, Location: How to Select the Best Site for your Business*. Central Point, OR: Oasis Press. This book analyzes how businesses should select the best location for their operation in order to maximize the number of customers they attract and the shopping experience they provide.

Websites

NAFTA. http://www.nafta-sec-alena.org/en/view.aspx. Visit the NAFTA website for more information on the North American Free Trade Agreement.

Notes and references

1. Kimes, S.E. and Fitzsimmons, J.A. (1990) 'Selecting profitable hotel sites at La Quinta Motor Inns', *Interfaces*, **20**(2): 12–20.
2. Hyer, N.L. and Brown, K.A. (2003) 'Work cells with staying power: lessons for processing operations', *California Management Review*, **46**(1): 27–52; Bohmer, R.M.J. (2010) 'Fixing health care on the front lines', *Harvard Business Review*, April: 62–9; Siebdrat, F., Hogel, M. and Ernst, H. (2009) 'How to manage virtual teams', *MIT Sloan Management Review*, **50**(4): 62–9; Swank, C.K. (2003) 'The lean service machine', *Harvard Business Review*, October: 123–30.
3. A useful overview of line balancing is provided in Mabs, G.H. (1990) 'Assembly line balancing – let's remove the mystery', *Journal of Industrial Engineering*, May.

Visit www.palgrave.com/business/hillom3e for self-test questions, guideline answers to some case study questions, useful weblinks and more to help you understand the topics in this chapter

Set back from the main road, the McDonald's in Christchurch, New Zealand is part of a large shopping area with ample parking for people wishing to take a break while they're out and about. From the outside it has all the usual hallmarks of a traditional McDonald's restaurant, but once you are inside it looks radically different. To improve sales revenue it recently introduced a McDonald's 'drive-thru' and then separated the inside of the restaurant into a traditional McDonald's 'in-store' area and a McCafé (see Figure 1). Although the sales revenue from the McDonald's 'in-store' area has remained constant over the past year, sales within the other two areas have increased significantly with 'drive-thru' sales up 43 per cent in the last eight months. Of the total restaurant sales, 44 per cent now come from the 'drive-thru' and 13 per cent from the McCafé.

STAFFING

Reporting to the Store Manager, two Senior Managers manage the three different parts of the restaurant. In addition, the McDonald's 'in-store' and 'McCafé' areas have a dedicated manager and assistant manager working with a team of full-time and part-time staff to prepare food and serve customers. In total, about 75 full-time and part-time staff work within the facility. To help meet the wide hourly and daily demand fluctuations, all staff are trained across a range of jobs enabling them to switch from food preparation to serving customers in busy times and to store cleaning-type tasks in more quiet times.

McDONALD'S 'IN-STORE' AND 'DRIVE-THRU'

The McDonald's 'drive-thru' facility was created by redesigning part of the rear car park. There are two customer order points and two collection hatches where food and drink are collected and paid for. The 'in-store' facility comprises a preparation area (that serves both the 'in-store' and 'drive-thru') and 'in-store' with small tables and chairs for about 36 customers (see Figure 1).

Hourly staffing requirements are based on sales forecasts. The store opens at 6am each day and closes at 11pm Sunday to Thursday and at 1am on Friday and Saturday. Customers enter the restaurant through the 'front entrance' or 'side entrance' and join a queue. When they reach the counter, they place their orders and the staff assemble the meal(s) from the items kept in the holding bins immediately behind the counter. In times of low demand some food items are prepared on request but typically the food is pre-prepared ahead of time to reduce customer waiting time. In recent years a breakfast menu has been added as well as a number of deli and 'lighter choices' (see Figure 2). Customers then choose to either take the food and drink away or eat in house.

Figure 1 Restaurant layout (not to scale)

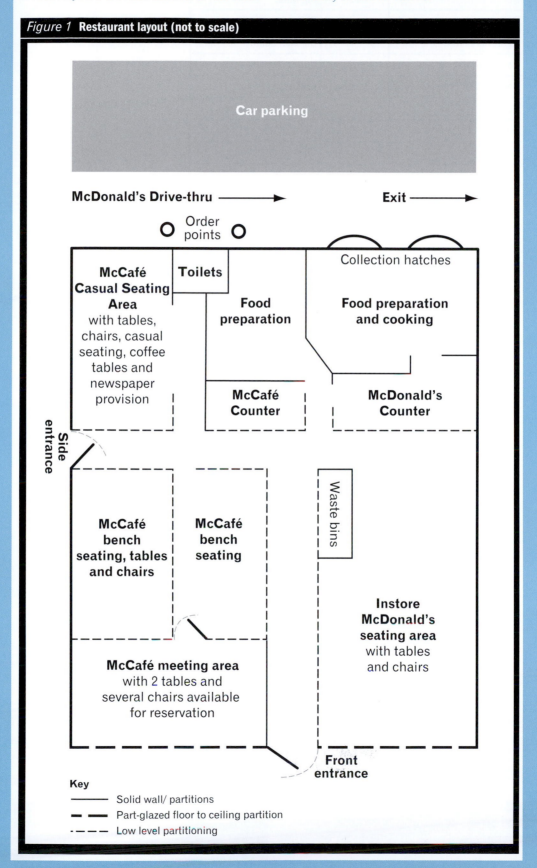

Figure 2 McDonald's 'in-store' and 'drive-thru'

Menu items	Quantity	Example
Beef and fish meals	12	Big Mac
Deli choices	8	BLT
Lighter choices	5	Chicken salad
Desserts	6	Hot fudge sundae
Breakfast options	12	Kiwi big breakfast
Hot drinks	6	Americano
Soft drinks	6	Coca Cola
Shakes	3	Chocolate shake

Figure 3 McCafé menu

Menu items	Quantity	Example
Sandwiches	8	Beef pastrami and salad
Wraps, paninis and melts	11	Mexican wrap
Cakes and muffins	16	Blueberry muffin
Quiche	2	Bacon and brie
Coffees	13	Latte
Other hot drinks	5	Pot of tea
Frappes	4	Mocha
Other cold drinks	16	Organic apple juice

McCAFE

Two staff start at 5.30am to set up the equipment and receive the daily fresh food deliveries. From 6am to 8am, the staff prepare the wraps and other food items while also serving customers. On entering the restaurant, customers queue at the McCafé counter, order their food and drink, pay and then choose where to sit. When their order is ready a member of staff takes it to them at their table. While some food items are pre-prepared, the wide choice on offer (see Figure 3) means that some have to be made-to-order along with the majority of the drinks.

The layout of the McCafé comprises three separate areas (see Figure 1). There is a casual seating area for customers with tables, chairs, casual seating and coffee tables with in-store local and national newspapers provided free-of-charge. The second area is a mix of bench seating and small tables and chairs for about 50 customers. The third area is an enclosed space that can be reserved by local businesses, societies and similar organizations for meetings or discussion groups at no cost other than the food and drink purchases made. When not in use for a meeting it is used by customers as an extra seating area.

Questions

1. Provide an overview of the three different restaurants – McDonald's 'in-store', McDonald's 'drive-thru' and McCafé – in terms of the service delivery system used in each.

2. Explain how the layouts within the restaurants – McDonald's 'in-store', McDonald's 'drive-thru' and McCafé – differ and why they meet the needs of each set of customers.

Lecturers: visit www.palgrave.com/business/hillom3e for teaching guidelines for this case study

No. _____

NAME _____

Week Ending _____

YOU ARE YOUR OWN TIMEKEEPER.
WE PAY BY THIS RECORD,
YOUR OWN RECORDING.

102115

	MORNING		AFTERNOON		OVERTIME		TOTAL
	IN	OUT	IN	OUT	IN	OUT	

Managing Capacity

8

ORDINARY TIME			
OVERTIME			
STAT. SICK PAY			
TOTAL WAGES			
LESS NAT. INSCE			
LESS INC.TAX			
LESS DEDUCTIONS			
AMOUNT PAID			

Learning objectives

After completing this chapter, you should be able to:

- Explain the role of operations management in an organization

- Understand the nature of capacity and the mix of resources involved

- Appreciate the purpose of managing capacity

- Explain how to define and measure capacity in different organizations

- Appreciate the differences between capacity, utilization and efficiency

- Know how to calculate utilization and efficiency levels and know how to use trend data to manage capacity

- Recognize the capacity-related implications for delivery system and manufacturing processes

- Understand the role, timescales and steps to be taken in resources planning and medium-term capacity planning

- Recognize the advantages and disadvantages of level capacity and chase demand capacity plans

- Understand the different ways to manage demand and capacity

Chapter outline

Executive overview

Introduction

An overview of managing capacity

Defining and measuring capacity
Defining capacity
Measuring capacity
Overall measurement
Using output to measure capacity
Measuring capacity in practice

Using utilization and efficiency data to manage capacity
Utilization
Efficiency

Factors affecting capacity management
Make-or-buy decisions

Introduction

Capacity – the resources (the people, systems and equipment) necessary to meet the demand for serving customers or making products.

Capacity is made up of the resources needed to serve customers, process information or make products, and is a mix of the people, systems and equipment needed to deliver the services or products involved. The purpose of managing capacity is to match an organization's resources to the demand for its services or products. For example, a bank needs staff to serve customers, IT systems to process transactions and ATMs to enable customers to draw out cash from their accounts, while a manufacturing company needs people and processes to make the products it sells. Having sufficient capacity ensures that customers are served and products are made in line with **schedules** and orders. Too little capacity results in delays and lost sales; too much incurs costs. Effective management of this key element of operations, therefore, underpins the short-term success and long-term growth of an organization.

Schedule – a timetable of jobs with start dates to meet customers' delivery requirements.

This chapter will provide an explanation of how capacity is measured and what statements of capacity look like, before addressing how to plan and manage capacity and the systems for doing this. First, we'll take a broad look at the task of managing capacity, and then we'll look at how capacity is measured. After that, we'll consider how service and product delivery systems affect capacity, and the demand- and capacity-related issues that need to be addressed when determining what level of capacity is appropriate. Next, the task and methods for planning capacity will be reviewed, together with the types of capacity plan that can be used. Finally, we'll look at ways of managing demand (for example, through changing demand patterns, using service or product design features and scheduling) and managing capacity (for example, through short-term adjustments and flexible work patterns).

An overview of managing capacity

When organizations develop their short- and long-term business objectives, they need to decide how they will provide the appropriate level of capacity to meet current and future demand. Decisions relating to capacity (staff skills, processes and systems) will need to take into account the:

- *Delivery system and process capabilities* – to ensure that the technical specification of the services or products can be met.

- *Volumes* – how many services are to be processed or products are to be made.

Simple though this seems, it is a challenging task. The types of capability required will vary depending on the nature and range of service and product designs involved. How much capacity is needed will be based on anticipated demand. However, the uncertainty of forecasts and the certainty of reality will continue to result in false starts, underused capacity or an inability to cope with actual demand. Furthermore, capacity considerations in service industries and the perishable nature of service capacity create their own set of difficulties. All in all, these variables and uncertainties create a challenging operations task that needs to be well managed both for its own sake (as it is sizeable and expensive) and to meet the needs of customers.

The costs incurred by investing forward (that is, investing in capacity for the future) when increased sales do not materialize and the lost sales that result from not being able to meet demand, support opposing sides of an argument over whether capacity investment should lead or follow demand. Even successful strategies place substantial strain on organizations as they attempt to change direction. Being successful, therefore, requires responses to be coordinated at both the strategic and the tactical levels.

> EXECUTIVE INSIGHT

A key business strategy decision is whether capacity investment should lead or follow demand.

The initial steps in capacity investment will always command corporate attention. New markets, new customer contracts, new services and new products are high profile by nature, while decisions concerning additional staff and new plant, equipment, buildings and site locations are characterized by investments of large size. As such, this phase is approached with thoroughness and care due to the vetting and control exercised in corporate investment appraisal systems and the level of executive responsibility to make sound decisions that normally accompany such proposals: and rightly so.

Similarly, when companies need to change existing capacity levels in either growth or downsizing scenarios, the same degree of rigour needs to be applied. While these decisions may not gain the same level of corporate attention as initial investments tend to attract, the outcomes are the same. Delays or inadequate reviews can result in an inability to respond to demand and lead to lost opportunities to retain or grow market share. Moreover, the need for rigorous reviews is also essential in times of downsizing. Cutting staff without either assessing the tasks that no longer need doing or re-engineering current practices will lead to responses that will inadequately support customers in times when retaining current sales is essential to business performance.

Defining and measuring capacity

There are several ways to define and measure how capacity is provided and used. Recognizing these is a necessary step to avoid confusion and to allow expressions of 'how much of' and 'how well' to be made with understanding and accuracy, as these definitions result in different insights.

Defining capacity

Before we look in more detail at how capacity is measured, it's important to note that two main definitions are used when managing capacity:

1. **Planned (or available) capacity** Although operations could theoretically run or be open 24 hours each day throughout the year, in reality this is not normally required, nor does it typically make sense. An exception to this is those companies using continuous processing (such as oil refineries), where the costs of stopping and starting a process are so high that the process is run continuously (see Chapter 6). Planned (or available) capacity is, therefore, a statement of the intended or planned number of hours that are to be made available in a given period.

2. **Actual capacity** Although a certain level of capacity is planned (or available), actual capacity refines this by taking into account the **utilization** (the number of hours actually spent working) and the level of **efficiency** achieved (the actual output compared with the expected output while working).

Planned (or available) capacity – a statement of the intended or planned number of hours to be made available in a given period.

Actual capacity – the measure of planned (or available) capacity, taking into account the number of hours actually worked (utilization) and the actual output compared to expected output (efficiency) while working.

Utilization – the actual capacity used out of the planned (or available) capacity.

Efficiency (or 'effective performance') – actual output compared with expected output.

As you can imagine, the variance between these two will differ from one operation to another. Before investing in extra capacity, an organization must first look for ways to increase the utilization and/or efficiency of its existing operation as these improvements are typically less expensive to make and easier to change.

Measuring capacity

There are two common denominators used in businesses to express, calculate and measure activities – time and money. In most parts of a business, money is the dimension used to express and evaluate activity, for example sales revenue and profit. In operations, however, the common denominator is time. Statements and measures of performance regarding capacity and output are calculated using time as the base. So all services and products will need to be measured in terms of the time taken to complete them. Checks can then be made to assess how much capacity is needed and how well it has been used. The second aspect to be clarified concerns whether a firm should use staff or plant/equipment as the basis of these capacity statements, particularly where both are used in providing its services and products. The sections that follow explain the factors affecting the process of measuring capacity but, before addressing the principles involved, it's useful to discuss capacity statements and measurements in general.

To illustrate why time is typically used as the basis for calculating the capacity required and assessing how well available capacity has been used, take a look at Figure 8.1. This shows how many units of two different products are made over two weeks by a manufacturing firm. If it takes 10 minutes to complete Product A and 5 minutes to complete Product B, the process should produce 6 and 12 items of Products A and B respectively, each hour. To assess how many products should be made or how efficient a process was in a given period, the data showing the number of services delivered or products made within that period needs to be converted from units (number of services or products) into time (the amount of standard hours delivered or made). For example, if the process was operated for 40 hours in a week and made the number of Products A and B as shown in Figure 8.1, how would you assess the performance in Weeks 1 and 2?

Figure 8.1 **Number of products A and B made per week**

Product	Week (units made)	
	1	2
A	205	50
B	70	375
Total	275	425

Based on the number of products made, Week 2 appears the much better week, with over 50 per cent more products made. But when the time taken per unit is introduced into the calculation (Figure 8.2), it shows a different and truer picture of output, with both weeks being almost the same.

Figure 8.2 **Time taken to make products A and B**

Weeks	Product A			Product B			Total	
	Units	Time (mins)		Units	Time (mins)		Units	Time (hrs)
		per unit	total		per unit	total		
1	205	10	2,050	70	5	350	275	40.0
2	50	10	500	375	5	1,875	425	39.6

> **EXECUTIVE INSIGHT**

Operations uses time as the common denominator to express and measure its activities. The rest of the business uses money.

Overall measurement

Statements and measurements of capacity will often differ within and between the various parts of an organization. Taking a hospital as an example, let us illustrate why this is so:

- *Overall size* A hospital will typically use the number of beds it has as one indicator of overall size as this is a key dimension of its capacity.

- *Emergency unit* Capacity in the emergency unit of the same hospital will reflect the expected levels of demand at different times throughout each day of a week. This will then be translated into the number and mix of staff (the ratio of doctors, nurses and support staff) who need to be on duty for different hours of each day, different days of each week and different weeks throughout the year.

- *Consultant clinics* Based on the average length of appointments, a clinic will be arranged on a number of days each week or each month. The number of clinics will reflect known and anticipated levels of demand (number of appointments), and this will be adjusted to reflect changes that occur in the future. Appointments will then be made in line with the times that the consultants' clinics have been scheduled.

In this way, expressions of capacity will differ, with each emphasizing the dimension that underlines the aspect of capacity that reflects the resource providing the services or making the products. However, you will notice from the three examples in the list above that the last two use a time base. Assessing how many emergency staff and how many clinics are required will use time as the means of calculating appropriate numbers.

As these examples demonstrate, statements and measures of capacity will vary because they need to be based on the resource that is most critical for delivering the service or product.

Figure 8.3 Capacity unit of measurement

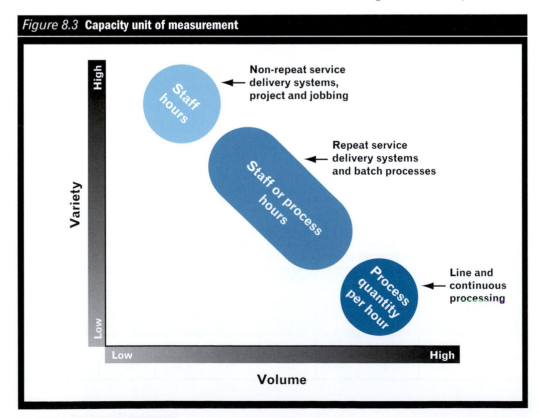

360

Figure 8.3 shows how staff hours, equipment hours and quantity can all be used as units for measuring capacity, depending on the type of product or service and as explained below:

- *Non-repeat service delivery systems, project and jobbing* In these businesses, skilled staff provide the service or product, with systems and equipment helping them to complete the task. Here, the measure of available capacity will be staff hours.

- *Line and continuous processing* With these processes, the process or equipment makes the product, and people support the process or equipment in this task. Although the speed of a line process can, within certain limits, be adjusted to reflect demand, the statement of capacity in these businesses will typically be based on the number of items the process is able to produce per hour.

- *Repeat service delivery systems* High-volume repeat service delivery systems are often more like line, with the equipment (for example, a cash machine or cheque-processing equipment) providing the service, so levels of capacity are typically expressed in terms of process or equipment hours. However, where staff provide the service, staff hours will be used to calculate capacity.

- *Batch processes* High-volume batch is more like line, so plant/equipment hours are typically the basis used for statements on capacity. Conversely, businesses that are more towards the low-volume end of batch processing will use staff hours as the basis of their capacity calculations. This is because people rather than equipment will be the factor governing output.

So the measure of capacity will reflect which input (people or equipment) into the service delivery system or manufacturing process is key to delivering the services and products involved.

Using output to measure capacity

How much operations capacity is needed will be assessed in relation to the size and type of expected demand, which is then translated into time as the way of comparing like with like. To explain this, let's look at a postal service delivering letters. The time taken to deliver letters in a town centre is considerably shorter than that taken for delivery in rural districts. Using the number of letters to be delivered would, therefore, not be a sufficiently accurate statement of demand or capacity. The time taken would need to reflect the number of deliveries, the distances involved and other variables. Using time as the basis for calculating demand and capacity is appropriate for most organizations as the services or products they provide will incur different amounts of staff or process time. But whereas the number of units (for example, letters delivered) is easily known, the time taken has to be calculated.

Although time is the underlying means of assessing capacity in most organizations, in some the number of units will, in fact, suffice. This will occur where the services or products are sufficiently similar to one another – here, units are an appropriate basis for calculating and assessing capacity. For example, the capacity of an oil refinery will be expressed as the number of litres processed per day, the capacity of an automobile plant by the number of vehicles assembled per day and the capacity of a fast-food restaurant by the number of meals served at given times in a day. These figures will then form the basis for statements of capacity and for calculations of utilization and efficiency.

Measuring capacity in practice

The two worked examples that follow are provided to help you understand the issues to be taken into account when measuring capacity in practice. They are based on real examples, although they have been simplified to help get the key points across.

'Should capacity **lead** or **follow** demand?'

WORKED EXAMPLE CONFORM

Conform is a small manufacturing business with five machines. One is normally fully used, but the other four machines always have spare capacity. Conform's business is subcontract work for a number of customers. The manufacturing process is simple, with all products being completed as a single operation on one of the five machines. Following machining, the products are packed before being despatched to customers to meet their order dates. Conform employs three machine operators who complete the necessary changeovers/set-ups on machines and undertake all the machining operations. In addition, there is one full-time and one part-time packer. The former is also responsible for despatch.

Planned machine operator capacity – from Monday to Friday, the three machine operators each work a single shift of seven and a half hours:

Planned capacity = Normal working hours
= 3 operators $\times$ 7.5 hours $\times$ 5 days = 112.5 hours

MACHINE OPERATOR UTILIZATION – WEEK 1

In Week 1, the company arranged overtime of one hour on each of four days for two of the machine operators. The utilization of operators in this week is shown below. As you will see, it compares total hours worked against planned capacity. In this way, it signals to the company that the number of hours required is higher than planned. and allows the company to monitor capacity and adjust if necessary.

$$\text{Machine operator utilization} = \frac{\text{Actual hours worked}}{\text{Planned hours of work}} \times 100$$

$$= \frac{41.5 + 41.5 + 37.5}{112.5} \times 100$$

$$= \frac{120.5}{112.5} \times 100$$

$$= 107 \text{ per cent}$$

MACHINE OPERATOR UTILIZATION – WEEK 2

In Week 2, no overtime was worked, and one operator had a period of three hours without any machining work. This operator was (as was normal in these circumstances) reassigned to packing. Machine operator utilization was, therefore:

$$\text{Machine operator utilization} = \frac{\text{Actual hours worked}}{\text{Planned hours of work}}$$

$$= \frac{37.5 + 37.5 + 34.5}{112.5} = \frac{109.5}{112.5}$$

$$= 97 \text{ per cent}$$

MACHINE UTILIZATION – WEEKS 1 AND 2

As we've already said, the company has five machines on which the three operators make a range of products, and the hours worked on each machine vary. The calculations for machine utilization highlight these differences, as shown in Figure 8.4.

Figure 8.4 Machine utilization at Conform		
Machine	**Week 1**	**Week 2**
1	41.5 hours worked / 37.5 hours available = 111 per cent	37.5 hours worked / 37.5 hours available = 100 per cent
2	9.0 hours worked / 37.5 hours available = 24 per cent	8.0 hours worked / 37.5 hours available = 21 per cent
3	22.0 hours worked / 37.5 hours available = 59 per cent	20.0 hours worked / 37.5 hours available = 53 per cent
4	35.0 hours worked / 37.5 hours available = 93 per cent	31.0 hours worked / 37.5 hours available = 83 per cent
5	13.0 hours worked / 37.5 hours available = 35 per cent	13.0 hours worked / 37.5 hours available = 35 per cent
Total hours worked on the five machines	**120.5**	**109.5**

WHAT DO THESE CALCULATIONS REVEAL?

- Higher or lower than 100 per cent utilization figures signal to the company that the number of hours used is higher or lower, respectively, than planned. Monitoring these figures over time will reveal whether or not this is an upward or a downward trend and allow appropriate adjustments to be made.

- Capacity often varies. Different staff skills and types of machine mean that the staff or machines in question can provide different services or products. Therefore, providing an average utilization figure for these five machines for Weeks 1 and 2 (in this instance 64 and 58 per cent, respectively) would lack meaning, whereas the actual utilization figure for each machine shows where capacity is available (as for Machines 2, 3 and 5), where there is some but not much capacity (as for Machine 4) and where capacity is fully used (as for Machine 1).

> EXECUTIVE INSIGHT
Utilization compares the actual hours worked with the planned hours of work.

Efficiency – operators

Standard output – the expected output for the hours worked.

Whereas utilization compares the number of hours worked with the number available or planned, efficiency (also known as 'effective performance') measures the amount of work produced in the hours worked and compares this figure with the amount expected (known as the '**standard output**'. In a business where the products are the same (for example, an automotive company), the calculation would be the number of cars produced in a day compared with the number expected. Where a company makes or provides several different services or products, comparisons are made by converting the latter into the hours of work they should have taken to complete and then comparing the total hours produced (that is, the number of units produced × the time per unit it should have taken to complete) with the total hours worked.

To illustrate let's look at the example given in Figure 8.5. Here, the three operators on machining each worked 7.5 hours on Day 1 of Week 1, with two operators also each working one hour of overtime. If during this day they made the products listed in Figure 8.5 then their overall efficiency would be calculated as shown below. Normally, this calculation would be made for a whole week.

Taking a single day keeps the example short yet still illustrates the principles and calculations involved.

Figure 8.5 **Calculating efficiency for machine operators at Conform on Day 1 of Week 1**

Product reference	# standard minutes to machine/complete	# produced	
		Products	Minutes
1612	10.0	14	140
4725	5.5	8	44
3408	25.0	3	75
0184	18.5	6	111
1229	36.0	4	144
4120	4.5	10	45
3678	12.0	30	360
2185	27.5	6	165
2766	3.0	25	75
Set-ups	15.0	9	135
Total minutes worked = 1294 = 21.6 hours			

Note: 1 As two operators on day 1 of the week each worked one overtime hour, this made a total hours worked of 3 × 7.5 + 2.0 = 24.5 hours.

$$\text{Efficiency} = \frac{\text{\# hours of work produced}}{\text{\# hours worked}} \times 100$$

$$= \frac{21.6}{24.5} \times 100 = 88 \text{ per cent}$$

> **EXECUTIVE INSIGHT**
Efficiency compares the actual output with the expected (known as the 'standard') output for the hours worked.

WORKED EXAMPLE JOHN MICHAEL

John Michael is a hairdresser in the centre of town. It employs seven part- and full-time staff and has seven hairdressing chairs – one allocated to each member of staff – that are used at different times during a week in line with expected demand, as shown in Figure 8.6. The working pattern illustrated reflects the mix of full-time (chairs 1 to 4) and part-time (chairs 5 to 7) staff, while the opening hours reflect the expected demand levels each day. Figure 8.6 shows that the four full-time staff work five days each week and take a different day off as arranged. The three part-time staff work at pre-arranged times, as shown.

Day	Planned opening hours	# Hours available per chair							Total hours
		1	2	3	4	5	6	7	
Monday	8	–	8	8	8	–	–	–	24
Tuesday	8	8	8	8	–	4	–	–	28
Wednesday	8	8	–	8	8	–	4	4	32
Thursday	8	8	8	–	8	4	4	–	32
Friday	10	10	10	10	10	8	8	8	64
Saturday	10	10	10	10	10	10	10	10	70

Figure 8.6 **Salon opening and hairdressing hours**

Note: Utilization on Monday $= \dfrac{\text{Hours used}}{\text{Hours available}} = \dfrac{8 + 8 + 8}{7 \times 8} = \dfrac{24}{56} = 43$ per cent

Hours available $= 7$ chairs $\times 8$ hours (the opening hours of the salon)

UTILIZATION – FACILITIES

As the facilities (that is, the chairs) are the same, calculating overall utilization is an appropriate statement. However, as capacity needs to match demand levels during each day, the planned capacity will be at different levels to reflect this. The John Michael salon opens for eight hours on Monday to Thursday, but on Friday and Saturday the planned capacity (that is, salon opening times) is ten hours (see Figure 8.6). During any week, the daily utilization calculations reflect this, as shown in Figure 8.7.

Figure 8.7 **Daily facilities utilization levels at John Michael**

Day	Utilization (%)
Mon	43
Tue	50
Wed	57
Thu	57
Fri	91
Sat	100

UTILIZATION – HAIRDRESSERS

Similar calculations assessing the utilization of each hairdresser during each day would also be appropriate. In John Michael's case, the schedule for a hairdresser was based on 15-minute booking slots, with longer jobs being allocated more than one 15-minute slot. A simple check on the number of slots not filled during each day gave the owner an adequate statement of the utilization of each hairdresser.

EFFICIENCY – HAIRDRESSERS

The efficiency of the seven hairdressers may be calculated in two ways. The first is based on standard times for each type of service – alternatives such as a trim, restyle, cut and blow dry, highlights and other forms of hair colouring will take different lengths of time. Calculations of efficiency will be similar to those outlined earlier in the Conform illustration under the section 'Efficiency – operators'.

A second method is available for businesses that are not complicated and where the services provided are similar to one another or tend to average out over a given period. This uses a simpler, broadbrush calculation such as the revenue generated by each hairdresser per hour worked. With prices reflecting, in part, the time involved and each hairdresser undertaking a similar mix of work, a 'revenue per hour worked' calculation would give a rule of thumb assessment of efficiency. It would be easy to calculate and yet provide a check on the level of efficiency achieved. In fact, the owner of the John Michael salon used this measure as follows, with net hours equalling staff hours minus the time not booked by clients:

$$\frac{\text{Revenue generated}}{\text{Net hours worked}} = \text{Revenue per hour worked}$$

Using utilization and efficiency data to manage capacity

The last section explained the way to calculate utilization and efficiency. Before moving on to capacity planning and the task of managing capacity and demand, let's first recap on the insights provided by utilization and efficiency data in helping a business to manage its capacity.

As highlighted at the start of the chapter, the importance of managing capacity concerns meeting customer requirements. Too little capacity means delays and possible lost sales: too much incurs unnecessary costs. Based on known or forecasted sales, companies calculate the staff or process capacity required. But this is often no easy task, especially in the front office of service delivery systems. Different services requiring different levels of skills complicates capacity provision. Add to this the fact that demand varies throughout a period, and capacity calculations need to reflect these hourly, daily, weekly and monthly patterns within the framework of uncertainty that characterizes forecasts.

> **EXECUTIVE INSIGHT**
>
> Too little capacity leads to delays and possible lost sales: too much incurs unnecessary costs.

Utilization

In the medium and longer term, demand will typically change. To help monitor this, information on utilization levels helps organizations to assess these trends and make any necessary adjustments so that they can maintain service levels while avoiding unnecessary costs. The options available to companies to change their capacity levels include the following:

- Short-term changes such as:
  - Overtime working, including at the weekend. This option increases the rate of pay per hour by what is known as the overtime premium – for example, the third and the half when the pay rate for each overtime hour increases to $1\frac{1}{3}$ and $1\frac{1}{2}$ the normal rate, respectively.
  - Employing temporary staff. This option often incurs training costs and using less-experienced and less-skilled staff.

- Longer term changes such as:
  - Recruiting additional full- or part-time permanent staff
  - Purchasing additional processes or equipment, together with the staff required
  - Recruiting an additional shift of either full- or part-time staff.

As you will see from these options, short-term changes are a more flexible alternative and, for this reason, tend to be preferred, especially as a first step.

Efficiency

Data on how long jobs take are an essential input into cost, price and capacity calculations. What efficiency checks do is to measure how well the service delivery system or manufacturing process is performing against set standards. Differences between actuals and standards alert an organization to changes in the task (for example, if the job is becoming more or less complicated, so the set standards need adjusting) or changes in the delivery system (for example, if additional staff training is required or the manufacturing process needs overhauling). Utilization and efficiency measures help to ensure that adequate levels of capacity are provided and that the service delivery system or manufacturing process is performing to the standards set. In this way, regular checks of 'how much' and 'how well' provide essential insights to help manage this key resource.

Factors affecting capacity management

Now that we know how capacity is measured and defined, let's move on to looking at some background factors that affect the management of capacity. In this section, we'll first look at make-or-buy decisions and how aspects of the service delivery system and manufacturing process design affect capacity, including the implications of an organization's chosen delivery system. We will then address how the level of capacity is determined, including the effect of various capacity- and demand-related issues.

Make-or-buy decisions[1]

Theoretically, every item, process or service currently purchased from an outside supplier is a candidate for in-house provision and vice versa. In reality, however, the choice is not so extensive, as sometimes buying from an outside supplier is the only option while in other times, making in-house is the only feasible alternative. Nevertheless, when choices are available, the make-or-buy decision needs to be considered at both the strategic and tactical levels. Apart from the level of capacity required, several other issues must be considered and these are now discussed.

Longer-term competitiveness needing operations support

In the pursuit of short-term financial improvements, some organizations decide to subcontract tasks traditionally completed within their own operations function. In some instances it makes sense, but there are issues to be checked before making such a change. For example, a decision to subcontract may be taken as a matter of expediency. Facing a difficult problem requiring managerial time and expertise to put right can often be the stimulus for subcontracting, without undertaking essential checks on the long-term impact. Similarly, some companies have painted themselves into the 'hollow corporation syndrome',[2] with the long-term consequence of an eroded operations base (both process and infrastructure) from which it will normally be more difficult to initiate change.[3]

Finally, companies may decide to subcontract parts of their business without carefully thinking through the long-term impact on customer retention. For example, Capital One, the US credit card company, has retained most aspects of its service delivery system in-house, including call centres. Its rationale is that this keeps it close to its customers, provides customer intelligence and clearly states the corporate importance of customer service within its business.

Delaying investment decisions by initially subcontracting

Process investment to meet the needs of new markets brings with it added uncertainty. One way of reducing the level of uncertainty is initially to subcontract operations until market demand is more clearly defined. A company making household products, for example, used subcontractors in the early stages of the life cycle of a new product range until it was able to ascertain the volumes involved. When the picture became clearer and volumes more certain, it could then choose from the following alternatives: allocate the new range to a part of its own manufacturing facility in keeping with forecast volumes; leave it with the existing subcontractor; or switch the contract to another subcontractor, again based on volume fit. In this way it was able to reduce the investment risk and better align processes and market requirements.

Handling technology uplifts

Stepped changes in technology often result in an organization having to buy in that technology. Although initially there may be no alternative, it is essential that organizations consider future make-or-buy positions once the technologies are more available and internal provision becomes an option.

Tactical issues

There are several tactical issues to be considered, including:

- The ease or difficulty of providing the internal technical or skill capability to meet service and product specifications

- The effect of make-or-buy decisions on overall lead-times

- The degree of dependence that results between a subcontracted item, process or service and the final service or product into which it goes

- Availability of suppliers over time to meet the volumes and specifications involved

- Comparative costings need to incorporate checks that the internal data used in making these decisions do, in fact, reflect the true costs, the real impact on internal overhead cost structures with volume changes and likely future actions by suppliers

- Decisions to make in-house result in increased aggregate volumes and consequently contribute to spreading overhead costs and help to balance demand and capacity over time

- The protection of service, product and process ideas

- Avoiding subjective decisions concerning beliefs about internal capabilities and cost structure costings that have not been checked.

How do service delivery systems and manufacturing process designs affect capacity?

Aspects of the service delivery system and manufacturing process design – the subjects of Chapters 5 and 6 – affect the provision of capacity within the operations process. Some key issues in relation to this are now discussed.

Customers as a source of capacity

The presence of customers within the front office of a service delivery system becomes a potential source of capacity. The extent to which this is taken advantage of is an important decision in terms of overall capacity, and this unique opportunity needs to form part of the delivery system design. The benefits of customer involvement include:

- It cuts costs.

- It helps to provide capacity at points in the delivery system where all or part of the service is consumed. For example, in a self-service restaurant, the job of the waiter is predominantly, if not totally, provided by the customer.

- Some customers prefer to be able to make their own choices. For example, self-service food shopping is now the norm, and salad bar provision in a restaurant is often preferred by customers.

Customers have proved willing to take part in the service delivery system if it can be shown to be beneficial, supportive of their needs, convenient or an enhancement of the sociable nature of the total process. Examples include self-service facilities of all kinds such as direct telephone dialling, purchases via the television, online shopping, investment brokerage services, other financial services (including cash machines) and travel arrangements. The impact of this upon the provision, type and cost of capacity can be considerable.

The perishable nature of service capacity

Service capacity is perishable. It cannot be put into inventory for use or sale in a future time period. In addition to the ways of changing capacity levels described earlier, companies can also seek to adjust demand patterns. The alternative ways available are discussed later in the chapter.

Back office vs. front office

Within a service business, a distinction needs to be made between the two basic parts of the process – the back office and the front office (see Chapter 4). A fundamental and distinctive factor between these two parts of the system concerns the customer interface. In the front office, customers are present, either in person or on the telephone, and the service system has to manage these customers during the delivery of the service. In the back office, customers are not present in the system, so there is no pressure to respond immediately. Consequently, capacity requirements, the opportunity to spread demand and to use technology to process cumulated volumes (thereby reducing costs) will differ between these parts.

Ensuring adequate capacity at each stage of a delivery system

Getting the capacity right significantly affects costs and customer support which, in turn, affect overall sales revenue and profits, as illustrated by Case 8.2. Where services or products require a single operation to complete them, the task of determining the capacity required is relatively easy. However, several steps and also differing amounts of time at each step are often involved in providing a service or making a product. This makes determining the necessary capacity a more difficult task as there are more stages and more combinations of stages, hence making it more complex.

Flexibility

The different dimensions of flexibility need to be recognized and reflected in capacity calculations. These include the ability to:

- Deliver a wider range of services and products

- Respond to any seasonal demand factors

- Meet shorter lead-times

- Cope with changes in a customer's specification during the process.

Skills and mix

The introduction of technology into parts or all of the operations process will lead to changes in skill requirements and staff mix. This alters the capacity requirements and so needs to be part of the decision process.

The impact of different delivery systems

Operations uses technology as part of its delivery system design, with the technical know-how to install, develop and maintain it being provided by specialists. It is essential, therefore, for operations to understand the business implications of the chosen delivery system or manufacturing process, several of which directly affect the definition, provision and management of capacity, as summarized in Figures 8.8 and 8.9.

CASE 8.1 INCREASING RESTAURANT CAPACITY

A restaurant experiencing high demand increased its capacity in two ways: it added more tables in its existing dining areas and it increased the speed of service in an attempt to improve throughput. Both provisions had a direct impact on the customer experience. Although the quality of the food remained the same, customers' perception of the service specification on offer changed. Bookings fell, and sales and profit declined.

Questions

1. What where the order-winners and qualifiers for the business?

2. Based on your answer to Question 1, assess the company's decision. What alternative decisions could it have made about its shortage of capacity?

Lecturers: visit www.palgrave.com/business/hillom3e for teaching guidelines for this case study

Case 8.2 DELL'S CUSTOMER SUPPORT

Dell believes its place in the top five PC manufacturers, with sales in excess of £2 billion, is due, in large part, to customer loyalty. More than 80 per cent of its custom is repeat business. Key to sustaining this is the company's strong field support for customers. Direct selling to customers instead of through dealers not only means lower prices but also removes those staff who traditionally supported a computer installation. To meet these needs Dell provides European sales and customer support through a telephone operation located close to Dublin. Highly trained multilingual staff offer 24/7 support for Dell users across Europe, with similar arrangements in place for other regions of the world. Providing a hotline with continuous support is key for customers with computer prob-

lems and is considered to be an essential part of Dell's success.

http://www.dell.co.uk

Questions

1. What are the key dimensions of customer support that help make Dell a success?

2. How did Dell handle the capacity requirements that it considered essential in its provision of customer support? Why?

Lecturers: visit www.palgrave.com/business/hillom3e for teaching guidelines for this case study

Service delivery systems

The factors in service delivery systems that affect the nature of capacity and its management and provision were highlighted earlier. They include the following:

- The nature of the service offering
  1. Non-repeat or repeat
  2. The level of volume for a repeat service
  3. The service/product mix

- What is being processed in the service delivery system – a customer, a customer surrogate (in car maintenance, for example, the car is the surrogate for the customer) or information
- Whether it holds a front- or back-office position in the delivery system
- Whether it is a single- or a multi-step service delivery system.

With these factors in mind, Figure 8.8 provides an overview of how some of the key dimensions of capacity differ in relation to the non-repeat/repeat and low/high volume dimensions of services, while the text will provide an explanation and highlights some differences.

Non-repeat services are delivered by skilled staff; consequently, capacity is based on the available working time of this key resource. As the services involved are non-repeat, the ability to define demand in terms of resource requirements will be low (the service has not been provided before), thus making the provision and control of capacity difficult. The flexible nature of the skilled staff, however, will facilitate the use of capacity in meeting the wide range of services on offer, the downside being that losing key staff through absence in the short term or moving to a new company in the longer term will impact capacity.

The transitional nature of these dimensions as the service delivery system shifts to one for a high-volume, repeat service is illustrated by the arrows in Figure 8.8. Calculating capacity in a fast-food restaurant involves a combination of staff and processes, whereas capacity in cash machine services is predominantly to do with the number (and location) of ATMs. Adding capacity is often stepped in nature (for example, adding a new outlet). In either case, the failure of the equipment involved in the system will have a significant impact on a company's ability to deliver services as the equipment is central to their provision.

Manufacturing processes

The implications for the management and provision of capacity overviewed in Figure 8.9 reflect the nature of the manufacturing process involved:

- *Project and jobbing* In both project and jobbing, the typical firms involved are relatively small in size, skilled staff are central to the process of making the products (equipment having the role of helping the skilled person complete the task), and the firm can offer a flexible response in terms of the range of products that the manufacturing process can handle. Changing from one product to another is an integral part of the manufacturing process and will involve short, inexpensive changes.

- *Line and continuous processing* Moving towards line and continuous processing brings with it a shift to the other end of each of these dimensions. Typically, companies are large in size, with processes rather than people making the products involved. Here, the role of people is to help the process complete the task. Demand is well defined as product knowledge is well established, and it is easy to calculate how much capacity is required. Capacity changes, on the other hand, are large scale in nature. Having

Figure 8.8 **Capacity-related implications of service delivery system choice**

CAPACITY-RELATED IMPLICATIONS		TYPICAL CHARACTERISTICS OF SERVICE DELIVERY SYSTEM CHOICE		
		Non-repeat services	Repeat services: Low volume	Repeat services: High volume
Service	type	Special	→	Standard
	range	Wide	→	Narrow
Number of customer orders		Few	→	Many
Capacity	basis for calculation	Staff	→	Staff/ process
	scale of changes	Incremental	→	Stepped
	control	Difficult	→	Easy
Demand - level of definition		Low	→	High
Delivery system flexibility		Flexible	→	Inflexible
Dominant factor in measuring capacity utilization		Staff	→	Staff/ process
Impact of	staff absence	High	→	Low
	equipment failure	Low	→	Significant

Figure 8.9 Capacity-related implications of manufacturing process choice

CAPACITY-RELATED IMPLICATIONS		Project	Jobbing	Batch	Line	Continuous processing
		TYPICAL CHARACTERISTICS OF MANUFACTURING PROCESS CHOICE				
Product	type	Special/standard	Special ⟶		Standard	Standard
	range	Wide	Wide ⟶		Narrow	Narrow
Number of customer orders		Few	Few ⟶		Many	Many
Capacity	basis for calculation	Staff	Staff ⟶		Process	Process
	scale	Small	Small ⟶		Large	Very large
	size of changes	Incre-mental	Incremental ⟶		Stepped	New facility
	control	Difficult	Difficult ⟶		Easy	Easy
Demand – level of definition		Variable	Low ⟶		Established	Established
Process flexibility		Flexible	Flexible ⟶		Inflexible	Very inflexible
Set-ups or change-overs	number	Many	Many ⟶		Unlikely	Unlikely
	expense per	Variable	Inexpensive ⟶		Expensive	Very expensive
Dominant factor in measuring capacity utilization		Staff	Staff ⟶		Process	Process
Bottle-necks	number	Few	Few	Often several	None	None
	position & nature	Random & movable	Random & movable	Fixed in the short & medium term	Not relevant	Not relevant
Impact of breakdowns		Variable	Little ⟶		Significant	Enormous

been designed to make a given product range, the process is rarely, if ever, changed, except at the end of a product's life cycle. As the process is designed to be balanced, bottlenecks are not a factor. However, the impact of breakdowns is significant as the process itself has stopped, and products cannot be made. In project and jobbing, on the other hand, the skilled staff simply switch to alternative tasks.

- *Batch* As shown in Figure 8.9, batch is a transition between the two extremes of process choice for most factors, as the arrows depict. The exception is bottlenecks, and we will now look at why this is. A bottleneck occurs where the capacity in one stage of a process is less than the capacity in the other parts of the process. To help visualize this, think of a wine bottle and the difference in size between the neck and the body. In multi-step batch processes, there are often differences in demand and capacity ratios at each stage (the neck and body factor). Some of these will invariably show bottleneck capacity characteristics, but it is a factor that will not usually change in the short and medium term.

Determining the level of capacity

Investment in plant and equipment is usually an irreversible decision. Also, staff capacity, once created, is expensive to change. As a result, growth and its associated capacity decisions present a challenging task, especially given the potential impact of these capacity decisions and those of competitors on sales revenue and market share.

The process of deciding on capacity levels is complex. Organizations are faced with a number of important considerations, such as:

- Anticipating the end of growth

- Avoiding overcapacity

- Choosing to plan ahead of growth or to follow growth – the lead or follow demand capacity alternatives

- What action to take in a situation of overcapacity – divest or diversify?

> **EXECUTIVE INSIGHT**
>
> Deciding on the level of capacity involves anticipating the end of growth, avoiding too much, deciding whether to lead or follow demand and deciding what to do with overcapacity – divest or diversify?

Similar dilemmas are also involved in downsizing. When and how much concern not only questions of cost, but also the potential impact on sales and market share, and, as with capacity investment, downsizing decision are costly to reverse.

To help manage capacity, companies consider a range of demand/capacity issues, and these are now discussed.

Demand-related issues

An organization focuses its capacity planning efforts towards meeting its customers' requirements. To do this, it needs to manage demand, which involves identifying the nature and size of the demand and determining how the company is best going to meet it. One characteristic of demand that further complicates this provision and makes managing it more challenging is that it is never the same twice over. Some of these variations are, however, more predictable than others, as explained below.

Predictable variations

Although demand levels will vary, there are very often characteristics of sales from which patterns can be identified, enabling such fluctuations to be predicted more easily. For example:

- *Seasonality* The seasonal nature of many services and products is well recognized. Defined as variation that repeats itself at fixed intervals, seasonal patterns are caused by many factors including the weather (for example, holiday bookings and sales of air conditioners and ice-cream) and time of the year (for example, the demand for air travel, types of clothing, gardening equipment, fireworks, training courses and tax processing).

- *Peaks* Whereas seasonality of demand occurs over a year, predictable variations in demand also occur at shorter intervals. To distinguish the two, the latter are normally known as peaks, and, as with seasonality of demand, they are caused by recurring factors that can be identified. For example, working hours affect traffic volumes, and the day of the week can affect demand – the emergency unit in a hospital will be busier than usual late on a Saturday night. Similarly, the time of day will affect the level of demand for sandwiches, and a firm's policies such as billing patterns and the push to meet sales targets will be reflected in the activity levels over a month.

- *One-off demands* Some services and products are subject to a predictable one-off peak in demand. This needs to be successfully managed to ensure that potential sales are maximized. Examples include film premieres, music festivals and book launches. However, there are risks if the certainty of a one-off demand is not guaranteed.

Unpredictable variations

Other demand characteristics are less predictable but still need to be managed. For example, airlines overbook on flights to protect against 'no-shows'. The same policy is also adopted by hotel operators, particularly those in locations where the unpredictability of bookings or the frequency of late cancellations brings uncertainty in the pattern of demand and a resulting loss of revenue from having turned business away.

Capacity-related issues

As with demand, there are issues in the provision of capacity that increase the difficulty of this management task. Again, some of these are more predictable than others, as explained below.

> **EXECUTIVE INSIGHT**
   Organizations need to separate the predictable from the unpredictable variations in demand and capacity.

Predictable aspects of capacity

Capacity is typically a mix of different staff skills and process types in order to handle the range of services and products and their associated volumes. Where this range is relatively wide, the demands placed on these different sets of skills and processes will vary and typically result in bottlenecks (the neck of the wine bottle referred to earlier) where the capacity in one phase of the delivery system is less than the demand placed on it. However, bottlenecks are short- to medium-term phenomena, so are predictable in terms of their position and extent. Knowing where they are enables a business to manage capacity within this constraint, while directing attention and resources to increasing capacity of the bottleneck, reducing demand on the bottleneck by using alternative skill sets or processes to deliver part of the service or product, redesigning the service or product to simplify its delivery or making the delivery system more efficient.

Unpredictable aspects of capacity

As with demand, some aspects of capacity are less predictable, and these introduce problems of a more ad hoc nature:

- *Absenteeism* People stay away from work for a number of reasons. Estimates place the direct and indirect costs for UK businesses as high as £16 billion, and absence rates are on average about 3.5 per cent. The short-term impact of this adds to the difficulty of managing capacity effectively. Ways of attempting to cope with this have centred on recognizing absenteeism as a management problem and attempting to reduce it to manageable levels. Lewisham Borough Council in the Greater London area was affected by absentee levels averaging 17 days a year for each employee, but better monitoring over a 24-month period helped bring this down to less than 11 days per employee per year. Others argue that unpaid sick leave encourages employees to believe that no one loses when they are away. Paying for sickness, including the penalty of taking away this benefit for abuse of the system, is part of why Nissan believes it has achieved absenteeism levels of less than 2 per cent at its plant in Washington in the north-east of England.

- *Short-term demand changes* Short-term demand variations can often result in a temporary shortage of capacity, with the difficulties this presents in managing capacity.

Successfully managing these capacity and demand issues is often central to the successful growth of a business and lies at the centre of the operations task.

Planning and managing capacity

The purpose of the chapter so far has been to introduce key definitions, provide an overall review of capacity and illustrate the purpose and outcomes of its provision. The rest of the chapter addresses the task of planning and managing long- and medium-term capacity. It will address the tasks of resource planning and medium-term planning, with short-term operations control and scheduling being covered in Chapter 9.

Capacity management is an essential responsibility of the operations function. The objective is to match the level of capacity to the level of demand, in terms of both quantity (how much) and capability (the skill mix to meet the service or product specifications). Simple though it sounds, meeting this basic requirement is a challenging task and concerns issues of:

- *Uncertainty* – demand is uncertain and can vary by the hour, day, week, month or year

- *Anticipating the future* – although they are much better than nothing, forecasts are, by definition, inaccurate

- *Timescales* – the scope of capacity management spans long-term planning through to day-to-day scheduling

- *Alternatives* – choosing from the different ways of providing capacity to meet demand

- *Execution* – fulfilling the plan.

The optimum approach to planning and managing capacity is to separate the task into its major elements and position these in terms of the time phases in which they need to occur. Figure 8.10 provides an overview of these tasks, showing their position in the overall planning and control system.

The level of detail involved will reflect the complexity of the services and products provided. As you will no doubt appreciate, managing a sandwich bar will be less complex than managing a large hotel, as would a small assembly shop compared with a large pharmaceutical plant making chemical formulations in a wide range of pack sizes and alternatives. In essence, though, the tasks are the same, as explained below:

- *Planning* Front-end planning provides key communication links between top management and operations. It helps to form the basis for translating strategic objectives and future market needs into operations plans and resources, and is essential in determining

Figure 8.10 Operations planning and control systems

TIMESCALES	PHASE		TASK
Years	Planning	Resource planning	Determines the resources to meet the aggregate demand forecasts for all services or products in a future timeframe, normally a period of between two and five years
		Medium-term capacity planning	Partially disaggregated demand forecasts are used to give a 'rough-cut' review of the necessary resources in terms of staff skills and process types. Will be for periods of six months to two years depending on the type of business involved
	Control	Scheduling	Detailed plans to determine the capacity (staff skills and processes) and materials to meet the service or product schedule, together with any contingency plans
Days/hours		Execution	Day-to-day (often hourly) control systems to manage the detailed capacity plans and material requirements to meet the scheduled delivery of services and products to customers

what can be achieved, the investments and decisions to be made and the timescales involved. It is during this phase that companies look toward and decide on the 'game plan' for the future. How far forward they look will depend on the investments and timescales involved, and these will be discussed in detail in the next section.

- *Scheduling* The scheduling phase determines capacity several weeks, months and sometimes up to one year ahead. It details how demand will be met from the facilities available and ensures that the capacity and material requirements are, or can be, put into place.

- *Execution* This phase of the system concerns executing day-to-day operations by determining and monitoring capacity and material requirements: this will ensure that customer demand is met and resources are used efficiently.

As Figure 8.10 shows, the planning phase is split into 'resource planning' and '**medium-term capacity planning**', and these are now reviewed. Discussion of the scheduling and execution phases of the system is covered in the next chapter.

> **Medium-term capacity planning (or 'aggregate' or 'rough-cut planning')** – capacity planning developed in broad terms to meet agreed output levels, where capacity is considered to be relatively fixed.

Resource planning

This strategic business task generally involves looking several years ahead. It aims to meet the long-term capacity requirements and resource allocations that will answer future organizational objectives, and it will do this by planning for capacity changes in line with anticipated increases in market share, the introduction of new services or products and the company's entry into new markets.

> **EXECUTIVE INSIGHT**
Resource planning looks several years ahead to provide future capacity requirements

Anticipating future demand in terms of its size (associated volumes) and nature (the service/product mix) involves an essential strategic decision that needs to address three critical dimensions:

1. *Amount* – how much is required?

2. *Timing* – when is the capacity needed?

3. *Location* – where should the capacity be located?

Capacity decisions for several years ahead are difficult to make because of the timescales involved and the fact that the above three dimensions are not stand-alone questions. All three impinge on each other. For example, determining size is not just a question of the total requirement but will need to address issues concerning size (how much capacity per hospital, office, retail outlet, manufacturing plant and so on), the location of this additional capacity and when it needs to be available. Consequently, these elements of operations planning need to be considered as an integrated whole.

Figure 8.10 shows resource planning as the first step in capacity planning. It is the most highly aggregated stage and has the longest planning horizon. It typically involves taking a two- to five-year timeframe and converting monthly and annual data from the operations plan into statements of aggregate resources such as total staff hours, office space and support equipment in a service organization, or staff hours, floor space and machine or process hours in a manufacturing firm. This level of planning potentially involves new capital investments such as buildings, warehousing and equipment that often have lead-times of months or years.

As Figure 8.10 explains, the operations planning task takes demand and resource planning information that details what is required and what is available, and then highlights possible constraints in terms of lead-times and levels of investment. These issues are large in size, complex in nature and concern the amount, timing and location, factors that are critical in terms of capacity.

Factors affecting the task of resource planning

The task of resource planning is complex in itself but several factors contribute to making the task more difficult as the next section explains.

General issues

Competition

As markets become more global and countries increasingly build up their own national capability to deliver services and make products, recognizing and incorporating these trends into long-term plans becomes more essential. In a world where demand is not growing as quickly as supply, overcapacity results. The impact on traditional industries such as steel, shipbuilding and automobiles is well reported. But, the same is happening in newer industries and segments of the service sector. Since the late 1980s there has been overcapacity in the semiconductor industry. The passenger airline industry is in a similar position. Over 90 per cent of airline passengers in the USA buy their tickets at a discount, paying on average about 35 per cent of the full fare. Although partly a response to deregulation, it is largely a reflection of the overcapacity in that industry.

Similar patterns have also emerged in the European passenger airline industry. Setting future capacity levels, therefore, needs to recognize the potential actions of competitors and possible new entrants and the result these will have on overall capacity within a given market.

Developing countries

The need for developing countries to increase the size of their wealth-creating sectors is fundamental to their own longer-term national prosperity. The resulting demand by governments to build local facilities increasingly affects the factors of location, size and timing in the capacity decisions of internationally based companies.

Technology

Changes in service, product, process and other technologies not only impact directly on levels of demand and capacity but also offer the opportunity to reposition capacity. The development of information technology allows companies to reposition the workplace of individual people (for example, home versus office) and also to outsource a range of business processes, from basic call centres to the complex back-office operations of merchant banks. For example, the support unit answering a customer query can be located anywhere in the world to reflect issues of cost and time of the day. Lower-cost countries in Europe (for example, Ireland) are increasingly being used as support unit locations. Similarly, as offices close for the day in Europe, calls are initially transferred to the east coast of the USA and then progressively westwards to be handled by staff working during their normal hours.

Being able to send data via satellite has enabled information-based service companies to relocate relevant processing capacity to anywhere in the world. Newspapers are often composed in one location but printed in sites close to their respective markets. The gains are not only the reduction in transport costs but also the speed of transfer that enables printing to be delayed until the very last moment. Similarly, companies involved in data processing are beaming the tasks to lower cost centres in countries such as India and South Africa without incurring the long lead-times that previously would have made such decisions impractical.

Amount of capacity

Deciding on the amount of capacity needs to incorporate forecasts of demand, make versus buy decisions and how much capacity a company intends to hold in relation to anticipated demand. The factors involved in these complex decisions are now discussed.

Forecasting demand for services and products

A prerequisite for capacity planning is a statement of demand. Organizations need to forecast demand in order to anticipate future capacity requirements as well as the other resources in a business (for example, buildings and facilities). But demand forecasting is difficult and no matter which method is used, it will not (by definition) be accurate. Despite this inaccuracy, it is essential to forecast demand, for the alternative is to have no forecast at all. Next, it is necessary to recognize the capacity planning horizon of different businesses. These will differ depending upon lead-times. Where capacity is staff-based (for example, in most service businesses and in a manufacturing company using a jobbing process), the relevant time horizon will normally be shorter than where investment in processes and equipment is involved. Manufacturing examples illustrating the dimension of long lead-times readily come to mind, for instance new vehicle assembly and petrochemical plants. Also, service industries with a similar dependency on equipment will experience longer lead-times, for example most elements of the transport industry.

While demand forecasts are often completed elsewhere in a business, it is necessary for those involved in capacity planning to understand the forecasting procedures used, the assumptions made and the implications for the operations function. To help appreciate these issues, some of the features involved are now described.

Operations issues in forecasting

A key operations issue in forecasting concerns accuracy. The more general the statement and the longer the time period covered by the forecast, the more accurate it will be. The annual forecast for all services or products sold is likely to be more accurate than the weekly or monthly total for each item in the range. But, at some point, projections have to be translated into the actual services and products to be provided and made. Establishing assumptions, forcing clarification and moving from the general to the specific in terms of mix, volumes and other key operational differences is an essential operations task in managing future capacity requirements.

The choice of forecasting method

The inherent difficulties of forecasting have led to many forecasting models being developed, and different models are based on different sets of assumptions. Understanding these assumptions, particularly those that may have an impact on operations, is an essential first step. Key factors to clarify so as to better understand forecast outcomes and signal aspects that need to be revisited at appropriate times within the long-term planning process include the following:

- The accuracy level of predictions sought and achieved and the trade-offs involved

- The extent to which a model assumes that past behavioural patterns and relationships will continue in the future: a continuous check on presumed levels of stability between the past and future has to be embodied in the forecasting procedure in order to evaluate this feature of a model

- Establishing the appropriate forecasting horizon that matches the capacity lead-time currently experienced

- The need to link the selected forecasting model and the data patterns that are present in a particular business. The most common patterns are described as being constant, trend, seasonal and cyclical. A business needs to ascertain its own data patterns to ensure that the model chosen reflects them appropriately.

Make vs. buy

The question of determining the make-versus-buy policy has already been signalled as a key step in the process of determining capacity. The issues and dimensions involved are discussed in detail in Chapter 12 and this subsection serves solely to restate its fundamental role in these decisions.

Size of operations units

How large to build an operations unit comprises many issues and the decision is made for a variety of reasons. The principal factor concerns scale – the size of operations units. The economies of scale argument is based on the premise that large units yield lower costs, as fixed costs are spread over more services or products. In some sectors (for example, petrochemical plants) there is a minimum size below which it is difficult to justify the necessary process investment. Scale economies are truly present in such situations. Whereas some companies follow the economies of scale principle, others limit the size of units in order to avoid what they consider to be the disadvantages of large scale, including remoteness, poor motivational climate for staff, increased complexity and the difficulties of managing a larger organization. For these reasons, some businesses put an upper limit on size after which a new unit would be built. Other factors include:

- **Catchment area** – in some industries and particularly in the service sector, units are built to serve a certain catchment area. Demand outside this area will be met by building another facility. Examples include retail chains, banks and restaurants.

- **Distribution costs** – products have different distribution cost-to-item-value ratios. Those companies where distribution costs are high in relation to the product value will tend to build more plants than where the ratio is low.

- **Innovation levels** – many companies wish to encourage innovation and tend to operate smaller units in order to avoid the bureaucracy and centralized control that comes with size but which usually militates against innovative behaviour.

The critical nature of scale and how this may need to be reassessed over time is illustrated in Case 8.3.

Timing of capacity

As levels of demand change over time, when to increase or decrease capacity is a key business issue for both long-term (five or more years ahead) and medium-term (up to two years ahead) planning horizons. This section deals with the former; the medium-term responses to this and other relevant aspects of capacity will be discussed later in 'Medium-term capacity planning'.

Businesses need to base capacity on demand forecasts. Using assumptions of average demand, an organization can choose to provide adequate capacity to meet peaks, meet average demand patterns or maximize its utilization of capacity. The choice will reflect the requirements of, and chosen responses in, the different markets in which it competes.

The essential question of timing is whether to lead or follow anticipated demand. How these alternatives work in practice are now described.

Proactive strategy

A proactive strategy concerns building capacity in advance of forecast levels of demand. This approach maintains a positive capacity cushion by aiming always to have capacity in excess of demand, while limiting the size of the excesses at any time.

Certain industries always adopt a proactive strategy to capacity provision by planning to ensure that customers' demands can always be met. Utility companies such as gas and electricity aim for this level of provision. Hospital emergency units have similar objectives. In the case of the former, long-term decisions on capacity are essential given the timescales involved. Examples in recent years where a sector failed to plan sufficiently far ahead to ensure that demand levels are met include water utilities in several Western countries. Increasing demand, changing weather patterns and the long timescales in provision have led to a growing shortage of water at certain times of each year. Similar scenarios have also been experienced in the timing of power generation capacity in many more developed economies in the first two decades of the new millennium.

Reactive strategy

A reactive strategy concerns building capacity to follow demand. This results in a negative capacity cushion where there is insufficient capacity to meet demand. As the gap grows, investments in additional capacity are made, with companies managing the gap in the meantime.

Walmart is a US supermarket chain that also owns ASDA in the UK and Bompreço in Brazil, and is one of the largest corporations in the world. Most new Walmart stores have an area of up to 200,000 square feet, the size of two (American) football fields, and are too big to be built anywhere other than on the edge of towns. But in 2003, Walmart opened its first Neighbourhood Market in Rogers, Arkansas – with a size of less than 40,000 square feet. The strategy was to limit the store size and thus allow the company to find sites in built-up urban areas, thus allowing it to compete head to head with the traditional supermarkets that dominated the cities. From its small beginnings in food sales in 1983, Walmart had become the biggest seller of food in the USA by 2001. Its sales revenues of $419 billion in 2011 was reportedly almost 50 per cent more than that of its five closest competitors combined.

Walmart's first foray into food was not, however, a success. Inspired by retail giants such as Carrefour and Le Clerc in France, Walmart built large, 260,000 square foot supermarkets. But these proved to be too big for customers to handle, and profits were low. Instead, it decided to move forward with its supercentres by adding groceries to its traditional discount stores and limiting the size to no more than 200,000 square feet. At the end of 2011, it had over 2,950 supercentres which, with Sam's Club, accounted for 25 per cent of the US grocery market.

Since 1998, Walmart has been tinkering with smaller store formats. The Neighbourhood Market offers about a fifth (24,000 against 120,0000) of the product items found in a supercentre, including a full assortment of food, health, beauty and household products. It includes a chicken rotisserie and home-made tortilla stand but lacks the extensive salad bars, delicatessens and meat and fish counters that competing supermarkets offer. Meat and fish arrive prepacked, ready for the shelf. There are also convenient extras – a drive-through service and a self-service coffee bar by the entrance. In addition, more than half the checkouts are self-scanning, which reduces queue lengths and staff costs.

Walmart is harnessing the same buying power and supply chain efficiency that enables it to offer food at prices some 10–15 per cent cheaper than its competitors. Its aim appears to be to provide convenience without the premiums that typically go with smaller size. By the end of 2011, Walmart had 188 Neighbourhood Markets.
www.walmart.com

Questions

1. How is Walmart using scale to compete in the US food market?

2. Why is Walmart pursuing its Neighbourhood Markets strategy?

Lecturers: visit www.palgrave.com/business/hillom3e for teaching guidelines for this case study

Many companies prefer to allow demand to grow and then invest in capacity in line with known demand. The reason is that follower strategies are less risky and many companies prefer to manage the problems of having too little capacity rather than being in a position of having too much capacity and the problems that this brings.

Combination strategy

A combination strategy is a mixed approach. Initially, capacity is allowed to move into a negative cushion position. Then, capacity investments are made that match, or more often exceed, current demand levels and so create a positive capacity cushion. Demand continues to grow and the cycle is repeated.

Strategic positioning

The decision when to build capacity may be driven by considerations of strategic positioning. Developments within the European Union (EU), for example, triggered decisions by many international companies to build manufacturing facilities or take over existing businesses in order to meet the EU criteria on imported goods. The growth in Japanese investments in Europe provides an example of this. Similarly, the decision to 'be in on the ground floor' has led to organizations entering countries and regions with high-growth economies. For example, companies from a diverse range of sectors from investment banks to automobiles and financial services to pharmaceuticals have made growth in Asia their top priority in the past 20 years. What drives the timing of these capacity decisions is primarily one of gaining position and helping to influence and shape developments rather than short-term profit.

Location

Where to position new or develop existing facilities is a key decision facing organizations. For companies involved in worldwide markets, the positioning of facilities concerns regional and country-level decisions as well as the more local concerns of where to locate within a given region. The significance of these decisions was highlighted in Chapter 7 where the issues involved in making location decisions at these different levels was addressed in full. Such considerations will need to be part of the decision and management of capacity, particularly where political pressure or incentives such as tax breaks and investment are significant factors in the overall scenario.

Medium-term capacity planning

Medium-term capacity planning (also referred to as aggregate or rough-cut planning), for periods up to two years[4] ahead, is used within the overall framework of the long-term plan. It involves medium-term plans to meet agreed output levels where capacity is considered to be relatively fixed. This step in the planning process is designed to look ahead and resolve, in broad terms, the approach that will best provide sufficient capacity to meet the levels of demand that have been forecast. It examines key areas of capacity (for example, skilled staff categories and equipment) to identify any capacity changes that would need to be made, how feasible these would be, the timescales involved and the steps to be taken.

> **EXECUTIVE INSIGHT**
> Medium-term planning looks up to two years ahead to resolve how to provide capacity to meet forecast demand.

Statements of demand (both forecast sales and known orders) are translated into operations requirements, and the medium-term capacity plan takes these and checks them against available capacity. Although small changes to demand forecasts can be accommodated from one period to another, it is necessary to develop medium-term capacity plans in order to know how to cope with an overloading or underloading of capacity in the longer term. In this way, an orderly and systematic adjustment of capacity can be made to meet any significant changes to the level and mix of demand while meeting both deliveries to customers and internal efficiency targets.

Steps in medium-term capacity planning

Figure 8.10 showed the position of the medium-term planning step within the planning phase. This subsection gives a more detailed explanation of what is involved, with the final one providing details of some of the ways in which the plan is achieved.

1. *Develop operations statements* Sales forecasts and known orders for each service or product within each time period are translated into statements of what operations needs to provide.

2. *Make-or-buy decision* Any changes to the make-or-buy decisions must be measured in capacity terms, initially through the medium-term capacity plans and, where major shifts occur, against resource plans.

3. *Select common measures of aggregate demand* The next step is to aggregate demand for all services and products into statements of similar capacity groups. For single-service or single-product organizations, this is typically not difficult. For the brewer, it could be gallons of beer; for the doctor, patient visits; for a coal mine, tonnes of coal. For multi-service or multi-product organizations, however, great care has to be used when selecting appropriate measures.

4. *Develop medium-term capacity plans* Medium-term capacity plans are then developed primarily to meet demand at the lowest cost while supporting other relevant order-winners and qualifiers.

5. *Select the planning horizon* The next step is to select an appropriate planning horizon for the medium-term capacity plan. Although this will cover several time periods, the plans will typically be considered on a month-by-month basis as decisions made in one time period will often limit the decisions that can be made in the next. Decisions that ignore future consequences will often prove costly.

6. *Achieving the medium-term capacity plan* This step involves choosing between a range of options to best achieve the plan. These include adjusting demand patterns and selecting ways of providing capacity. The next subsection discusses these in detail.

7. *Select the medium-term capacity plan* The final step is to select the most suitable medium-term capacity plan to meet the agreed corporate objectives.

Achieving the medium-term capacity plan

As the pattern of demand for services and products will vary over time and within a given period, it is not possible to provide services or make products in one time period that exactly match the pattern of demand in the same period. To handle this companies choose between:

- Making products ahead of demand and holding items in inventory for sale in a future time period. For example, summer clothes will be made several months ahead of time.

- Holding orders in a queue (known as order backlog or forward load) waiting to be processed.

In both instances, changes in demand levels will alter the amount of inventory or the length of the queue, with both approaches helping to manage the uncertainty of demand and the relatively fixed nature of capacity that characterize this task. Figures 8.11 to 8.13 provide a more detailed explanation of how this works.

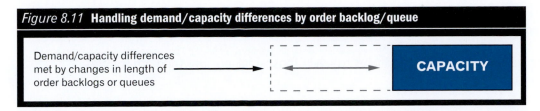

Figure 8.11 Handling demand/capacity differences by order backlog/queue

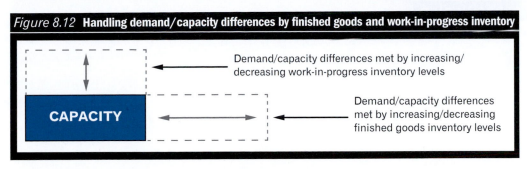

Figure 8.12 Handling demand/capacity differences by finished goods and work-in-progress inventory

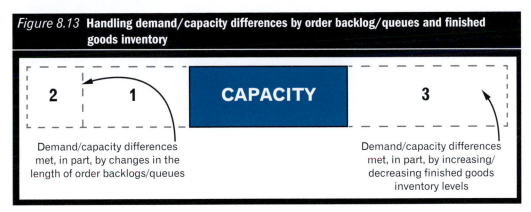

Figure 8.13 Handling demand/capacity differences by order backlog/queues and finished goods inventory

Companies working on a make-to-order basis will use the length of their order backlogs or queues as a mechanism for coping with variable demand patterns. Where demand exceeds capacity, the order backlog will lengthen and vice versa. If demand continues to grow, increasing capacity will need to be considered to reduce the lengthening lead-times that result and the impact of these on customer delivery requirements.

Companies using this approach will normally be handling special and low-volume standard services and products. However, some high-volume businesses (for example, Western car companies) also manage demand and capacity in this way.

Companies working on a make-to-stock or assemble-to-order basis will use finished goods or work-in-progress inventory levels respectively as a mechanism for coping with variable demand patterns. Where demand is greater than capacity, one or both forms of inventory will increase and vice versa. Companies using this approach will be those handling higher-volume services and products where future demand is more predictable and products are made in anticipation of future sales. In service companies, decisions to make ahead of demand will invariably concern the product content of the sale – for example, publishers printing books and restaurants part-preparing menu items.

Companies making standard products can also use a mixed approach to handle demand/capacity differences. In Figure 8.13, the company allows order backlog/queues to grow to the equivalent of four weeks of sales (Position 1). At this point a production order equivalent to 12 weeks of sales is initiated. During the process lead-time, two further weeks of order backlog/queues accumulate (Position 2). When the order quantity is completed in production, the six weeks of backlog orders are met and the balance creates finished goods inventory to meet future sales (Position 3).

Companies using this approach will be typically those making low-/medium-volume standard products.

Types of capacity plan

The second key decision concerns which capacity plan a business decides to adopt. The alternatives are:

- Level capacity

- Chase demand

- Mixed plan

and these are now described.

Level capacity plans

In a **level capacity plan**, operations capacity is set at the same level throughout the planning period, irrespective of the forecast pattern of demand. In this way, companies uncouple capacity and demand rates. Whether companies choose to make-to-order or make-to-stock, alternative mechanisms are available to adjust demand/capacity imbalances as they occur:

- *In make-to-stock situations* levels can be smoothed throughout by transferring the capacity available in low-demand periods to higher-demand periods in the form of inventory. This smoothing can be used by manufacturing companies to create stability in their capacity requirements and has several attendant benefits, especially in terms of continuity of employment. Figure 8.14 provides an illustration of this for a 12-month, medium-term planning period.

- *In make-to-order situations* the level of the queue or order backlog becomes the adjusting mechanism used to enable capacity levels to remain level. Figure 8.15 provides

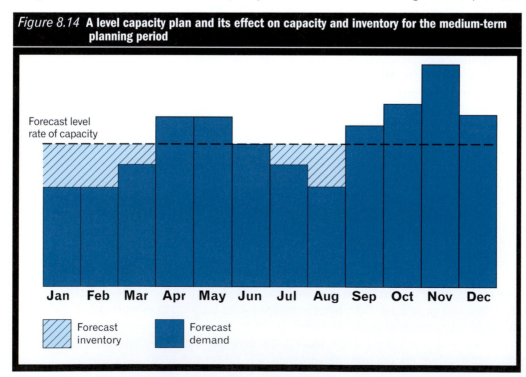

Figure 8.14 A level capacity plan and its effect on capacity and inventory for the medium-term planning period

Forecast level rate of capacity

Jan Feb Mar Apr May Jun Jul Aug Sep Oct Nov Dec

Forecast inventory

Forecast demand

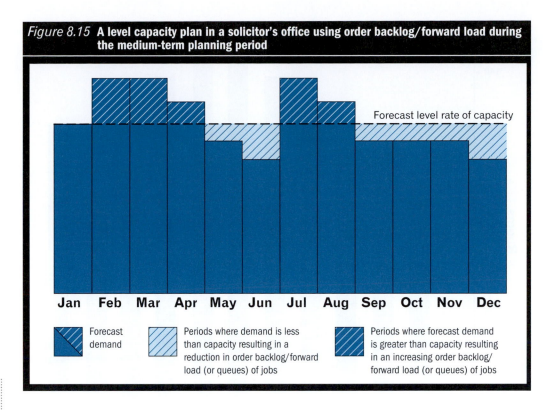

Figure 8.15 A level capacity plan in a solicitor's office using order backlog/forward load during the medium-term planning period

Jan Feb Mar Apr May Jun Jul Aug Sep Oct Nov Dec

Forecast level rate of capacity

| | Forecast demand | | Periods where demand is less than capacity resulting in a reduction in order backlog/forward load (or queues) of jobs | | Periods where forecast demand is greater than capacity resulting in an increasing order backlog/forward load (or queues) of jobs |

Chase demand capacity plan – involves changing capacity levels from one period to another by adjusting some combination of staff numbers, working hours and available equipment.

an example of this. Here a solicitor's office uses the order backlog/forward load of client jobs to balance the capacity/demand requirements for a 12-month, medium-term planning period.

Chase demand capacity plans

The opposite of a level capacity plan is one designed to adjust capacity in line with anticipated changes in demand. Known as a **chase demand capacity plan**, this involves changing capacity levels from one period to another by adjusting some combination of staff numbers, working hours and available equipment. This approach is more complex and the task factors that make this approach more difficult to manage than a level capacity plan include ensuring the availability, training and retention of staff and the potential impact of less-experienced staff on quality conformance.

Manufacturing companies making standard products can take advantage of a level or mixed plan (explained in the next section) by using inventory as part of the means to manage imbalances, whereas service organizations and manufacturing businesses making special products usually cannot. Because most services cannot be stored and special products, by definition, cannot be made ahead of demand, chase demand (Figure 8.16) and order backlog (see Figure 8.15) are the options available to these organizations.

With a chase demand plan, the decisions concern not only by how much to increase capacity, but also demand issues such as:

- Timing – when to increase capacity

- The extent to which a business is prepared to carry excess capacity (and the costs involved) as an alternative to the costs and concerns of repeatedly changing capacity levels

- The possibility of not being able to meet customer lead-times due to lengthening backlog of orders/queues.

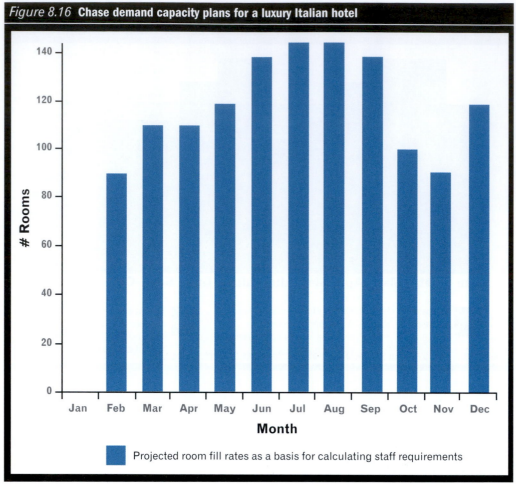

Figure 8.16 Chase demand capacity plans for a luxury Italian hotel

Projected room fill rates as a basis for calculating staff requirements

Note: The hotel has a total of 153 rooms.

Mixed capacity plans

The third option to handle capacity/demand differences is to choose a **mixed capacity plan**. Here, some inventory is accumulated to make effective use of existing capacity, and some capacity changes are made to reflect changes in demand. The example in Figure 8.17 shows an increase in capacity during the months of September to December that resulted from introducing a temporary evening shift (18.30–22.00 hrs) to help meet demand in the build-up to peak sales at Christmas.

Managing demand and capacity

So far, we have discussed the concept and role of medium-term capacity planning and the alternative approaches from which a business may choose. This section discusses the options for adjusting levels of demand and capacity within the overall plan. These will fall within the control of an organization and are designed to help fine-tune capacity plans to better meet the business's objectives as well as the market's needs.

Managing demand

Demand is inherently variable at all times. That is the nature of market demand and the challenging task that operations needs to manage and discharge. Within its overall approach, however, an organization can select from alternatives to help manage demand so that it can better meet the needs of the business and its customers. These alternatives fall within a number of categories, as described below.

> **Mixed capacity plan** – involves some inventory being accumulated to make effective use of existing capacity and some capacity changes being made to reflect changes in demand.

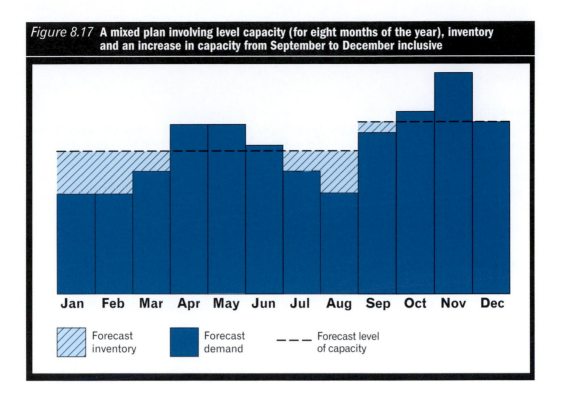

Figure 8.17 A mixed plan involving level capacity (for eight months of the year), inventory and an increase in capacity from September to December inclusive

Legend:
- Forecast inventory
- Forecast demand
- – – – Forecast level of capacity

Changing the pattern of demand

One way of adjusting demand and capacity differences is to change the pattern of demand. Examples include:

- *Altering price levels* to differentiate, for example, between peak and off-peak periods. In this way, some customers are persuaded to choose periods where demand levels are normally lower in exchange for paying less, for example off-season holidays, matinee cinema and theatre prices, factory discounts for early or late season purchases, off-peak rail travel and early evening menu discounts at restaurants. The purpose of these pricing schemes is to help level out demand through different time periods.

- *Advertising* can be used to stimulate demand. Often working hand-in-hand with price changes, one purpose of advertising can be to stimulate demand in periods of otherwise low demand and, in that way, change the pattern of demand to help improve the capacity/demand balance for an organization.

- *Complementary services and products* can be developed for counter-cyclical, seasonal trends. In this way, demand for the complementary services and products will occur in the periods of lower sales for current services and products. Examples include the use of hotels in the winter for conferences, coach tour operators providing school bus services, fast-food restaurants offering breakfast menus, and garden tractor and mower companies developing a range of blowing equipment to handle autumn leaves and winter snow.

Scheduling

A second way is to develop elements of the scheduling procedure that are aimed specifically at modifying demand patterns. These include the following:

- *Reservations and appointments* are an effective way to help manage demand. In essence, they are a way to pre-sell capacity within a service delivery system. When preferred slots are already taken, demand can be deflected into other available time slots. Many service delivery systems use this mechanism, including hospitals, dental and other health practices, passenger airlines, hairdressing and beauty salons, hotels and restaurants.

- *Fixed service schedules* are often used by companies to increase the effective use of capacity by forcing customers to adapt their requirements to the capacity schedule available. All forms of public transport use fixed service schedules as one way to help manage capacity.

Managing uncertainty

Demand is uncertain. To reduce this uncertainty, companies use a range of approaches. For example, pre-payment coupled to pre-booking which gets round the problem of late cancellations resulting in lost sales. In other systems, cancellations incur penalties. The passenger airline approach is to offer from a 'no change' deal through to a totally flexible ticket depending upon the level of price discounting the passenger accepts. Those passengers buying a non-discounted ticket have complete freedom to change, while those with a discounted ticket receive no refund if they cancel.

Managing capacity

The other principal way in which companies can take steps to handle the differences in demand and capacity is to consider different ways of managing capacity. These include the following.

Short-term capacity adjustments

These adjustments can be made in two ways – overtime and temporary staff. Although the use of overtime is being reduced in many developed economies, the use of temporary labour is increasing.

Temporary staff have long been used in many businesses as a way to handle marked changes in demand when overtime working is not a sustainable option. As companies continue to restructure to help cope with today's competitive climate, they have slimmed down in an effort to reduce overall costs, and they are often left with a core of permanent staff that represents an insufficient capacity to cope with demand at peak times. Temporary and contract staff are increasingly being used to provide for such capacity shortfalls on a need-to-have basis, and this approach is proving to be a way of providing capacity to meet predictable and random demand patterns while helping companies to better control their costs and respond quickly to fluctuations in demand.

Flexible capacity

The last subsection dealt with ways of adjusting planned capacity levels. This one considers ways of being able to change capacity within the existing plan:

- *Flexible staff* provide the option of moving existing capacity around within the system or process to reflect changes in demand. Training to increase each person's range of skills is fundamental to this alternative. Switching staff in line with forecast sales and known orders has been an integral part of manufacturing businesses for many years, but is now more important than ever because of the increase in product options on offer and the shorter lead-times often expected by customers.

This approach is also widely used in service delivery systems. In fast-food restaurants, for example, staff switch from serving to cleaning tasks during periods of low demand and vice versa. Similarly, moving front-office staff to and from back-office tasks is increasingly used by financial service companies to provide better support for customers while managing overall staff capacity within agreed budgets.

- *Arranging different capacity levels* within the same time period is also used to change capacity to reflect different patterns of demand. Part-time staff, temporary staff, shift patterns and staggered working hours (including break times) are some of the more common ways that organizations use.

One of BMW's key tasks when it took over the Mini car plant in Oxford was to increase productivity and bring the levels of output per worker up to those of its factories in Germany. BMW estimated the gap at some 30 per cent and explained in discussions with local management and staff, that the options were to close the gap or face significant job cuts. The changes sought concerned working practices that had transformed BMW's shop floor into one of the world's most productive.

Among the important changes that BMW was looking to introduce was flexible working. In its own plants, BMW had dispensed with the standard eight-hour day and five-days-a-week shifts. Instead, BMW staff work varied shift patterns (including a regular requirement to work on Saturday at no extra pay) that, on average, added up to four days a week. The shift patterns were very varied (about 250 models) to meet different sets of needs. For instance, at one factory in rural Bavaria there is one model for a handful of workers who are also farmers that takes into account their need to leave early to tend their livestock.

The result is that BMW's expensive plants run longer and are not idle at weekends, thereby cutting the actual costs per car by one-quarter compared with traditional work patterns. With machines and processes costing as much as $250 million, the savings are substantial.

Another element of flexible working that BMW has introduced is the time accounting module. This allows the company to increase or decrease a person's hours (up to a maximum at any time of 200 hours) in line with demand, and with workers later taking time off or working longer, again at no extra cost.

www.bmw.com

Questions

1. Explain how these arrangements have helped BMW to become more competitive.

2. Give an example of when a company would use flexible working and the time accounting model.

Lecturers: visit www.palgrave.com/business/hillom3e for teaching guidelines for this case study

Staff at Lloyds Banking Group (one of the major UK banks) are encouraged to work flexibly. Under the Work Options initiative, staff no longer have to explain to their managers why they want to change their working hours: their case will be decided purely on whether it makes sense for the business. One outcome is that about one-third of Lloyds group staff work flexible or reduced hours. From now on, the bank is adapting practices used successfully in the USA and the rest of Europe to allow staff to work differently. Under this new system employees choose from a menu of options: job sharing, reduced hours, a compressed working week (for example four longer days), variable starting and finishing times and working off-site for one to three days a week. Staff can also propose alternative arrangements.

Applicants need to explain how they will fulfil their duties, how colleagues and customers will be affected, how the bank could benefit and how they propose to detect and handle any problems.

The approach was triggered after the merger of Lloyds and TSB in the mid-1990s, and an environment characterized by increasing competition (for example from supermarkets), the trend to 24-hour banking for which staff had to provide extended cover and the growing need to recruit and retain staff in a more competitive labour market. The new system aims to make flexible working a mainstream business practice, not an entitlement or a benefit. Past arrangements were recognized as being too dependent on individual relationships between employee and manager. The aim is to move these arrangements from the category of 'a favour' and to give everyone more control over when work was done, with the emphasis switching to output rather than the time spent at work. Employees need to think through how this will work for them and how they and their respective managers will review how well the process is working.

Part of the launch involved briefing managers on the new perspectives of work as well as the taboos of flexible working, for example that teleworking is impractical for managers. Working at home gives a greater opportunity to allocate more time to the activities of thinking and planning than is often available in the workplace. While each arrangement has to be supported by a business case, a change in attitude to work and work practices and the emphasis on the outputs and work contributions made will bring benefits to employees and the business alike.
www.lloydsbankinggroup.com

Questions

1. How will flexible working help Lloyds Banking Group run its business better?

2. What benefits do you see for employees?

3. Make a business case for working a condensed week of four longer days.

Lecturers: visit www.palgrave.com/business/hillom3e for teaching guidelines for this case study

Changing the form and nature of capacity

To meet the dynamic nature of markets and the varying patterns and fluctuations in demand that follow on from this, companies have been changing the form and nature of their capacity. Some of the more commonly used approaches are now discussed:

- *Annualized hours* entails calculating working time on an annual rather than a weekly or monthly basis, with employees contracted to work, for example, 1,748 hours per year rather than 38 hours per week. (This example comprises 52 weeks less 6 weeks of holidays x 38 hours per week.) The system gives companies more flexibility when scheduling work, allowing for longer hours at some periods and shorter hours at others. Overtime is not ruled out in these arrangements, but being able to match capacity to seasonal patterns of demand leads to marked reductions in overtime and in the attendant costs. Case 8.4 describes BMW's approach, while Case 8.5 provides a look at the different elements used by Lloyds Banking Group.

- *Substituting capacity* can be achieved by increasing the use of technology and/ or customers in the delivery system. Both these alternatives reduce the number of employed staff and thereby the overall size of the task of managing capacity, whereas using the customer as part of the delivery system (for example, with ATMs and other self-service arrangements) means that the 'capacity' to serve will always be on hand as customers comprise both the source of demand and the source of capacity.

- *Subcontracting* similarly allows companies to spread the task of handling capacity/ demand differences by having suppliers manage part of the capacity implications resulting from changes in demand.

- *Sharing capacity* is a concept designed to spread the cost of expensive equipment or highly skilled staff resources that would normally be underutilized. For example, hospitals may agree to share expensive medical equipment. Similarly, smaller passenger and freight airlines reach agreement on sharing a range of facilities with other airlines, from check-in terminals and staff to baggage handling equipment and ground personnel.

> **EXECUTIVE INSIGHT**

Taking actions to change demand patterns and adjust and change the shape of capacity are your key tasks when managing these resources.

Making capacity in practice

- Capacity levels need to change to meet uncertain and variable levels of demand. But, given the relatively long timescales involved in changing capacity, operations needs to identity the timeframes and cut-off points involved and force the key capacity decisions onto the business agenda.

- Although companies can reduce risk by making capacity investments that 'follow' rather than 'lead' demand, they will find it difficult to regain market share once it has been lost.

- Forecasts, by definition, are inaccurate but having a forecast is better than no forecast at all. The key task for operations then is to understand the assumptions on which the chosen forecast model is based and to question whether all the key issues affecting operations have been recognized and taken into account.

- Invariably sales forecasts are presented as a single figure. To help manage capacity, operations should ask for:
  - Three or four sales forecast levels with appropriate probabilities of their being accurate
  - As sales levels start to slow, all the functions within the businesses (especially sales, marketing, operations and customer service) need to review to work out why this has happened and determine the new forecast that they need to support
  - Often, capacity does not match demand because of decisions made by functions other than operations, such as inaccurate sales forecasts from sales and marketing and an unwillingness to invest in new capacity by finance. Operations needs to record and analyze these reasons to ensure that the business clearly understands why capacity did not match demand so that better decisions can be made in the future.

- Operations needs to assess the role of delivery reliability for key customers and use this as part of the discussion on capacity planning. Understanding the impact of failing to meet customers' requirements needs to be an integral part of these capacity decisions.

- It is essential to direct sales efforts to services and products where adequate, or even excess, capacity is available. Otherwise, the demand will not be met and the door will be left open for the competition. It is significantly more difficult to regain market share once it has been lost.

Driving business performance

One of operations' prime tasks is delivering the services and making the products sold to or provided for customers. Managing the capacity (staff and premises) to meet these requirements is a key factor in meeting these needs and consequently is a key factor affecting business performance in the following ways.

Managing capacity to release cash

Sufficient capacity underpins sales performance and so helps cash flow. Too little capacity leads to lost sales and attendant lost cash flows. Where manufacturing companies choose source inventory as one way to manage capacity, the cash flow consequences will invariably be significant. Too much capacity will not only increase capacity, but may also lead to an increase in work-in-progress and finished goods inventory because most organizations would not want to see this investment (people and equipment) underutilized.

Managing capacity to improve market support

Operations uses a mix of staff, processes and systems to provide the services and make the products it sells in the marketplace. Having sufficient capacity then, both in terms of mix and level, is a key factor in meeting demand while also helping to ensure that customers return. If operations has too little capacity to meet customer due dates it is likely that next time around these customers will go elsewhere and also tell others.

In many markets, delivery reliability is an order-losing qualifier and sufficient capacity must be available to support this. Companies using a 'chase demand' strategy reduce the risk of costs being too high, but increase the risk of reduced sales and the subsequent cost of trying to regain them.

Managing capacity to reduce costs

While having sufficient capacity to meet demand is essential in terms of sales growth, having too much incurs unnecessary costs. In the service sector this leads to excess costs for the business. In the manufacturing sector, the choice facing a company is one of incurring excess costs or making products ahead of demand and holding them in inventory with its attendant costs and cash flow implications.

Critical reflections

Managing operations capacity is both complex and challenging owing to the size of the task and the need for all facets of capacity to work well both in themselves and together, in an environment where demand is increasingly dynamic and less predictable.

For example, the data in Figure 8.18 provide an illustration of the size and interrelated nature of capacity. This is what it takes an American airline to feed one day's passengers from Atlanta airport and well illustrates the forward-looking as well as the day-to-day nature of capacity management.

Figure 8.18 **What it takes an American airline to feed its passengers from Atlanta airport on one day**

Aspects		Quantity
Number of	passengers	36,800
	flights	274
	trucks	60
	assembly lines	16
Kilograms of	chicken	1,130
	pasta	535
	broccoli	23
	spinach	100
	tomatoes	140
	lettuce	1,120
	butter	235
	coffee	420
Number of	dinner rolls	18,500
	apples	5,800
Litres of	olive oil	86
	wine	6,320

But all this is happening in an environment characterized by high levels of risk. As markets open up, decisions on capacity and location, for instance, will have an impact on future market positions and opportunities. As an example, several major car companies have built assembly plants to help position themselves early in relation to potential market opportunities in China. China and India are two such examples where forecast gross domestic product (GDP) will exceed that of the USA in less than ten and 25 years, respectively. As a consequence, companies in different sectors have sought to get an early foothold, but all have found it tough going.

Take, for example, pharmaceutical companies that have set up manufacturing facilities in China. Inherent in their decisions to do so are several concerns including moves by the national government to protect the local drug industry, fresh restrictions on a foreign company's ability to sell drugs and serious problems experienced by foreign investors concerning the protection of intellectual property as patents are broken and substitute products are made locally. Although some companies, such as Xian-Janssen and GlaxoSmithKline, have earned good profits, others are below target. It has been forecast that, by 2018, annual pharmaceutical sales in China will have reached around $133 billion. With predictions that spending on drugs as a percentage of GDP will more than double between 2009 and 2013, companies believe they cannot afford not to be present and are thus planning not only to stay, but to expand. Companies such as Bristol-Myers Squibb. GlaxoSmithKline, Janssen (part of Johnson & Johnson), Novo Nordisk, Pfizer and Pharmacia & Upjohn are prepared to take the risk and gamble on the end game.

For any business, deciding whether to increase or decrease capacity is typically a major question. Capacity comprises not only the level of permanency involved, but also the issue of timing. A loss in market share always goes to a competitor. The competitor who adds capacity first does not necessarily make a profit. But the competitor who trails behind on the growth/capacity path will find great difficulty in regaining its future market share position, whether or not it decides to increase capacity at a later date. On the other hand, adding capacity that is subsequently underused is bound up with unnecessary costs and high exposure. There are few areas of decision-making where the outcomes are under such an intense spotlight. Buying capacity that does not get used or having insufficient capacity to meet demand will always be viewed with a level of incredulity by those outside a company due to the fundamental nature of capacity provision in transacting business.

The example given earlier concerning China reflects the size and nature of the dilemma. Furthermore, the dimensions underpinning these decisions are becoming more difficult to embrace as the timescales become shorter and the risks get bigger. As this chapter has highlighted, the issues impacting demand and capacity have an increasing measure of these characteristics. The dynamic nature of today's markets is matched by developments in technology, the issue of where work needs to be undertaken, and repositioning in terms of the make/buy mix and the impact of all these factors on capacity. The outcome serves only to reinforce the key decisions involved in the choice and management of capacity. A challenging task indeed!

Summary

- Managing capacity is central to the basic business task of providing services and products in line with customer demand. As the elements of staff, delivery systems and processes contribute to operations' capacity, its central role is further emphasized by the size and interrelated nature of its provision. Key elements of effectively managing capacity include:
  - Determining the way in which capacity is most appropriately measured to reflect the nature of the business involved
  - Measuring output needs to distinguish between the dimensions of utilization (a comparison of actual hours worked with planned hours) and efficiency (a comparison of the work produced to the number of hours worked)
  - The desired position is to have neither too much nor too little capacity. But corporate decisions concerning make versus buy, service/product range, process design and the perishable nature of capacity (particularly in the service sector) are among the several variables that make this a difficult call.

- Within an environment where definitions of capacity are characterized by uncertainty, operations needs to reduce the planning and managing task in several ways, including:
  - Identifying those parts of total demand that can be predicted (for example, seasonality and peaks) as opposed to those which cannot be predicted, and thereby reducing the truly uncertain aspects when forecasting demand
  - Influencing demand to reduce the peaks and troughs that characterize demand profiles.

- The remainder of the chapter addressed the long-term horizons of capacity provision and the ways to help when managing demand and capacity. Key points included the approaches to resource planning (often two to five years ahead) and medium-term planning (typically from six months to two years ahead).

- The sections on resource and medium-term planning also provided illustrations of alternative approaches that may be used. In resource planning, the amount, timing and location of capacity were central to the discussion. In medium-term planning, the steps used to provide a plan were detailed, together with alternative approaches to achieving the plan – level capacity, chase demand or a mixed plan.

- The final section in the chapter introduced alternative ways of managing demand (including changing demand patterns and scheduling) and managing capacity (for example, short-term adjustments, forms of flexible capacity and changing its basic form).

Study activities

Discussion questions

1. How do the capacity considerations in a hospital, wine bar and a company making lawnmowers differ?

2. Discuss the major differences between a call centre and a soft drinks company producing own-label products for major retailers with respect to:
   - Capacity provision
   - Facilities location.

3. Should an organization always attempt to match its capacity to its forecast and known demand patterns? Give two examples to illustrate your views.

4. Discuss the advantages and disadvantages of the following approaches for meeting demand:
   - The build-up and depletion of finished goods inventory
   - Subcontract work
   - Using part-time workers.

5. Which approaches to capacity management would you favour using in an Italian ski resort hotel? Explain your choice.

6. Which approaches (order backlog/queues or work-in-progress/finished goods inventory or a mix of the two) would the following organizations use to help handle the rough-cut capacity plan issues discussed in the chapter:
   - An architect's office?
   - A high-quality, reproduction furniture manufacturer?
   - A management consultancy company?

Assignments

1. A fully integrated oil company would be involved in the following major steps in the business process:
   - Searching for new oilfields
   - Drilling for oil
   - Building a new or extending an existing oil refinery
   - Managing an oil refinery
   - Delivering different fuel grades to petrol stations
   - Managing the sale of non-fuel goods at a petrol station.

What are the likely capacity planning time horizons for each of the above activities? Then, fit them into the long-, medium- and short-term time frames introduced in this chapter.

2. Compose and contrast the alternative ways in which the following businesses might manage demand and manage capacity to help in managing operations.
   - A restaurant
   - A local bakery with three outlets – one unit in town and the other two in nearby towns.

Exploring further

TED Talks

Leadbeater, C. (2005) *Innovation*. In this deceptively casual talk, Charles Leadbeater weaves a tight argument that innovation isn't just for professionals anymore. Passionate amateurs, using new tools, are creating products and paradigms that companies can't. **www.ted.com/talks/charles_leadbeater_on_innovation.html**

Journal articles

Adler, P., Hecksher, C. and Prusak, L. (2011) 'Building a collaborative enterprise', *Harvard Business Review*, **89**(7/8): 94–101. Organizations must learn to: (1) Define a shared purpose (2) Cultivate an ethic of contribution (3) Develop scalable procedures (4) Create an infrastructure that values and rewards collaboration.

Katz, K.L., Larson, B.M. and Larson, R.C. (1991) 'Prescription for the waiting-in-line blues: entertain, enlighten and engage', *Sloan Management Review*, **32**(2): 44–53. Examines customer perceptions of waiting in line and the methods for making waiting more tolerable.

Klassen, K.J. and Rohleder, T.R. (2002) 'Demand and capacity management decisions in services: how they impact on one another', *International Journal of Operations and Production Management*, **22**(5/6): 527–49. The article's findings are based on modelling the impact of automation, customer participation, cross-training employees, informing customers about the operation, and other factors.

Ramaswamy, V. and Gouillart, F. (2010) 'Building the co-creative enterprise', *Harvard Business Review*, **88**(10): 100–9. The article examines how a company can use its stakeholders including customers, employees and distributors to determine HR practices and design and market its services and products.

Books

Chase, C. (2009) *Demand-driven Forecasting: A Structured Approach to Forecasting*. Hoboken, NJ: Wiley/SAS Business Services. This practitioner-focused book is filled with real-life examples and case studies looking at how to improve business forecasting.

Morlidge, S. and Player, S. (2010) *Future Ready: How to Master Business Forecasting*. Chichester: John Wiley & Sons. A thought-provoking look at how businesses need to rethink the way they forecast in order to navigate through turbulent times. A combination of 'good enough' forecasts, wise preparation and timely action is critical within business.

Notes and references

1. This issue is also discussed in Chapter 12.
2. Eg. see 'The hollow corporation', Special Report, *Business Week*, 3 March 1986.
3. The strategic aspects of this issue are dealt with in some detail in Alex Hill and Terry Hill, *Manufacturing Operations Strategy*, 3rd edn, Palgrave Macmillan (2010) Chapter 9.
4. Although the timescales for resource and medium-term capacity planning are classically referred to as two to five years and six months to two years ahead respectively, many organizations do not need to plan that far ahead as the lead-times involved to change capacity are not that lengthy. Many organizations may well need to look only one to two years ahead without limiting their options and opportunities.

Visit www.palgrave.com/business/hillom3e for self-test questions, guideline answers to some case study questions, useful weblinks and more to help you understand the topics in this chapter

It's a cold December lunchtime and Minkies is buzzing. 'It always brightens up my day,' explained one customer. 'I love popping in for a coffee, something to eat or just to say hello. They're so friendly and the food is amazing! What more could I ask for? With so much variety I can eat here seven days a week without getting bored. I love the "minx" on rye, but I'm also always tempted by all the other food they have. The roast chicken I had last week was wonderful and the salads are truly delicious!'

Doron Atzmon set up Minkies four years ago as a local deli serving a wide range of tasty, nutritious and healthy products. It has been a great success and he has just opened a butcher across the street from it too. 'People love the food we sell,' he explained. 'We offer a wide range of products, sandwiches, salads and hot dishes. If customers want something that's not on the menu (see Figure 1), we'll prepare that too! Some people love this and are happy to wait for what they want. However, I think other customers who have less time would be happy with less choice, if it means they could get their lunch more quickly.'

PRODUCTS
The deli currently stocks over 400 different items sourced from 30 local suppliers and Doron constantly travels around the

Figure 1 Deli Menu

Breakfast

Minkies Breakfast – organic free-range eggs, (scrambled, fried, or omelette), bacon or smoked salmon, toast, freshly squeezed orange juice, coffee, tea or hot chocolate

Kensal Rise Breakfast – muesli or porridge, fresh fruit salad, yoghurt and fresh orange juice

Create your own breakfast – eggs, bacon, smoked salmon, toast, jam, marmalade, honey, marmite, peanut butter, bagel, cream cheese, fresh fruit salad, cereal, porridge, freshly squeezed juice, croissant, almond croissant, pain au chocolate or fruit danish

Sandwiches

Sabich – grilled aubergine, houmous, pickled cucumber, hard boiled egg & parsley

Clare Bear – grilled aubergine, goat's cheese, tahini & baby leaf

Sunday Deluxe – salt beef, picked cucumber, horseradish & mayonnaise

The Minx – salami, tahini, houmous, grilled vegetables & baby leaf

TLC – organic smoked back bacon, baby leaf & tomato

Italian Job – Parma ham or salami, cheese, tomato & baby leaf

Mozzarella – mozzarella, pesto, tomato & baby leaf

Halloumi – grilled halloumi cheese, pesto, rocket & tomato

Classic – smoked salmon & cream cheese

Too Nice – tuna, avocado & hard boiled egg

Avo – brie, avocado, baby leaf & tomato

Omelette – omelette, cream cheese, tomato & green onion

Gorgeous Nicola – bacon, melted mozzarella, mayonnaise, baby leaf, tomato & mustard

Hot dishes

Roasted Chicken – marinated with thyme, olive oil & garlic

Organic Meat Balls – in red sauce

Organic Grilled Chicken

Organic Salmon – on a bed of sweet potato, carrot and red sauce

Meat Lasagna

Vegetable Lasagna

Salads	Sweet treats	Side orders
Feta Goat's Cheese	**Banana Loaf**	**White rice**
Baby Leaf	**Almond & Orange Cake**	**Brown rice**
Cooked Carrot	**Chocolate Cake**	**Mashed potato**
Cooked Spinach	**Clementine Mini-loaf**	**Hand-cut chips**
Moroccan	**Triple Choc Brownies**	**Couscous**
Green Tahini	**Cup Cakes**	**Quinoa**
Chopped Mixed	**Blueberry Muffin**	
Babaganoush	**Banana Muffin**	
Home-made Houmous	**Banana & Raisin Mini-loaf**	
Grilled Vegetables	**Butter Biscuits**	
	Cannoli Flapjack	
	Pecan Pie	
	Petit Fours	

Drinks

Coffee – latte, cappuccino, americano, espresso or macchiato

Tea – English breakfast, Earl Grey, chamomile, mint, green or fennel, or hot chocolate

Fresh juice – orange, apple, beetroot, ginger or a combination of your choice

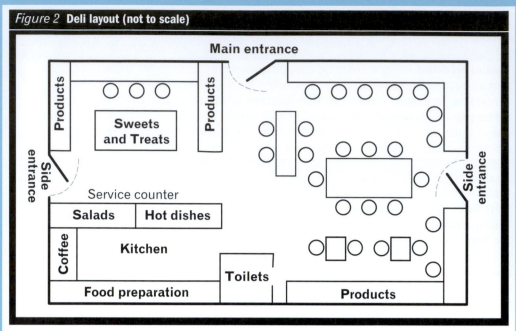

Figure 2 Deli layout (not to scale)

Notes: 1. The areas marked 'Products' contain pre-packed items that customers can select and purchase and buy at the service counter.
2. The three sides of the building with entrances are predominantly glazed.
3. Customers can select cakes, muffins etc. from the sweet treats area and pay for them at the service counter.
4. Customers queue in the outlet from the 'Service counter' towards the 'Main entrance'.

country in search of new and interesting products. 'The products that we sell in the deli are also the ones we use in our sandwiches, salads and hot dishes,' he explains. 'All our stock is on display and we simply cook up items that are starting to reach their best-before date. For instance, we recently bought some Spanish calasparra brown rice. Its wonderful stuff, but no one bought it! I ended up cooking it up and selling it in the deli instead. Only having a small storage area means we keep track of everything and only buy what we need.'

KEEPING UP WITH DEMAND

'The original idea was to sell great products and serve fresh food to customers eating in the deli,' Doron continues. 'However, customers also want to take it away to eat either at home or at work. Although we're easily able to cope with the steady flow of customers during the day, lunchtime is a challenge! Increasingly, people take food away and we get at least two large orders each day from local businesses. As well as myself, there is one other person serving customers during the day and two at lunchtime. These two work well

together preparing drinks and serving customers. However, I'm struggling to keep up with demand in the kitchen as everything is made to order. Although the large takeaway orders are great for business, they don't come in until the last minute and mean other customers have to wait while I prepare them. I don't really know what to do as we're unable to expand the physical area (see Figure 2) and I can't afford to employ any more staff.'

www.minkiesdeli.co.uk

Questions

1. What are the order-winners and qualifiers in Minkies' markets?

2. What is the level of demand in these markets? Assess its impact on capacity.

3. How could Minkies manage demand and capacity in its growing business?

Lecturers: visit www.palgrave.com/business/hillom3e for teaching guidelines for this case study

	MARCH	APRIL	MAY	JUNE
6	6 13 20 27	3 10 17 24	1 8 15 22 29	5 12 19 26
7 14 21	7 14 21 28	4 11 18 25	2 9 16 23 30	6 13 20 27
1 8 15 22	15 22 29	5 12 19 26	3 10 17 24 31	7 14 21 28
26 2 9 16 23	30	6 13 20 27	4 11 18 25	1 8 15 22 29
20 27 3 10 17 24	3 10	7 14 21 28	5 12 19 26	2 9 16 23
21 28 4 11 18 25	4 11 18 2	8 15 22 29	6 13 20 27	3 10 17 2
15 22 29 5 12 19 26	5 12 19 26	16 23 30	7 14 21 28	4 11 18

JULY	AUGUST	SEPTEMBER		NOVEMBER
3 10 17 24 31	7 14 21 28	4 11 18 25	2 9	6 13 20 27
4 11 18 25	1 8 15 22 29	5 12 19 26	3 10 17	7 14 21 28
19 26	2 9 16 23 30	6 13 20 27	4 11 18 25	22 2
27	3 10 17 24 31	7 14 21 28	5 12 19 26	3 10
4 11 18 25	1 8 15 22 29	6 13 20 27	
12 19 26	2 9 16 23 30	7 14 21 28	4 11
20 27	3 10 17 24	1 8 15 22 29	5

After completing this chapter, you should be able to:

• Appreciate the key role of operations control (the tasks of scheduling and execution) within a business

• Recognize the different types of operations scheduling systems and for which business each is appropriate

• Explain the elements of a materials requirements planning system

• Appreciate how manufacturing resource planning and enterprise resources planning have developed and how they supplement a materials requirement planning system

• Understand the different categories and options that can be used to cushion a delivery system from the inherent instability of markets

• Recognize the difference between independent and dependent demand

• Understand the just-in-time approach both in terms of its role as a scheduling system and as a philosophy of operations management

• Understand how optimized production technology works

Chapter outline

What is the role of scheduling and executing operations?

- Scheduling concerns the detailed plans to determine the capacity and materials to meet customer orders or the service and product output plans for the business

- Execution comprises the day-to-day (often hourly) control systems to manage the resources to meet the schedules and ensure that customer demands are met and resources are used effectively

Why are scheduling and execution important?

- Needing to meet both customer requirements and business performance targets makes operations scheduling and execution a difficult task, principally because the different nature of these tasks places different sets of demands on operations

- Whereas demand is, by its nature, unpredictable as markets are inherently unstable, operations needs to maintain a stable delivery system

- Changing or disrupting plans and schedules invariably incurs costs, reduces efficiency and results in delays

- The task of scheduling and execution is to help cushion the delivery system from the inherent instability of markets, thus fulfilling the dual task of meeting customer order dates and business performance targets

How do scheduling and execution impact business performance?

- Providing the services and products sold to customers is the very essence of the operations task. Scheduling the staff and resources to meet these requirements lies at the heart of this provision and underpins the well-being of an organization

- Repeat customers are the key to sales revenue growth

- Using resources effectively ensures that the cost structures that underpin profit targets are sustained

What are the key issues to consider when choosing how to schedule and execute operations plans?

- The scheduling and execution phases convert the plans into detailed schedules

- These are then managed to meet customer requirements and delivery dates

- The factors that influence the choice and design of the system to be used include:
  - Service/product complexity. Organizations offering a narrow range of services often deliver them as a single transaction. As neither the customer nor information needs to be processed at a second step, these require much simpler systems
  - Standard services and products with their known tasks and typical high volumes lend themselves to using a system to schedule and execute operations plans. With special (non-repeat) services and products there are few, if any, repeat orders and little, if any, knowledge of how to provide or make them and so typically organizations rely on their skilled staff to schedule the work in line with customer delivery dates
  - Decisions on how much an organization proactively manages demand and capacity. The more these are managed, the easier the scheduling and executing tasks are.

Introduction

The challenge confronting organizations is how best to meet customers' requirements as well as day-to-day performance targets such as output, efficiency and costs. The former underpins sales revenue, while the latter underpins profits in a commercial business, or ensures that budgets are well spent in non-profit organizations and the public sector. In this regard, scheduling is a vital element of managing operations, as it ensures that both customer requirements and day-to-day performance targets are met.

This chapter will first define scheduling and discuss its role in the operations process. It will then go on to look at project management and outline the various operations scheduling systems, the processes for introducing them and their relative benefits. To begin with, informal systems (such as bar charts) are described. After that, systems for more complex operations and repeat services and products are explained, including **network analysis**, **material requirements planning (MRPI)**, manufacturing resources planning (MRPII), **enterprise resource planning (ERP)**, **just-in-time (JIT)** and **optimized production technology (OPT)**.

What is operations scheduling?

In the last chapter we looked at resource and medium-term planning and set these in the context of the planning and control systems used in operations. The overview provided in Chapter 8 is reintroduced here as Figure 9.1 so as to reinforce the links between the planning phase (covered in the last chapter) and the operations control, scheduling and execution task (the subject of this chapter).

The operations control task concerns the tactical decisions that involve detailed operations activities to ensure that customer demands are met and resources are used effectively.

Before examining why scheduling is essential to operations, let's define the term itself and consider the types of tasks involved in it. A schedule is a timetable of jobs with start dates arranged to meet customers' delivery requirements or a business's output targets and timescales while taking into account the availability of materials and short-term capacity (staff, systems and equipment). The schedule determines the sequence of jobs and then manages and controls these jobs through the service delivery system or manufacturing process. In some businesses, such as rapid-response service operations where customers arrive in an unplanned way, the scheduling of orders is linked to the arrival of customers. Here, the key scheduling tasks concern managing short-term capacity and any materials and services purchased ('bought-out') from suppliers. Detailed scheduling is built around the front-office phase of a service delivery system, where servers and customers interface in a stimulus-response manner. Even so, the task of matching short-term capacity to uncertain patterns of demand is difficult, and companies alleviate this by reshaping demand and varying their capacity, as discussed in Chapter 8.

Network analysis – a means of scheduling complex operations that involves planning (establishing all the activities or steps to be completed), scheduling (applying limiting factors such as time and cost) and controlling (updating the plan using feedback obtained during the process).

Material requirements planning (MRPI) – the system that determines the final services and products (in terms of which ones and how many) that a company will provide during a future period and then specifies the necessary inputs (in terms of volumes and timing) to meet that demand.

Enterprise resource planning (ERP) – a software system that integrates operations planning and scheduling systems with all the other functions in a company, such as finance, sales and marketing, logistics and human resources.

Just-in-time system (JIT) – a system in which small quantities of services or products are produced just in time to be sold.

Optimized production technology (OPT) – a scheduling system based on loading work in line with the available capacity at stages in the process that have less capacity than others (known as bottlenecks).

Figure 9.1 Operations planning and control systems

TIMESCALES	PHASE		TASK
Years ↓ Days/hours	Planning	Resource planning	Determines the resources to meet the aggregate demand forecasts for all services or products in a future timeframe, normally a period of between two and five years
		Medium-term capacity planning	Partially disaggregated demand forecasts are used to give a 'rough-cut' review of the necessary resources in terms of staff skill and process types. Will be for periods of six months to two years depending on the type of business involved
	Control	Scheduling	Detailed plans to determine the capacity (staff skills and processes) and materials to meet the service or product schedule, together with any contingency plans
		Execution	Day-to-day (often hourly) control systems to manage the detailed capacity plans and material requirements to meet the scheduled delivery of services and products to customers

The role of scheduling in managing operations

Providing the services and products sold to customers is the very essence of the operations task. Scheduling the staff, materials and other resources to meet these requirements lies at the heart of this provision and is essential to the well-being of an organization, as repeat customers are the key to sales revenue growth. This is because:

- Dissatisfied customers don't come back (and often they tell others they're unhappy with the service!).

- Satisfied customers return and repeat buy.

Needing to meet both customer requirements and business performance targets can make scheduling operations a complex task, because customer requirements and business performance targets place differing demands on operations. Whereas markets are inherently unstable, operations needs to maintain a stable delivery system, as changing or disrupting plans and schedules invariably incurs costs, reduces efficiency and results in delays.

Given the nature of markets, organizations need to find ways to handle the unstable nature of demand. As Figure 9.2 illustrates, businesses cushion the delivery systems from the unstable markets into which they sell in a number of ways:

- *Basic mechanisms* Organizations choose order backlog (or queues) or inventory or a combination of the two as the basic mechanism in this cushioning task.

- *Secondary mechanisms* Again as explained in the previous chapter, organizations can use several additional methods including planned capacity, forecasting and demand management in addition to the basic mechanisms described in the previous point. Furthermore, organizations also use process improvement (the subject of Chapter 13) and scheduling (the subject of this chapter) to help in the cushioning task.

- *Supplementary mechanism* Finally, companies may often use reactive capacity (in the form of overtime working) to supplement demand/capacity imbalances that have slipped through the net.

> **EXECUTIVE INSIGHT**
Operations scheduling helps to cushion the delivery system from the instability of the market.

As shown in Figure 9.1, the scheduling and execution phases of operations planning and control systems convert the plans into detailed schedules and then manage these to meet customer requirements. The principal activities of these phases are to create the schedules and instructions to undertake the necessary tasks and ensure that all is available as and when needed.

Not all companies require the same operations scheduling system. The factors that influence the choice they make and the design of the system to be used include:

- *Service/product complexity* The complexity of the service or product directly affects the choice and design of the scheduling system. Service businesses offering a limited and narrow range often deliver a service as a single transaction. Neither the customer nor any information thus needs to be processed at a second stage, and this clearly simplifies the overall scheduling task. At the other extreme, scheduling a range of multi-step services or products completed in different parts of the total delivery system will result in the need for more complex scheduling systems.

- *Special versus standard services and products* In the case of standard services and products, the task is known (as it has been done before), and this provides the opportunity to develop a scheduling system (and, in addition, the repeat volumes involved justify such an investment). Where services and products are specials and hence are not repeated, the steps are less defined and the scheduling system used is less detailed, relying on the skilled staff to undertake the day-to-day scheduling tasks.

- *Make or buy decisions* The extent to which a company makes or provides internally the parts that comprise the services or products it sells will directly affect the complexity of the operations scheduling task. The more it purchases from outside, the simpler the task of scheduling the steps of the internal systems or processes. Similarly, the more it purchases from outside, the greater the orientation of the execution phase, towards managing the supply chain (covered in Chapter 12).

- *Decisions on managing demand and capacity* The decisions taken by a business regarding the extent to which it proactively manages demand and capacity will directly affect the complexity of the scheduling task. The more demand and capacity are managed, the easier the scheduling task and its execution are.

Operations scheduling systems

As we have just explained, services and products differ in factors such as complexity (the number of steps involved to provide a service or make a product), the one-off or repetitive nature of the demand and the range of services or products offered. The simpler the task,

Figure 9.2 **Cushioning the delivery system – categories and options[1]**

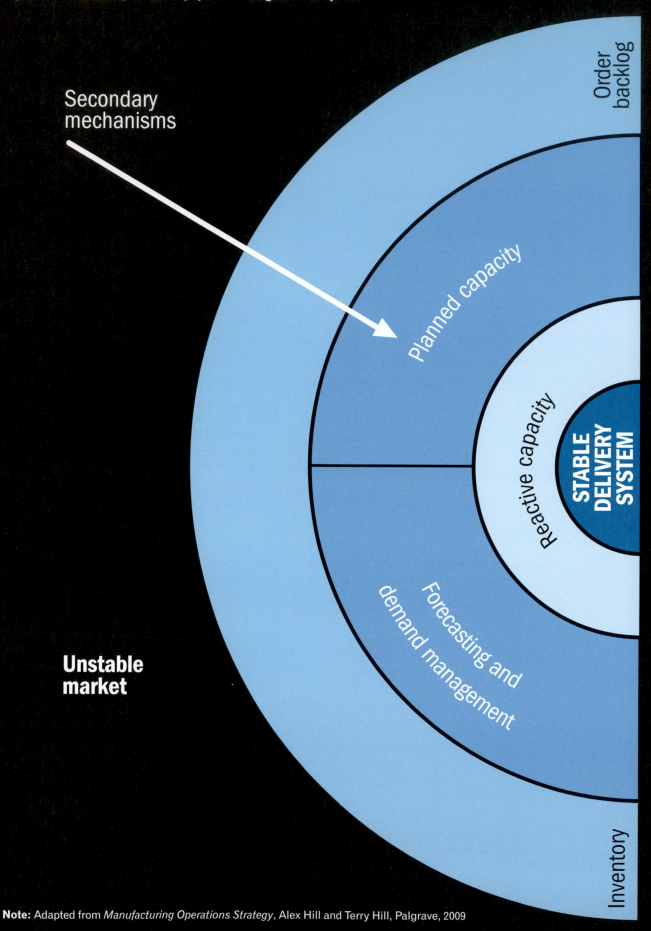

Secondary
mechanisms

Unstable
market

Order backlog

Planned capacity

Reactive capacity

STABLE
DELIVERY
SYSTEM

Forecasting and
demand management

Inventory

Note: Adapted from *Manufacturing Operations Strategy*, Alex Hill and Terry Hill, Palgrave, 2009

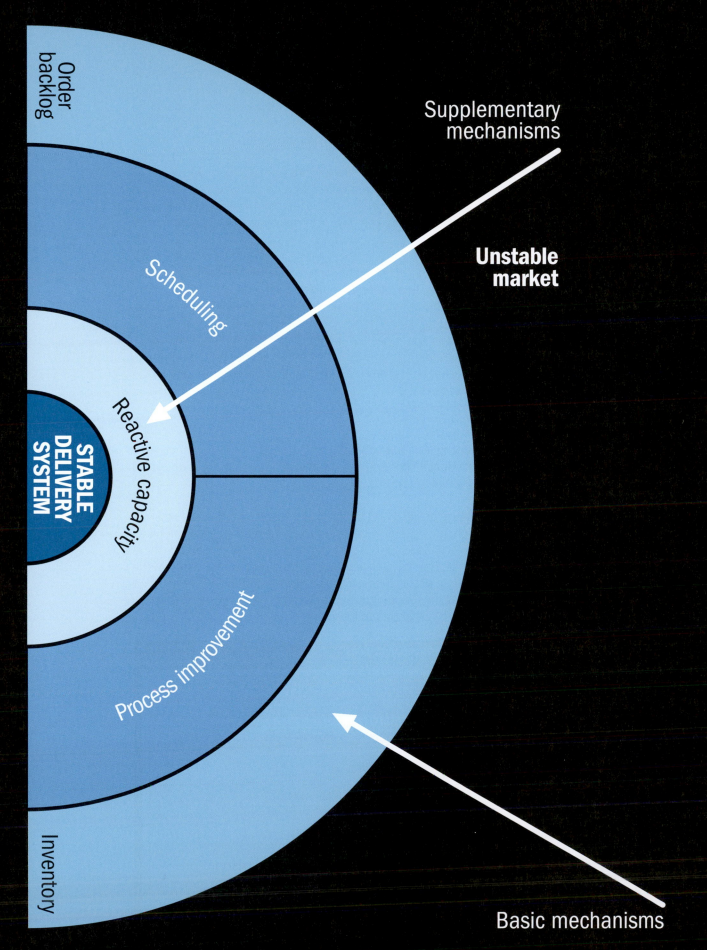

Order backlog

Supplementary mechanisms

Scheduling

Unstable market

Reactive capacity

STABLE DELIVERY SYSTEM

Process improvement

Inventory

Basic mechanisms

the simpler the scheduling system. In businesses with a very simple level of system-based scheduling, capacity and materials will be scheduled against expected levels of demand, but hour-by-hour control will be exercised on an as-needed basis.

Take, for example, a café on a main street that has a limited number of seats inside but space for more on the pavement, while also offering a take-away service. The fresh food requirements will reflect the day of the week and time of the year. Staffing will be scheduled in line with each hour of the day, as will decisions regarding the preparation of some food (for example, salads and sandwich fillings) ahead of time to meet demand in peak periods. Staff training to handle the various tasks (for example, fresh coffee and hot food preparation) will facilitate staff flexibility during busy times. Then, within these dimensions, decisions on who does what will be handled by a combination of allocating the principal tasks to staff that is supplemented by an ad hoc reallocation of work depending upon the level of demand during the day. Attempting to schedule in a more detailed way would be inappropriate.

In other businesses, the level of operations scheduling will be more detailed as the services/products are more complex and more varied and customer demand is more manageable in that it has a longer duration profile than in the example of the café above.

The rest of the chapter describes the types of scheduling systems that are used. Simpler and more informal scheduling systems are sometimes adequate to meet these requirements. These simpler systems are now outlined and are then followed by an explanation of the more complex ones.

Bar charts

One of the simplest methods of operations scheduling is a bar chart. In essence, this method shows the elements of capacity (for example, staff or process) on the vertical axis with time represented as a bar on the horizontal axis (see Figure 9.3).

Selecting the appropriate dimension of time (for example, hours, days or weeks) will reflect the nature of the operations system to be scheduled. Figure 9.3 uses weeks as this best suited this company's scheduling needs. In professional companies, there is often an additional aid in the form of a calendar that runs horizontally below the chart to show the schedule against actual dates, in this instance scheduling consultant availability against the start times for new assignments. Finally, a description of the task (the name of the client in Figure 9.3) is added to the chart.

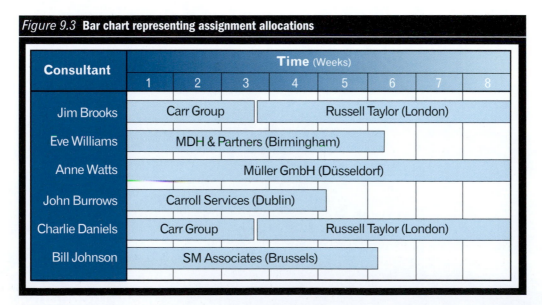

Figure 9.3 **Bar chart representing assignment allocations**

Consultant	Time (Weeks)							
	1	2	3	4	5	6	7	8
Jim Brooks	Carr Group			Russell Taylor (London)				
Eve Williams	MDH & Partners (Birmingham)							
Anne Watts	Müller GmbH (Düsseldorf)							
John Burrows	Carroll Services (Dublin)							
Charlie Daniels	Carr Group			Russell Taylor (London)				
Bill Johnson	SM Associates (Brussels)							

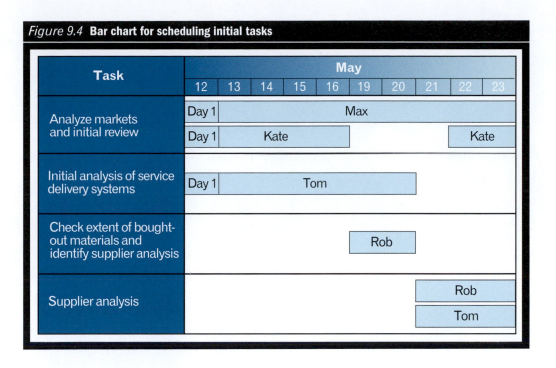

Figure 9.4 **Bar chart for scheduling initial tasks**

Task	May									
	12	13	14	15	16	19	20	21	22	23
Analyze markets and initial review	Day 1	Max								
	Day 1	Kate						Kate		
Initial analysis of service delivery systems	Day 1	Tom								
Check extent of bought-out materials and identify supplier analysis						Rob				
Supplier analysis								Rob		
								Tom		

Bar charts are also used to schedule and control more complex operations tasks, particularly where choices can be made. Figure 9.4 represents an overview of consultant allocations to clients. Within an assignment, the various elements are covered by the team of consultants allocated to that job. The lead consultant typically controls the allocation of tasks to the team to reflect their skills and experience, individual loadings and completion times. Figure 9.4 shows a bar chart to represent this. You will see that it covers the tasks at the start of the assignment. Other tasks will be identified as the assignment continues, and these will then be introduced into the schedule of work, and allocated a team member(s) and a start and finish date. Typically, a weekly review will check the team's progress against the schedule. The bar chart is then updated in terms of the work completed, with any revisions to the schedule being incorporated at the review meeting.

Some services and products comprise several steps, each completed by a different part of the process or delivery system. Again, bar charts can be used to schedule these jobs through the system to meet the required delivery dates. A bar chart identifies and helps to resolve potential capacity problems, provides short-term orders and the control over the progress of work and allows a business to assess whether or not operations is able to take on additional sales orders within existing capacity levels and delivery timescales. Figure 9.5 provides part of a schedule showing jobs loaded on different processes within the sequence necessary to complete the task. Here the products comprise a number of steps that, in turn, need to be completed on different processes. The resulting task is more complex and includes the need to determine priorities between jobs that require the same process.

In this way, a bar chart identifies potential capacity problems, provides short-term control over the progress of the work and allows a business to assess whether or not operations is able to take on additional orders in the light of its existing capacity levels and delivery commitments. Bar charts can be used to manage scheduling tasks of differing complexity in terms of variety and detail, but IT-based systems are typically used to manage more complicated schedules. In many businesses, however, the demands on and requirements of the operations control system lead to other systems being used to meet these more difficult control tasks. The sections that follow describe these.

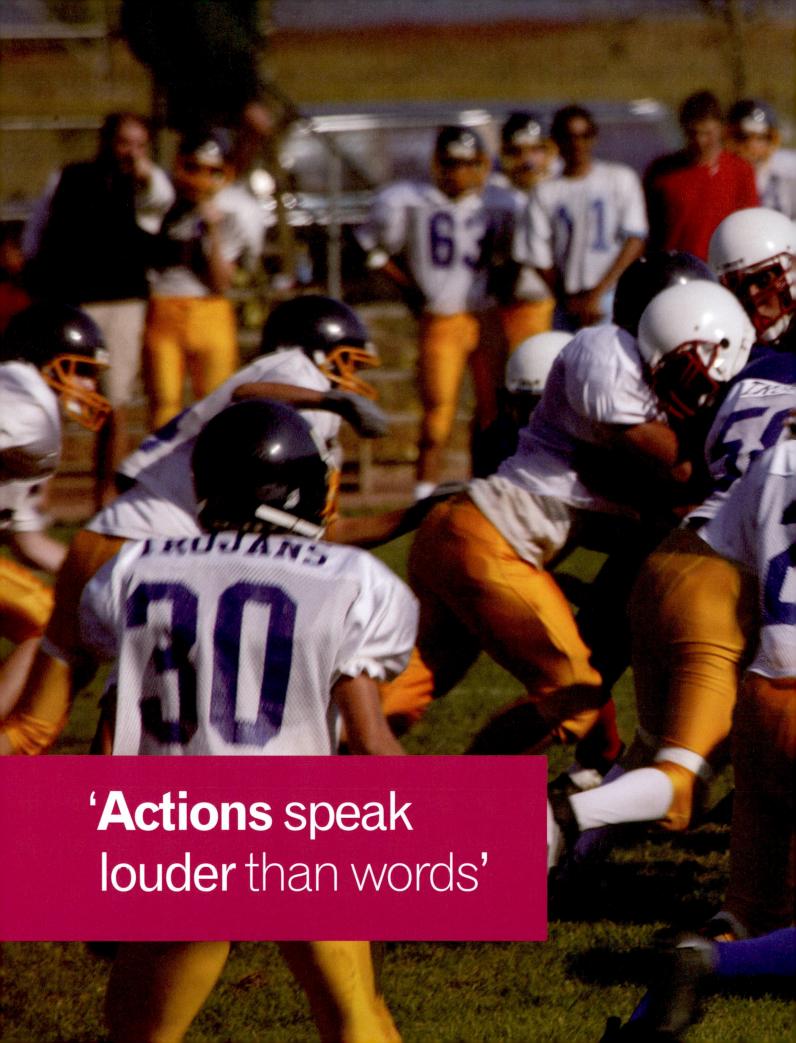

'**Actions** speak
louder than words'

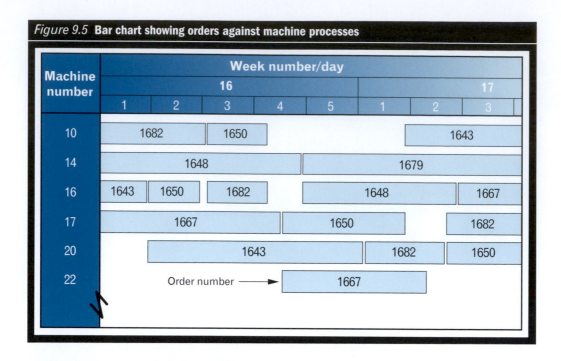

Figure 9.5 **Bar chart showing orders against machine processes**

Scheduling systems for complex services or products

As has already been explained, where the delivery system contains only a relatively few activities, an informal scheduling approach can be used. More complex, non-repeat services or products involving many interrelated activities, however, require a different scheduling approach. One of these is termed network analysis, and the principles underlying it are now explained.

Network analysis

The first task here is to determine the level of detail on which the network will be based. For large projects, an overall network will often be developed to provide a control system to overview the whole task, with more detailed subnetworks to schedule different parts of the task.

In a network, the service or product is broken down into a series of 'activities', all of which have to be completed for the task to be finished. When drawing the network, these activities are shown in the order in which they have to occur. It is, therefore, necessary to establish, for each activity, any other activity or activities that have to be completed before it can begin. This is called 'dependency'. One or more activities will, however, be independent of any other activity being completed before they can start, and these are obviously the ones to be completed at the beginning of the process. When these independent activities have been completed (which in network language is called an 'event'), any activity that can start only when these have been completed can now commence, and so on. In this way, a network is developed. Those activities which follow others are said to be 'sequential', while those that can be completed at the same time as others (that is, they are independent of one another) are said to be 'parallel'. The language and symbols used in constructing networks are explained in Figure 9.6.

When constructing a network, the following steps are used:

1. *Planning* Establish all the activities or steps to be completed, determine the dependency between these activities and draw the network.

2. *Scheduling* Apply to the network any limiting factors such as time, cost and the availability of materials, bought-out services, equipment and staff. These factors will

Figure 9.6 **The principal building blocks used to construct networks**

Type	Description	Symbol
Activity	Activities are tasks that have a time duration At the start and finish of each activity, there will be, in network language, an event	→
Event	Events occur instantaneously and state that the preceding activity (or activities) is (are) now complete, and that other activities that depend on its (their) completion can now start As this is instantaneous, it has no time duration	○
Dummy activity	Dummy activities are used in two ways · As an aid to drawing the network · As a way of extending the dependency of one or more activities to other activities	----→

often lead to redrawing some parts of the network to accommodate the constraints they impose.

3. *Controlling* Obtain feedback during a project to ensure that the activities are being completed on time, and to update the plan in the light of any changes.

Planning

The first step is to list the activities necessary to complete a project and determine their dependency on each other. Then draw the network using the following guidelines:

- All activities start and end with an event.

- An activity is a time-consuming task.

- An event is instantaneous; its occurrence means that all activities entering that event have now been completed and, therefore, all activities leaving that event can now be started.

- Any number of activities can go into and out of an event.

- Activities, wherever possible, should go from left to right when drawing the network.

- Activities occurring on the same path are sequential and, therefore, directly dependent on each other.

- Activities on different paths are parallel activities: they are independent of other sets of parallel activities and can, therefore, take place at the same time.

- Dummy activities are not time-consuming (as the time involved has already been registered with the original activity), hence their name. They are used in two ways:
  1. As an aid to drawing a network – as such, they form part of the set of conventions to be followed. One of these conventions is that two or more activities cannot leave one event sign and enter the next event sign. In order to accommodate such situations, dummy activities are used (see Figures 9.7 and 9.9).
  2. To extend the dependency of one or more activities to other activities (see Figures 9.7 and 9.9).

To explain using a practical example, Figure 9.8 lists the activities to be undertaken to complete a task and indicates those activities on which an activity is dependent.

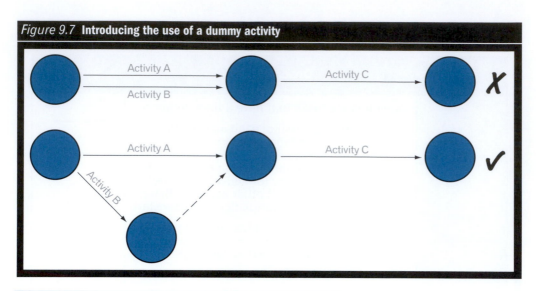

Figure 9.7 **Introducing the use of a dummy activity**

Figure 9.8 **Activities undertaken to complete a task**

Activity	Activities on which it is dependent
A	–
B	A
C	B
D	B
E	A
F	C and D
G	E
H	F and G

Figure 9.9 **Network representing the task in Figure 9.6**

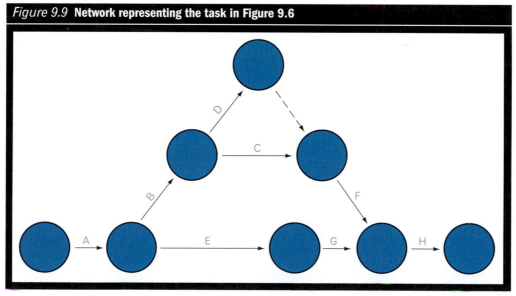

Notes: Activities A, E, G and H are examples of sequential activities.
Activities B, C, D and F are parallel to activities E and G.

Therefore, Activity B cannot start until Activity A has been completed, and so on. The resulting network is shown as Figure 9.9. It starts with Activity A as this is the only activity that does not depend upon any other activity before it can start. The rest of the activities are then built into the network to represent the statement of the task.

Scheduling

The next step is to schedule the network. This involves applying to it limiting factors such as time and cost. In the example given in Figure 9.10 the activities for putting up a sign are listed. Staffordshire County Council asked Claymore Construction to tender to erect 1,275 signs throughout the county. To maximize the use of vehicles to travel to these different locations, the company decided to use a team of three, and developed the network diagram shown in Figure 9.11 to establish the shortest time for doing the job.

Figure 9.10 **Activities to erect a road sign**		
Activity	**# People**	**Duration (minutes)**
Dig hole	1	35
Hold sign and backfill hole	3	15
Add water to concrete and mix	1	10
Assemble sign onto post	1	30
Unload sign, equipment and materials	3	15
Mix concrete	1	25
Position sign into hole	1	10
Clear site and reload vehicle	3	10

There are three additional points to note from Figure 9.11:

1. Activity descriptions, often abbreviated, are written above the arrows. It is important where possible to avoid using, for example, numbers that then need to be checked to understand what activity is taking place because it makes reading the network laboured and may lead to errors.

2. The time duration for an activity is written below the relevant arrow.

3. The event signs (often known as 'nodes') have been used to provide additional information. This is explained in Figure 9.12.

The earliest time for a particular event to take place is calculated from the beginning of a network by adding together the times taken for all the sequential activities before it. It also expresses the earliest time by which any activity leaving a particular event can start. Where two or more activities enter an event, the activity to finish last will establish the

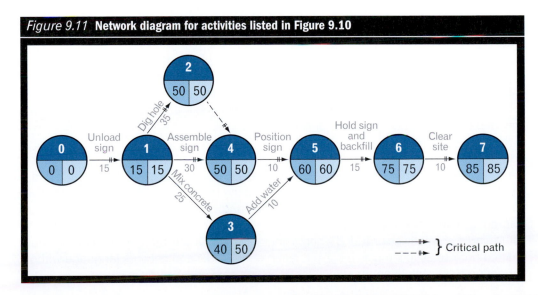

Figure 9.11 **Network diagram for activities listed in Figure 9.10**

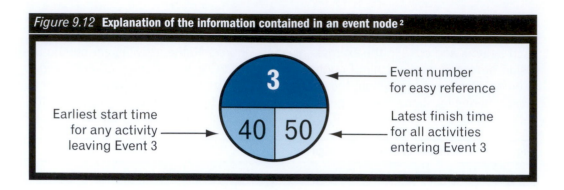

Figure 9.12 Explanation of the information contained in an event node [2]

Event number for easy reference

Earliest start time for any activity leaving Event 3

Latest finish time for all activities entering Event 3

earliest start time for any activities subsequent to that event taking place. Thus in Figure 9.11, two activities enter Event 5. Activity 'Add water' between Events 3 and 5 will result in an earliest start time for activities leaving Event 5 of 40 + 10 = 50 minutes. However, activity 'Position sign' between Events 4 and 5 results in an earliest start time of 50 + 10 = 60 minutes. Consequently, activity 'Hold & backfill' can only start after 60 minutes, so '60' is recorded as the 'earliest start time' for activities leaving Event 5. The same is true for activities 'Dig hole' and 'Assemble sign' that both enter Event 4.

The planned finish time for a project is recorded in the final event sign for a project. In Figure 9.11, this is 85 minutes, and this is recorded in Event 7.

The latest finish time is calculated from the end of a network. The same cumulative time as that entered in the earliest start time segment of the final event node is also entered in the latest finish time segment of that node – for example, 85 in Figure 9.11. Then the duration of activities is successively subtracted from this finish date and entered into the appropriate event sign. Where two or more activities back into one event, the earliest of the cumulative times will determine the latest finish time for all previous activities.

For example, look at Event 1 in Figure 9.11. Activities from Events 2, 3 and 4 back into this event. While the calculation for Event 3 would be 50 – 25 = 25, and that for Event 4 would be 50 – 30 = 20, that for Event 2 would be 50 – 35 = 15. Thus, the 'latest finish time' for Event 1 is recorded as 15. The reason is that unless the 'latest finish time' requirement of 15 minutes is met at this point in the network, more time than originally planned will need to be added into the sequence of activities, and this, in turn, will result in the overall time for the job being increased.

The minimum length of time to complete a project is an essential aspect of scheduling. This is determined by finding the longest path through a network, which represents the **critical path**. Each task on this path is known as a 'critical activity' because delays to any of these activities will increase the overall length of the project. The critical nature of these tasks is shown by the fact that the earliest start and latest finish times recorded in the series of events on the critical path are the same. There is no flexibility for these activities: if the start of any of them is delayed, the whole project will be delayed. The critical path is then marked in one of several ways (see Figure 9.11, for example).

However, a delay in activities that do not fall on the critical path will not immediately affect the project's completion time. The extent of the delay before the overall time is affected is the difference between the earliest start time and the latest finish time minus the activity duration. This is known as **slack** (or total float) and is usually entered on the network diagram as part of the information necessary for the control phase of a project. This level of detail would normally be provided when using network analysis but has been purposefully omitted here so as to simplify the explanation of networks and network language without detracting from explaining the principles on which network analysis is based.

Critical path – the longest sequence of activities through a network, so any delay on these activities is deemed 'critical'.

Slack (or total float) – the extent of the delay before the overall time taken to complete a project is affected.

Controlling

A network is a control mechanism. Information on the tasks completed and delays anticipated or incurred needs to be fed back so that the network can be updated. Knowledge of these changes and the impact they have on a project as a whole are essential for three important reasons:

1. This is a prerequisite for effective control.

2. Throughout the life of a project, decisions need to be made on the best course of action to take in the light of changing circumstances, and networks readily help managers to appreciate the impact of delays. In turn, this allows them to consider in advance the action to take as they have knowledge of the impact on aspects such as cost and completion dates and so will not have to take decisions in a crisis situation with insufficient time to evaluate alternative courses of action.

3. Out-of-date networks soon fall into disrepute and managers stop using them.

Scheduling systems for repeat services or products

Where a business provides repeat services or products, it needs a scheduling system that can handle the control requirements involved. The purpose of this subsection is to introduce these systems before explaining them more fully later.

As we mentioned earlier, operations scheduling systems start with a statement of demand. Where services and products are standard (that is, they repeat), a key dimension to take into account is the principle of independent and dependent demand:

> **Independent demand** – services and products for which the pattern of demand has to be forecast or based on known orders.

> **Dependent demand** – services and products for which the pattern of demand is directly linked to the use of other items.

> **EXECUTIVE INSIGHT**
> Requirements for services or products with an independent pattern of demand have to be forecast or based on known orders.

- Requirements for services or products with an **independent pattern of demand** have to be forecast or based on known orders. Examples include finished goods and services, such as automobiles, or pre-prepared sandwiches sold in a coffee bar.

- **Dependent demand** describes services and products for which the pattern of demand is directly linked to the use of other items, for example tyres that go onto automobiles and the bread and fillings that make up sandwiches. Such items do not have to be forecast as they can be calculated.

> **EXECUTIVE INSIGHT**
> You can calculate requirements for items with a dependent demand pattern.

In a fast-food restaurant, the daily demand for each type of main item, fries and other items on the menu is classed as being independent. The demand for burgers, buns, other ingredients and packaging is classed as dependent. Similarly, the oil and packaging for fries would have a dependent pattern of demand and, as with all such items, would not need to be forecast as they can be calculated.

With these principles now in place, let us turn our attention to the various scheduling systems to help manage these requirements.

Material requirements planning

The role of a scheduling system is to translate demand into statements of requirements for capacity (staff and/or process), materials and bought-out services, in terms of how much is needed and when. The starting point is to establish the statement of demand for all the services and products that have an independent pattern of demand. In make-to-order businesses, the requirements for services and products (that is, customer orders) will have been received beforehand. In make-to-stock businesses, the statement of demand may comprise both known orders and forecast requirements, or solely the latter.

Material requirements planning (MRPI) is a system that determines the services and products with an independent pattern of demand (in terms of which ones and how many) that a company will provide during a future period and then specifies the inputs that are needed to meet that demand. For example, the demand for engines, wheels, body panels and other parts that go into vehicle assemblies is linked to the demand for those vehicles. To determine the number of engines, wheels, body panels and other parts, we have first to determine the number of vehicles to be built in different time periods and then calculate the requirements for all such dependent items.

With MRPI then, the first task is to determine the future demand for all independent items. For each final service or product, an MRPI system contains a recipe (or **bill of materials (BOM)** in systems language) of the inputs necessary to make one unit. The system then simply multiplies the number of finished services or products required by the values in the recipe. This results in a statement of the requirements to meet known and/or forecast orders. Any existing inventory of dependent items will then reduce the final requirement to give a net requirement figure.

> **EXECUTIVE INSIGHT**
> MRPI determines the future demand for independent items and then calculates the requirements for dependent items.

What makes MRPI attractive is that it is straightforward and is practical to use. Reality, of course, brings issues of uncertainty (for example, suppliers meeting agreed delivery dates and whether the actual internal capacity matches the plan), but the fundamental logic of MRPI offers many advantages. Now let's look at MRPI in more detail.

The master schedule

As described above, MRPI starts with a statement of demand for independent items, determined from known and/or forecast orders and modified by any existing inventories of the independent items. This forms what is known as the **master schedule** and normally spans one or more time periods. It is then used as the input into MRPI which, by means of a **parts explosion**, calculates the requirements for all dependent items by generating statements of the materials, services, components and subassemblies necessary to complete the master schedule.

This is known as a 'push' system (as opposed to a 'pull' system, such as JIT, which is described in a later section), in that statements of requirements are made in line with agreed delivery dates, and the necessary materials, components and subassemblies are 'pushed' into the process. In order to keep inventory as low as possible and the associated inventory control task as simple as possible, the dates on which orders are due (referred to as 'due dates') are checked to ensure that materials are available. Materials are then 'pushed' through the process to meet these due dates. As explained earlier, MRPI is based on the independent and dependent demand principles, and as such, only one forecast is necessary. Requirements for all dependent items are, as highlighted earlier, then calculated based on the known and/or forecast demand for the independent services and products in which they are used.

For organizations with a range of services and products, MRPI is practical only with some form of data-processing. Without this, it would normally be too difficult to recalculate requirements with each schedule change.

The development of a master schedule needs to be completed no matter what type of control system is chosen to manage the operations scheduling task. Without a master schedule, operations cannot function. But how a business then schedules and executes the operations control task will depend upon which system it chooses, a decision that should reflect its own business needs and characteristics.

A master schedule (or operations statement) is completed for each service or product, and is a management commitment to provide or produce certain quantities of services or products in particular time periods. To do this, the system takes the statements of demand (both forecast sales and known orders) and tests them against statements of capacity and resources (medium-term capacity plans and short-term elements of capacity) for the same period(s). As such, this is a statement of operations output and not of market demand. However, by taking into account capacity limitations as well as the desire to utilize capacity fully, the master schedule will optimize the position by resetting planned output levels to match capacity, and this forms an important communication link between sales and operations. The schedule states requirements in terms of service or product specifications (for example, part numbers or service/product descriptions) for which bills of materials (the 'recipes') exist. The detailed schedule that is produced then drives the MRPI system that, in turn, drives the operations and purchasing records and procedures.

The master schedule (or operations statement) thereby leads to an agreement between marketing and operations on what to provide or produce, and the financial implications that result from these decisions. Accurate information is essential if this task is to be performed well. Information requirements include inventory records, the quantity and timing of current operations schedules, outstanding purchase orders, up-to-date bills of materials ('recipes') and clear information about existing customer requirements, current

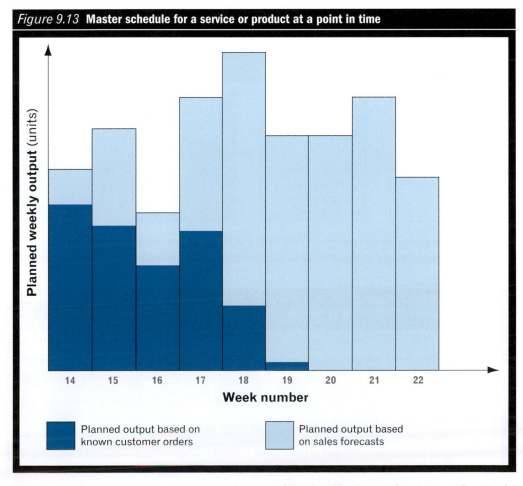

Figure 9.13 **Master schedule for a service or product at a point in time**

Planned weekly output (units)

Week number

Planned output based on known customer orders

Planned output based on sales forecasts

orders and sales forecasts. It is likely that the schedule will contain a major proportion of firm customer orders in the more immediate time periods and will be based mostly on forecasts in the later periods of the planning horizon, as shown in the example given in Figure 9.13.

The length of the planning horizon is determined by calculating the operations lead-time for an item (materials lead-time plus process lead-time) and adding a period of time to allow the purchasing function a window of visibility over what might happen in the future so that price and delivery advantages can be secured (Figure 9.14).

For many companies, the resulting planning horizon will be several months. It would, therefore, be impractical not to allow changes to the master schedule, particularly for time periods well into the future. One method of controlling changes to the master schedule is to split the planning horizon into time zones, each of which has different rules concerning acceptable levels of change (see Figure 9.15).

Service/product structure records

Service/product structure records provide information on materials and components (the bill of materials) and how each service or product is made. The bill of materials is a file or set of files that contains the 'recipe' or 'formula' for each finished service or product (Figures 9.16 and 9.17).

Depending upon the complexity of the structure for the particular service or product, there will be a number of levels within a bill of materials. The end-item itself is termed level 0. The components (subassemblies, parts and materials) that together make the end-item will be listed in the parts explosion and designated level 1. Any level 1 components that themselves have a components list will, in turn, be exploded as level 2 and so on (Figure 9.16). This calculation will be completed for all components across all services and products.

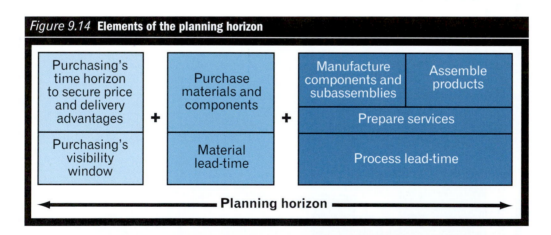

Figure 9.14 **Elements of the planning horizon**

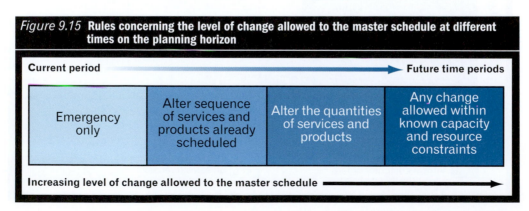

Figure 9.15 **Rules concerning the level of change allowed to the master schedule at different times on the planning horizon**

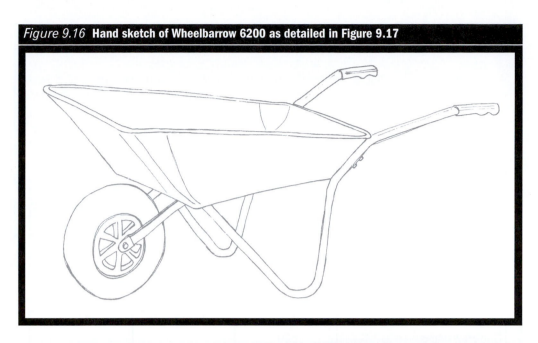

Figure 9.16 Hand sketch of Wheelbarrow 6200 as detailed in Figure 9.17

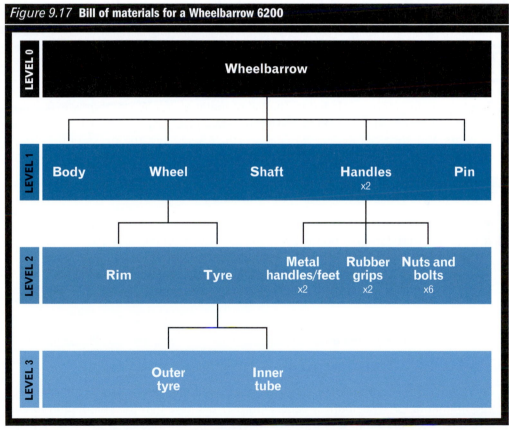

Figure 9.17 Bill of materials for a Wheelbarrow 6200

LEVEL 0 — Wheelbarrow

LEVEL 1 — Body | Wheel | Shaft | Handles x2 | Pin

LEVEL 2 — Rim | Tyre | Metal handles/feet x2 | Rubber grips x2 | Nuts and bolts x6

LEVEL 3 — Outer tyre | Inner tube

Inventory status records

The inventory status file records all transactions (receipts and issues) and inventory balances. Adjustments to recorded balances will also be made as a result of inspection reports identifying rejects and physical inventory checks revealing balances different from those recorded on file.

The main requirements of inventory information are accuracy and timeliness. These are critical to the running of an MRPI system and form the basis of the operations and purchasing plans.

WORKED EXAMPLE AN MRPI SYSTEM

As explained in the last sections, the master schedule, inventory status and service/product structure records comprise the inputs into an MRPI system. Figure 9.18 shows the master schedule for Wheelbarrow 6200 given in Figures 9.16 and 9.17. This schedule was completed for Period 7 (hence the firm programme in that period) with a forward look for Periods 8 and 9.

Figure 9.18 **Master schedule for Wheelbarrow 6200**			
Product – Wheelbarrow 6200			
Period	**7**	**8**	**9**
Forecast sales	550	600	700
Forecast end of period inventory	125	140	150
	675	740	850
Opening inventory	114	125	140
	561	615	710
Firm programme	600[1]		

Note: Any known orders for delivery in Period 7 would be noted and taken into account when determining the 'firm programme' quantity. If (say) an order for 150 Wheelbarrow 6200 had been received in Period 6 for delivery in Period 7, the 'firm programme' quantity would probably be adjusted upwards to take account of this. The reason is to ensure that the forecast end of period inventory of 125 units would be achieved at the end of Period 7.

This schedule is then exploded by the bill of materials for Wheelbarrow 6200 and the firm requirements are netted down by existing inventory levels of relevant components and subassemblies (see Figure 9.19). This shows the gross and net requirements for Wheelbarrow 6200. To help you follow the calculations completed in Figure 9.19, notes on the columns are now provided:

- **Inventory** – the current inventory holding (number of units).

- **Scheduled receipts** – the quantity (number of units) of an item already scheduled to be received during Period 7. This could be from a supplier (for example as with the Wheelbarrow body) or a subassembly made internally but currently in WIP waiting to be completed (for example as with the wheel, see Figure 9.17).

- **Gross requirements** – the quantity required without taking account of any inventory.

- **Net requirements** – the quantity required when inventory and scheduled receipts are taken into account.

So now let's look at Figure 9.19 and see how the figures are derived. First, the net requirements for Wheelbarrow 6200. Figure 9.18 shows that the calculation to arrive at a 'firm programme' for 600 of the Wheelbarrow 6200 includes deducting the opening inventory figure of 114 wheelbarrows, hence a quantity of 600 is the net requirement. For all these parts, the 'net requirement' is calculated by deducting any existing inventory and schedules receipts in the period from the 'gross requirements'. Thus, the 'net requirements' for Body 6201 is 600 − (70 + 500) = 30. Similarly, a rim and tyre go together to make a wheel. So, when calculating the net requirements for these two parts existing inventory and 'scheduled receipts' for wheel 5010 as well as that for Rim 5011 and Tyre 5012 respectively are included in the calculation. Hence, for Rim 5011 the 'gross requirement' is 600 less the wheel 5010 inventory of 280 and then this is again reduced by the existing inventory of

Rim 5011 itself. Thus, the 'gross requirements' for Rim 5011 is 600 − 280 = 320 while the 'net requirement' is 320 − 190 = 130.

Similarly the gross requirements for Outer Tyre 5015 and Inner Tube 5016 are calculated by taking into account the inventory for Wheel 5010 and Tyre 5012 as shown below.

Initial gross requirements		600
Less – Wheel 5010 inventory	280	
Tyre 5012 inventory	135	415
Actual gross requirement		185

And so on.

Figure 9.19 **Gross and net requirements for Wheelbarrow 6200 for Period 7**

Part		Inventory	Scheduled receipts	Requirements	
Description	Number			Gross	Net
Wheelbarrow 6200	6200	114	–	–	600
Body	6201	70	500	600	30
Wheel	5010	280	–	600	320
Shaft	6215	180	300	600	120
Handle	6220	240	400	1,200	560
Pin	0030	2,800	2,500	600	–
Rim	5011	190	–	320	130
Tyre	5012	135	–	320	185
Metal handle/feet	6221	140	400	1,200	660
Rubber grips	6224	320	1,000	1,200	–
Nuts and bolts	0220	7,280	1,500	3,600	–
Outer tyre	5015	–	1,000	185	–
Inner tube	5016	–	1,000	185	–

Note: Part numbers 0030 and 0220, as the above quantities suggest, are common to other products. Hence, the relatively large inventory held and 'scheduled receipts' quantities recorded here. The system would aggregate the demand for these parts from all relevant products and complete a calculation similar to that above in order to determine the total Period 7 requirements.

As you will see from these examples, a key element of the system is the gross to net calculation for both specific and common parts (see the footnote to Figure 9.19). The gross to net relationship is both the basis for calculating appropriate quantities for the programme of work and the communication link between part numbers.

Manufacturing resource planning

When the scheduling activities of material requirements planning are tied in with purchasing, sales, engineering, accounting and other relevant functions of the business, the result is known as **manufacturing resource planning (MRPII)**. As both systems have the same initials, they are abbreviated to MRPI and MRPII, respectively.

> **EXECUTIVE INSIGHT**
> When the scheduling activities in MRPI are tied in with the activities of other relevant functions, the result is MRPII

Increasingly powerful desktop computing and the advent of local area networks that link personal computers, servers and the like provided both markedly higher levels of processing power and the opportunity to increase communications within a business. With these available, MRPII was in a position to be developed.

The organizational needs that stimulated MRPII developments include the following:

- *The need for integration* In today's dynamic business environment, integrating different parts of a business brings major gains as it ensures that all aspects of a business are taken into account when reaching an effective corporate decision. One principal facet of MRPII is an integrated system with one database used by the whole business according to individual functional requirements. This allows the aspects of a business managed by individual functions (for example, inventory and capacity in operations, and cash flow controlled by accounting and finance) to form part of the corporate decision-making process. A single database reduces inconsistencies, facilitates updating and allows multifunctional perspectives to be taken into account when making decisions.

- *Time-based competition* Key order-winners in many markets increasingly include delivery speed and the need for shorter operations lead-times. More sophisticated IT systems provide managers with timely and essential data to help support customers' changing demands and to respond more quickly to decisions and enquiries in a more informed manner.

- *National and international communications* Many companies currently support their markets using a national and international provision. Information embracing the whole supply chain enables operations executives to better coordinate worldwide operations and purchasing activities. Satellite-based communications displaying real-time information from around the world enable operations to respond to changes and react quickly even with widely dispersed systems and operations locations.

Powerful computer-based systems with large storage capacities enable expanded MRPII systems to support companies' wide-ranging needs for real-time data and comprehensive reviews. Information on corporate activities and resources is continuously updated, and this leads to decisions being made on the basis of the business as a whole, with real-time information providing an up-to-date picture.

Enterprise resource planning

With the complexities of modern business, the global nature of today's commercial activities and the increasingly competitive and dynamic nature of current markets, companies continue to seek better ways of integrating the planning and execution of their activities so that the efforts of the whole organization can be coordinated. To help address these issues, **enterprise resource planning (ERP)** systems evolved out of MRPII and are designed to provide the information backbone to cope with these requirements. These systems provide a seamless integration of all the information that was previously dispersed throughout a company, and turn it into a tool that managers can use. This

Manufacturing resource planning (MRPII) – evolved from MRPI, it provides a planning and monitoring system, not only for the planning and scheduling of operations and materials but all the resources of a business, including marketing, finance and technical support.

Enterprise resource planning (ERP) – a software system that integrates operations planning and scheduling systems with all the other functions in a company, such as finance, sales and marketing, logistics and human resources.

includes information from the supply chain, customers, human resources, finance and accounting and management reporting.

As shown in Figure 9.20, ERP is designed to embrace the whole organization and shows a common database, allowing integration between the different parts of the company without duplicate information systems running in parallel.

As the software communicates across all functions, everyone can see what is happening in different parts of a business, along with the capability to link customers and suppliers into a complete supply chain.

In the late 1970s, the Germany company SAP (Systeme, Anwendungen und Produkte in Datenverarbeitung, or Systems, Applications and Products in Data Processing) released an early version of ERP software referred to as R/2. However, businesses did not begin investing in ERP systems until the mid-1990s when SAP released R/3, the next generation of software, which marked a shift in the technology platform from the mainframe to the increasingly popular UNIX-based client-server architecture. Since then, sales by providers such as SAP (with over one-third of world sales), Oracle, Infor Global Solutions, PeopleSoft and JD Edwards have grown significantly.

Software characteristics

Each provider has a unique approach to packaging ERP software. To ensure that these packages provide the system with its intended gains, they need to have the following characteristics:

- The software should be multifunctional in scope, thereby meeting the day-to-day needs of system users. In this way, the information on which to base decisions and

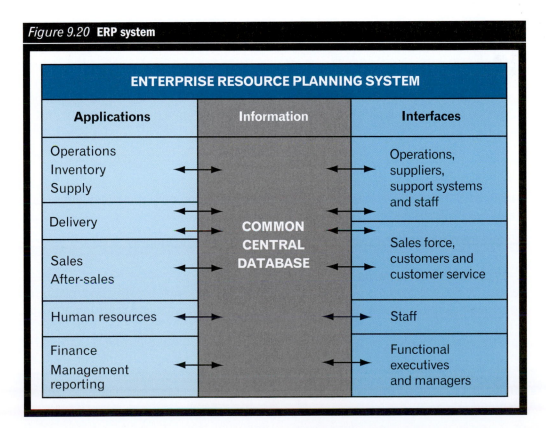

Figure 9.20 ERP system

the outcomes of the decisions made is expressed in terms that reflect each function's requirements. So for example, the software should be able to track financial results in monetary terms, sales in units and value, operations in time and cost, and so on.

- The software should have a modular structure, enabling the parts to be combined into a single system on the one hand, while allowing it to be easily expanded on the other.

- The software needs to be integrated so that if a transaction or change is made by one part of the business, the data are automatically amended in related functions.

- The software must encompass the essential operations planning and control activities, including forecasting, operations planning, operations scheduling and inventory management, in order to provide a business-wide set of tools to help manage demand and capacity in line with customers' requirements and business performance objectives.

There are several benefits for companies implementing ERP, four of which are discussed here.

1. A common systems platform

ERP can trace its origins back to the MRPI systems that provided control over operations processes. MRPI became MRPII with the addition of more supply chain activities, such as distribution and other related activities in a business. These developments then broadened into ERP to take in financial control, human resource management and the international and diverse activities and locations that characterize today's companies.

Companies collect, generate and store vast quantities of data, but in many instances this is undertaken by separate computer systems that cannot talk to one another – each of these so-called 'legacy' systems provides invaluable support for the individual functions, business units, regions, factories or offices for which they were developed. The source of this disconnection is simple – IT developments have been undertaken in businesses over many years. The initial choice would have reflected individual sets of needs and while the decision was sound in itself, it was taken, understandably, to meet a set of specific requirements. This piecemeal growth of IT accepted the inherent lack of system interfacing, and the need to start again with a common system would have been postponed until some later, often unspecified, time. The growing internationalization of business and the flurry of takeovers and mergers in the past 25 years has heightened the size of this incompatibility problem. ERP, however, meets today's needs and in particular:

- Avoids future duplication of systems, thereby reducing costs and avoiding mis-understandings

- Integrates the business with the external phases of the supply chain including Tier 2 and Tier 3 customers and suppliers

- Improves the speed of responding to customer queries and requirements.

2. Process improvements

Having multiple systems in place made a firm's underlying information platforms highly inefficient, expensive to maintain and update, and unreliable. An integral part of introducing an ERP system has been the opportunity to improve processes such as logistics and scheduling by standardizing and re-engineering the business activities in these areas, both to take out costs and to enable them to respond to market challenges. In this way, an ERP system leads to best practice being agreed, implemented and maintained as it becomes integrated into management routines and used throughout the organization.

3. Data visibility

The highly integrated nature of ERP systems increases data visibility and provides an end-to-end view of the supply chain. As common databases are continuously updated, accurate and consistent information is shared across the business, leading to more informed decision-making. Furthermore, the online, real-time transactions that characterize ERP systems provide current as opposed to historical data, thereby improving a firm's response to customers' needs and making better use of its internal resources.

4. Web-integrated ERP

ERP provides the opportunity for a business to link up with the outside world through e-commerce. Although a company may currently be restricted in terms of such developments due to the practical problems of integrating different systems, the potential for this next move is built into the system and can be developed as and when the opportunity arises. The expansion of internet-based trading in the future is a given, and ERP systems provide the basis for taking these developments forwards.

How would an ERP-based system work?

Let's say that a Milan-based sales team of a US-based software house is preparing a quotation for a customer. With an ERP system, basic information about the customer's requirements will be entered and a formal contract, in Italian, will be produced, specifying the product and service configuration, the range of applications and locations involved, the lead-times concerning the pre-application review, development phase and installation, post-development support, training and price. After contract discussions, any modifications will be made on the system and quotations updated as required. When the customer accepts the quotation, the order is recorded in the system, credit checks are made, and all functions within the business are brought into the loop. Relevant functions check proposed lead-times, capacity allocations are verified and recorded, schedules are revised, materials are ordered, and the whole operations system is brought up to date and into line. The benefits that user companies enjoy are wide-ranging:

> **Computer aided design (CAD)** – when computer technology is used in the product or service design process.

- Autodesk, a leading US maker of **computer aided design (CAD)** software, reduced its delivery lead-times from a two-week average to 24 hours for 98 per cent of orders.

- The storage systems function at IBM reduced the time to re-price all its products from 5 days to 5 minutes, the time to deliver a replacement part from 22 to 3 days, and the time to complete a credit check from 20 minutes to 3 seconds.

- Fujitsu Microelectronics reduced its order fill time from 18 to 1.5 days and halved the time to close its financial records to 4 days.

- Owens Corning replaced its grand total of 211 existing systems with an ERP system that has coordinated order management, financial reporting and the company's diverse, worldwide supply chain. It is now able to track its finished goods inventory daily in all parts of its delivery systems and has cut its spare parts inventory by some 50 per cent.

However, as with all applications, success is bound up with fitting the system to a business's needs, including its strategic positioning. Two areas of concern, which reflect the size of ERP undertakings, are noted by companies:

1. *Failed or out-of-control applications* The cost of ERP projects in larger organizations can run from $50 million to over $500 million. The issue, however, is not just the investment costs but the fundamental nature of such sizeable developments. FoxMeyer Drug, a US pharmaceutical company, alleges that its ERP system installation helped drive it into bankruptcy. Mobil Europe spent hundreds of millions of dollars on its ERP system only to abandon it when it merged with Esso/Exxon. Dow Chemicals spent seven years

and $0.5 billion implementing a mainframe ERP system before deciding to start all over again on a client-server application. In 2010, Waste Management took SAP to court claiming $500 million compensation for a failed ERP implementation. Case 9.1 outlines Dell's experience.

2. *ERP systems: standard versus customized offering* Clearly, ERP systems offer substantial benefits. However, with past IT systems, organizations would first decide on what the business needed and then choose a software package that would support those needs. They often rewrote large portions of the software to provide a better fit. With the size (investment and timescale) of ERP systems, the sequence is reversed, and the business often needs to be modified to fit the system.

Just having good data does not mean that a business will improve. To gain the most from ERP systems, companies need to recognize the full business implications. Organizations may have good reasons to change: they may have struggled for years with incompatible information systems and may see ERP as a quick fix. However, before moving forwards, organizations need to address some key questions, including:

- How might an ERP system strengthen our competitive position?

- How will the system affect our organizational structure?

- Do we need to extend the system across all functions, or across all regions, or only to implement certain modules and reflect differences in need by differences in approach?

Because of the profound implications for a business, any ERP developments must be assessed in terms of meeting the needs of a business and the way an organization works. There is no one right answer. For instance, take Monsanto and Hewlett-Packard. After studying the data requirements of each business unit, Monsanto's managers placed a high priority on achieving the greatest possible degree of commonality across the whole company even though they knew it would be difficult to achieve and that it would not be possible to standardize fully on more than 85 per cent of the data used. At Hewlett-Packard, a company with a strong tradition of business unit autonomy, applications specific to each part of the business were developed. With little sharing of resources, the estimated investment was over $1 billion, but autonomy, a recognized corporate strength, was preserved.

Just-in-time control system

An alternative approach to the operations control task that originated in the Japanese automobile industry and has since gained much support in other industrial countries and types of business is the JIT system. Whereas MRPI is a plan-push system, JIT is a demand-pull system (Figure 9.21).

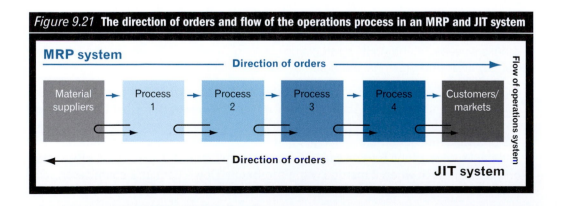

Figure 9.21 The direction of orders and flow of the operations process in an MRP and JIT system

CASE 9.1 IT SYSTEMS CHANGES AT DELL

© Felix Alim

Dell spend two years implementing SAP's R/3 to run its operations and then found that its ERP system did not fit its new decentralized management structure. SAP was found to be 'too monolithic' to be altered for its changing organizational needs when its business model changed from a worldwide focus to a regional focus.

Some time later, Dell chose an i2 Technologies system to manage raw materials, an Oracle system for order management and a Glovia system for operations. Putting in a piece at a time has worked for Dell.
www.dell.co.uk

Questions

1. What appeared to be the principal reasons why the SAP R/3 application failed at Dell?

2. Why is the IT systems approach that Dell later installed working?

Lecturers: visit www.palgrave.com/business/ hillom3e for teaching guidelines for this case study

The JIT operations system is relatively simple, requires little use of computers and, in some sectors, can offer far tighter levels of control than computer-based alternatives. The idea is to produce and deliver goods and services just-in-time to be sold, subassemblies just-in-time to be assembled into finished goods, parts just-in-time to go into subassemblies, and purchased materials just-in-time to be transformed into parts.[3] The aim is for all materials to be in active use within the total process. In this way, materials are always a productive element within the operations system, which avoids incurring costs without any corresponding benefits. Thus, the JIT system is based upon the concept of producing small quantities just-in-time, as opposed to many alternative philosophies that are based on making inventory to optimize process capacity utilization or 'just-in-case' it is required.

JIT control systems are based on the principle that each part of the total operation (including suppliers as well as a company's internal processes) delivers to the next stage the exact quantity needed for the following period's requirements. The period involved varies. In some instances, the quantities equate to one or more days' requirements, whereas in others there may be several deliveries a day. The outcome is that each stage in the process receives sufficient from the previous stage just-in-time to enable it to complete a given quantity. The more deliveries during a day, the less inventory is held in the operations process. The number of deliveries is, however, typically not the same between all stages. Factors such as length of the process set-up time for a part, the physical size of the part and, in the case of suppliers, the travelling distance will affect this decision. However, the procedure used to call for an order quantity is similar:

- Parts, components or materials are delivered from one stage in a process to the next in agreed quantities and in a designated container, together with a card or document relating to that part or material.

- When a container of parts, components or materials is taken by the next stage in the process, the card (the most well-known system being *kanban*, which means visible record or sign board in Japanese) or similar signal is sent to the previous stage in the operations system. This signal now authorizes that part of the system to make an agreed order quantity.

- In turn, this stage uses materials, components and subassemblies, and this triggers its own signal(s) to the previous part(s) of the process, and so on. In this way, all parts of operations supply the next stage just-in-time.

For suppliers, the frequency of deliveries is bound up with the distance between locations and the (monetary) value of the parts involved. Normally, the longer the distance and the lower the (monetary) value of a part, the less frequent the deliveries. To help to increase the number of deliveries and hence reduce inventory, suppliers are encouraged to build smaller facilities close to a plant. For example, Johnson Controls, the Milwaukee-based international manufacturer with automobile sector sales alone of $20 billion in 2011, has 260 car-seat plants mainly in North America and Europe serving all the major car companies including Fiat, Ford. GM, Honda, Mazda, Mitsubishi, Nissan, Peugeot Renault, Toyota and Volkswagen. Although the seat plant is off-site, it is typically connected to the car plant by an overhead conveyor system that transports the seats directly onto the assembly line to exactly match the build programme.

Similarly, several suppliers to the Nissan car plant in Washington, UK, are located just a few miles away. To keep inventory as low as possible, deliveries are made every two hours throughout the day. To ensure that delivery times are met, Nissan has agreed three different routes for suppliers' vehicles. These need to be used in a preferred order, thus providing alternatives in case of difficulty. Case 9.2 provides more detail.

CASE 9.2 JIT SYSTEM DEVELOPMENTS AT NISSAN

Nissan's JIT system developments include synchronizing supplier deliveries with its own car assembly programme. One such link is between Nissan and Sommer-Allibert, a French-owned carpet and trim manufacturer that has a satellite plant 3 km away from the car factory. As each car starts its journey through Nissan's manufacturing system, a special coding tag triggers a message to Sommer-Allibert that specifies which of the 120 variations of carpet and trim is needed for that particular vehicle, a factor that reflects colour, right- or left-hand drive, engine size and option selection. At Sommer-Allibert, the correct set of requirements (including carpets, parcel shelves and boot (trunk) linings) is selected, trimmed and finished before being stacked in sequence and loaded onto a vehicle in reusable carriers. On ar-

rival (which can be as many as 120 times a day), the driver takes the sets straight to the assembly line.

www.nissan-global.com

Questions

1. Why is a car assembly plant particularly well suited to JIT scheduling system?

2. What developments in this example have been important in making the system work?

3. What advantages and disadvantages are inherent in these arrangements?

Lecturers: visit www.palgrave.com/business/hillom3e for teaching guidelines for this case study

For a JIT system to work, end users need to fix their own output programme that cannot then be altered. Only with this certainty of requirements can a JIT control system be introduced and maintained with the result that inventory is kept to a minimum at all stages of a supply chain.

The main features of JIT systems and some prerequisites for their introduction are now summarized:

- JIT systems reverse the flow of information concerning parts and materials so that each stage calls up requirements from the previous stage as needed.

- Work-in-progress (WIP) inventory is kept to a minimum.

- Bottlenecks need to be eliminated. As WIP is now minimized, there is no longer a cushion of inventory between the stages. Process uncertainty, therefore, has to be kept to a minimum.

- Changeover or set-up times need to be reduced so that smaller order sizes become practical. For example, the set-up time for a hood and fender stamping operation in other automobile plants was estimated by Toyota as follows: USA 6 hours, Sweden and Germany 4 hours, while Toyota's time was 0.2 hours.

The concept of JIT is very appealing, but there are several prerequisites if it is to be achieved. These include:

- It is most suited to situations with high-volume, low-variety and repetitive operations.

- It must be end-user driven. The business making the final services and products must take responsibility for instigating this development and liaise with its suppliers accordingly.

- Operations schedules must be fixed. The desired state in JIT is for no excess material in the system. Consequently, scheduled quantities cannot be increased (as there is no material) or decreased (as unnecessary inventory would be the by-product).

- Suppliers must be geographically close to customers, thereby enabling regular deliveries to be made. Where the geographical distance is long, frequent deliveries of small quantities are not feasible. Larger amounts at longer intervals will be the alternative and inventory will result.

Key factors for this system to work effectively are stable schedules (which are fixed and cannot be changed inside the agreed material lead-times of a supplier's supplier) and developing close relationships with suppliers. In many companies, however, control systems more typically have to handle the impact of inherent market instability and a lack of close liaison with suppliers. Customers desiring the benefits of JIT sometimes introduce or demand a JIT materials or parts provision, yet are unable to keep suppliers' schedules stable. The outcome is that suppliers hold inventory, with all its attendant costs, as a practical way of meeting the resulting short lead-time demands of their customers.

Physical changes

Several physical changes need to become an inherent part of the JIT process:

- *High-volume, low-variety demand* needs to underpin operations. This justifies the investment and allows the creation of a series of processes that are as near to the coupled nature of a line process as possible. In was not just chance that JIT was first developed in the automobile industry – the conditions there provided many of the prerequisites (especially the high volume) necessary for JIT control systems. Ways to increase volumes include simplifying products in terms of width of range, and using standard parts in as many products as possible.

- *Set-up reduction* will, in turn, allow order quantities to be reduced. There are no set-ups in a line process. If processes need to be reset when a different product is to be made, reducing the time this takes will allow smaller order quantities to be made.[4] This is necessary to enable quantities of components, subassemblies and final assemblies to be made in line with demand rather than in terms of the length of time it takes to reset the process.

- *Layouts* are changed so that the flow of products consistently follows the preferred routing (Figure 9.22).

- *Operations arrangements* are often based on autonomous cells, each responsible for its own tasks and for the supply to and from adjacent cells.

- *Balanced flow of materials* occurs throughout the processes.

- *Standard containers* that hold predetermined quantities are used to fix material levels, and also as partial substitutes for a control system and paper-based procedures.

- *Improved levels of quality conformance* are achieved throughout the process. This is based on the use of statistical process control techniques and is explained more fully in Chapter 11.

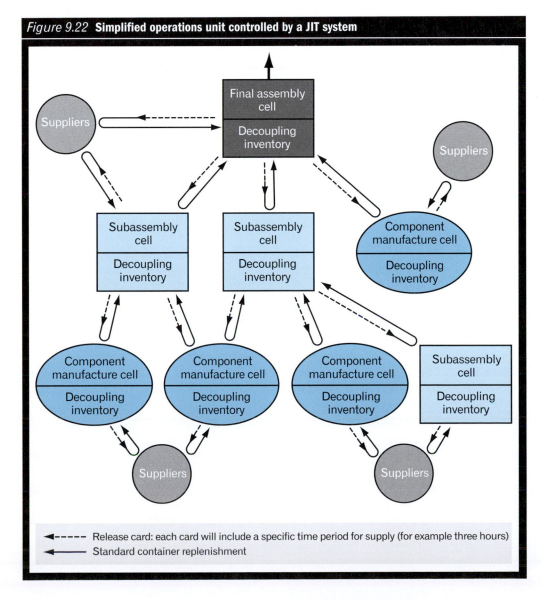

Figure 9.22 Simplified operations unit controlled by a JIT system

- - - - → Release card: each card will include a specific time period for supply (for example three hours)
———→ Standard container replenishment

Staff involvement

The role of staff in the process is also radically changed, in the following ways:

- *A broader, day-to-day role in terms of job content* This includes cross-training with a range of tasks often now involving indirect work such as improving operations and scheduling. This not only improves job interest, but also means that when there are no products to make (remember that in JIT the authority to make an order quantity must be received before work can commence), staff can undertake indirect tasks that add value.

- *Responsibility for quality conformance* As part of the last point, staff assume responsibility for the quality conformance checks completed during the process (see Chapter 11). This typically includes the authority to stop the process if a product defect is discovered.

- *Continuous improvement* The increased involvement of staff is also designed to use their knowledge to improve the system as part of the drive for continuous improvement (covered in detail in Chapter 13).

Control system changes

JIT impacts all aspects of scheduling but principally within the operations and purchasing systems. These have already been overviewed and now a more detailed description of a JIT control system is provided.

The objective of a JIT system is to ensure that all materials in the process are active. In order to do this, steady schedules need to be supported by shorter set-up times so that appropriate quantities of parts can be delivered to each stage of the process. To enhance this basic quantity factor, standard containers designed to hold agreed quantities are introduced. Lastly, a card-type system (*kanban* was mentioned earlier – other systems have their own signal, for example 'action plate' at Nissan and 'DOPS' at Honda) forms the basis of all transactions. This document is the authority to produce, and only on receipt of it can work be started. Figure 9.22 provides an outline chart illustrating materials flow in a simplified manufacturing business. The last module in this illustration is the final assembly cell which makes the end product. In a demand-pull, material flow system, final assembly will withdraw a standard container of work from a small quantity of decoupling inventory (see Chapter 10). Part of this transaction includes sending the release card to the previous, appropriate cell. In turn, this latter cell is now authorized to make a standard quantity of components or subassemblies. To do this it withdraws, from its own small quantity of decoupling inventory, a standard container of components or subassemblies. As part of this transaction, this cell also releases a card to its material supplier, as illustrated in Figure 9.22 and so on.

By striving continuously to reduce set-ups and work-in-progress inventory, the operations system is simplified in control terms, requires less inventory material to support transactions and has fewer inter-process dependencies. As a result, inventory levels continue to decline and the basis of control is simplified still further.

However, given the unstable nature of the marketplace, to achieve the high level of stability necessary to underpin a JIT system, the 'operations delivery system' has to be effectively cushioned (see Figure 9.2) by fixing the schedule so that what is to be produced cannot be changed within the lead time it takes to make changes to material purchases. This prerequisite needs to be end-user driven and will take one or a combination of the following:

- Finished goods inventory is held. Thus, when demand is lower than output, the schedule is not changed accordingly but inventory will be created to sell in a later period. Figure 9.23 shows the inventory holding at a car manufacturer's outlet.

- Adopt a make-to-order approach which means that products are only made on receipt of an order and will result in an order backlog or forward load preceding the delivery system. Now the system works on known orders and material is scheduled accordingly. Most European car makers produce on a make-to-order basis (that is, all automobiles have been sold to the company's distributors) and hence are able to use JIT control systems.

From these general requirements it can be deduced that JIT applications are suitable for the regular schedules of repetitive manufacturing and not for the irregular work demands associated with jobbing or low-volume batch processes used to provide the needs of markets with uncertain and intermittent demands.

Finally, there are a number of prerequisites to be met at the operating level in order to support the conceptual base of a JIT system. These include:

- Level schedules – schedules of work must be level. That is, within a given period, daily workloads need to be the same size.

- Frozen schedules – work schedules must be frozen over a time period.

- Frequent set-ups – a large number of set-ups will be completed each day to support the basis of making only as required. Consequently, set-ups must be of short duration.

- Order quantities – order quantities for parts must be small and fixed in size.

- Quality conformance – quality conformance levels must be high to reduce rework and increase the certainty of the output level of a process.

- Process breakdowns – processes must function. This requires diligent preventive maintenance to reduce breakdowns.

- Labour utilization – the principle of labour utilization should not be the basis on which schedules are determined. This requires that those involved are trained to cope with a wide range of tasks (including indirect work) in order to provide the necessary flexibility to meet both a wide range and times when output is not required.

Figure 9.23 **Finished goods outlet**

© Michael Bodmann

- Employee involvement – employees must participate in making improvements in order to monitor the existing system to ensure that quality conformance levels are maintained in the short term and achieve continuous improvements in the future. The goal is, therefore, correct rather than hurried work.

Lean – a philosophy of operations management

The introduction and development of JIT within businesses involves a set of approaches that are integral to its success as an operations scheduling system. This overall approach has, over the years, been extended into many aspects of operations management, to the point that it is now appropriately referred to as **lean management**, signalling a fundamental change of approach to managing operations.

Lean management – has developed from JIT to become a philosophy of operations management which focuses on eliminating waste and reducing inventory.

Many of the techniques that underpin JIT are now in general use as stand-alone approaches while also forming part of several other areas of operations management, such as continuous improvement. These approaches, which emanate directly from lean management itself, are now briefly reviewed, with a fuller coverage provided in Chapter 13.

Asset emphasis: inventory versus process

In the past, a driving force for many businesses was the high utilization of fixed assets. Prior to the mid-1960s when, in most sectors, world capacity was less than world demand, a high utilization of fixed assets (such as manufacturing processes) was the way for a business to maximize its output and profit. This view continued to be held even in sectors where the imbalance between capacity and demand had been reversed. Lean management, however, challenged this approach by trading off the objective of high utilization of processes for lower levels of inventory and the elimination of waste, as shown in Figure 9.24.

Figure 9.24 **The different orientation of traditional and lean approaches**			
Aspects		**Traditional approach**	**Lean approach**
Focus		Make so as to keep processes and staff working – the objective is high utilization	Make only when needed – the objective is low inventory
Uses of inventory[a]	cycle	Large order quantities to reduce the impact of set-ups on the net available capacity	Make as little as possible – reduce set-ups or leave processes pre-set until the next order arrives
	decoupling	Allow processes to make to and draw from WIP inventory, so decoupling the dependency between processes and thus allowing them to operate independently of one another	Minimize inventory between processes. This increases their mutual dependency and the need for cooperation and coordination throughout the delivery system
	overall	Make inventory just in case it is needed	Make inventory just at the time it is required
Operations emphasis		Process throughput speeds. Inventory facilitates high process utilization and supports a high level of efficiency objectives	Reduce set-ups or hold excess capacity to allow small order quantities to be scheduled and low inventory levels to be maintained

Note: [a] These types of inventory are explained in Chapter 11.

The advantages of scheduling material using a lean approach are not restricted to those associated with the investment and cash benefits inherent in having lower levels of inventory. There are additional and sizeable gains concerning an easier scheduling task, simpler and less expensive systems and controls, and lower overhead costs to manage the material system. The downside is that, as products are made only on an as-required JIT basis, spare process capacity typically exists throughout the system.

Improvement through exposing problems

The lean approach is designed to deliberately expose problems and use this as a vehicle for improvement. Figure 9.25 illustrates this point. It shows how excessive inventory (in the form of water depth) allows the delivery system (in the form of a ship) to operate with a whole range of problems going undetected. It creates a situation where management is unaware of the type and size of the inefficiencies that exist in the operations system and the improvements that need to take place. By reducing inventory (water) levels, the problems (depicted in Figure 9.25 as rocks) are exposed, the ship will now founder (management is alerted to issues), and the areas for improvement are highlighted. In more traditional approaches, problems are viewed as being a sign of inefficient management, are not deliberately sought and often are covered over (for example, with excess inventory as depicted in Figure 9.25). The opportunity to identify areas for improvement is thereby lost.

Incorporating indirect activities into the remit of direct staff

In traditional organizational approaches, direct staff are employed to undertake direct work. Thus, direct staff's sole task is to provide services or make products. There are several consequences that result from this traditional approach:

- In circumstances where there is no demand for a service or product, operations managers either have to make inventory or record direct staff as an excess cost (that is, they are not working). Most corporate performance measures make the latter less preferable than the former.

- The experience and capability of direct staff is limited to providing services or making products. Indirect activities such as scheduling, quality conformance and improvement are not an integral part of the role of direct staff and, consequently, are neither provided for as part of their job nor seen as part of the direct staff's contribution to a business.

One element of the lean approach is to increase the involvement of direct staff (supported by appropriate training) in indirect areas of work such as day-to-day scheduling, quality conformance and the drive for continuous improvement. By incorporating indirect tasks

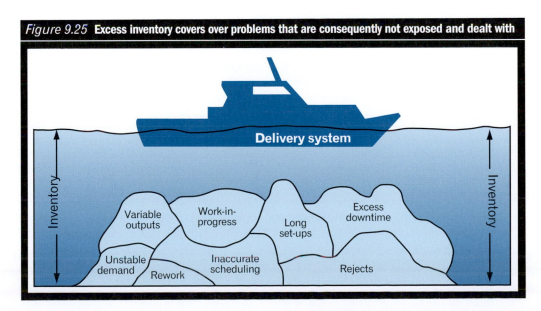

Figure 9.25 **Excess inventory covers over problems that are consequently not exposed and dealt with**

into the role of direct staff, the new mix of work will then be reflected in the time allocations and expectations related to the performance and output of those involved. This approach not only secures the contribution of all staff in areas such as continuous improvement, but also eliminates the 'make inventory' or 'no work' scenario. If there is no direct work on hand, staff now have 'legitimate' indirect tasks to undertake.

Eliminating waste

Waste is any activity that does not add value. One of the cornerstones of the lean approach is to identify and reduce or, where possible, eliminate waste that occurs throughout the operations system. Examples of waste include the following:

- *Inventory* The drive to reduce inventory has already been highlighted. The benefits of lower investment, the release of cash to be used elsewhere in a business, the simplification of systems and the reduction in the overhead costs associated with the level of material control needed will result in significant gains for a business.

- *Movement* The unnecessary movement of materials and people results in unproductive activity and introduces uncertainty into a system. While the waste element of un-necessary movement is easy to visualize, it is not often appreciated how common it is in operations systems, or indeed the size and extent to which it occurs. Changing layouts to reduce movement and improving systems and procedures to eliminate the need to check, ask questions or fetch necessary materials that should have been on hand are common improvements that result in significant gains.

- *Lead-times* One by-product of waste is that operations lead-times are extended. Unnecessary movement has already been highlighted. Other causes include waiting time (as having material in the operations system that is not being worked on results in delay and additional lead-time), set-ups (lengthy changeover times increase lead-times) and process failures (equipment breakdowns introduce delays and lengthen lead-times).

Set-up reduction

Making products as required and using JIT implies making smaller quantities on a more frequent basis. Reducing set-up times allows this to happen while keeping the ratio between set-up times and the length of a production run to complete an order quantity at an acceptable level. For example, a one-hour changeover to make an order quantity equivalent to six hours of processing time offers the same ratio as a ten-minute changeover and an order quantity taking one hour.

Optimized production technology

Over the last two decades, much attention has been focused on a proprietary system called **optimized production technology (OPT)**. In essence, OPT addresses the following issue.

> **Optimized production technology (OPT)** – a scheduling system based on loading work in line with the available capacity at stages in the process that have less capacity than others (known as bottlenecks).

> **EXECUTIVE INSIGHT**
> Capacity constraints govern the rate of flow in operations.

With multi-step delivery systems, there will typically be some parts of the total system that have less capacity to handle the work required than other parts of the same delivery system. These are known as bottlenecks. What OPT recognizes is that these capacity constraints or bottlenecks will limit how much work can flow through the total system, and that consequently it is necessary to schedule the amount of work into operations in line with these constraints. The level of throughput that bottleneck processes can handle will determine the amount of product that can be completed and made available to sell. Companies, particularly in the past, have often followed a policy of maximizing the utilization of all available resources. Where this policy is adopted, a business will generate part-completed work at some stages in the process that cannot be worked on at other stages (that is, the bottleneck processes) because of a lack of capacity. The result is work-in-progress (WIP) inventory.

Loading in line with the available capacity at bottleneck (or scarce resource) processes enables companies to manage the flow of work so as to achieve maximum saleable output. Leading on from this, OPT prioritizes attention on increasing capacity at these bottlenecks by improvements such as reducing set-ups and improving process yields. Thus, any improvements will result in increasing saleable output and with it greater profits.

In line with these central features, the OPT literature highlights other points to reinforce the logic and provide direction on which actions to follow when adopting an OPT system:

- The aim is to balance flow rather than capacity. Reducing bottlenecks will increase the total flow through the system.

- As a consequence of the above, an hour lost at a bottleneck is an hour lost for ever, but an hour saved at a non-bottleneck is of no consequence. Thus, reducing set-ups at a bottleneck increases capacity and throughput of the whole process, while additional set-ups at a non-bottleneck process do not affect output but do minimize WIP inventory.

- The order quantity transferred from one stage to the next may not be equal to the order quantity being processed. This recognizes the fact that a company needs to determine order quantities at a bottleneck process with a view to both reducing the number of set-ups and hence increasing available capacity (the concept of cycle inventory – see Chapter 10) and then reducing the order quantity it transfers to the next process in line with demand rather than to maximize the utilization of subsequent processes. Thus, order quantities to be processed should be recognized to be variable not fixed.

Theory of constraints

The principles underlying the OPT philosophy have universal applicability. Consequently, they can be used to enhance many existing control systems as well as provide useful insights into the more effective management of operations. To this end, the general use of the concepts introduced in the last section on OPT is encapsulated in the term 'theory of constraints', where a constraint is anything that limits an organization's ability to provide services or products. Constraints can be physical (for example, process capacity or resource availability) or non-physical (for example, procedures or systems) in nature. It is the effective management of these constraints that makes the OPT approach such a useful tool in managing a range of functions. The six-step process below can help managers to get the most out of an organization's resources:

1. Identify a system's constraints, whether physical or non-physical.

2. Ascertain those which affect the overall throughput of that part of the organization (the idea of bottlenecks and non-bottleneck processes described earlier).

3. Decide how to get the best possible throughput within the limits imposed by the current constraint(s).

4. Avoid keeping non-constraint resources busy as this produces unneeded work that sits in the form of WIP inventory or part-completed tasks.

5. Evaluate a system's constraints and take actions to reduce the effects of these constraints, such as reducing existing capacity losses, increasing available capacity and offloading demand or parts of demand to another part of the system. It is important here to make everyone aware of these constraints and their effects in order to focus attention on the problem and its solutions.

6. Where constraints are relaxed in Step 5, go back to Step 1.

Scheduling and executing operations in practice

- The call for and attraction of having a 'modern' IT-based scheduling system will always be strong. Proactively evaluating the current and proposed alternatives is a critical task as such investments are expensive and disruptive to install.

- Just having good data does not mean a business will improve. However, inaccurate data leads to unsound decisions, unnecessary failures and mistakes and adds to waste in a business.

- Before deciding to invest it is essential that companies evaluate the current system in terms of what it does well, to what extent any under-performance is down to inaccurate data or design flaws, what the system cannot provide and the cost of updates, developments and improvements. Similarly, any proposed system needs to be reviewed critically in terms of what it can offer, the fit with the needs of the business, the downsides of the proposed alternative and investment (time and money) involved.

- Inaccurate data leads to avoidable problems. Whether you intend to keep the existing or invest in a new system, updating the data is a task common to both alternatives.

- As business units (and often one business unit) can often provide different services and products and need to support different order-winners and qualifiers, then the choice of scheduling system needs to reflect these differences.

- Ensuring that the prerequisites for introducing a system are in place is an essential task. Beware the allure of the benefits associated with alternatives – there is no such thing as a free lunch.

- Scheduling is at the heart of providing services and products in line with agreed delivery dates. As a qualifier in many businesses, delivery reliability is a key factor in retaining customers which, in turn, underpins sales revenue growth.

- *Western view* Although displaying the appropriate characteristics of a high volume and a stable product mix, Western companies have introduced JIT control systems without creating the environment for JIT to be developed in its optimum form. Two of the more critical dimensions essential to the introduction of a JIT system that Western companies often fail to provide are:

  1. Not fixing forward schedules. As a consequence, the end user, while requiring a JIT response from its suppliers, still retains the 'right' to change call-offs within material lead-times. The only option for a supplier wanting to meet such schedule changes in terms of quantity and/or delivery date is to hold inventory, thus undermining the underlying principle of minimizing inventory throughout a supply chain.

  2. Overlooking the technical and staffing changes described earlier that are necessary to bring about reductions in WIP inventory. This is often because of the greater corporate influence exerted by accountants relative to that exerted by operations.

The central role of scheduling within a business rightly attracts attention and discussion. Furthermore, it is an aspect of the field of operations management that has undergone regular development over the years in keeping with the importance of the scheduling task and the increasing demands placed on operations in facing up to more complex business requirements, more competitive markets and more demanding customers. The developments leading from MRPI to ERP, which we covered earlier, are a testament to this. Add into this the tendency to evaluate existing systems by what they do not provide while evaluating alternatives by the gains they bring, and companies may too often look to an all-in-one, quick-fix type of change without sufficient analysis of what the current system does well and less well, the alternatives for improvement (both fixing the old and investing in the new), the prerequisites for the successful introduction of the new approach and the costs and timescales involved. Operations needs to be at the forefront of these reviews and evaluations of alternative approaches as the role of scheduling in the selling process is a key factor in retaining and growing market share.

Summary

In many markets, meeting customers' on-time delivery needs is a prerequisite for getting and staying on a customer's shortlist, and providing this qualifier is a key operations management task.

- Businesses use a number of ways to cushion the delivery system from the instability of their markets. These ways are classed as basic, secondary and supplementary mechanisms.

- Although the need is the same in all organizations, the way of scheduling operations to meet this requirement differs from business to business and needs to reflect those dimensions which alter the control task and the control design system. These include the complexity of the service or the product, and whether the services and products are specials or standards.

- The main section of the chapter introduced the alternative scheduling systems that are available, explained these in detail and illustrated their use with examples. These were:
  - Bar charts – recording capacity (for example, processes or staff) against a timescale. Figures 9.2 and 9.3 illustrated some of the applications.
  - Network analysis – organizations often use this method to plan, schedule and control complex, one-off tasks. The simple example in Figure 9.6 is then followed by a slightly more complex, real-life example in Figure 9.8.
  - MRPI and JIT – two of the most widely used systems to schedule standard products and services. Referred to as a push and a pull system, respectively, these two systems, and how they differ, are explained in detail.

- All operations control systems start with a statement of demand, produced from data on known and/or forecast sales. One other key reminder at this time is the principle of independent and dependent demand. Whereas assessing demand levels by known and/or forecast orders is a fundamental task for independent demand items, requirements for dependent items can be calculated as they are directly related to the pattern of demand of the independent items to which they relate.

- Once the master schedule for a service or product has been established, the scheduling task of determining material requirements and process/staff capacities can be completed. These, in turn, provide the inputs for the day-to-day execution of the plan. Detailing the MRPI and JIT systems then completed this section of the text.

- Next came sections on MRPII and ERP. Where scheduling activities in MRPI are tied in with the tasks of other relevant functions, the result is known as MRPII. ERP evolved out of MRPII and is designed to embrace the whole organization using a common database, thus allowing integration between the different parts without the use of duplicate information systems. The section on ERP outlined the benefits and concerns relating to it while highlighting the key dimensions to ensure its successful application.

- Finally, OPT and its finite scheduling role in refining existing control systems were explained. The final section addresses the developments in ERP systems, outlining the benefits and concerns and highlighting the key dimensions to ensure their successful application.

Study activities

Discussion questions

1. Give an example of a business that would use a push and one that would use a pull operations control system. Explain your choice and briefly describe how the system would work.

2. What is the difference between independent and dependent demand? Give two manufacturing and two service examples to illustrate your answer.

3. Under what conditions should a company refuse a customer order that it is technically able to provide?

4. Your local dry cleaner always specifies a two-day lead time, no matter what items of clothing you take in to be cleaned. Suggest reasons why the outlet is able to do this and how it works.

5. Describe a service application where the principles of the theory of constraints can apply.

6. In operations priorities manifest themselves in a conflict between meeting customers' lead times and due dates, and the productivity and efficiency goals of the operations system staff. Discuss and provide examples to illustrate your points.

Assignments

1. A small business consultancy company has three specialists in one area of its work. Furthermore, each of these three is further specialized to undertake certain phases of an assignment. Jim Brown handles phase 1, Anne Dewar phase 2 and Jean Holden undertakes phase 3.

   Details of the work to complete each of these assignments together with agreed completion dates are given below. In all cases the phases need to be completed in the order 1, 2 and 3.

Client	Phase			Agreed completion (No. of days'[1])
	1	2	3	
McCanley	10	16	8	49
Williams	3	9	16	46
Beattie	12	10	10	45

Note: 1. Calculated from day 1 as start date.

The three consultants can complete other, non-fee-paying work during the period.

Using day 1 as the start date, draw a bar chart to schedule the above tasks in order to meet the agreed completion dates and release each consultant as early as possible to take on other fee-paying work when their part of these three jobs has been completed.

2. A piece of equipment requires the following times to manufacture.

Activity	No. of days	Activity	No. of days
1 Purchasing	15	5 Assembly	7
2 Fabrication	5	6 Controls	6
3 Hydraulics	5	7 Test	3
4 Electronics	18	8 Packaging	1

Each of the activities must be completed sequentially except that fabrication can be started 10 days after purchasing begins and the hydraulics and electronics steps can be completed in parallel. Draw a bar chart for this job.

If the hydraulics and electronics steps could also be started 10 days after purchasing begins, draw a network for this job and calculate the critical path.

Exploring further

Journal articles

Davenport, T.H. and Glaser, J. (2002) 'Just-in-time-delivery comes to knowledge management', *Harvard Business Review*, **80**(7): 107–11. Knowledge workers could benefit from a just-in-time knowledge management system tailored to delivering the right supporting information for the job at hand. An analysis of the knowledge management initiative at Partners HealthCare System is provided to illustrate the potential gains.

Ramaswamy, V. and Gouillart, F. (2010) 'Building the co-creative enterprise', *Harvard Business Review*, **88**(10): 100–9. The article examines how a company can use its stakeholders including customers, employees and distributors to determine HR practices and design and market its services and products.

Shapiro, B.P., Kasturi Rangan, V. and Sviokla, J.J. (2004) 'Staple yourself to an order'. HBR Classic. *Harvard Business Review*, **82**(7): 162–71. The article is based on a detailed analysis of how an order was processed in 18 companies and highlights the findings.

Books

Dennis, P. (2007) *Lean Production Simplified*, 2nd edn. New York: Productivity Press. This book provides a simple introduction to the application and benefits of lean production.

Heerkens, G.R. (2007) *Project Management: 24 Steps in Helping you Master a Project*. McGraw Hill. This provides a short (128 pages) practical overview of project management.

Hill, A. and Hill, T. (2009) *Manufacturing Operations Strategy: Text and Cases*, 3rd edn. Basingstoke: Palgrave Macmillan. The text provides a useful supplement to Essential Operations Management by outlining an in-depth approach for developing and implementing operations strategy within manufacturing organizations.

Hill, A. and Hill, T. (2011) *Essential Operations Management.* Basingstoke: Palgrave Macmillan. The text provides a useful supplement to *Operations Management* by focusing on the essential aspects for managing operations within service and manufacturing organizations.

Jacobs, F.R., Berry W.L., Whybark D.C. and Vollman T.E. (2011) *Manufacturing Planning and Control Systems for Supply Chain Management*, 6th edn. McGraw-Hill. This provides a detailed review of the MRPI, MRPII, ERP and JIT systems.

Liker, J.K. (2004) *The Toyota Way*: *14 Management Principles from the World's Greatest Manufacturer*. McGraw Hill. This book lists the key principles that underpin Toyota's approach to managing operations.

Phillips, J. (2010) *IT Project Management*, 3rd edn. McGraw Hill. This addresses the practical issues when managing and implementing IT projects, emphasizing the key aspect of final completion.

Notes and references

1. This figure is developed from Exhibit 10.11, p. 319, in Alex Hill and Terry Hill *Manufacturing Operations Strategy*, 3rd edn (2009) Palgrave Macmillan, Basingstoke.
2. In more complex networks, the event node often contains more information.
3. One of the earliest statements providing this definition comes from Schonenberger, R.J. (1982) *Japanese Manufacturing Techniques: Nine Hidden Lessons in Simplicity*. New York: Free Press, p. 16.
4. If a 30-minute set-up time is reduced to 10 minutes, the order quantities to be provided can be reduced to one-third while maintaining the ratio between the length of set-up and the length of the run time.

Visit www.palgrave.com/business/hillom3e for self-test questions, guideline answers to some case study questions, useful weblinks and more to help you understand the topics in this chapter

ASH ELECTRICS

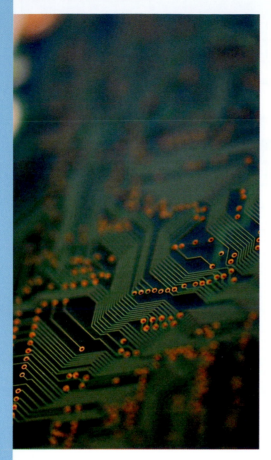

Ash Electrics (AE) makes doorbells, door chimes, switches, industrial alarms and a range of small transformers. Producing over five million units per year (from a 38 cm diameter bell to a replacement bulb in a light switch), the company sells to electrical wholesalers throughout its domestic and export markets. One of its important selling features is its 'same-day' delivery service.

The range of manufacturing activities includes coil winding, simple cropping and punching, and other operations such as bending, forming and crimping simple components for later assembly. The principal activity, however, is the assembly, testing and packing of products made from the bought-out and made-in-house components, mouldings and parts (Figure 1). To reduce material costs and inventory levels, the company has standardized many product components, from fixing screws through to clips, bobbins, coils, lamps and multilingual instruction leaflets. Apart from the metal bars or domes that produce the sound of the bell, the principal material used is plastic. Plastic bases, front pieces and components are bought in from outside suppliers to meet demand forecasts for each final product.

The company schedules production based on 13 four-week periods (starting in January each year) and forecasts for each product both sales and end-of-period finished goods inventory levels for several periods ahead. When setting the production schedule, any anticipated differences between actual and forecast sales and any known large orders for delivery in the next or subsequent periods will be taken into account so that actual end-of-period finished goods inventory is as close as possible to the forecast level. These adjustments are made at the start of each period when firm production outputs are agreed.

Figure 1 Outline of the operations process

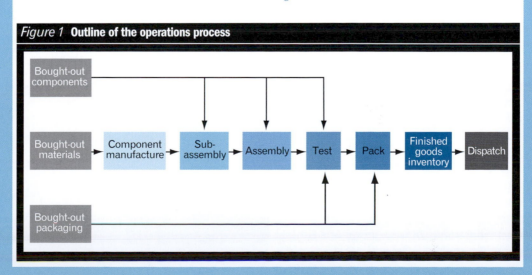

Figure 2 **High tone data**

Period	10	11	12	13
Forecast sales	8,500	9,500	10,000	8,500
Forecast end of period inventory	2,100	2,000	2,000	2,350
End of Period 9 inventory	1,960			

Figure 3 **Zig-Zag data**

Period	10	11	12	13
Forecast sales	10,500	12,000	14,000	9,000
Forecast end of Period 9 inventory	2,800	2,100	2,100	3,700
End of period inventory	2,390			

Notes: 1. The 13 four-week periods start in January.
2. Order from Australia for 3,400 Zig-Zag units to be delivered in Week 2 of Period 10.
3. Order from Germany for 2,800 Zig-Zag units to be delivered in Week 1 of Period 11.
4. Period 9 has just been completed.

The sales revenue of the company has grown year on year, particularly in its export markets, which now account for 58 per cent of total sales. The company recognizes that its order-winners are product design and delivery speed. To maintain its position as market leader, it frequently introduces new designs, some to add to its range, others to replace existing products. Delivery speed is provided by holding finished goods inventory. This enables AE to send out products for home orders on the same day the order is received, while for export orders it sends out products to catch the next available container ship or container train or in line with a customer's delivery date. The result is that AE's customers can, in turn, hold only a limited amount of inventory themselves, knowing that their order will be met quickly.

The qualifiers in AE's markets are quality conformance (products are made to specification every time), delivery reliability (AE always delivers to the promised date) and price. Given the design and delivery speed advantages it has created, AE is able to price its products at the top end of the market, resulting in high profit margins that fund its design investment and the costs of holding inventory.

As an illustration of how operations scheduling is completed, Figures 2 and 3 provide data for two representative products. The High Tone is a long-established product that enjoys steady demand and has fairly accurate forecast sales. The Zig-Zag, on the other hand, is a new product whose demand has so far been greater than AE's initial forecasts. The export market for Zig-Zag is also taking off and, as shown in the notes to Figure 3, two large orders need to be delivered in the next period (note that Period 9 has just finished). Meeting the 'end of period inventory forecasts' is obviously a key performance target for operations as it underpins the company's ability to always meet the short lead-time promises that it has set itself to support its customers and win more business.

Questions

1. What are the critical features of operations scheduling in Ash Electric?

2. What is the key operations scheduling task?

3. Develop a schedule for Period 10 for both the High Tone and the Zig-Zag products. Explain your decisions.

Lecturers: visit www.palgrave.com/business/hillom3e for teaching guidelines for this case study

Managing Inventory

10

After completing this chapter, you should be able to:

- Explain the different types of inventory and their roles

- Show and explain the presence of the different types of operations inventory in service delivery systems and manufacturing processes to address the key inventory questions relating to:
  - what items to hold in stock
  - how much to hold, and how much and when to order

- Identify which of the different inventory systems should be used for different types of business

- Understand the principles that underpin an ABC analysis of inventory

- Complete such an analysis and identify the actions that should follow

- Understand how to complete a causal analysis of inventory, appreciate the outcomes and identify the actions to take

Chapter outline

What is the role of inventory?

- The underlying purpose of inventory is to uncouple the various steps of the service delivery systems/manufacturing processes in order to allow each to work independently of the other parts

- In addition, there are other roles including to guard against supply failures, to meet customers' short lead-times and to enable operations to improve efficiency

- It also gives the convenience of having material to hand, enables you to take advantage of price discounts by purchasing larger volumes of material and reduces the material element of operations' lead-time

Why is managing inventory important?

- Managing inventory is typically a large financial investment

- It helps organizations to run smoothly and efficiently

- It affects the supply of services and goods to customers

How does managing inventory impact business performance?

- On the one hand, inventory is a large asset and a sizeable financial investment

- Unlike other large assets such as buildings and equipment, inventory is a by-product of day-to-day activity and, as it all looks the same, can go unnoticed

- Without sound control, increases can go unchallenged

- The unfavourable impact on cash flow can be marked

- On the other hand, inventory directly affects operations lead-times and consequently can impact a company's response to the delivery speed and delivery reliability dimensions of its markets

What are the key issues to consider when managing operations?

- The issues listed below reflect the key factors to consider when deciding how to manage inventory:
  - Most organizations describe inventory as comprising the categories of raw materials/components, work-in-progress and finished goods
  - This is due to the needs of the finance functions when completing profit and loss statements and balance sheets
  - While these categories meet the finance function's needs, they offer little insight into why the inventory is there and the role it provides for the business

- To provide the insights to help manage this sizeable investment, organizations should undertake a causal analysis of inventory that recognizes the broad categories of corporate and operations inventory together with the various sub-categories in each

- When managing inventory key background issues include:
  - The independent/dependent demand principle
  - The Pareto Principle or 80/20 rule.

Introduction

In Chapter 8, we dealt with managing capacity (the capability to provide services and make products). This chapter will cover issues surrounding the management of the materials that go into the services and products at different points in the conversion process from input to output, otherwise known as **inventory**. Inventory management is a key operations task because it is typically a large financial investment, helps operations to run smoothly and efficiently and also affects the supply of services and goods to customers.

Inventory – the inputs (materials) into the delivery system or manufacturing process, part-finished items (services or products) within the service delivery system or manufacturing process and outputs (finished items) to be sold or supplied to customers.

This chapter will discuss why inventory is kept, the level of inventory involved and its management and control. First, the forms and functions of inventory are explained and the division between corporate and operations inventory is defined as part of the way to effectively manage this important asset. Second, background issues relating to the management and control of inventory are discussed. These include the independent/dependent demand principle, the Pareto Principle, the use of economic order quantities (EOQs), and how reorder levels are calculated and used. Third, the key questions of what and how much to hold and to order are discussed, including the approaches to follow and the concepts to use when resolving these key questions. Finally, the different systems to manage inventory are explained. The chapter then goes on to give a detailed review of analyzing inventory by cause and using this as the basis for reducing its levels.

What is inventory?

What are the roles of and why do organizations hold inventory? Before answering these questions, let's first discuss what we mean by inventory. In the context of this chapter, it comprises the inputs (services or materials) used, any part-finished items (services or products) in a process (called work-in-progress inventory) and the outputs (finished items) to be sold or supplied to customers. On the other hand, it does not comprise the equipment or fixtures and fittings (for example, the tables, chairs, tablecloths, napkins, cutlery, plates, dishes and glasses in a restaurant) needed to provide services or make products. These are classed as the **fixed assets** of a business as they do not form a direct part of what it sells.

Fixed assets – assets that are held in the short-term and are intended to be sold or transformed into products and/or services.

Perhaps the easiest way to explain and illustrate these differences is to ask you to reflect on the inventory you keep and why you keep it. You hold stocks of food and other items that you use as part of day-to-day living. In addition, you have other assets such as cooking utensils, a mobile telephone, IT equipment and clothes that are used and reused as part of everyday living. The former set of items are used and replenished, while the latter items are purchased and consumed (that is, the functions they provide are used) over a much longer period. This chapter concerns the management and control of a company's equivalent of the stocks of food and other consumables you keep. And, just like you, the company needs to make decisions about which items to hold, how much of each item (that is, inventory) to carry, when to replenish these items and how much to buy at any one time.

However, before addressing the management and control of inventory, let's first consider its roles, the types of inventory and the functions they provide.

The role of inventory

The underlying purpose of inventory is to uncouple the various phases of a service delivery system or manufacturing process and thereby allow each phase to work independently of the other parts. Hence, keeping food in the kitchen allows you to prepare a meal without first having to shop. In reality, however, there are many other issues and dimensions involved. For example, you may need fresh milk only for your breakfast coffee, but you have to buy milk in larger quantities as prescribed by the retail store from which you buy it. Similarly, you may buy a larger box of food or more than the one item that you need for a meal in order to reduce costs as the direct result of a price deal offered by the food store or to avoid the inconvenience and time taken to purchase a particular food item each time you need it.

> **EXECUTIVE INSIGHT**
> The underlying purpose of inventory is to uncouple the various phases of a service delivery system or manufacturing process and thereby allow each phase to work independently of the other parts.

In the context of operations, Figure 10.1 shows the forms in which inventory is present throughout the three phases of operations – inputs, operations process and outputs – in two different types of organization.

As the flow of materials into and through a process invariably differs from the pattern and rate of customer demand, inventory will be held to help cushion the operations delivery system from these changes. How much inventory there is will depend upon the relative rates of demand and supply, as illustrated in Figure 10.2. This depicts the relationship between the rate of supply, the rate of demand and the level of inventory, using the analogy of a water tank. In this example, the rate of inflow and outflow of water

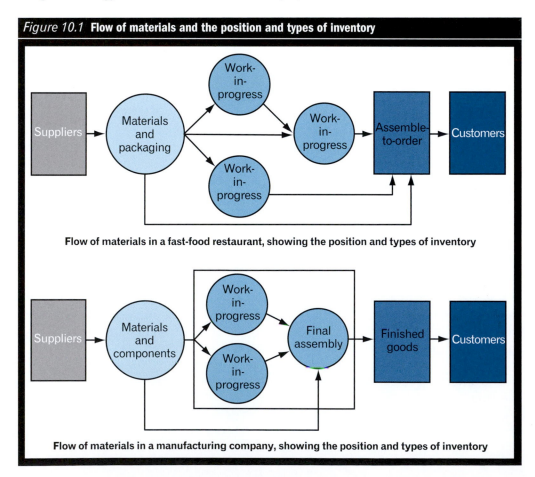

Figure 10.1 **Flow of materials and the position and types of inventory**

Flow of materials in a fast-food restaurant, showing the position and types of inventory

Flow of materials in a manufacturing company, showing the position and types of inventory

will directly affect the level of inventory (stored water) in the tank (which represents the conversion process).

These dimensions of inventory management will be addressed later, but they need to be recognized early on.

Types of inventory

There are two principal categories of inventory – process and support:

1. **Process inventory** comprises items directly used in providing the services and making the products sold by a business. Thus, the ingredients to bake bread and pastries form part of the process-related inventory for a bakery, as will the foodstuffs used to prepare meals in a restaurant. The chassis, wheels, subassemblies, windscreens, engines and other parts that go into a motor vehicle are, similarly, examples of process-related inventory. All items going into the services or products, from raw materials through to packaging, fall within this category.

2. **Support inventory** comprises items that are not an integral part of the service or product but are essential to the overall running of any organization. Maintenance and office supplies (such as spare parts for equipment and stationery) are examples for the bakery and car assembly illustrations earlier. Cleaning materials for kitchen utensils, ovens and the like are examples for the restaurant.

Generally, businesses with activities centred on products and manufacturing processes have more inventory and need to develop more controls and systems than organizations where the service/product mix is oriented more to the service end of the service/ product continuum described earlier in Figure 1.7. This is principally because the fewer operations materials that are involved, the less inventory there will be in the system to control. For example, in a bank, most services are consumed as they are generated, and the material content is negligible. In fact, the forms and other paperwork used in a bank's delivery system are examples of support inventory. The control of support inventories is an important task for all organizations, but more emphasis will be given here to process inventories because these are an integral part of the service and product provided and also involve a much higher investment.

> **EXECUTIVE INSIGHT**
> There are three categories of process inventory – raw materials and components, work-in-progress and finished goods.

Finally, within process inventory, there are three categories – raw materials and components, work-in-progress and finished goods. Figure 10.3 shows how these link to the stages in the process and provides a brief explanation of each. These categories offer an essential insight into the management and control of inventory and will feature throughout the rest of the chapter.

Functions of inventory

Why, then, does an organization invest so much in inventory? Why does it exist, and what are the benefits? Earlier, the underlying purpose of inventory was identified as one of uncoupling the various phases of the service delivery system or manufacturing process. This is a common, overall function, but there are also important advantages that relate more to one type of inventory than to another, as outlined in Figure 10.4.

As you read the detail in Figure 10.4, you will notice that some advantages relate to operations issues, while others relate to the business as a whole. To help identify these

Figure 10.2 **Rate of supply and demand and level of inventory**

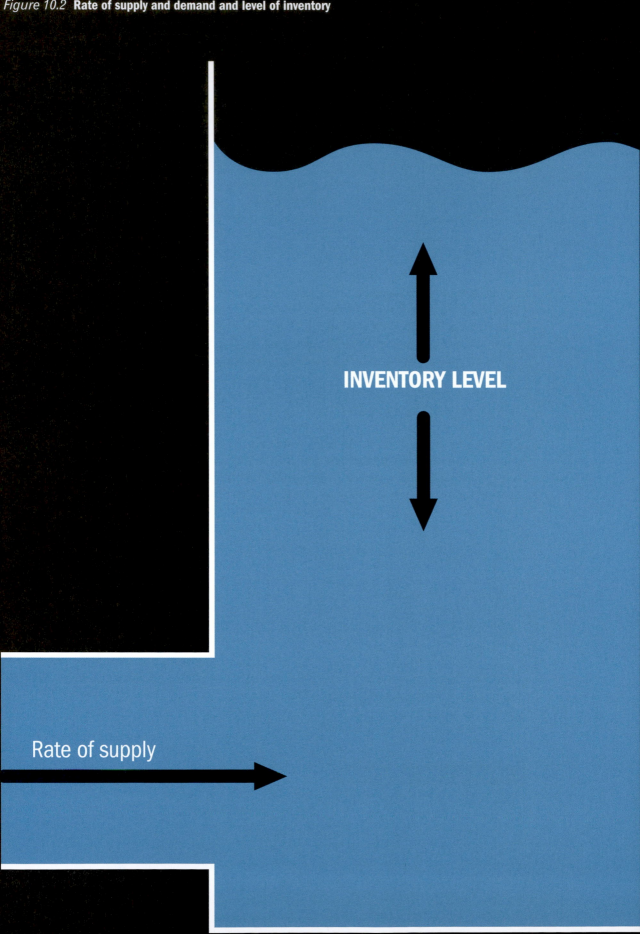

INVENTORY LEVEL

Rate of supply

INVENTORY LEVEL

Rate of demand

Figure 10.3 Process stage, types of inventory and examples

PROCESS STAGE	PROCESS INVENTORY		SUPPORT INVENTORY
	TYPES	**EXAMPLES**	
Inputs	Raw materials	**Sandwich bar** Sandwich fillings – e.g. a range of meats and cheeses, green salad and tomatoes Beverage ingredients – e.g. coffee, tea and milk Other foodstuffs - e.g. bread, cakes, pies, pasties and bought-out salads	Supplies that are not central to the services or products provided.
		Toy manufacturer Plastic granules and other materials Bought-out components Packaging Instruction leaflets	
Operations process	Work-in-progress	**Sandwich bar** Sandwich fillings – e.g. chicken, egg mayonnaise and tuna with sweetcorn Soup Range of salad dishes – e.g. mixed and green	These include maintenance and office supplies and consumables such as cleaning materials.
		Toy manufacturer Components made in-house Subassemblies – e.g. wheels attached to axles Assembled toys awaiting packing	
Outputs	Finished goods	**Sandwich bar** Range of completed and packaged sandwiches Pastries, pies and pasties Packaged snacks – e.g. crisps and nuts Bottled drinks	
		Toy manufacturer Packaged toys Packaged spare parts	

Corporate inventory – inventory that does not provide an operations function, but is held to provide advantages for other parts of an organization.

Operations inventory – inventory held to undertake the basic tasks of operations.

different functions, it is necessary to categorize them into two broad types of inventory, each of which comprises a number of subfunctions. These two types are known as **corporate inventory** and **operations inventory**. Whereas the latter directly helps operations to undertake its basic tasks, the former comprises inventory that is held to provide advantages for other parts of the organization. These two categories and their assorted subcategories form a useful way to help manage and control inventory, and will be used in some of the sections later in the chapter.

Corporate inventory

Corporate inventory is inventory that does *not* provide an operations function. The types of corporate inventory are numerous and reflect the nature of the organization involved.

One dimension of corporate inventory is, however, a common feature – typically it accounts for 20–25 per cent of the total. Examples include:

- Sales inventory to support customer agreements

- Sales inventory owing to actual sales being lower than forecast sales, and where operations has produced to agreed schedules

- Corporate safety inventory due to the uncertainty of supply (for example, in anticipation of national or international strikes)

- Purchasing inventory incurred to take advantage of quantity discounts

- Marketing inventory to support a service or product launch

- Inventory to reduce operations lead-time as a strategic response by the business to market needs; this can be held at the raw material, work-in-progress and finished goods stages or at all three.

Figure 10.4 **Role of different types of inventory**

Raw materials and bought-out parts inventory allow an organization to:
- Cater for the variability of supply
- Reduce costs by taking advantage of quantity discounts or market prices
- Provide holdings of parts that could in future be in short supply due, for instance, to an anticipated increase in world demand
- Form an investment when price increases are anticipated
- Reduce operations lead-times

Work-in-progress inventory helps to maintain the independence of stages in the process by uncoupling the steps involved. This leads to:
- Orders being easier to schedule
- Stabilizing the different output rates at each part of a process
- Reducing the total delivery lead-time to supply customer demands
- Facilitating a higher utilization of plant, processes and staff

Finished goods inventory enables an organization to:
- Provide fast, off-the-shelf delivery
- Achieve a steady delivery of goods to customers in the face of intermittent production or supply
- Cope with fluctuations in demand, particularly in the case of seasonal products
- Provide an insurance against equipment or process breakdowns and, in some instances, against suppliers' strikes

Note that when categorizing the types of corporate inventory, the function or business-based decision is specified. So, 'sales inventory to support customer agreement' refers to the fact that the sales function negotiated the holding of this inventory as part of a customer's contract.

> **EXECUTIVE INSIGHT**
Corporate inventory typically accounts for 20–25 per cent of the total inventory held.

Operations inventory in manufacturing processes

Regardless of whether the operations inventory under review is at the raw material, work-in-progress or finished goods stage, it may be further described as one or more of decoupling, cycle, pipeline, capacity-related or buffer inventory, with each fulfilling a specific function. Figures 10.5 and 10.6 illustrate these, and below is an explanation of how they relate to both the category of inventory and the particular choice of manufacturing process.

> **EXECUTIVE INSIGHT**
The five functions in operations inventory are decoupling, cycle, pipeline, capacity-related and buffer.

Figure 10.5 Inventory functions related to categories of inventory in manufacturing

Inventory function	Inventory category		
	Raw materials	Work-in-progress	Finished goods
Decoupling		✓✓✓ a	
Cycle		✓✓✓	✓
Pipeline		✓✓✓	✓
Capacity-related		✓✓	✓✓✓
Buffer b	✓✓	✓✓	✓✓✓

Figure 10.6 Inventory functions related to the type of manufacturing process

Inventory function		Type of manufacturing process				
		Project	Jobbing	Batch	Line	Continuous processing
Decoupling		✓		✓✓✓		
Cycle		✓✓		✓✓✓		
Pipeline			✓✓	✓✓		
Capacity-related	Work-in-progress	✓✓		✓		
	Finished goods	✓		✓✓	✓✓✓	✓✓✓
Buffer	Raw materials	✓		✓	✓✓	✓
	Finished goods			✓✓	✓✓✓	✓

Notes: a ✓, Degree of function typically provided.

b Concerns variation in supply or demand around the average, essentially to cover instances when supply delays or actual levels of demand are above average. However, where inventory is held for reasons such as uncertainty of supply, it should be identified under a relevant category within corporate inventory.

Decoupling inventory

Decoupling inventory – this inventory is used to 'decouple' or detach one process from another.

In project processes, the use of decoupling inventory varies. When the task involves a single product (for example, a bridge or tunnel), the use of decoupling inventory is either restricted or unwarranted. However, where a number of houses are being built at the same time, work on one stage may be scheduled ahead of time so that other skilled tradespeople are not kept waiting.

In jobbing, there is no decoupling inventory as the skilled person will always be progressing the job. Similarly, in line and continuous processing, there is no decoupling inventory as they are both sets of coupled processes.

It is in batch processes that the function of decoupling inventory is best illustrated. As a batch process is designed to be used and reused by different products, having inventory to decouple processes from one another facilitates scheduling and ensures that processes (specifically those with high utilization levels) are fully used. Having part-finished (work-in-progress) inventory waiting means that processes always have materials on which to work.

Decoupling inventory – this inventory is used to 'decouple', or detach, one process from another.

Cycle inventory

The rationale behind using **cycle inventory** in the operations system is to reduce the number of set-ups (the time taken to stop work on one item and make ready the delivery system or process or get everything together to start the next task). This increases the amount of capacity that can be used to make saleable output, while also spreading the costs of a set-up over the number of products made (the order quantity), which thereby reduces the set-up costs per unit.

Cycle inventory is a feature of batch processes where set-ups are an inherent feature of this process. The principle here is to make more than one item at the same time, thus reducing the loss of processing time when a set-up occurs and also spreading the cost of a set-up over all the products made in the order quantity. Whereas the time when products are being made is termed 'saleable productive time', the time taken to complete a set-up is termed 'non-saleable productive time'. The role of cycle inventory, therefore, spreads the non-saleable productive time over more products. How many are to be made at one time will take into account the length of the set-up time, the value and physical size of the products and the time needed to make a product.

In a project process, where a number of houses (say) are being built at the same time then, for similar reasons to those explained above, a stage in the build (for example, putting in the foundations, laying down the concrete floor, plastering the walls or installing the plumbing and electrics) will often be completed on several houses one after the other. In this way, costs such as the hire of special equipment and contractors' time (for example, travelling to the site) is reduced in overall terms.

In jobbing, there is little need for this inventory function as the skilled person will set up for each job individually and is often making an order quantity of one. Similarly, cycle inventory has no function in line or continuous processing as these are set up to manufacture an agreed range of products and are not reset – see Figures 10.5 and 10.6.

Pipeline inventory

The decision to subcontract that results in **pipeline inventory** is often made part way through the operations process. Examples during the process include a manufacturer having the finishing processes (for example, plating and painting) completed by a subcontractor.

In both jobbing and batch processes, companies may decide to subcontract a particular step part way through the manufacturing process and, in so doing, create pipeline inventory in support of that decision. Subcontracting an operation(s) in project, line, or continuous processing is typically infeasible, so pipeline inventory is not a feature of these processes.

Capacity-related inventory

Capacity-related inventory transfers work from one time period to the next in the form of inventory and provides one way of stabilizing operations capacity in an environment of fluctuating sales levels. For example, the seasonal demand for fireworks to celebrate national festivals and the high demand for toys and gifts at peak periods such as Christmas are accommodated, in part, by capacity-related inventory.

In jobbing, products are made to order, and hence capacity-related inventory is not typically used. The same is true for make-to-order (MTO) products using a project process. However, where building firms construct several houses at the same time, they may well use capacity-related inventory in the form of both work-in-progress and finished goods to help balance out changing patterns of demand and the efficient use of their skilled workforce. For similar reasons, capacity-related inventory is used in batch, line and continuous processing.

Cycle inventory – relates to the decision to make a quantity of products (referred to as an order quantity or 'batch size') at the same time in order to reduce the loss of processing time when a set-up occurs.

Pipeline inventory – (also referred to as 'transit inventory') is the inventory that exists as a result of companies deciding to subcontract one or more operations to an outside supplier at some time during the operations process.

Capacity-related inventory – transfers work from one time period to the next in the form of inventory and helps to stabilize operations capacity against fluctuations in the market.

Buffer inventory

Buffer inventory relates to the fact that average demand, by definition, varies around the average. In order to cope with situations where demand exceeds the average, businesses hold buffer inventory. The function of this inventory holding is to help cushion the manufacturing process against unpredictable variations in demand levels or supply availability. The higher the delivery on-time performance level set by a business or the lower the level of **stockout** risk it is willing to endure, the higher the size of buffer inventory it must carry. However, note that inventory exceeding buffer levels falls into the category of corporate inventory known as 'safety stock'.

You will see by looking back at Figure 10.6 that all process types other than jobbing will typically use buffer inventory for these reasons. On the other hand, jobbing, with its MTO position, will order materials as required and linked to the start date of a job.

Buffer inventory – is inventory held to cover situations where demand exceeds the average.

Stockout – is a situation where available inventory is not sufficient to meet demand.

Operations inventory in service delivery systems

Now let's review the use of inventory in service delivery systems. As the roles and rationale are the same in service delivery systems as in manufacturing processes, this part of the discussion will not be repeated. So first let's clarify what constitutes inventory in a service company. A delivery system can involve the processing of:

- Customers

- Customer surrogates (a car being serviced is a surrogate for the customer)

- Information

- Materials that go into the product element of the service/product offering.

Although inventory in the form of customers, customer surrogates or information does not have a direct cost or investment dimension, it will impact the ability of operations to meet certain order-winners or qualifiers, such as delivery speed and delivery reliability. The sections that follow illustrate how the five functions of operations inventory form part of the service delivery systems of different organizations – see Figure 10.7.

Figure 10.7 **Inventory functions in relation to different service delivery systems**			
Inventory function	**Type of service delivery system**		
	Non-repeat	**Single-step repeat**	**Multi-step repeat**
Decoupling			✓✓✓
Cycle		✓✓	✓✓✓
Pipeline	✓✓		✓✓
Capacity-related		✓✓	✓✓
Buffer	✓	✓	✓✓

Decoupling inventory

Decoupling inventory in a service delivery system allows steps in the system to work independently of one another and thereby facilitates the efficient use of resources (staff or equipment). For these reasons, decoupling inventory is typically found in multi-step delivery systems where information or customers wait for the next step in the system to be available. Thus, a patient in a hospital typically waits at each step in the delivery system (for example, for a hospital consultant or X-ray facility) before being processed at that step. Similarly, in a garage handling bodywork repairs, cars will often have to wait for the next stage (for example, one of the spray booths) to become available.

Cycle inventory

Cycle inventory relates to a decision to hold back information or customers and then process a large quantity or number at the one time. In most delivery systems, information and customers are processed singly, but there are examples where an organization clusters two or more together before starting the next step. Examples of cycle inventory being used include back-office processing such as cheque clearance and the preparation of personal or business bank statements, and customer clustering during a conducted tour of a museum or art gallery, where some customers wait until the group is sufficiently large for that stage in the system to begin.

Pipeline inventory

Pipeline inventory within services is used to provide the same role as in manufacturing. Examples of pipeline inventory in service delivery systems include a dentist subcontracting the manufacture of a crown for a patient's tooth and a doctor having blood samples analyzed off site. In both instances, the completion of the service for a customer is put on hold while the subcontracted dimension of the total service is finished.

Capacity-related inventory

An example of capacity-related inventory is where a city centre sandwich bar prepares the fillings and garnish for its products (or the finished items themselves) in the hours before its peak demand periods (say) around lunch time. Fast-food outlets and restaurants do the same, using work-in-process (part-finished) and finished goods inventory to transfer staff capacity in low demand periods to be sold in high demand periods. In addition, by changing a service delivery system from one based on **making-to-order (MTO)** to one based on **assembly-to-order (ATO)** or **making-to-stock (MTS)**, service delivery system lead-times are reduced.

Buffer inventory

Where products are involved and demand is uncertain, companies may decide to use buffer inventory by increasing the inventory levels of some items to avoid being out of stock should demand substantially exceed forecasts.

Managing and controlling inventory – general issues

This and the next section concern some general and specific issues regarding the management and control of inventory. Their purpose is to provide essential context in which these tasks have to be implemented and set the scene for the sections that follow.

One factor influencing the size of the inventory investment is the pressure applied by the various key functions within a business, each of which will have a different view of what is a desirable inventory level (see Figure 10.8). The result is a conflict of views over where the company's funds should or should not be invested, and these are outlined below.

Making to order (MTO) – when operations delivers services and makes products only on receipt of an order. Often this approach is used for special (non-repeat) services and products.

Assembly to order (ATO) – when part-finished items are made and held, then assembled and completed on receipt of an order.

Making to stock (MTS) – when operations completes items ahead of demand and then meets orders from finished goods inventory.

Figure 10.8 **General preferences of three key functions towards the level of holding by type of inventory**

Type of inventory	General preference by function		
	Finance/ accounting	Operations	Sales and marketing
Raw materials	Low	High	Indifferent
Work-in-progress	Low	High	Indifferent
Finished goods	Low	Indifferent	High

Inventory and its impact on profit levels

So far this chapter has looked at inventory as a part of working capital. However, it is not just in this form that pressure is applied to inventory levels. Consider the situation facing managers where a company is going through a period of reduced sales. It is difficult to shed costs quickly in the short-term by reducing either variable or fixed costs. Such a course of action would normally be expensive. On the other hand, if all the overhead costs are carried by a level of throughput set in line with the current, lower sales activity, the profits for that period would be considerably reduced. Instead, management often decides to carry over some of the costs from the current to a future period. A classic response here is to use capacity to make products to the work-in-progress or finished goods stage for which there are no sales but for which it is anticipated there will be sales in the future. In this way, a proportion of the costs from one time period can legitimately be absorbed into the inventory value of that period and carried forward to a future period when the work-in-progress or finished goods inventory is sold. Thus, costs incurred in one time period are transferred to a future time period in the form of inventory, as the value of the inventory includes the associated direct and overhead costs involved.

One result of this action is that profits will not fall as much as they would otherwise have done and the value of the company will be upheld. With an upturn in sales, the inventory will be sold and the associated costs of the inventory incurred earlier will be recovered.

If the upturn in sales does not come about, then a company will often be reluctant to sell the excess inventory at a low price in order to recover at least some of the investment. Such an action would usually lead to further reduced profits and a further reduction in the value of the company. This aspect of inventory can, therefore, frequently result in organizations operating with too much inventory and yet being reluctant to remedy the situation.

Inventory cost structures

The management of this sizeable asset is, in part, to provide the roles of inventory on the one hand, while controlling the cost of inventory on the other. One important prerequisite to undertaking this task is understanding the make-up and structure of the associated costs of inventory investment. These are:

- *Item costs* concern the cost of buying or producing the individual items held in inventory. Volume often affects the cost of an item, as quantity discounts can be secured for purchased items and services and non-variable costs such as overheads can be spread over more items; operators' costs can be lowered if a greater number of items are produced.

- *Ordering and set-up* costs relate to the ordering and provision of a given quantity. Any costs associated with arranging and providing services or products fall into this category. They include order preparation and placement, monitoring the order, transport, receiving and invoice reconciliation and payment.

- *Carrying costs* concern the costs of holding inventory. These include the cost of the inventory investment itself, the storage costs including management, space and insurance, and the costs of deterioration, obsolescence and losses that occur during the period in which the inventory is held awaiting its use in the process or sale to a customer.

- *Stockout costs* reflect the economic consequences of running out of inventory. These concern the lost profit on a particular sale and any loss of customer goodwill occasioned by the late or non-delivery of a service or product.

Corporate issues

At the corporate level in organizations, there are a number of key decisions that affect the competitive stance of a business which, in turn, impact inventory requirements. These include:

- Service levels are statements concerning the targets set by a business with regard to meeting the expectations of its customers. Those concerning shorter lead-times and service or product range support will have a direct impact on the levels of inventory to be maintained. The impact on inventory of agreed targets must be recognized and assessed as part of a company's review of its competitive positioning and the role that inventory investment makes in meeting these targets.

- Lead-times are directly affected by decisions concerning whether a company:
  - makes to order (MTO)
  - assembles to order (ATO)
  - makes to stock (MTS).

  Progressively, lead-times are reduced as companies move from MTO to MTS, with an increasingly larger part of the service or product being undertaken before a sale is made, held as inventory and thereby reducing the lead-time required to fulfil a customer order.

- Supplier relations concern the level of cooperation between customers and their suppliers. This entails accurate and timely information with regard to demand schedules and also a mutual understanding of the services, products and processes involved in both the customer's and supplier's organizations. As suppliers are part of the total supply chain, customers need proactively to involve them in order to help reduce materials in the system. These issues are addressed in detail in Chapter 12, which covers managing the supply chain.

Models and approaches to managing inventory

This section first covers some of the broader approaches to managing inventory. Once these have been explained, the key decisions relating to inventory (what to order, how much, and when to order it) are then discussed in detail.

The independent/dependent demand principle

The starting point for the management and control of inventory is customer demand. Companies translate their forecasts of demand or actual orders received into statements of operations requirements, such as the capacity and materials needed. In completing this task, companies use the principle of dependent/independent demand.

> **EXECUTIVE INSIGHT**
> Dependent demand items are the components or materials used to provide a service or make a product. They are, therefore, dependent on the number of services or products provided. Consequently, the quantity required can be calculated.

- *Dependent demand items* These are the components or materials used in a process to provide a service or make a product. They are, therefore, dependent on the number of final services or final products sold. Hence, an automobile company will need four wheel rims and five tyres for each vehicle it makes, and the total quantity of these and other parts directly relates to the number of automobiles made. The wheel rims, tyres and other components and materials can be calculated based on the number of vehicles to be made and are said to be dependent demand items. Similarly, a fast-food restaurant will calculate the number of fillings, buns, frozen French fries and other items based on its sales forecast for each type of meal on the menu.

'Many profitable companies go **bankrupt** because they run out of **cash**'

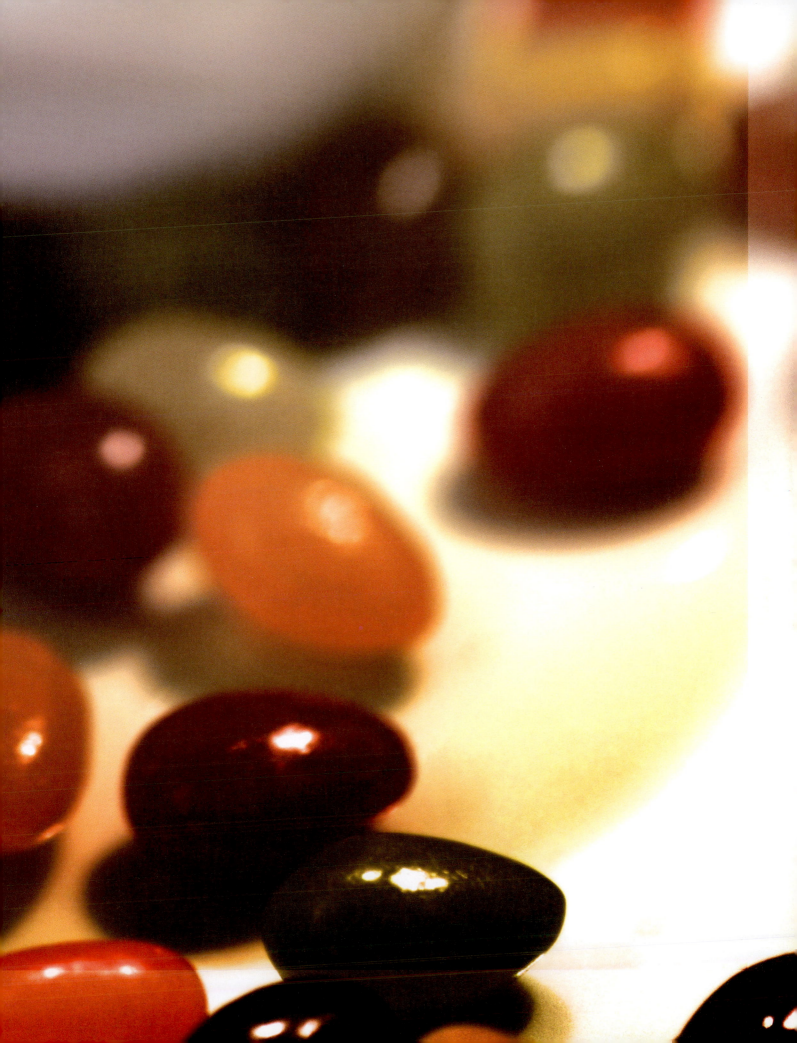

- *Independent demand items* These are, on the other hand, the final services provided or products made. They are independent because they are not linked to the demand pattern of other items. Thus, the demand for automobiles and meals is classed as having an independent pattern of demand. The choice of inventory management system reflects whether an item has a dependent or independent pattern of demand, as will be explained later. The key difference here is that with independent demand items, the number of services or products is either known (that is, orders have already been received) or has to be forecast. With dependent demand items, the number can be calculated.

> ### EXECUTIVE INSIGHT
> Final services or products sold have an independent pattern of demand in that they are not linked to any other service or product. Here the number of items required is either known (they have already been ordered) or has to be forecast.

Pareto analysis[1]

The size and importance of items will vary, and the relationship between the relative value or importance of a range of items will typically reflect what is known as the 80/20 rule or the Pareto principle. A review of inventory will typically show support for this principle. The 80/20 rule states that 80 per cent of the inventory value will be accounted for by 20 per cent of the items in stock.[2] Given this relationship, most of the effort in managing inventory should be concentrated in the areas of high value. In that way, the number of items to carefully manage is reduced, but most of the inventory value is under control.

> ### EXECUTIVE INSIGHT
> The **Pareto principle** (or 80/20 rule) highlights the fact that 20 per cent of items typically account for 80 per cent of the total value of inventory. Concentrating time and resources on these items is a key factor in managing inventory.

Where to direct effort is derived from a Pareto analysis based on the **annual requirement value (ARV)** of each item. To calculate this for each item of inventory, two facts are needed: unit value and annual usage. The product of these two figures is known as the ARV.

The inventory items are now placed in order, that with the largest ARV first, then the next largest, and so on. Figure 10.9 lists a representative sample of 30 items. Such a list is typical of many organizations. Because of the wide range of ARVs, it does not make sense to spread the inventory control effort equally over each part. Pareto's 'vital few' and 'trivial many' idea, or the 80/20 rule, applies here, as illustrated by Figure 10.10. The summary in Figure 10.10 shows that 74 per cent of the total ARV is accounted for by as little as 23 per cent of the total items held in inventory.

This approach to inventory control can then be further extended into an ABC analysis. Here, the high-ARV items are classed as A items, the middle range as B items and the low-ARVs as C items (Figure 10.11). Once this has been determined (bearing in mind that the ARV for an item may change over time and so, therefore, will its classification), the approach used to control items in each of these categories will differ to reflect the varying levels of inventory value.

It stands to reason that A items should be checked and controlled, and requirements calculated, in order to keep inventory levels in line with forecast usage. It is worth the administrative and management costs involved. C items, on the other hand, will be managed with less control and effort, as explained later in the chapter. B items fall in the middle ground, and the level of control and attention to be assigned needs to be considered individually for each item in this category.

Pareto analyses – show the frequency and cost associated with a quality problem. Problems are listed in descending order to highlight those that are causing the greatest cost to a business.

Pareto Principle (also known as 80/20 rule) – a rule which summaries the concept of the 'vital few' and the 'trivial many' and is used to describe instances where 80% of the outputs originate from 20% of inputs.

Annual requirement value (ARV) – is calculated by multiplying the unit value (£) of an item by its annual usage. The higher the ARV of an item, the greater the level of control is called for.

Figure 10.9 A representative sample of inventory items in order of decreasing annual requirement value

Part number	Unit value (£)	Annual usage (units)	Annual requirement value (£) Actual	Annual requirement value (£) Cumulative
303-07	58.50	6,000	351,000	351,000
650-27	2.46	80,000	196,800	547,800
541-21	210.00	500	105,000	652,800
260-81	164.11	450	73,850	726,650
712-22	2.39	25,000	59,750	786,400
054-09	5.86	10,000	58,600	845,000
097-54	136.36	300	40,908	885,908
440-18	17.30	2,000	34,600	920,508
440-01	337.35	100	33,735	954,243
308-31	136.20	200	27,240	981,483
016-01	12.89	2,000	25,780	1,007,263
305-04	45.30	475	21,518	1,028,781
155-29	38.02	500	19,010	1,047,791
542-93	62.91	300	18,873	1,066,664
582-34	32.08	500	16,040	1,082,704
323-34	71.30	200	14,260	1,096,964
412-27	23.01	600	13,806	1,110,770
540-80	24.76	500	12,380	1,123,150
137-29	12.31	1,000	12,310	1,135,460
401-53	30.64	400	12,256	1,147,716
418-51	168.86	65	10,976	1,158,692
418-50	168.80	65	10,972	1,169,664
390-02	17.47	500	8,735	1,178,399
037-41	24.05	200	4,810	1,183,209
402-50	22.00	600	4,400	1,187,609
900-01	41.64	100	4,164	1,191,773
543-61	15.10	200	3,020	1,194,793
900-11	46.80	50	2,340	1,197,133
003-54	11.41	200	2,282	1,199,415
691-30	0.41	5,000	2,050	1,201,465

Figure 10.10 Summary of items in Figure 10.8

Percentage of total items	Percentage of total ARV
23	74
44[a]	21
33	5[a]
Total 100	**100**

Note: [a] Figures have been rounded up.

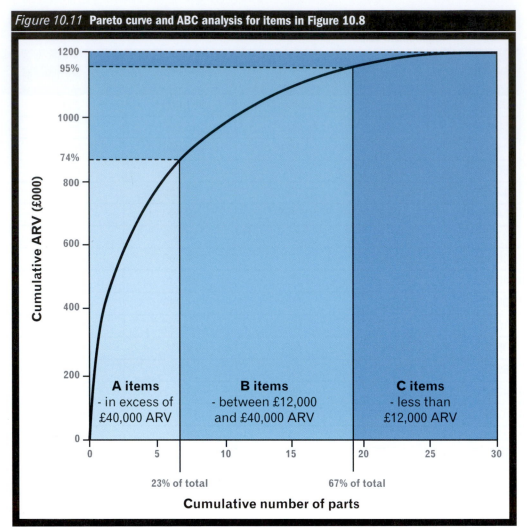

Figure 10.11 Pareto curve and ABC analysis for items in Figure 10.8

A items
- in excess of £40,000 ARV

B items
- between £12,000 and £40,000 ARV

C items
- less than £12,000 ARV

23% of total

67% of total

Cumulative number of parts

Cumulative ARV (£000)

Note: ARV is annual requirement value.

Economic order quantity and economic batch quantity/economic lot size

One of the fundamental decisions in inventory management concerns how much to order in terms of securing the lowest total cost. The order quantity decision, therefore, needs to relate the various costs of placing an order and carrying the inventory to the value of the quantity ordered. The economic order quantity (EOQ) and economic batch quantity (EBQ)/economic lot size (ELS) models address the question of how much to order so as to minimize the total cost of holding inventory. The formula for each of these is given below:

$$EOQ = \sqrt{\frac{2zC_s}{cC}} \text{ for instantaneous replenishment}$$

and

$$EBQ/ELS = \sqrt{\frac{2zC_s}{cC}} \times \frac{p}{p-d} \text{ for replenishment at rate } p$$

where z = total annual usage, C_s = cost of placing an order, c = unit cost of the item, C = carrying cost rate per year, p = production provisioning rate (units) per day and d = demand rate (units) per day.

However, it is important to note that these models make the following simplifying assumptions:

- The rate of demand is constant.

- Costs remain fixed.

- Operations capacity and inventory holdings are unlimited.

Yet despite these assumptions, the models provide a useful guideline for ordering decisions in most operating conditions.

Determining the reorder level

A key question in any inventory system concerns when and how much to order (something we'll look at in more detail in the next section). In some situations, these decisions are made in response to another event. For example, ordering dependent items is typically linked to the decision of when and how many independent items are to be provided. The same goes for companies working on an MTO basis as explained earlier. Here, customers' orders trigger the subsequent decisions about when and how much to order.

In other situations, companies need to deal with the question, when should an order to replenish inventory be placed? Assuming that a company does not wish to run out of inventory, the level at which it must reorder is calculated by multiplying the time it takes to get an order into the company from an outside supplier (the material lead-time) by the number of units of this particular item used during the same period. So, if the material lead-time for an item is one week and the weekly usage is 100 units, the **reorder level** is 1 x 100 = 100 units.

But the rate of usage will vary with demand, often considerably. Furthermore, it is only where demand/usage rates are higher than average that stockouts will occur. To avoid this, it will be necessary to carry inventory to cater for the above-average demand during a lead-time. This extra quantity is called buffer inventory, as explained earlier. Hence, the reorder level calculation can now be modified as follows:

Reorder level = average usage in a material lead-time + buffer inventory

So far, we have discussed inventory levels without stating what they mean. As Figure 10.12 illustrates, physical inventory levels need to be adjusted for both allocations and material on order.

Figure 10.12 **Calculating the level of available inventory**		
Product 1260		
Actual physical inventory	125	= the actual number of items in inventory
Less allocated inventory	38	= items needed to fulfil any existing sales orders
Available inventory	87	= physical less allocated inventory
Plus material on order	100	= the quantity on any outstanding purchase orders
Total	187	= available inventory plus outstanding purchase orders

Reorder level decisions are normally based on 'available inventory' figures (87 items for Product 1260 above), any 'material on order' quantities and their expected delivery dates, as well as the anticipated pattern of future demand for the item.

Key inventory decisions – what to stock and when to order

Once the models for managing inventory on a broader scale have been applied, key decisions can be made relating to inventory, including:

- What items to hold in stock

- How much to hold, and how much and when to order.

The answer to these questions will relate to the background issues that we've just covered, as well as other agreements with customers and suppliers and any internal decisions made within a business. One of the fundamental factors affecting the decisions to be made, systems to use and approaches to follow is the independent/dependent demand principle, which was explained earlier.

Call-off – an agreed future delivery to a customer.

Deciding which items to hold in stock

Companies will decide to complete services or make products ahead of time for a number of reasons. The known orders or scheduled **call-offs** (agreed future deliveries) required to fulfil customer contracts will often be produced or provided in advance to ensure that due dates are met. Similarly, inventory to meet future demand peaks or known seasonality patterns, and to level out operations capacity requirements over a period of time, are practical inventory responses used by companies to manage these different circumstances. The factors affecting the decision of which items to hold in stock are now discussed.

Make-to-order, assemble-to-order or make-to-stock

A major factor influencing the decision of what to hold in stock is whether a company selects an MTO, ATO or MTS response to meeting customer needs:

- *MTO* businesses are usually involved in the provision of special (that is, not to be repeated)[3] services and products. In addition, some companies decide to meet demand for standard (that is, repeat) items only on an MTO basis. Either way, an MTO response means that inventory will not be held as either part-finished or finished items. What may be held in stock, however, are the materials and components that form all or part of an item.

- *ATO* businesses are those that part-finish an item beforehand and then complete it on receipt of an order. The stage to which an item is part-completed reflects the associated value of inventory and process lead-time reduction that results. Fast-food restaurants prepare beforehand the individual items in the range (for example, French fries and different types of burger) and then assemble these to customers' requirements. Similarly, top restaurants part-prepare some food (for example, desserts and vegetables) ahead of time.

- *MTS* businesses are those that complete or purchase items ahead of demand and then meet orders from finished goods inventory. Examples include all retail outlets and manufacturers making finished goods. Others such as newspaper shops can only sell this way – if a newspaper is not available on the day, the sale is simply lost.

80/20 rule

Based on the 'vital few' and 'trivial many' phenomenon, companies typically decide as follows:

- For high-ARV items – maintain a low inventory holding (high total value) and purchase in line with demand

- For low-ARV items – maintain a high inventory holding (low total value) and purchase in bulk (lower purchasing costs but with a relatively small increase in inventory value).

Independent/dependent demand items

Decisions to hold items in stock are affected by whether or not they fall within the independent or dependent demand categories. As explained earlier, the former are end-items and are open to the choice of whether or not to hold them in stock. However, as the usage for dependent items is linked directly to the demand for independent items, there is no requirement to hold inventory for these until a decision is made to provide relevant independent items. Exceptions to this are holding inventory for dependent items for reasons such as safety (to guard against uncertainty of supply) and buffer (to reflect the variance within suppliers' delivery times), as well as EOQ benefits, purchasing discounts, reduced transaction costs, and so on. Holding dependent demand item inventory to gain lower costs or improve a company's ability to support its markets and customers makes for sound management practice.

Corporate inventory

Companies often hold inventory for non-operations reasons. Classic categories include customer agreement and corporate safety stock:

- *Customer agreement inventory* – where a company agrees with a customer to hold a given level of inventory at all times in anticipation of an order. This may also be provided as **consignment inventory** held on a customer's own premises.

- *Corporate safety stock* is held due to the uncertainty of supply, for example to guard against national or international strikes or in anticipation of a general national, regional or world shortage.

Illustrations of corporate decisions on inventory that reflect the nature of a company's business or to meet market needs are now provided. First, though, take a look at Case 10.1 and reflect on what has been covered so far.

> **Consignment inventory** – inventory held at a customer's site but not invoiced until used. The customer houses and manages the physical inventory but the responsibility for replenishing what is used remains with the supplier.

Deciding how much inventory to hold, and how much and when to order materials

The three issues of how much inventory to hold and how much and when to order materials make up an integral set of decisions and so the factors that affect these questions are addressed here together.

Make-to-order – special services and products

Companies providing special services and products will use customer orders already received (known as order backlog or forward load) together with forecast sales profiles to estimate capacity and determine material requirements. Decisions regarding how much and when to order the necessary materials will be made depending on the size and start dates of the orders on hand. In some instances, particularly where expensive materials are involved, customers will, as part of the contract, provide materials on a 'free issue' basis (that is, a customer buys the materials and has them delivered to the supplier). Companies will often hold inventory for some non-specific materials that are in general use and replenish these as necessary, while for materials that are specific to an order, companies will typically purchase as required. In summary then, in MTO situations, items to fulfil an order will be purchased:

- Solely for a given order (typically high value and/or seldom used)

- To meet the requirements of several orders and consequently kept as inventory (typically low value and frequently used).

In MTS conditions, items are made ahead of demand in line with sales forecasts.

RETAIL OUTLETS

Retail outlets need to hold inventory in order to sell products and display the extent and nature of a range of goods. Where the purchase price is low or a lack of inventory will lead to a lost sale (for example, a newsagent or food store), the policy will be to hold inventory in line with forecast sales and to reflect demand fluctuations. Where the items are of high value (for example a suite of furniture, china dinner service or set of cut-glass wine glasses), examples of the range (typically those that sell the most), supported by fabric choices or catalogues and the like in terms of dinner services and wine glasses will be the basis for which items are held in inventory.

PRE-PREPARED FOOD IN RESTAURANTS

Restaurants hold the basic food and other ingredients in stock and part or fully prepare food in line with the menu and anticipated sales of the various menu options. The extent to which materials are part-prepared will reflect the level of choice provided and the speed of service offered or expected by customers.

BALANCING INVENTORY APPROACHES

A company selling a range of household items used two approaches to holding inventory of its products. Products classed as Category 1 were made in anticipation of sales and on a make-to-stock basis. Orders for products classed as Category 2 were allowed to go into arrears and then a quantity of a product would be made that covered:

a. outstanding sales orders
b. sales orders received during the process time to make the order quantity
c. inventory to cover a given number of weeks of future sales.

When the quantity was made, outstanding orders in a. and b. would be met. Future sales were then met from the finished goods inventory that remained. Eventually the company would go into an outstanding order position for its Category 2 products and the procedure outlined above would be repeated.

Questions

1. What is the role of inventory in these three illustrations?

2. Explain in detail how inventory would be used in each delivery system.

Lecturers: visit www.palgrave.com/business/hillom3e for teaching guidelines for this case study

Make-to-order or make-to-stock – standard services and products

Companies providing standard services and products can do so using either an MTO or MTS approach. Using MTO as the basis for scheduling means that companies provide services and products only in line with actual customer orders or contract call-offs. This means that the timing and quantity of materials required are known and built into the scheduling procedure.

Companies choosing to provide services and products on an MTS basis convert sales forecasts of demand into statements of operations requirements. These are then, in turn, converted into schedules and material call-offs.

Approaches to managing inventory

To help manage decisions on how much inventory to hold and how much and when to order materials, companies use a number of approaches, as follows.

1. Reorder point

Companies use the principle of reorder levels as the basis for deciding how much inventory to hold and when to reorder. This system can be used for finished items as well as for raw material and component inventory. The logic of an order point system is to trigger the reorder of a part or item every time the inventory level of that part or item falls to a predetermined level. The item illustrated in Figure 10.13 is for material sourced from an outside supplier. It shows how the timing and quantity of the reorder level need to take into account the average usage in the delivery lead-time plus the agreed buffer inventory as follows:

Delivery lead-time for an item	1 week
Average weekly usage delivery	100 units
Average usage in the delivery lead-time	1 x 100 = 100 units
Agreed buffer inventory	25 units
Reorder level	125 units

Note: For finished items, lead-time is the time taken to make a product (known as process lead-time) assuming that the required materials and components are held in inventory. If not, the lead team to replenish is material lead-time plus process lead-time which together are known as 'operations lead-time'. For raw materials and components, lead-time is the time taken for a supplier to deliver (known as material lead-time), while the next section explains how to calculate the level of buffer inventory.

Figure 10.13 shows the importance of recognizing that only usage patterns after the reorder level has been reached are of consequence in terms of stockouts, so the period following an order point is known as 'being at risk'. Let's explain this important point more fully. Demand patterns above a reorder point will only result in inventory falling to this level either more quickly or more slowly than average, depending upon whether actual demand is higher or lower, respectively. As far as potential stockouts are concerned, demand patterns above the reorder point are not a factor.

However, above-average demand patterns experienced after a reorder point has been reached influence whether or not stockouts occur. Above-average demand will result in a stockout if the amount of buffer inventory is insufficient to cover the level of actual demand experienced. Hence the term 'being at risk', as illustrated in Figures 10.14 and 10.15. In Figure 10.14, above-average demand is followed by a period of below-average

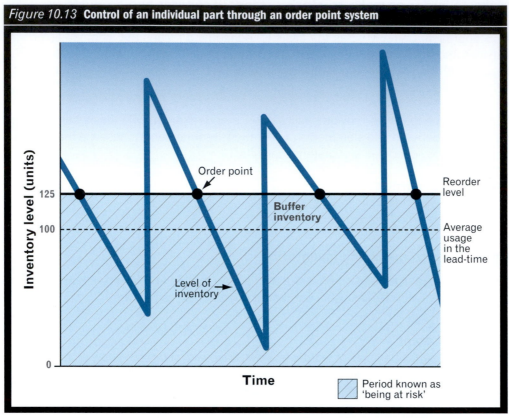

Figure 10.13 **Control of an individual part through an order point system**

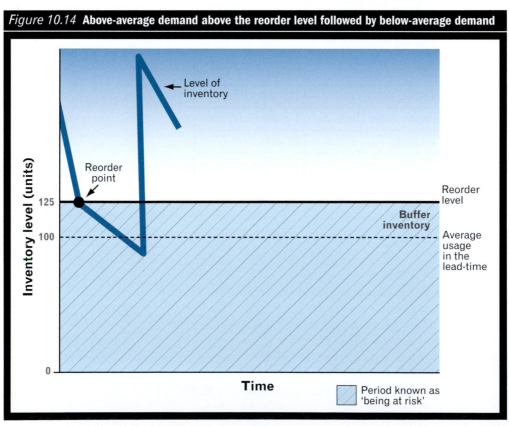

Figure 10.14 **Above-average demand above the reorder level followed by below-average demand**

demand, whereas in Figure 10.15 the reverse demand pattern is shown and its impact on inventory levels and stockouts is illustrated.

2. Buffer inventory

The function of buffer inventory is to provide a safeguard against periods of above-average demand and thereby avoid or reduce the number of stockouts. Where there is sufficient

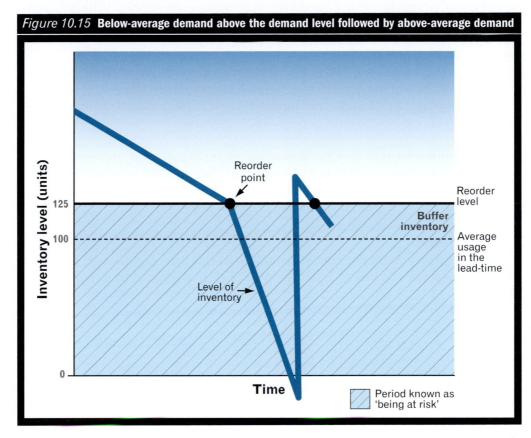

Figure 10.15 **Below-average demand above the demand level followed by above-average demand**

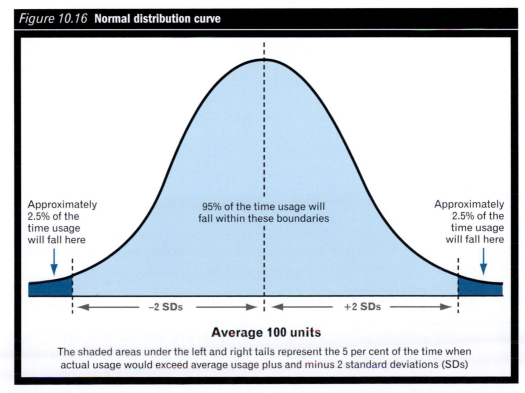

Figure 10.16 **Normal distribution curve**

information, buffer inventories can be calculated using basic statistics. The first step is to calculate the average usage for an item and the standard deviation of usage around that average. For example, assume that an item has an average weekly usage of 100 units and that this is normally distributed with a standard deviation of 12 units. By applying normal distribution curve theory (Figure 10.16), the individual weekly usage would be within two standard deviations either side of the average for 95 per cent of the time (the mathematical explanation is not given here, but for those interested it will normally be available in any textbook on inventory control). Of the 5 per cent of the time that usage does not fall within two standard deviations, half can be expected to be less than average and half to be more than average. Now, an organization is concerned only with instances where usage is above average and, therefore, it can expect that only for 2.5 per cent of the time will usage exceed the average plus two standard deviations, that is $100 + 2(12) = 124$. In this situation, if the reorder level were set at 124, a stockout would not be expected more than 2.5 per cent of the time, or once in 40 occasions.

Calculating buffer inventory in this way, however, normally applies only to A and possibly some B items (see Figure 10.11). In these instances, the high ARV and resulting impact on inventory levels would make the time and cost worthwhile. For other B and all C items, buffer inventory levels will be determined using much cruder methods.

3. Service levels

A further measure that may be used to gauge the level of customer support are service levels. The level of service that an organization wishes to maintain can be established, and the level of buffer inventory needed to yield acceptable service levels can be calculated. One commonly used way of expressing service levels is given below:

$$\text{Service level (percentage)} = \frac{\text{No. of customers served without delay}}{\text{Total orders received}} \times 100$$

4. Economic order and economic batch quantities

The EOQ and EBQ or ELS models were explained earlier. They are, as their full titles suggest, directed towards helping to determine the quantity that will give the lowest total cost outcome. Although these models are built on a number of simplified assumptions, they are useful in providing guidelines on how much to order or provide.

Some companies use different criteria for arriving at the order quantity to be processed. For example, a company making high-specification reproduction furniture restricted its order quantity to that equating to no more than two days of work for their staff. For this company, limiting the amount of time spent working on the same piece of furniture helped to ensure that conformance to the very high specification demands of its product range would best be met by varying the task frequently to help to maintain job interest for its skilled staff.

5. Consignment stock

Consignment stock is inventory held at a customer's premises that is not paid for until it is used. Suppliers typically retain the responsibility for checking inventory levels and replenishing stock as needed. In these instances, how much to hold on a customer's site and when to replenish are based on actual usage and agreed minimum inventory levels.

6. Corporate inventory

The level of inventory for items can also be directly influenced by corporate decisions on a range of issues. As mentioned earlier, these are classified as corporate inventory that comprises many categories such as 'customer agreement' and 'safety' inventory that have already been explained. Other illustrations of corporate inventory include purchase discount inventory (that held at above-normal levels to acquire the price discounts on offer) and marketing inventory (that held at above normal levels to support a marketing initiative, for example, promotions).

Inventory control systems and analysis

The models and approaches described so far to help control inventory have simplified the size of the problem. Coping with thousands of stock items, supplied by many different suppliers and supporting the needs of numerous customers, results in a complex and dynamic operations task. To cope with this, operations managers need to:

- Recognize that the level of control to be provided reflects the ARV of an item

- Select and develop an inventory control system in line with other existing systems and the nature of the item itself (for example, dependent versus independent items)

- Undertake checks on current inventory levels to verify the system, test how well it is working and identify changes in working practices, customer demands and other business issues, and how they affect inventory.

Regular stocktaking is an integral part of managing inventory and helps to check on the current position.

Inventory control systems

Companies use a variety of systems to help manage and control inventory. Which to use will reflect the nature of their business and take into account several background issues, as discussed earlier and listed below:

- *Operations scheduling systems* are linked to the control of inventory. The task of inventory control is an integral element of the material schedules that form part of the operations control system. High-volume, MTS or MTO businesses (for example, motor vehicles) typically use just-in-time systems that dictate material call-offs and help to control and maintain low levels of inventory. Where companies adopt an MTO policy for scheduling standard services and products, actual customer orders and call-offs will trigger the operations schedule that, in turn, activates the demand for materials.

- *Dependent demand items* are, by and large, calculated in line with requirements for independent demand items, as described earlier. In addition, for low-value ARV items simple systems would be used and managed on the principle of ensuring no stockouts.

- *The 80/20 rule* should determine the level of control that companies provide. The selection of appropriate systems for low-ARV items is concerned with keeping the management and control costs low while ensuring that stockouts are avoided (as highlighted in the last point). Calculating and ordering small quantities of these items would not make sense. For high-ARV items, the reverse is true.

Corporate inventory control

In most companies, some 20–25 per cent of inventory is held for corporate rather than operations reasons. Several categories of these have been given earlier. Companies will need to assess the investment in terms of its (monetary) value and return (what advantages and functions the inventory provides). Each category will need to be assessed item by item (see the later subsection on 'Causal analysis').

Operations inventory control

Operations inventory typically accounts for 75–80 per cent of the total. This inventory exists for operations reasons and provides a number of the functions described earlier. The systems used to control operations inventory are now discussed. Several of the aspects and issues introduced earlier in the chapter are included, which enables us to refer to them without going into detail.

Continuous review systems

In a **continuous review system** (or Q system for short), the inventory level is monitored after each transaction (that is, continuously). When the inventory drops to a predetermined level (or reorder point), a fixed quantity is placed on order. Since the order quantity is fixed, the time between orders will vary in line with the pattern of demand. Figure 10.12 earlier provided an example of this principle and showed the following characteristics:

- A fixed quantity (that incorporates the EOQ principle) is purchased.

- The material lead-time (the time between an order being placed and its delivery) is deemed to be the same.

- The gap between purchase orders will vary in line with the different patterns of demand.

Expensive items are best managed using this approach as it helps to keep the value of inventory to a minimum. The increase in costs associated with these systems and the management of higher ARV items is justified by the greater control of expensive items that is provided and the associated lower inventory levels that result.

Periodic review systems

While the virtue of the continuous review system is that it can make use of EOQs, monitoring and checking inventory levels continuously (even when using computer-based systems) is time-consuming and expensive. An alternative and similar approach is the periodic review system, also known as the 'fixed order period system' (or P system for short). In a **periodic review system**, the inventory position is reviewed at fixed intervals and a reorder quantity is then placed that constitutes the difference between the actual level and the target level of the inventory. The target level is set to cover demand until the next periodic review plus the delivery lead-time of the item. As usage varies, so the amount ordered will vary, and hence one disadvantage of this system is that the EOQ principle cannot always be used.

Using P and Q systems in practice

Both P and Q systems together with modified versions of them are widely used for the management of independent demand items. The choice between the two is not an easy one and will be made on the basis of management practices as well as costs. Conditions that favour the use of one system as opposed to the other include the following:

- Timing of replacement inventory – when orders must be placed or material delivered at specified intervals, a P system should be used. Weekly deliveries of items to a retail store would be an example of this condition.

- Multiple item shipments from the same supplier would follow a P system in order to secure the gains of consolidating items into a single shipment and the resulting reduction in delivery and paperwork costs.

- Inexpensive items not maintained on inventory records should use a P system. Low-value items such as fasteners (for example nuts, washers and bolts) could be stocked in bins and periodically checked and replenished to a given target quantity. No records of use or receipts of inventory would be made, in keeping with the low-cost management approach for such items.

- Expensive items are best managed using a Q system that helps keep inventory to a minimum. To safeguard against stockouts, P systems require higher buffer stocks which makes them less suited to expensive items. The increase in costs associated with Q systems, and the management of higher ARV items is justified by the greater control provided and associated lower inventory levels that result.

Continuous review system (Q system) – when inventory is monitored after each transaction and a predetermined quantity is reordered when inventory falls to a given level.

Periodic review system, also known as 'fixed order period system' (or P system) – here the stock position is reviewed at fixed intervals and the reorder quantity is placed that constitutes the difference between the actual level and target level of inventory.

Supplementary systems and approaches

Companies also use a number of supplementary systems and approaches to manage different inventory requirements. Two of the more common requirements are:

1. *Managing low ARV items* The costs involved in managing and controlling inventory can be high. For low ARV independent and dependent items, we need systems that ensure there are no stockouts but are not costly to maintain. Two of the more commonly used systems that provided this low-cost requirement are now described:
   - *Single-bin systems* involve periodically filling up a shelf, bin or tank. Examples are shelves in retail outlets, and bins holding commonly used nuts and washers in repair shops. These are examples of P systems. Individual records of receipts and usage are normally not made. Control is provided by checking expected usage levels over a period compared with the level of purchases made during this time.
   - *Two-bin systems* comprise inventory held in two bins. The one in current use is open and the second is sealed. When the first container is empty, the second is opened and this act triggers a replacement order. This is a Q system, with the quantity in the second container being equal to the reorder level. As with single-bin systems, records of individual transactions are not kept, with control provided by periodic checks similar to those described for single-bin systems.

2. *Seasonal demand* Demand patterns for many businesses have a seasonal element. Some companies alter capacity to meet these changing requirements. Where companies can make products in one period to sell in the next, meeting seasonal demand by using capacity-related inventory is an alternative to changing capacity levels, While the downside of using inventory is the investment and cost involved, advantages include maintaining a stable and experienced workforce, reducing the costs of training and avoiding the lower productivity levels associated with temporary staff.

Companies that use capacity-related inventory as a way to balance fluctuating demand levels must establish the different ratios between the staff content (number of hours used) of inventory and its overall value. Calculating the ratio between inventory value and standard hour content will enable a company to elect to produce for inventory those items with the most favourable ratios. In this way it will be able to absorb 'spare capacity' for the lowest inventory value increases. Figure 10.16 provides an example of this approach. Representative items for a company show the inventory value (column 3) and also the number of standard hours required to make the item (column 4). Dividing the inventory value by the standard hours to make an item gives the value of inventory made per standard hour used (column 5). In low-demand periods companies can then absorb the overcapacity in operations but restrict increases in inventory value.

Let us look at Figure 10.17 to see how it works. While item E180 has a unit inventory value of £25.80, in effect it uses 6.3 standard staff hours to produce each item. Consequently its inventory/staff ratio is only £4.10/hour. On the other hand, E150 and WD162 both have unit values less than E180 at £13.50 and £18.65 respectively. However, their inventory/staff ratios are significantly higher than that for E180 at £19.30/hour and £23.30/hour respectively. Thus, using this calculation as one factor in planning inventory at times when capacity is greater than sales will enable companies to keep inventory increases to a minimum while effectively using the capacity on hand.

Inventory analysis

Inventory is an integral part of business activity, which helps companies in the provision and sale of services and goods. However, it's a costly investment, so it is pertinent to ask: 'Is the amount of inventory that the company is currently holding necessary?'.

To evaluate how well their control systems are working, companies need also to analyze inventory as part of this review process. In most businesses, the recording and valuation of inventory leads to statements that separate the total inventory into the categories of raw materials and components, work-in-progress and finished goods. Typically, this is done once or twice a year, in line with the need for the accounting function to prepare a profit and loss account and balance sheet. But although this analysis meets these requirements, it does not provide enough useful information to help in the task of managing inventory. The insights on inventory provided by categorizing it as raw materials and components, work-in-progress and finished goods relate to the state and position of material within the system. In other words, material has not been processed (raw materials and components), the processing of material is now complete (finished goods) or the material is somewhere between these two positions (work-in-progress). While this is adequate as a basis for assessing the value of inventory, it fails to provide the key insight to help manage and assess inventory levels; that is, why is it there in the first place? To provide this key insight, a review of inventory is necessary to determine why it is there, or what caused the inventory.

Figure 10.17 **Inventory/staff hour ratios**						
Products		**Inventory value (£s)**	**Staff content (standard hours)**	**Inventory made per standard staff hour used**	**Product rankings – to minimize inventory value (£) increases per standard hour of staff used**	
Reference	**Inventory**	**Per unit**		**£ p**	**WIP/ finished items**	**Overall**
WB674	work-in-progress	66.05	13.2	5.00	2	3
WA321		35.50	2.6	13.70	8	13
WC193		32.85	3.2	10.30	5	10
WB280		21.15	4.1	5.20	3	4
WB055		19.00	1.4	13.60	7	12
WD162		18.65	0.8	23.30	10	18
WD610		6.35	0.4	15.90	9	16
WB405		4.25	0.9	4.70	1	2
WE350		3.54	0.4	8.90	4	8
WC184		1.15	0.1	11.50	6	11
G163	finished items	150.10	10.1	14.90	7	15
D114		122.50	8.0	14.20	6	14
A195		93.75	3.2	29.30	9	19
B680		65.00	12.5	5.20	2	4
B008		33.60	5.5	6.10	3	6
D710		28.00	2.9	9.70	5	9
E180		25.80	6.3	4.10	1	1
E150		13.50	0.7	19.30	8	17
B160		11.50	1.3	8.80	4	7
D109		6.75	0.2	33.75	10	20

> **EXECUTIVE INSIGHT**
  Causal analysis asks the question, why is the inventory there? These insights allow any necessary changes to be made, so stopping inventory at source.

Causal analysis

It is not necessary to undertake this task at the same time for all the inventory held as parts can be reviewed at different times. The first step is to select a portion of the inventory holding for review and then ask the question, why is it there? The answers are then categorized into:

- One of the many categories of corporate inventory that exist

- One of the five functions of operations inventory explained earlier.

At the same time, the position and value of the inventory in the operations process is recorded. 'Position' here identifies the stage through which the inventory was last processed and the stage it is waiting to enter. Where inventory is recognized as providing more than one category or function, the value of the holding is split between the categories or functions provided and recorded as separate entries.

In this way a picture of inventory is developed that shows clusters of inventory by category or function and stage in the operations process. Large clusters are then checked to see why they exist. This allows the rules and procedures involved to be reviewed and modified such that the changes would still meet the relevant corporate or operations needs but would reduce the amount of inventory involved. This approach is based on a recognition that changing a rule or interpretation of a rule or procedure that allows inventory to be made will reduce the level of inventory entering the system, thereby lowering inventory holdings.

Let us consider the examples in Case 10.2, one involving corporate and the other involving operations inventory.

REDUCING THE LEVEL OF CUSTOMER SUPPORT INVENTORY

Corporate inventory – support inventory for a customer was agreed and was to be held at the equivalent of three weeks-worth of sales. On reviewing the current position it was found that weekly sales of this item to the customer had reduced but the inventory holding had not been recalculated to reflect this lower sales position. As a result, the inventory holding at the time of the analysis was much higher than the equivalent of three weeks of sales. Discussions with the customer also included revising the agreement. The overall result was that the level of customer support inventory was reduced to one week of sales at current levels.

REDUCING THE LEVEL OF OPERATIONS INVENTORY

Operations inventory – a review of inventory highlighted a large cluster of work-in-progress inventory waiting to enter a given process. The resulting analysis led to the purchase of additional equipment as it was found that there was currently insufficient capacity at this stage. The alternatives to handling this bottleneck were considered but as the process investment costs were low it was decided that purchasing additional equipment was the most effective solution. Once the additional capacity was in place, associated inventory levels were systematically reduced.

Question

How did causal analysis help the companies in these two examples?

Lecturers: visit www.palgrave.com/business/hillom3e for teaching guidelines for this case study

Managing inventory in practice

- Inventory is invariably a sizeable asset. Unlike other assets (such as land, buildings and equipment) it is intended to be converted into services and products, sold and converted back into cash: the cash to work to cash cycle. Controlling inventory then is a major factor in managing cash flow both in terms of the size (how much) and the length of time it sits within the 'work' element of the cash flow cycle.

- Inventory is unique in that increases are typically not authorized ahead of time. Unlike purchases of equipment, buildings and other assets which undergo a stringent review, inventory is a by-product of activity and increases are not subject to review ahead of time or sometimes not at all.

- For reasons of size and the impractical nature of requesting authorization on an as-required basis, sound management and control systems supported by regular and frequent checks needs to be in place.

- All too often attention to inventory and the need to manage and control it results from what are, in fact, unexplained or unanticipated increases in inventory levels. Too often it is a case of 'closing the stable door after the horse has bolted'.

- Inventory checks are typically restricted to annual, bi-annual or quarterly stocktakes undertaken to meet the financial tasks of preparing profit and loss accounts and balance sheets. The outcomes separate inventory into raw materials and components, work-in-progress and finished goods. While such a split fulfils the accounting practice requirements to separate inventory in this way, as an aid to managing and controlling inventory it offers little. To know that the processing of material/use of components has not started (raw materials and components), it is finished (finished goods) or is somewhere in between is of little value in the task of managing and controlling this asset. Knowing where it is in the process is not a basis of control. What you need to know is, why is it there and what rule, interpretation, decision, custom and practice or procedure triggered inventory to be made.

- Causal analysis fulfils such a role as it answers this question and the answer then points to the change(s) to be made.

- Principles such as the 80/20 rule and independent/dependent demand are key to pointing the approach to take and the level of effort (and associated costs) to apply.

Driving business performance

Inventory is invariably a large asset, facilitates operations in its scheduling task and helps meet customers' desired lead times. Managing inventory, therefore, impacts business performance in the following ways.

Managing inventory to release cash

- Inventory is a large asset. Whereas other large assets such as equipment and buildings are single purchases using stringent controls that assess costs and returns, inventory is a by-product of a company's day-to-day activity. Consequently, inventory needs constant monitoring to ensure that its level is kept to a minimum. While inventory provides many roles and advantages to a business, the task of managing it well is to keep any unnecessary inventory to a minimum.

- Inventory provides many business benefits and offers a sound return on such investments. The aim here then is to identify and then reduce that portion of inventory that offers no or an inadequate return thereby releasing the tied up cash!

- The outcome of reducing or eliminating the 'unnecessary' inventory and then keeping it to desired levels is that cash is released to be used elsewhere in the business. As the level of unnecessary inventory is reduced businesses are better able to make the cash 'work in the business'. As a result the cash to work to cash cycle will be speeded up while the cash tied up in the 'work' element of this cycle is reduced.

Managing inventory to improve market support

- Two factors that frequently provide a qualifying or order-winning role in many markets are delivery reliability and delivery speed. Holding inventory directly affects both these factors as follows:
  - Material and component inventory reduces or eliminates material lead-time
  - Work-in-progress inventory reduces process lead-time, while
  - Finished goods inventory reduces or eliminates operations.

In addition to reducing and making lead-times more manageable, holding inventory also helps ensure that customer due dates are met.

- Delivery-related benefits offer sound returns to a business especially given the increasing pressure by customers to shorten lead-times. But checking to see if inventory levels can be reduced without impairing customer support is a necessary and essential operations management task.

Managing inventory to reduce costs

- Holding inventory incurs a range of costs including the value of the goods or materials, staff, storage and insurance costs together with losses through obsolescence and damage.

- Eliminating unnecessary inventory lowers these intrinsic costs, while employing the Pareto Principle helps keep the management and system costs to a minimum.

- In addition to the tangible costs listed here, the cost of not being able to use the cash that is being unnecessarily tied up in inventory for alternative investments should not be overlooked.

Critical reflections

Inventory is a significant asset in most organizations, and its effective management is a key task within operations. But controlling inventory is far from easy and represents a challenging task. It involves a complex set of decisions due to the many forms that inventory takes and the many functions it provides. In addition, inventories are the result of functional policies within an organization as well as the short- and long-term decisions taken by the purchasing, operations and sales functions. There is, therefore, a need for the decisions on how much inventory to hold to be taken at the highest level, as well as the appropriate control systems and procedures to be used lower down in an organization. The all-embracing and interrelated nature of this investment necessitates that all concerned share its provision and control.

Corporate attitudes

The way an organization uses its funds and then manages and controls these investments is a key executive task. A glance at the balance sheet of any organization will show that inventory typically represents a sizeable part of its working capital and, as such, needs to be efficiently managed and controlled. Although the size of the inventory holding in many organizations is significant in itself and also in relation to other assets, the key task of managing and controlling inventory is typically not allocated sufficient resources or given adequate executive attention. While decisions to use funds for plant and equipment purchases are usually carefully judged and monitored, the efforts to manage and control inventory levels normally come too late. Increases in inventory invariably happen first and a company becomes concerned about controlling them later. A case, too often, of closing the stable door after the horse has bolted.

Although investments in equipment/processes and inventory are both sizeable typically, as mentioned earlier, the former is better managed than the latter. There are several reasons for this, including the following:

- Inventory is an inherent part of a company's operations. When output exceeds sales, purchases exceed output or purchases exceed sales, inventory increases or vice versa. Thus changes to the level of inventory are a consequence of a company's day-to-day activities, but are usually not specifically addressed each time these events take place. With equipment purchases, the investment is a one-off event and invariably made following a conscious decision to address a particular proposal to buy an item of equipment. Control in this instance is easier to effect.

- Inventory all looks the same and there are normally large but acceptable quantities of it; more of the same is not easy to detect. However, new equipment, no matter how small, draws attention, questions and thereby control.

- The control of inventory investment needs to be ongoing. Plant investment on the other hand is a one-off decision and over a period is often not so demanding of management's time.

- Inventory control is often not seen as a senior executive task. It has no qualities or characteristics that give it inherent attraction or bring it to the attention of top management. It is not dynamic. It is a task of day-to-day detail seen by most as mundane. The content, issues and discussions on inventory all appear to be the same. As a consequence, it is not normally an agenda item for a management meeting (unless the horse has bolted), whereas fixed asset investment usually is.

- Companies fail to distinguish between records and control. Consequently, the inventory information provided is typically in the form of a record – a statement of the past and often for historical, financial purposes. However, companies mistakenly interpret this as control data, whereas it merely expresses the value of inventory in a format required for financial statements. One outcome is that ongoing controls necessitated by the size of this asset are not developed, often contributing to unnecessarily high levels of inventory.

Records versus controls

The challenging task facing operations is to ensure that the amount of inventory held is sufficient to provide the many benefits and functions that come with holding inventory while ensuring that no more than necessary is held in order to minimize the level of investment involved. Accomplishing this requires sound and appropriate systems, supplemented by analysis. While businesses typically have inventory systems in place, the information necessary to help control and keep inventory to a minimum is often limited.

Evaluating inventory as raw materials/components, work-in-progress and finished goods, although necessary to prepare profit and loss accounts and balance sheets, is of little help in checking and controlling inventory levels for the following reasons:

- They are a record (reflecting a stage in the process) and not a control

- The information fails to address the questions of why the inventory is there and how much is necessary.

Causal analysis supplements inventory systems as it provides answers to these questions and so enables a business to keep inventory low while retaining the benefits and functions that inventory provides and that are so essential to the business overall. Finally, inventory is an integral part of a business. As such, it reflects the dynamics that characterize the organization. It facilitates meeting customers' needs, oils the wheels of the organization, is the outcome of corporate and functional decisions, is sizeable and is subject to change over short timeframes. As a result, managing inventory is a complex but key task. The maxim that prevention is better than cure fits well here but relates as much to meeting market requirements as to keeping levels in check. As such, it needs to be well managed throughout the business.

Summary

- Inventory is not only sizeable in asset terms, but is also complex to manage and control.

- Companies wish to keep the investment in inventory as low as possible. Nevertheless, inventory is an integral part of a company's activities and central to the workings of its processes and delivery systems, so it must be efficiently managed and controlled within the context of the overall business and market requirements.

- One overriding principle is that of distinguishing between independent and dependent demand items. As usage rates of the latter are linked to the levels of demand of the former, requirements for dependent demand items can be calculated and scheduled in line with demand for the independent items to which they relate.

- The principle of calculating requirements for dependent demand items is central to managing and controlling this type of inventory. However, it may make more sense for a company to hold inventory of some of these dependent demand items at a level that is not tied to a calculated rate of requirement. Reasons for severing this link are to do with issues of overall cost. For items that have a low unit cost (for example, C items), buying in quantities that exceed demand patterns may lower the total unit cost (price per unit plus related inventory costs). Buying or making in large quantities will almost always lower the actual cost per unit, and such items lend themselves to the use of systems such as two-bin type controls that are simple to operate and inexpensive to manage.

- The approaches to managing and controlling independent items need to reflect the several issues and dimensions that were introduced and discussed throughout the chapter. Foremost will be the choice of whether to provide services or make products on an MTO, ATO or MTS basis.

- In MTO businesses, material and work-in-progress inventory will reflect the delivery dates of customer orders for the services and products provided. When they are finished, items will go straight to customers.

- Where items are part-made and then assembled or finished in line with customer orders and where items are MTS, what and how much is made and when and how much to order need to take into account issues such as the 80/20 rule, corporate inventory commitments, the reorder point, buffer inventory requirements and EOQs.

- The key throughout is fitting the decisions to the characteristics and requirements of an organization. Knowing the alternatives that can be used and incorporating relevant dimensions into the decision-making process should always form the basis of the management and control outcomes.

Study activities

Discussion questions

1. How does inventory contribute to the value-adding activities of a firm? When should inventory be considered a symptom of a waste?

2. What types of material inventory would you find in the following businesses:
   - A retail pharmacist
   - A petrol station
   - A coffee bar
   - A stone and gravel extraction company?

3. What activities add to the cost of inventory and which functions are responsible for incurring them?

4. What aspects of the delivery system in service companies need to accommodate their inability to convert capacity into inventory?

5. How realistic are the assumptions of the EOQ model? Why is this model still being used in both textbooks and businesses?

6. Describe the difference between independent and dependent demand and give two examples of each for a pizza restaurant.

7. Explain the ABC classification system and detail its advantages.

8. Referring back to Chapter 9, how does JIT influence inventory holdings?

9. Textet Computing sells software through the internet. With each purchase, the company includes a computer manual and currently it is rethinking whether it should outsource the preparation of these manuals or continue to make them in-house. Below are the cost estimates for the options:

Outsourced	total cost per manual £0.50
Make-in-house	variable cost per manual £0.03 annual fixed costs £75

   a. Which alternative has the lower total cost if annual demand is 30,000 copies?
   b. At what annual volume do these alternatives have the same cost?

c. Textet Computing estimates that its sales of software next year will increase to 55,000 units. The outside supplier will drop the price per manual to £0.43 on these volumes. At what quantity are the cost of making in-house and the cost of outsourcing at £0.43 equal?

10. In making reservations for services, a common approach where demand is uncertain is to 'overbook' to avoid the cost of no shows.
    a. Using a passenger airline and a good quality restaurant, discuss the pros and cons of this approach.
    b. How ethical is this practice?

11. Some top restaurants part-prepare some food ahead of time. How is this both an example of assemble-to-order and the use of capacity-related inventory?

Assignments

1. Choose one service and one manufacturing company and extract the following information from their latest balance sheet:
   • Inventory
   • Each category of fixed assets
   • Total fixed assets.

   Compare your findings to the observations made in this chapter.

2. What difficulties are, in general, forced on service organizations as a result of their inability to convert their capacity into inventory, if required?

3. How do organizations attempt to manage the difficulties identified in Question 2? Illustrate your answer using the following businesses:
   • Sandwich bar
   • Passenger airline
   • Bank
   • Call centre.
   Following your analysis, compare and contrast the approaches you identified.

4. Electro Supplies assembles a range of items and is seeking to improve its inventory systems. Below is a sample of components that it buys in from outside suppliers.

Items	Annual demand	Unit price (£)
1100	5,000	0.10
1174	750	2.45
1219	1,000	1.10
1220	600	0.95
1235	950	3.15
1340	1,850	4.00
1600	1,700	0.61
1605	1,700	1.05
1685	1,350	3.40
1690	400	0.60

Item	Annual demand	Unit price (£)
1810	2,000	1.15
1845	10,000	0.30
1855	1,400	6.50
1915	1,890	8.20
1920	680	16.50
1965	2,850	0.35
1980	9,050	0.70
1900	7,100	2.20
2010	600	1.15
2020	280	3.45

a. Calculate the annual requirement value (ARV) for each item.
b. Classify the items as A, B or C.
c. Taking the highest and lowest ARV items, advise Electro Supplies on the inventory approach it should adopt.

Exploring further

Journal articles

Abernathy, F.H., Dunlop, J.T., Hammond, J.H. and Weil, D. (2000) 'Control your inventory in a world of lean retailing'. *Harvard Business Review*, **78**(6), pp. 169–76. Despite demanding retailers and product proliferation, manufacturers have stayed with indiscriminate production schedules and sourcing strategies. Manufacturers tend to treat every stock-keeping unit (SKU) within a product line in the same way. The article argues that, by differentiating SKUs according to their actual demand patterns, inventories on some can be reduced and on others increased, thereby improving overall profitability.

Arnold, D. (2000) 'Seven rules of international distribution'. *Harvard Business Review*, **78**(6), pp. 131–37. Companies entering markets in developing countries quickly learn that they need to work with local distributors. Some guidelines are provided to help multi-nationals anticipate and correct potential problems in these arrangements.

Chopra, S. and Lariviere, M.A. (2005) 'Managing service inventory to improve performance'. *MIT Sloan Management Review*, **47**(1), pp. 56–63. This article shows how service inventories allow firms to buffer their resources from the variability of demand and reap benefits from economies of scale while benefiting customers. It discusses how inventory can be used as a strategic lever in designing and managing service offerings.

Books

Donath, R., Mazel, J. and Dublin, C. (2002) *The Ioma Handbook of Logistics and Inventory*. Chichester: John Wiley & Sons. This book provides practical insight when planning logistics strategies as ways to reduce inventories and logistics costs.

Hill, A. and Hill, T. (2009) *Manufacturing Operations Strategy: Text and Cases*, 3rd edn. Basingstoke: Palgrave Macmillan. The text outlines an in-depth approach for developing and implementing operations strategy within manufacturing organizations.

Hill, A. and Hill, T. (2011) *Essential Operations Management.* Basingstoke: Palgrave Macmillan. The text provides a useful supplement to *Operations Management* by focusing on the essential aspects for managing operations within service and manufacturing organizations.

Wild, T. (2002) *Best Practices in Inventory Management*, 2nd edn. Oxford: Elsevier Science. This text offers a useful overview of the basis and reasons for inventory and practical approaches to successfully reducing inventory while meeting customer requirements.

Notes and references

1. In 1906, Vilfredo Pareto observed that a few items in any group contribute the significant proportion of the entire group. At the time, he was concerned that a few people in a country earned most of the income. The law of the significant few can be applied in many areas, including inventory. See Pareto. V. (1969) *Manual of Political Economy*. Fairfield, NJ: Augustus M. Kelley.
2. The 80/20 relationship implied in the rule is only intended as an indication of the size of the actual figures involved, as shown in Figures 10.9 and 10.10.
3. Special services and products are non-repeat items or ones for which the time gap between one order and the next is so long that investment will not be made.

Visit www.palgrave.com/business/hillom3e for self-test questions, guideline answers to some case study questions, useful weblinks and more to help you understand the topics in this chapter

In January 2007, Michael Dell was reinstated as CEO of Dell. The company he had lovingly built over the previous 25 years was in trouble and its shareholders were getting nervous. Market share had fallen and it was rapidly losing share to Hewlett-Packard (HP), now the world's largest PC manufacturer. Analysts felt that its 'direct' business model no longer gave it a competitive edge and its lack of focus on product innovation and customer experience was causing it to lose market share. As the analyst Matt Raine explains, 'Demand for desktop PCs is falling as notebooks and mobile devices become more popular. As product innovation grows, life cycles shorten and choice widens and then customers increasingly want to touch a product and talk to someone about its features before buying it. Dell's current business model doesn't allow for this.'

THE EVOLUTION OF DELL

In 1983, Michael Dell was studying at the University of Texas and selling custom-ers cost-effective computers by buying components and assembling them. Three years later, he was running a company with $34 million annual sales, 100 employees and a 3,000 square-foot facility. To meet the growing demand, he established retail agreements with CompUSA, Staples, BestBuy, Costco, Business Depot and PC World to serve small businesses and individual consumers. This was working well, but then problems struck. In 1994 inaccurate sales forecasts left the business with high inventories and it lost $36 million. To rectify this situation, Dell exited the retail market and went back to selling products directly to customers.

Eliminating middlemen and distributors allowed Dell to better understand customer needs, which it then passed on to its suppliers. As a result, it reduced component inventory from 70 to 20 days and average lead-time from 45 to 10 days. Finished goods inventory was eliminated as products were now made to order within

Figure 1 Percentage total sales by product group (2004–10)

Product group	% total annual sales					
	2004	2005	2006	2007	2009	2010
Desktop PCs	45	42	38	34	28	24
Notebooks	23	24	25	27	31	31
Software and peripherals	12	14	15	16	17	17
Servers and networking	10	10	10	10	11	12
Services	7	8	9	9	9	12
Storage	3	3	3	4	4	4
Total	**100**	**100**	**100**	**100**	**100**	**100**

Figure 2 Financial performance (1998–2010)

Performance	1998	2000	2002	2004	2006	2007	2008	2009	2010
Sales revenue ($m)	18,243	31,888	35,404	49,205	57,420	61,133	61,101	52,902	61,494
Gross profit ($m)	4,106	6,443	6,349	9,015	9,516	11,671	10,957	9,261	11,396
Inventory year end ($m)	273	400	306	459	660	1,180	867	1,051	1,301
Share price year end ($)	73.19	26.12	23.86	41.76	24.22	20.04	9.50	12.90	13.16
Dividend per share ($)	0.58	0.89	0.79	1.20	1.15	1.33	1.25	0.73	1.36

five days from receipt of an order. The cash released by the inventory reduction was invested in higher quality products to compete with Compaq and IBM. To help to sell products directly to customers, Dell launched its website www.dell.com in 1998 and by 2000 over half its sales were through the internet. It then started to expand its product range by selling refurbished PCs, notebooks, scanners and printers along with serviced network servers, workstations and storage systems (see Figure 1). A year later, it became the largest PC manufacturer in the world, with annual sales of $32 billion (see Figure 2), of which 72 per cent were in North and South America, 20 per cent in Europe and 8 per cent in Asia Pacific. The company grew from strength to strength and in 2004 it broke the worldwide industry record by shipping 8 million PC units in the first quarter. At the same time, Michael Dell stepped down as CEO to become Chairman of the board.

DELL'S DIRECT BUSINESS MODEL

Using the 'direct' business model summarized in Figure 3, Dell continually looks for ways to reduce inventory and delivery lead-times. In 2004, its inventory turned over 107 times compared to 8.5 times at HP and 17.5 times at IBM. This means it does not have to discount products as they become obsolete and new products are introduced almost two months faster than competitors because it does not have existing component inventory to sell before new products can be introduced. Its direct customer interface helps link product and service innovation to customer needs, reduces distribution costs and allows its sales force to focus on end users rather than distributors.

One key to Dell's success is the way it manages its supply chain. Products and information flow through a variety of relationships and partnerships (Figure 4) and across a number of regions (Figure 5). It

Aspect	Description
Figure 3 Dell's direct business model	

Product selection	· The website caters for different market segments: individuals, home office computers, small businesses, medium businesses, large businesses and public sector companies
	· Customers customize their order on the website by selecting:
	  – **Features** – such as processors, display screen, memory, hard drive, video card and audio card
	  – **Accessories** – such as printers, power options, TV tuner, batteries and carrying case
	  – **Software** – such as Microsoft Office
	  – **Services** – such as warranty, installation and internet
	· At every step, customers are warned if shipping could be delayed due to components being unavailable

Sales order processing	· Orders are received by telephone, email or downloaded from the internet every 15 minutes (50 per cent from the internet) · Customer credit and order configuration are checked · Orders are then sent to the order management system, which reviews component inventory, generates material requests and sends these to the relevant suppliers
Production planning	· All products are made to order · Once all the components are available, a barcode is printed and attached to them · Production lines in all factories around the world are rescheduled every two hours · Dell only assumes ownership of the components when they reach the assembly line · Once the production plan has been established, a message is sent to the relevant supplier logistics centre(s) telling it which components it should deliver and to which 'delivery dock' they should go · Suppliers are given 90 minutes to deliver components to the 'delivery dock' and Dell has 30 minutes to move them from here to the assembly line before the next production cycle starts · Production is planned on a first-in-first-out basis · All orders are planned to be fulfilled within five days from receiving the customer order · All factories have flexible assembly lines that can be used for desktop PCs, notebooks or servers · Activities within a factory are rescheduled if defective units need replacing or if there is a large corporate order

Assembly	· Once all the components for an order are received at the delivery dock, the barcode is scanned and parts are sent on a conveyor belt to the assembly line
	· The assembly process consists of a number of steps:
	  1. Computer system is assembled by a single worker in a single location
	  2. Software is loaded onto it
	  3. Authenticity labels such as Intel and Microsoft are added
	  4. System is cleaned and placed into a box
	  5. Inspection is completed on a random selection of 10 per cent of the systems
	  6. A separate box containing the keyboard, documentation and mouse (all supplied by one subcontractor) is added to the existing box
	  7. The order is packaged and sent to distribution

Distribution	· Using the barcode on the box, orders are sorted depending on their final destination · Products are then shipped to the relevant distribution hub before travelling on to the final customer
After-sales service	· All subsequent technical and after-sales services is handled by Dell through its call centres

collaborates closely with suppliers and bases procurement decisions on four criteria: cost (30 per cent weighting), quality conformance, service and flexibility (70 per cent weighting). Kevin Kettler, chief technology officer at Dell, explained that the product features, functions and performance are important, but we also need to know if they [suppliers] can meet our quality conformance and volume requirements. They must be able to quickly diagnose and respond to any customer-related issue and, if necessary, trace it back to the component-level. We have to work together to ensure we are both successful.

Dell separates procurement activities, with price negotiations, contract terms and sourcing of major components managed by a global team in Texas, while purchase order release, delivery management, payment and sourcing of consumables managed within the local manufacturing units. All suppliers must have a warehouse called a supplier logistics centre (SLC) located within a few miles of each Dell factory so as to reduce transport costs and lead-times. In fact, some small component suppliers actually have premises within the Dell factory next to the production lines. Several suppliers typically share an SLC and use it to either produce or stock components. Dell schedules its production lines every two hours and the SLC then supplies components to meet these requirements. Suppliers have to maintain 8–10 days of inventory for each component and most suppliers replenish the SLC stock three times a week. In 2005, radio frequency identification (RFID) was installed in some facilities and some suppliers so as to

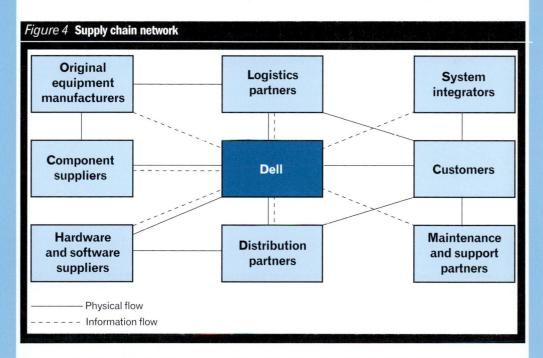

Figure 4 Supply chain network

- Physical flow
- - - - - Information flow

Figure 5 Location of suppliers and level of spend

Region	Country locations		% total supplier spend
US and Latin America	United States Mexico	Costa Rica Brazil	27
Europe	Germany Ireland	Italy Spain	1
Asia	China Indonesia Japan Korea Malaysia	Philippines Singapore Taiwan Thailand	72

allow tagged component kits to be routed through production thus ensuring that the correct type of customization occurs and the correct software is installed. This greatly reduces production stops, order cancellations and incorrect product shipping.

Dell maintains close supplier relationships and shares information regarding inventory levels, demand expectations and long-term plans. In turn, suppliers share information on capacity and new technology drivers. With some suppliers, Dell has purchase agreements in place to ensure there is adequate supply in high demand periods. Dell holds monthly sales and production planning meetings to review changing product strategies, competitive factors and constraints. Dell's marketing department generates 75 per cent accurate sales forecasts based on new product developments, purchasing patterns, budget cycles and seasonality trends, such as the end of a government department's financial year, the beginning of the academic year or the Christmas holiday period. Commodity teams break down the forecast to component levels and create six-month forecasts that are updated every week and passed on to suppliers with a firm commitment for the following week's order. Suppliers immediately confirm their ability to meet this forecast and real-time requirements are placed on suppliers through the extranet site valuechain.dell.com.

Dell holds a weekly lead-time meeting with sales, marketing and supply chain executives to interpret demand trends, resolve supply issues and manage delivery lead-times to customers. If component lead-times increase, then orders are expedited, additional suppliers are brought in or customers are encouraged to buy substitute products. Within hours, the marketing team creates advertisements for computers for which it has abundant components and these are then posted on Dell's own and other popular websites. Similarly, if component inventory accumulates, then customers are provided with incentives to buy those products that use these components. Pricing is changed from week to week to reflect the balance between demand and supply, and lead-times are updated on a daily basis.

Daily performance figures for each supplier against price, quality conformance, delivery speed and delivery reliability are posted on valuechain.dell.com to show a comparison within each component sector. Performance feedback and future expectations are outlined at quarterly supplier meetings. Based on their performance, suppliers are awarded a percentage of Dell's purchases for the next quarter. Thirty of its 250 suppliers are used to provide 75 per cent of the demand for its 3,500 components and, based on the previous year's performance, 'Best Supplier' awards are given at the annual suppliers' conference.

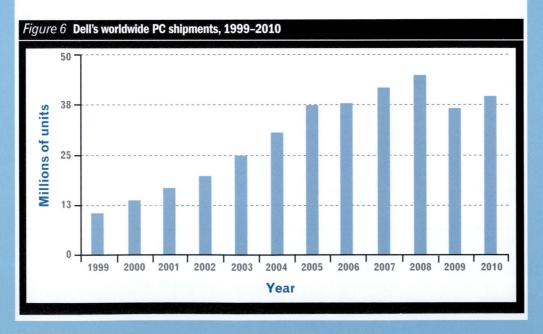

Figure 6 **Dell's worldwide PC shipments, 1999–2010**

Figure 7 **Comparison of market share for major PC vendors, (1995–2010)**

Vendor	Market share (% total)						
	1995	2001	2004	2006	2008	2009	2010
HP	4	7	16	17	18	19	18
Dell	3	13	18	18	15	12	13
Acer	–	–	4	5	11	13	12
Lenovo	–	–	2	6	7	8	10
Toshiba	3	3	3	4	5	5	5
Asus	–	–	–	–	–	3	5
Apple	8	3	2	2	3	3	4
Compaq	10	11	–	–	–	–	–
Fujitsu Siemens	5	5	6	–	–	–	–
IBM	6	6	6	–	–	–	–
Gateway	2	2	2	2	–	–	–
Other	59	50	41	46	41	40	33
Total (million units)	**89**	**128**	**189**	**239**	**302**	**306**	**308**

Notes: 1. HP acquired Compaq in 2002.
2. IBM sold its PC business to Lenovo in 2005.
3. Acer acquired Gateway in 2007.

Supplier engineers often work with Dell's new product development teams to understand customer requirements, develop products and solve problems. Collaborative supplier projects are also used to raise awareness of working hours, health and safety and environmental issues and improve business processes.

COMPETITIVE PRESSURES

By 2006, Dell had been successful for a number of years and it couldn't seem to put a foot wrong. Its worldwide PC shipments had grown threefold in the previous seven years to 38 million units for the year (Figure 6). Then, competitive pressures caused a sudden drop in market share (Figure 7). HP took over as world number one with a very different strategy to Dell by focusing on product innovation, outsourcing product assembly and selling both directly and through retailers. Customers could order products through HP's internet site, but the majority of orders came from retailers through its extranet site. Both types of order are assembled and delivered within five days by one of HP's manufacturing partners. Retail partners forecast their own demand, manage their own stock and provide a variety of technical and after-sales services. HP develops long relationships with a few suppliers, selected for their performance against price, quality conformance, security, service, capacity and technology. In order to get competitive prices, it has more than one supplier for each product, but 85 per cent of components come from only 35 suppliers. HP buys components centrally to achieve economies of scale and then sells them on to its manufacturing partners at a slightly higher price.

HP's success meant that many analysts were now questioning Dell's strategy. Matt Raine explains, 'Although Dell has low inventory and distribution costs, it has high support costs to service customer requests, queries and orders. Its competitors have offloaded these tasks to their distribution partners and retailers and they are now also benefiting from falling component prices and automated manufacturing. Customers increasingly want to touch and feel a product, buy it and then walk away with it. You can't do this with a Dell product. On top of this, Dell's wide product range results in diseconomies of scale while the product features aren't innovative and there are no after-sales service centres.'

NEW DIRECTION

Shortly after being reappointed as CEO in 2007, Michael Dell put in place a new executive team and brought in Michael Cannon as head of the global operations organization to consolidate the company's manufacturing, procurement and supply chain activities. He immediately started to integrate supply chains, eliminate overlapping activities, laid off 1,000 employees in existing factories and set up new plants in India, Poland and Brazil. Dell also started to move away from its direct-only model by opening retail stores in Dallas, New York and Russia and launched a 'PartnerDirect' programme with a number of 'value added resellers' in North America (Walmart, Sam's Club and Macy's), Europe (Carphone Warehouse, Carrefour, BestBuy and Staples), Asia (Bic Camera Inc. and Gartner Group) and online (Shoplet.com). Customers can see products, touch them and place orders, but cannot take them away as no inventory is actually held at these retailers. However, some resellers will assemble products themselves and have installed software to ensure they are delivered in five days.

Dell's new strategy received a mixed response. As Matt Raine explains, 'This represents a significant change and I'm not sure its supply chain is geared up for it. Inventories need to be managed differently and its cost advantage is weakened. Any company jumping from a direct to a channel-based model cannot expect a soft landing. This model caused so many problems for Dell in the early 1990s, why should it be any different now?'.

Questions

1. How does Dell manage inventory within its supply chain?

2. How has it used inventory management to drive the performance of its business?

3. How well is Dell positioned for the future?

Lecturers: visit www.palgrave.com/business/hillom3e for teaching guidelines for this case study

Managing Quality

11

After completing this chapter, you should be able to:

- Explain what quality is and why it is important

- Understand the stages involved in managing quality conformance

- Apply alternative tools and techniques to improve quality conformance

- Critically evaluate the quality conformance levels within your organization and suggest improvements

- Understand the alternative approaches to managing quality and select the one appropriate for your organization

- Propose and substantiate quality improvements within your organizational context

What is the role of managing quality within the business?

- Quality concerns:
  - Designing – services and products to meet customer requirements, and
  - Consistently delivering – services and products in line with this design specification

- Improving quality levels within an organizations helps:
  - Improve market support – as quality conformance is either an order-winner or qualifier in most markets
  - Reduce operating costs – as poor quality results in high internal, external, appraisal and prevention costs
  - Increase employee motivation and engagement – as most people want to do a good job and take pride in doing this

Why is managing quality important?

- Good quality is an essential foundation for a business and it is often impossible to manage a business where poor quality is considered an acceptable way of working

- The cost of quality within many organizations is 15–20 per cent of sales

- Over 80 per cent of quality problems are caused by poor management

How does managing the supply chain impact on business performance?

- **Improving market support** – by ensuring that service and product designs meet customer requirements, and that these services and products are then consistently delivered in line with these designs

- **Reducing costs** – by systemically reducing the internal, external, appraisal and prevention costs of poor quality

- **Releasing cash** – the main objective of improving quality would not be to release cash. However, better matching service and product designs with customer needs should, in turn, help reduce finished inventory levels obsolescence. Equally, more predictable delivery systems enable lower levels of buffer inventory to be held

What are the key issues to consider when managing quality?

- A quality management philosophy should include:
  - **Measuring the cost of quality** – to prioritize investment and track improvement
  - **Meeting or redefining customer requirements** – aim to either meet customer requirements with a market-driven strategy or challenge and redefine them with a market-driving strategy
  - **Benchmarking performance** – against other organizations to identify areas for improvement
  - **Proactively looking for ways to improve quality** – so that potential problems are prevented before they occur. Reactive quality improvement must only be seen as a short-term solution
  - **Using statistical tools and techniques** – to manage and improve quality levels
  - **Using breakthrough projects** – to focus resources on fixing chronic problems
  - **Putting in place quality controls and programmes** – to ensure breakthrough improvements are maintained and a quality habit is developed throughout the organization

- Typically, internal and external costs account for 50–80 per cent of the total cost of quality, so these are initially the main areas to be improved

- Quality improvement involves two key steps:
  1. **Control** – delivery systems and processes by removing unpredictable variation, then
  2. **Improve** – quality levels by reducing predictable variation

- All staff must be trained to use quality improvement tools and techniques

- Implementing a Total Quality Management (TQM) philosophy within your organization requires you to broaden your skills and be more innovative

- The Baldrige Award is a good target for your US facilities and operations

- The EFQM Excellence Award is a good target for your European facilities and operations

- When managing quality within your business, you must:
  - Publish, recognize and reward supplier performance
  - Assess supplier capabilities before purchasing services and products
  - Continually review and adjust the sampling plans you use to reduce inspection costs without increasing consumer risks (accepting poor quality services or products) or producer risks (rejecting good quality services or products)
  - Control delivery systems (reducing unpredictable variation), before looking for ways to improve them (reducing predictable variation)

Introduction

A range of quality philosophies, approaches, tools and techniques have been developed to help companies measure, control and improve quality. This chapter examines how to do this by looking at the following aspects:

- What is quality and why is it important?
- What are the different philosophies about managing quality?
- What are the steps to managing quality effectively?
- What tools and techniques are available to help improve quality?
- How should businesses manage quality?
  - What management philosophy should they use?
  - What systems and procedures need to be in place?
- What are the issues with managing quality in practice and how can these be overcome?
- How can managing quality be used to drive business performance?

What is quality and why is it important?

Quality conformance is either an order-winner or qualifier for most customers. However, before 'quality' can be measured and improved, it must be defined. Within operations, 'quality conformance' means consistently delivering services and products in line with their **design specification** that, in turn, reflects customer needs. Figure 11.1 shows how these different aspects interact, and **gaps** between what customers want and expect, what a company sells, how services and products have been designed and what operations delivers, which all need to be constantly managed.

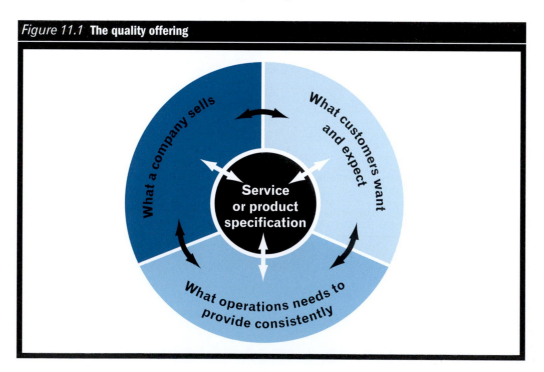

Figure 11.1 The quality offering

Design specification – this provides precise and explicit information about the requirements for a service or product design including its nature and scope (such as speed of delivery, durability, length and weight), its user group and its overall purpose.

Quality gaps – these occur when customer expectations of the level of service or product quality to be delivered is not met by their perceptions of service or product delivery.

Quality concerns two aspects:
1. Designing services and products to meet customer requirements
2. Consistently delivering services and products in line with this design specification.

This second aspect is called 'quality conformance'.

Effective quality management can help organizations attract and retain customers. For example, the Anstruther Fish Bar (see Case 11.1) continually alters the recipe of its batter to reflect the changing specification of the fish it catches throughout the year. As a result, it attracts over 2,000 customers a day, with daily takings exceeding £10,000 and queues of up to 1.5 hours at busy times. Equally, the Royal Bank of Scotland (see Case 11.1) found that customers with efficiently resolved problems were more likely to buy RBS products in the future than those who had not experienced a problem.

By modifying the service or product specification, companies can also reduce delivery costs and increase customer and staff loyalty. For example, Hampton Inns hotel chain changed its service and product specification by guaranteeing refunds for dissatisfied customers, empowering staff to grant refunds and putting an iron and ironing board in each of its rooms. As a result, sales revenue increased, staff turnover reduced and it eliminated the cost of moving the irons between different rooms (see Case 11.2). Equally, Zebra Technologies, increased sales by 50 per cent by introducing a basic, no-frills bar code printer (see Case 11.2) and United Parcel Services (UPS) increased sales by encouraging drivers to spend 30 minutes per day with customers building relationships and give them advice on how best to ship their products (see Case 11.2).

As you can see from the examples in Case 11.2, effectively managing the quality of services and products, and changing the specification when necessary, is essential to maintaining customer satisfaction and securing repeat sales. But how does an organization go about selecting which characteristics make up a specification, and how are standards for quality set and met? The next sections will look at these questions in more detail, but first let's review the work of some key pioneers in the field.

Quality philosophies: the work of Deming, Juran and Crosby

The drive to improve quality in European and North American organizations stemmed from the superior levels of quality conformance achieved by Japanese and South East Asian companies from the 1960s onwards that had changed the competitive dimension of quality conformance from a qualifier into an order-winner. The figureheads of this response were provided by three principal contributors whose work is now briefly reviewed. The four main principles of all these philosophies are:

1. **Measure the cost of quality** – to prioritize areas for improvement and track progress. These include:
   - Internal cost of failure – defects, rework, yield losses, reinspection and disposal
   - External costs of failure – after a service or product has been delivered, such as complaints, returns, after-sales support and repairs
   - Appraisal costs – associated with assessing services and products, including inspection, checks, quality assurance and the cost of test equipment
   - Prevention costs – including quality planning, new service and product reviews, process controls and data collection, analysis and reporting.

2. **Meet customer requirements** – the first step is always understanding customer requirements before designing services and products to meet these needs. Without this, everything else is a waste of time.

ANSTRUTHER FISH BAR

How was Ian Whyte able to sell his small fish and chip shop, housed in a modest building overlooking the harbour in Fife – a quiet Scottish fishing town – for £1.6 million? Because it attracts over 2,000 customers a day, with daily takings exceeding £10,000 and queues of up to 1.5 hours at busy times.

The Anstruther Fish Bar has managed to win customers and keep them coming back by consistently giving them what they want. The secret to perfect fish and chips is the consistency of the batter and the quality of the fish. This may seem obvious, but it's not always easy to get right. Whyte noticed that the quality of haddock varied considerably throughout the year. For example, fish caught in early spring, the spawning season, are much thinner, and haddock caught in early summer are more oily as they feed on herring and land

eels at that time of year. Ian discovered that quality could be managed by altering the batter recipe to suit the changing specification of the haddock caught throughout the year to ensure that it always only lightly coats the fish fillet and literally drops off when it is broken. Then, it must be fried consistently to create fish and chips to die for!

www.anstrutherfishbar.co.uk

THE ROYAL BANK OF SCOTLAND

As the financial services sector becomes more competitive, companies must work out how they can maintain and grow their market share. For example, the Royal Bank of Scotland (RBS) made a surprising discovery when it analyzed the satisfaction of its existing customers. It divided them into three categories:

1. Those with a problem that was not resolved
2. Those with a problem that had been efficiently resolved
3. Those whose experience with the bank had been problem-free.

It was surprised to find that, of the three groups, customers with efficiently resolved problems were most likely to buy RBS products in the future with a score of 80 per cent compared to 40 per cent for the dissatisfied group and 60 per cent for the problem-free group.

www.rbs.co.uk

Questions

1. What are the similarities between the two examples?

2. What are the implications of these findings for maintaining and growing sales within a business?

3. How should service recovery be managed within a business?

Lecturers: visit www.palgrave.com/business/hillom3e for teaching guidelines for this case study

CASE 11.2 CHANGING THE QUALITY OFFERING

ZEBRA TECHNOLOGIES

The US bar code printer manufacturer had a reputation for high-quality, top-of-the-line printers. It saw a potential for also selling products at the lower end of this market, but was concerned that this might affect its top drawer image and cannibalize its existing product line. It decided to introduce a basic, no-frills version at a 25 per cent lower selling price that was slower, could not print on different types of materials and, most importantly, could not be upgraded. As a result, total sales increased by 50 per cent and, as the margins for these new products were the same as its original ones, so did its profits.

www.zebra.com

HAMPTON INNS

The US-based chain decided to offer guaranteed refunds to customers who were in any way dissatisfied with their stay. Subsequent research showed that implementing this policy persuaded people to stay and brought in additional sales revenue at a level almost 11 times that of the refunds paid out. By also empowering all staff to grant refunds, job satisfaction increased with staff turnover falling from 117 to 50 per cent over the following three years. The refund programme also helped to identify aspects that most annoyed guests. One of the biggest issues was the lack of irons and ironing boards in their premium 'Embassy Suite' rooms. As a result, it spent $0.5 million putting an iron and ironing board in each room and found that it saved more than this in the first year by no longer having to move them between rooms.

http://hamptoninn1.hilton.com/en_US/hp/index.do

UNITED PARCEL SERVICES

United Parcel Services (UPS) had always assumed that on-time delivery was critical for its customers and it defined 'quality' as meeting its delivery promise, for example all 'next-day packages' had to be delivered by 10.30 the following morning. Its operations were prioritized and measured accordingly with elevator times and delays in customers answering their doorbells measured and included in schedules. Drivers even shaved the corners off their van seats to help reduce the time getting in and out of the van! Frequent customer surveys showed that customers were happy with its delivery performance, but surveys didn't ask customers what they actually wanted. When they finally looked at customers' wants and expectations, they were surprised to find they wanted more contact with their drivers to discuss aspects such as how best to ship their products. As a result, UPS drivers are now given 30 minutes each day to spend with customers to build relationships and bring in new sales. The programme costs UPS over $4 million in drivers' time but additional sales are many times higher. Drivers are also encouraged to visit customers with UPS sales staff for their regular customer reviews.

www.ups.com

Questions

1. Review these three cases and identify the elements of the quality offering that the companies changed or improved.

2. What benefits did these companies and their customers receive and what disadvantages or costs were involved?

Lecturers: visit www.palgrave.com/business/ hillom3e for teaching guidelines for this case study

3. **Deliver error-free services and products** – services and products must be delivered in line with their design specification right first time and every time. Errors are not acceptable. However, if they do occur then the root cause needs to be identified and changes made to prevent them from occurring again.

4. **Proactively manage quality** – quality must be managed in a proactive rather than a reactive way. This involves identifying what could go wrong and having checks in the delivery system to ensure that potential problems are identified before they occur so that action can be taken to prevent them from happening.

Market-driven strategies – aim to meet existing customer requirements.

> **EXECUTIVE INSIGHT**
>
> The following principles are common to all quality philosophies:
> - Measure the cost of quality – to prioritize investment and track improvement
> - Meet customer requirements – with a **market-driven strategy** or try to challenge and change customer requirements with a market-driving strategy
> - Deliver error-free services and products
> - Proactively manage and improve quality levels – so that potential problems are prevented before they occur.

W. Edwards Deming

Deming is widely credited with leading the Japanese quality revolution. He exposed Japanese managers to the fundamental tools and techniques they needed for this (and which are dealt with later in this chapter), such as statistical process control, with the Japanese government recognizing his contribution by creating, in 1951, the Deming Prize.

Deming summarized his views for quality management using 14 points:

1. Managers need to improve services and products by promoting a clear vision for the firm, its customers and the role of quality in that provision.

2. A philosophy should be introduced in which mistakes, inadequate training and ineffective supervision and management are unacceptable, and in which putting systems and procedures right is essential.

3. A dependence on mass inspection should be replaced with a drive to eliminate errors and defects.

4. The practice of awarding purchasing contracts on the basis of lowest price should be ended, with a move to building long-term relationships with fewer suppliers.

5. Waste should be reduced throughout a company's delivery systems and processes by never-ending quality improvements.

6. Training needs to be centred on the concept of acceptable work.

7. The job of management is not supervision but leadership.

8. People must be encouraged to ask questions, report failures and come up with solutions.

9. The barriers between functions should be broken down by developing a team-based approach throughout the organization.

10. Instead of slogans and posters exhorting improvements, management should ensure that people have the right tools and training to do the job and improve the process.

11. Quotas and targets should focus on the quality and not the quantity of output.

12. Barriers that hinder pride in one's work should be removed.

13. Continuous training will keep people up to date with new developments, design and process improvements, new tools and innovative techniques.

14. To accomplish these steps, management needs to work continuously on the other 13 points.

Deming used his 14 points to highlight the central role of managers in bringing about essential changes. He saw managers as the real obstacle to improvement, pointing out that 85 per cent of quality problems could be traced to management actions and failures. To help managers change, he advocated that they needed to address five 'deadly sins':

1. A lack of constancy of purpose

2. An emphasis on short-term results

3. The use of performance evaluation and annual reviews that reinforce short-term actions and goals

4. The practice of moving managers every two or three years, thus promoting short-term approaches to improvement and change

5. The practice of measuring corporate performance using visible, financial numbers, thus again promoting short-term actions.

Joseph M. Juran

Juran defines quality as 'fitness for use'. His work on quality spanned over 30 years and his approach to quality management is based on an analytical approach centring on the cost of quality where all costs needed to be allocated to one of the following four categories:

1. Internal cost of failure, including defects, rework, yield losses, reinspection and disposal

2. External failure costs, such as detection after despatch to a customer, complaints, returns, field service support and repairs

3. Appraisal costs, associated with assessing services and products, including inspection, checks, quality assurance and control and the cost of test equipment

4. Prevention costs, including quality planning, new service and product reviews, process control and data collection, analysis and reporting.

Juran highlighted the first two categories as they typically account for 50–80 per cent of the total costs. Juran's goal was to bring about a fundamental shift in which quality management became a 'quality habit'. To this end, he advocated a four-stage approach:

1. **Goals** – establish specific goals for the organization

2. **Plans** – detail ways to achieve these goals

3. **Responsibilities** – assign tasks for executing the plans

4. **Rewards** – base rewards on results.

Proactively improve quality

Juran proposes that quality should be proactively improved using three steps:

1. **Breakthrough projects** – in the early stages of a quality improvement programme, break-through projects need to be used to solve chronic problems (see Figure 11.2). He suggests that:

   a. *Pareto analysis* – should be used to identify the chronic problems, and then a

   b. *Dedicated improvement team* – should be given dedicated time (away from their day jobs) to understand and solve the problem.

2. **Quality controls** – to ensure the gains from the breakthrough projects are maintained. This allows companies to further reduce the cost of quality by moving from the 'improvement projects zone' to the 'reappraisal zone' shown in Figure 11.3.

3. **An annual quality programme** – should then be introduced to help build the quality habit within the organization and ensure that complacency does not set in.

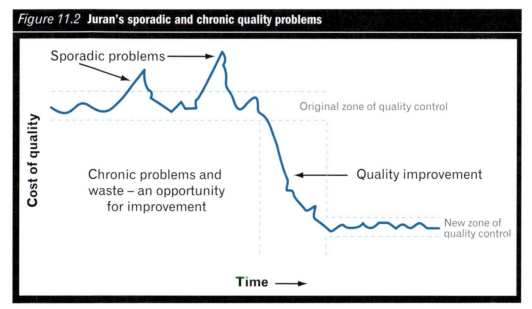

Figure 11.2 Juran's sporadic and chronic quality problems

Source: Adapted from J.M. Juran and F.M. Gryna *Quality Planning and Analysis*, New York, McGraw-Hill (1993), p. 10.

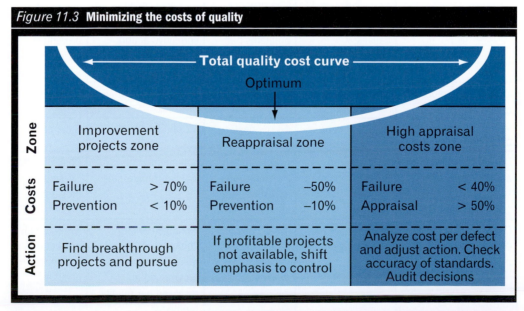

Figure 11.3 Minimizing the costs of quality

Zone	Improvement projects zone	Reappraisal zone	High appraisal costs zone
Costs	Failure > 70% Prevention < 10%	Failure –50% Prevention –10%	Failure < 40% Appraisal > 50%
Action	Find breakthrough projects and pursue	If profitable projects not available, shift emphasis to control	Analyze cost per defect and adjust action. Check accuracy of standards. Audit decisions

Source: Adapted from J.M. Juran and F.M. Gryna *Quality Planning and Analysis*, New York, McGraw-Hill (1993), p. 26.

Juran believes that quality should be improved by:

- **Using breakthrough projects** – to focus resources on fixing chronic problems
- **Putting in place quality controls** – to ensure breakthrough improvements are maintained
- **Developing an annual quality programme** – to help build a quality habit throughout the organization.

Philip B. Crosby

Crosby believes that the cost of quality is as high as 15–20 per cent of sales within many organizations. He has developed a 'maturity grid' to help companies analyze the level of quality awareness within their organization. The grid identifies five levels of maturity

Figure 11.4 **Crosby's quality management maturity grid**

Crosby's quality management maturity grid		Stages				
		1 Uncertainty	**2 Awakening**	**3 Enlightenment**	**4 Wisdom**	**5 Certainty**
Management understanding and attitude		Fails to recognize quality as a corporate issue	Supports quality management in theory but does not allocate resources	Embraces quality management and actively supports it	Participates personally and provides leadership in quality activities	Recognizes quality as necessary for corporate survival and growth
The organizational status of the quality function		Quality limited to the operations and technical functions and largely comprises inspection and checking activities	Quality leader appointed but otherwise activities remain similar to those in Stage 1	Quality function reports to top management and its leader actively involved in company management	Quality manager is a top management appointment and activities reoriented to prevention	Quality manager is on the board of directors. Prevention now the main activity and zero defects the management goal
Approach to handling problems		Fire-fighting approach. Symptoms, not causes, addressed	Teams established to resolve problems but still short term in nature	Problems resolved in an orderly fashion and involves corrective action	Problems identified at an early stage and preventive action taken	Problems are prevented at the design and development stage
Cost of quality as percentage of sales	reported	Unknown	5 per cent	8 per cent	6 per cent	2–3 per cent
	actual	0–40 per cent	18 per cent	12 per cent	8 per cent	2–3 per cent
Quality improvement actions		No organized activities	Actions based on exhortation and short term in nature	Implements the 14-step programme	Continues the 14-step programme	Quality improvement is a regular ongoing activity
Overview of corporate position on quality management		'We don't know why we have problems'	'Do we always have to have quality problems?'	'Management's commitment and quality improvement programme is resolving our quality problems'	'We routinely prevent quality problems from occurring'	'We no longer have quality problems, we know why, and we aim to do better'

Source: Adapted from P.B. Crosby *Quality is Free*, New York, McGraw-Hill (1979), pp. 32–3.

based on the status of the quality function within the business, the level and type of problem-solving procedures used and the costs of quality within the business, as shown in Figure 11.4. Once companies have positioned themselves on the maturity grid, Crosby suggests a 14-point programme for quality improvement:

1. Management must be clearly committed to the importance of quality

2. Quality improvement programmes need to be supported by a multifunctional team

3. Quality measures need to be in place

4. The cost of quality needs to include the price of non-conformance as well as the price of conformance so as to help prioritize action

5. Quality awareness needs to be promoted throughout the organization

6. Improvements and ideas need to be actioned at the appropriate level of an organization

7. The goal is to achieve a position of zero defects

8. Education and training should form the basis of any quality programme

9. A specific future date should be established as zero-defects day

10. Management need to set goals

11. Everyone is to be responsible for identifying the source of defects and errors

12. A quality programme should receive public, non-financial recognition

13. A quality council should be formed to help share experiences, problems and ideas

14. To highlight the never-ending process of quality programmes, companies then need to return again to Step 1.

> **EXECUTIVE INSIGHT**
Crosby believes that companies should:
- **Benchmark** – themselves against other organizations using his 'maturity grid'
- **Aim for 'zero-defects'** – to focus on proactively improving quality
- **Set up a 'zero-defects day'** – to signal the start of their move towards this goal.

The steps to effectively managing quality

To manage quality, firms must first control it through a number of steps:

1. **Determining quality characteristics** – the first step is to determine the characteristics that make up the service or product to be provided. These must cover all aspects of the **service package** and need to be defined in such a way that enables them to be measured and controlled, as shown in Figure 11.5 for a restaurant:
   - **Explicit services** – such as the design of the food or how it is served in a restaurant
   - **Implicit services** – such as the level of attention and recognition given to regular customers by restaurant staff
   - Supporting structural facilities – such as the quality of the table linen, plates, glasses and cutlery in a restaurant.

2. **Measuring quality characteristics** – the characteristics that describe quality fall into two groups as shown in Figure 11.6 for the varying characteristics of a teapot:
   - **Variables** – can be measured on a numerical scale. For example, the length of a product or the time taken to serve a customer.
   - **Attributes** – are measured by using the qualitative conditions of a process. These can be based on judgement or checks without detailed measurement with a service or product simply passing or failing its requirement. For example, a **go/no-go gauge** indicates if the specification has been met without taking an exact measurement.

Service package
– the collection of individual services and products provided by an organization which includes both explicit and implicit services and products.

Explicit services
– are the primary services delivered to a customer such as the food or the level of service within a restaurant.

Implicit services
– the secondary services delivered to a customer such as the atmosphere within a restaurant.

Variables – quantitative service or product characteristics that can be measured on a numerical scale such as the length of a product or the time taken to serve a customer.

Attributes
– qualitative characteristics of a service or product that are measured judging if a service or product passes a requirement.

A **go/no-go gauge**
– can be used to judge if a service or product characteristic meets its qualitative requirement.

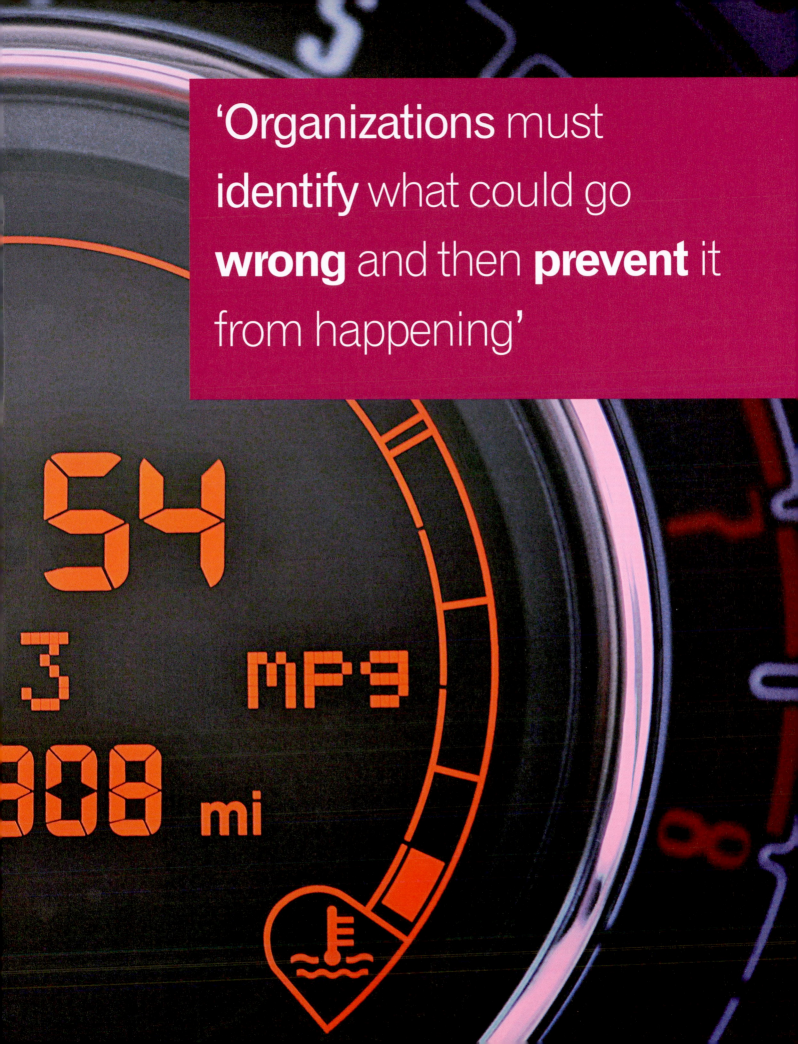

'Organizations must identify what could go **wrong** and then **prevent** it from happening'

Figure 11.5	Defining quality characteristics for a restaurant
Dimension	**Example quality characteristics**
Explicit service	• Minimizing delays at different stages in the delivery system – for example greeting guests, taking pre-dinner drinks orders, offering menus and taking orders for dinner in a timely manner • Food ingredients – for example freshness by food type, and size of portions • Food presentation – such as layout on a plate, spacing and colour combinations
Implicit service	Regular guests: • Identified by name • Staff advised ahead of time • Table preferences noted and allocated
Supporting structural facilities	• Table spacings • Table layout • Glassware and cutlery checked and polished with a dry cloth

Figure 11.6	Teapot quality characteristics		
Characteristic	**Variable**	**Attribute**
Dimensions/shape Durability Availability	• • •	
Surface appearance Design/styling Performs as a teapot Ease of use Value for money Packaging		• • • • • •

3. **Setting quality standards** – defining the level of quality for each characteristic that defines the boundary between acceptable and unacceptable. For example, a retail outlet might decide that customer queues should, for 95 per cent of the time, be no longer than three minutes, which would then become the quality standard for this service package.

4. **Deciding how to monitor quality levels** – once quality levels have been set, a company must decide how to measure conformance across the service system or process in order to ensure consistency in delivering quality. To monitor quality conformance effectively, two decisions must be made:
   1. *Where in the process to check* – conformance to agreed standards – these can be made at various points within the delivery system as shown in Figure 11.7
   2. *How many services or products should be checked* – to guarantee that the quality level is met: this is a key decision as checking everything is expensive and increases operations lead-times.

> **EXECUTIVE INSIGHT**
   Quality improvement involves two key steps:
   1. **Remove unpredictable variation** – so that delivery systems and processes are predictable and controlled, then
   2. **Reduce predictable variation** – so that quality conformance levels are improved.

Once the level of quality conformance is consistent and under control, it can then be improved by:

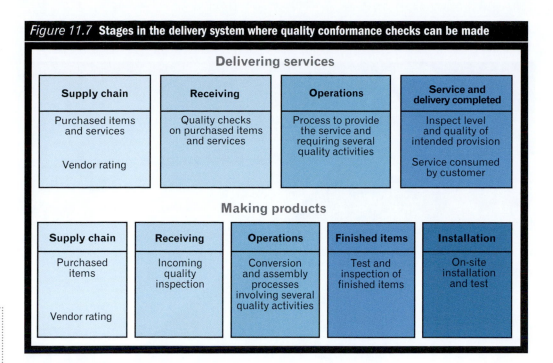

Figure 11.7 **Stages in the delivery system where quality conformance checks can be made**

Delivering services

Supply chain	Receiving	Operations	Service and delivery completed
Purchased items and services Vendor rating	Quality checks on purchased items and services	Process to provide the service and requiring several quality activities	Inspect level and quality of intended provision Service consumed by customer

Making products

Supply chain	Receiving	Operations	Finished items	Installation
Purchased items Vendor rating	Incoming quality inspection	Conversion and assembly processes involving several quality activities	Test and inspection of finished items	On-site installation and test

Quality failures – occur when the service or product delivered does not meet its design specification.

5. **Correcting and improving quality** – by recording instances of below-standard quality conformance and identifying their causes, the more common reasons for **quality failure** can be identified and corrected. Once quality problems have been identified, companies need to react quickly so as to maintain market share and consumer confidence. For example, Coca-Cola and Perrier both lost significant market share when they delayed recalling faulty products (see Case 11.3).

6. **Continue to make improvements** – once an organization has eliminated the quality problems within its operation then it can start to take a more **proactive approach** to improving quality by preventing errors from occurring in the first place. This involves identifying what could go wrong before it does and having in place appropriate **preventive action** and backup plans. It will, in turn, mean that customer requirements are more consistently met in the long run. Case 11.4 shows how the US Department of Transport monitors the on-time performance of US airlines to improve quality conformance by identifying the percentage of flights that are late due to the air carrier, weather, the national aviation system, security or the aircraft. Publishing these figures helps identify areas for improvement by benchmarking performance between airlines and identifying common issues within the industry.

Proactive approach – involves anticipating quality problems that may occur and taking action to prevent them from occurring.

Preventive action – involves improving how a service or product is designed or delivered before a quality failure has occurred.

> **EXECUTIVE INSIGHT**

Organizations must aim proactively to improve quality by continually identifying what could go wrong before it does and then preventing these problems from occurring. Reactive quality improvement must only be seen as a short-term solution.

Tools and techniques

Quality management tools and techniques are used statistically to measure and improve quality within all functions and levels of an organization. Applying these tools and techniques requires collecting both variable and attribute service, product and process data:

• Attribute data – attribute data measures qualitative conditions such as the accept or reject decision. Figure 11.8 gives an example of a department that receives and checks incoming products by taking a sample of 40 from each delivery. If there are four or less ($\leq$10 per cent) defects, then the delivery is accepted. Otherwise, the whole delivery is rejected. Using the attribute data in column 3, we can see that 12 of the 15

CASE 11.3 REGAINING CONSUMER CONFIDENCE AT COCA-COLA AND PERRIER

COCA-COLA

In 1999, Coca-Cola spent several days assuring customers that its products were safe, while dozens of children were hospitalized following complaints of stomach cramps, dizziness and vomiting. When it finally admitted that they had been tainted by an accidental injection of 'defective' carbon dioxide, it planned only to partially withdraw its products. However, the Belgium and Luxembourg governments and some major supermarkets (for example Carrefour in France) banned the sale of all its products to avoid confusion. The media also attacked Coca-Cola, with one paper showing its trademark polar bear doubled up in pain and another renaming it 'Coca-Colic'.

PERRIER

In 1990, Perrier, the French sparkling water producer reacted slowly and begrudgingly to traces of benzene found in its products. After tarnishing its reputation and losing market share, it was eventually forced to recall every bottle at a cost of $200 million.

Sources: Abelson, R. (1999) 'In a crisis, Coke tries to be reassuring', *New York Times*, 16 June.

BBC News 'The company file European warning over Coca-Cola'. Available from http://news.bbc.co.uk/1/hi/business/the_company_file/369684.stm.

Collins, G. (1995) 'Tobacco Giant Recalls 8 Billion Faulty Cigarettes', *New York Times*, 27 May.

Rehak, J. (2002) 'Tylenol made a hero of Johnson & Johnson: The recall that started them all', *New York Times*, 23 March.

Questions

1. Describe the reaction of these two companies to the quality conformance problems they faced.

2. Was quality conformance an order-winner or qualifier in these companies and how did it affect their markets?

3. What role would operations have in each situation? Give details to explain your points.

Lecturers: visit www.palgrave.com/business/hillom3e for teaching guidelines for this case study

CASE 11.4 ON-TIME PASSENGER FLIGHTS: IMPROVING QUALITY

Airline	# flights	Percentage of flights					
		On time	Air carrier delay	Weather delay	National aviation system delay	Aircraft late	Cancelled
Alaska Airlines	12,481	78.6	5.3	0.2	5.7	7.5	2.0
American Airlines	57,000	75.0	4.6	1.9	10.2	6.1	2.1
American Eagle	35,762	74.4	4.9	0.8	9.0	8.4	2.5
Continental Airlines	23,741	79.9	2.8	0.2	13.3	3.2	0.4
Continental Express	27,795	80.4	3.0	0.3	11.8	4.0	0.4
Delta Airlines	54,423	70.9	5.3	0.5	14.5	6.7	2.0
Hawaiian Airlines	3,743	89.6	4.2	0.4	0.1	4.4	0.9
JetBlue Airlines	6,726	88.2	2.8	0.1	5.4	3.0	0.1
Northwest Airlines	39,750	77.4	5.5	0.8	11.9	2.6	1.5
Southwest Airlines	77,190	82.2	3.6	0.3	3.4	9.0	1.2
United Airlines	42,675	81.9	3.4	0.2	9.4	4.3	0.7
US Airways	32,019	83.8	3.3	0.2	6.7	5.0	1.2
Total[1]	553,876	77.5	4.8	1.1	9.0	5.7	1.7

Note: 1. Total is for 19 airlines from which the above 12 have been selected.
Source: Bureau of Transportation Statistics (US Department of Transport).

Customers want their flights to arrive on-time. To ensure that their needs are met, relevant overseeing organizations (such as the Association of European Airlines and the US Department of Transport) monitor the on-time performance of airlines as shown above for 12 US airlines:

www.transtats.bts.gov

Questions

1. Why is this level of detail collected by the Bureau of Transportation Statistics?

2. What reasons can you suggest for the different level of on-time flights for the 12 carriers?

Lecturers: visit www.palgrave.com/business/hillom3e for teaching guidelines for this case study

deliveries were accepted and 3 were rejected in Quarter 1, which results in an 80 per cent acceptance rate for that period.

- Variable data – measures quantifiable delivery system conditions, which can be measured and tracked over time. Using the variable data shown in column 2 of Figure 11.9, we can see the # defects within each batch showing that this was higher (between 15 and 25 per cent) in the early part of Quarter 1.

Figure 11.8 **Attribute and variable quality conformance data on 15 deliveries received in Quarter 1**

Delivery date	# defects per batch of 40 units	Decision: accept (✓) or reject (✗)
3 Jan	6	✗
6 Jan	2	✓
11 Jan	10	✗
24 Jan	4	✓
3 Feb	7	✗
17 Feb	0	✓
19 Feb	3	✓
28 Feb	3	✓
3 Mar	2	✓
6 Mar	2	✓
12 Mar	1	✓
18 Mar	1	✓
24 Mar	3	✓
26 Mar	4	✓
30 Mar	4	✓

A number of **tools and techniques** have been developed to help organizations improve the level of quality conformance within their business by improving how services and products are designed or delivered:

- **Designing services or products** – design tools help staff develop services and products that better meet customers' needs and expectations.

- **Delivering services or products** – process tools help staff to assess the conditions and capabilities of existing delivery systems by drawing pictures of the process, monitoring existing quality conformance levels and identifying areas for improvement.

> **EXECUTIVE INSIGHT**
> Quality conformance can be improved by changing how services or products are either designed or delivered.

Some of the principal tools and techniques available to companies are now discussed and it is shown how they can be applied and the insights they give. As Case 11.5 illustrates, it is important to motivate and support employees to improve quality conformance, but they must have the right tools for the job and be able to use them properly.

Checklists

A **checklist** is a simple, common tool used to collect information in a form that records the size and other dimensions of quality (and other) problems. Figure 11.9 shows an

A **quality tool or technique** – can be used to visually display quantitative or qualitative information to help identify the number of times a quality problem occurs and the reasons for them occurring.

Checklists – collect real-time data at the location where the data is generated to show how frequently a quality problem occurs.

example of a checklist at a retail outlet recording the frequency of quality conformance problems that have occurred in a month. This shows that two of the five problems account for 71 per cent of the total problem occurrences. Therefore, the outlet needs to focus on reducing the number of times the length of checkout queue exceeds the target (42 per cent) and ensuring that there are goods on the shelf (29 per cent).

> **EXECUTIVE INSIGHT**
Checklists record how often a problem occurs.

Figure 11.9 **Checklist showing frequency of quality conformance problems at a retail outlet**

Problem	Frequency	Total	Percentage of total
Shelf display differs from bar code record	1111 1111 1111 1	16	14
No goods on shelf	1111 1111 1111 1111 1111 1111 1111	34	29
Goods out of stock	1111 1111	10	8
Length of checkout queue exceeds target	1111 1111 1111 1111 1111 1111 1111 1111 1111 1111 1111	49	42
Items returned faulty	1111 111	8	7
Total		**117**	**100**

Sampling

When 100 per cent inspection is not an integral part of a delivery system, then a sample of services or products has to be selected for checking or inspection. There has been much written about the subject of sampling and **tables** are available to show the inferences that can be drawn from the different sampling procedures and outcomes. Should you wish to review these aspects in more detail, suggested readings are included in the Exploring Further section at the end of this chapter. However, the following principles apply when using the concept of sampling:

- Random or stratified – the samples must be representative of the variety of activities undertaken within a relevant period of time.

- Size – the sample must be large enough to be sufficiently representative of the whole.

- Preserved – the identity of the total quantity from which the sample has been taken should be preserved so it is clear what it is a sample of.

Once the sample has been identified for checking or inspection, then an **acceptable quality level (AQL)** must be agreed for a sample to pass on to the next stage in the delivery system. Key to this is ensuring that the **sampling risk** is minimized so that an unacceptable batch is not accepted (the consumer's risk) or an acceptable batch is rejected (the producer's risk). To achieve this, a single, double, multiple or sequential sampling plan can be used depending on the nature of the delivery system being used and the characteristic being inspected:

- **Single sampling plan** – is essentially a go/no-go procedure where the total quantity delivered is accepted if a single sample meets the specified AQL.

- **Double sampling plan** – where one or two samples can be used. An example of a double sampling plan is shown in Figure 11.10. Following this plan, a batch of services or products would be accepted or rejected using the following steps:

Statistical tables – in the UK, the British Standards Institute provides a range of sampling plans, which include OC curves, AQLs, single, double and multiple sampling plans and cover both attributes and variables – see BS 600 (1991, 1993, 1994 and 1996) and BS 6002 (1993 and 1994).

Acceptable quality level (AQL) – the maximum percentage of defective items that can be considered acceptable for a step within a delivery system.

Sampling risk – the risk that either an unacceptable batch will be accepted (known as the consumer's risk) or an acceptable batch will be rejected (known as the producer's risk).

The Nashua CEO, Bill Conway, was addressing some top management visitors from Ford. He started the meeting with a challenge:

'Suppose I ask two of you successful vice-presidents at Ford to enter a contest. The winner will win a trip around the world for his whole family. I know that both of you are totally motivated and dedicated by virtue of your exalted positions at Ford. The contest is to see who can drive a nail into this wall. One of you will get a hammer, the other nothing but management encouragement. Who do you think will win?'

The answer was obvious. Motivation and management support are important, but employees must have the right tools to do the job.

www.nashua.com

Questions

1. What point is Bill Conway, the Nashua CEO, trying to make?

2. Why it is important for people to realize this when they are trying to manage quality within their business?

Lecturers: visit www.palgrave.com/business/hillom3e for teaching guidelines for this case study

a. Take the first sample – of 100 services or products from the whole batch.
b. **Accept** – if there are two or less errors in the first sample, then the whole batch is accepted.
c. **Reject** – if there are seven or more errors in the first sample, then the whole batch is rejected.
d. Take the second sample – if there are between three and six errors in the first sample, then take a second sample of 100.
e. **Accept** – if the cumulative number of errors from both samples of 100 is seven or less, then the whole batch is accepted.
f. **Reject** – if the cumulative number of errors from both samples of 100 is eight or more, then the whole batch is rejected.

Figure 11.10 **An example of a double sampling plan**			
Sample		**Number of errors or defective items**	
#	**Size**	**Acceptable quality level**	**Unacceptable quality level**
1st	100	≤ 2	≤ 7
2nd	100	≤ 7	≤ 8

> **EXECUTIVE INSIGHT**
> Each sampling plan involves a different set of trade-offs between the:
> • **Cost** – of checking and inspecting the services, products and/or delivery systems, and the
> • **Risk** – of accepting bad services or products (the consumer's risk) or rejecting good services or products (the producer's risk).

• Multiple sampling plan – the principle of the double sampling plan can be extended into a multiple sampling plan. In this case, there is an AQL and an **unacceptable quality level (UQL)**. An example of a multiple sampling plan is shown in Figure 11.11. Following this plan, up to four samples are taken until the cumulative results of all the multiple samples fall into either the accept or reject category shown in Figure 11.11.

Unacceptable quality level (UQL) – the percentage defective level at which the total quantity would be rejected.

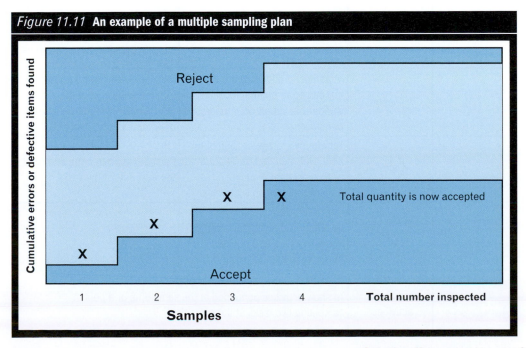

Figure 11.11 **An example of a multiple sampling plan**

- **Sequential sampling plan** – is similar to a multiple plan, but the sample size is one. As with multiple sampling, the results are normally plotted on a graph until sufficient information has been gained on which to make a decision.

Process mapping

A process needs to be mapped to understand how it currently operates before determining how to improve it. In reality, a number of these tools will be used to understand a process before identifying areas for improvement:

- **Process charts** – the principal activities within a process are operations (completing tasks), checks or inspections, transportation, delays and storage (as shown in Figure 11.12). A process chart is used to show the sequence of steps that occur and the time taken to complete each step. As with other analyses, it must be checked using actual information and evidence.

....

> EXECUTIVE INSIGHT

Mapping processes help you to understand how a business currently operates. Until this is known, it is not possible to identify areas for improvement.

....

- **Service maps** – these are used to map the movement of customers, information and materials through a process using the symbols shown in Figure 11.13. As discussed in Chapter 5, a key feature of service delivery is determining the number of customer interfaces, and therefore the line of visibility that separates front-office from back-office activities.

- **Information and material flow charts** – these trace the flow of information and/or materials through the process. It is important to show both physical and electronic

Figure 11.12 **Process chart symbols**

Symbol	Activity	Used to represent	
		Material or information	**Person doing the task**
◯	Operation	Materials, products or information are modified or acted upon during the operation	Person completes an operation or task. This may include preparation for the next activity
▢	Inspection	Materials, products or information are checked and quality, quantity or accuracy is verified	Person checks and verifies for quality, quantity or accuracy at this stage in the process or procedure
⇨	Transport	Materials, products or information are moved to another location without being part of an operation or inspection	Person moves from one position to another as part of the process or procedure without being part of an operation or inspection
◗	Delay	Temporary storage or filing of an item. Not recorded as 'in store' or filed and not requiring authorization for its withdrawal	Person unable to complete the next part of the task
▽	Storage	Controlled storage, governed by authorized receipt and issue; document filed and retained for future reference	Not used
◎	Combined activities	To show activities performed at the same time or a person competing two tasks at the same time	

Figure 11.13 Symbols used in service maps

Symbol	Used to represent
●●●●● ●●●●●●●●●	*Line of visibility* – used to divide the part of the operations visible to the customer (including telephone and written communication) from the rest of the service delivery system
△	*Fail points* – points in the process where there is a high level of service failure
➡	*Service paths* –the optimal and 'when things go wrong' service paths are shown as follows: – Optimal service path – Path where things go wrong
P	*Problem* – indicates where problems occur in a process
D	*Dialogue* – indicates where customer interface with the delivery system takes place - the line of interaction

documents as well as computer screenshots showing the level and type of information used within a process, system or procedure.

- **Person flow charts** – these map the movements of staff as they carry out a task. As with information or material flow process charts, these flow charts show all the operations and inspections that take place, together with any movements and delays.

- Videoing – as well as charting a process, it is useful to video it to see what happens. Videoing has a number of advantages over the other charting methods as it:
  - *Is more accurate* – it provides a complete record of the activities that take place.
  - *Helps process analysis* – it is often easier to assess the process as it can be reviewed many times and allows any number of people to review what happens.
  - *Increases acceptability that problems exist* – those involved in the process more readily accept the record of events (as the camera shows things as they really are) as well as their role within it.

> **Pareto analysis** (the 80/20 rule) – shows the frequency and cost associated with a quality problem. Problems are listed in descending order to highlight those that are causing the greatest cost to the business.

Pareto analysis

As shown in Figure 11.14, we often find that 80 per cent of quality conformance problems result from 20 per cent of causes. This is referred to as the **80/20 rule** and it implies that companies must focus on improving the causes that result in the highest number of problems. To help identify these, companies can use a Pareto analysis listing the quality problems identified, how often they occurred and the costs (for example rectification or reject) associated with each problem. Placing the highest number of occurrences, or total costs depending on which dimension was perceived to be the more relevant, at the top of the list, the second highest next and so on gives a Pareto analysis as shown in Figure 11.14. The principle here is to direct time and resource at the top 20 per cent (or so) that typically accounts for 80 per cent (or so) of the problems. In the example shown in Figure 11.14, this involves not 'accepting late passengers' that accounts for 39 per cent of flight departure delays. Once this problem has been solved, the airline then needs to reduce the number of times a plane is 'waiting for a tug pushback', and so on. As each problem is eliminated, the percentage of incidences caused by the other problems increases.

Figure 11.14 **Pareto analysis of reasons for flight departure delays**

Problem	Percentage of incidents	Cumulative percentage
Accepting late passengers	39	39
Waiting for tug pushback	24	63
Waiting for refuelling	14	77
Late weight and balance sheet	9	86
Cabin cleaners take longer than scheduled	8	94
Waiting for food services	4	98
Other	2	100

Scatter diagrams

Scatter diagrams can be used to graphically illustrate the bivariate relationship between two variables, such as 'percentage of rejects' and the 'length of a production run' as shown in Figure 11.15. From this diagram, we can see that as the run length increases, the percentage of rejects decreases and this decline follows a consistent pattern.

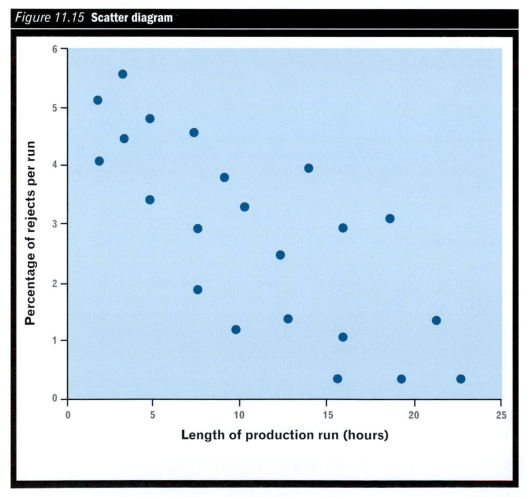

Figure 11.15 **Scatter diagram**

> **EXECUTIVE INSIGHT**
> Scatter diagrams identify the relationship between two variables.

Cause and effect diagrams

Cause and effect (or fishbone) diagrams – identify the potential causes of quality failure to help identify the root cause of a problem, identify relationships between causes and determine which ones to address first.

Also known as **fishbone diagrams** (due to their shape) or Ishikawa charts (after the person who developed them), cause and effect diagrams identify potential causes and help direct improvement efforts to the most likely causes of quality conformance problems. These diagrams are built through the following steps:

1. **Identify the problem to be addressed** – this becomes the label for the root effect arrow. For example, Figure 11.16 looks at the potential reasons why a flight departure is delayed.
2. **Identify the major categories of causes** – the second step is to identify major categories of causes for the problem identified in step 1. These are then drawn at an angle to the root effect arrow. For example, in Figure 11.16 flight delays could be

Figure 11.16 **Cause and effect diagram used to ascertain the cause of flight delays**

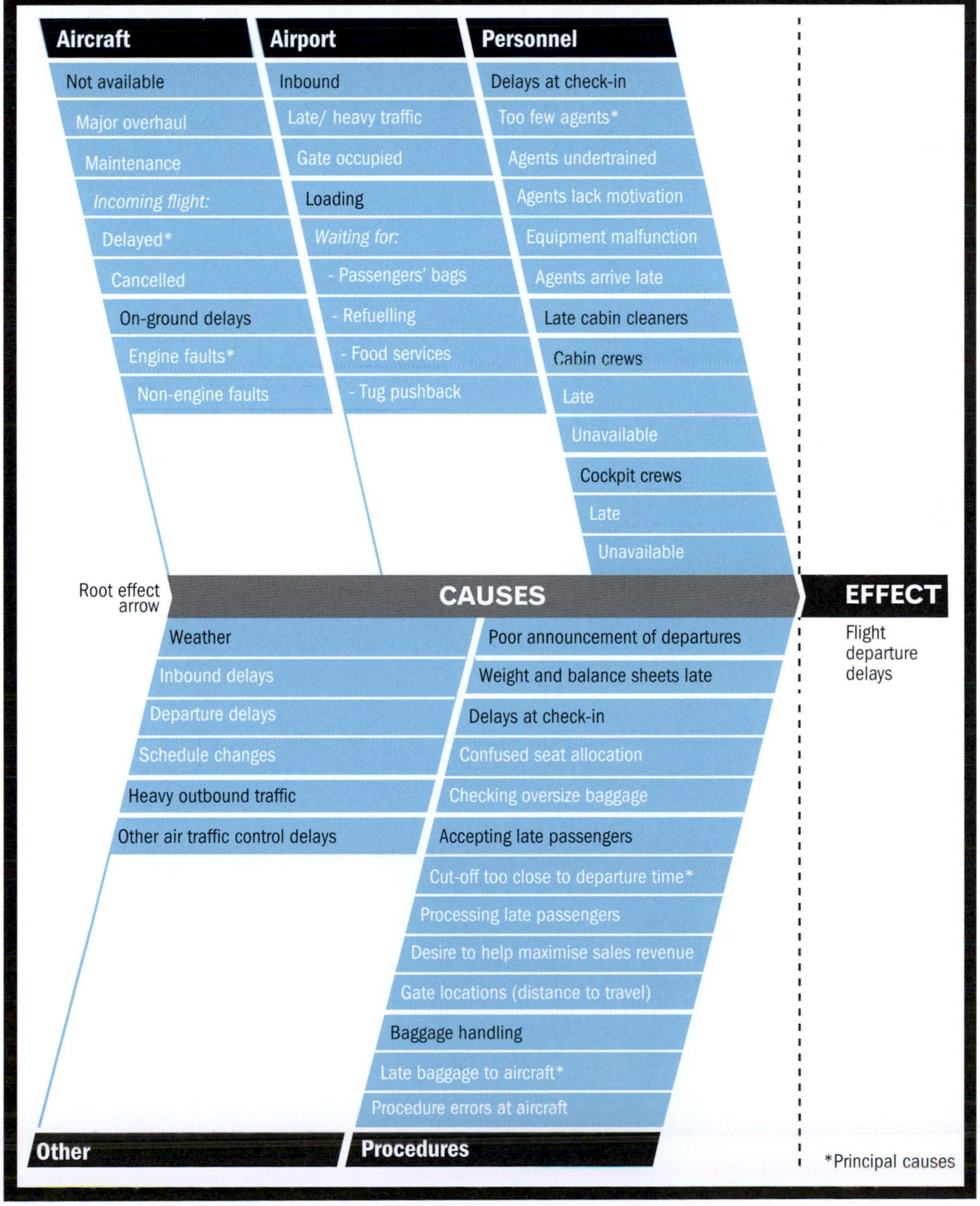

caused by problems with the aircraft, airport, personnel, procedures or other factors such as weather, outbound traffic and air traffic control.

3. **List all the detailed causes** – the next step is to list all the detailed causes within each of the major categories. For example, personnel problems can result from delays at check-in, late cabin cleaners, cabin crews and cockpit crews (see Figure 11.16).

4. **Identify the principal causes** – the final step is to identify the principal causes within the list of detailed causes based on frequency data that might have been gathered through a checklist or a Pareto analysis. For example, the major causes of flight departure delays are incoming flight delays, engine faults, too few agents at check-in, agreeing to accept late passengers too close to the departure time and baggage arriving late to the aircraft (see Figure 11.16).

This process helps to identify the root cause of a problem, to identify relationships between causes and to determine which ones to address first. So, based on the information in Figure 11.16, airlines need to focus on: increasing the reliability of their aircraft engines; having more agents at check-in; stopping late passengers from being accepted onto the plane; and ensuring the baggage arrives earlier to the aircraft.

> **EXECUTIVE INSIGHT**
Cause and effect diagrams should be used to identify the root cause of a problem so that it can be solved and prevented from recurring.

Gap analysis

The gap model, initially developed by Parasuraman, Zeithaml and Berry[1], can be used to understand why a **customer's perception** of a service or product does not match the **expectations** that they had. As Figure 11.17 shows, the overall gap between customer expectations and perceptions of a service or product (Gap 5) is an accumulation of four other gaps that may exist:

1. **Knowledge gap** – Gap 1 occurs when there is a difference between customer expectations and management's concept of the service or product. For example, this would occur if a hotel manager does not know what customers expect from their room or any additional services they may require. Aspects that can cause this are poor communication between customers and top management, too many management layers within the business and inadequate customer research.

2. **Design gap** – Gap 2 occurs when the service or product design does not match management's perceptions of customer expectations. For example, a restaurant manager may realize that customers expect to be served within 20 minutes of ordering, but may not have an operation designed to do this. This gap can result from aspects such as inadequate service design or delivery.

3. **Performance gap** – Gap 3 occurs when the service or product delivery does not match its design (quality conformance). Aspects that can cause this include inadequate employee skills, lack of training, lack of responsibility and poorly defined roles.

4. **Communication gap** – Gap 4 occurs when the service or product delivery does not match what customers have been promised. For example, a hotel may show beautiful rooms, swimming pools and lobbies in its adverts that are different to those actually used by its customers. This gap can result from factors such as over-promising and poor communication with the advertising agency a company uses.

Customer perceptions – these come from customers' actual experience of the quality of a service or product delivered to them.

Customer expectations (of the quality of a service or product) – these come from what customers have been promised by communication from the company (such as advertising) or other customers who previously experienced the service or product.

As with the cause and effect diagram, this technique can be used to identify the root cause of a problem by looking at the relationships between different causes and determining which ones to address first.

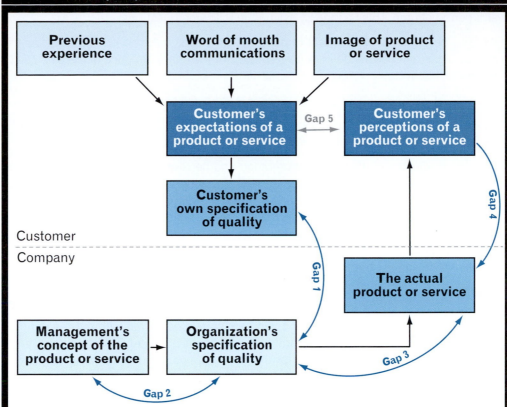

Figure 11.17 The gap model for understanding the difference between customers' expectations and perceptions

Source: Slack, N., Chambers, S. and Johnston, R. *Operations Management*, 6th edn. Pearson Education Limited. Adapted from Parasuraman, A., et al. (1985) 'A conceptual model of service quality and implications for future research'. Reproduced with permission of the American Marketing Association.

Kaizen – Japanese for 'improvement' or 'change for the better' and occurs when everyone in the organization continually looks for ways to improve how it operates.

Kaizen blitz events – focused improvement activities used to address a particular issue within five days or less, such as changing the process, layout or procedures used within an operation.

> **EXECUTIVE INSIGHT**
> Gap analysis identifies exactly why a customer's perception of the quality of a service or product is less than their expectations, so that this problem can be solved and prevented from recurring.

Breakthrough projects

Breakthrough projects (often known as '**Kaizen blitz events**') occur when a small group of employees (usually five or six) are taken out of their day jobs for a short period (usually 2–5 days) to analyze part of the business, identify changes and make improvements. By dedicating employee time in this way, significant changes can be made to procedures, paperwork, process activities, layout, roles, responsibilities and the like within a few days while often leading to subsequent projects working with IT and engineering. The advantage of this approach is that changes are made quickly by people who work within the process and have an incentive for making it work better.

> **EXECUTIVE INSIGHTS**
> Breakthrough projects involve taking employees out of their day jobs and dedicating them to improvement activities for 2–5 days. These can be very effective in:
>
> • Starting an improvement process
> • Understanding major problems, and
> • Making significant improvements.

Control charts

Control charts can be used to monitor a process and ensure that it performs consistently over a period of time. This is done by asking the following questions:

- *What?* – determine which aspect of performance needs to be controlled, such as the output of the process, its delivery performance or the characteristics of the services or products it delivers.

- *Where?* – at which points within the delivery system will performance be measured.

- *How?* – which control charts will be used to measure performance, how frequently performance will be measured and what sample size will be taken.

- *By whom?* – who will measure performance and be responsible for taking corrective action for improving performance when it moves either above the upper control limit or below the lower control limit (Figure 11.18). It is usually best if the person delivering the service or product is also responsible for measuring and improving its quality.

Using this approach, control charts can be used to ensure that a process performs within specified limits against both its variable and attribute characteristics:

- *Control charts for variables* The original design of a service or product usually specifies the mean (average) and acceptable levels of deviation for each of its characteristics. For example, a retailer may specify that customers should be served within three minutes on average, but that between two and four minutes is acceptable. In this case, three minutes is the mean performance for this process, two minutes is the lower control limit and four minutes the **upper control limit**. The level of time to serve a customer should then be monitored by selecting an agreed sample of customers (for example, 20 per cent) at agreed intervals (such as every half an hour). The level of time to serve a customer could then be measured over the day and plotted on a chart similar to that shown in Figure 11.18. If a customer was served within less than two minutes or more than four minutes, the cause of this would need to be identified and, if necessary, corrective action taken (here it could be to reduce or increase the number of staff in certain time periods) to stop this from recurring.

- *Control charts for attributes* Similarly, performance against attribute characteristics can also be measured and plotted on a control chart, as shown in Figure 11.19. For example, a restaurant may measure whether customers are satisfied with the level of service they have received by simply using a 'yes' or a 'no' tick box on a compliment slip. The level of customer satisfaction could then be measured for an agreed sample

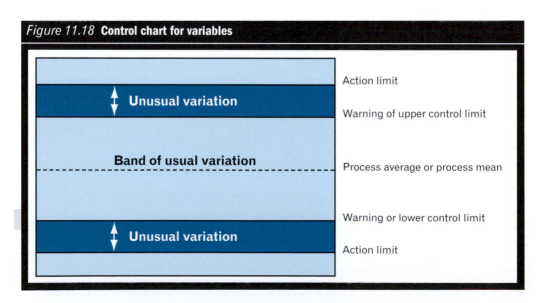

Figure 11.18 **Control chart for variables**

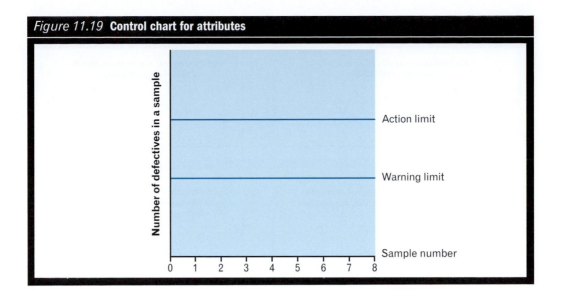

Figure 11.19 **Control chart for attributes**

of customers (such as 80 per cent or possibly even all customers) at agreed intervals (for example, every half an hour) and plotted on a chart similar to that shown in Figure 11.19. If a customer was not satisfied, the cause of this would need to be identified and, where necessary, corrective action taken to stop this from recurring.

Statistical process control

Statistical process control involves methodically using control charts across a business similar to those shown in Figures 11.18, 11.19 and 11.20 to help employees identify areas of underperformance and take corrective action. It is important to recognize that the purpose of this is not simply to achieve a situation where all sample points are within the upper and lower control limits. Once this happens, the control limits then need to be reviewed and brought closer to the average value, so setting new targets to further improve performance. Typically, a business should aim to have two-thirds of the points within the limits as this means it is continuously looking for ways to reduce variability and improve the overall performance of its processes.

> **EXECUTIVE INSIGHT**
> Control charts can be used to control any aspect of a process to ensure that it performs within specified limits. These limits need to be continually reviewed to ensure that the performance of the process is being continually improved.

Six-sigma quality

Some companies have chosen to take statistical process control one step further and set a 'six-sigma' quality target for their organization. For example, in the late 1980s Motorola's Semiconductor Products Division challenged itself to make only 3.4 defective products within every million it made (the target by setting a goal of six-sigma quality), and then set a similar target for its product design, sales and service functions. Most companies currently fall well short of such a target, typically generating about 35,000 defects per million, which sounds (and is) a lot and constitutes, in statistical terms, three-and-a-half-sigma quality (Figure 11.21). As such, pursuing this sort of initiative will help a company to gain a competitive advantage that can be used to drive a market in a new direction. Examples of companies who have managed to do this are: General Electric; 3M (Case 11.6), which makes a wide range of products from dental fillings to Scotchguard tape; Sun Microsystems, a manufacturer of servers and software; Carlson Companies, whose businesses include the Radisson hotel chain; and Home Depot, the US retailer.

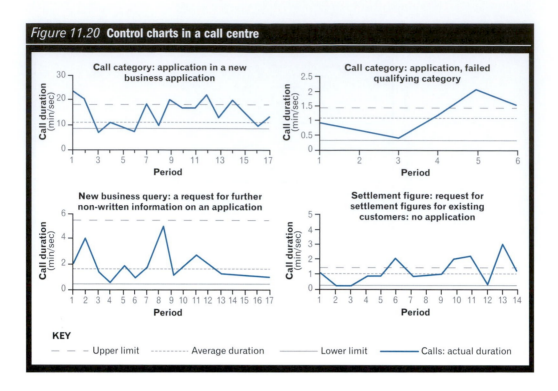

Figure 11.20 Control charts in a call centre

Figure 11.21 Specification limits and their corresponding percentage of good quality and defects per million

Specification limit	# Defects per million	Percentage good quality
±one sigma	691,000	31.00
±two sigma	308,700	39.13
±three sigma	66,810	93.32
±three and a half sigma	35,900	96.41
±four sigma	6,210	99.37
±five sigma	233	99.98
±six sigma	3.4	99.99

> **EXECUTIVE INSIGHT**

Six sigma involves using control charts to measure, control and improve all aspects of performance within your business with the ultimate aim of having less than 3.4 defects per million for all the activities completed and services or products delivered by your business.

Tools and techniques in practice

This section looks at how you would apply some of the tools and techniques identified earlier to manage quality in the supply chain, checking bought-in services and products and delivering services and products to customers.

Managing the supply chain

Companies need to control the quality of the services, products and processes they have outsourced. It is impossible to control their own in-house delivery systems and processes if the quality of these inputs is out of control. To do this, companies must follow seven key steps:

1. **Develop a precise service and/or product specification** – explaining what suppliers need to deliver in terms of the variable and attribute characteristics that have to be met, as outlined earlier. Having a detailed and accurate purchasing specification is critical when the service or product is:
   - Expensive
   - Bought in large quantities
   - Critical to the service or product mix that is subsequently delivered to the customer
   - Expensive or difficult to rework after it has been delivered.

2. **Do not base the purchase decision on price alone** – all of the market order-winners that the company has to support should be used in the supplier selection criteria, such as service design, after-sales support, delivery reliability and quality conformance.

3. **Develop a vendor appraisal system** – to assess the ability of a supplier to deliver services and/or products at the required level of quality conformance before an order is placed.

4. **Evaluate supplier performance** – to determine the total cost of quality for the services and products they deliver.

5. **Benchmark suppliers** – against each other in terms of their performance.

6. **Publish benchmarks** – so that suppliers can see how they are performing against each other.

7. **Reward and recognize suppliers for good performance** – by giving them more business and recognizing them through methods such as non-financial rewards.

Proactively managing bought-out service and product quality

When service design, product design and/or quality conformance are an order-winner or qualifier for an organization's end customer, then it is critical that the quality levels of bought-in services and products are evaluated before deciding to use them. However, most organizations only check the quality levels of services or products once they have been purchased. Examples of how this is done in different industries are:

- **Passenger airline** – as described in the end of chapter case in Chapter 1, Southwest Airlines uses its customers to help select and interview its new employees before they are recruited.

- **Consultancy services** – senior consultants are often financially rewarded for finding new employees and suppliers. These consultants then form part of an extensive selection procedure used to evaluate the employee's or supplier's capability before they start working with them.

- **Executive education** – senior academics will interview part-time staff and observe their teaching before they employ them.

- **Aerospace** – sophisticated quality assurance procedures are used to meet the high safety and traceability requirements of their end customers. These must be in place before services and products can be supplied.

Reactively managing bought-out service and product quality

Even with these proactive checks in place, it is also often necessary to check the quality of a service or product after it has been delivered. Critical decisions here concern:

- **Determining number of samples** – to be checked and/or inspected

- **Determining size of sample(s)** – to be checked and/or inspected

- **Setting acceptance quality level (AQL)** – the maximum percentage of defective services or products that can be accepted

- **Setting unacceptable quality level (UQL)** – the percentage of defective services or products that would be rejected.

Essentially, this involves a trade-off between cost and risk where the business has to try to reduce the cost of checking and inspection without increasing the risk of either accepting an unacceptable batch (the consumer's risk) or rejecting an acceptable batch (the producer's risk). To help make this decision, it is useful to plot an operating characteristic (OC) curve as shown in Figure 11.22 using statistical tables that have been developed for each particular situation. In the case of Figure 11.22, we can see that having an AQL of 2 per cent and a UQL of 15 per cent would result in:

- **Producer's risk** – 5 per cent probability of good services or products being rejected.

- **Consumer's risk** – 10 per cent probability of bad services or products being accepted.

To decrease or increase this risk, the OC curve can be changed by moving to a sampling plan with different numbers of samples, sample sizes, AQL or UQL. For example, Figure 11.23 shows the reduced producer and consumer risk of moving from a single to a double sampling plan.

Delivering services and products

Variability is inherent in all delivery systems and processes. However, before this variability can be managed, controlled and reduced, the variations need to be split into:

- **Predictable variations** – caused by known and predictable reasons, and

- **Unpredictable variations** – caused by random and unplanned events.

Once the variations in the delivery system have been identified and classified, then the unpredictable variations have to be investigated so that they eventually become predictable. All predictable variations can then be planned for and eliminated if the investment required to do this is justified.

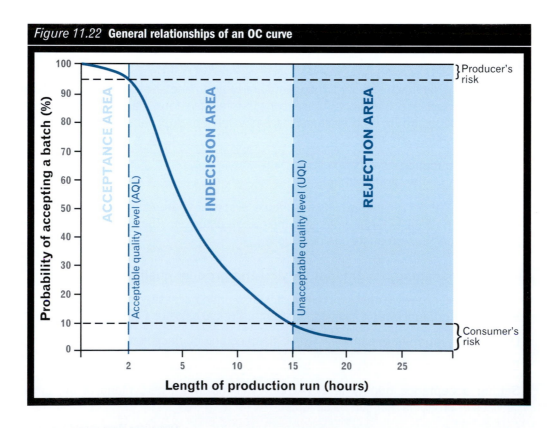

Figure 11.22 **General relationships of an OC curve**

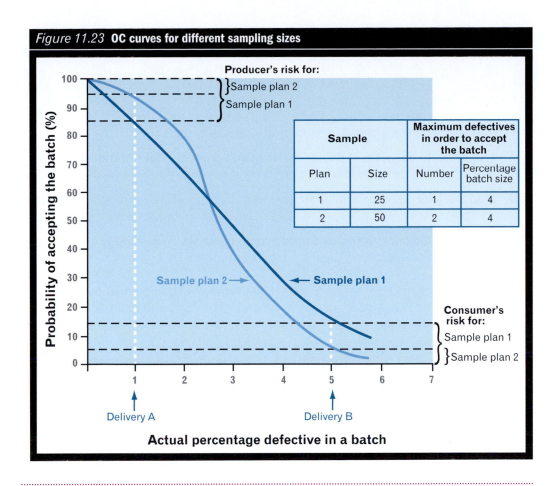

Figure 11.23 OC curves for different sampling sizes

Sample		Maximum defectives in order to accept the batch	
Plan	Size	Number	Percentage batch size
1	25	1	4
2	50	2	4

Approaches to managing quality

This section looks at the management philosophies (such as total quality management) and systems and procedures (such as ISO 9000, the Baldrige Award and the EFQM Excellence Award) that can be used to manage quality within an organization.

Total quality management philosophy

Total quality management (TQM) is a philosophy and set of guiding principles for managing quality within an organization. It embraces a number of management theories, approaches, tools and practices that can help a business improve performance by increasing the level of service and product quality conformance and decreasing costs by focusing on seven key elements:

1. **Understand and work out how to meet customer needs and expectations** – understand the key order-winners and qualifiers and how these should be met.

2. **Cover all functions** – all functions must be involved in improving quality.

3. **Involve all levels** – everyone in the organization must be involved.

> **Total quality management (TQM)** – a philosophy and set of guiding principles for managing quality within an organization.

4. **Examine the current cost of quality** – this is done in order to determine the impact of the existing level of quality conformance and the key areas to improve first, by looking at the following sources of cost (see the earlier section on Juran):
   - External failure – loss of custom, warranty costs and customer complaints
   - Internal failure – scrap, rework and lost production time
   - Appraisal – inspection, quality control and customer surveys
   - Prevention – quality systems, design costs and quality training.

5. **Work out how to design and deliver services and products right first time** – to help reduce the quality costs identified above.

6. **Develop a quality management approach** – doing this will allow a company to manage quality conformance, as discussed in more detail in the following section.

7. **Continuously look for ways to improve the business** – the organization must continuously assess its capabilities, looking for improvements through all its activities.

TQM requires a broadening of outlooks and skills, an innovative approach to improvement, a more sophisticated application of quality management tools and approaches and an increased emphasis on people and their involvement. A number of aspects are required to make these changes, including:

- **Develop a quality strategy** – that integrates into the overall business strategy and covers all the functions and levels within an organization. Quality conformance needs to be built into all aspects of service and product design and delivery and form part of the way their performance is measured.

- **Get top-management support** – as with many approaches, the belief and commitment by those at the top of an organization is critical to its success. TQM will not succeed unless it is prioritized and given the appropriate time and resource from the business.

- **Use a TQM steering group** – to guide its implementation, prioritize areas for improvement and allocate time and resources to improvement projects.

- **Use improvement teams** – managers need to release and empower people to form improvement teams to identify and make improvements. This helps gain the commitment and participation necessary to implement this initiative.

- **Recognize success** – improvements must be recognized and encouraged through regular communication, feedback and support. For example, communicating performance against targets; and benchmarking them against other parts of the business.

- **Use quality tools and approaches** – to identify problems, facilitate improvements, implement solutions and sustain the new ways of working.

- **Train staff in TQM aims and tools** – everyone needs to have a general awareness of quality management aims, tools and techniques. A formal education programme is required to help people identify and make improvements.

For many organizations, a TQM approach requires significantly different attitudes, behaviours and working practices for it to be adopted throughout the organization. Case 11.6 illustrates that although James McNerney launched a corporate-wide quality initiative when he arrived at 3M, he knew that it would take 10–15 years to change the **DNA** of the organization. In fact, it took Japanese companies more than 30 years to change their reputation for producing poor quality products! However, to start this journey, companies need to make:

- Everyone responsible for their own quality

- Improvement part of everyone's job

- Everyone focus on meeting customers' needs

TQM steering group – a cross-functional group or committee that guides the implementation of TQM initiatives within an organization by prioritising areas for improvement and allocating time and resource to improvement projects.

DNA – the DNA of an organization can be described as its values, philosophy, personality and behaviour.

Case 11.6 3M: COMMITTING TO QUALITY IMPROVEMENT

In 2001, James McNerney became CEO at 3M (the multi-national conglomerate corporation behind a wide range of brands in the fields of technology, stationery and health care). He immediately launched a corporate-wide quality initiative by introducing a one-week training programme for all 28,000 employees and selecting 500 up-and-coming managers to work full time on quality programmes over the first two years. However, he knew that things were not going to change overnight and saw this as the first step in a 10–15-year journey to change the DNA of the 3M organization. Joseph M. Juran was a management consultant (see also the earlier section outlining his contribution) who was well known for his many books on quality management. He believed that it takes at least six, and more usually 10, years for companies to become quality leaders within their industries. Because of this, companies must not use top management-led programmes that aim to change the whole company at once. The Harvard professor Mike Beer has argued that it is a mistake to think that a large company can be changed all at once, something he terms 'the fallacy of programmatic change'. To make improvements, organizations must bring about change unit by unit in order to get real buy-in from the organization as a whole.

www.3m.com

Sources: Beer, M., Eisenstat, R.A., and Spector, B. (1990) 'Why change programs don't produce change', *Harvard Business Review*, **68**(6), pp. 158–66. Juran, J.M. (1989) *Juran on Leadership for Quality: An Executive Handbook*. New York: Free Press.

Questions

1. What do these examples say about how firms should introduce TQM?

2. What do you think of James McNerney's approach to introducing TQM at 3M?

Lecturers: visit www.palgrave.com/business/hillom3e for teaching guidelines for this case study

- Suppliers and customers part of the improvement process

- Any mistakes made be viewed as opportunities for improvement rather than reasons for criticism.

Quality management frameworks: ISO 9000, Baldrige Award and EFQM Excellence Award

Although most companies have developed their own approaches to managing quality, a number of formal national and international systems are also available to help organizations consistently design and deliver services and products in line with their specifications. The three most widely used programmes – ISO 9000, the Baldrige Award and the EFQM Excellence Award – are now discussed in more detail.

ISO 9000

Established in 1947, the International Organization for Standardization (ISO) is a non-government body that secures international agreements on key topics and publishes these as international standards in over 100 countries. In 1987, it published the ISO 9000 series as a set of internationally accepted standards for business quality and certifications have now been awarded to over 400,000 firms in 158 countries. Most countries have their own equivalent, if not identical, standards, but accept ISO 9000 as the internationally recognized and accepted certification. They provide a framework that governs the activities and procedures that help companies control their processes within a variety of aspects of their business such as:

Traceability records – show the complete history of a service or product by recording the person, material or information used in each step of its design or delivery.

- Designing and developing new services and products

- Controlling materials and keeping **traceability records**

- Controlling processes for delivering services and products

- Inspecting, measuring and testing services and products

- Handling, storing and packing products

- Servicing products after they have been installed

- Maintaining and auditing quality records for all of the above aspects.

Baldrige Award

In response to the competitive challenges it faced in the early 1980s, the US government developed the Baldrige Award to recognize and encourage quality and productivity improvements by:

Best practice – the most effective way of designing or delivering a service or product.

- Stimulating companies to attain excellence in quality

- Recognizing outstanding companies and helping disseminate experience and **best practice** across companies

- Establishing guidelines for organizations on how to assess and manage quality

• Gathering information on how to change **corporate cultures** and practices to help develop best practice.

The award is administered annually by the National Institute of Standards and Technology with companies being reviewed by independent outsiders, onsite visits and judges. The award examines a business using the seven categories outlined in Figure 11.24 with the emphasis placed on business results which account for 450 of the 1,000 total points awarded. Companies can apply for the award in the service, manufacturing or small business (less than 500 staff) categories. Up to two companies in each category are given the award each year and past winners include Motorola, Xerox, Federal Express, Ritz-Carlton Hotels, AT&T, Cadillac and Texas Instruments.

> **EXECUTIVE INSIGHT**
The Baldrige Award is a good target for the US facilities and operations within your organization.

Figure 11.24 **Baldrige Award criteria for performance excellence**

Categories and items	Points	
1 Leadership		**120**
· Organizational leadership	70	
· Social responsibility	50	
2 Strategic planning		**85**
· Strategy development	40	
· Strategy deployment	45	
3 Customer and market focus		**85**
· Customer and market knowledge	40	
· Customer relationships and satisfaction	45	
4 Measurement, analysis and knowledge management		**90**
· Measurement and analysis of organizational performance	45	
· Information and knowledge management	45	
5 Human resource focus		**85**
· Work systems	35	
· Employee learning and motivation	25	
· Employee well-being and satisfaction	25	
6 Process management		**85**
· Value creation processes	50	
· Support processes	35	
7 Business results		**450**
· Customer-focused results	75	
· Product and service results	75	
· Financial and market results	75	
· Human resource results	75	
· Organizational effectiveness results	75	
· Governance and social responsibility results	75	
Total		**1,000**

Source: Baldrige National Quality Programme, 2009–2010, www.baldrige.nist.gov.

EFQM Excellence Award

The EFQM was founded in 1988 and now has over 850 members. In 1992, it launched its Excellence Award (initially called the European Quality Award) to recognize quality achievement, with companies applying each year for a national award with the top firms

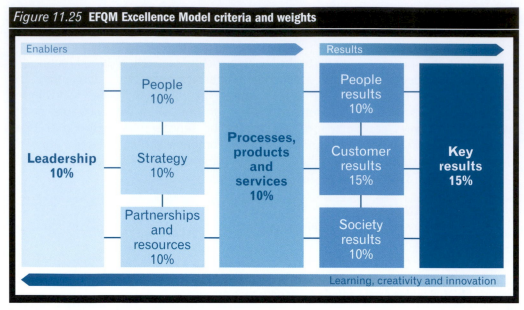

Figure 11.25 **EFQM Excellence Model criteria and weights**

Source: www.efqm.org, © EFQM 2009.

from each country competing for a European award. Figure 11.25 shows how 1,000 points are awarded across nine aspects:

1. **Leadership** – how its leaders inspire, support and promote a quality culture

2. **Policy and strategy** – how it formulates, deploys, reviews and implements its quality policy and strategy

3. **People** – how it realizes the potential of its people

4. **Partnerships and resources** – how effectively and efficiently it manages resources

5. **Processes** – how it identifies, manages, reviews and improves its processes

6. **Customer results** – how satisfied are its external customers

7. **People results** – how satisfied are its employees

8. **Society results** – how satisfied are the local, national and international communities within which it operates

9. **Key performance results** – is it meeting its planned objectives and satisfying the needs and expectations of everyone with a financial interest or stake in the organization.

> **EXECUTIVE INSIGHT**
  The EFQM Excellence Award is a good target for the European facilities and operations within your organization.

Managing quality in practice

When managing and improving the levels of quality in your business, it is important to consider the following aspects:

- **Developing a business case for quality improvement** – to win management support for investing time and money in managing and improving quality. Otherwise, the quality improvement budget will be cut as soon as there is pressure to use this time and money elsewhere in the business. In particular, it is important to show the expected financial impact of the initiatives, such as:
  - *Reduced costs* – the cost of quality is typically 15–20 per cent of a company's sales revenue. You need to understand this in detail by identifying the current internal, external, appraisal and prevention costs and showing how they can be reduced. Typically, internal and external costs account for 50-80 per cent of the total cost of quality, so these are initially the main areas to focus on.
  - *Increased sales revenue* – quality conformance is usually an order-winner or qualifier in most markets. It is therefore important to show how increasing quality conformance levels will impact sales revenue by helping to win new customers and retain existing customers.

- **Understanding market requirements** – quality conformance is usually an order-winner or qualifier in most markets. However, it is important to understand how its level of importance varies within the current and future markets that the business wishes to support as this will determine its role in retaining and increasing sales revenue.

- **Developing a quality programme** – to create a quality habit within the organization by:
  - *Proactively improving quality* – use statistical tools and techniques to identify potential problems so you can prevent them from occurring. Reactive quality improvement must only be seen as a short-term solution.
  - *Controlling then improving* – once the level of quality conformance is consistent and under control, it can then be improved. It is impossible to improve a delivery system or process that still has 'unpredictable variation'.
  - *Using breakthrough projects* – to fix chronic problems.
  - *Publishing and recognizing good performance* – achieved by both your own employees and also those within your suppliers.

- **Realize this is a long journey** – it takes 10–15 years to change the DNA of an organization.

Driving business performance

Releasing cash

The main objective of improving quality would not be to release cash. However, cash may be released as a result of quality improvement. For example:

- **Finished goods inventory** – better matching service and products designs with customer needs should, in turn, help reduce finished inventory levels and obsolescence.

- **Buffer inventory** – lower levels need to be held as the quality levels of external suppliers and internal delivery systems becomes more predictable.

Improving market support

Quality conformance is either an order-winner or qualifier in most markets. Some examples of how different tools and techniques can be used to improve quality conformance are:

- **Measuring existing quality levels** – using checklists and sampling plans

- **Understanding existing processes** – using process charts, service maps, information and material flow charts, person flow charts and videoing

- **Identifying improvement areas** – using Pareto analysis

- **Determining causes of poor quality** – using scatter diagrams, cause and effect diagrams, and gap analysis

- **Making improvements** – using breakthrough projects

- **Controlling improved processes** – so that the improvements are maintained using control charts, statistical process control and six-sigma quality.

Reducing costs

The cost of quality within many organizations is 15–20 per cent of sales. Significant cost reductions can be made by reducing the various costs of quality within the business including:

- **Internal cost of failure** – defects, rework, yield losses, re-inspection and disposal

- **External costs of failure** – complaints, returns, after-sales service and repairs

- **Appraisal costs** – inspection, checks, quality assurance and the cost of test equipment

- **Prevention costs** – quality planning, new service and product reviews and data collection, analysis and reporting.

Typically, internal and external costs account for 50–80 per cent of the total cost of quality, so these are initially the main areas for improvement.

The evolution of quality management

The evolution of quality management has, to some extent, come full circle. In times before the Industrial Revolution, skilled craftsmen were responsible for both delivery (making services and products) and quality (ensuring they met their design specification). After the Industrial Revolution, production volumes increased and firms decided to make different individuals and departments responsible for delivery and quality. However, as Figure 11.26 shows, systems for monitoring and managing quality have evolved rapidly since the 1970s with simple inspection activities first replaced by quality control, then enhanced by quality assurance, with many organizations now working towards a TQM philosophy where everyone in an organization is again responsible for the quality of the work they produce.

Applying quality approaches to other aspects of business performance

The need for quality improvement to be applied at all levels and all aspects of a business has been recently highlighted by the scandals at WorldCom, Enron, Tyco, Parmalat and the banking activities that led to the recent world recession. As a result, the Baldrige Award now includes 'Governance and social responsibility results' (Figure 11.24) and the EFQM Excellence Model also includes 'Society results' (Figure 11.25). Quality tools, techniques and approaches could easily be used to improve executive board performance by looking at factors such as how the organization uses independent directors, governs the business, complies with accounting regulations and compensates its executives. Companies that start applying quality approaches to other aspects of their business may be the ones that succeed and prosper or, at least, will not be the ones that stumble and fall.

Summary

- Quality conformance is either an order-winner or a qualifier in most markets. However, the word 'quality' needs to be defined before it can be measured. For operations, quality conformance means consistently delivering services and products in line with their design specifications, which, in turn, reflects customer needs.

- To manage quality, firms must first control it by determining which quality characteristics need to be delivered, deciding how to measure each of these quality characteristics, setting the required level of quality for each characteristic, and monitoring quality levels to ensure that these standards are met.

- Once the level of quality conformance is consistent and under control, it can then be maintained by correcting quality if it falls below the required standard, and continually improving the management of quality levels.

- A number of tools and techniques have been developed to help organizations improve their level of quality conformance for designing or delivering services and products. Some of the main tools used to improve quality are:
  - **Checklists** – for collecting information recording the size and other dimensions of quality (and other) problems
  - **Pareto analysis** – for identifying the frequency of causes of quality conformance problems
  - **Cause and effect diagrams** – for identifying the root cause of a problem, identifying the relationships between causes and determining which ones to address first
  - **Gap analysis** – for understanding why there is a gap between customers' expectations and perceptions by identifying whether there is a gap in knowledge, design, performance or communication
  - **Control charts** – to control a process and ensure that it performs within specified limits.

Figure 11.26 **The evolution in managing quality**

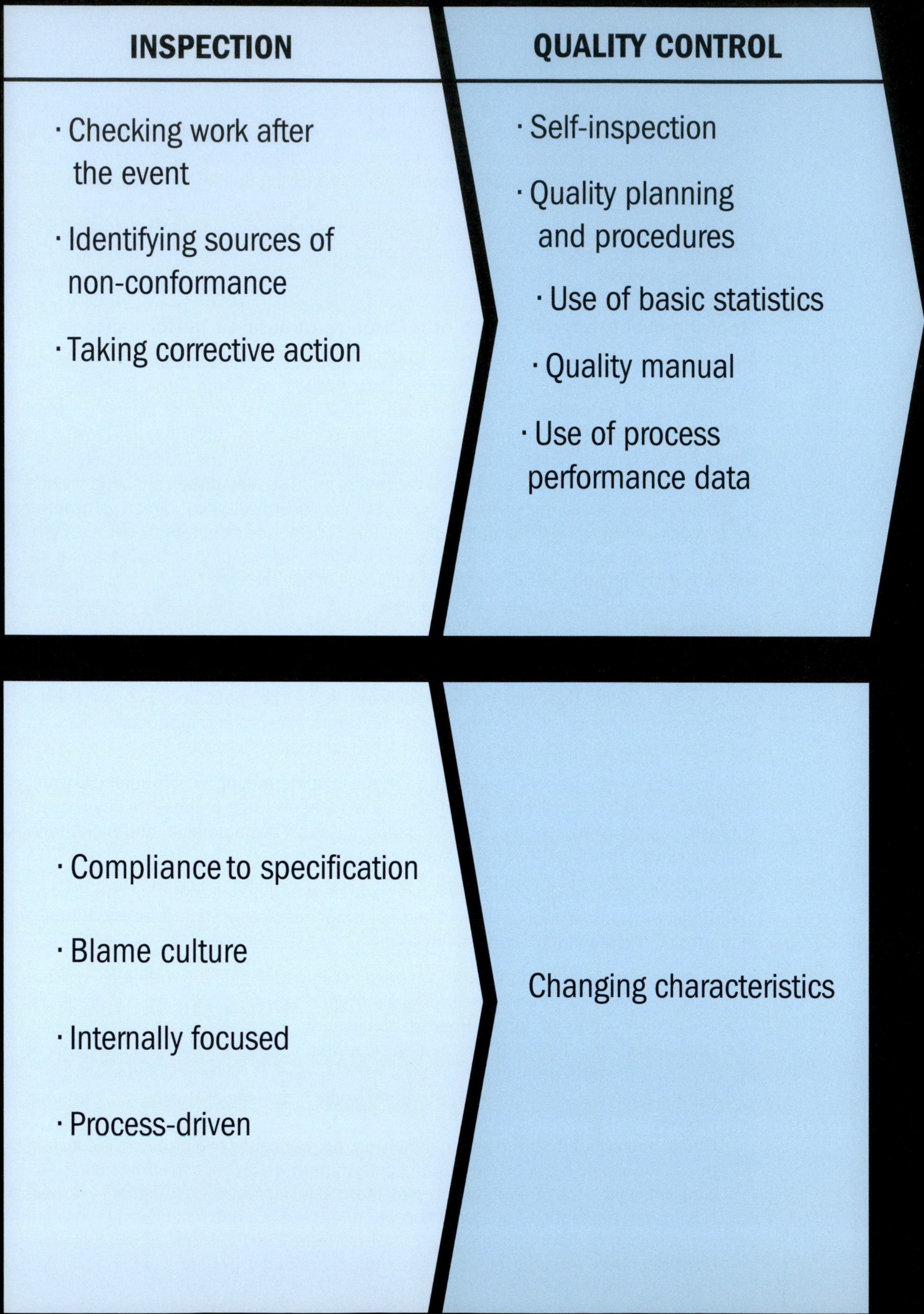

INSPECTION	QUALITY CONTROL
· Checking work after the event	· Self-inspection
· Identifying sources of non-conformance	· Quality planning and procedures
· Taking corrective action	· Use of basic statistics
	· Quality manual
	· Use of process performance data

· Compliance to specification	
· Blame culture	Changing characteristics
· Internally focused	
· Process-driven	

QUALITY ASSURANCE	TQM
· Develop quality systems	· Teamwork
· Use of quality cost data	· Employee involvement
· Quality planning	· Process management
· Use of statistical process control	· Performance measurement
· Involve non-operations functions	· Involves: - all operations - suppliers and customers

	TQM
and switch in orientation	· Continuous improvement
	· Involvement
	· Ownership of issues
	· Empowerment of people
	· Externally focused
	· Customer driven

- TQM is an approach and set of guiding principles for managing quality within an organization by focusing on seven key elements:
  1. Meeting customers' needs and expectations
  2. Covering all parts of the organization
  3. Involving everyone in the organization
  4. Examining all quality costs
  5. Getting things right first time
  6. Developing quality systems and procedures
  7. Continuously making improvements.

- TQM can be implemented by:
  - Developing a quality strategy and getting top-management support
  - Using a steering group
  - Using improvement teams
  - Recognizing success
  - Using quality tools and approaches
  - Training staff in the aims and tools of TQM.

- The successful implementation of TQM often requires a culture change. It is necessary for employees to be responsible for their own quality and for the task of making improvements to become part of everyone's job. Employees must focus on meeting customers' needs, and suppliers and customers should be involved in the improvement process. A working culture needs to be developed where mistakes are seen as opportunities for improvement rather than reasons for criticism.

- Although most companies have developed their own approaches to managing quality, a number of formal national and international frameworks are also available to help organizations consistently design and deliver services and products in line with their specifications. The three most widely used programmes are ISO 9000, the Baldrige Award and the EFQM Excellence Award.

Study activities

Discussion questions

1. The table below lists data concerning the errors in an account management function in the financial services sector.

Error type	Frequency in last period	Estimated costs involved (£s)
A	40	12,500
B	4	2,800
C	33	36,000
D	56	15,500
E	22	7,500
F	12	5,750
G	16	23,000
H	28	116,000

Prepare two Pareto lists – the first based on frequency and the second on estimated costs. Comment on these rankings.

2. Discuss the advantages and disadvantages of staff recording their own performance data in the form of a control chart and analyzing the outcomes for the delivery system for which they are responsible.

3. Explain what is meant by acceptance sampling.
   Give an example of each of the sampling plans included in this chapter.

4. The evolution in how best to manage quality has been described as follows:

Product reliability ⟶ Process reliability ⟶ People reliability ⟶ Total quality management

Comment on these rankings.

5. What are the advantages and disadvantages of 100 per cent inspection?

Assignments

1. Draw a fishbone diagram to represent why your car might be two hours later than the promised completion time at an auto service centre.

2. To access part of its service delivery system, a fast-food chain undertakes regular checks on certain elements of the system. One such check at an outlet revealed the control data below.

Aspects	Product freshness (minutes)	Queue length (# customers)	Time to serve (# minutes)	Cleanliness	
				Floor (# items)	# Tables not cleaned
Upper control limit	7.0	8.0	3.0	10	6
Average	3.0	4.0	2.0	5	4
Lower control limit	1.0	2.0	0.5	0	0
Sample #					
1	6.5	3.0	1.5	8	3
2	4.5	7.0	3.0	6	5
3	5.0	6.0	3.0	2	1
4	3.5	2.0	1.5	4	5
5	2.0	8.0	1.5	3	4
6	6.0	5.0	2.0	7	6
7	3.0	6.0	3.5	9	3
8	2.5	10.0	1.5	12	8
9	6.0	4.0	1.0	2	1
10	6.5	3.0	2.5	4	0
11	5.5	2.0	2.5	6	2
12	1.5	9.0	3.5	8	4

Notes: 1. Product freshness – length of time (to the nearest half-minute) since any of the next-to-be-used main item products were made. Any product made eight or more minutes before is discarded.

2. Queue length – number of customers waiting: assessment above was made on all customer queue lengths in the service delivery system.

3. Time to serve – worst and best times in a 10-minute period for a selected server to serve a customer (to the nearest half-minute).

4. Cleanliness – floor: number of items (for example food, packaging and cutlery) on the floor; tables: number of free tables that have not been wiped down since the last customers left.

3. An operations manager records the daily output and number of rejects on a bag-making line that runs for a single eight-hour shift with occasional overtime on a Saturday. The data for the last 40 days are given overleaf.

a. Construct a control chart for these data
b. What does the data analysis tell you?
c. What management action should be taken?

Day #	Day	Output (# Bags)	Rejects	Day #	Day	Output (# Bags)	Rejects
1	Mon	2,040	24	21	Wed	2,440	36
2	Tue	2,210	28	22	Thu	2,290	30
3	Wed	2,090	34	23	Fri	2,180	26
4	Thu	2,235	20	24	Sat	2,260	31
5	Fri	2,050	14	25	Mon	2,095	37
6	Sat	2,240	32	26	Tue	2,080	19
7	Mon	2,080	39	27	Wed	2,290	22
8	Tue	2,280	34	28	Thu	2,260	38
9	Wed	2,260	30	29	Fri	2,125	41
10	Thu	2,260	41	30	Sat	–	–
11	Fri	2,150	38	31	Mon	2,235	37
12	Sat	2,290	18	32	Tue	2,140	38
13	Mon	1,970	29	33	Wed	1,985	24
14	Tue	2,285	41	34	Thu	2,195	31
15	Wed	2,265	26	35	Fri	2,180	37
16	Thu	2,160	32	36	Sat	–	–
17	Fri	2,165	37	37	Mon	2,165	41
18	Sat	2,365	20	38	Tue	2,265	37
19	Mon	2,100	26	39	Wed	2,280	44
20	Tue	2,190	24	40	Thu	2,165	39

4. Casual Elegance is a mail order business selling clothes for the younger business person. From time to time, customers complained about errors in their orders – wrong style, wrong size, and so on. The company wishes to keep order errors to less than 2 per cent. To check how well the system was working, a sample of 50 orders was taken several times over a representative period. The results are shown below.

a. What type of control chart is appropriate for checking the process capability of the ordering operation?

b. Construct a control chart using these data. What observations can you make about the process?

#	OK	Problem	#	OK	Problem
1	50	0	11	47	3
2	47	3	12	50	0
3	49	1	13	45	5
4	48	2	14	48	2
5	48	2	15	47	3
6	46	4	16	46	4
7	50	0	17	48	2
8	50	0	18	50	0
9	49	1	19	50	0
10	48	2	20	49	1

Exploring further

TED talks

Goetz, T. (2010) *It's time to redesign medical data*. Your medical chart: it's hard to access, impossible to read and full of information that could make you healthier if you just knew how to use it. Thomas Goetz looks at medical data and makes a bold call to redesign it.
www.ted.com/talks/thomas_goetz_it_s_time_to_redesign_medical_data.html

Johnson, S. (2010) *Where good ideas come from*. People often credit ideas to individual 'Eureka!' moments, but Steven Johnson tells a different story, from the 'liquid networks' of London's coffee houses to Charles Darwin's long, slow hunch to today's high-velocity web.
www.ted.com/talks/steven_johnson_where_good_ideas_come_from.html

Leadbeater, C. (2005) *Innovation*. In this deceptively casual talk, Charles Leadbeater weaves a tight argument that innovation isn't just for professionals anymore. Passionate amateurs, using new tools, are creating products and paradigms that companies can't.
www.ted.com/talks/charles_leadbeater_on_innovation.html

McCandless, D. (2010) *The beauty of data visualization*. David McCandless turns complex data sets (like worldwide military spending, media buzz, Facebook status updates) into beautiful, simple diagrams that tease out unseen patterns and connections. Good design, he suggests, is the best way to navigate the information glut and it may just change the way we see the world.
www.ted.com/talks/david_mccandless_the_beauty_of_data_visualization.html

Journal articles

Hall, J.M., and Johnson, M.E. (2009) 'When should a process be art, not science?', *Harvard Business Review*, **87**(3): 58–65. The purpose of this article is to help executives understand which processes should not be standardized and how to manage 'artistic' and 'scientific' processes in the same organization.

Heskett, J.L., Jones, T.O., Loveman, G.W., Sasser, W.E. Jr and Schleringer, L.A., (2008) 'Putting the service–profit chain to work', *Harvard Business Review*, **86**(7/8): 118–29. This article puts hard values on soft measures so that managers can calibrate the impact of employee satisfaction, loyalty and productivity on the value of products and services delivered. Managers can then use this information to build customer satisfaction and loyalty.

Jones, T.O. and Sasser, W.E. Jr (1995) 'Why satisfied customers defect', *Harvard Business Review*, **73**(6): 88–99. Companies that excel in satisfying customers excel both in listening to customers and in interpreting what customers with different levels of satisfaction are telling them. If companies are good at recovery, would-be defectors can be transformed and can become apostles: customers who are so completely satisfied that they feel inspired to spread the word.

Markey, R., Reichheld, F. and Dullweber, A. (2009) 'Closing the customer feedback loop', *Harvard Business Review*, **87**(12): 43–7. Many companies devote a lot of energy to listening to the voice of the customer, but few are very happy with the outcome of their effort. The Net Promoter Score categorizes customers into promoters, passives and detractors, and shows whether a customer experience was a success or a failure, and why.

Mitra, D. and Golder, P.N. (2007) 'Quality is in the eye of the beholder', *Harvard Business Review*, **85**(4): 26–7. A discussion of 'actual quality' versus 'perceived quality' of products, suggesting consumers are slow to react to changes in quality of familiar products.

Reichfield, F.F. and Sasser, W.E. Jr (1990) 'Zero defections: quality comes to services', *Harvard Business Review*, **68**(5): 105–11. As companies reduce customer defection rates, amazing things happen to their financials. Although the magnitude of the change varies by company and industry, the pattern holds: profits rise sharply. Reducing the defection rate by 5 per cent generates 85 per cent more profits in one bank's branch system, 50 per cent more in an insurance brokerage, and 30 per cent more in an auto-service chain.

Reinartz, W. and Kumar, V. (2002) 'The mismanagement of customer loyalty', *Harvard Business Review*, **80**(7): 4–12. Not all loyal customers are profitable, and not all profitable customers are loyal. Traditional tools for segmenting customers do a poor job of identifying that latter group, causing companies to chase expensively after initially profitable customers who hold little promise of future profits. The authors suggest an alternative approach, that more accurately predicts future buying probabilities.

Books

The British Standards Institute provides a range of suitable sampling plans, with explanations on how to use them. They include OC curves, AQLs, single, double and multiple sampling plans and cover both attributes and variables – see BS 600 (1991, 1993, 1994 and 1996) and BS 6002 (1993 and 1994).

Dodge, H.F. and Romig, G.H. (1959) *Sampling Inspection Tables – Single and Double Sampling*, 2nd edn. London: John Wiley & Sons. This discusses the factors to be considered when setting up inspection plans to minimise the amount of inspection conducted. It also outlines the mathematical tables to be used when 'double sampling' and discusses how these can be applied within a business.

Evans, J.R. and Lindsay, W.M. (2007) *The Management and Control of Quality*, 7th edn. Cincinnati, OH: South-Western. This provides a comprehensive review of quality issues that is well supplemented by a range of business illustrations.

Heskett, J.L., Sasser, W.E. Jr and Schleringer, L.A. (2003) *The Value Profit Chain: Treat Employees Like Customers and Customers Like Employees*. New York: Free Press. The authors show how the loyalty, trust and satisfaction of customers, employees, partners and investors leads, in turn, to increased profit and growth within an organization.

Zeithaml, V.A. (2009) *Delivering Quality Service: Balancing Customer Perceptions and Expectations*. New York: Free Press. Looks at how the SERVQUAL measurement tool can identify and reduce the gap between customers' expectations and perceptions of service quality.

Websites

The Baldrige Award: www.baldrige.nist.gov The European Foundation for Quality Management: www.efqm.org
Terry Tate, Office Linebacker: www.returnofterrytate.com

Notes and references

1. Parasuraman, A., Zeithaml, V.A. and Berry, L.L. (1985) 'A conceptual model of service quality and its implications for further research', *Journal of Marketing*, 49: 41–50.

Visit www.palgrave.com/business/hillom3e for self-test questions, guideline answers to some case study questions, useful weblinks and more to help you understand the topics in this chapter

THE IPSWICH HOSPITAL NHS TRUST

'It all began after I attended a one-day Quality for Hospital Pharmacists course,' explained the Head of Pharmacy at the Ipswich Hospital. 'This not only fired me up, but also confirmed that the problems we faced were not unique to our organization. More importantly, it also provided a simple and practical approach for improving quality. Since then, everyone in the department has attended a similar programme and continuous improvement teams have been set up to improve how we work and how we deliver services to the other departments in the hospital.'

BACKGROUND

The Ipswich Hospital NHS Trust has over 800 beds and handles more than 100,000 in-patients and new out-patients with over 150,000 follow-up out-patients visits in a typical year. The Pharmacy Department provides a range of core and non-core services (see Figure 1) to the rest of the hospital (see Figure 2) between 8.30am and 5.30pm on weekdays with an additional on-call, out-of-hours service.

Figure 1 Core and non-core services provided by the Pharmacy Department

Level of provision		Service
Core services provided to all departments	Clinical services	Drug information Prescription monitoring Patient counselling Stock 'top up' Ward stock control Therapeutic drug level Monitoring
	Procurement	Purchasing Invoice reconciliation Clerical Financial data provision
	Manufacturing	Licensable manufacturing Pre-packaged drugs Resuscitation box Provision Quality control Extemporaneous dispensing
	Dispensing	In-patient Out-patient Discharge prescription dispensing Distribution Portering
Non-core services provided to some departments		• Education and training to nursing and other health care staff • Ward round participation • Self-medication scheme • Centralized intravenous additive scheme (CIVAS) • Cytotoxic drug reconstitution

Figure 2 Hospital departments, wards and specialist units

Departments	# wards	# specialist clinics
General medicine	7	–
surgery	6	–
Elderly services	6	–
Maternity and gynaecology	5	1
Trauma and orthopaedics	4	–
Paediatrics	2	–
Specialist surgery	1	–
Oncology and haematology	1	–
Anaesthetics	–	1

THE CONTINUOUS IMPROVEMENT INITIATIVE

When the Head of Pharmacy returned from the one-day Quality for Hospital Pharmacists programme, he called a meeting with the other Senior Pharmacists to discuss the idea of launching a continuous improvement initiative within the department. They agreed to the proposal and all the staff within the department (see Figure 3) then attended a similar day's training over the following month.

Figure 3 Pharmacy Department staff	
Grade	**# Full-time equivalents**
Pharmacists	13.5
Technicians	16.0
Assistants	5.0
Clerical	3.5

'Sending everyone on a similar one-day programme really helped get them all on board,' explained the Head of Pharmacy. 'A third of the department attended the workshop each time, which meant the rest of the team had to manage without them. This meant staff had to work together and cooperate to handle the extra workload, which also started laying the foundation for launching this type of initiative.'

The one-day programmes looked at many aspects of quality improvement including the role of improvement initiatives and an introduction to the various tools and techniques for improving quality (such as brainstorming and cause-and-effect diagrams). Once everyone had attended the workshop, the Continuous Improvement Programme (CIP) was officially launched with a CIP coordinator and four Sectional Improvement Teams (SITs) as shown in Figure 4. Together, these teams organized the programme, identified areas for improvement and suggested a team to investigate these areas and make improvements. One member from each SIT, the Head of Pharmacy and the CIP Coordinator then became the Steering Group to manage the overall initiative.

Many of the improvements identified were very simple and easy to implement, but still resulted in a significant improvement. For example:

- **Clinical services** – the team found that the service provided varied according to the pharmacist delivering it. Drawing on the approaches used by different staff, the team agreed a specification for each clinical service activity. The result was a higher specification service that was consistently delivered in line with this specification.

- **Manufacturing** – staff rotate in the manufacturing department on a three-month basis. To help refresh and/or update staff joining the department, the team developed an outline of 'good manufacturing practice', which highlighted procedures that had recently changed.

- **Dispensing** – technicians undertake the initial dispensing, which is then checked by a pharmacist before being given to a patient. As the pharmacists are involved in several tasks, the benches where the dispensed prescriptions wait for their final check can become very congested.

Figure 4 Section Improvement Team (SIT) members		
Team	**Department**	**# staff in team**
Clinical services	Pharmacy Manager	1
	Pharmacists	2
	Technicians	1
	CIP Coordinator	1
Manufacturing	Pharmacists	2
	Technicians	3
	CIP Coordinator	1
Dispensing	Pharmacists	2
	Technicians	3
	CIP Coordinator	1
Stores and distribution	Pharmacy Resource Manager	1
	Technicians	3
	CIP Coordinator	1

As a result, the improvement team suggested putting each prescription on a separate plastic tray and colour coding them to indicate their level of urgency.

- Stores and distribution – the value and cause of out-of-date stock was analyzed by the improvement team. To prevent out-of-date stock from recurring, the minimum stock levels to be held of individual items were adjusted. They also put in place a regular review of expensive items and a weekly monitoring of short shelf-life items.

REVIEWING PROBLEMS

To help the improvement teams review problems and take appropriate action, the CIP Cordinator held various discussion sessions. This involved categorizing problems into one of three types:

1. Internal type 1 problem – concerning only one section in the Pharmacy Department

2. Internal type 2 problem – concerning two or more sections in the Pharmacy Department

3. External problem – involving one or more departments outside the Pharmacy Department.

'Each SIT chose an internal type 1 problem to focus on first as they were easier to improve,' explained the CIP coordinator. 'Once we had got a few quick wins under our belt, then we started to look at the internal type 2 problems, and so on.'

THE PORTERS' PROBLEM

An example of one of these more complex problems is now discussed. A group was set up to look at the effective use of the porters' time. The team comprised one person from each of the four SITs, the two departmental porters and the CIP coordinator.

They found that the pharmacy department receives requests for inpatient drugs in four different ways:

1. **Stock items** – for wards where orders come in a black box brought back by one of the porters from the ward.

2. **Non-stock items** – for individual patients that come either directly from a ward pharmacist or in red bag brought back by one of the porters from the ward.

3. **Medication requests** – for individual patients that have been discharged and will go back to their own home. Again these come either directly from a ward pharmacist or in a red bag brought back by one of the porters from the ward.

4. **Urgent items** – nursing staff telephone requests for urgently needed drugs and then bring down the relevant prescription to collect the drugs. Figure 5 shows the number of times this usually occurs within a 4-week period. In general, 15 per cent of all requests for 'urgent items' are required immediately, 80 per cent for delivery that day and 5 per cent for the following day.

Figure 5 Average number of calls by nursing staff for urgently needed drugs	
Time of day	Average number of calls by nursing staff per day
08.30 – 09.30	3.1
09.30 – 10.30	6.9
10.30 – 11.30	10.0
11.30 – 12.30	10.2
12.30 – 13.30	29.5
13.30 – 14.30	22.0
14.30 – 15.30	16.4
15.30 – 16.30	6.6
16.30 – 17.30	32.4
17.30 onwards	26.8

Figure 6 Tasks undertaken and service provided by the pharmacy porters

General information
The two porters share the wards. The split of wards on a porter's round reflects both their distance from the pharmacy department and the size of the wards in terms of its number of patients and range of illnesses.

All wards have one red bag and one black box that are marked with the name of the ward.

Controlled drugs (for example, pethidine and morphine) have to be signed for on receipt by one of the nursing staff on the relevant ward.

The daily routine
- Boxes and bags are collected from the wards between 08.00 and 09.30 each day and returned to the pharmacy department.

- The pharmacy staff then dispense the requirements for the wards.

- One set of boxes is delivered back to the wards with the required drugs in them at 10.45.

- The second set of boxes and bags is then delivered to the remaining wards at 11.30.

- Between 13.45 and 14.30, the porters again collect the bags from the wards and the procedure in the morning is replicated, with the afternoon deliveries (which are typically fewer) taking place between 16.00 hours and the end of the working day at 17.00.

- In between collecting and delivering boxes and bags, the two porters undertake general work in the department and make special journeys to deliver the one-off requests for drugs and other medicines as required.

The principal role of the porters was to collect the 'black boxes' and 'red bags' containing drug requests from the various wards, return them to the pharmacy department and then distribute them back to the wards later that day with the dispensed drugs inside. However, the pharmacy department (including the porters) felt that the porters' time could be used more efficiently and effectively to improve the level of service offered to the wards within the hospital.

Over several months, data were collected to analyze the tasks undertaken by the pharmacy porters and the level of service they provided, as described in Figure 6. Using this information, a fishbone analysis was then developed to show why the porters' time is inefficiently used, as shown as Figure 7 with accompanying notes in Figure 8.

'It would really help the rest of the hospital if we could increase the number of porter deliveries to three or even four a day,' explained the team leader of this improvement project. 'If we're able to do this, then 60 per cent of the "urgent orders" could wait until the next porters' round. This would save everyone a lot of extra work, especially the nurses who currently have to come to the pharmacy department to pick them up. Fitting in another delivery would not add to the dispensary workload as these drugs have to made up anyway. We just need to change how the porters work so as to make this possible.'

THE FUTURE
'Although the improvement programme hasn't actually been running for that long, everyone is really motivated and the results so far are very encouraging,' explained the Head of Pharmacy. 'We have attempted to keep the improvement activity to a "sensible" level so it doesn't impact the rest of our work, but the porters' problem is still

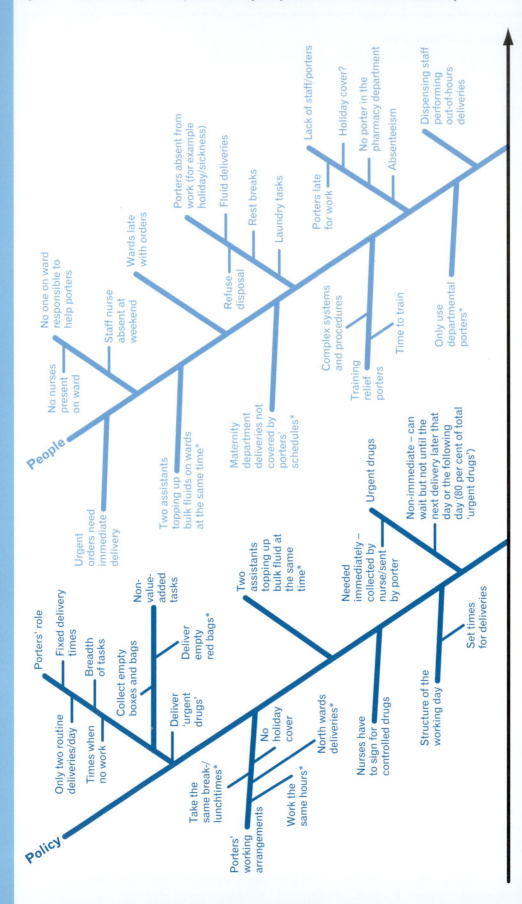

Figure 7 **Fishbone analysis completed on 'why the porters' time is not used effectively'**

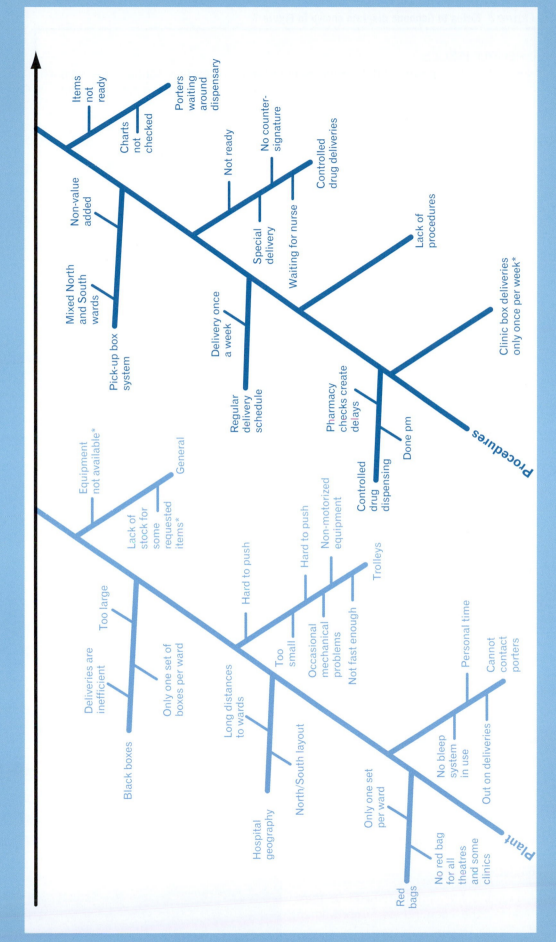

Procedures

Items not ready

Charts not checked

Porters waiting around dispensary

Non-value added

Mixed North and South wards

Pick-up box system

Not ready

No counter-signature

Special delivery

Waiting for nurse

Controlled drug deliveries

Delivery once a week

Regular delivery schedule

Lack of procedures

Pharmacy checks create delays

Controlled drug dispensing

Done pm

Clinic box deliveries only once per week*

Plant

Equipment not available*

General

Lack of stock for some requested items*

Too large

Hard to push

Hard to push

Non-motorized equipment

Trolleys

Deliveries are inefficient

Only one set of boxes per ward

Long distances to wards

Too small

Occasional mechanical problems

Not fast enough

Personal time

Cannot contact porters

Black boxes

Hospital geography

North/South layout

Only one set per ward

No bleep system in use

Out on deliveries

Red bags

No red bag for all theatres and some clinics

Figure 8 **Notes to fishbone diagram shown in Figure 7**

PEOPLE ISSUES

- **Maternity department deliveries are not covered by porters' schedules** – the porters don't deliver or collect from this department as part of their normal schedule.

- **Only use department porters** – the current policy is to use only pharmacy department porters to undertake the collection and distribution of boxes and bags. Previously, when short, porters from other departments or those with general hospital duties were used, but due to a current lack of knowledge and experience this no longer happens.

PROCEDURES

Clinic boxes are delivered only once per week – clinic boxes are collected and delivered only once a week, unlike the ward boxes and bags that are collected and delivered twice a day. The once-a-week deliveries have to be planned in around an already very busy schedule.

PLANT

- **Lack of stock for some requested items** – sometimes the pharmacy department does not having sufficient inventory to meet the wards' requests for stock items and has to deal with these on an 'on-demand' basis.

- **Equipment not available** – equipment (for example boxes) is only checked at the time of use.

POLICY

- **Two assistants top up bulk fluids on wards at the same time** – the pharmacy department provides a 'top-up' service for bulk fluid items (for example, one litre bags of dextrose and sodium chloride) that does not require technical know-how to complete.

- **Take the same break-/lunchtimes** – the two porters take the same break-times and lunchtimes.

- **Work the same hours** – the two porters start and finish work at the same time.

- **Deliver empty red bags** – there is only one red bag per ward. Therefore, porters sometimes have to deliver an empty red bag so that the ward can put its waste into it.

- **North Ward deliveries** – deliveries to the North Ward are made first. However, as clinical pharmacists visit these wards later in the day, many of the drugs required by these wards are not known or completed in time for the porters' delivery. This then results in a second delivery later in the day, which falls under the category of 'non-immediate urgent drugs'.

causing us a headache. If we fix this problem, then not only could we significantly reduce the costs of running the department, but we could also improve the service that we offer to the rest of the hospital.'
www.ipswichhospital.org.uk

Questions

1. Examine the approach used to introduce the continuous improvement programme within the pharmacy department at the Ipswich Hospital and comment.

2. Analyze the 'porters' problem' explained in the case. What recommendations would you make?

Lecturers: visit www.palgrave.com/business/hillom3e for teaching guidelines for this case study

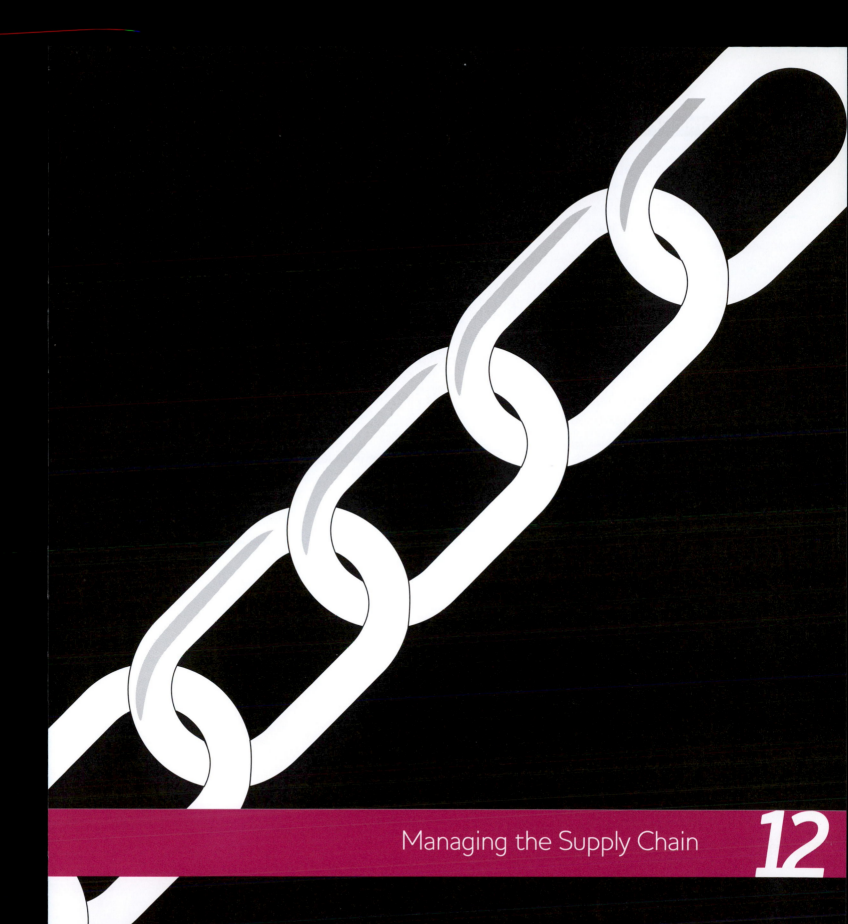

Managing the Supply Chain **12**

After completing this chapter you should be able to:

- Define the supply chain within your business and outline the steps that make up the chain

- Understand how supply chains should be designed, including identifying what to make or buy, the alternatives to making or buying and the issues surrounding outsourcing, both domestically and offshore

- Identify and challenge inappropriate make or buy decisions

- Manage and develop supply chains more effectively and understand the techniques used to do this

- Outline the benefits of managing supply chains effectively

Chapter outline

Executive overview

What is the role of managing the supply chain within the business?

- The primary role of businesses is to develop and deliver services and products to meet customer requirements

- To do this, they need to manage material and information flows across supply chain networks

- To attract and retain customers, all the steps within the supply chain need to be aligned to support the key market order-winners and qualifiers

- Not only are integrated, coordinated and synchronized supply chains more effective at supporting market needs, but they are also more efficient and easier to manage

Why is managing the supply chain important?

- Deciding which services, products and processes to make in-house and which ones to buy from outside has significant short- and long-term implications for a business

- The whole chain is only as strong as its weakest link. Therefore, businesses need to develop the internal parts of the chain, and also work with their suppliers to help them develop the external parts of the chain

- Businesses need to realize that as they choose to outsource certain activities they start to compete as supply chains rather than as individual organizations

- Integrated, coordinated and synchronized supply chains are more effective and more efficient. They are, therefore, critical in helping companies to retain and grow market share while also meeting their other business objectives

How does managing the supply chain impact business performance?

- Choosing to make in-house provides a business with increased control over processes, material supply and service/product knowledge, as well as a greater opportunity for differentiation and cost reduction

- Deciding to buy from outside makes it easier to manage costs, allows an increased focus on critical tasks and increases access to external sets of capabilities

- Aligned and synchronized supply chains are more effective in meeting customer needs, more efficient to run, easier to manage and tie up less cash

What are the key issues to consider when managing supply chains?

- The first step in designing a supply chain is to decide what to make and what to buy

- Making in-house provides increased control over processes and service/product knowledge together with a greater opportunity for differentiation and cost reduction

- Companies should keep in-house the services, products and processes that help them to:
  - Understand customer requirements and build customer relationships
  - Retain core capabilities so safeguarding the future of the business
  - Identify, develop and manage supplier relationships

- Deciding to buy makes it easier to manage costs, provides an increased focus on critical tasks and increases access to external sets of capabilities. However, it is difficult to reverse the decision once a process has been outsourced

- To reduce the potential disadvantages of deciding to buy, businesses can instead use joint ventures, strategic partnerships or co-source services or products

- When managing the supply chain, businesses must:
  - See suppliers as an integral part of the total supply chain and realize that the whole chain is only as strong as its weakest link
  - Build strong relationships with those suppliers that are most strategically critical to their aim to create sustainable supply chains that have a positive economic, social and environmental impact within all parts of the chain
  - Continually look for opportunities to move from physical to digital supply chains that can give customers access to a wider range of less-expensive products, are easier to manage and enable suppliers to reduce cash holdings and supply costs

- When developing supply chains, businesses must:
  - First integrate activities across the chain, and then look for ways to coordinate them, before finally working out how to synchronize them
  - Look for ways to improve customer support, change attitudes to suppliers, increase the use of IT, develop strategic partnerships and work more closely with customers

Material flow –
how materials
move through
processes in order
to be transformed
into services and
products.

Information flow –
how information
moves through
a business to
provide details
including customer
requirements,
delivery dates and
invoicing information
to relevant parts of
the organization.

Introduction

Companies rarely, if ever, own the resources and activities to provide a service or make a product from start to finish, including delivery to customers. Consequently, they need to decide what to provide or make internally and what to buy. Furthermore, whether a company makes or buys an element of the eventual service or product it sells, it needs to manage effectively the internal and external phases of the supply chain, both in terms of parts and as an integrated whole.

Businesses need to recognize that they are at the centre of networks of **material flows** and **information flows**. These flows extend from the customer interface through operations to the building of relationships with suppliers. The operations role, however, is not just the integration and management of the parts of the supply chain but also the constant reviewing and alignment of these closely linked networks to meet better the changing needs of the organization's markets and help achieve its sales revenue and profit goals. This chapter first defines the supply chain, and explains how the types and locations of the suppliers used affects the design of the overall network. The advantages and disadvantages of making in-house and sourcing externally are then outlined. After this, the process of managing suppliers is described, including the tools and techniques that can be used and how factors such as corporate social responsibility and the growth of digital supply chains affect the task of supply chain management. Finally we'll look at the importance of continuing to improve the supply chain, and the benefits that this can bring to organizations.

> **EXECUTIVE INSIGHT**
> Businesses have to manage flows of material and information across a supply network to provide services and products to their customers.

What is a supply chain?

The supply of any service or product involves a number of steps that are known as a supply chain. These steps start with the original request from a customer for a service or product and finish with the delivery of the order to that customer. Organizations undertake some of the steps in the chain themselves and buy in the other steps in the form of materials and/or services from other businesses. Figure 12.1 shows a supply chain for a sandwich bar and a consumer products manufacturer. As you can see from these examples, all the steps necessary to provide a service or product will have to be completed. What is done externally (the decision of what to buy from an external supplier) and what is done internally (the decision of what to make or provide in-house) will not alter the total number of tasks to deliver the service or product but will alter the internal/external mix and the size of the task of managing suppliers. The decision on this split will be based on many factors and these, together with the task of managing suppliers, are dealt with in later sections.

> **EXECUTIVE INSIGHT**
> A supply chain comprises all the steps required to supply a service or product to a customer. However, it is more accurate to call this a 'network' rather than a 'chain'.

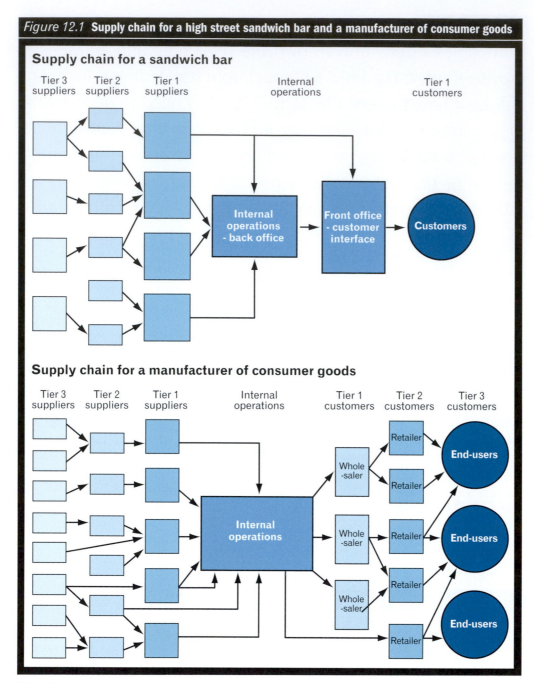

Figure 12.1 Supply chain for a high street sandwich bar and a manufacturer of consumer goods

Supply chain for a sandwich bar

Tier 3 suppliers · Tier 2 suppliers · Tier 1 suppliers · Internal operations · Tier 1 customers

Internal operations - back office → Front office - customer interface → Customers

Supply chain for a manufacturer of consumer goods

Tier 3 suppliers · Tier 2 suppliers · Tier 1 suppliers · Internal operations · Tier 1 customers · Tier 2 customers · Tier 3 customers

Internal operations → Whole-saler → Retailer → End-users

Note: The above diagrams are not to scale, and the number of customers and suppliers are illustrative.

As you can imagine, the number of tiers of suppliers and customers varies depending on the complexity of the service or product being supplied and how many steps in the chain are bought in from outside. Managing a supply chain effectively is a considerable challenge and requires a shift away from traditional functional thinking to managing a set of integrated processes across multiple functions as shown in Figure 12.2.

Designing the supply chain

Developments and improvements to the supply chain need to be made based on a vision of the entire supply chain that reflects a company's market and business requirements. As we'll learn in the following section the decision about what to make and what to buy affects how much of the supply chain is internal and how much is external to an organization; the task is then to integrate these internal and external parts so they work as one. As Figure 12.2 illustrates, to achieve this requires that the material, information and financial details all flow across the whole supply chain enabling all the activities to be synchronized with each other and thereby working, in effect, as a single entity using the same data and timeframes. **Integrated** and **synchronized supply chains** thereby allow companies to respond better to market opportunities and competitive pressures by:

- Collaborating throughout the supply chain

- Exchanging information to ensure end-user needs are met

- Working on the same timeframes

- Operating as a **demand chain** rather than a supply chain by using customer requirements as the basis on which to provide services or make products.

In this way, companies compete as a supply chain rather than as a number of individual organizations.

> **EXECUTIVE INSIGHT**
> Businesses must integrate and synchronize all the steps in a supply chain to both retain and grow market share.

Deciding whether to make or buy

The first step in the design and management of supply chains is to decide what to make and what to buy. This key decision will be based on the following business-related factors:

- The market order-winners and qualifiers supply chains have to support

- How best to understand customer requirements

- If they need to maintain supplies of key materials

- Which core capabilities need to be retained in-house

- How they could create barriers to entry

- Which external capabilities they need to access from elsewhere

- How they wish to take advantage of reduced trade barriers.

Integrated supply chains – the internal and external parts of a supply chain are developed so as to work as one.

Synchronized supply chains – the internal and externals parts of a supply chain will work on the same frames, thereby ensuring they work together.

Demand chain – a reference back to JIT systems – where customer demand is the trigger for activities to start.

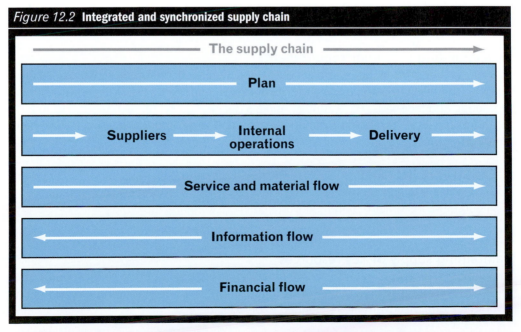

Figure 12.2 Integrated and synchronized supply chain

The supply chain

Plan

Suppliers → Internal operations → Delivery

Service and material flow

Information flow

Financial flow

Although in theory every service or product can be provided internally or bought from outside, in reality the choice is far more restricted. In many instances, organizations have no alternative other than to outsource materials, components, products or services because they lack the in-house technical capability or the high levels of investment required cannot be justified. However, companies should consider a number of aspects when deciding whether to make or buy as outlined below. Case 12.1 looks at some of the strategic outsourcing decisions used by the US credit card company Capital One and the US airline Delta.

Supporting market order-winners and qualifiers

Make-or-buy decisions need to be made within the strategic context of a business. In particular, how they will affect its ability to support its market order-winners and qualifiers (for example price, delivery reliability, delivery speed and quality conformance). For example:

- Dell – developed the capability to assemble personal computers quickly in response to customers' orders, but found that this was constrained by component suppliers' long lead times.

- LEGO – the privately owned Danish toy manufacturer concentrates its production in Europe and the USA, arguing that this best satisfies its design and quality conformance customer requirements.

- Benetton – the Italian clothes manufacturer decided to source garments locally, rather than in a low-cost region such as Southeast Asia or Eastern Europe, to meet the fast response needs of its fashion-conscious customers.

Understanding customer requirements

As well as integrating backwards, companies can also integrate forwards. As this happens, they start to better understand customer requirements through greater contact, knowledge and feedback. For example, Apple's decision to set up its retail stores in 2007 has increased its understanding of how customers use its products and what they might want from future developments.

Backward integration – the decision to make (instead of buying) activities that take place earlier in the supply chain and move the internal part of a supply chain backwards towards the source of supply.

Maintaining supply of key resources

Companies may choose to make, rather than buy, to ensure supply of key components or materials. As with all forms of **backward integration**, this decision brings its own set of advantages and disadvantages that need to be considered.

CASE 12.1 CAPITAL ONE AND DELTA: STRATEGIC OUTSOURCING DECISIONS

© kizilkayaphotos

When an organization decides to serve its customers using a telephone, rather than face to face, it first needs to consider if this should be in-house or outsourced. Should it hand over something as important as customer relations to an external provider? And, if so, where should the facility be located?

It is cheaper to outsource call centre services as specialist organizations have greater call volumes, lower costs, cheaper staff and can manage variable staff capacity requirements more easily. However, some companies still prefer to set up and run their own call centres. For example, the US credit card company Capital One outsources only a few specialized parts of its service, such as debt collection from customers who are very late in making payments, as it believes effective customer management is key in its market. Equally, the US airline Delta sited its European customer reservation centre in London, where labour costs are high and competition for staff is fierce, as it believes the access to staff speaking a wide range of languages makes it worthwhile.

www.capitalone.com
www.delta.com

Questions

1. Why are most companies subcontracting call centre facilities?

2. What reasons would make a company elect to set up and manage its own call centre?

Lecturers: visit www.palgrave.com/business/hillom3e for teaching guidelines for this case study

Retaining core capabilities

Companies must keep their core capabilities in-house, so they maintain control of those processes that create value for customers. These are the key processes to support the critical order-winners and qualifiers within their markets. In manufacturing firms, they are often the assembly-onward production processes, whereas in service businesses they are usually the final link with customers. For example, in the late 1990s NatWest Bank considered subcontracting the back-office cheque processing and account management activities for its retail and corporate customers. In the past these activities were an integral part of its in-house operation, but now options to subcontract were available. In the end, NatWest decided to keep these activities in-house as they provided an essential link with its customers. Similarly, Fidelity, one of the world's largest fundraisers, considers administrative systems to be a core part of its business and has, therefore, kept them in-house through significant systems technology investment over several decades.

Creating barriers to entry

Keeping processes in-house and developing them over time can create strong **barriers to entry** due to the high levels of investment and managerial resources required to replicate this capability.

Accessing external capabilities

As well as wishing to retain **core capabilities**, companies may also find that they need to access capabilities from elsewhere that they do not have in-house. As a result, a company buys in the capability in the form of materials, components, products or services from external suppliers. For example, in 2005 a US fund manager had to reduce the time it took to settle trades from three days to one day. This could only be done through large IT investment and upgrades. Instead of developing this capability in-house, it chose to buy it in from outside. Similarly, an upmarket ladies' clothes outlet makes minor garment alterations in-house, but outsources more complex modifications for which it does not have the in-house capability.

Taking advantage of reduced trade barriers

Trade barriers across much of the world have declined sharply over recent years. For example, in 1998 the average tariff was 94 per cent less than in 1960. This has made **global manufacturing** more commercially feasible, which has in turn reduced the need for local manufacturing plants as companies can now easily import goods from overseas. For example, in Australia the **tariff** on imported cars dropped from 57.5 per cent in 1987 to 10 per cent in 2005. As a result, imported cars rose from 15 to 70 per cent of the market in that period and domestic car plants started to close.

> **EXECUTIVE INSIGHT**
> Make-or-buy decisions need to be reviewed on an ongoing basis as markets change, products move through life cycles and new business opportunities become available.

Deciding how much to make or buy

Once a firm has decided in which steps of the supply chain it wishes to be involved, it then has four options in terms of determining how much to make or buy. It can complete all steps in-house (fully internal), it can outsource all steps (fully external), it can outsource its non-value adding steps or it can use both internal and external capabilities for some or all of the steps in the supply chain. These options are now discussed in more detail.

Fully internal

At one extreme, firms may decide on a fully integrated strategy, where all service and product requirements are provided internally using fully owned subsidiaries. This alternative works best when:

Barriers to entry – factors (for example size of investment and technical know-how) that make it difficult for new competitors to enter a market.

Core capabilities – capabilities which create value for customers and influence the decision to buy.

Trade barriers – a way of deliberately restricting trade, for example by using import tariffs.

Global manufacturing – refers to the increasing integration of manufacturing activity around the world.

Tariff – a tax levied by a government on imports and, more occasionally, exports.

- Price is not an order-winner and so the company does not have to pursue the lower-cost alternatives.

- The customer relationship is a key market order-winner.

- The knowledge and expertise required to perform all the steps in the chain is critical in winning and retaining customers.

- The opportunity for creating competitive advantage and building barriers to entry comes from completing all of the steps in the chain in-house.

- Capacity can be incrementally increased in line with demand.

Fully external

At the other extreme, firms may decide to outsource all their product and service requirements by simply only handling the customer order processing activities themselves. This alternative works best when:

- A commodity service or product is being provided.

- Price is an order-winner and so the company has to pursue the lowest cost alternative.

- The business is completely dependent on an external capability that it is not possible to develop in-house.

Outsource non-value adding steps

The most common option is where companies determine the value-adding activities required to support their key market order-winners and then outsource their non-value adding activities. This works well when:

- There is a clear distinction between those activities which add value (support key order-winners and qualifiers) and those that do not.

- There are a number of suppliers who can provide the non-value added activities.

> **EXECUTIVE INSIGHT**
  Normally, the right strategy is for companies to outsource their non-value adding activities and focus their time and money on developing the value-adding activities that help them attract and retain customers.

Use both make and buy options for some or all the steps in the chain

The final option is to adopt a 'taper-integrated strategy' where firms use both in-house and external capabilities to supply some or all of the steps in the chain. This works well when:

- The business wants to ensure that its internal capacity is fully utilized and, therefore, enables it to reduce costs and compete more effectively in price-sensitive markets.

- The business needs to respond quickly to demand fluctuations and short lead-time customer requirements, and does not wish to maintain excess capacity in-house to do this.

However, there are a number of disadvantages associated with this strategy. It may:

- Prevent good customer and supplier relationships from being developed that, in the long run, may result in losing customers or alienating suppliers.

- Make it more difficult for both internal and external providers to reduce costs as the volume of orders is split between them.

- Increase the cost of outsourcing as suppliers charge a price premium to cope with the low and unpredictable volume of demand that they have to meet.

Advantages and disadvantages of make or buy

The decision to make or buy brings with it a number of advantages and disadvantages, which are summarized in Figure 12.3 and discussed in more detail below.

Figure 12.3 **Advantages and disadvantages of make or buy**

Option	Advantages		Disadvantages	
Make in-house	Increased control over	· Processes and capabilities · Supply of materials · Market and service/product know-how	More difficult to manage costs	· More difficult to control cost · Increased overhead costs
	Increased opportunity to	· Differentiate and customise services or products · Reduce costs	Less focus	· More complex task · Less focus on core issues · Investment spread over a wider set of tasks
			Reduced access to	· External capabilities · Up-to-date technologies
Buy/ outsource	Easier to manage costs	· Easier to control as the unit price is known · Lower overhead costs	Increased risk	· More vulnerable to supply problems · Expose intellectual property to others · Less control of processes, capabilities and developments
	Increased focus	· Frees up resources to focus on core issues	Difficult to reverse	· Inherent skills lost · Stepped investment to buy in capabilities in the future
	Increased access to	· Capacity · Up-to-date technology · World-class capabilities	New skills required	· To manage supply chain
			Less flexible	· No longer own the skills or capabilities

Advantages of making in-house
Making in-house brings with it several advantages including:

- Increased control over
  - Processes and capabilities – that support the key market order-winners and qualifiers
  - Supply of materials – backward integration reduces dependency on suppliers
  - Market and service or product knowledge – **forward integration** allows better business forecasts (from demand patterns to identifying technology and cost changes) to be made that help strengthen a firm's competitive position.

- Increased opportunity to
  - Differentiate services or products – including customization, by using alternative materials and designs to meet varying market requirements
  - Reduce costs – by increasing internal demand. For example, Japanese semiconductor manufacturers such as Fujitsu, Hitachi, Mitsubishi, NEC and Toshiba are able to make their products at increasingly lower costs than their competitors due to the high-volume base created by internal, corporate demand-making semiconductors along with everything else from robots to cars and satellites. As a result, Japan currently has over 50 per cent of the world semiconductor market.

Forward integration – the decision to make (instead of buying) activities that take place later in the supply chain and move the internal part of a supply chain forwards towards the end customer.

Disadvantages of making in-house

Making in-house, however, also brings with it several disadvantages including:

- More difficult to manage costs
  - More difficult to control costs – the costs of all the resources (including staff, materials and overheads) used to produce a product have to be estimated, measured and controlled
  - Increased overhead costs – making in-house requires additional overheads in management and development staff and resources and these costs are difficult to assess, evaluate and control.

- Less focus
  - Making in-house leads to more tasks, more complexity and consequently makes it more difficult to focus on core issues
  - Having more tasks in-house spreads the available investment (both time and money) across more tasks and dilutes the focus on core issues.

- Reduced access to
  - External capabilities and up-to-date technologies – specialist suppliers invest and develop in their specific area of expertise. Making in-house reduces access to these external capabilities and up-to-date technologies.

> **Outsourcing** – one of the terms used to describe the process of hiring out or subcontracting some of the work that a company needs to do.

Advantages of deciding to buy

Deciding to buy, or **outsourcing**, brings with it several advantages including:

- Easier to manage costs
  - Easier to control costs – as only a supplier's quoted price for a service or product needs to be checked and controlled instead of all the different costs associated with making in-house
  - Lower overheads – as the associated support costs are reduced.

- Increased focus
  - Not making in-house simplifies the operating task and frees up resources that can focus on core issues.

> **World-class capabilities** – having the staff, processes and equipment that rank among the best in the world.

- Increased access to
  - Capacity – outsourcing allows access to capacity across the supply chain that can be used to absorb demand fluctuations
  - Up-to-date technology – outsourcing enables a company to access the technology developments made by suppliers in their own specialist areas
  - **World-class capabilities** – all companies strive to develop world-class capabilities to remain competitive in their markets. Outsourcing allows a firm to access these capabilities and the benefits they bring. As shown in Case 7.2, Fender International used outside expertise to enhance the delivery of its products to customers.

CASE 12.2 FENDER INTERNATIONAL: CREATING A POSITIVE RETAIL EXPERIENCE

Fender International, the US manufacturer of world-famous electric guitars such as the Stratocaster, Telecaster and precision base, set an objective to double market share in Europe, the Middle East and Africa. Part of its strategy to achieve this was to create a 'positive retail experience' that meant a guitar must be playable when taken out of its box. It was able to achieve this in the USA, but was struggling in Europe, the Middle East and Africa until it set up a partnership with UPS.

The UPS European Distribution Centre at Roermond in the Netherlands now receives guitars from Fender manufacturing sites around the world and then uses local professional and amateur musicians to tune them prior to final distribution. All guitars, from standard models to some of the most expensive and elite guitars in the world, are now inspected by players before being sent to customers. UPS also handles the return of damaged guitars for repair and the central facility manages inventory for the whole region. This has led to lower inventories in the whole supply chain, shorter distribution lead times and enabled Fender to get closer to distributors, retailers and customers. One unexpected outcome is that many distributors are ordering products that they never ordered before.

www.fender.com

Questions

1. What is the significance for Fender International of the guitar tuning service offered by UPS?

2. Why do you think distributors are now ordering products that they never ordered before?

Lecturers: visit www.palgrave.com/business/hillom3e for teaching guidelines for this case study

Disadvantages of deciding to buy

Outsourcing, however, also brings with it several disadvantages including:

- **Increased risks**
  - More vulnerable to supply problems – as a company becomes more dependent on its suppliers
  - Exposing **intellectual property** to others – the more suppliers used to provide a service or product, the greater the exposure of its intellectual property and the potential loss of a technical advantage over its competitors
  - Less control of processes, capabilities and developments – as these are now provided by suppliers.

- **Difficult to reverse**
  - Once a product or service has been outsourced, it is rarely brought back in-house due to a reluctance to change direction on a previous decision and the level of time and investment required to re-create the necessary in-house capability.

- **New skills required**
  - Managing a supply chain is different, and often more demanding, than managing an in-house process.

- **Less flexible**
  - When market requirements change, it may be more difficult to modify its processes and capabilities as it no longer owns them.

The potential risks that come with only having a single supplier are clearly shown in Case 12.3.

> **EXECUTIVE INSIGHT**
> Deciding to buy makes a business more vulnerable to supply problems, exposes intellectual property and reduces control over capabilities. It is also difficult to reverse, requires new skills and can make a business less flexible.

Similarly, a review of the data in Figures 12.4, 12.5 and 12.6 illustrates the mix of advantages and disadvantages when sourcing from domestic as opposed to overseas suppliers, while the advantage of lower costs (higher discounts) when outsourcing to suppliers in Central America, Asia and similar regions has to be set against the disadvantage that such suppliers are less willing to respond to changes in quantities and order mix once an order has been placed.

> **EXECUTIVE INSIGHT**
> Although there are cost advantages of sourcing services and products from low-cost regions such as Central America and Asia, these suppliers are often less willing to change quantities and mixes once orders have been placed.

Figure 12.4 **Percentage discount by supplier location agreed with North American and UK retailers**

Retailer	% Discount by supplier location					
	Asia	Africa	Central America	Europe	North America	UK
North America	20–30	10–15	20–25	5–10	0	–
UK	25–35	15–20	–	10–15	1–5	0

Source: Based on Lowson, R.H. (2001) 'Offshore sourcing: an optimal operational strategy?', *Business Horizons*, Nov–Dec, 61–6.

UPF-Thompson, the sole chassis frames supplier for Land Rover's Discovery model, went bankrupt in 2001. Critics said Land Rover should never have single sourced such a crucial component for the car range that accounts for 35 per cent of its sales revenue. KPMG, the receivers brought in to run UPF, poured fat on the fire by demanding that Land Rover should pay off UPF's debt of £50 million to guarantee chassis supply for the next year. Land Rover took them to court and won a High Court injunction to guarantee supply for the following year.

Single sourcing is now the norm for most car manufacturers as it reduces the investment cost in tooling and equipment, which was £12 million for the Land Rover chassis frame. Land Rover and KPMG came to a compromise, but this incident demonstrates how vulnerable they have become with over 90 per cent of their components single sourced from 900 suppliers.

www.landrover.com
www.kpmg.com

Questions

1. Comment on KPMG's role in this dispute with Land Rover.

2. What would you advise Land Rover to do in general about its single sourcing policy?

Lecturers: visit www.palgrave.com/business/hillom3e for teaching guidelines for this case study

Figure 12.5 Percentage of suppliers not allowing any change to order volume once orders have been placed before and after the season has started

Relative to start of season	% Suppliers not allowing any change to order volume once orders have been placed					
	Asia	Africa	Central America	Europe	North America	UK
Before	66	58	41	29	16	9
After	70	66	52	35	39	19

Source: Based on Lowson, R.H. (2001) 'Offshore sourcing: an optimal operational strategy?', *Business Horizons*, Nov–Dec, pp. 61–6.

Figure 12.6 Percentage of suppliers not allowing any change to order mix once orders have been placed before and after the season has started

Able to change products ordered	% Suppliers not allowing any change to order mix once orders have been placed					
	Asia	Africa	Central America	Europe	North America	UK
Before	70	62	46	37	21	21
After	86	73	63	41	47	28

Source: Based on Lowson, R.H. (2001) 'Offshore sourcing: an optimal operational strategy?', *Business Horizons*, Nov–Dec, pp. 61–6

As the figures show, deciding where to outsource greatly affects an organization's ability to support its own customer needs. However, rather than outsourcing, a company can also choose to set up its own offshore facilities. These developments typically occur within four main phases as summarized in Figure 12.7 and some examples of how companies have used offshore facilities are shown in Figure 12.8:

1. **Offshore** – normally used to reduce cost and supply a specific service or product to either external customers or other operations that it owns.

2. **Server** – established to overcome tariff barriers, reduce taxes, minimize logistics costs and cushion the business from exposure to foreign exchange fluctuations. However, they are limited to serving a specific geographical market.

3. **Contributor** – established to gain access to knowledge, expertise or capability within a region. As a result, their responsibilities grow as they use this local capability to develop new services, products and/or processes that are then used to supply services or products to internal or external customers.

4. **Lead** – as with Phase 3, these operations are established to gain access to knowledge, expertise or capability within a region. However, they now also take on the responsibility of implementing these developments within other operations in the company. As such, they start to lead innovation within the business, playing a key role in selecting and developing suppliers to be used throughout the business. They also start to become responsible for managing relationships with external stakeholders such as customers, suppliers and research centres.

Alternatives to outsourcing

The discussion so far has implied that companies must either make or buy. However, other alternatives are also available including:

Figure 12.7 Progressive roles of offshore facilities

Development phase	Characteristics
1 Offshore ↓	• Operation typically established to reduce cost • Supplies a specific service or product to regional, national or global markets • Technical and managerial investments are kept to a minimum • Low local autonomy

2 Server ↓	• Operation typically established to:
	  – Overcome tariff barriers
	  – Reduce taxes
	  – Minimize logistic costs or
	  – Cushion the business from exposure to foreign exchange fluctuations
	• Supplies services or products to specific national or regional markets
	• Provides a base from which to launch products into a market (for example the European Union)

3 Contributor ↓	• Operation typically established to gain access to local knowledge, expertise or capabilities
	• Supplies services or products to specific national or regional markets
	• Responsibilities extend to:
	  – Developing new services, products and processes
	  – Selecting and developing local or offshore suppliers
	• Often used as a site for testing new services, products, process technologies and computer systems

4 Lead	• Operation typically established to gain access to local knowledge, expertise or capabilities
	• Creates new services, products, processes and technologies that are then used by other operations in the company
	• Responsibilities extend to:
	  – Collecting local knowledge and technical resources
	  – Developing new services, products and processes
	  – Selecting and developing suppliers to be used within other operations in the company
	  – Managing external relationships with customers, suppliers and research centres
	  – Leading and implementing developments within other operations in the company

Figure 12.8 Examples of companies seeking and gaining additional roles from offshore operations

Company	Location	Roles
Hewlett-Packard	Guadalajara (Mexico)	• Designs memory boards • Assembles computers
3M	Bangalore (India)	• Designs computer software • Writes computer software
Motorola	Singapore	• Designs pagers • Makes pagers

> **Co-sourcing –** occurs when two or more competitors collectively source a service or product.

• **Co-sourcing** – this occurs when a company works with one or more of its competitors to collectively source a service or product. For example, in 2003 Barclays and Lloyds Banking Group (at the time known as Lloyds TSB), the UK's third and fourth largest banks respectively, decided to both source their cheque processing service and set up

Joint ventures – are where two or more companies set up a separate organization to provide a range of capabilities for those companies involved.

a new company to be managed by Unisys, the US consultancy firm. The new company, in which each bank has a 24.5 per cent stake, expects to generate £500 million in sales revenues during the next 10 years and now competes for business from other banks. This solution meant Barclays and Lloyds could take advantage of outsourcing without losing complete control of these operations.

- **Joint ventures** – these are a useful alternative when two or more organizations wish to exploit similar opportunities, particularly in areas such as applied technology and research. These companies can set up a separate entity that draws on the strengths of their owners, taps into the synergy of such a relationship and improves the competitive capability of all the organizations involved. Over the past three decades, the number of joint ventures has increased substantially, particularly in the communication, IT and service industries. As Figure 12.9 shows, most companies see joint ventures as a viable alternative and one that they will increasingly look to use. However, joint ventures should not be seen as a way to hide weaknesses. If used effectively, they can help develop internal capabilities, share and utilize resources, allow them to focus on the activities where they can add the most value, reduce risk and increase opportunity. Figure 12.10 summarizes the operational and strategic reasons why a joint venture may be an appropriate business decision.

> **EXECUTIVE INSIGHT**
> Joint ventures should not be seen as a way to hide weaknesses within a business. When used effectively, they can develop internal capabilities, share and utilize resources, allow them to focus on the activities where they can add the most value, reduce risk and increase opportunity.

Non-equity-based collaboration – when two or more companies collaborate to provide a range of capabilities for those companies involved without setting up a separate company to do this.

- **Non-equity-based collaboration** – this is a useful alternative when companies are unwilling or unable to enter a joint venture arrangement. However, such collaborations need to be viewed as a long-term strategy if they are to yield meaningful and useful results. Examples of such arrangements include:
  - Research and development collaboration – to increase the level of innovation and the exploitation of new service, product or process developments
  - Cross-marketing collaboration – to widen product lines and share distribution channels
  - Cross-operations collaboration – to avoid duplication of facilities, provide vertical integration opportunities and transfer knowledge between operations
  - Purchasing collaboration – to increase buying power and supplier allegiance.

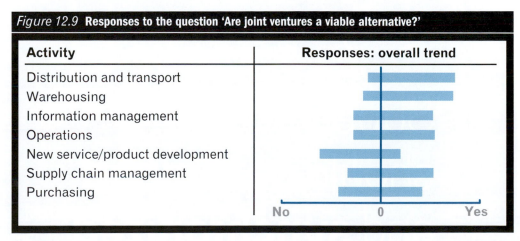

Figure 12.9 **Responses to the question 'Are joint ventures a viable alternative?'**

Activity	Responses: overall trend
Distribution and transport	
Warehousing	
Information management	
Operations	
New service/product development	
Supply chain management	
Purchasing	

Source: Hill, T. (2005) *Operations Management*, 2nd edn. Basingstoke, Palgrave Macmillan

'Supply chains should be **aligned** and **synchronized**'

Figure 12.10 **Reasons for forming joint ventures**	
	Advantages
Strategic	• Strengthen current strategic position: – pioneer developments into new segments – rationalize existing segments
	• Pre-empt competitors: – facilitate access to new markets and customers – support market share growth – gain access to global markets
	• Augment current strategic position: – create and develop synergies – technology and skill transfers
	• Widen service/product range
Operational	• Share investment and risk
	• Process capacity sharing: – increased utilization – avoids process/skill duplication
	• Share facilities in other parts of the supply chain, for example distribution channels and outlets
	• Increase technological know-how by: – facilitating information exchange – potentially creating critical mass in areas such as research and development – broadening expertise, for example in IT systems
	• Help retain key staff: – increased job scope – improved job opportunities

Source: Developed from Harrigan, K.R. 'Managing joint ventures – Part I', *Management Review*, February (1987), p. 29.

> **EXECUTIVE INSIGHT**

To reduce the potential disadvantages of deciding to buy, your business can use joint ventures, non-equity collaborations or co-source services, products and processes instead.

Reasons for making inappropriate make-or-buy decisions

Despite the different advantages and disadvantages of making or buying, many organizations fail to consider the strategic and operational implications that this decision will have on their business. Instead, they simply choose to make or buy because it is what they have always done; they only looked at the capability and cost implications of this decision; they wanted to outsource difficult tasks; they did not consider all of the costs associated with outsourcing; or there was political pressure within the organization to either make or buy.

> **EXECUTIVE INSIGHT**

The make-or-buy is a critical strategic and operational decision. Too often though, businesses make this decision by simply continuing what they have always done, only looking at capability and cost, trying to shed difficult tasks and responding to political pressure within the organization.

Continuing yesterday's decisions

Make-or-buy decisions taken in the past are often not reconsidered at a later date because a level of inertia develops as executives do not want to take on more work and are worried about the possible short-term problems of changing this decision. However, these decisions need to be periodically reviewed as markets change, products move through their life cycles and different make-or-buy alternatives become available.

> **EXECUTIVE INSIGHT**

Make-or-buy decisions need to be reviewed on an ongoing basis as markets change, products move through life cycles and new business opportunities become available.

Considering only the capability and cost of making or buying

Too often businesses decide to make or buy first by only asking if they have the capability to deliver the service or product themselves and then how cheaply it can be bought from elsewhere:

1. **Is the company capable of delivering the service or product themselves?** If not, then businesses too often choose to buy in from outside rather than developing the internal skills or process capabilities, which might be better, long-term strategic decisions.

2. **What is the cost of delivering the service or product?** Where skill or process capability is not a barrier, the next decision is often one of cost. If the service or product can be bought less expensively from elsewhere, then the decision is made to buy it rather than make it in-house. However, this might not be the best strategic decision. For example, it is often better to support market order-winners such as customer relationship, service/product design and delivery speed by making in-house. Equally, if price is an order-winner then it might strategically be more important to live with higher costs in the short-term so that, in the long-term, a low-cost capability can be developed in-house.

Case 12.4 shows how a firm can damage both its short-term and long-term strategic position by using capability and cost as the only criteria for choosing to make or buy.

Outsourcing difficult tasks

Too often, companies simply outsource difficult operations tasks rather than working out how to do them efficiently and effectively in-house. When doing this they focus too much on the investment in both time and money required to:

- Develop new services or products

- Develop new in-house personnel capability to deliver these services or products

- Develop new in-house process capability to deliver these services or products

- Refurbish equipment that needs updating or repairing to deliver these services or products.

However, although choosing to buy overcomes these short-term investment problems, it may not be the right long-term strategic decision: the business may end up losing control of a key value-adding activity, which will reduce its opportunity to differentiate itself in the market and build barriers to entry. It is worth remembering that anyone can do the easy tasks well. The high profit margins are made by doing the difficult tasks well.

> **EXECUTIVE INSIGHT**

The opportunity for gaining real competitive advantage and creating barriers to entry lies in doing the difficult tasks well. Anyone can do the easy tasks well.

CASE 12.4 RAWLINS INDUSTRIES: THE DOMINANCE OF THE COST ARGUMENT

© istockphoto.com/Georgiy Shpade

Part of a large, US-based conglomerate, Rawlins Industries (RI) manufactures and assembles pumps for a wide range of chemical, oil refining and mining customers. Three years ago RI split its UK-based facility into a number of business units to reflect the industries in which its customers competed. Each unit was performing well and supporting the needs of its different markets until the Group set up an operation in Asia to make castings for its products at a cheaper cost.

All of the business units were told to purchase their castings from the new operation in Asia. However, while their previous casting supplier was able to provide castings within four weeks, the new Asian facility had fixed its production schedules to reduce its manufacturing costs and therefore needed 16–20 weeks' notice for a new order.

By choosing to buy castings from the new Asian facility, RI then found that it started to lose market share because its customers needed their pumps within six weeks. Therefore, although it could now make it products more cheaply than before, customers no longer wanted them.

Questions

1. Why did Rawlins Industries start to lose market share?

2. What can other businesses learn from this?

Lecturers: visit www.palgrave.com/business/hillom3e for teaching guidelines for this case study

Ignoring some of the costs and investments of outsourcing

Companies often fail to look at the total costs and investments associated with the decision to outsource a service, product or process: for example, the investment required to develop a supplier, rework costs for poor quality services and products, and inventory that may subsequently need to be held to buffer against supply uncertainty or reduce delivery lead times. By not looking at the overall picture, the outsourcing option may appear more attractive than it actually is.

Political pressure

Within some companies there is often political pressure either to keep work in-house or outsource it. However, these decisions need to be the right strategic ones for the long-term future of the business. For example, in 2007 Volkswagen decided to cut thousands of jobs at its Spanish, Portuguese and Belgian factories even though they were less efficient than its German facilities. However, this might not be the right decision for the long-term future of the business.

Managing supply chains

The balance of internal and external parts that make up an organization's supply chain is determined by the make-or-buy decision. Once the balance between making in-house and buying from external sources has been decided, it is necessary to manage these external and internal parts as an integrated and synchronized whole, which is able to support customer requirements as emphasized earlier (see Figure 12.2 and the accompanying narrative).This is especially important in a business environment where, increasingly, companies compete as supply chains rather than individual organizations.To successfully integrate the supply chain, organizations need to re-think the relationship they have with suppliers and realize that they must be proactive in encouraging improvement and change when it is required.

First and foremost, organizations must realize that their suppliers are an integral part of the total supply chain and are, in many ways, partners in the task of competing effectively. For the best results, suppliers have to be involved early on (for example, on new service/ product introductions and design changes) and essential information (including sales trends and financial data) has to be shared in a timely fashion. Only then can the benefits of a totally integrated supply chain be effectively used to compete in today's markets.

> **EXECUTIVE INSIGHT**
> Businesses must see their suppliers as an integral part of the total supply chain and realize that the whole chain is only as strong as its weakest link. In some cases, it may be more important to help your suppliers develop their capability to support you rather than simply focusing on developing your own in-house capability.

As Case 12.5 shows, the integration of the supply chain, and the need for collaboration between organizations and their suppliers, can lead to a fundamental rethink of the objectives, structure and style used within an organization as well as affecting its position on broader issues such as **corporate social responsibility** (a topic that is introduced later in this chapter and covered in detail in Chapter 15).

In the 1980s and early 1990s, companies focused on fixing problems within their internal operations. However, by the mid-1990s, they were starting to look across the whole of the supply chain to meet shorter service and product life cycles, wider customer choice, reduced lead times and growing world competition. The challenge of managing supply chains effectively continues to grow as more companies outsource operations. A key factor in managing supply chains is the type of supplier relationship that an organization decides to adopt. The alternatives and how they differ are now explained.

Corporate social responsibility (CSR) – refers to the activities undertaken by an organization to meet the social, environmental and economic responsibilities of their various stakeholders including employees, suppliers, customers and the societies in which they operate.

Recently, Chiquita, the global food company, moved its main purchasing team from the USA to Costa Rica to forge closer links with its fruit-growing producers. Chiquita Fresh (one of the world's largest banana producers) transferred its 20-strong procurement team from Ohio, plus several staff from the US head office in Cincinnati, to San José, one of its seven Latin American export locations. As well as procurement skills, buyers must also speak Spanish and understand local cultures.

The move was part of a wider initiative to integrate procurement, which had previously been seen as a support function, within the wider supply chain operation. The relocation provided the opportunity for procurement specialists to provide direct, on-the-spot support to the people who buy fresh fruit for its world markets – more than half of Chiquita's products are sold in Europe.

The company is also stepping up its corporate social responsibility policy by getting its materials and services suppliers to adhere to its own code of conduct in all future contracts.

www.chiquita.com

Questions

1. Why did Chiquita move its main purchasing team to Costa Rica?

2. What opportunities did the relocation offer?

Lecturers: visit www.palgrave.com/business/hillom3e for teaching guidelines for this case study

Types of supplier relationship

The relationship between customers and suppliers is influenced by the level of dependency on each other as shown in Figure 12.11. Companies can manage these relationships in a number of ways:

- **Trawling the market** – suppliers are kept at arm's length and transactions are often completed over the internet. For example, General Electric (GE) in the USA increasingly purchases components over the internet by posting the contract details and then asking **pre-qualified vendors** to quote. These internet auctions have little face-to-face interaction and products are bought on price alone with on-time delivery and quality conformance (the order-winners) as qualifiers for becoming a potential supplier. GE estimates it has also reduced order processing costs by 90 per cent using this method. However, this approach is only appropriate for **commodities** and **non-value-adding** services and products.

- **Ongoing relationships** – establish medium-term contracts with suppliers to help develop relationships and share information.

- **Partnerships** – establish long-term contracts with suppliers to further develop relationships, share information and build trust. For example, US auto makers have doubled the average length of supplier contract since 1988.

- **Strategic alliances** – establish strategic alliances to further increase depth and breadth of the relationship. Strategic alliances usually have long timescales and require extensive information sharing, increased trust, and joint service, product and process development. Boeing has strategic alliances with GE, Rolls-Royce and Pratt & Whitney to reduce the financial risk of new aircraft programmes and better manage new product development between the different parts of an aircraft. A prerequisite for establishing strategic alliances is to dramatically reduce the number of suppliers used. For example, Xerox has reduced its suppliers from over 5,000 to about 400. However, if managed

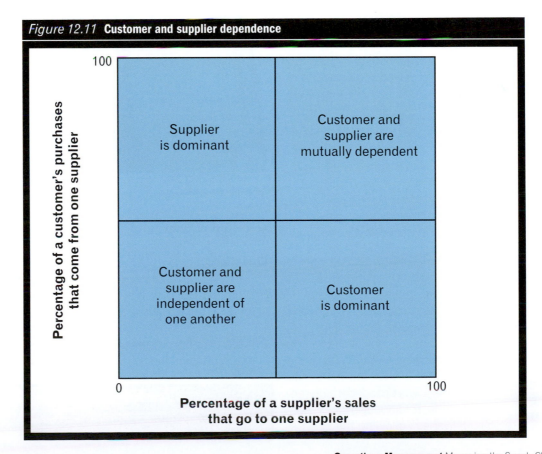

Figure 12.11 **Customer and supplier dependence**

CASE 12.6 FEDEX AND KINKO JOIN FORCES TO INCREASE DELIVERY SPEED

Companies can use the internet to bypass existing layers of the supply chain or engage new participants in the delivery of a service or product. For example, FedEx and Kinko (the US-based visual communication and document copying service company) created a new document delivery flow path that bypassed FedEx's own air-transport fleet. Both companies could receive documents electronically from customers and immediately route them to printers close to the intended recipients. Same-day delivery was provided which cost far less than the traditional two- or even three-day deliveries Following the success of this alliance, FedEx decided to acquire Kinko.

www.fedex.com

Questions

1. What did FedEx and Kinko 'bring to the table' in this strategic alliance?

2. What benefits did the individual companies gain from these new arrangements?

Lecturers: visit www.palgrave.com/business/ hillom3e for teaching guidelines for this case study

correctly, this can have significant benefit. For example, Chrysler has saved more than $0.5 billion from supplier-generated ideas. Case 12.6 also shows how Fedex developed an alliance with Kinko to increase the delivery speed of documents to its customers.

- **Backward integration** – the final step is to change from relationship to ownership by acquiring the supplier. This leads to full information and creates consistent objectives and culture, if managed correctly.

> **EXECUTIVE INSIGHT**
> Businesses must build strong relationships with the suppliers that are most strategically critical to their business and help them support their key order-winners and qualifiers.

Corporate social responsibility

The need to rethink corporate norms in the context of outsourcing does not stop with the sharing of information. Other corporate values will also come under scrutiny when selecting which supplier to use. High on this agenda is that of corporate social responsibility (CSR). The issues to be considered when managing supply chains are covered in more detail in Chapter 15.

> **EXECUTIVE INSIGHT**
> Your business must aim to create sustainable supply chains that have a positive economic, social and environmental impact within all parts of the chain.

Digital supply

Developments in IT have changed the format of some services and products together with the supply chain used to deliver them. One recent change is in the form of digital supply. Digital supply chains initially evolved from the delivery of digital media (such as music or video) by electronic means from the point of origin (content provider) to a destination where it is then consumed (such as a computer, mobile phone or television). One outcome has been to simplify the provision of services and products and with it the task of managing the associated supply chain.

The growth in digital supply was triggered by a couple of significant IT developments, as shown in Figure 12.12:

- **Increase in electronic and more mobile devices** – such as mobile phones and portable electronic devices (for example iPods and iPhones)

- **Faster and more mobile internet access** – through faster broadband speeds and more wi-fi hotspots and 3G mobile networks.

These developments provide the opportunity for companies to restructure their service and product provision.

Figure 12.12 **Factors affecting growth in digital media markets**							
Key indicators (millions)	**2003**	**2004**	**2005**	**2006**	**2007**	**2008**	**2009**
Broadband lines	104	151	209	280	350	411	471
Mobile phone subscriptions	1,185	1,350	1,817	2,017	2,500	3,087	3,700
3G mobile phone subscriptions	–	25	90	137	614	895	1,153
Portable music player sales	2	12	84	120	140	160	176

> **EXECUTIVE INSIGHT**

The continued development of mobile electronic devices and faster internet connections creates the opportunity for companies to move from physical to digital supply chains.

By moving from physical to digital products companies can deliver these through digital supply chains. This has led to a number of benefits for both the supplier and the customer including:

- Customer benefits
  - Increased delivery speed – products can be consumed within seconds of being ordered
  - Wider availability – products can be downloaded from anywhere
  - Ease of use – products are simpler to find and purchase than through a traditional retail channel
  - Cheaper products – products are cheaper to buy than through traditional retail channels.

- Supplier benefits
  - Lower cash holdings – companies do not have to hold product inventory: instead, they can put one digital version of the product into a data centre and sell this a million times over
  - Lower costs – no excess or obsolete inventory and no physical supply chain
  - Supply chain is easier to manage – no physical inventory, no inventory management systems, no quality issues and no physical purchase orders.

> **EXECUTIVE INSIGHT**

Digital supply chains give customers access to a wider range of cheaper products that they can access more quickly. They are also easier to manage, enabling suppliers to reduce cash holdings and supply costs.

Such developments are well illustrated by the digital recorded music industry, the growth of which is show in Figures 12.13 and 12.14 with Apple's iPod and iTunes retail stores driving the revolution (see Case 12.7) as they offer an increasingly diverse range of products and services. In fact, PricewaterhouseCoopers forecasts that revenues from the global media industry will rise by 5.7 per cent per year to $1.9 trillion in 2015. However, these ideas are also starting to impact other industries and consultancy firms such as Hewlett-Packard and Capgemini now offer digital supply chain services.

Figure 12.13 **Growth of digital recorded music market**

Digital recorded music	2003	2004	2005	2006	2007	2008	2009	2010
Revenues ($m)	20	380	1,125	2,174	2,900	3,712	4,243	4,636
% total industry	–	2	5	11	15	20	27	29

Figure 12.14 **Example growth of digital media markets**

Global digital revenues (% total)	2003	2004	2005	2006	2007	2008	2009	2010
Recorded music	–	2	5	11	15	20	27	29
Newspapers	–	–	–	–	2	4	6	8
Films	–	–	–	–	3	4	5	7
Books	–	–	–	–	2	4	8	12

Source: PWC Global Entertainment and Media Report (2011).

The iTunes software was created in 2001 to let customers manage the music on their iPods. Two years later, the iTunes music store was launched selling 200,000 songs that could each be downloaded for $0.99. It took three years to sell one billion songs, but then things started to take off and by February 2008 iTunes had sold more than 4 billion songs, owned 70 per cent of the worldwide digital music market and was the third-largest US music retailer behind Walmart and Best Buy. Profits are low on sales (about 9 per cent), but Apple's iPod sales grew seven-fold when iTunes was first introduced in 2003 and it keeps customers locked in to using their iPods.

By June 2010, 300 million iPods had been sold. Apple still owned 70 per cent of the MP3 player market with competitors getting fewer and fewer as rivals decided to leave the market. Estimates show each iPod customer spends another 30 per cent of the iPod value on accessories. In June 2007, Apple launched the iPhone combining its iPod touch with a mobile smartphone. By January 2010, it had sold 45 million iPhones and had 16 per cent of the smartphone market. Building on this success, it launched the iPad in April 2010, as a tablet computer running a similar operating system to the iPod touch and iPhone. By June 2010, just 60 days after its launch, it had sold 2 million iPads averaging one every three seconds.

www.apple.com/iTunes

Questions

1. What is Apple's business model?

2. How has its digital supply chain contributed to its recent success?

(Answer these questions in relation to how to manage the supply chain.)

Lecturers: visit www.palgrave.com/business/hillom3e for teaching guidelines for this case study

Developing supply chains

The goal of supply chain management is to more efficiently and effectively align customers, distribution channels, operations and suppliers to better support market needs. As outlined earlier, many companies focused on fixing their own operations problems in the 1980s, but few looked across the whole supply chain. However, in the 1990s this changed as a European-based survey in 1996 showed.[1] Of the companies reviewed, 88 per cent had significantly overhauled their supply chains and saw this as key to improving their overall performance. However, this is not radically different from Ralph Borsodi's observation in 1929[2] that the cost of distributing necessities and luxuries had nearly trebled between 1870 and 1920, while production costs had come down by one fifth… and what we are saving in production we are losing in distribution. The same scenario exists today: consequently companies need to look both upstream and downstream if they are to improve overall supply chain performance and market support. Supply chain activities require integrating, coordinating and synchronising across the whole chain.

> **EXECUTIVE INSIGHT**
> Supply chains can be developed to more efficiently and effectively support market needs by integrating, coordinating and synchronising activities across the chain.

Stages of development

This section reviews the origins and evolution of supply chains and examines the steps typically involved in their development.

Origin and evolution of supply chains

The functional management and control used to manage organizations in the past results in fragmented supply chains by focusing on managing **vertical** rather than **horizontal processes**, as illustrated in Figure 12.15. The figure shows how functions within an organization have their own self-contained reporting structures and systems. This results in artificial barriers being created between the different steps of the supply chain, which causes fragmentation, delay or unnecessary inventory to be locked in the system.

Integrating activities

The first step in developing a supply chain is to integrate activities within the **internal supply chain**, as illustrated in Figure 12.16. To do this, companies must align all the activities involved from initial customer contact to final service or product delivery. Forging cooperation across all these steps will create an integrated internal chain and identify opportunities to reduce costs and improve customer support.

Vertical processes – resulting from hierarchical reporting structures.

Horizontal processes – managing across the processes within and between businesses.

Internal supply chain – that part of a supply chain that is managed within a business.

Figure 12.15 **Phase 1 – fragmented supply chains**

Figure 12.16 Phase 2 – integrating supply chain activities within a business

Suppliers | Internal supply chain | Distribution | Customers

Delays/inventory

Coordinating activities

Once the internal supply chain has been integrated, companies can start coordinating activities between the different businesses within the chain (i.e. the **external supply chain**). As shown in Figure 12.17, this coordination is across all parts of the chain – Tier 2 suppliers, **Tier 1 suppliers**, **Tier 1 customers** (such as wholesalers/retailers or distributors/dealers) and Tier 2 customers (such as end users) – to ensure there is collaboration across the whole of the chain.

Synchronizing activities

The final phase is to synchronize all the activities across the supply chain as shown in Figure 12.18. This requires partnership and strategic alliances to help create real-time information flows across the chain regarding aspects such as customer management, order placement, service or product design, payment and final delivery. This necessitates dramatic changes in roles and responsibilities across the chain with suppliers, distributors and customers often being involved in service or product design and deciding how much and when to dispatch, and is significantly different to the original supply chain design shown in Figure 12.15. However, companies must address a number of issues to achieve this:

- **Overcome the barriers to integration** – functions within organizations and organizations themselves create barriers to integration. Businesses must view the supply chain as a whole before thinking about how best to use it to better improve performance and market support.

- **Respond to short lead time** – delivery speed is an order-winner or qualifier for many customers. To reliably support this requires developing lean logistics and managing the supply chain as an integrated whole. A study completed by Ernst & Young and the University of Tennessee showed that average order cycle times fell from 6.3 to 3.5 days when they were outsourced.[3]

- **Eliminate costs** – integrated and synchronising the supply chain lowers costs by reducing inventory, simplifying procedures, eliminating duplication and removing other non-value-added activities together with associated overheads. In the same Ernst & Young and University of Tennessee study, outsourcing in participating businesses led to average logistics costs and average logistic assets falling by 8 and 22 per cent respectively.

- **Move information, not inventory** – focusing on moving information rather than materials enables companies to reduce delays and deliver against **real-time needs** rather than using inventory to cushion against uncertain demand.

> **External supply chain** – that part of the supply chain managed by suppliers.
>
> A **Tier 1 supplier** supplies directly to an organization, a Tier 2 supplier supplies materials to a Tier 1 supplier and so on.
>
> A **Tier 1 customer** is supplied directly by an organization, a Tier 2 customer is supplied by a Tier 1 customer and so on.

> **Real-time needs** – the immediate requirements of a customer.

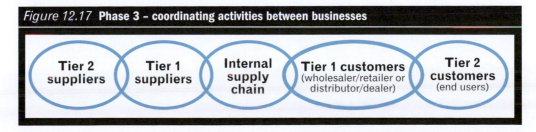

Figure 12.17 Phase 3 – coordinating activities between businesses

Tier 2 suppliers | Tier 1 suppliers | Internal supply chain | Tier 1 customers (wholesaler/retailer or distributor/dealer) | Tier 2 customers (end users)

Figure 12.18 **Phase 4 – real-time planning and execution of activities across the supply chain**

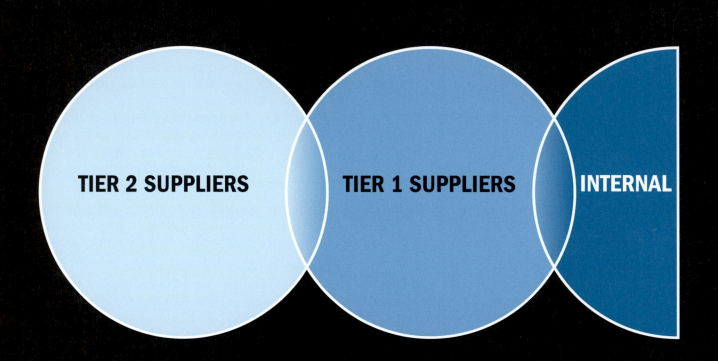

TIME INFORMATION FLOWS

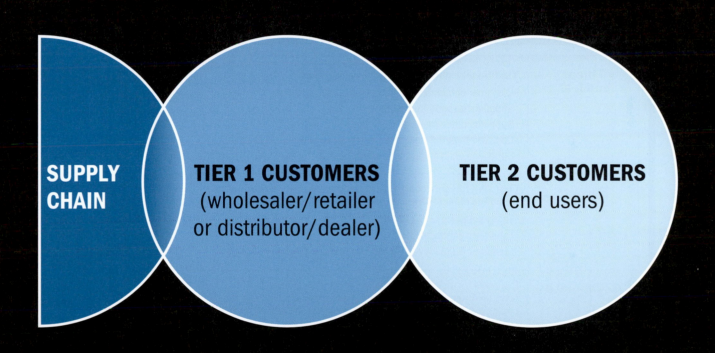

SUPPLY CHAIN

TIER 1 CUSTOMERS
(wholesaler/retailer
or distributor/dealer)

TIER 2 CUSTOMERS
(end users)

> **EXECUTIVE INSIGHT**

To develop a supply chain, you must first integrate activities across the chain, then look for ways to coordinate them before finally working out how to synchronize them.

An example of **lean supply chain management** is the revolutionary changes brought to high peak climbing by Reinhold Messner described in Case 12.8.

Tools and techniques for developing supply chains

Making the changes outlined in the last section involves addressing a number of critical issues within the business and the key ones are now discussed.

> **EXECUTIVE INSIGHT**

Businesses can develop their supply chains by improving customer support, changing attitudes towards suppliers, using IT, developing strategic partnerships and working with customers to better understand their needs.

Lean supply chain management – extending JIT principles to the whole supply chain so as to eliminate waste and reduce inventory throughout; typically based on close, long-term relationships with a small number of suppliers.

Figure 12.19 **Phases in changing attitudes to suppliers**

Threat and fear	**Traditional stance. Perceptions based upon:** · Customer dominates the relationship with suppliers · Suppliers respond to demands · Suppliers pitted against each other · Constant threat of purchases being given to other suppliers · Supplier's ongoing fear of losing contract
Reward	**First step towards cooperation and moving from a reactive to a proactive stance. Characterized by elements such as:** · Fewer suppliers · Long-term contracts · Customer is proactive in building a relationship with suppliers
Collaborate	**Progressive move towards fuller and more cooperative relationships, the pace of which is set predominantly by the customer. Evolution through a series of steps such as:** · Customer identifies improvements that a supplier can make · Customer provides support and resources (for example, technical capability) to undertake improvements within supplier's delivery systems · Customer gives actual help to improve supplier's capabilities, including training supplier's staff · Customer takes into account the processes of its suppliers when designing services and products to help them improve their support · Customer focuses attention on Tier 2 suppliers as a source of improving Tier 1 suppliers' support (see Figure 12.17)
Integrate and synchronize	The final step is to integrate activities achieving benefits typically associated with ownership – the concept of virtual ownership. Based upon mutual respect and trust, these include suppliers' access to real time information, with customers harmonising their suppliers' work and synchronizing their support. These changes range from: · Access to design-related information and responsibility for service/product design · Suppliers' responsibility for deciding when and how much to despatch

Reinhold Messner, the Italian climber, is one of the great sports heroes of Europe. His claim to fame is not so much that he has climbed all 14 of the world's highest peaks, but that he introduced a totally new way of climbing – the direct alpine approach – which uses little equipment and no oxygen support to reach the top.

Conventional mountaineering strategy is based on massive support, including extra oxygen, thought essential for climbs over 25,000 feet. Climbers such as Sir Edmund Hillary and Chris Bonington relied on hundreds of guides who carried food, oxygen and supplies. In fact, in 1963 one American expedition to climb Everest included 900 porters carrying 300 tonnes of equipment. Messner argues that under this strategy, the slowest man sets the pace. His goal is speed of execution. Although assisted by guides up the base of the mountain,

Messner makes the final assault by himself, or with one other person, in a single day. When Hillary and Tenzing first climbed Mt Everest in 1953, they took seven weeks. On 22 May 2004, Pemba Dorji Sherpa took 5 hours 10 minutes using the direct alpine approach!

www.reinhold-messner.de

Questions

1. Review the stages in the supply chain represented in Figure 12.15 with that of the conventional mountaineering strategy described above. What similarities can you draw?

2. Repeat the analysis for Figure 12.18 and Messner's approach to mountaineering.

Lecturers: visit www.palgrave.com/business/hillom3e for teaching guidelines for this case study

Improving consumer support

There is more to supply chain management than hard-nosed procurement and tight inventory control. While effective management concerns eliminating delays and reducing resources along the way, such improvements also need to create more effective support. To do this, customers/companies need to understand market requirements and how best to support them rather than simply aiming to reduce cost.

Changing attitude to suppliers

Traditionally, companies have not cooperated with suppliers with the aim of building long-term relationships. Instead, they have ruled through threat and fear by maintaining control over product or service design and order scheduling and then pitting suppliers against each other to meet their requirements. To change this attitude, companies must bring suppliers on board much earlier in the design process and even invite them to help in identifying future services and products. They need to understand how to reward and collaborate with them if they are to build integrated and synchronized supply chains, and to recognize that this is a lengthy development process that goes through the series of phases shown in Figure 12.19. The approach required to make this change is described in Figure 12.20. Case 12.9 explains the approach that some Japanese companies use when working with their suppliers.

Figure 12.20 Changing approach to managing supply chains

Dimensions		Approach	
		From	To
Customers and suppliers		Contractural relationships	Harness the power of partnerships
Basis for competition		Manufacturer	Supply chain
Organisation relationships		Functional/corporate orientation	Cooperation
Focus		Individual contract	Relationship
Communication		Primarily one way	Two way and balanced
Performance measures	Focus	Individual parties	Partnership
	Development	Independently	Jointly
	Results	Might be shared	Joint performance
Risk/reward evaluation		By transaction	Over the life of the relationship

Identifying potential suppliers

It is important to keep up to date with current developments and potential suppliers. Sources of supplier information include:

- **In-house information** – files showing the range of services and materials previously delivered by suppliers, their historical delivery reliability and quality conformance performance and their ability to handle long-term and short-term changes in demand

- **Supplier catalogues** – various supplier catalogues should be gathered and put into an in-house library to highlight potential sources of services and materials

- **Trade registers, directories and journals** – registers, such as the Kompass Publications, provide technical and general background on potential suppliers, while trade journals give current information on suppliers related to the technical areas covered by that journal

- **Trade exhibitions** – provide opportunities to identify potential suppliers and discuss the services and products that they can deliver

CASE 12.9 JAPANESE COMPANIES: APPROACH TO SUPPLIERS

Reproduced with the permission of Canon (UK)

Viewed in the past merely as purchasing, supply chain management is now recognized as a strategic part of operations that stretches from suppliers to end-customers. Suppliers are no longer transient providers selected solely on the basis of lowest cost but partners contributing to the continuous improvement of the supply chain that delivers value to customers. While Japanese buyer–supplier relationships vary from firm to firm and sector to sector, companies as diverse as Nintendo, Canon and Toyota display certain common aspects in their different approaches to suppliers.

Once selected, component suppliers are retained during the life cycle of the specific model. Staff from the buyer will typically train supplier's staff on their operations and quality procedures and other aspects of the organization. Finally, the buyer firm will evaluate the supplier organization to test the viability of a long-term relationship by ensuring the robustness of the whole organization.

www.nintendo.com
www.canon.com
www.toyota.com

Questions

1. Review the common aspects in the Japanese companies' approach to suppliers.

2. How do these illustrate the 'change in attitude' highlighted above?

Lecturers: visit www.palgrave.com/business/hillom3e for teaching guidelines for this case study

- **Professional colleagues** – other professional colleagues whose judgement you respect and trust can be a good source of potential suppliers.

Evaluating potential suppliers

From the long list of potential suppliers, companies need to evaluate prospective providers by conducting an initial evaluation, visiting the supplier's facilities and reviewing its ability to help you support your markets, reduce your cash holdings and reduce your costs. Each step in this process is now explained in more detail:

1. **Initial evaluation** – the first step is to conduct an initial evaluation of the potential suppliers looking at their:
   - *Financial stability* – looking at a supplier's credit rating, does it have the necessary resources to support you both now and in the future?
   - *Technical capability* – is it able to meet the specifications of your current and future service and product requirements?
   - *Managerial capability* – will it undertake self-initiated developments and improvements, make changes and investments to help support your needs and be willing potentially to develop a partnership with you in the future?
   - *Operations capacity* – does it have the capacity to support your anticipated levels of demand and any plans for future growth?
   - *Market support* – how well does the supplier support the relevant order-winners and qualifiers of its current customers? This will help in understanding its ability to support your own markets.

2. **Visit supplier facilities** – once a shortlist has been identified, these suppliers can then be visited to understand in more detail each ones:
   - *Technical capability* – what level of process, equipment and system investment has been made within its facilities? What is the competence of the technical and operations management teams? What customers does it currently support? What services and products does it currently provide?
   - *Managerial capability* – how professionally was the visit handled? What is the attitude and stability of the top and middle management teams? What is the level of staff morale within the business? Are staff willing to work with you to meet your goals and support your current and future customers?
   - *Operations capacity* – how much capacity does it currently have? How much spare capacity is available? Does it have access to other in-house or external capacity? Is it planning on investing in more capacity in the future?
   - *Market support* – how does it measure its performance? How appropriate are these measures given the order-winners and qualifiers that it has to support? How appropriate are these measures to the order-winners and qualifiers that you have to support in your current and future markets? How well has it performed against these measures over the past few months?

3. **Review ability to help you support your markets** – a number of checks then need to be made to understand if a supplier is capable of supporting your current and future order-winners and qualifiers. These include:
   - *Price* – what price has it quoted for the services and products you require? Is it making investments to reduce its future material, labour and overhead costs? What is its current mix of production volumes? What are its current levels of efficiency and productivity? What are its current production volumes and run lengths?
   - *Quality conformance* – what are its current quality conformance levels for the services and products it delivers? Does it have any quality systems in place such as ISO 9000? Has it won any quality awards recently such as EFQM?
   - *Delivery reliability* – what are its current levels of delivery performance for services and products similar to the ones that you require? What are its current operations lead-times? What are the current levels of waiting time within its existing operations processes? Would it be prepared to hold inventory in its process to reduce the operations lead-time?

- *Delivery speed* – what is its current operations lead-time? What are the current levels of waiting time within its existing operations processes? What are its current material lead-times? Would it be prepared to hold inventory in its process to reduce the operations lead-time?
- *Service or product range* – what is the current range of services and products that it delivers? What other services and products is it developing? How much of its sales revenue is historically invested in research and development?
- *Demand fluctuations* – is it able to make short-term increases in its operations capacity? What percentage of the people working in the business are on part-time contracts? How much spare capacity is available? Does it have access to other in-house or external capacity? Is it planning on investing in more capacity in the future?
- *Speed of new service or product development* – how long has it previously taken to develop and launch new services or products? How much of its sales revenue has it historically invested in research and development?
- *Technical support* – what levels of technical support are currently provided to its customers? How many people currently provide technical support to its customers? Is it making any investments to increase the level of technical support offered?

4. **Review ability to help you reduce your cash holdings** – once its ability to support your markets has been reviewed, then you need to understand how each supplier could help you reduce your cash holdings:
- *Payment terms* – what are the payment terms for the services and products it delivers?
- *Minimum order quantities* – what are the minimum order quantities for the services and products that it provides? What are the prices associated with ordering different quantities of its services and products?
- *Managing your inventory levels* – what inventory management services does it currently offer to its customers? How many people currently provide inventory management services to its customers? It is making any investments to increase the level of inventory management support offered to its customers?
- *Holding inventory for you* – does it currently hold consignment inventory for its customers? If so, then where is this inventory located? Would it hold consignment inventory for you?

5. **Review ability to help you reduce your costs** – finally you need to understand how each supplier could help you reduce your costs:
- *Material costs* – what price has it quoted for the services and products you require? Is it making investments to reduce its future material, labour and overhead costs? What is its current mix of production volumes? What are its current levels of efficiency and productivity? What are its current production volumes and run lengths?
- *Labour costs* – what services does it offer that could help you reduce your labour costs? What inventory management services does it currently offer to its customers? What delivery arrangements does it currently have in place with its customers? Is it prepared to develop customer-specific packaging to help you manage and process its products? Is it prepared to develop services that will help reduce your transportation and logistics costs?
- *Overhead costs* – what services does it offer that could help you reduce your overhead costs? What inventory management services does it currently offer to its customers? Does it currently hold consignment inventory for its customers?

Selecting suppliers

Suppliers should be selected using a weighting system showing how well each of them performs against the relevant criteria used to review them using the following three steps:

1. **Agree selection criteria** – however, it is always important to consider the impact on market support, cash and costs.

2. **Weighting importance of selection criteria** – to reflect:
   - *Market support* – the level of importance of different market order-winners and qualifiers that have to be supported in your own markets
   - *Cash* – the need to release cash within the business so that it can be invested elsewhere
   - *Costs* – the need to reduce costs within the business.

3. **Rate each potential supplier** – against these selection criteria. Figure 12.21 shows an example of how this approach can be used to compare four potential suppliers, with Supplier C coming out on top due to its better technical capability, ability to support long-term capacity requirements, delivery speed and ability to hold and manage inventory levels.

Figure 12.21 **The weighted-factor approach for selecting suppliers**

Aspect	Criteria	Importance	Weighting for potential supplier			
			A	B	C	D
Financial stability	Current stability	10	10	10	10	10
	Ability to support future requirements	20	20	20	20	20
	Subtotal	**30**	**30**	**30**	**30**	**30**
Managerial capability	Current capability	10	5	5	10	10
	Ability to support future requirements	20	10	10	20	20
	Subtotal	**30**	**15**	**15**	**30**	**30**
Technical capability	Current capability	40	30	40	40	40
	Ability to support future requirements	60	40	40	50	50
	Subtotal	**100**	**70**	**80**	**90**	**90**
Operations capacity	Current capacity	20	20	20	20	20
	Ability to increase in short term	10	0	0	10	5
	Ability to meet long-term requirements	50	30	40	45	40
	Subtotal	**80**	**50**	**60**	**75**	**65**
Support markets	Delivery speed	80	40	40	70	50
	Delivery reliability	60	50	60	60	50
	Technical support	40	30	30	35	30
	Quality conformance	40	40	35	35	35
	Price	30	30	30	20	30
	Subtotal	**250**	**190**	**195**	**220**	**195**
Release cash	Payment terms	10	10	10	10	10
	Minimum order quantities	10	5	5	10	10
	Managing your inventory levels	20	5	5	20	10
	Holding inventory for you	20	5	5	20	10
	Subtotal	**60**	**25**	**25**	**60**	**40**
Reduce costs	Material costs	10	10	10	5	10
	Labour costs	10	5	5	10	5
	Overhead costs	10	5	5	10	5
	Subtotal	**30**	**20**	**20**	**25**	**20**
Total		**580**	**400**	**425**	**530**	**470**

Measuring and improving supplier performance

The supplier selection process is based on expected performance against a number of criteria as shown in Figure 12.21. However, once a supplier has been selected then its actual performance against these same criteria needs to be measured and improved. When doing this, it is important to:

- **Agree measures with suppliers** – with an explanation of why and how they will be used.

- **Both customer and supplier measure performance** – and meet regularly to discuss trends and improvement opportunities. Keeping separate records will ensure they are both focusing on achieving these objectives and reveal any discrepancies that might occur.

- **Regular performance meetings** – to discuss current levels, identify improvements and discuss any future developments that might affect customer requirements or supplier performance.

Distribution and transportation systems

Distribution is a key element within a supply chain and often accounts for 20 per cent of its total cost. For certain retail service companies it can be even higher. For example, LL Bean (the US-based retailer) despatches 11 million packages a year (an average of 650,000 each week) and fills a 40-foot trailer every 20 minutes during peak times. Distribution and transportation costs depend largely on:

- **Location** – where a company is located relative to its customers, and the

- **Transportation system** – which reflects how quickly its services or products need to be delivered, how many have to be delivered and the physical nature of the product being delivered. For example, oil will be piped from oil well or oilfield to a refinery. However, once refined, these oil products (such as petrol and diesel) will be taken to petrol or gas stations by road.

The five principal commercial modes of transportation are rail, road (trucking), water, air and pipeline. The options have different pricing structures and speed factors as shown in Figure 12.22. However, some of these relative positions would change if the distance travelled was lengthened or shortened.

Each option is now discussed in more detail:

- **Rail** – is best for transporting low-value, high-density, bulk products such as raw materials over long distances. Examples include coal, minerals and ores. Although it transports products quickly between two points, the overall transportation lead-time is long because the products have to be transported to the rail station first and then onto the customer's facility afterwards, usually by road.

- **Road** – provides a flexible point-to-point service for delivering small quantities of products over both short and long distances. As a result, it is the most popular way

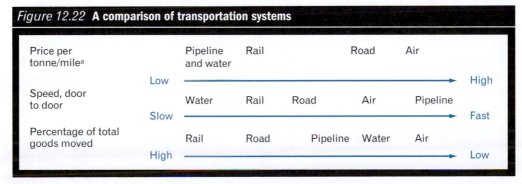

Figure 12.22 **A comparison of transportation systems**

Price per tonne/mile[a]		Pipeline and water	Rail		Road	Air	
	Low	→					High
Speed, door to door		Water	Rail	Road	Air	Pipeline	
	Slow	→					Fast
Percentage of total goods moved		Rail	Road	Pipeline	Water	Air	
	High	→					Low

Note: [a] price per tonne/mile = one tonne of freight carried one mile.

of moving freight particularly given the increased emphasis on reducing the levels of inventory within a supply chain. In more developed economies, road haulage systems are extensive and the service provided is typically fast, reliable and less prone to damage than some alternatives. The growing use of articulated vehicles (in which the trailer detaches from the front pulling unit) and containers allows vehicle loading to be completed while the front pulling unit (and high investment part of a truck) can be used elsewhere.

- **Airfreight** – can be used to deliver relatively small packages quickly and reliably using providers such as UPS, Federal Express and DHL. Examples of the types of product shipped by airfreight include medical supplies, electronic components, perishable products such as flowers, fruit and vegetables, and documents. However, it is more expensive than the other alternatives and is not much quicker than road haulage for distances less than 500 miles due to the increased time spent collecting, handling, loading, unloading and delivering the products.

- **Water** – most countries have a wide range of rivers, canals, lakes, coastlines and oceans that can be used for transporting products. However, while it is a low-cost alternative, it is also a very slow and inflexible system. It is particularly suited to moving heavy bulk items such as raw materials, ores, grain, chemical, mineral and petroleum products. To help reduce the delivery time and handling costs, a number of Transocean shipping companies have developed intermodal transport systems combining trucks, railroads and ships. During this process, goods are packed into standardized containers and remain in these for their entire journey.

- **Pipelines** – are used to transport liquids or gases from one point to another, for example crude oil, natural gas, petrol, diesel, water and slurry products that have been pulverized and transformed into liquid (such as clay and coal). Although pipelines require a high level of initial investment, they have a long life and are low cost to operate. They are also able to transport materials over terrains where other transportation systems could not cope (such as the trans-Alaskan and North Sea oil pipelines).

Increasing the use of IT

Since the early 1960s four major IT developments have transformed the way companies conduct business and are able to better manage their supply chains from suppliers through to end users.

- **Mainframes** – in the early 1960s companies began using mainframe computers to manage their businesses. Business applications included material requirements planning (MRPI) and manufacturing resource planning (MRPII), which enabled companies to standardize and systemize their day-to-day tasks. However, this emphasized the functional divisions within organizations as people became systems experts within their own business area.

- **Personal computers** – in the 1970s personal computers started to be used within companies to run applications such as word processors, spreadsheets and presentation software. This development started to put the power of computing back into the hands of employees and helped break down functional barriers by creating cross-functional processes.

- **Network computing** – in the mid-1980s computer networks were introduced with customer/supplier applications, **electronic data interchange (EDI)**, **electronic point-of-sale (EPOS)** and electronic mail. This significantly reduced the costs of handling information and increased its speed of exchange allowing companies to develop real-time systems and responses as illustrated by Case 12.10.

- **E-commerce** – in the early 1990s, the internet was developed providing a universal infrastructure that facilitates the interchange of information between businesses. This further helped cooperation across the supply chain enabling priorities and performance

Electronic data interchange (EDI) – a system using remote computer networks to exchange business data between companies within a supply chain without going through any intermediaries.

Electronic point-of-sale (EPOS) – a system that records sales and payment transactions at cash terminals in retail stores as and when they happen and typically used to track sales trends on which to base purchase orders and to replenish goods in stores.

E-commerce – the use of the internet to transfer information across the supply chain, or to buy or sell services and products.

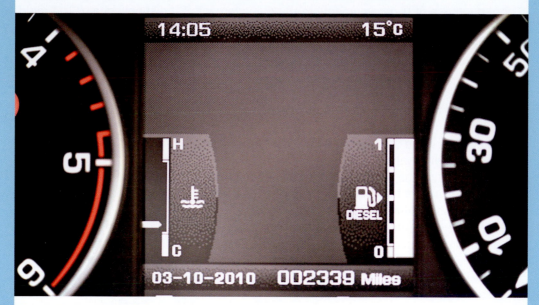

Caterpillar, the giant US earth-moving equipment manufacturer, has developed electronically based systems that identify ahead of time when equipment needs servicing. An electronic message is relayed to the Caterpillar centre. The local dealer is alerted as well as the necessary parts to complete the servicing requirement being sent. Dealers agree appropriate dates with customers and the specified work is then completed.
www.caterpillar.com

GAP, the US-based apparel company, is currently achieving 14 inventory turns a year while also being able to change the stockholding in all its outlets 13 times per year and on the same day. The data requirements and real-time systems that underpin these arrangements include accurate inventory data, electronic point-of-sale (EPOS) facilities and synchronized logistics.
www.gap.com

© istockphoto.com/Jon Schulte

Question

Explain how IT developments have enabled Caterpillar and GAP to change their business model.

Lecturers: visit www.palgrave.com/business/hillom3e for teaching guidelines for this case study

to be managed across the chain through better communication and interchange of information between companies. The earlier section on digital supply highlights the continued use of IT developments in the management of the supply chain. The rapid growth of e-commerce has, however, brought with it some concerns that originate from both the delivery system that underpins the system and the speed of its use within commercial activities and transactions:

– *Fraud* – the Fraud Advisory Panel (the UK government's Serious Fraud Office) estimates that fraud could be costing £5 billion a year and is likely to increase. US data from the National Consumers' League supported this trend. Its reports showed that incidents of internet fraud in 1996 were 689 and by 1999 these had increased to 10,660 at a value of $3.2 million. The rise has continued, with 37,183 incidents with a corresponding value of $20.5 million by 2003.

– *Vulnerability* – the level and nature of vulnerable outcomes inherent in the growing use of the internet are being highlighted in a series of incidents throughout the world from bomb-making to arranging and managing gang violence.

– *Focusing on non-value-added activities* – increasingly companies have focused attention on minimizing non-value-added activities while providing information and communication tools that allow employees to focus on the value-added and strategic activities within a business. As firms reduce non-value-added activities, they redirect those newly released resources to the value-added and strategic dimensions of their business. For example, companies are increasingly using electronic intranet catalogues that enable office staff (the actual consumer) to order non-operations goods (for example office supplies and computer software) directly from agreed suppliers. Not only does this break down barriers but also eliminates non-value-added activities such as data re-entry and checking, thus allowing more time for purchasing staff to focus on their value-added activities such as developing supplier relations and contract negotiations.

> **E-procurement** – the use of the internet to enable everyone in an organization to buy services or products online.

• Introducing e-procurement – empowers everyone in the organization to buy online with the traditional purchasing forms, counter-forms and authorizations replaced by checks and controls within the software. However, this requires a significant culture change and the whole purchasing system has to be re-engineered to create a new way of working. As shown in Figure 12.23, electronic catalogues are at the heart of these developments. These catalogues are either managed in-house by the purchasing function or outsourced to a third-party provider. Once someone in the organization

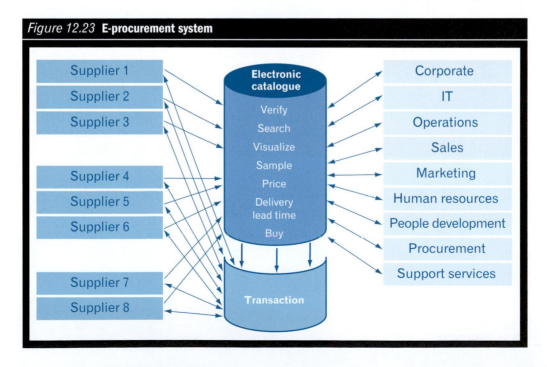

Figure 12.23 E-procurement system

has completed an electronic purchasing application, the system checks the service or product specification, price and delivery dates and offers other alternatives. Once the person has decided on the service or product they want, the system then places the order and monitors its progress. Estimates suggest that companies can save up to 11 per cent of indirect purchasing costs by introducing e-purchasing systems for dealing with the procurement of indirect services and products. This is a significant saving given that companies can spend up to 15–20 per cent of sales revenue on indirect services and products. Other benefits include:

- *Increased in-contract compliance* – due to increased use of preferred suppliers, reduced off-contract spending and reduced processing errors
- *Reduced material costs* – increased visibility and understanding of the actual spend by supplier, service or product gives the business greater purchasing power when negotiating discounts
- *Lower processing costs* – for example, Cisco Systems reduced its cost of procurement from an average of $130 to $40 per order due to faster processing times, lower number of faxes and telephone calls and reduced errors
- *Increased involvement of people* – staff throughout the business feel more involved and responsible for the purchase decision. They are also more aware of the process behind the decision and the alternatives that are available
- *Helps introduce an e-commerce system* – these initiatives tend to cover non-business critical items such as stationery. As such, they are low risk and usually result in a quick financial payback. This makes them a good initial step in introducing an e-commerce system.

Order fulfilment – all the steps involved in completing a customer's order.

Over the past 30 years, these IT developments have continually broken down the barriers between individuals, functions, businesses and corporations within supply chains, as shown in Figure 12.24. E-commerce presents some businesses with new opportunities and poses a significant threat to those who ignore it. Many sectors have seen the increasing and competitive impact of the internet. For those ready to adapt to the new technology, it represents an opportunity to rethink all aspects of **order fulfilment**, from order entry to distribution, as shown in Case 12.11.

Figure 12.24 **The evolving role of IT in managing supply chains**	
Phase	**Aspects of change**
1. Cross-individuals	Broke down barriers between functional experts themselves and between these and the executives responsible for managing core parts of a business, particularly operations
2. Cross-functional	Facilitated links between functions by requiring and helping the interchange between different parts of the same business
3. Cross-businesses	Impacted on the way companies conduct business by removing barriers within an organization and between parts of the immediate supply chain
4. Cross-corporate	Continued the cross-corporate changes by facilitating cooperation of businesses within a supply chain including Tier 2 suppliers

As Figure 12.25 shows, businesses are increasingly using IT to grow sales revenue rather than reduce costs. For example, putting internet-based information in front of consumers is transforming US pharmaceutical supply chains where, unlike Europe, companies are allowed to advertise their products. Putting information about their drugs on the internet means patients can quickly find out about new treatments and more proactively look for ways to use them. For example, GlaxoSmithKline's new treatment for diabetes, Avandia, outsold rival products in its first six months on the market as a result of its more effective e-commerce strategy.

CASE 12.11 DELL: SUPPLY CHAIN INTEGRATION

One company that is building on its current history of excellent supply chain management is Dell Computer Corporation. Dell uses supply chain management to continuously improve its direct business model by sound supply chain integration as follows:

- Dell only makes-to-order – no resources are committed until a customer order is received.

- Dell purchases components on a JIT basis, thus benefiting from the latest (that is, lowest) component prices.

- By holding little inventory, Dell is able to respond to component developments quickly and without incurring inventory losses through obsolescence.

- Short component lead-times also allow Dell to meet the delivery speed characteristics of its market with minimum investment in inventory.

Dell continues to develop and improve the capabilities of its supply chain in several ways. In 2009, the Dell website was generating daily revenues of more than $25 million. The website makes online ordering quick and convenient by allowing customers to specify the product features they want and instantly receive a quoted price.

In the corporate sales market, Dell has also created 'Premier Pages'. These are websites dedicated to corporate clients that can be accessed by a client's authorized employees to research, configure and price personal computers before purchase. Each website page holds client-specific data such as preferred configurations, specifications and prices. This development increases the accuracy of orders and simplifies Dell's customer ordering process resulting in the overall cost of buying PCs being greatly reduced. For example, the Ford Motor Company estimates that using Premier Pages saves it up to $2 million annually.

www.dell.com

Questions

1. Explain how Dell integrates its supply chain.

2. How does the Dell website feature in these integrative developments?

3. How is the Ford Motor Company able to save up to $2 million annually by using Dell's Premier Pages?

Lecturers: visit www.palgrave.com/business/hillom3e for teaching guidelines for this case study

Figure 12.25 **The main goal of IT investment for organizations**

Period	Goal (% total)	
	Cost-cutting	Sales revenue growth
1991–92	69	31
1996–97	37	63
2001–02	20	80

Source: The *Economist* survey of electronic commerce.

Equally, the UK supermarket Sainsbury's has built a web-based supply chain, planning and collaboration system, which allows suppliers and buyers to work through every detail of a product promotion in advance and track its success in real time. This enables it to better plan and support its special promotions, which account for about 10 per cent of sales revenue. Similarly, Chrysler developed an online system for customer purchases to help customers make better car-purchasing decisions. It now has over $15 billion online sales.

As sales revenue growth adds value to a business, current e-commerce developments are reflecting this potential core contribution. Whereas currently e-commerce typically allows customers to order from a specified range of services and goods, increasingly customers will be asked 'What is your need?' The requirement for supply chains to be able to cope with exceptions is the next phase of development. To do this the supply chain will move from a passive to a more dynamic mode, responding to customer demands, advising if it has the capability to meet the requirement, at what price and in what lead time. The impact that such developments will have on the supply chain will require fresh approaches to how services and products are managed in operations.

> **Virtual integration –** when an organization works with other companies in the chain as if they were part of their own company and so enabling the whole chain to become more competitive.

Developing strategic partnerships

The ultimate aim is for companies to move to the level of strategic partnering This embodies a conscious decision to **virtually integrate** the supply chain by working with other companies in the chain as if they were part of one's own business and so enabling the whole chain to become more competitive. However, this requires a major change in customer–supplier relations to synchronize activities across the chain so that it becomes vertically integrated (see Figure 12.19 earlier). How far customer attitudes to suppliers can be changed depends not only on the companies involved, but also the evolution of the industry within which it operates. For example, in the early days of the computing industry the major players had no option but to make all their components in-house. However, as the sector grew, companies emerged that produced specific components giving new industry entrants the opportunity to buy rather than make. As Michael Dell (founder of Dell) explained:

'As a new start-up, Dell couldn't afford to create every piece of the value chain. But more to the point, why should we want to? We concluded we'd be better off leveraging the investments others have made and focusing on delivering solutions and systems to customers... It's a pretty simple strategy, but at the time it went against the dominant "engineering-centric" view of the industry. The IBMs, Compaqs and HPs subscribed to a "we-have-to-develop-everything" view of the world. If you weren't doing component assembly you weren't a real computer company.'[4]

Some other examples of strategic partnership developments made by Volkswagen, Mercedes-Benz and Skoda are described in Case 12.12.

CASE 12.12 STRATEGIC PARTNERSHIP DEVELOPMENTS AT VOLKSWAGEN, MERCEDES-BENZ AND SKODA

Components account for over 60 per cent of the cost of a new car. Yet the component makers have traditionally not shared the risk of launching a new car. The car makers, on the other hand, have to meet large fixed investments, such as factories and capital equipment, in what are increasingly uncertain markets. Part of the move to strategic partnering is now based on shared costs and shared uncertainty. At Volkswagen's bus and truck plant in Resende (some 150 km from Rio de Janeiro, Brazil), about 35 per cent of the fixed costs have been met by component suppliers. Resende is also managed by VW and its suppliers under a profit-sharing consortium.

www.volkswagen-vans.com

The Hambach plant in eastern France, which builds the two-seater Mercedes-Benz sports car, provides another example of the changing relationships within strategic alliance developments. Ten suppliers preassemble important sections. For example, steel bodies come from Magna International (the Canadian group), fully assembled cockpits come from VDO (the German electronics maker) and complete door assemblies come from Ymos (the German component specialist). But that's not all. The 10 suppliers invested almost $300 million in the project.

www3.mercedes-benz.com

The assembly plant for Skoda's Octavia saloon is designed with six zones adjacent to the production line. The zones are also positioned on an outside wall so that the suppliers involved have direct truck access. The component suppliers are responsible for supporting the production schedule that includes the pre-assembly of parts just before they are required to go onto the car.

www.skoda-auto.com

Questions

1. What are the benefits of the supplier partnerships used by Volkswagen, Mercedes-Benz and Skoda?

2. What could other companies learn from these approaches?

Lecturers: visit www.palgrave.com/business/hillom3e for teaching guidelines for this case study

Work more closely with customers

On the delivery end of the chain, companies can work with their customers to better understand their needs. For example, some retail stores share electronic point-of-sale (EPOS) data with their suppliers to help them meet market trends and changes. On the sourcing end of the chain, suppliers can deliver more frequently, keep consignment stock in a customer's warehouse (and only invoice when it is used) and manage stock replenishment. This frees up customer resources while providing the supplier with a longer-term commitment, increased barriers to entry that reduce its sales and marketing expense and firm data to plan and schedule its own operations and supply chain. One illustration of increased partnering is provided in Case 12.13.

The benefits of improving supply chains

Supply chain developments can improve the performance of the whole chain by reducing costs, increasing access to technical expertise, shortening lead-times and reducing inventories as explained in the next section.

> **EXECUTIVE INSIGHT**
> Your business can develop its supply chains to reduce costs, reduce lead-times, reduce cash holdings and give greater access to technical expertise.

Reduced costs

As supply chains develop, the overall cost of supplying services or products through these chains reduces. A.T. Kearney Inc., a Chicago based consulting firm, estimates the cost of purchased parts and services can be reduced by up to 30 per cent by incorporating suppliers into their service or product development process. Large savings can also be made by encouraging suppliers to suggest cost-cutting ideas and design innovations for existing services and products.

Increased access to technical expertise

Suppliers can also be a great source of technical expertise as the following examples illustrate:

- Honda and Toyota – the Japanese car makers do not source much from low-wage countries as their supplier technical capability is seen as being more important than low labour costs.

- Dell – the US PC manufacturer recently increased its procurement spend with Taiwanese suppliers from to US$8 billion to US$12.5 billion on the agreement that they deliver the 'newest, greatest technology'.

Shorter lead-times

Improving supply chains can greatly reduce the overall lead-time of the chain by getting suppliers to become more than just parts providers. Involving suppliers and using their expertise provides several different ways to shorten the time it takes to supply a customer, as the following examples illustrate:

- A.W. Chesterton Co. – a US family-owned seal, pump and packing manufacturer found customers now wanted its products in days or even hours compared with 12–16 weeks a decade ago. To meet this requirement, it installed computer systems allowing customers to transmit drawings and engineering specifications directly to its manufacturing plant that was geared up for fast-response. However, this only reduced its in-house lead-time. To ensure customer needs were met, it then also reduced the number of suppliers it worked with from 1,300 to 125 and gave delivery reliability, delivery lead-times and quality conformance twice as much importance as price when evaluating with which suppliers to partner.

Calyx and Corolla, a US-based company, pioneered the delivery of fresh cut flowers direct to customers from the growers. Using Federal Express (FedEx), customers' orders are relayed to one of 25 suppliers (the flower growers) who assemble the chosen bouquet from one of 150 products.

Within the supply chain FedEx visits all suppliers to train their staff on the best ways to pack the flower arrangements and ensures that the delivery phase of the chain synchronizes with the work schedules and product availability of individual growers. Direct supply results in the flowers lasting 9–10 days longer than competitors' product offerings.

For Calyx and Corolla, this not only results in a no-inventory arrangement but the delivery speed and quality conformance advantages allow the company to price its products at a 60 per cent premium. Sales revenues in the period 1992–98 grew from $10 million to $25 million when the company was acquired by the Vermont Teddy Bear Company.

www.calyxflowers.com
www.vermontteddybear.com

Questions

1. How has Calyx and Corolla synchronized its supply chain?

2. What advantages has the company gained from these developments?

Lecturers: visit www.palgrave.com/business/hillom3e for teaching guidelines for this case study

- IKEA – the Swedish home furnishings retailer has also worked with its suppliers and made a number of in-house developments to meet the delivery speed needs of the fashion market it serves. This has been achieved through long-term relationships with 1,800 suppliers and a sophisticated in-house logistics and warehouse system. Electronic point-of-sale (EPOS) information from its 100 retail stores in over 50 countries provides online sales data to the nearest warehouse and the operational head office in Almhult, where information systems analyze sales patterns worldwide. In turn, the warehouses work with retail stores to anticipate demand and eliminate shortages while keeping inventory and floor space low.

- Acer – the Taiwanese PC maker meets the short product life cycles of its market by working on a 10-month rolling product life cycle: three months for product development, six months for sales of the product and one month to sell old inventory before the next cycle begins.

- Dana Corporation – a major supplier of truck axles has an entire 60-engineer laboratory near Toledo dedicated to U-joints. Using a computer-aided design (CAD) system, Dana can design new products cheaply and build prototypes for customers in just a few hours.

Lower inventories

Managing supply chains as a whole means moving to a 'one-firm concept' where external providers are treated like partners as if they were inside the company, as illustrated in Figure 12.26. For example:

- Eastman Chemical – uses 1,500 different raw materials provided by 850 suppliers. To make sure there is as little idle inventory as possible, Eastman uses a 'stream inventory management' system where the whole supply chain is treated as a single pipeline: 'When an order comes in from the customer, we take one pound of product out of the tail end, with the raw material function working with the supplier to put another pound in on the other end. We want to achieve continuous flow.' Eastman monitors inventory at its suppliers and uses accurate production forecasts to reduce excess inventory across the whole supply chain. As a result:

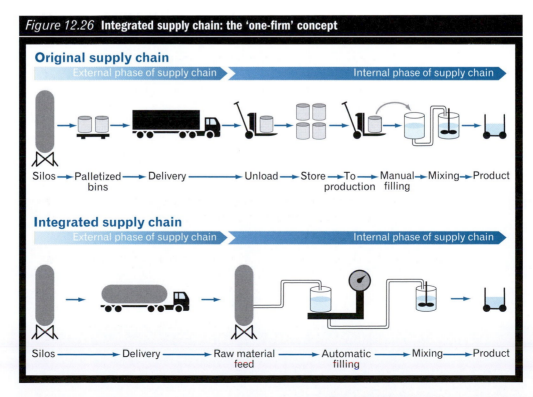

Figure 12.26 **Integrated supply chain: the 'one-firm' concept**

Original supply chain

External phase of supply chain   Internal phase of supply chain

Silos → Palletized bins → Delivery → Unload → Store → To production → Manual filling → Mixing → Product

Integrated supply chain

External phase of supply chain   Internal phase of supply chain

Silos → Delivery → Raw material feed → Automatic filling → Mixing → Product

- Total inventories halved in the last decade and are now 9 per cent of sales, with raw materials and supplies at less than 2 per cent
- Wood pulp stock reduced from three-months to nine-days supply, with the next target set at four-days
- Paraxylene, a material for polyethylene terephthalate (PET) plastic soda bottles, reduced from 18 million pounds held 20 years ago to 14 million pounds today even though production volume is three times higher.

Dell – the US PC manufacturer significantly reduced costs and inventories by selling direct to customers rather than through a third-party retailer. To do this, it has used technologies and information to 'virtually integrate' the chain and blur the traditional boundaries in the supply chain between suppliers and customers. This enables it to tap into the benefits of a coordinated supply chain traditionally only available through vertical integration while also tapping into the benefits of **specialization** where each company within the chain (Dell and its suppliers) focuses on what it is good at. Keeping inventories low is critical in the fast-changing technology business to protect the business from falling material prices and reduce the time for launching new products. For these reasons, Dell works closely with its suppliers to keep inventories low. For example, Airborne Express and United Parcel Services (UPS) collect computers from Dell and then match them with the same quantity of monitors from Sony's plant in Mexico before delivering them directly to Dell's customers. To do this, Dell has developed **real-time information** on its own demand profile and links this into its suppliers, sometimes every few hours. 'The greatest challenge in working with suppliers is getting them in sync with the fast pace we have to maintain. The key to making it work is information,' explained Michael Dell.[5] As a result, Dell's total inventory is less than 10 per cent of sales.

Specialization – concentrating on a limited area of expertise.

Real-time information – data that represents the current position.

Managing supply chains in practice

When managing supply chains in practice, it is important to consider the following aspects:

- **Increase flow of information** – to integrate and synchronize all of the steps within the chain so that they can compete effectively together towards the same goal. Information will only start to flow if companies trust and have relationships with each other. You need to develop this with your suppliers by starting to trust and share information with them. It is also important to look for ways to do this with your customers although this may be more difficult as you might have less power over this relationship.

- **Compete as a supply network** – the network is only as strong as its weakest link, so you need to find this link and focus your efforts on helping them better support your markets, manage your cash and reduce your costs.

- **Keep value-adding activities in-house** – normally, the right strategy is for companies to outsource their non-value-adding activities and focus their time and money on developing the value-adding activities that help them attract and retain customers. However, it is also important to keep in-house those activities that help you better understand customer requirements, maintain supply of key resources, retain core capabilities, create barriers to entry and take advantage of reduced trade barriers.

- **Consider alternatives to outsourcing** – to reduce the potential disadvantages of deciding to buy, you should also consider using joint ventures, non-equity collaborations or co-sourcing services, products or processes instead.

- **Challenge previous decisions to make or buy** – make-or-buy decisions need to be reviewed on an ongoing basis as markets change, products move through life cycles and new business opportunities become available. Also, inappropriate make-or-buy decisions are made as organizations often simply continue yesterday's decisions, outsource difficult tasks, ignore some of the costs and investments associated with outsourcing and respond to political pressure to make or buy.

- **Create sustainable supply networks** – you must aim to create networks that have a positive economic, social and environmental impact within all parts of the networks. Critical within this is to understand the expectations of all your stakeholders, in particular the ones with high levels of power and influence over your organization.

- **Look for opportunities to move from physical to digital networks** – it will not always be possible to do this, but when you can there will be huge benefits to you, your suppliers and your customers. If your initial reaction is 'this is not possible', then challenge yourself to understand how you could do this for at least part of your business.

- **Create opportunities for open innovation** – as discussed in more detail in Chapter 14 on improving operations, it is important to look outside of the organization to other stakeholders such as suppliers and customers to help you innovate and improve your supply networks. To do this, you must give them more power than they usually have. However, this will only be successful if open, honest and trusting relationships are in place.

Driving business performance

Releasing cash

Significant levels of cash can be released by integrating, coordinating and synchronising supply chains. For example:

- **Internal inventory** – improving information and material flow throughout the chain reduces the suppliers' lead-times and increases their delivery reliability. As a result, lower levels of inventory need to be held within the in-house steps of the chain.

- **External inventory** – improving information and material flows across the chain also means that suppliers are able to reduce their own inventory holdings as demand becomes more certain and predictable.

Improving market support

Some examples of how different market order-winners and qualifiers can be better supported through improved supply chains are:

- **Delivery speed** – increasing the flow of information helps suppliers reduce their lead-times and improve their ability to meet customers' short lead-time requirements. This often means helping suppliers reduce their order-backlog lead-time by providing them with more accurate sales forecasts and giving them firmer delivery commitments.

- **Delivery reliability** – by working with suppliers to identify and eliminate causes of supply variability.

- **New service and product development** – by identifying the suppliers that have responsibility for the key value-adding activities within the chain and working with them to develop new services and products.

- **New product introduction** – by reducing the levels of inventory throughout the chain so that new products can be introduced more quickly and more cheaply as existing products within the chain do not have to be sold first.

- **Service or product design** – by working with both customers and suppliers to help develop new products that better match customer requirements and better utilize suppliers' knowledge, experience and expertise.

Reducing costs

Significant cost reductions can be made by integrating activities across the chain and then finding ways to coordinate and synchronize them. For example, reducing:

- **Research and development costs** – by developing strategic partnerships with critical customers and suppliers.

- **Labour costs** – by outsourcing certain steps within the chain to countries with low labour costs, such as India (for services) and China (for products).

- **Material costs** – by developing long-term supplier relationships and using single sourcing policies. Businesses often also demand a year-on-year price reduction from a supplier where high-volume services or products are singly sourced.

- **Overhead costs** – by integrating, coordinating and synchronising the supply chains, companies can reduce the level of overhead that is required to manage them. As this management process becomes simpler, it is also possible to ask suppliers to take on managing inventory levels and reordering services and products as required.

- **Inventory costs** – integrating, coordinating and synchronising supply chain will reduce both inventory holdings and levels of product obsolescence.

Critical reflections

Increasingly, businesses must recognize that they are at the centre of material networks and information flows. These flows extend from the customer interface through operations to the building of relationships with suppliers. The operations role involves the constant reviewing and alignment of these closely linked networks to better meet the changing needs of the company's markets and to help achieve the sales revenue and profit goals of the organization.

Increased outsourcing is creating more complex supply networks

Since the mid-1980s, companies have chosen to outsource more services and products from an outside provider. As a result, supply chains are becoming more complex and have evolved into supply networks. For example:

- Dell, Cisco (a US-based networks solution company) and Walmart have all outsourced their logistics functions.

- Amazon relies on publishers for product development, Visa and Mastercard for revenue collection and UPS for logistics.

- Xerox uses GE Capital for customer financing, revenue collection and billing.

- Cable & Wireless (a leading telecommunications company) has outsourced its human resource processes to e-Peopleserve, a joint venture between Accenture (a global consultancy and technology services company) and British Telecom.

- BP (an international petroleum products company) and Bank of America have outsourced their human resource administration processes to Exult (a California-based provider of business services related to human resources).

- The Royal National Institute for the Blind uses Arval PHH (an international contract hire and fleet management business) to manage its vehicle fleet.

Significant opportunity for improving supply networks

There are significant improvement opportunities within most supply networks to release cash, improve market support and reduce costs. For example:

- **Release cash** – Figure 12.27 shows the level of inventory held within the top 20 manufacturing companies in the 2010 Fortune 500. This shows the huge opportunity for releasing cash within their own organizations, let alone the amount of inventory within their entire supply chains.

- **Improve market support** – it is important to understand the key order-winners and qualifiers within the markets that you serve. Recent research shown in Figure 12.28 shows the increasing importance of managing a supply network well to support customer service level, flexibility and delivery requirements.

- **Reducing costs** – with global gross domestic product estimated to be in the order of $30 trillion, and the cost of loading, unloading, sorting, reloading and transporting goods to be some 12 per cent (or about $3.5 trillion) of this total, the opportunities for making cost savings provide an overwhelming case for supply chain development even when it is not an order-winner.

Developing and managing relationships

The main ingredient of a supply network is trust, not technology. If suppliers trust each other, then they will share information previously regarded as confidential. Once companies have decided to share information then they can use technology such as EDI systems and internet portals to communicate it across the network.

Figure 12.27 Current inventory holding in the top 20 manufacturing companies in the 2010 Fortune 500

Company	Inventory held in 2010		
	$billion	% sales revenue	% current assets
Boeing	24.3	38	60
Archer Daniels Midland	7.6	12	42
Procter & Gamble	6.4	8	34
United Technologies	7.8	14	33
Kraft Foods	5.3	11	33
Caterpillar	9.6	23	30
Dow Chemicals	7.1	13	30
General Motors	12.1	9	19
Pepsi	3.4	6	19
Lockheed Martin	2.4	5	19
Johnson Controls	1.8	6	17
Abbott Laboratories	3.2	9	14
Pfizer	8.4	12	14
Intel	3.8	9	12
Hewlett Packard	6.5	5	12
IBM	2.5	3	5
Verizon Communications	1.1	1	5
Ford Motor	5.9	5	5
Dell	1.3	2	4
General Electric	11.5	8	2

Once trust is in place, then relationships can be developed. However, the true strength of these relationships is often only revealed when sales revenues start to decline. For example, even though Toyota's total production has dropped 25 per cent since the early 1990s, none of its suppliers have closed down in the last decade. But the spirit and practice of customer–supplier relations need to fundamentally change for this to happen, as illustrated in Figure 12.29. While the potential benefits are considerable, the necessary time and investment need to be recognized by top management as a corporate priority, and this must be demonstrated by commitment throughout the organization.

Integrating supply networks

Once trust and relationships are in place, then supply networks can start to be integrated by first integrating the internal steps within the network and then extending these developments to external suppliers and customers. This is achieved using practices such as collaborative planning and vendor-managed inventory. These approaches signal a critical change in organizations as they now begin to see and manage business processes as they truly are – networks of activities performed by different organizations.

Empowering customers

E-commerce provides the opportunity to not only change the EPOS procedure but can also increase sales for a number of reasons:

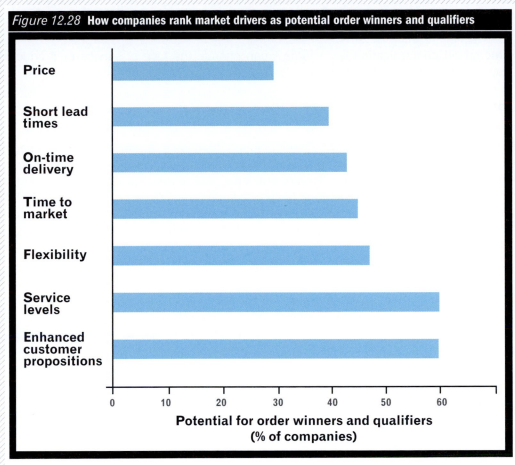

Figure 12.28 How companies rank market drivers as potential order winners and qualifiers

Potential for order winners and qualifiers
(% of companies)

Source: PricewaterhouseCoopers 'Shaping the value chain for outstanding performance: meeting the challenge of global supply chains' (1998), p. 6.

Figure 12.29 Changing nature of customer–supplier practices

Dimension		Customer–supplier practice	
		Traditional	**New millennium**
Strategic role		Price, price and price	Help meet end-customer needs
Customer orientation		Make	Buy
Suppliers	number	Many	Few
	length of relationship	One-night stand	Long-term partner
	customers' role	Reactive	Proactive
	basis of relationship	Threat and fear	Collaboration
	selection	Functional level	Board level
Customer support	training	None	Ongoing
	technical help	Little and reactive	Ongoing and proactive

- **Additional services and products** – companies are able to sell additional services by giving customers and potential customers more information about the services or products on offer.

- **Increase delivery speed** – of both the services and products delivered, which helps conclude a sale and reduces the subsequent product delivery lead time.

- **Increased choice** – customers have more insight into what is on offer thus increasing choice.

- **Increased customization** – customers can change the type of service or product delivered and when it is delivered.

Competing as supply networks

It is important that businesses start to look for ways to compete as supply networks rather than individual businesses. Developing and managing relationships, integrating supply networks and empowering customers will help to do this. For example, in the late 1990s Boeing's significant delivery problems resulted in lost sales revenue with customers turning to its competitors. To build a large passenger jet such as a 747, 767, 777 or A340 you need about 6 million parts, which is complex in itself. Between 1992 and 1999 Boeing also increased production (from 228 to 620 aircraft per year) and reduced its delivery lead time (from 36 to 8–12 months). However, Boeing failed to ensure that suppliers could meet these new requirements and ended up having to reengineer its supply chain while its sales were booming. Suppliers were unable to match demand and, as a result, Boeing delivered its aircrafts late. Customers went elsewhere and Airbus took over as the number one aircraft manufacturer in 2004.

Summary

- When designing their supply chains, companies need first to decide what to make and what to buy based on:
  - The market order-winners and qualifiers they have to support
  - How they could create barriers to entry
  - If they need to maintain supply of key materials
  - How best to understand customer requirements
  - Which core capabilities need to be retained in-house
  - Which external capabilities they need to access from elsewhere
  - How they wish to take advantage of reduced trade barriers.

- However, in reality these decisions are governed by other factors such as continuing yesterday's decisions, meeting cost targets, shedding difficult tasks or meeting political requirements. Choosing to make or buy brings a number of advantages and disadvantages. But, some of these can be altered by choosing from other alternatives to outsourcing such as joint ventures and co-sourcing.

- Making in-house offers firms greater control over its processes, capabilities and business environment. It also increases market knowledge, product knowledge, technological innovation and product differentiation while providing greater opportunity to reduce product cost. However, it can reduce the focus on core tasks and reduced access to capacity, up-to-date technology and world-class capability. Equally, it can increase operating costs and make them more difficult to control.

- To some extent, the advantages and disadvantages of outsourcing are the inverse to those of making in-house. If used appropriately and managed well, outsourcing can free resources and increases the focus on the core tasks that add value to the customer. It can reduce operating costs and make them easier to control, while improving design and market perception of services and products by giving greater access to capacity, up-to-date technology and world-class capabilities. However, it can also result in loss of control of key processes and capabilities and make the business more vulnerable by potentially exposing intellectual property to outside organizations. Equally, once a process has been outsourced, it is then difficult to move back in-house as the knowledge is no longer within the organization.

- Too often, businesses make inappropriate make-or-buy decisions by simply doing what they have always done, outsourcing difficult tasks, not considering all the costs associated with outsourcing or responding to political pressure within the organization to either make or buy.

- Make-or-buy decisions need to be reviewed on an ongoing basis as markets change, products move through life cycles and new business opportunities become available.

- Increasingly, companies compete as supply chains rather than individual organizations. Totally integrating a supply chain from material producer through to end customer greatly improves how a business operates and supports its customers. However, effective collaboration and fuller relationships across the chain are required to achieve this. Other corporate values will also come under scrutiny such as its approach to corporate social responsibility and the environment as discussed in Chapter 15.

- Where companies develop the long-term supplier relations that go hand in hand with supply chain management developments, one test of the new depths of these joint working arrangements is their response in times of reduced sales. For example, Toyota's commitment to its suppliers is underlined by the fact that no supplier has closed down in the past decade even though Toyota's total production has dropped 25 per cent since the early 1990s. Western companies, as part of developing more effective and more responsive supply chains, are moving into closer collaborative relationships and agreements than in the past.

- With global GDP estimated in the order of $30 trillion and the cost of loading, unloading, sorting, reloading and transporting goods some 12 per cent (or about $3.5 trillion) of this total, the opportunities for savings provide an overwhelming case for supply chain development. But the spirit and practice of customer–supplier relations needs to fundamentally change. While the potential benefits are considerable, the necessary time and investment need to be recognized by top management as a corporate priority and demonstrated by commitment throughout the organization.

- To develop the supply chain, companies must focus on improving consumer support, change their attitude to suppliers, invest in IT and create strategic partnerships with companies upstream and downstream within the chain. The first step is to integrate activities within the internal supply chain by aligning all the activities from initial customer contact to final service or product delivery. Once the internal supply chain has been integrated, companies can start coordinating activities between the different businesses within the chain.

- Finally, the supply chain can be synchronized using partnerships and strategic alliances to help create real-time information flows across the chain regarding aspects such as customer management, order placement, service or product design, payment and final delivery. This requires dramatic changes in roles and responsibilities across the chain with suppliers, distributors and customers often being involved in key decisions from service/product design through to delivery schedules. To achieve this, companies must overcome barriers to integration and focus on moving information rather than inventory across the chain.

- Integrated and synchronized supply chains allow companies to better respond to market opportunities and competitive pressures by competing as a supply chain, rather than as a number of individual organizations, and collaborating with other parts of the chain to improve their efficiency and effectiveness. They also allow information to be exchanged, ensuring end user needs are met.

- Operating as a demand chain rather than a supply chain allows organizations to reduce inventory levels across the chain while making them more responsive to changing customer requirements.

Discussion questions

1. What factors should be taken into account when making make-or-buy decisions? Illustrate your answer with examples from a service and a manufacturing organization.

2. Given the increasing importance of environmental concerns, how would a company incorporate these issues into the make-or-buy process? Give two examples to illustrate your views.

3. How will e-commerce continue to impact the supply chain?

4. What benefits do suppliers receive from developing closer ties with major customers?

5 A major company decides to move to a more collaborative stance with a supplier. What would be the first key changes it would need to make? What possible initial responses might be made by the supplier?

6. Give two examples (with reasons) for both a service and manufacturing company where outsourcing a service:
   - Makes sense
   - Does not make sense .

7. What type of call centre service providers lend themselves and do not lend themselves to overseas provision?

8. What benefits would a company derive from introducing e-procurement? What are the obstacles you would expect to hinder this development?

Assignments

1. What criteria do you think the owner of each of the following independent outlets would use to evaluate and select key suppliers?
   - A restaurant
   - A stationer
   - A coffee shop.

Now visit an independent outlet for each of these types of company and ask the owners how they evaluate and select key suppliers. Compare the results and explain any significant differences.

Exploring further

TED talks

Iyengar, S. (2010) *The art of choosing*. Sheena Iyengar studies how we make choices and how we feel about the choices we make. She talks about both trivial choices (Coke v. Pepsi) and profound ones, and shares her groundbreaking research that has uncovered some surprising attitudes about our decisions.
www.ted.com/talks/sheena_iyengar_on_the_art_of_choosing.html

Jacques, M. (2010) *Understanding the rise of China.* Martin Jacques asks why the West often puzzles over the growing power of the Chinese economy, and offers three building blocks for understanding what China is and will become.
www.ted.com/talks/martin_jacques_understanding_the_rise_of_china.html

Mitra, S. (2010) *The child-driven education*. Education scientist Sugata Mitra tackles one of the greatest problems of education: the best teachers and schools don't exist where they're needed most. In a series of real-life experiments from New Delhi to South Africa

to Italy, he gave children self-supervised access to the web and saw results that could revolutionize how we think about teaching.
www.ted.com/talks/sugata_mitra_the_child_driven_education.html

Journal articles

Aron, R. and Singh, J.V. (2005) 'Getting offshoring right', *Harvard Business Review*, **83**(12): 135–43. In the past decade, many companies in North America and Europe have experimented with offshoring and outsourcing business processes, hoping to reduce their costs and gain a strategic advantage. According to several studies, however, many have failed to generate the expected financial benefits. The article presents a three-part methodology that can help improve the current success rate.

Gottfredson, M., Puryear, R. and Phillips, S. (2005) 'Strategic sourcing: From Periphery to the core', *Harvard Business Review*, **83**(2): 132–9. Outsourcing has become strategic, but many executives still treat 'sourcing' as 'procurement' rather than an opportunity to redesign their business. To do this, however, requires a new set of managerial skills.

Lee, H.L. (2004) 'The triple-A supply chain', *Harvard Business Review*, **82**(10): 102–12. This article puts forward the view that supply chains that focus on speed and costs tend to deteriorate over time. It argues that only companies building supply chains that are agile, adaptable and aligned get ahead of their rivals. All three components are essential; without any one of them, supply chains break down.

Lee, H.L. (2010) 'Don't tweak your supply chain. Rethink it end to end', *Harvard Business Review*, **88**(10): 62–9. The article suggests organizations need to use a holistic approach to introduce sustainable practices into their supply chains.

Lewin, A.Y. and Peeters, C. (2006) 'The top-line allure of offshoring', *Harvard Business Review*, **84**(3): 22–4. The article reports a study of offshore arrangements and concludes that not only are there gains of lower costs, but also that 73 per cent of offshore arrangements support companies' growth strategies, with 32 per cent of those initiatives involving product innovation and design, research and development, or engineering.

Narayanan, V.G. and Raman, A. (2004) 'Aligning incentives in supply chains', *Harvard Business Review*, **82**(11): 94–102. An analysis of more than 50 supply networks demonstrates that companies often look after their own interests while giving far less attention to those of their suppliers. The article argues that a supply chain will work well only if the risks, costs and rewards of doing business are distributed fairly across the network.

New, S. (2010) 'The transparent supply chain', *Harvard Business Review*, **88**(10): 76–82. This article discusses how technologies such as radio frequency identification, online databases and webcasting can be used to make information on products more transparent for both managers and consumers.

Pande, A. (2011) 'How to make on-shoring work', *Harvard Business Review*, **89**(3): 30–33. Companies can make onshore IT service centres successful by locating near quality local colleges, focusing on specialist skills, and having a clear employee retention plan.

Prokesch, S. (2010) 'The sustainable supply chain', *Harvard Business Review*, **88**(10): 70–2. It is vital for corporations to renew their identities as communities of human beings as well as merely machines for the creation of profit.

Ramaswamy, V. and Gouillart, F. (2010) 'Building the co-creative enterprise', *Harvard Business Review*, **88**(10): 100–9. The article examines how a company can use its stakeholders including customers, employees and distributors to determine HR practices and design and market its services and products.

Slone, R.E., Mentzer, J.T. and Dittmann, J.P. (2007) 'Are you the weakest link in your company's supply chain?', *Harvard Business Review*, **85**(9): 116–27. This article identifies the key areas in which CEOs can influence their supply chains and shows them how to assess the influence they currently exert.

de Treville, S. and Trigeorgis, L. (2010) 'It may be cheaper to manufacture at home', *Harvard Business Review*, **88**(10): 84–7. Locating a factory near the company's headquarters can offer greater savings than moving it out of the country.

Books

Christopher, M. (2010) *Logistics and Supply Chain Management*. London: Financial Times. This looks at how to develop and manage supply chain networks in order to gain sustainable advantage in today's turbulent global markets.

Cousins, P., Lamming, R., Lawson, B. and Squire, B. (2007) *Strategic Supply Management: Principles, Theories and Practice*. Harlow: Prentice Hall. This book traces the development of purchasing and supply management from its origins as a tactical commercial function into a key strategic business process.

Nassimveni, G. and Sartor, M. (2006) *Sourcing in China*. Basingstoke: Palgrave Macmillan. Comments on the types of strategy and critical issues when outsourcing in China.

Patel, A.V. and Aran, H. (2005) *Outsourcing Success: The Management Imperative*. Basingstoke: Palgrave Macmillan. This addresses the practical issues in developing a sourcing strategy, the risks involved and the guidelines for choosing outsourcing partners.

Films

Black Gold. Directors: Marc Francis and Nick Francis. Documentary looking at the world of coffee and global trade.
blackgoldmovie.com
Made in Britain. TV documentary 2011. Evan Davis looks at the British economy and asks what it is good at and how it can pay its way in the world.
www.bbc.co.uk/programmes/b0125v5k

Notes and references

1. Economist Intelligence Unit and KPMG Management Consultants Report (1996) *Supply Chain Management: Europe's New Competitive Battle Ground*. London.
2. Borsodi, R. (1929) *This Ugly Civilization*. New York: Simon & Schuster.
3. As reported in Allen, E. (1999) 'One-stop shop is no cure-all', *Financial Times*, 17 June p. 16.
4. Margretta, J. (1998) 'The power of virtual integration: an interview with Dell Computer's Michael Dell', *Harvard Business Review*, March–April, pp. 78–84.
5. Margretta, J. (1998) 'The power of virtual integration: an interview with Dell Computer's Michael Dell'. *Harvard Business Review*, March–April, pp. 78–84.

Visit www.palgrave.com/business/hillom3e for self-test questions, guideline answers to some case study questions, useful weblinks and more to help you understand the topics in this chapter

ZARA

The Zara boutique-clothing store on Calle Real in the northern Spanish city of La Coruna is buzzing. Customers have made the journey here on a rainy Saturday morning to see what new exciting styles are available this week. The red tank tops and black blazers seem to be a hit, but customers also really like the beige and bright purple ones too. Faced with this problem most fashion companies would normally have to spend months retooling and restocking their range. Not Zara, however. Each store manager is able to spot these changes in trends and then type them into their handheld computer on Saturday in the safe knowledge that they will arrive on Monday or Tuesday the next week.

There is a very strong link between store managers and the central design team based at Zara's head office in La Coruna in northern Spain. Each store is electronically linked back to head office so that they can view and assess sales on a real-time basis. This allows the company to make sure that they can adapt quickly to customer wants and desires. One example of this was a new khaki skirt that the company initially just stocked in Spain to see how it would sell. In the Coruna store it was sold out af-ter only having been on the shelves for a couple of hours. After speaking to Barcelona, it was apparent that sales were brisk there too. It was then decided that the skirt should be tested out elsewhere, so overnight Zara sent out 7,800 skirts to more than 1,300 stores worldwide. The results were clear, the skirt was a hit and within the next few days stores in Europe, Asia, and North and South America were being stocked with the khaki skirt.

It is this mix of intelligence gathering, fashion instinct and technological *savoir-faire* that is allowing Zara to set in motion something unique in the clothing trade. The combination of being able to translate the latest trends into products in less than 15 days and delivering them to its stores twice a week means that it is able to catch fashion trends while they are hot and so respond quickly to the fast changing tastes of young urban consumers. 'Nobody else can get new designs to stores as quickly,' says Keith Mortimer, European-retail analyst. 'Unless you can do that, you won't be in business in 10 years. It continuously analyzes its value chain and seeks to achieve control of as many sections of it as possible. By focusing on reducing time between design and sale, it has developed an operations cycle that is entirely different from fashion sector norms. The design team is working throughout the season studying everything from what clothes are worn in hit TV series to how clubbers dress. This means there is a continuous stream of new designs that ensures customers keep coming back to see what's new. Its clothing has filled an untapped niche: Prada at moderate prices.'

Customers seem to love the results of this high-velocity operation. They are often known to queue up in long lines at Zara's stores on designated delivery days, a phenomenon that has been dubbed in the press as 'Zaramania'. And this popularity is generating tangible, bottom-line results as well as admiration from the fashion world (see Figure 1). Over the last five years it grew profitability at a 30 per cent average annual rate, which is 45 per cent faster than its four industry rivals during that period.

A GLOBAL SUCCESS

Founded in 1963 as a maker of ladies' lingerie, Zara opened its first store in 1975 as a retail clothing company with a single location in the city of La Coruna, northwest Spain. By 1989, the company had 98 retail shops and production facilities distributed around Spain and in the same year the company started its international expansion by opening a shop in Lisbon, Portugal. This was only the beginning of what became a huge expansion plan across the world. It is now the largest and most profitable unit of Inditex SA, the Spanish clothes manufacturer and distributor, with over 1,400 stores distributed throughout Europe, Middle East, Asia Pacific and the Americas (see Figure 2).

As Jonathon May, retail consultant comments, 'This rapid expansion has meant that Zara now has three characteristics that distinguish it from its competitors. Firstly, they are the fastest-growing retail business not only in Europe but also across the world. Secondly, they have been able to export their formula internationally exceedingly well at a time when many other clothing companies in the middle and lower-middle market have found it difficult. Next, for example, is a fantastic company, but has always struggled to export its particular format. And thirdly, they have created a simple, singular message for all their customers. The shopping experience is upscale, while the product offering is very much good quality, but not best quality, at a good price. They might well have sacrificed a little bit of technical quality but they have more then made up for it through how products are designed in terms of fabrics, colours, patterns and styles. If you go into a store this immediately hits you and then when you look at a garment you will see that their price tags are big and colourful, emblazoned with the flags of a dozen countries, each accompanied by a local-currency price that is the same for that item around the world, from Madrid to Riyadh to Tokyo.'

CHALLENGING THE COMPETITION

In times when a combination of the recession and some merchandising mistakes have forced Gap and comparable European stores like Sweden's H&M to retrench, Zara continues to expand. Much of the success is due to its unusual structure.

Figure 1	Net store openings, number of company-managed and franchised stores, selling area, net sales and operating income (2000–10)					
Data	**2000**	**2002**	**2004**	**2006**	**2008**	**2010**
Stores						
Net openings	53	85	97	174	61	123
Company-managed	382	487	649	1,077	1,099	1,544
Franchised	24	44	74	98	193	179
Selling area (000s m²)	408	562	811	1,138	1,447	1,688
Performance						
Net sales (€M)	2,044	2,913	3,760	5,534	6,824	8,088
Operating income (€M)	327	540	654	911	1,048	1,534

Region	Country	# stores	Region	Country	# stores
	Andorra	1	Middle East	Bahrain	2
	Austria	12		Egypt	3
	Belgium	27		Israel	19
	Bulgaria	4		Jordan	2
	Croatia	5		Kuwait	5
	Cyprus	5		Lebanon	5
	Czech Republic	6		Oman	1
	Denmark	2		Qatar	2
	Estonia	2		Saudi Arabia	23
	Finland	4		Syria	1
	France	113		UAE	9
	Germany	65	Asia-Pacific	China	71
	Greece	46		Hong Kong	7
	Hungary	6		Indonesia	10
	Iceland	2		Japan	63
	Ireland	9		Korea	17
	Italy	84		Malaysia	6
	Lithuania	2		Philippines	6
Europe	Luxembourg	4		Singapore	7
	Malta	1		Thailand	5
	Monaco	1	Americas	Argentina	9
	Montenegro	1		Brazil	30
	Norway	3		Canada	19
	Poland	32		Chile	7
	Portugal	61		Columbia	9
	Romania	13		Costa Rica	2
	Serbia	4		Dominican Republic	2
	Slovakia	2		El Salvador	2
	Slovenia	5		Guatemala	2
	Spain	333		Honduras	2
	Sweden	8		Mexico	50
	Switzerland	10		Panama	2
	The Netherlands	18		Puerto Rico	1
	Turkey	27		United States	49
	Ukraine	7		Uruguay	2
	United Kingdom	64		Venezuela	11
			Other	Morocco	4
				Russia	47
				Tunisia	2

Figure 2 **Current stores by region and country**

For decades now, the majority of clothing retailers have outsourced their manufacturing to Third World countries in the pursuit of lower costs and greater efficiencies. However, Zara bucked this trend and took a different stance. It felt that it would be better off developing a business that was able to respond quickly to shifts in consumer tastes and thus made the decision to set up a vertically integrated business model spanning design, just-in-time production, marketing and sales. As such, it now produces more than half of its own clothes at its ultramodern factory in northern Spain rather than relying on a network of disparate and often slow-moving suppliers. H&M, for instance, has 900 suppliers and no factories, whereas Zara makes 40 per cent of its own fabric and produces 60 per cent of its merchandise in-house. 'Vertical integration has gone out of fashion in the consumer economy,' says David Johnston, a retail consultant in London. 'Zara is a spectacular exception to the rule.'

The result is that Zara has more flexibility than its rivals to respond to fickle fashion trends. It can make a new line from start to finish in three weeks, against an industry average of nine months. It is able to introduce 10,000 new designs into its stores each year, none of which stay there for over a month. This constant refreshing of the store offering creates a sense of excitement that attracts new shoppers and ensures that old ones return. It is also radically changing the way that people shop. As David Johnston explains, 'If customers see a product that they like in the store, they know that it will only be there for four weeks, not four months, and that they will

probably not be able to find it after that. It stimulates customers to buy now, creating a greater velocity of shopping. This is quite a different situation to the high streets of old and more and more retailers are finding it difficult to compete. For example, C&A chose to exit the UK market and the Japanese basics retailer Uniqlo has closed all but five of its UK stores here. Boring, staple clothing is being killed off!' However, its not just the traditional high street chains that have been affected. Even supermarket clothing retailer George at Asda has been inspired to react, by producing a collection called 'Fast Fashion'.

KEEPING UP WITH FASHION

Fashions and trends can have a short lifespan. Being quick allows Zara to reduce to a minimum the risk of making a mistake with their collections. With this in mind, the designers at Zara work hard to constantly update, mix and match popular styles (rather than simply flooding the market with a single item), with no product available for more than four weeks. As David Johnston explains, 'No one wants to dress like everybody else. It is important always to have fresh fashion. Zara's business model not only allows them to offer mid-market chic at downmarket prices, but it also protects them against slip-ups. Whereas most retailers have already committed to 60 per cent of their production at the start of the season, at Zara the figure is only 15 per cent. This makes it easier for them to drop a range that turns out to be unpopular.'

Although mistakes can happen, Zara tries to minimize them by pushing its designers onto aeroplanes in search of new trends, spending their time looking through fashion magazines, attending fashion shows and frequenting fashionable cafes, restaurants and bars. 'Zara realize how important it is to listen to their customers as they know better than anyone what they want,' David Johnston explains. 'Their designers act like sponges soaking up information about fashion trends from all over the world and translating them into new ideas. They are constantly travelling, watching catwalk shows and even music videos to find the next look, which can then be in the stores within a month. Traditionally, fashion col-

lections are designed only four times a year, but Zara produce over 10,000 different designs each year. Whilst the style and shape of the garments don't vary significantly, they are produced in a wide variety of different fabrics, colours and patterns.'

From the beginning of its international expansion in 1989, Zara has always focused on developing products for the global market. This has helped it reduce costs (such as product development, manufacturing, logistics and inventory) and create a consistent product and brand image across all its markets. These global products are developed by the design team at its head office in Spain, which contains people with fashion, marketing and retailing experience. Drawing on these different backgrounds and using information gathered through regular field research and computerized store data, the team develop and launch new products, working out which products to develop, when they should be launched, how many should be made, how many should be shipped to each country and what price they should be sold for.

All of its garments are displayed in stores with an international price tag showing the different prices in each country. Prices are globalized, taking into account the differences in local market conditions and the potential problems of parallel imports.

PRODUCTION AND DISTRIBUTION

For a fashion business, Zara is also unique in the way that it is driven by consumer feedback. In many ways, its store managers are the most important people in the business. Selecting from over 10,000 lines a year, they are responsible for placing orders with the factory and central office in Spain.

These orders are placed twice a week and determine the type and quantity of products that will be stocked in their store. They rely on their ability to understand and monitor how well products are selling in order to ensure that they have the right stock at the right time in the right place.

Each store manager receives information via a handheld computer showing images of the products that can be ordered. Based on sales over the last few days and trends that seem to be emerging in each of the local stores, they then decide which products and how many to order. In the head office in Spain, there is a section dedicated to each country and the store manager will usually talk to them once or twice a day and three to five times on order days. The firm's commercial sections then liaise with the designers and factories to make sure that the products meet the needs of the local customers for each store. While there is an initial trend framework set up at the beginning of each season, modifications are continually made as required in response to the reaction of customers to each range.

As well as operating its own worldwide distribution network out of its facility in Spain, Zara also designs and manufactures products there too. Lead times for new designs average from about four to six weeks, but may be as little as two. Zara achieves this by holding fabric in stock and then cutting and dyeing it at the last minute. With its team of designers identifying new fashions while keeping in constant contact with store managers, the company can spot and react quickly to trends, including taking something stylish off a music video that has just been released. Other retailers, in contrast, need an average of six months to design a new collection and then another three months to manufacture it. A store manager will send in a new idea to the La Coruna head office. The 200-plus designers decide if it is appealing, and then come up with the specifications. The design is scanned into a computer and zapped to production computers in manufacturing, which cut and dye the material and this is then assembled into clothes by outside workshops. The in-house manufacturing plant is futuristic, with large clothes-cutting machines that are run by a handful of technicians in a laboratory style computer control centre. The dying part of the process occurs in small units in another part of the factory. By dying products after they have been cut, they are able to minimize the quantities of dye used and help to control costs.

For most garments, the company owns every part of the production process, apart from the sewing. Fabric comes from places like Spain, the Far East, India, and Morocco and is cut and coloured at the company's state-of-the-art factory. Using information gathered from stores, production managers decide how many garments to make and which stores will get them. Then the fabric is sewn together at 400 cooperatives run by local seamstresses before being shipped around the world. This combination of real-time information sharing and internalized production means that Zara can work with almost no stock and still have new designs in the store twice a week, as opposed to the six weeks that it traditionally takes most competitors. The twice weekly deliveries help keep Zara stores seeming fresh, and store clerks heighten the sense of rapid turnover by changing the location of key items.

RETAIL STORES

In keeping with the philosophy of the rest of the business, the stores themselves are designed by an in-house team of architects with a 'white box' style that evolves as it goes along in terms of signage and lighting or, for instance, the introduction of escalators. They are very minimal in design and the way in which clothing is presented. However, the constantly rapid turnover of products and changing the position in the store of key items results in keeping customers curious and keen to see the latest styles. They find that this in itself is sufficient to draw shoppers into the store and thus, again unlike the majority of its competitors, Zara has an approach to advertising that is as minimal as its store interiors. It consists of only taking a full-page local newspaper advert twice a year, the night before it has a sale.

Zara's main media sources are the store locations and the shop windows. Its business model is based on the premise that it doesn't need to persuade customers to buy its products as they already want them. Because of the short production and distribution lead times, there is less need to discount, except at those two sale periods each year. In fact, they do not really have to have a sale at all, but we find that it works well as a promotional tool.

THE FUTURE

'In terms of the future for Zara,' reflects Keith Mortimer, European-retail analyst, 'the question now is how far can it go with the concept of design-on-demand retailing, which it runs with almost no advertising outside its biannual storewide sales. There is nothing wrong with it taking advantage of its rivals' weaknesses to gain market share. Zara's still entirely Spanish management team will have to be careful not to indulge in the over-expansion that has undermined so many rivals in the past. The further the Group gets from its heartland, where it has faced only modest competition, the more its model will be stretched. The chain is now well known in South America and Europe, but less so in the USA where it is still establishing itself. Yet again this year, they will be pursuing a very aggressive expansion plan claiming that the only restraining factor is the availability of suitable real estate. Its decision last year to start selling clothes online makes sense as finding new store sites has become more difficult. This may help to boost its profile in the United States where customers are less reluctant to buy online than in its homeland of Southern Europe.'

Questions

1. What underpins the success of Zara in its chosen markets?

2. How has it designed its supply chain?

3. How does its supply chain meet the needs of its markets?

Lecturers: visit www.palgrave.com/business/hillom3e for teaching guidelines for this case study

Analyzing Operations

13

After completing this chapter, you should be able to:

- Explain why companies need to analyze their operations

- Understand how to analyze the business context of an operation in term of its stakeholder requirements and corporate objectives

- Analyze the 'health' of a business

- Analyze how well an operation supports its current and future market requirements, where cash is currently trapped within an operation and its current operating costs

- Determine the potential for releasing cash, improving market support and reducing costs within an operation

- Understand the issues involved when analyzing operations in practice

Chapter outline

What is the role of analyzing operations within the business?

- Operations can be used to either support existing market requirements (market-driven) or create new markets with new requirements (market-driving)

- However, current performance needs to be analyzed and understood before strategies can be developed and implemented

- Operations need to be analyzed before they can be improved to release cash, improve market support or reduce costs

Why is analyzing operations important?

- **Large function** – operations is a large function and typically manages the largest number of assets, costs and people within a business. It therefore needs to be understood in detail if a business wants to work out how to release cash, improve market support or reduce costs

- **Key to supporting markets** – operations is either solely or partly responsible for supporting one or more of the key order-winners and qualifiers in all its markets

- **Key to building barriers to entry** – operations is key to developing barriers to entry as its capabilities can often be difficult to imitate easily

- **Need to challenge and check executive opinion** – use analysis to collect data that can be used to check executive opinion and ensure business decisions are not biased by functional and hierarchical perspectives

- **Insights often surprising** – the data gathered often gives insights that are different to the myths and beliefs that currently exist within the business

- **Increases focus on improvement** – the data gathered stops management discussing and debating facts and, therefore, focuses their time on working out how to improve performance and implement these actions

How does analyzing operations impact business performance?

- Operations must be analyzed before it can be improved to understand where:

  - **Cash is trapped** – in terms of inventory, accounts receivables, properties, buildings and equipment, before inventory can be reduced, customer payment terms can be changed and equipment can be sold, leased and/or outsourced
  - **Markets are not supported** – by identifying relevant order-winners and qualifiers, translating these into strategic tasks, reviewing current performance against these tasks and identifying areas for either improving existing market support (market-driven) or creating new markets (market-driving)
  - **Costs are too high** – by reviewing and reducing actual material, direct labour and overhead costs, mapping activities, identifying areas of waste, reviewing service and product mixes and reviewing service and product prices

- Once this is understood, then improvements can be made to release cash, improve market support and reduce costs

What are the key issues to consider when analyzing operations?

- Analyzing operations involves balancing gut feeling with in-depth analysis so that action is not delayed, but also focuses on areas of maximum impact given the strategic objectives of the business and the investment funds (money) and resources (time) that are available

- Operations can be analyzed by following five main steps:

  1. **Understand the business context** – by identifying the stakeholder requirements and corporate objectives that need to be met and understanding the current health of the business (such as sales, profits, operating costs and customer satisfaction trends)
  2. **Analyze current and future markets** – by identifying the business's current and future markets and determining the order-winners and qualifiers that need to be supported in these markets
  3. **Analyze market support** – for the current and future order-winners and qualifiers that it has to support
  4. **Analyze cash holdings** – by understanding the reasons for cash currently being tied up in accounts receivable, financing receivables or inventory (current assets) and property, buildings and equipment (fixed assets)
  5. **Analyze operating costs** – by reviewing actual material, direct labour and overhead costs

- When analyzing operations, it is important to:

  - **Visit the business** you are analyzing
  - **Visit customers** – if possible, visit a representative sample of the customers it serves
  - **Observe service delivery and product manufacture** – to understand how the business operates and the issues it faces
  - **Be a customer** – both of the business you are analyzing and also a customer of all its major competitors to compare their front-office processes, the customer journey, the layout of the front office, how customer interactions are managed, how complaints are handled and how customers are handed over between different steps and functions within the delivery system
  - **Be a service, product or customer order** – of the business you are analyzing to understand the back-office steps in the delivery system to understand what happens at each stage, how handovers are managed, the delivery system layout and the eventual delivery to a customer
  - **Challenge and check executive opinion** – by comparing it with other opinions and data
  - **Challenge and check data collected** – by comparing with other data, observation and executive opinion
  - **Triangulate your findings** – by looking at everything from at least three different perspectives
  - **Test your findings and conclusions** – as they start to emerge using data and executive opinion
  - **Collect more data than you think you need** – but, in your final report or presentation, you should only include the data that help explain your analysis, show how you have reached your conclusions and show the expected cost and benefit of your proposed recommendations

Introduction

Operations strategies can be market-driven or market-driving. Even with a market-driving strategy, it is first important to know what customers currently want and the level of support they currently receive before these requirements can be driven to create new markets.

Why analyze operations?

It is important to analyze operations for a number of reasons:

- **Large function** – operations is typically responsible for managing the largest number of assets, costs and people within a business.

- **Key to supporting markets** – in all markets:
  - Operations is either solely or partly responsible for supporting one or more of the key order-winners and qualifiers.
  - If operations is not aligned to its markets, then the business will struggle to attract and retain customers.

- **Key to building barriers to entry** – operations is key to developing barriers to entry as its capabilities can often be difficult to imitate easily.

- **Challenge and check opinion** – it is always critical to find data to challenge and test executive opinion as this helps remove functional and hierarchical bias and often leads to greater and more in-depth insights.

- **Insights often surprising** – often the insights obtained through analysis are surprising and different to the myths and beliefs that exist within a business.

- **Increases focus on improvement** – too much time is spent discussing and debating the facts within a business such as where and why cash is tied up, the significant operating costs and how orders are won. Once you have the data that show these issues then management time and effort can focus on how to improve them rather than trying to determine them.

> **EXECUTIVE INSIGHT**
> Operations needs to be analyzed because it is:
> - A large function with high assets and costs
> - Key to supporting markets
> - Key to building barriers to entry
> - Important to check executive opinion with data
> - Insights are often surprising
> - Critical for focusing management on action rather than discussion.

How to analyze operations

Operations can be analyzed by going through five main steps:

1. **Understanding the business context** – by identifying the stakeholder requirements and corporate objectives that need to be met and understanding the current health of the business (such as sales, profits, operating costs and customer satisfaction trends).

2. **Analyzing markets** – by identifying the business's current and future markets and determining the order-winners and qualifiers that need to be supported in these markets.

3. **Analyzing market support** – for the current and future order-winners and qualifiers that it has to support.

4. **Analyzing cash holdings** – by understanding the reasons for cash currently being tied up in accounts receivable, financing receivables or inventory (current assets) and property, buildings and equipment (fixed assets).

5. **Analyzing operating costs** – by reviewing actual material, direct labour and overhead costs.

These steps are described in more detail in the rest of the chapter. However, when analyzing the business, there a number of key principles that you must follow:

- **Visit the business** – there is nothing quite like visiting the business that you are analyzing to watch how it works and speak to the people that work there. You will get a sense of how it operates and some of the issues it faces simply by seeing it. Trying to analyze a business without seeing it is the same as talking about a country without visiting it. You can talk about its issues at a broad level, but you will not have a true grasp of it.

- **Visit customers** – where possible, there is also huge benefit in visiting customers to get a real understanding of how they operate, the issues they face and the benefit they receive from the services and products delivered by the business you are analyzing.

- **Observe service delivery and/or product manufacture** – where possible, it is also important to watch services being delivered and products being made. Again, this will give you an insight into the business, how it operates and the issues it faces.

- **Be a customer** – to understand the front-office steps in the delivery system, you should be a customer of the business you are analyzing and also of its competitors, if possible. Again, this gives you a different insight into the business, enabling you to understand and compare it with its competitors by considering:
  - The front-office processes used to serve customers
  - The journey a customer has to take
  - The layout of the front office and how a customer moves through this
  - How customer interactions are managed
  - How complaints are handled – to analyze this, you will have to complain about the service you have received
  - How customers are handed over between different steps and functions within the delivery system.

- **Be a service, product or customer order** – to understand the back-office steps in the delivery system, you should walk through the different steps of the delivery system as if you were a service, product or customer order being processed through the business to understand what happens at each stage, how handovers are managed, the delivery system layout and the eventual delivery to a customer.

- **Challenge and check executive opinion** – constantly look for ways to challenge and check the opinions of the different executives you interview by:
  - *Comparing with other opinion* – from executives within the same function and other functions
  - *Comparing with data* – that will either verify or contradict their point of view.

For example, if a marketing executive tells you that a particular market segment is price sensitive, then you need to ask other marketing executives the same question and also compare this with the view of executives from other functions such as sales, customer service and operations. You also then need to look at the actual profit margins of orders for a representative sample of customers within each segment. Low margins would confirm that price is an order-winner. Whenever you find a difference between opinion and data, then you need to try to work out why this has occurred. For example, is that executive's view of the business or the market skewed for some reason or is there a functional bias that is affecting their judgement?

- **Challenge and check data** – equally, when you collect data you need to challenge and check them with opinion. This can be done by:
  - *Comparing with other data* – from, for example, other services, products, customers, markets, delivery systems or processes to see if your findings are either similar or dissimilar, but for predictable reasons.
  - *Comparing with observation* – visit, for example, the delivery system or facility to see if your observations of how it works in practice agree or disagree with the insights you have gained from the data you have collected.
  - *Comparing with opinion* – show your insights to executives to see if they are consistent with their opinion. Again, it is useful to test against multiple executives working in different functions.

- **Triangulate your findings** – implicit within the last two points is the need to triangulate your findings by looking at something from at least three different perspectives, which will usually be a combination of opinion, data and observation.

- **Test your findings and conclusions** – as your findings start to emerge then look for ways to test them against opinion or data. This will not only allow you to test your logic and understanding, but also confirm whether your ideas are practical and can be implemented.

- **Collect more data than you present** – your data analysis should be wide to explore all aspects of the business, understand the issues it faces and the opportunities that exist. However, you should not present all of this information in your final report or presentation. Instead, you should only present the data that help explain your analysis, show how you have reached your conclusions and show the expected cost and benefit of your proposed recommendations.

> **EXECUTIVE INSIGHT**
  When analyzing operations, it is important where possible to:
  - Visit the business you are analyzing
  - Visit representative customers of its current and future markets
  - Observe service delivery and/or product manufacture
  - Be a customer of the business you are analyzing and also of its competitors
  - Be a service, product or customer order that is being processed by the operation
  - Challenge and check executive opinion
  - Challenge and check data as you collect them
  - Triangulate your findings
  - Test your findings and conclusions
  - Collect more data than you think you need.

Understanding the business context

The first step in your analysis is to understand both the external and internal business context. The purpose of doing this is to identify the overall corporate objectives that need to be met, the overall health of the company, the requirements of the key stakeholders, the opportunities and threats that exist within its markets and the culture within the organization. Analyses that can help you do this are now discussed.

Stakeholder requirements

The requirements of the different **stakeholders** of the business need to be understood using the following steps:

1. **Identify the key stakeholders** – typical stakeholders would include shareholders, employees, suppliers, customers and the societies in which they operate. However, there may be others to consider as well, such as governments and legislative or environmental bodies.

2. **Identify their power and influence** – over the decisions made within the business and **map** them onto the power and interest matrix shown in Figure 13.1 where:

   - **Power** – is the ability of individuals or groups to persuade, induce or coerce others into following a certain course of action.
   - **Interest** – how interested is each group in impressing its expectations on an organization's purpose and the choices it makes?

Figure 13.1 **Mapping stakeholder power and interest**

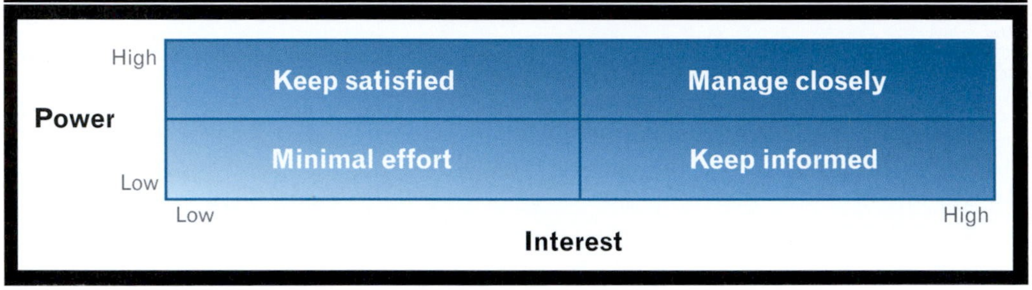

3. **Identify their needs and requirements** – in particular, it is important to look for any potential areas of conflict that might exist. For example, shareholders may purely be concerned about the short-term financial performance of the business whereas employees are more concerned about its long-term social and environmental impact.

Corporate objectives

What are the overall objectives of the business? For example,

- **Sales revenue growth** – is it trying to increase its sales revenue within its existing markets? Or is it trying to move into new markets?

- **Survival** – is it simply trying to survive within its existing markets?

- **Profit** – is it trying to increase the profitability of its existing services and products? Or it is trying to develop new, more profitable services and products?

- **Return on investment** – what return needs to be gained to secure investment and funds within the business? What expectations do shareholders and investors have in terms of getting a return on the equity they have invested in the business?

- **Inventory turns** – how often do inventory levels need to be 'turned' within the business. This is critical in helping to prevent too much cash from being tied up within the business.

- **Debtor (or Accounts Receivable) levels** – how much of the sales revenue has not yet been paid by customers? Again, this is critical for managing cash levels within the business.

- **Environmental targets** – is the business trying to reduce its **environmental footprint**?

- **Social targets** – is the business trying to improve the impact it has on the societies in which it operates, such as customer safety, staff safety, fair employment policies within its supply chain, fair pricing and non-exploitation of developing countries?

Stakeholders – individuals or groups who depend on an organization to fulfil their own goals and on whom, in turn, the organization depends.

Stakeholder mapping – identifies the interest and power of stakeholders and helps identify which ones can or should be used to identify and make improvements.

Inventory turns – the number of times inventory is turned within a year. It is calculated as: annual sales revenue ($) divided by inventory level ($).

Debtor (or Accounts Receivable) levels – the value of invoices that have not yet been paid by customers.

Environmental footprint – of an organization is the impact that it has on the earth's natural resources through the design and delivery of its services and products.

Business health check

What is the overall health of the business? A number of different analyses can be completed to look at the sales, revenue, sales volume, profit, operating costs and customer satisfaction trends within the business. Examples of these analyses are now completed using the data shown in the Southwest Airlines case study at the end of Chapter 1.

> **EXECUTIVE INSIGHT**
The health of a business can be checked by looking at its sales revenue, sales volume, profit, operating costs and customer satisfaction trends compared with its competitors.

Sales revenue trends

Are sales increasing or decreasing? How does this vary by market segment and compare with competitors? Useful analyses include:

Figure 13.2 **Southwest Airlines' sales revenue compared with its major competitors (1999–2009)**

Airline	Sales revenue ($bn)						
	99	01	03	05	07	08	09
Delta	14.9	13.2	14.2	16.1	14.5	22.7	28.1
American	16.1	15.6	17.4	20.7	17.2	23.8	19.9
United	18.0	16.1	14.9	17.4	20.1	20.2	16.3
Continental	8.0	8.0	7.3	11.1	10.6	15.2	12.6
US Airways	8.5	8.2	6.8	7.2	6.5	12.5	10.5
Southwest	4.7	5.6	5.9	7.6	9.9	11.0	10.4
Alaska	1.8	1.8	2.0	2.4	3.1	3.2	3.4
Northwest	9.9	9.6	9.2	12.3	9.5	13.6	–
America West	2.2	2.0	2.2	3.4	2.7	–	–

Note: Delta merged with Northwest in 2008.

Figure 13.3 **Market share as a percentage of sales revenue (1999–2009)**

Airline	Market share (% of sales revenue)						
	1999	2001	2003	2005	2007	2008	2009
Delta	18	16	18	16	15	19	28
American	19	20	22	21	23	19	20
United	21	20	19	18	20	17	16
Continental	10	10	9	11	11	12	12
US Airways	10	10	8	7	6	10	10
Southwest	6	7	7	8	10	9	10
Alaska	2	2	3	2	3	3	3
Northwest	12	12	11	13	10	11	–
America West	3	3	3	3	3	–	–

Figure 13.4 Sales revenue analysis (1999–2009)							
Airline	Sales revenue (% of Southwest's 1999 sales revenue)						
	1999	2001	2003	2005	2007	2008	2009
Southwest	100	117	125	160	208	233	219
Competitors							
United	381	341	315	367	425	426	345
American	340	330	367	436	484	502	421
Delta	315	279	300	340	306	479	593
Northwest	208	203	194	260	202	287	0
US Airways	179	174	143	152	136	263	221
Continental	169	168	155	235	224	322	267
America West	46	43	47	72	58	–	–
Alaska	37	37	43	51	65	68	72
Competitor average	**209**	**197**	**195**	**239**	**238**	**293**	**240**

- Company sales revenue trend – Figure 13.2 shows that Southwest Airlines has the sixth largest sales revenue in its market.

- Company market share (% sales revenue) trend – Figure 13.3 shows how Southwest's market share has increased by 4 per cent in the last 10 years, but it is still a relatively small player in terms of sales revenue.

- Sales revenue compared with competitors – Figure 13.4 then analyzes this information by showing all the figures as a percentage of Southwest's performance in 1999. From this, we can see that it has doubled its sales revenue over the last 10 years while the sales revenue of its competitors, on average, has not changed dramatically. In fact, Delta is the only other airline to have significantly increased sales and this is only the result of it merging with Northwest in 2008.

Sales volume trends

Are sales volumes increasing or decreasing? How does this vary by market segment and compare against competitors? Useful analyses include:

- Company sales volume trend – Figure 13.5 shows Southwest has the second largest sales volume in its market. Its sales volume has remained constant for the last three years, but the overall market size has fallen over the last 10 years.

- Sales volume market share against competitors – Figure 13.6 shows Southwest's market share has almost doubled in the last 10 years, but has remained constant for the last three years.

- Sales revenue per customer – Figure 13.7 shows that Southwest's sales revenue per customer is significantly lower than its competitors. This is appropriate given that its strategy is to compete on price. However, this would be a concern if this wasn't its strategy.

- Sales volume against competitors – Figure 13.8 shows that its sales volume has increased by 55 per cent in the last 10 years. While this is significantly better than its competitors, it is concerning that it hasn't grown in the last three years. Given its strategy to compete on price, sales volume is critical for reducing its operating costs.

Figure 13.5 Number of domestic passengers (1999–2009)

Airline	Millions of domestic passengers carried						
	1999	2001	2003	2005	2007	2008	2009
Delta	106	94	84	86	73	71	161
Southwest	65	74	75	88	102	102	101
American	82	78	89	98	98	86	86
United	87	75	66	67	68	63	56
US Airways	56	56	41	42	42	55	51
Continental	44	43	39	43	49	47	46
Alaska	14	14	15	17	17	16	16
Northwest	55	52	52	57	54	49	–
America West	19	20	20	22	16	–	–
Total	**528**	**506**	**481**	**520**	**519**	**489**	**517**

Figure 13.6 Market share as a percentage of domestic passengers (1999–2009)

Airline	Market share (% sales volume)						
	1999	2001	2003	2005	2007	2008	2009
Delta	20	19	17	17	14	14	31
Southwest	12	15	16	17	20	21	20
American	16	15	19	19	19	19	17
United	16	15	14	13	13	13	11
US Airways	11	11	9	8	8	11	10
Continental	8	8	8	8	9	9	9
Alaska	3	3	3	3	3	3	3
Northwest	10	10	11	11	10	10	–

Figure 13.7 Sales revenue by passenger (1999–2009)

Airline	Sales revenue per passenger ($)						
	1999	2001	2003	2005	2007	2008	2009
United	207	215	226	259	296	321	292
Continental	182	185	188	258	217	324	274
American	196	201	196	211	234	256	232
Alaska	126	126	135	142	181	189	213
US Airways	151	147	165	172	154	227	205
Delta	141	141	169	187	199	320	174
Southwest	73	75	79	86	97	108	102
Northwest	179	184	177	216	177	277	–
America West	114	102	111	154	171	–	–

Profit trends

Are profits increasing or decreasing as a percentage of sales revenue? Again, how does this vary by market segment and compare against competitors? Useful analyses include:

Figure 13.8 Sales volume analysis (1999–2009)							
Airline	**Sales volume (% Southwest's 1999 sales volume)**						
	1999	**2001**	**2003**	**2005**	**2007**	**2008**	**2009**
Southwest	100	114	115	135	157	157	155
Competitors							
Delta	163	145	129	132	112	109	248
United	134	115	102	103	105	97	86
American	126	120	137	151	151	143	132
US Airways	86	86	63	65	65	85	78
Continental	68	66	60	66	75	72	71
Alaska	22	22	23	26	26	26	25
Northwest	85	80	80	88	83	75	–
America West	29	31	31	34	25	–	–
Competitor average	**89**	**83**	**78**	**83**	**80**	**76**	**80**

- **Company profit trend** – Figure 13.9 shows that Southwest is the only airline to have consistently made a profit for the last 10 years. However, it also shows the impact of its sales volumes not growing for the last three years.

- **Company profit trend as a percentage of sales revenue** – again Figure 13.10 shows that Southwest consistently makes a profit and performs better than its competitors. However, these are very low profit figures compared with other industries. For example, Dell also competes on price, but it made a 18 per cent profit margin last year. Therefore, part of your further analysis would be to try and understand why these margins are so low throughout the industry and if anything can be done to change this.

Figure 13.9 Operating profit (1999–2009)							
Airline	**Operating profit ($M)**						
	1999	**2001**	**2003**	**2005**	**2007**	**2008**	**2009**
Southwest	782	631	298	548	791	449	262
Competitors							
Alaska	(12)	(65)	(11)	(8)	123	(22)	267
US Airways	202	(1,181)	(421)	(213)	543	(1,800)	118
Continental	480	(342)	30	(94)	552	(378)	(144)
Delta	1,730	(972)	(1,157)	(1,198)	1,040	(8,314)	(324)
United	1,358	(3,743)	(1,554)	(241)	360	(5,396)	(651)
American	1,004	(2,558)	(1,444)	(351)	842	(2,054)	(1,004)
America West	198	(423)	24	(121)	(19)	–	–
Northwest	769	(797)	(277)	(895)	1,124	(541)	–
Competitor average	**716**	**(1,260)**	**(601)**	**(390)**	**571**	**(2,644)**	**(290)**

Operating cost trends

Are operating costs increasing or decreasing as a percentage of sales revenue or sales volume? Again, how does this vary by market segment and compare against competitors? Useful analyses include:

- **Company operating cost trend** – Figure 13.11 shows Southwest's operating costs per available seat mile (i.e. as a percentage of sales volume).

Figure 13.10 Operating profit as a percentage of sales revenue (1999–2009)							
Airline	**Operating profit (% sales revenue)**						
	1999	**2001**	**2003**	**2005**	**2007**	**2008**	**2009**
Southwest	17	11	5	7	8	4	3
Competitors							
Alaska	(1)	(4)	(1)	0	4	(5)	8
US Airways	2	(14)	(6)	(3)	8	(14)	1
Continental	6	(4)	0	(1)	5	(2)	(1)
Delta	12	(7)	(8)	(7)	7	(37)	(1)
United	8	(23)	(10)	(1)	2	(27)	(4)
American	6	(16)	(8)	(2)	4	(8)	(5)
America West	9	(21)	1	(4)	(1)	–	–
Northwest	8	(8)	(3)	(7)	12	(4)	–
Competitor average	**8**	**(13)**	**(6)**	**(3)**	**6**	**(18)**	**(2)**

- Operating cost compared with competitors – Figure 13.11 shows that Southwest's operating costs are significantly lower than its competitors'. In 2008, they were 58 per cent of the competitor average.

Figure 13.11 Operating costs (1999–2008)						
Airline	**Operating costs per available seat mile (in cents)**					
	1999	**2001**	**2003**	**2005**	**2007**	**2008**
Southwest	6.6	7.5	7.9	8.3	9.1	10.2
Competitors						
US Airways	12.4	14.2	14.0	13.9	10.9	20.8
Northwest	9.3	11.3	11.4	15.2	10.4	19.3
Delta	9.0	10.1	12.9	13.1	10.6	18.7
Continental	9.0	10.3	9.8	13.1	10.2	17.1
United	9.7	12.4	12.4	12.9	11.4	15.7
Alaska	10.2	10.2	9.8	10.9	12.2	14.5
American	9.4	11.9	11.5	12.0	11.4	13.9
American West	7.3	9.3	7.9	11.5	12.9	–
Competitor average	**9.5**	**11.2**	**11.2**	**12.8**	**11.3**	**17.1**

Customer satisfaction trends

These trends can start to give some indication of the future financial performance of the business as satisfied customers will usually lead to increased sales in the future. Key questions to ask are: what customer satisfaction measures exist within the business? Does it simply measure complaints, or is it more proactive than that? How are these satisfaction levels changing over time? How do these compare with its competitors? Useful analyses include:

- Customer satisfaction trend against competitors – Figure 13.12 shows that Southwest's are consistently more satisfied than its competitors'. Also, they are more satisfied than they were 10 years ago.

Figure 13.12 Customer satisfaction as a percentage of customers surveyed (1999–2010)

Airline	% customers satisfied							
	1999	2001	2003	2005	2007	2008	2009	2010
Southwest	72	70	75	74	76	79	81	79
Competitors								
US Airways	61	60	64	57	61	54	59	62
Continental	64	67	68	70	69	62	68	71
Delta	68	61	67	65	59	60	64	62
United	62	59	63	61	56	56	56	60
American	64	62	67	64	60	62	60	63
Northwest	53	56	64	64	61	57	57	61
Competitor average	**62**	**61**	**66**	**64**	**61**	**59**	**61**	**63**

> **EXECUTIVE INSIGHT**
> Poor market support and customer satisfaction will eventually result in:
> • Reduced sales revenues – as customers leave or
> • Reduced profits – as customers will not pay high prices for your services and products.

Overall health of the business

From all of these analyses we can make a number of conclusions about the overall health of Southwest Airlines:

• **Customers like its services and products** – that is why customer satisfaction is the highest within its industry and its sales revenue and sales volume has increased significantly over the last 10 years.

• **Good cost control** – it manages its operating costs well. This enables it to compete on price, but still make a profit.

• **Strong financial position** – compared with its competitors, it is in a strong financial position and has returned a profit every year for the last 10 years.

• **Competitive and declining market** – however, despite all the good points outlined above, there is still a concern that its market is declining and becoming increasingly competitive. As a result, although it is the most profitable airline in this market, these profit margins are significantly lower than those for successful businesses competing in other markets.

Given these findings, we would now want to analyze Southwest's market and operation to understand if it has any options for:

• **Improving market support** – so that it can gain more market share, move into new markets that are more profitable or start to increase its prices for certain services or products.

• **Reduce costs further** – so that it can make its current market share more profitable.

> **EXECUTIVE INSIGHT**
> The health check:
> • Identifies strengths and weakness – within a business, and
> • Guides subsequent analysis – of markets, market support, cash holdings and operating costs to identify areas of improvement.

Analyzing markets

Once the business context is understood, then the next step is to identify the business's current and future markets and determine the order-winners and qualifiers that need to be supported in these markets. While undertaking this analysis, it is important to follow a number of key principles:

> **Customer voice** – is what customers tell you they want.
>
> **Customer behaviour** – shows you what customers actually want.

- **Analyze both 'customer voice' and 'customer behaviour'** – it is important to understand both what customers say they want (customer voice) and what they actually want (customer behaviour) as:
  - *Appealing to customer voice* – is important for winning new business.
  - *Supporting customer behaviour* – is necessary for retaining existing business.

- **Analyze multi-functional perspectives of the market** – all functions interact with customers in different ways and, therefore, have different perspectives of their needs. The process of identifying the order-winners and qualifiers must therefore involve interviewing executives from a range of business functions. For example, Sales and Marketing often hear the voice of the customer, whereas Customer Service and Operations see their behaviour.

- **Test executive opinion with data** – the different functional market perspectives then need to be tested against data to see if they are correct.

- **Realize order-winners and qualifiers may vary by customer order** – not only may the order-winners and qualifiers demanded within a market vary by customer, but they may also vary by the services and products they demand and even vary by the different customer orders for the same service or product. It is important to identify these differences and the varying demands they place on the business.

- **Realize that order-winners and qualifiers within a market will change over time** – hence, you need to identify the order-winners and qualifiers required today and show how the criteria that have to be met and their level of importance will change over time for different markets, customers, services or products and customer orders.

> **> EXECUTIVE INSIGHT**
>
> When analyzing markets it is important to:
> - Analyze both 'customer voice' and 'customer behaviour'
> - Analyze the market from different functional perspectives
> - Test executive opinion of market needs with data showing how customers actually behave
> - Realize that order-winners and qualifers may vary by customer, service, product and even customer order
> - Realize that the order-winners and qualifiers required today will change over time.

Identify current and future markets

The first step in analyzing markets is to identify which ones the business wishes to compete in today and in the future. It is important to remember here that the most important orders are the ones to which you say 'no', as these mark the boundaries of the market in which you wish to compete. Without this level of clarity, the business will try to be 'all things to all people', which means that it will not support any of its markets effectively.

> **> EXECUTIVE INSIGHT**
>
> The most important orders are the ones to which you say 'no' as these determine the boundaries of the:
>
> - Market in which you wish to compete and the
> - Capabilities that you need to develop.

'Measure **twice**,

Identify executive opinion of current and future order-winners and qualifiers

Once the current and future markets of the business have been developed, then the current and future order-winners and qualifiers for these markets need to be identified. The first step is to understand marketing's view of the market, before testing it with other functional perspectives and then finally testing all of these views with data showing how customers actually behave. The following sections describe how you would do this and give examples of analyses that you might complete. To illustrate how this works, an example of a completed market analysis is shown in Figure 13.13 for a graphic designer. This example will be referred to in the following sections.

> **EXECUTIVE INSIGHT**
>
> Markets will naturally become more price-sensitive as:
> - **Competition increases** – so more services and products are available and
> - **Customers' knowledge increases** – of the alternative services and products that are available and the differences between them.

Understand marketing's view of the market

The first step is to ask marketing executives to:

1. **Segment the market** – from a marketing point of view and choose customers, services or products that represent each segment. In Figure 13.13, the graphic designer has chosen two customers to look at: Customer A and Customer B.

2. **Determine an appropriate planning horizon** – for each segment so that the current and future order-winners and qualifiers can be identified. In Figure 13.13, the graphic designer has decided to look two years ahead.

3. **Select and weight the order-winners and qualifiers** – for each segment in both the current and future time periods using customers, services or products that represent each segment. Again, using the example in Figure 13.13, we can see that Customer B is currently more price-sensitive than Customer A who requires more technical support. However, this is expected to change over the next three years as Customer B becomes less price-sensitive and requires more technical support.

Test marketing's view with other functional perspectives of the market

Once marketing's view of the market is understood, it needs to be tested against the other functional perspectives in the business. This then leads to an improved understanding of the market. During this process, either the order-winners and qualifiers or their weightings identified before may change. However, it is important to remember that one functional perspective is not more or less important than another. All are valid and important. Instead, you need to keep asking yourself the question: 'What data do I need to collect to test this opinion and see if it is true?' At all times, you must remember that the purpose of this discussion and debate is to:

- **Improve market understanding** – debating and testing markets enables key distinctions between customers, orders and products to be understood. In this way, a company's view of its markets is improved.

- **Review markets, customers, services, products and customer orders** – so that key differences can be understood.

- **Identify market segment importance** – for the business in terms of generating revenue and profit and understanding the capabilities that need to be developed to support it both now and in the future.

- **Prioritize investment and development** – the order-winners and qualifiers within a company's markets define the capabilities that it needs to develop.

- **Help align functional strategies** – functions typically develop strategies independently of one another. Debating and testing markets allows essential differences and perspectives to be exposed and explored. This creates a cross-functional perspective of markets that, in turn, helps align the different functional strategies within the business.

Test executive opinion with data

Once you understand the different functional perspectives in the business, you then need to test these opinions with data showing how customers actually behave. However, when you complete this analysis it is important to remember that:

- **Analysis is difficult** – some may be difficult to undertake if data are not readily available. In this instance, a decision needs to made about how to capture the data so that they can be analyzed. Instead of trying to analyze all customers, services, products and customer orders within a segment, it is often easier to identify a representative sample of customer orders and analyze those in detail.

- **Analysis may give limited insight** – some will give little or no insight. When this occurs, you need to go back to the data and see if it needs to be segmented further. It may be that it looks at too broad a range of requirements.

- **Try to look at both won and lost customer orders** – this will help you understand the importance of order-winners and qualifiers in markets not currently supported by the business.

Examples of analyses that can be used to test the importance of order-winners and qualifiers within different markets are summarized in Figure 13.14 and are now discussed in more detail.

> **EXECUTIVE INSIGHT**
> To prevent markets from becoming more price-sensitive, you need to develop new services, products, processes and business models that:
> - **Differentiate your services and products** – from competitors' and
> - **Create barriers** – to entry and to exit within your existing markets.

Price

To determine if price is an order-winner or qualifier, you need to review the actual costs and margins for those customers, services, products or customer orders. Contribution will be low if it is an order-winner and high if it is a qualifier. In many instances, companies will use their own form of standard costs to determine these margins. However, these cost calculations are invariably inaccurate. It is essential, therefore, to identify the actual costs involved in delivering a service or product to a customer.

Quality conformance

The importance of quality conformance within a market can be determined by identifying the actual number of times a service or product is delivered in line with its design specification and reviewing the level of customer satisfaction and complaints within a market segment.

Delivery reliability

Before measuring delivery reliability, the definition of 'on time' needs to be agreed. For some customers this may mean a service or product being delivered within a couple of minutes, whereas for others it could be any day within a given week. Equally, some may not want it delivered before a given time, while others may require all the items in the order to be delivered at the same time. Once this has been defined, then the actual

CRITERIA	CUSTOMER A BY YEAR			CUSTOMER B BY YEAR		
	Current	1	2	Current	1	2
Product design	40	40	40	30	40	50
Price	Q	Q	Q	40	20	Q
Delivery reliability	QQ	QQ	QQ	QQ	QQ	QQ
Delivery speed	30	20	Q	30	20	Q
Quality conformance	QQ	QQ	QQ	QQ	QQ	QQ
Technical support	30	40	60	–	20	50

delivery of a service or product needs to be compared with the delivery time promised by the business for each customer, service, product or customer order.

Delivery speed

The importance of delivery speed within a market can be determined by comparing the date and time a customer places an order with the date and time they requested the delivery of a service or product. When undertaking this analysis it is important to:

- **Review delivery request amendments** – sometimes customers pull forward their requested delivery date after the order has been placed

- **Check short lead-time requirements** – contact customers with short lead-time requirements to check that this is when they actually need the service or product. In some cases, they may have shortened the lead-time to help buffer against poor performance or may simply have inaccurate standard service or product lead-times in their computer ordering system.

Service or product range

Review the number of service or product types and the dates when they were requested by customers within that segment. It is then possible to assess how ranges have increased or decreased over an appropriate time period for the services and products requested by different customers.

Service or product design

The importance of service or product design can be reviewed by:

- **Reviewing service or product design specifications** – higher specifications with tighter tolerances would mean that design is more important.

- **Benchmarking design against competitors** – again higher levels would indicate more importance.

- **Review lost orders** – speak to sales executives to try to estimate how many times orders were lost because the competition had a better designed service or product.

Demand fluctuations

Analyze how both the 'volume of customer orders placed' and the 'volume of services and products requested' varies over an appropriate time period. This will show if demand fluctuates in either the order entry or order fulfilment part of the process. As with all other analyses, this must be done for specific products, or customers, to highlight the differences between them.

Speed of new service or product introduction

Review the level and speed of a new service or product introduction for different customers over an appropriate time period. It would also be worth speaking to sales executives to understand if more new services and products had been requested than were introduced and also where orders were lost because new services or products were unavailable.

Other market order-winners and qualifiers

There are many different order-winners and qualifiers besides those discussed above. Once again it is important to test executive opinion with data showing how customers actually behave by analyzing a representative sample of services, products and customer orders. Without this analysis, it is not possible to understand fully how the business wins and qualifies for orders in its markets.

ORDER WINNER OR QUALIFIER
Price
Quality conformance
Delivery reliability
Delivery speed
Service or product range
Service or product design
Demand fluctuations
Speed of new service or product development

EXAMPLE ANALYSES FOR REVIEWING LEVEL OF IMPORTANCE

- Review actual material, direct labour and overhead costs for delivering services and products to those customers
- Using these actual costs, review the actual profit margins

- Review actual quality conformance levels
- Review customer satisfaction levels
- Review customer complaints and returns

- Define what constitutes 'on time' for each customer
- Compare the actual day/time of service or product delivery with the day/time of promised delivery

- Review customer requested delivery lead-times
- Review customer delivery request amendments
- Check short-lead-time requirements are actually needed by customers

- Review the range or services and products requested by a customer within an appropriate time period

- Review the design specifications of the services and products delivered to a customer
- Benchmark the level of design specification against competitors
- Estimate how many customer orders were lost because the design of the service or product was not as good as the competition

- Review how the volume of customer orders varies over an appropriate time period
- Review how the volume of services or products ordered varies over an appropriate time period

- Review the level of new service or product introduction for different customers over an appropriate time period
- Estimate how many customer orders were lost because new services or products were not available

> **EXECUTIVE INSIGHT**

You must constantly look for ways to use data to challenge and check:
- **Executive opinion** – of order-winners and qualifiers, and
- **Your own opinion** – of how orders are won.

Analyzing market support

Once the current and future order-winners and qualifiers for current and future markets are understood, then the next step is to review the current level of support for these market requirements. Figure 13.15 gives some examples of how performance can be reviewed against order-winners and qualifiers typically supported by operations. This involves an analysis of the services and products delivered to meet customer orders and also, where possible, a review of customer orders that were not won to understand why this happened. Both Chapter 11 on managing quality and Chapter 14 on improving operations discuss a number of tools and techniques that can help in this analysis, such as:

- **Benchmarking** – comparing business practice and performance against other parts of the same organization, direct competitors, companies within the same sector who are not direct competitors, latent competitors and/or companies outside of the industry

- **Mapping the customer journey** – to help understand the journey that customers take and identify the points of interaction that they have with the business

- **Mapping processes** – to understand how they currently operate using tools such as process charts, service maps, information and material flow charts, person flow charts and videoing

- **Pareto analysis** – to help identify the frequency of problems

- **Cause and effect diagrams** – to help identify the causes of poor performance

- **Why-why reviews** – to get to the root cause of a problem.

> **EXECUTIVE INSIGHT**

Managing quality and improving operations tools and techniques can be used to analyze the level of support for the current and future market order-winners and qualifiers.

Price

Operations must check its current performance on a number of aspects to understand if price is being supported. Analyses that help highlight current or potential problems and typical areas for improvement are:

- **Review actual material, direct labour and overhead costs** – while all aspects of cost must be reviewed, materials and overheads are usually the main areas on which to focus as they tend to account for 70–90 per cent of total costs. Trends should be reviewed to understand historical and forecasted changes.

- **Review activity costs** – as well as splitting costs by type, it is also useful to separate them into different activities. To do this, you should map the entire business process from customer order placement through to customer payment. Then work out the cost of each activity within this process.

- **Review staff and process efficiency** – by estimating the **standard time** to complete a task using:
  - **Time studies** – for short, repetitive tasks as described in Figure 13.16 and illustrated visually in Figure 13.17, and
  - **Estimates** – for long, non-repetitive tasks as illustrated in Figure 13.18.

Then compare this against the actual performance for completing the activity.

Standard time is the time it typically takes a qualified person to complete an activity at a defined level of performance. This will include an allowance for tasks not directly related to the job, such as rest time.

Time study – break an activity down into its key tasks and then observe how long it takes a trained person to complete each task.

Estimates – assess the time required to carry out an activity based on knowledge and experience of a similar type of activity.

Figure 13.15 Examples of performance reviews for different order-winners and qualifiers

Order-winner or qualifier	Example performance reviews
Price	· Review actual material, direct labour and overhead costs · Map current processes and identify areas of material and labour waste · Review mix of production volumes · Review process efficiency and productivity · Review annual production volumes within a product range · Review production run lengths · Review contribution per machine hour · Review product pricing
Quality conformance	· Review quality conformance levels for products, orders, customers and market segments
Delivery reliability	· Review delivery performance for products, orders, customers and market segments · Analyze and compare customer requested and operations actual delivery lead times · Compare actual processing with overall operations lead-time
Delivery speed	· Analyze and compare customer requested and operations actual delivery lead-times · Map actual operations process and identify long lead-time activities · Compare actual processing lead-time with overall operations lead-time · Work with suppliers to understand their lead-times
Service or product range	· Review the process capability to meet required current and future service or product range
Service or product design	· Review current service and product design specifications · Compare them with customer expectations · Benchmark them against competitors
Demand fluctuations	· Assess ability of capacity to respond to known or anticipated demand changes
Speed of new service or product development	· Map new product development process and identify areas of waste · Determine length of activities and their dependency on other activities or key resources · Identify activities for which operations has responsibility

Figure 13.16 Using a time study to estimate the standard time for a short, repetitive task

Step	Description
1	Select the task to be reviewed
2	Break the task down into the following elements: · Repetitive – occur every time the task is completed · Occasional and contingent – only occur when a particular event happens · Rest and personal needs – that also occur during the working day
3	Observe a person undertaking the task and measure the time that it takes to do this. It is useful to video them so that it can be viewed again if required
4	Rate the level of competence of the person to complete these tasks
5	Adjust the time recorded for the task based on the level of competence of the person observed to create a 'basic' or 'normal' time
6	Add to the 'basic time' estimates for: · Occasional and contingent elements · Rest and personal needs to determine the overall 'standard time' for the task

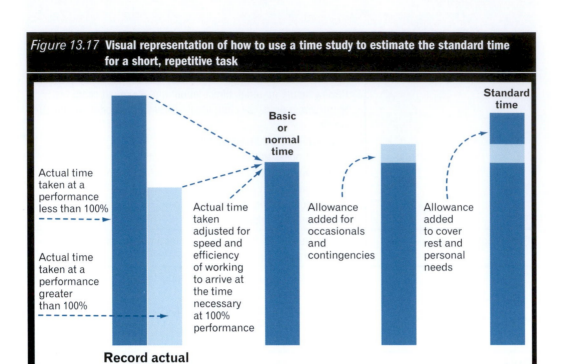

Figure 13.17 Visual representation of how to use a time study to estimate the standard time for a short, repetitive task

Standard time

Actual time taken at a performance less than 100%

Actual time taken at a performance greater than 100%

Record actual times

Actual time taken adjusted for speed and efficiency of working to arrive at the time necessary at 100% performance

Basic or normal time

Allowance added for occasionals and contingencies

Allowance added to cover rest and personal needs

Figure 13.18 An example of how basic, analytical and comparative estimates can be used to determine the standard time for cleaning an office

Estimating method	Application of approach
Basic	The estimator could estimate the time it would take to empty all the waste bins and then vacuum and dust the office based on their own experience of similar work
Analytical	The estimator could break the activity down into a number of tasks such as: · Empty 10 waste bins · Dust 10 desks · Dust 10 chairs · Dust 20 filing cabinets · Dust 50 metres of skirting board · Dust 10 window ledges · Dust 5 doors · Vacuum 150 square metres of carpet with a high level of furniture congestion The estimator could then estimate the time it would take to complete each activity based on their own experience of similar work
Comparative	The estimator could identify a number of categories that reflect the different types of offices and how long they take to be cleaned as shown below:

Type of office	Time to clean (hours)	Example
A	0.5	Partner's office
B	1.0	Purchasing department
C	1.5	Drawing office
D	2.0	Housing department
E	3.0	Main open-plan office

An estimate of the time to clean each type of office could then be established using either a basic or analytical estimate as described above

All future jobs would then be allocated to a category and compared against the benchmark for that type of job

- Review staff and process productivity – by comparing the output of a person or process with the amount of time that they work. Examples of productivity measures for different types of operations are shown in Figure 13.19.

- Review mix of service or product volumes – cost efficient operations typically focus on a narrow range of high-volume services or products. However, as markets mature, product ranges widen and production volumes decrease. Therefore it is important to review the service/product and volume mix within operations to understand if this is preventing it from reducing costs.

- Review service or product pricing – supporting price involves not only having the right level of costs, but also then making sure the services and products are priced effectively. Therefore, the pricing of services and products over an appropriate time period needs to be reviewed to see if they are increasing or decreasing and if they vary by market. Equally, it is important to understand how these services and products are priced and the standard costing methods used, as these may not reflect the true costs of delivering a service or product.

Figure 13.19	Examples of single-factor and multiple-factor productivity measures in different businesses	
Business	**Single-factor measure**	**Multi-factor measure**
Law firm	# briefs filed	# briefs filed and court attendances undertaken
	Lawyer	Lawyer
Bookshop	# customers served	# customers served, deliveries handled and despatches sent
	Full-time equivalent staff	Full-time equivalent staff
University	# student contact hours	# student contact hours, research assistants supervised (hours) and administrative tasks (hours)
	Faculty member	Faculty member
Consultancy firm	# consultancy days billed	# consultancy days billed, training undertaken (days) and administrative tasks (days)
	Total consultancy days available	Total consultancy days available
Engineering design firm	# design projects completed	# design projects completed, tenders submitted and site visits undertaken
	Engineering staff days	Engineering staff days

Quality conformance

Actual quality conformance levels for different customers, services, products and orders must be reviewed and compared against market requirements. Again, it is useful to understand if previous poor performance has resulted in the loss of customers or the inability to win them in the first place. Tools such as Pareto analysis, cause and effect diagrams and why-why reviews can then help identify the causes of these problems.

Delivery reliability

Collect and analyze delivery performance data to see if they vary by customer, service, product or order. Comparing delivery on-time performance with aspects such as order size, customer lead-times, delivery lead-times and supplier lead-times helps identify causes of above or below average delivery reliability performance and highlights areas and actions for improvement.

Delivery speed

Analyze actual delivery lead-time by breaking it down into the relevant elements of service or product delivery and then compare this with customer expected delivery lead-time. It is useful here to map again the entire operations process from customer order placement through to final delivery and identify the lead-time of each part of the process. This may also involve working with suppliers to understand the lead-time for the services and products that they supply and to see if these can be improved.

Other order-winners and qualifiers

Examples of how the support for other order-winners and qualifiers could be reviewed are:

- **Service or product range** – review the capability of operations to process the current range on offer and any future proposed changes. This needs to be completed for all steps involved in delivering a service or product.

- **Service or product design** – review current service and product design specifications, compare them with customer expectations and benchmark them against competitors.

- **Demand fluctuations** – assess the ability of the current operations process capacity to respond to known or anticipated demand changes.

- **Speed of new service or product development** – map the current new service or product development process to understand how it works. Determine the length of each activity and its dependency on other activities or key resources and identify the activities for which operations has responsibility.

> **EXECUTIVE INSIGHT**
> It is impossible to identify and justify business improvements until:
> - Market requirements are known, and
> - The current level of market support is understood.

Analyzing cash holdings

Releasing cash enables investments to be made elsewhere in the business, dividends to be given to shareholders and creditors to be paid back. Within most businesses, the highest levels of cash are tied up in accounts receivables, inventories, properties, buildings and equipment. Figures 13.20 and 13.21 analyze the cash holdings within Dell, the case study at the end of Chapter 10. Two main points emerge from these analyses:

- **Current assets are increasing in relation to sales** – this is of particular concern given the sharp increase in sales in 2010.

- Main areas that cash is tied up in are:
  - Accounts receivable – 39 days of sales and $6.5 billion
  - Financing receivables – 22 days of sales and $3.6 billion
  - Property, buildings and equipment – 12 days of sales and $1.9 billion
  - Inventory – 8 days of sales and $1.3 billion.

> **EXECUTIVE INSIGHT**
> The main areas where cash usually gets tied up are:
> - Accounts receivable and inventory (current assets)
> - Property, buildings and equipment (fixed assets).

Some examples of how to analyze the current and fixed asset holdings within a business are now discussed.

Performance	Value ($m)							
	1999	2002	2003	2005	2007	2008	2009	2010
Annual sales revenue	25,265	31,168	41,444	55,908	61,133	61,101	52,902	61,494
Current assets								
Cash and cash equivalents	3,809	3,641	4,317	7,054	7,764	8,352	10,635	13,913
Accounts receivable	2,608	2,269	3,635	4,082	5,961	4,731	5,837	6,493
Financing receivables				1,366	1,732	1,712	2,706	3,643
Inventory	391	278	327	588	1,180	867	1,051	1,301
Short-term investments	323	273	835	2,016	208	740	373	452
Other	550	1,416	1,519	2,688	3,035	3,749	3,643	3,219
Total	**7,681**	**7,877**	**10,633**	**17,794**	**19,880**	**20,151**	**24,245**	**29,021**
Fixed assets								
Goodwill	–	–	–	–	1,648	1,737	4,074	4,365
Property, buildings and equipment	765	826	1,517	1,993	2,668	2,277	2,181	1,953
Purchased intangible assets	–	–	–	–	780	724	1,694	1,495
Long-term financing receivables	–	–	–	325	407	500	332	799
Investments	2,721	4,373	6,770	2,686	1,560	454	781	704
Other	304	459	391	454	618	657	345	262
Total	**3,790**	**5,658**	**8,678**	**5,458**	**7,681**	**6,349**	**9,407**	**9,578**
Total assets	**11,471**	**13,535**	**19,311**	**23,252**	**27,561**	**26,500**	**33,652**	**38,599**

Figure 13.20 **Dell's annual sales revenue, current assets and fixed assets (1999–2010)**

Review current assets

The level of current assets needs to be reviewed within the business to see if the current levels of cash holdings can be reduced. For example:

Analyzing inventory

As explained earlier in Chapter 10 on managing inventory, companies need to understand:

- **Where inventory is held** – within the operations process, and

- **Why it is held** – by grouping it into one of the following categories: corporate, decoupling, cycle, pipeline, capacity-related and buffer.

This analysis then identifyies how inventory levels can be reduced without negatively impacting market support. An example of a causal analysis for an engineering company is shown in Figure 13.22. This shows that the main reasons for holding inventory are:

- **Decoupling** – 34 per cent enables different steps in the process to work independently of each other.

- **Capacity-related** – 22 per cent results from products being made ahead of demand.

- **Customer agreement** – 17 per cent is to meet customer contractual agreements.

- **Supplier agreement** – 10 per cent results from supplier minimum order-quantities.

Assets	Days of sales							
	1999	2001	2003	2005	2007	2008	2009	2010
Current								
Cash and cash equivalents	55	43	38	46	46	50	73	83
Accounts receivable	38	27	32	27	36	28	40	39
Financing receivables	–	–	–	9	10	10	19	22
Inventory	6	3	3	4	7	5	7	8
Short-term investments	5	3	7	13	1	4	3	3
Other	8	17	13	18	18	22	25	19
Total	**111**	**92**	**94**	**116**	**119**	**120**	**167**	**172**
Fixed assets								
Goodwill	–	–	–	–	10	10	28	26
Property, buildings and equipment	11	10	13	13	16	14	15	12
Purchased intangible assets	–	–	–	–	5	4	12	9
Long-term financing receivables	–	–	–	2	2	3	2	5
Investments	39	51	60	18	9	3	5	4
Other	4	5	3	3	4	4	2	2
Total	**55**	**66**	**76**	**36**	**46**	**38**	**65**	**57**
Total assets	**166**	**159**	**170**	**152**	**165**	**158**	**232**	**229**

Figure 13.21 **Dell's current and fixed assets as days of sales (1999–2010)**

Using this information, inventory can then be reduced by making improvements such as re-engineering the process, reducing process set-up times, reducing operations lead-times, improving delivery reliability and renegotiating customer agreements.

Analyzing accounts receivables

The level of **debtor days** should be calculated for different markets and customers. This will help understand where cash is getting trapped to:

- Focus customer payment chasing resources

- Identify where customer payment terms need to be renegotiated, or

- Identify which customers are unable to pay their invoices.

Review fixed assets

As well as trying to release cash from current assets, it is also useful to look at fixed assets such as property, buildings and equipment. Once the significant assets have been identified, then a casual analysis can be completed to understand why they are being used. It may be that decisions can then be made to help reduce them, such as selling or leasing equipment or outsourcing processes requiring high building or equipment investment. However, as discussed in Chapter 12 on managing the supply chain, the strategic implications of making such decisions need to be reviewed first.

Analyzing operating costs

Even when price is not an order-winner, it is still important when analyzing the operating costs of a business to see if they can be reduced. These reviews are similar to those used for investigating whether price-sensitive markets are supported. Useful analyses include:

Debtor days – the number of days before a customer pays you. It is calculated as the level of outstanding customer invoices ($) divided by the typical daily sales revenue ($) for that customer.

Figure 13.22 Causal analysis of inventory held within an engineering company						
Type	Cause	Decision made by	% raw material inventory	% work-in-process inventory	% finished goods inventory	% total inventory held
Corporate	Customer agreement: contractual requirement	Sales	–	–	41	17
	Supplier minimum order quantity	Operations	41	–	–	10
	Inaccurate sales forecast	Sales	–	–	12	5
	To meet planned future sales	Marketing	6	–	–	2
	Total		**47**	**–**	**53**	**34**
Operations	Decoupling: enabling process steps to work ndependently of each other	Operations	53	62	–	34
	Capacity-related: made ahead of demand	Operations	–	15	41	22
	Cycle: different production cycles at each process step	Operations	–	12	3	5
	Pipeline: being transported between process steps	Operations	–	11	–	4
	Buffer: against demand uncertainty	Operations	–	–	3	1
	Total		**53**	**100**	**47**	**66**
	Total		**100**	**100**	**100**	**100**

- Review actual material, direct labour and overhead costs – focusing on materials and overheads as they tend to account for 70–90 per cent of total costs and reviewing trends to understand historical and forecasted changes

- Review activity costs – by mapping the entire business process from customer order placement through to customer payment and working out the cost of each activity within this process

- Review staff and process efficiency – by comparing the actual time against the standard time for completing an activity

- Review staff and process productivity – by comparing the output of a person or process with the amount of time that they work

- Review mix of service or product volumes – as a wide mix will make it difficult to reduce costs

Analyzing operations in practice

When analyzing operations in practice, it is important to consider the following aspects:

- **It is not possible to analyze everything** – as it would take too much time and money to do this. Therefore, you need to identify the critical issues to focus on given the stakeholder requirements, corporate objectives and current health of the business.

- **Analyze representative samples** – as it is not possible to analyze everything, when analyzing markets you will need to identify a representative sample of:
  - Customers for each market segment
  - Services and products for each customer
  - Customer orders for each service and product and then analyze these in detail.

- **Analyze representative time periods** – as it is not possible to analyze everything, when analyzing market support, cash holdings and operating costs you will need to identify a representative time period of production orders and then analyze these in detail.

- **Split out different market segments** – when analyzing markets, if:
  - Customers within a market segment have different requirements
  - Services or products delivered to a customer have different requirements, or
  - Customer orders for a service or product have different requirements
  then you need to separate them into different market segments.

- **Look at both won and lost customer orders** – as this will help understand the importance of order-winners and qualifiers in markets not currently supported by the business.

- **The critical areas to analyze keep changing** – if market requirements change or you make improvements, then the areas you need to improve in the business will change.

- **Challenge and check executive opinion** – you need constantly to look for ways to check executive opinion by comparing it with other opinions and data.

- **Challenge and check data collected** – you need constantly to look for ways to check the data you have collected by comparing with other data, observation and executive opinion.

- **Data is not always available** – so you will need to put 'traps' in place to capture it. For example, you may need to ask a person to record why a service or product is delivered late or a piece of inventory has been generated. These data will have to be recorded for a representative period of time before they can be analyzed.

- **Balance gut feeling with in-depth analysis** – analyzing operations involves balancing gut feeling with in-depth analysis so that action is not delayed, but also focuses on areas of maximum impact given the strategic objectives of the business and the investment funds (money) and resources (time) that are available.

Driving business performance

Releasing cash

Cash can be released from an operation by:

- **Reducing inventory** – held within operations through a causal analysis asking why it is necessary, why it is there and what caused it. The systems, procedures and rules that created the inventory can then be challenged, reviewed and changed to reduce it.

- **Changing supplier payment terms** – companies can delay paying suppliers. However, this will negatively affect their suppliers' cash flow, which could have a disastrous impact on a small supplier. In fact, one way to help persuade suppliers to make improvements and take on more responsibility (such as managing inventory) is to improve their payment terms.

- **Selling or leasing equipment** – non-essential equipment can be sold and essential equipment can be leased. Although leasing will probably increase the overall cost of the equipment, it spreads it over a longer period of time. Equally, it is often easier to update leased equipment as it does not have to be sold before new equipment can be bought.

- **Outsourcing** – processes that require a high investment in equipment or inventory. However, it is critical to make sure this does not have a negative long-term strategic impact on the business.

Improving market support

The operations function of a business is critical in winning and retaining customers. Some examples of how different market order-winners and qualifiers can be better supported through improved operations are:

- **Price** – by reducing material, direct labour and overhead costs that, in turn, enable selling prices to be reduced without lowering profit margins. This can be done by modifying service and product designs, finding cheaper materials, eliminating process wastes, reducing the mix of volumes and improving staff and process efficiency and productivity.

- **Quality conformance** – by reducing the quality gaps that exist between what customers want and expect, what a company sells, how services and products have been designed and what operations delivers.

- **Delivery reliability** – by reducing the gap between promised and actual delivery. This can be done by collecting and analyzing delivery performance data to understand how it varies by service, product, order, customer, order size, customer lead-time, delivery lead-time and supplier lead-time.

- **Delivery speed** – by reducing the gap between requested and actual delivery. This can be done by:
  - Analyzing actual expected customer lead-time – to see if it matches their real requirement, and
  - Mapping the actual operations process – to determine the actual operations lead-time and identify areas for improvement.

- **Service or product range** – by improving the capability of staff and the processes they use to deliver the current and future ranges proposed.

- **Demand fluctuations** – by improving the ability of the delivery system to respond to known or anticipated demand changes.

- **Speed of new service or product development** – by reducing the current development lead-time. This can be done by mapping the current development process, determining the length of each activity and its dependency on other activities or key resources, and identifying areas for improvement.

Reducing costs

Significant cost reductions can be made within an operation, for example reducing:

- **Research and development costs** – by developing strategic partnerships with critical customers and suppliers.

- **Labour costs** – by getting customers to serve themselves, outsourcing activities to suppliers, modifying service and product designs, eliminating non-value-adding activities, reducing the range and mix of volumes delivered and improving staff and process efficiency and productivity.

- **Material costs** – by modifying service and product designs, developing long-term supplier relationships, using single sourcing policies and finding cheaper alternatives.

- **Overhead costs** – by making the operation easier to manage, getting customers to serve themselves and outsourcing management tasks to suppliers, such as managing inventory.

- **Inventory costs** – by reducing inventory levels within the operation.

Critical reflections

Businesses constantly need to look for ways to improve how they operate. If a company isn't moving forwards, it's actually moving backwards as there is always someone else looking for ways to take its customers. Therefore operations must be continually analyzed to:

- **Monitor and track the health of the business** – and identify any potential problems before they occur by monitoring aspects such as the level of customer satisfaction, employee satisfaction, research and development, costs, sales revenue, market share and profits.

- **Understand current market requirements** – as markets are constantly evolving and changing, it is critical that businesses continually track both customer voice and customer behaviour to identify the order-winners and qualifiers that need to be supported within its current markets.

- **Predict future market requirements** – a deep understanding of customers' current needs will help predict future market requirements and trends.

- **Identify areas of poor market support** – by understanding if it has the ability to support both current and future market requirements.

- **Identify areas of trapped cash** – that can potentially be released and invested elsewhere within the business such as new equipment or research and development. Within most businesses, the highest levels of cash are tied up in accounts receivables, inventories, properties, buildings and equipment.

- **Identify areas of high costs** – that could be reduced as long as they do not negatively impact a firm's ability to support its current and future market requirements. In most businesses, material and overhead costs tend to account for 70–79 per cent of total costs.

When completing this analysis, it is important to look continually for ways to check executive opinion with data. In many cases, the data may not currently be available so you will need to put in place 'traps' to capture them. During this process, you will need to develop the ability to 'zoom in' on a particular problem to understand how to solve it and then 'zoom out' to see if it is relevant to the strategic issues faced by the business. It is also critical to develop the ability to learn from success as well as failure. Too often we only analyze operations when things are not working rather than trying to understand why something has gone well so that we can repeat this again in the future.

Summary

This chapter has looked at why organizations should analyze operations, how they should do this and how they should understand the business context before analyzing markets, market support, cash holdings and operating costs. It then considers the practical implications of analyzing an operation.

Why analyze operations?

It is important to analyze an operation because it is:

- A large function – with high assets, costs and people

- Key to supporting markets – as it is critical to winning and retaining customers

- Key to building barriers to entry – as its capabilities are often difficult to imitate

- Important to challenge and check executive opinion – with other opinion and data.

In addition:

- Insights are often surprising – and often contradict the myths and beliefs that exist within a business.

- Analysis increases the focus on improvement – by focusing management on action rather than discussion.

How to analyze operations?

Operations can be analyzed by going through five main steps:

1. **Understanding the business context** – the stakeholder requirements and corporate objectives that need to be met and the current health of the business.

2. **Analyzing current and future markets** – and the order-winners and qualifiers that need to be supported in these markets.

3. **Analyzing market support** – for the current and future order-winners and qualifiers that it has to support.

4. **Analyzing cash holdings** – understanding why cash is currently tied up in accounts receivable, inventory, property, buildings and equipment.

5. **Analyzing operating costs** – reviewing actual material, direct labour and overhead costs.

When doing this, it is important to:

- **Visit the business** – to observe how it operates.

- **Visit customers** – to understand what they need.

- **Observe service delivery and product manufacture** – to understand its delivery systems.

- **Be a customer** – to understand the front-office steps in the delivery system.

- **Be a service, product or customer order** – to understand the back-office steps in the delivery system.

- **Challenge and check executive opinion** – by comparing it with other opinions and data.

- **Challenge and check data collected** – by comparing them with other data, observation and executive opinion.

- **Triangulate your findings** – by looking at everything from at least three different perspectives.

- **Test your findings and conclusions** – as they start to emerge using data and executive opinion.

- **Collect more data than you think you need** – but only present the data that explains your analysis and supports your conclusions and recommendations.

Understanding the business context

The first step in your analysis is to understand the external and internal context of the business by:

- **Identifying stakeholder requirements** – identify the key stakeholders, their power and influence over the business, and their needs and requirements.

- **Identifying corporate objectives** – such as the sales revenue, profit, return on investment, inventory turns, debtor levels and environmental or social targets that need to be met.

- **Checking the health of the business** – by comparing its sales, revenue, sales volume, profit, operating costs and customer satisfaction trends against those of its key competitors.

The findings from these analyses are then used to:

- **Identify strengths and weakness** – within the business, and

- **Guide the subsequent analysis** – of markets, market support, cash holdings and operating costs to identify areas of improvement.

Analyzing markets

Once the business context is understood, then a company's current and future markets need to be analyzed by:

- **Identifying current and future markets** – remembering that the most important orders are the ones to which a company says 'no'.

- **Identifying executive opinion of current and future order-winners and qualifiers** – within these markets start with the marketing function before testing this with other functional perspectives.

- **Test executive opinion with data** – showing how customers actually operate.

While undertaking this analysis, it is important to follow a number of key principles:

- **Analyze both 'customer voice' and 'customer behaviour'** – to understand what customers say they want (customer voice) and what they actually want (customer behaviour).

- **Analyze multi-functional perspectives of the market** – as they all interact with customers in different ways and have different perspectives of their needs.

- **Test executive opinion with data** – showing how customers actually operate.

- **Realize order-winners and qualifiers may vary by customer order** – and identify how these orders place different demands on the business.

- **Realize that order-winners and qualifiers within a market will change over time** – so you need to identify current market needs and show how these are expected to change over time.

Analyzing market support

Once the current and future order-winners and qualifiers for current and future markets are understood, then the next step is to review the current level of support for these market requirements. This involves an analysis of the services and products delivered to meet customer orders and also, where possible, a review of customer orders that were not won to understand why this happened.

A number of tools and techniques that are discussed in more detail in Chapter 11 on managing quality and Chapter 14 on improving operations can be used to start identifying potential areas for improvement. For example:

- **Benchmarking** – against other parts of the organization, direct competitors, other companies within the same industry and/or companies outside of the industry

- **Mapping the customer journey** – to identify the points of interaction with the business

- **Mapping processes** – using tools such as process charts, service maps, information and material flow charts, person flow charts and videoing

- **Pareto analysis** – to help identify the frequency of problems

- **Cause and effect diagrams** – to help identify the causes of poor performance

- **Why-why reviews** – to get to the root cause of a problem.

Analyzing cash holdings

Releasing cash enables investments to be made elsewhere in the business, dividends to be given to shareholders and creditors to be paid back. Within most businesses, the highest levels of cash are tied up in accounts receivables, inventories, properties, buildings and equipment. Causal analyses need to be completed to understand why cash is tied up in these areas and how it can be released.

Analyzing operating costs

Even when price is not an order-winner, it is still important to analyzing the operating costs of a business to see if they can be reduced. Useful analyses include:

- **Reviewing actual material, direct labour and overhead costs** – focusing on materials and overheads as they tend to account for 70–90 per cent of total costs

- **Reviewing activity costs** – for each activity and step within a delivery system

- **Reviewing staff and process efficiency** – by comparing the actual time against the standard time for completing an activity

- **Reviewing staff and process productivity** – by comparing the output of a person or process with the amount of time that they work

- **Reviewing mix of service or product volumes** – as a wide mix will make it difficult to reduce costs.

Analyzing operations in practice

When analyzing operations in practice, it is important to consider the following aspects:

- **It is not possible to analyze everything** – as it would take too much time and money to do this

- **Analyze representative samples** – of customers, services, products and customer orders

- **Analyze representative time periods** – of production orders

- **Split out different market segments** – if customers, services, products or customers have different requirements, then you need to separate them into different market segments

- **Look at both won and lost customer orders** – as this will help understand the importance of order-winners and qualifiers in markets not currently supported by the business

- **Critical areas for analysis keep changing** – as market requirements change and business improvements are made

- **Challenge and check executive opinion** – with other executive opinions and data

- **Challenge and check data** – with other data, observation and executive opinion

- **Data are not always available** – so you will need to put 'traps' in place to capture data

- **Balance gut feeling with in-depth analysis** – so that action is not delayed, but also focuses on the areas of maximum impact.

Exploring further

TED talks

McCandless, D. (2010) *The beauty of data visualization*. David McCandless turns complex data sets (like worldwide military spending, media buzz, Facebook status updates) into beautiful, simple diagrams that tease out unseen patterns and connections. Good design, he suggests, is the best way to navigate the information glut and it may just change the way we see the world.

www.ted.com/talks/david_mccandless_the_beauty_of_data_visualization. html

Journal articles

Gouillart, F.J. and Sturdivant, F.D. (1994) 'Spend a day in the life of your customers', *Harvard Business Review*, **72**(1): 116–25. The article argues that a senior executive's instinctive capacity to empathize with and gain insight from customers is the single most important skill that can be used to direct a company's strategic posture approach. Yet most top managers retain only limited contact with consumers as their organizations grow, relying instead on subordinates' reports to define and feel out the market for them. To get a true sense of the market, senior executives should consider the wants and needs of every step in the distribution chain, right down to the end user of a finished product.

Kahneman, D., Lovallo, D. and Sibony, O. (2011) 'Before you make that big decision', *Harvard Business Review*, **89**(6): 50–60. This article proposes a 12-question checklist to help leaders examine whether a team has explored appropriate alternatives, gathered all the right information and used well-grounded numbers to support its case.

Kanter, R.M. (2011) 'Zoom in, zoom out', *Harvard Business Review*, **89**(3): 112–16. The best leaders can zoom in to examine problems and then zoom out to look for patterns and causes. The point is not to choose one over the other but to learn to move across a continuum of perspectives.

Martin, R.L. (2011) 'Don't get blinded by the numbers', *Harvard Business Review*, **89**(3): 38. Business leaders need to be able to analyze and interpret data.

Shapiro, B.P., Kasturi Rangan, V. and Sviokla, J.J. (2004) 'Staple yourself to an order', *Harvard Business Review*, **82**(7): 162–71. The article is based on a detailed analysis of how an order was processed in 18 companies and highlights the findings.

Books

Cahill, M. (2010) *Making the right investment decisions*, 2nd edn, *Financial Times*. This book looks at how the stock market examines companies and values shares. It helps you understand the factors that drive long-term wealth creation as well as highlighting the key risks that lead to value being destroyed.

Hill, A. and Hill, T. (2009) *Manufacturing Operations Strategy: Text and Cases*, 3rd edn. Basingstoke: Palgrave Macmillan. The text provides a useful supplement to the current book by outlining an in-depth approach for developing and implementing operations strategy within manufacturing organizations.

Hill, A. and Hill, T. (2011) *Essential Operations Management*. Basingstoke: Palgrave Macmillan. The text provides a useful supplement to this book by focusing on the key, essential aspects to consider when managing operations within a service or manufacturing organization.

Hill, T. (1998) *The Strategy Quest: Releasing the Energy of Manufacturing Within a Market Driven Strategy: A Dynamic Business Story*. Available from AMD Publishing, 'Albedo', Dousland, Devon, PL20 6NE, UK; e-mail: amd@jm-abode.tiscali.co.uk; fax: +44 (0)1822 882863. This book (written as a novel) describes how an art business and a manufacturing organization restructure themselves to meet the changing demands of their customers.

Films

Big Chef Takes on Little Chef. TV documentary, 2009. This documentary describes how the Little Chef Restaurant management team bring in Michelin three-star award-winning chef Heston Blumenthal to help it try to recapture the commercial success it once had.
www.channel4.com/programmes/big-chef-takes-on-little-chef/4od

Heston's Mission Impossible. TV documentary, 2011. This documentary describes how Heston Blumenthal uses his maverick culinary genius to dramatically reinvent food production at British Airways, the NHS, the Royal Navy and Cineworld Cinemas.
www.channel4.com/programmes/hestons-mission-impossible

Made in Britain. TV documentary, 2011. Evan Davis looks at the British economy and asks what it is good at and how it can pay its way in the world.
www.bbc.co.uk/programmes/b0125v5k

Visit www.palgrave.com/business/hillom3e for self-test questions, guideline answers to some case study questions, useful weblinks and more to help you understand the topics in this chapter

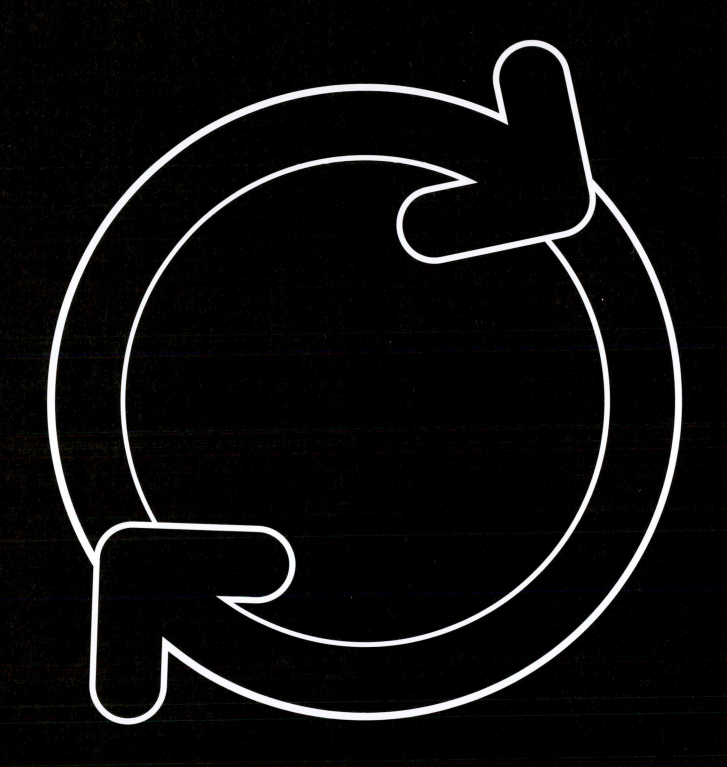

Improving Operations **14**

Executive overview

What is the role of improving operations within the business?

- Operations needs to be improved to meet a variety of different corporate objectives, but the most common reasons are to:
  - **Release cash** – so it can be invested elsewhere within the business, given to shareholders or used to reduce debtors
  - **Improve market support** – to increase sales revenue by attracting, retaining and growing customers and increase profits by allowing higher prices to be charged
  - **Reduce costs** – so that margins can be improved or the business can compete more effectively in price-sensitive markets

- It is also key in helping ensure the long-term future of a business by meeting the requirements of all its stakeholders, such as shareholders, customers, employees, suppliers and the societies in which it operates

Why is improving operations important?

- **Large function** – operations is typically responsible for managing the largest number of assets, costs and people within a business

- **Key to supporting markets** – in all markets:
  - Operations is either solely or jointly responsible for supporting one or more of the key order-winners and qualifiers
  - If operations is not aligned to its markets, then a business will struggle to attract and retain customers

- **Barriers to entry** – operations can be key to developing barriers to entry as its capabilities can often be difficult to imitate

How does improving operations impact business performance?

- **Releasing cash** – by reducing inventory, changing supplier payment terms, selling or leasing equipment and/or outsourcing

- **Improving market support** – by identifying relevant order-winners and qualifiers, translating these into strategic tasks, reviewing current performance against these tasks and identifying and implementing improvements

- **Reducing costs** – by reviewing and reducing actual material, direct labour and overhead costs, mapping activities, identifying and eliminating areas of waste, reviewing and reducing the mix of volumes within operations, reviewing and increasing the price of services or products, and choosing to no longer supply some services or products

What are the key issues to consider when improving operations?

- When identifying problems that need improving, start with your 'gut feeling', but then dig the data to really understand the type of problems that occur, how often they occur and the impact they have on the business

- The two main barriers to improving operations are a lack of time and money

- Overcome the problem of a lack of time by allocating dedicated time for working on improvement projects

- Overcome the problem of lack of money by identifying low cost, easy ways to release cash from the business

- Your role in the improvement process will initially be directive and then become more supportive

- A proactive approach is better for driving improvement within an organization as it enables you to better control and drive change

- It is best to use a combination of incremental and breakthrough changes as they both have advantages and disadvantages

- An improvement culture is critical in driving and maintaining changes and developments

- A wide range of tools and techniques is available to help make improvements

- Improvements can be made by anyone who is interested in the business, as long as they are given the power to do this

- An improvement culture can be created by establishing self-managed teams, sharing information and creating time for improvement activities

- Using suppliers to help identify and make improvements requires moving to a situation where you are both mutually dependent on each other for developing new services or products and improving how they are delivered

- Using customers to help improve services, products and processes can increase customer loyalty, reduce research and development costs and help tailor services or products to customer needs

Introduction

Organizations must continually look for ways to improve as markets constantly change and competition continually grows. Operations managers can help companies improve by releasing cash to be invested elsewhere, improving market support to grow sales revenue and reducing costs to increase profits. The process of making these improvements involves going through a never-ending cycle of four steps: plan, do, check and review. This can be done using either a 'passive' or 'proactive' approach to make 'incremental' or 'breakthrough' improvements or **innovations**. A variety of tools and techniques is available to benchmark performance, map the customer journey, understand processes, identify the causes of problems, generate improvement ideas and reengineer business processes. Traditionally, companies have only used the people who worked for them to identify and make changes, but they are now also starting to use other stakeholders such as suppliers and customers. This can lead to significant benefits, but requires a radically different way of working.

> **Innovations** involve changing something established by introducing a new method, idea, business model, service or product.

Why improve operations?

As discussed in Chapter 2, operations can be improved to better meet a variety of different corporate objectives. However, the most common reasons for improving operations are to release cash, improve market support and/or reduce costs.

> **EXECUTIVE INSIGHT**
> Operations can be improved to:
> * **Release cash** – so that it can be invested elsewhere in the business, given to shareholders or used to pay back debtors
> * **Improve market support** – to increase sales revenue by attracting and retaining customers and increase profits by allowing higher prices to be charged
> * **Reduce costs** – so that margins can be improved and the business can compete more effectively in price-sensitive markets.

Releasing cash

One of the reasons for improving operations is to release cash that can then be invested elsewhere, either in another aspect of operations or another function of the business. This can be done through a number of actions:

* **Reduce inventory** – held within operations. As explained in Chapter 9, companies need to conduct a causal analysis to understand why inventory is being held by grouping it into one of the following categories: corporate, decoupling, cycle, pipeline, capacity-

related and buffer. When the reason for holding the inventory has been identified, then questions can be asked, such as: is it necessary? Why is it there? And, what caused it? Once this is known, the systems, procedures and rules used can be challenged, reviewed and changed.

- **Change supplier payment terms** – another way to release cash is to delay paying suppliers. However, when doing this, companies must remember that although they will benefit from this strategy, it will negatively affect their suppliers' cash flow. For small suppliers, this could have serious implications as they tend not to have much cash in their business anyway.

- **Sell or lease equipment** – equipment that is not essential to the business can be sold off. Equally, equipment that is essential could be leased rather than bought. Although this would probably increase the overall cost of the equipment, it would reduce the negative impact on cash flow by spreading it over a longer period of time.

- **Outsource** – processes requiring a high investment in equipment or inventory could be outsourced. However, as discussed in Chapter 12, companies need to review the strategic implications of making such decisions.

> **EXECUTIVE INSIGHT**
Releasing cash enables:
- **Investments** – to be made elsewhere in the business
- **Dividends** – to be given to shareholders or
- **Creditors** – to be paid back.

Improving market support

The second reason for improving operations it to increase the level of market support leading, in turn, to greater sales revenue by increasing market share, establishing a new market or enabling a company to raise the price of its service or product. Case 14.1 gives examples of improvements made by Ritz-Carlton, Steinway & Sons and Massachusetts General Hospital. The process of making these improvements involves the following steps:

1. **Identify the order-winners and qualifiers** – that operations must support from the market review, as discussed in Chapter 2.

2. **Translate these into strategic tasks** – for example, if price is a key order-winner, then costs must be reduced throughout the operation; or if quality conformance is a key qualifier then errors must be reduced and quality built into the process rather than checked after the event.

3. **Review current performance** – against each of these strategic tasks. Figure 14.1 gives examples of how to check current performance against order-winners or qualifiers.

4. **Identify and implement changes** – to improve performance against each strategic task. Again, see Figure 14.1 for examples of how this can be done.

> **EXECUTIVE INSIGHT**
Improving market support leads to:
- **Increased sales revenue** – by attracting and retaining new customers, establishing new markets or enabling prices to be raised
- **Increased profits** – by enabling prices to be raised.

Examples of performance reviews and typical improvements are now discussed for some of the main order-winners and qualifiers typically supported by operations.

CASE 14.1 IMPROVING PROCESSES: RITZ-CARLTON, STEINWAY & SONS AND MASSACHUSETTS GENERAL HOSPITAL

RITZ-CARLTON

After decades of asking employees to serve customer using a 20-point list, Ritz-Carlton's managers realized it was no longer meeting the wide-ranging expectations of its customers, who had become younger, more diverse, more tech savvy, and often travelled with children and other family members. Instead of trying to expand the list to cover every possible situation, they created a simpler 12-point set of values and encouraged employees to use their own judgement and improvise. Tightly defined process dictums like 'always carry a guest's luggage' and 'use phrases like "good morning", "certainly, I'll be happy to", and "it's my pleasure"' were replaced with looser value statements such as 'I build strong relationships and create Ritz-Carlton guests for life' and 'I am empowered to create unique, memorable, and personal experiences for our guests'. As a result, they found customer satisfaction improved dramatically.

www.ritzcarlton.com

STEINWAY & SONS

Steinway & Sons uses feedback from demanding concert pianists to help design, manufacture and tune its pianos. However, the company promotes the fact that its pianos all have different 'personality', as it believes this indicates the richness of the materials and craftsmanship that go into producing a piano, just as master winemakers know that their job is to make the most of the distinctive qualities of each year's harvest.

www.steinway.com

MASSACHUSETTS GENERAL HOSPITAL

Massachusetts General Hospital continually looks for ways to reduce costs and improve quality by standardizing its patient care. With complex procedures like coronary bypasses, it standardizes most of the pre-op and post-op treatment, but then allows surgeons technical judgement over the detailed procedure. It then measures and evaluates 'standardized processes' against hard rules and metrics, but assesses 'artistic processes' through patient feedback.

www.mgh.harvard.edu

Questions

1. Should processes always be standardized?

2. When should companies manage their processes more creatively?

Lecturers: visit www.palgrave.com/business/hillom3e for teaching guidelines for this case study

Figure 14.1 **Examples of how to review performance and typical improvements to meet alternative order-winners and qualifiers**		
Order-winner or qualifier	**Reviewing current performance**	**Typical improvements**
Price	• Review actual material, direct labour and overhead costs • Map current processes and identify areas of material and labour waste • Review the mix of operations volumes • Review annual operations volumes within a service/product range • Review production run lengths • Review the contribution per machine hour • Review product pricing	• Reduce large areas of costs –70–90 per cent of the total cost is usually accounted for by materials and overheads • Reduce material and labour waste • Reduce changeover and set-up times for the manufacturing process • Reallocate products across operations • Focus each operation on a particular market or resource
Quality conformance	• Review quality conformance levels for the following areas: services, products, orders, customers and market segments	• Reduce quality conformance errors • Build quality control into the system rather than checking conformance after the event
Delivery reliability	• Review the delivery performance for services/products, orders, customers and market segments • Analyze and compare the delivery lead-times that customers have requested against the actual delivery lead-times that operations supplies • Compare the actual processing with the overall operations lead-time	• Improve the scheduling of activities • Improve process reliability • Hold inventory at varying stages in the process
Delivery speed	• Analyze and compare the delivery lead-times that customers have requested against the actual delivery lead-times that operations supplies • Compare the actual processing with the overall operations lead-time • Map the actual operations process and identify any areas of material and labour waste	• Eliminate any waiting time between the steps in the process • Reduce the lead-time of steps in the process • Eliminate wasteful activities
Service or product range	• Review the capability of the process to meet the service or product range required now and in the future	• Develop the capability of the system to cope with the service or product range • Develop employee skill levels • Reduce changeover and set-up times
Demand fluctuations	• Assess the ability of the available capacity to respond to known or anticipated changes in demand	• Invest in capacity or inventory
Speed of new service or product development	• Map the new service/product development process and identify waste • Determine the length of activities and their dependency on other activities or key resources • Identify activities for which operations has responsibility	• Eliminate wasteful activities • Increase the capacity of any constraining resources • Reschedule activities so they are completed in parallel (rather than in sequence) with other parts of the process

Price

Operations must check its current performance on a number of aspects to understand if price is being supported. Analyses that help highlight current or potential problems and typical areas for improvement are now discussed:

- **Review actual material, direct labour and overhead costs** – while all aspects of cost must be reviewed, materials and overheads are usually the main areas on which to focus as they tend to account for 70–90 per cent of total costs. Trends should be reviewed to understand historical and forecasted changes and, in some instances, companies may wish to stabilize cost fluctuations with supplier or employee agreements.

- **Map activities and identify areas of waste** – as well as splitting costs by type, companies must also separate them into different activities. To do this, the entire business process from customer order placement through to customer payment is mapped. Waste such as unnecessary process steps, movements, inventories, paperwork or inspection can then be eliminated, and working practices for the remaining value-adding activities can then be improved. Both sets of actions will help lower costs.

- **Review mix of volumes in an operation** – cost-efficient operations typically focus on a narrow range of high-volume services or products. However, as markets mature, service or product ranges widen and operations volumes decrease. Businesses must review the service/product and volume mix within operations to help retain a focused approach.

- **Review staff and process efficiency** – the first step in improving staff and process efficiency is to estimate the standard time to complete a task. This is completed using time studies for short, repetitive tasks and estimates for long, non-repetitive tasks. Once the 'standard time' for a task has been established, actual performance against this standard can then be measured and efficiency improvements made.

> **EXECUTIVE INSIGHT**
>
> Businesses use two dimensions to control their activities:
> 1. **Time** – is used to plan, estimate, cost and manage operations activities.
> 2. **Money** – is used to trade with customers and suppliers and report the costs and investments associated with delivering services and products.

- **Review staff and process productivity** – by comparing the output of a person or process with the amount of time that they work. Examples of productivity measures for different types of operations are shown in Figure 14.2. These can be improved in a number of ways such as:
  - Reduce non-value-adding activities – this is normally the most effective method of improving productivity as most individuals are competent at completing their tasks.
  - Understand customer requirements – to further reduce non-value-adding activities and levels of rework.
  - Train staff – to increase their competence at completing a task.
  - Improve information and material design – used in the process to make them easier to transform into services and products.
  - Improve information and material quality conformance – to increase the consistency and reliability of the process.

- **Review service or product pricing** – the range of profit margins typically generated from different services, products or customers is not always due to varying operations costs. It can often result from how the services or products are priced. The standard costing methods used may often not reflect the true costs of all services or products. Also, once a price is set it is rarely reviewed and increased or decreased to reflect volume, material cost and other cost changes. Once services or products with low profit margins have been identified then improvements and developments can be made to reduce costs, higher prices can be negotiated with customers, or the service/product deleted from the range offered.

Figure 14.2 Examples of single-factor and multiple-factor productivity measures in different businesses

Business	Single-factor measures	Multi-factor measure
Law firm	$\dfrac{\text{\# briefs filed}}{\text{Lawyer}}$	$\dfrac{\text{\# briefs filed and court attendances undertaken}}{\text{Lawyer}}$
Bookshop	$\dfrac{\text{\# customers served}}{\text{Full-time equivalent staff}}$	$\dfrac{\text{\# customers served, deliveries handled and despatches sent}}{\text{Full-time equivalent staff}}$
University	$\dfrac{\text{\# student contact hours}}{\text{Faculty member}}$	$\dfrac{\text{\# student contact hours, research assistants supervised (hours) and administrative tasks (hours)}}{\text{Faculty member}}$
Consultancy firm	$\dfrac{\text{\# consultancy days billed}}{\text{Total consultancy days available}}$	$\dfrac{\text{\# consultancy days billed, training undertaken (days) and administrative tasks (days)}}{\text{Total consultancy days available}}$
Engineering design firm	$\dfrac{\text{\# design projects completed}}{\text{Engineering staff days}}$	$\dfrac{\text{\# design projects completed, tenders submitted and site visits undertaken}}{\text{Engineering staff days}}$

> **EXECUTIVE INSIGHT**
> Profit is created differently in price-sensitive and non-price-sensitive markets:
> - Price-sensitive markets – by reducing costs. So you can charge a low price, but still be profitable.
> - Non-price-sensitive markets – by increasing price. So you need to invest to develop factors such as the capabilities and customer relationships that enable you to charge a high price for your services and products.

Quality conformance

Quality conformance measures how consistently a service or product is delivered in line with its design specification. These levels need to be reviewed for services, products, orders and customers to assess how well markets are being supported. Steps must then be taken to reduce the quality gaps that exist between what customers want and expect, what a company sells, how services and products have been designed and what operations delivers (as described in more detail in Chapter 11).

Delivery reliability

Collect and analyze delivery performance data to understand how delivery reliability varies by service, product, order or customer. Comparing delivery on-time performance with aspects such as order size, customer lead-times, delivery lead-times and supplier lead-times helps identify causes of above or below average delivery reliability performance and highlights areas and actions for improvement.

Delivery speed

Several analyses can be used to identify causes of poor performance and identify where improvements need to be made. These include:

- **Analyze the total customer lead-time** – from receipt of order to point of payment.

- **Map the actual operations process** – to determine all the steps that make up the operations lead-time.

- **Analyze operations actual delivery lead-time** – and break it down into the relevant elements of service or product delivery.

- **Analyze customer expected lead-times** – and compare them to actual delivery lead-times.

- **Identify areas for improvement** – by comparing lead-time for each process step with the actual time it takes to deliver a service or product.

Other order-winners and qualifiers

Companies often have to support several other order-winners and qualifiers besides those discussed above. In all instances, current operations performance must be reviewed against each to check how well they are supported and to identify areas for improvement. For example:

- **Service or product range** – review the capability of operations to process the current range and any future proposed changes to the range. This needs to be completed for all the steps involved.

- **Demand fluctuations** – assess the ability of the current operations process capacity to respond to known or anticipated changes in demand.

- **Speed of new service or product development** – map the current new service or product development process and identify areas of waste. Determine the length of each activity and its dependency on other activities or key resources and identify the activities for which operations has responsibility.

Reducing costs

Even when price is not an order-winner, costs often have to be reduced to increase profit margins. These reviews are similar to those identified in the section entitled 'Price' above and companies need to:

- Review where they can reduce actual material, direct labour and overhead costs.

- Map activities to identify and eliminate areas of **waste**.

- Review and reduce the mix of volumes within operations.

- Review and, where appropriate, increase the price of services or products.

- Review and, where appropriate, delete services or products from the range.

Methods and approaches for analyzing costs are discussed in Chapter 13 on analyzing operations.

> **> EXECUTIVE INSIGHT**
> The role of reducing costs is different in price-sensitive and non-price-sensitive markets:
> - Price-sensitive markets – it makes them more efficient and enables them to compete more effectively within their markets.
> - Non-price-sensitive markets – it only makes them more efficient and they need to ensure these changes do not damage the capabilities that create differentiation and enable them to charge a higher price for their services and products.

Process of improving operations

Improving any aspect of operations involves going through four key steps and these are shown in Figure 14.3 and discussed below.

1. Plan

The first step is to identify a problem or aspect that needs to be improved. In other words: where do you want to release cash, improve market support and/or reduce costs? It is

> **Waste** – or 'non-value-adding' activities are those which a customer is not willing to pay for such as waiting for resources, transportation between operations or unnecessary paperwork and documentation.

'Organizations must **continually** look for ways to **improve** operations'

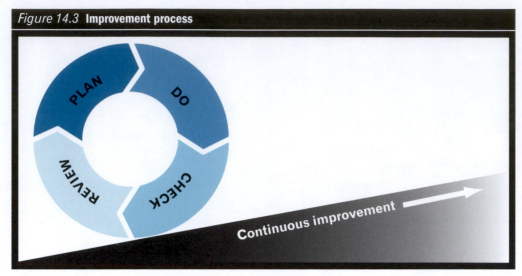

Figure 14.3 **Improvement process**

Note: This is often referred to as the Deming improvement cycle.

important to involve the managers and employees who work in the area being reviewed as they have a better idea of the issues faced, the areas for improvement and how best to fix them. Initially, this can be a 'gut feeling' analysis, but it must then be supported with data or evidence clearly showing the type of problems that exist and how frequently they occur. Based on this analysis, improvement and development areas can be identified and then prioritized before action is taken. Assessing each potential improvement using the following criteria can help prioritize where to start:

- **Cost of implementing the improvement** – the cost of making the change, the amount of investment involved (cash that will be tied up) and the reduction in day-to-day operating costs all need to be considered.

- **Ease of implementing the improvement** – the time and resource required for implementation will reflect the size of the change, type and number of stakeholders involved and whether they agree on the course of action suggested.

- **Impact of making the improvement** – how much cash will be released, the ongoing costs of operating differently and the benefits achieved such as improved market support, increased sales and increased profits.

Again, this analysis can start as a 'gut feeling' with each aspect rated out of five, where five is low cost, high impact and easy to implement. The scores for each action can then be totalled and improvement teams can be set up to look at each action in more detail. Once a more detailed analysis has been completed and the cost, ease and impact are better known, then an organization can decide which improvements to make. Two key aspects that help create focus when prioritising actions and allocating resources to implementing them are:

- **Impact of doing nothing** – how much cash will be tied up, the ongoing 'unnecessary' cost of the current operation and the result of current market support in terms of reduced sales and profits

> **EXECUTIVE INSIGHT**
> When identifying problems that need improving:
> - **Start with your gut feeling** – regarding areas that cause significant problems and will be relatively cheap and easy to improve
> - **Then dig the data** – to really understand the type of problems that occur, how often they occur and the impact they have on the business. These data will help to really focus your resources and justify the investment required to make step-change improvements.

- **Speeding up implementation** – how many resources are required and how these need to be used to implement the improvement actions in less time.

2. Do

Once the improvement plan has been developed, it needs to be implemented. Involving employees in the first step helps this to occur as they feel more empowered, more involved and more responsible for the improvement. The next section explains how companies can choose to take a 'passive incremental', 'proactive incremental', 'passive breakthrough' and/or 'proactive breakthrough' approach to improving operations.

> ### > EXECUTIVE INSIGHT
> Examples of how you can overcome the initial barriers to change are:
> - Time – allocate dedicated time for working on improvement projects either by pulling people out of their day jobs for between one and five days or using overtime working
> - Money – start with low-cost improvements (say less than £500) and then look for ways to release cash that can then be re-invested in the business.

3. Check

Once a change has been made, it is important to check if the anticipated level of improvement was achieved. In other words, the impact of the actions made in Step 2 must be measured against the improvement objective identified in Step 1. The measures identified earlier in Figure 14.1 can be used to review the change in performance against different order-winners and qualifiers.

4. Review

Finally, the checks must be reviewed to determine if the improvement objectives have been met and sustained. This will highlight gaps that, in turn, identify further problems or aspects to be improved that then lead back to Step 1.

> ### > EXECUTIVE INSIGHT
> Improving operations should be a continual, ongoing process. However, your role within this process will change over time:
> - **Initially directive** – to drive the process and overcome the initial inertia to change
> - **Then supportive** – as your team members start to drive the process themselves, you will ensure they are focusing on the right strategic objectives and share good practice.

Approach to improving operations

Once the necessary improvements have been identified, then an organization needs to decide the approach to take. Although improving any aspect of operations involves going through the same four key steps, these improvements can be stepped or incremental and made on a passive or proactive basis as shown in Figure 14.4. In reality, companies will use a variety of approaches to improve their business as they all have a number of different features as described in Figure 14.5.

Companies must first decide if they want to take a 'passive' or 'proactive' approach to improvement where:

> A **passive approach** – this occurs when operations managers allow the improvement process to be driven by other functions or levels within the business without trying to create or control it.
>
> A **proactive** approach – this occurs when operations managers create or control the improvement process rather than responding to it after it has happened.

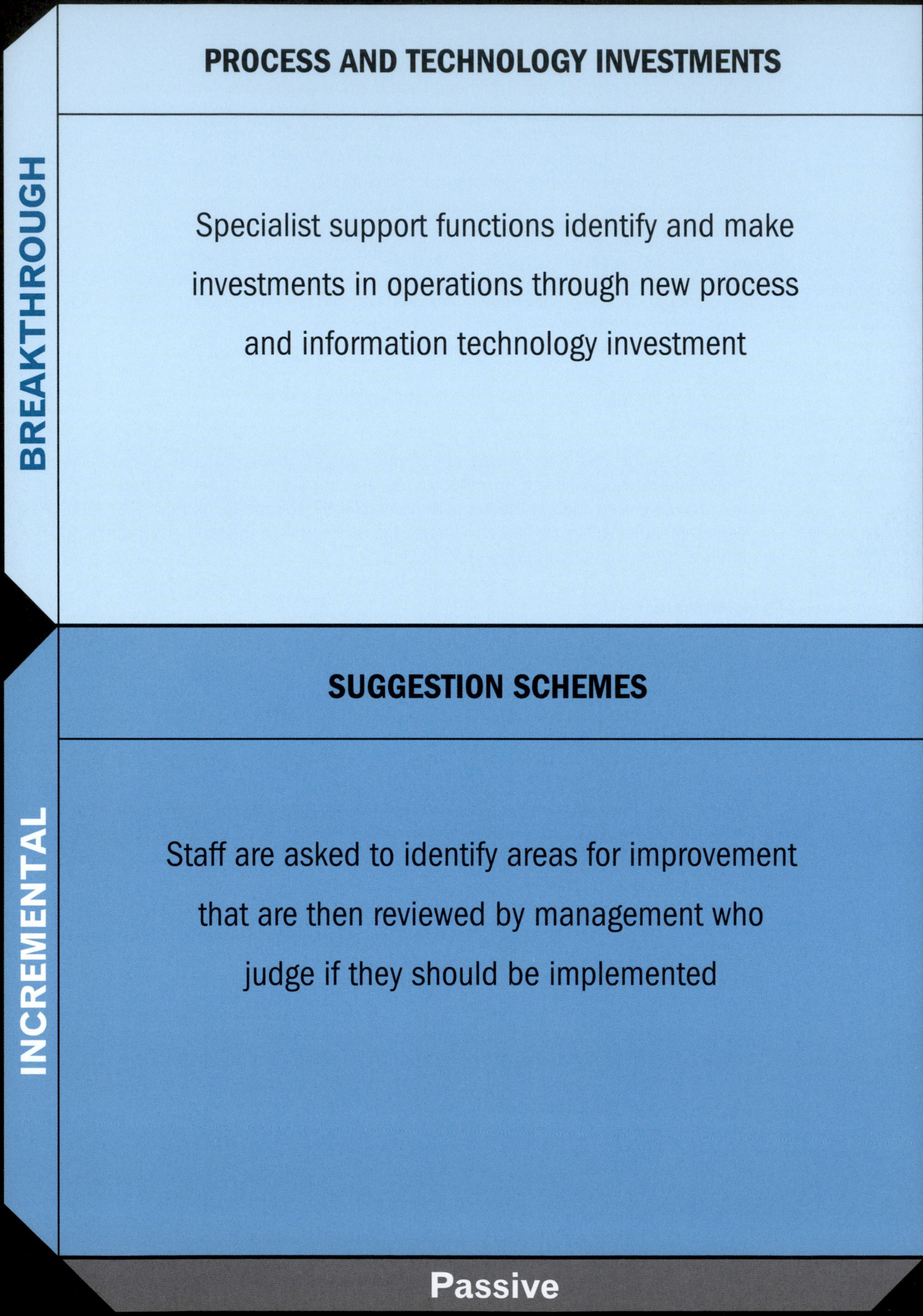

Figure 14.4 **Examples of alternative approaches to improving operations**

BREAKTHROUGH

PROCESS AND TECHNOLOGY INVESTMENTS

Specialist support functions identify and make investments in operations through new process and information technology investment

INCREMENTAL

SUGGESTION SCHEMES

Staff are asked to identify areas for improvement that are then reviewed by management who judge if they should be implemented

Passive

KAIZEN BLITZ EVENTS

Operations resource is taken out of
day-to-day activities for a concentrated
period of time (normally up to 5 days)
to identify and make improvements

IMPROVEMENT CULTURE

Staff are trained to use improvement tools
and techniques. Part of their working week is
then allocated for analyzing existing working
methods and making improvements

Proactive

Figure 14.5 Typical features of alternative approaches to improvement

Typical features			Incremental		Breakthrough	
			Passive	Proactive	Passive	Proactive
Level of investment in	Assets	Low	●	●		●
		High			●	
	Employee time	Low	●			
		High		●		●
Improvement typically changes		Procedures	●	●		●
		Process activities	●	●		●
		Process technologies		●	●	
		Layouts		●		●
		Roles and responsibilities		●		●
Timeframe to develop and implement the improvements		Short-term	●	●		●
		Medium-term	●	●		
		Long-term			●	
Type of improvement		One-off			●	●
		Ongoing	●	●		
Number of people involved		Few			●	●
		Many	●	●		
Led by		Operations	●	●		●
		Specialist function			●	
When benefits occur from improvement		Occur during activity	●	●		●
		Require further actions			●	
Ease of sustaining improvement activity		Easy		●		●
		Difficult	●		●	

- **Passive** – improvements are identified and implemented through activities such as 'suggestion schemes' and 'process and technology investments' made by support functions such as IT and engineering.

- **Proactive** – operations takes control and drives change by developing an 'improvement culture' and using 'kaizen blitz events' to make improvement.

> **EXECUTIVE INSIGHT**
  A proactive approach is better for driving improvement within an organization as it enables you to better control and drive change.

The next step is then to decide whether to take an 'incremental' or 'breakthrough' approach to improvement where:

- **Incremental** – improvements come from a larger number of smaller, more frequent improvements that often involve low investment through sources such as 'suggestion schemes' or establishing an 'improvement culture'.

- **Breakthrough** – improvements result from major changes to existing practices and normally involve large investment either in assets (for example, process, technology or equipment) or the time of the people who work within operations for 'kaizen blitz events'.

> **EXECUTIVE INSIGHT**
  Organizations should improve their operations through a combination of incremental and breakthrough changes.

Kaizen – Japanese for 'improvement' or 'change for the better', which occurs when everyone in the organization continually looks for ways to improve how it operates.

Figure 14.6 shows the improvement in performance resulting from 'breakthrough' and 'incremental' change. However, in reality most companies use a combination of 'passive incremental', 'proactive incremental', 'passive breakthrough' and 'proactive breakthrough' approaches as they vary in terms of the:

- Level of investment required

- What the approach typically changes

- The time taken to develop and implement the improvement

- The type of improvement that occurs

- The number of people involved

- Who leads the improvement

- When the benefits of the improvement occur and

- How easy the improvement activity is to sustain after it has been started.

Case 14.2 gives examples of different types of 'breakthrough' and 'incremental' improvements that have been made by Sheffield City Council, South African gold mines and Metro, and the advantages and disadvantages of each different improvement approach are now discussed in more detail.

Passive incremental

A 'passive incremental' approach to improvement involves activities such as 'suggestion schemes' where employees are asked to identify improvements within their working area. These suggestions are then typically reviewed by managers or an improvement group to determine if they should be implemented. The advantages of this improvement approach include its low level of investment in assets and employee time. The disadvantages include its typical focus on small changes in procedures or process activities, and the difficultly of sustaining employee engagement for a long period of time. Some organizations try to use financial incentives for improvement ideas, but this can actually end up preventing the flow of ideas from staff as they want to be paid for them and it can build resentment between employees by suggesting that 'one idea is worth more than another'.

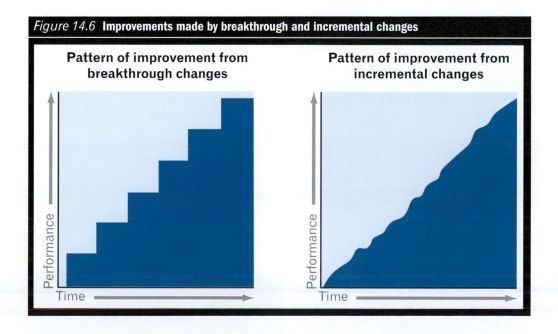

Figure 14.6 Improvements made by breakthrough and incremental changes

Pattern of improvement from breakthrough changes

Pattern of improvement from incremental changes

CASE 14.2 BREAKTHROUGH VS INCREMENTAL IMPROVEMENT: SHEFFIELD COUNCIL, GOLD MINING, METRO AND McDONALD'S

SHEFFIELD COUNCIL

Sheffield City Council (UK) introduced a new geographic information system. By inputting details from over 1,350 maps on property holdings, road details and 'street furniture' (such as road signs and traffic lights), it has significantly reduced the time to answer queries. For example, to complete a land and property deed search now takes one day rather than four weeks. Also, giving information on any property, planning temporary diversions, modifying existing routes and assessing the impact on school numbers by altering catchment areas can be reviewed and refined within minutes.

www.sheffield.gov.uk

GOLD MINING

South African gold mines have dramatically increased their productivity by applying stone quarrying methods. Instead of using dynamite to blast the rock, they now use a steel cable studded with industrial diamonds to cut it into large chunks. Although it costs $290 per metre, the cable can operate 24 hours a day, requires less labour, minimizes the amount of rock wasted and eliminates the 900,000 blasts it previously made each day.

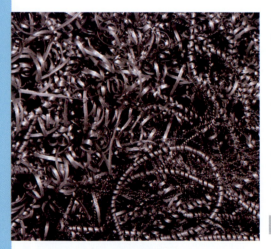

METRO

In 2003, the German retailer Metro launched its 'Future Store'. Customers have a computer on their shopping trolley that directs them to where the product is located in the store, scans it as it enters the trolley, shows the total cost of the items in the trolley and signals any special offers as you walk around the store. It also has a built-in camera for identifying and pricing fruit and vegetables. All of these initiatives have helped reduce Metro's costs and simplified their customers' shopping experience.

www.future-store.org

McDONALD'S

McDonald's is constantly looking for ways to reduce cost. For example, recently negotiations with its electricity suppliers have enabled it to reduce costs by £1.4 million, from £18 million, in England and Wales; and by 30 per cent in Scotland.

www.mcdonalds.com

Question

How do the four examples given here illustrate different improvement approaches?

Proactive incremental

DNA – the DNA of an organization can be described as its values, philosophy, personality and behaviour.

If companies want to start driving incremental change within their business, then they need to establish an 'improvement culture' by training everyone in the use of improvement tools and techniques and then allocating time within their working week for them to analyze parts of the business, identify improvements and implement change. As discussed earlier in Case 11.6 on 3M, creating an improvement culture requires significant changes in attitude, behaviour and working practices throughout an organization. Most experts believe it takes 10 to 15 years to achieve this, but it tends to be easier to sustain improvement activity once it has become an established part of an organization's **DNA**. Compared with a 'passive incremental' approach, this requires more investment in employee time and will eventually lead to larger structural changes such as improving layout and modifying employee roles and responsibilities.

> ### EXECUTIVE INSIGHT
> An 'improvement culture' is critical in driving and maintaining improvement. It is okay for a small team to start the process, but they will quickly run out of energy and make inappropriate decisions unless everyone becomes involved in the improvement process and starts to drive it themselves.

Case 14.3 shows how Porsche has established an improvement culture within its business and Case 14.4 describes how Microsoft, Volvo and Ricoh are constantly looking for ways to improve their businesses. These sorts of approaches are guided by the following three key principles:

1. **Process reviews** – the processes across the whole supply chain are reviewed from the initial design of a service or product through to its delivery to a customer.

2. **Success comes from people** – success relies on people's knowledge and insight of the systems and procedures they use and their ability to identify and make improvements. High levels of skill, employee participation and management support for these programmes are also an essential factor in bringing about these changes.

3. **Constant need for change** – the current processes within the business, however good, must never be considered adequate. Employees must constantly want to improve, look for aspects to change and make improvements.

> ### EXECUTIVE INSIGHT
> Proactive improvement requires the participation and involvement of all employees throughout the different levels and functions within the business.

Passive breakthrough

A 'passive breakthrough' approach is where operations relies on support functions such as IT and engineering to identify and make process and technology improvements. Unlike the incremental approaches to improvement, these can lead to significant performance improvements, but tend to take a long time to develop and implement. The benefit of such improvements are often not realized until sometime after the change has been made due to the further staff training and changes in working practices required. In fact, the benefits on which an investment was initially justified are sometimes never fully achieved due to the poor selection or implementation of the new process technology.

Proactive breakthrough

'Proactive breakthroughs' involve activities such as 'Kaizen blitz events' where small groups of operations employees (usually five or six) are taken out of their day jobs for a small period (usually two to five days) to analyze part of the business, identify changes

In 1993, the car manufacturer Porsche was on the verge of bankruptcy as sales had fallen dramatically from 53,254 cars in 1986 to fewer than 13,000 in 1993. Since then, however, it has used a mix of breakthrough and incremental change to turn the business around. For example, it has introduced new working methods that have helped it to reduce its workforce by 34 per cent, halve the time to produce a car from 120 to 60 hours and reduce its inventory by over 50 per cent. In addition, Porsche has slashed the number of suppliers it uses from 900 to fewer than 300, and it also now uses parts across a number of its cars. For example, around 36 per cent of the parts used in its 911 cars are now identical to those used in its Boxsters. The impact of these improvements has been dramatic, with sales increasing to 98,652 cars in 2008. Equally, it now can produce 8.6 cars per employee compared with 2.4 in 1994.

www.porsche.com

Questions

1. How do the improvements at Porsche show the need to drive improvement continuously?

2. Check on the Porsche website www.porsche.com to see how well the company is currently doing.

Lecturers: visit www.palgrave.com/business/hillom3e for teaching guidelines for this case study

CASE 14.4 CONTINUOUSLY DRIVING IMPROVEMENT: MICROSOFT, VOLVO AND RICOH

MICROSOFT

In the 1990s, Microsoft and IBM managed their businesses very differently. IBM measured its engineers by the number of lines of code they wrote per day, whereas Microsoft encouraged them continually to identify and make improvements. For example, when they worked together on one project a Microsoft engineer found he could rewrite an IBM code using 200 rather than 33,000 characters, meaning it took 99 per cent less time to read and process. However, the IBM managers claimed that this was 'rude' and that, by their standards, he had not written enough code that day!

www.microsoft.com

©Ermin Gutenberger

VOLVO

Five employees competing for Volvo Group's Internal Environmental Award came up with a simple way to save energy. Instead of using heat to dry newly painted engine blocks before they were assembled into their vehicles, the company now uses dry air. As a result, parts of the same quality are now produced using 90 per cent less energy: 70 rather than 650 kW per hour.

www.volvogroup.com

RICOH

At Ricoh's copier plant in Shenzhen, China, the 3,500 staff are encouraged to come up with suggestions to cut costs. On average, 18 suggestions are made per day. For example, one worker recently suggested narrowing the distance between two work stations from 120 to 90cm, the distance of one stride. This might not seem that significant, but implementing changes helps motivate people, demonstrates the importance of their contributions and the cumulative impact of all of these changes is essential as the company's profit margin is less than 2 per cent.

www.ricoh.com

Question

Use these examples to illustrate the three points guiding continuous improvement.

Lecturers: visit www.palgrave.com/business/ hillom3e for teaching guidelines for this case study

and make improvements. Essentially, this is a more focused and concentrated version of the 'proactive incremental' approach. By dedicating employee time in this way, significant changes can be made to procedures, paperwork, process activities, layout, roles, responsibilities and the like within a few days while often leading to subsequent projects working with IT and engineering. The advantage of this approach is that changes are made quickly by people who work within the process and have an incentive for making it work better.

> ### EXECUTIVE INSIGHT

'Kaizen blitz' events are just 'kaizen events' completed in a compressed timescale by taking employees out of their day jobs and dedicating them to improvement activities for two to five days. These can be very effective in:
- Starting an improvement process
- Understanding major problems, and
- Making significant improvements.

Improvement tools and techniques

Some of the various tools and techniques that can be used to analyze and improve operations are now discussed. These can be used by organizations to benchmark their performance against other businesses, map the journey of their customer, review the processes used within their business to deliver services and products, identify problems, generate improvement ideas and reengineer their business.

Benchmarking

Benchmarking involves comparing business practice and performance between companies. It can be used to help start or maintain an improvement process by identifying, setting and measuring improvement targets against:

- Other parts of the same organization

- Direct competitors

- Companies within the same sector who are not direct competitors

- Latent competitors; and/or

- Companies outside of the industry.

> ### EXECUTIVE INSIGHT

Benchmarking helps to:
- Start an improvement process – by showing people that there are other ways of working
- Maintain improvements – by sharing best practice between and within organizations.

Case 14.5 shows how Ford improved its 'accounts payable' department by benchmarking itself against Mazda. Some other examples of improvements resulting from benchmarking are:

- **Rover Cars** – halved its test times after benchmarking against Honda.

- **British Rail** – reduced the time taken to clean a train to eight minutes after benchmarking against British Airways.

- **McDonald's** – reduced the lead-time for building a restaurant from 18 to 10 days after adopting best practice from the British Airports Authority.

CASE 14.5 FORD MOTORS: BENCHMARKING ITS 'ACCOUNTS PAYABLE' DEPARTMENT AGAINST MAZDA

After reviewing its 'accounts payable' department, Ford felt it could reduce staff from 500 to 400 employees. It was very enthusiastic about this until it realized Mazda only employed five people in its 'accounts payable' function. Further analysis showed that Ford's 'account payable' department spent most of its time checking, querying and investigating 14 bits of information on three different documents that it received from purchasing, goods inwards and suppliers. Instead Ford decided to use a paperless system with automatic checks. It also asked goods inwards to simply only accept goods in line with the information on the computer system; and told suppliers it would pay on receipt of goods.

www.ford.com

Question

How did benchmarking help Ford improve its business?

Lecturers: visit www.palgrave.com/business/hillom3e for teaching guidelines for this case study

Mapping the customer journey

Another useful tool to help organizations consider which services and products to deliver and how to deliver them is to map the **customer journey** through the following steps:

1. **Map the journey that customers take** – the steps customers go through from becoming aware of the need for a service or product through to final delivery and subsequent after-sales service.

> The **customer journey** is the stages that a customer travels through from awareness, consideration, inquiry, selection, payment to service/product delivery and after-sales support.

Figure 14.7 **Customer journey for business class air passengers and examples of service developments made by British Airways and Virgin Atlantic**

Customer journey	Examples of developments on certain long haul flights	
	British Airways	**Virgin Atlantic**
Select and purchase flight	• Book online or over the telephone • Frequent flier programmes record customer preferences and use these to tailor the service (such as meal and seat preferences)	
Checking in	• Check in online • At airport using self-service points or dedicated business class desks	
Travel to airport		• A limousine collects passengers from any destination within 75 miles of the airport
Check in baggage	• Checking in of baggage is at 'fast bag drop' points or dedicated business class desks	• Not required – baggage is checked in when placed in the boot of the limousine
Travel through immigration and security	• Dedicated business class areas speed up the process	

Wait for flight	• A dedicated lounge for business class customers with a number of areas in which they can work or relax	• A dedicated lounge for business class customers with more relaxation options, including:
		  – A delicatessen, brasserie, bar or roof garden
		  – Games or a cinema
		  – A beauty and hair salon, spa pool, sauna, steam rooms and showers

Board flight	• A dedicated business class area to speed up the process	

Fly to destination	• A number of features to help customers work or relax including:
	  – Flat beds
	  – Flexible eating times
		• A wider variety of options to help customers relax, including:
		  – Bar and dining areas
		  – Massages
		  – Flat beds

Collect baggage	• Baggage belonging to business class and first-class customers is unloaded first	
Travel through immigration and security	• A dedicated business class area to speed up the process	

Freshen up	• A dedicated lounge for business class customers with:
	  – Showers
	  – Clothes pressing service
	  – Hot/cold breakfast	

Travel to destination		• A limousine takes passengers to any destination they wish within 75 miles of the airport

2. **Identify the points of interaction that they have with the business** – where on their journey do customers interact with the business? Where are they **picked up**, **dropped off** and passed between departments within the business?

3. **Determine where on the journey you wish to interact with customers** – should the customer be picked up earlier, should the customer be dropped off later and why?

4. **Determine how best to manage these interactions** – should customers be passed between different departments and, if so, how should these hand-offs be managed within the business? How should information about the customer be managed and communicated across the organization?

> **EXECUTIVE INSIGHT**
> Mapping the 'customer journey' helps:
> * Identify services and products – to deliver to a customer as they go through their journey
> * Determine how to deliver them – to add value to a customer's journey.

Customer satisfaction tends to increase when customers are in contact with a business for a longer part of their journey and when the interactions meet their needs. For example, Figure 14.7 shows the typical journey of a business class traveller. British Airways and Virgin Atlantic interact with customers at different points of their journey and have made different developments at each interaction. A key difference is the limousine service used by Virgin to collect customers at the start of their journeys and deliver them to their final destinations. Being customers for more of their journey and offering more relaxation options within the lounge and on the flight have led to Virgin recently surpassing British Airways to win the Business Traveller Award for 'Best Business Class' service.

Mapping processes

A process needs to be mapped to understand how it currently operates before determining how to improve it. In reality, a number of these tools will be used to understand a process before identifying areas for improvement:

* **Process charts** – the principal activities within a process are operations (completing tasks), checks or inspections, transportation, delays and storage (as shown in Figure 14.8). A process chart is used to show the sequence of steps that occur and the time taken to complete each step. As with other analyses, this can initially be by gut feeling, but must then be checked against actual data and evidence.

* **Service maps** – are used to map the movement of customers, information and materials through a process using the symbols shown in Figure 14.9. As discussed in Chapter 5, a key feature of service delivery is determining the number of customer interfaces and, therefore, the line of visibility that separates front-office and back-office activities.

* **Information and material flow charts** – trace the flow of information and/or materials through the process. It is important to show both physical and electronic documents as well as computer screenshots showing the level and type of information used within a process, system or procedure.

* **Person flow charts** – map the movements of a person as they carry out a task. As with information or material flow process charts, they show all the operations and inspections that take place together with any movements and delays.

* **Videoing** – as well as charting a process, it is useful to video it to see what happens. Videoing also has a number of advantages over the other charting methods including:
  - *More accurate* – it provides a complete record of the activities that take place.
  - *Helps process analysis* – it is often easier to assess the process as it can be reviewed many times and allows any number of people to review it.

– Increases acceptability that problems exist – those involved in the process more readily accept the record of events (the camera shows it as it is) and their role within it.

Figure 14.8 Process chart symbols

Symbol	Activity	Used to represent	
		Material or information	**Person doing the task**
 ○	Operation	Materials, products or information are modified or acted upon during the operation	Person completes an operation or task. This may include preparation for the next activity
□	Inspection	Materials, products or information are checked and quality, quantity or accuracy is verified	Person checks and verifies for quality, quantity or accuracy at this stage in the process or procedure
 ⇨	Transport	Materials, products or information are moved to another location without being part of an operation or inspection	Person moves from one position to another as part of the process or procedure without being part of an operation or inspection
 ◗	Delay	Temporary storage or filing of an item. Not recorded as 'in store' or filed and not requiring authorization for its withdrawal	Person unable to complete the next part of the task
 ▽	Storage	Controlled storage, governed by authorized receipt and issue; document filed and retained for future reference	Not used
 ▣	Combined activities	To show activities performed at the same time or a person competing two tasks at the same time	

Figure 14.9 Symbols used in service maps

Symbol	Used to represent
 ●●●●● ●●●●●●●●	_Line of visibility_ – used to divide the part of the operations visible to the customer (including telephone and written communication) from the rest of the service delivery system
 △	_Fail points_ – points in the process where there is a high level of service failure
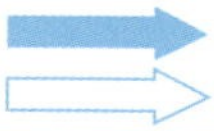 ⇒ ⇨	_Service paths_ – the optimal and 'when things go wrong' service paths are shown as follows: - Optimal service path - Path where things go wrong
 ⌂ P	_Problem_ – indicates where problems occur in a process
 ⬡ D	_Dialogue_ – indicates where customer interface with the delivery system takes place – the line of interaction

Identifying causes of problems

Once a process has been mapped, the root cause of the problems can be identified using a number of tools and techniques:

- **Cause and effect diagrams** – these help solve problems by identifying the causes and effects involved (as discussed earlier in Chapter 11). Figure 14.10 shows an example of a cause and effect analysis of a company that is unable to supply products on time and in line with the agreed design specification. This detailed and systematic analysis enabled the company to identify where improvements needed to be made.

- **Why-why reviews** – this approach starts with the problem and then asks why it occurred. This process is then repeated again by asking why each reason occurred. The logic is that continually asking 'why' (usually seven or more times) will get to the root cause of the problem.

Generating improvement ideas

Once the root causes of the problems have been identified, then improvement ideas can be generated. Most people, because of their training and background, are good at analytical thinking, but few are good at divergent or creative thinking. Some barriers that often prevent the generation of ideas are:

- Self-imposed limits to possible solutions

- An inherent belief that there is one right answer

- Fear of being wrong

- Conformity to behavioural norms

- Unwillingness to challenge the obvious.

Analytical approaches restrict imagination as they often prevent the development of ideas outside of apparent norms or perceived boundaries. Creative thinking, on the other hand, encourages ideas that were previously unrelated by consciously suspending judgement and evaluating ideas at a later stage. This allows the mind to think laterally by going through five different steps:

1. **Preparation** – collecting the known facts, defining the problem in different ways and restating/clarifying the problem

2. **Generation** – concerns the need to generate ideas, both in themselves and as a stimulus to creating other perspectives

3. **Incubation** – leaving the problem in the subconscious state as a way of creating new thoughts, the process of 'association'

4. **Insights** – linking ideas to possible solutions

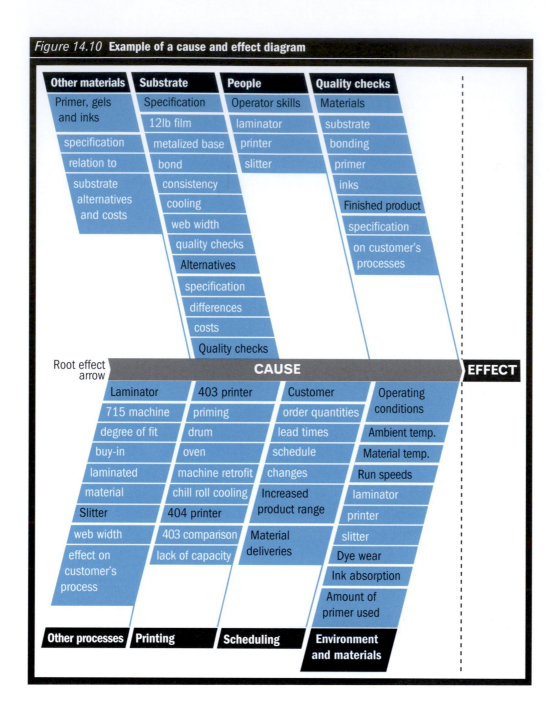

Figure 14.10 Example of a cause and effect diagram

Other materials	Substrate	People	Quality checks
Primer, gels and inks	Specification	Operator skills	Materials
specification	12lb film	laminator	substrate
relation to	metalized base	printer	bonding
substrate alternatives and costs	bond	slitter	primer
	consistency		inks
	cooling		Finished product
	web width		specification
	quality checks		on customer's processes
	Alternatives		
	specification		
	differences		
	costs		
	Quality checks		

Root effect arrow — **CAUSE** — **EFFECT**

Other processes	Printing	Scheduling	Environment and materials
Laminator	403 printer	Customer	Operating conditions
715 machine	priming	order quantities	Ambient temp.
degree of fit	drum	lead times	Material temp.
buy-in	oven	schedule	Run speeds
laminated	machine retrofit	changes	laminator
material	chill roll cooling	Increased product range	printer
Slitter	404 printer		slitter
web width	403 comparison	Material deliveries	Dye wear
effect on customer's process	lack of capacity		Ink absorption
			Amount of primer used

5. **Evaluation** – analyzing all the facts on which to base evaluations of the possible solutions.

While stages 1 and 5 are based on analytical approaches, the other three (stages 2, 3 and 4) are based on creative thinking. Deliberately separating these two phases is key with the creative stages (2, 3 and 4) best done in groups, with the aim of creating quantity not quality of ideas. By creating large numbers of ideas, new ideas are sparked off. To help achieve this, it is important to:

• **Suspend judgement** – criticism of ideas is not permitted. Evaluation comes after the creative stage. Bringing these two phases together will lead to implied criticism and a reluctance to contribute. The key is to discourage self-evaluation from entering the process.

• **Freewheel** – wild ideas are deliberately fostered as they lead to better results.

- **Cross-fertilize** – at set stages, give participants the task of combining and improving on the ideas of others.

In addition, the generation of ideas can be helped by using a number of techniques including:

- **Brainstorming** – 6–20 people take a problem and, working with the above rules, seek solutions. All ideas are written down to remain visible throughout. Typically, stages 1–5 form the basis for using this technique.

- **Reverse brainstorming** – asks, of an idea being considered, 'In how many ways can this idea fail?'.

- **Listing attributes** – lists the main attributes of the idea or object and examines how it can be changed.

- **Forcing relationships** – lists the ways in which ideas or objects can be combined. These approaches generate what is referred to as 'effective surprise'. The eventual improvements are typically not of an 'off-the-map' nature but, in fact, have the quality of obviousness. The element of surprise is that, in retrospect, the solutions/improvements were obvious, in fact 'How else would the problem have been solved?' The role of creative thinking is to push down the self-imposed barriers to alternatives so that we can access all the options.

An example of how to do this is described in Case 14.6 for IDEO, the US design consultancy.

Reengineering business processes

Once improvement ideas have been generated, then processes can be reengineered. Essentially, this involves developing processes that provide the highest value for customers by eliminating waste and then reconstructing management structures and functions around them. This involves going through a number of steps as shown in Figure 14.11:

> **Value-adding activities** – those services, products or features that a customer is willing to pay for.

1. **Map the process** – to establish facts rather than perceptions of how the business currently operates.

2. **Identify value-adding activities** – for which activities would a customer be prepared to pay? For example, they are not really interested in the internal procedures and controls within the business as long as the service or product delivered meets their expectations.

3. **Eliminate waste** – remove the unnecessary procedures and processes within the business.

4. **Make the value-adding steps flow** – once you are left with the essential, value-adding steps that a customer is prepared to pay for, then these must be made to flow by reengineering the interfaces between successive steps, operating them in parallel rather than sequentially, and removing any delays between each step.

5. **Repeat the cycle** – once this point has been reached, the new process needs to be mapped and the reengineering process started again.

Rule	Practice
Defer judgement	• Don't dismiss any ideas • Any idea is good, no matter how crazy • Nothing can kill the spirit of a brainstorm quicker than judging ideas before they have a chance to gain legs
Encourage wild ideas	• Embrace the most out-of-the-box notions because they can be the key to solutions • The whole point of brainstorming is coming up with new and creative ideas
Build on the ideas of others	• No 'buts', only 'ands' • Sometimes people say crazy and bizzare things, like 'make it on Mars', but there is some element of truth in it. When you build on the ideas of others, you might bring those crazy ideas back down to earth and make them real innovations
Stay focused on the topic	• Always keep the discussion on target. Otherwise you can go beyond the scope of what you are trying to achieve
One conversation at a time	• No interrupting, no dismissing, no disrespect, no rudeness • Let people have their say
Be visual	• Use yellow, red and blue markers to write on big 30-inch by 25-inch 'Post-it' notes that are put on a wall • Nothing gets an idea across faster than drawing it. It doesn't matter how terrible a sketcher you are
Go for quantity	• Aim for as many new ideas as possible. In a good session, up to 100 ideas are generated in 60 minutes • Crank the ideas out quickly

Founded in 1991, IDEO is considered to be the most successful design consultancy in the world. By 2009, it had won over 300 design awards, held over 1,000 patents and had developed solutions for over 4,000 clients from a variety of industries including health care, fast-moving-consumer-goods (FMCG), hospitality, financial services, automobiles and charities. Unlike other design firms who keep their design processes and methodologies secret, it believes in open source innovation and discloses its secrets to encourage clients to think creatively and foster innovation within their own organizations. It runs educative workshops for its clients and encourages brainstorming using the above rules.

www.ideo.com

Questions

1. How is IDEO's approach different to other design consultancies?

2. Why are the rules it suggests so important when brainstorming new ideas?

Lecturers: visit www.palgrave.com/business/hillom3e for teaching guidelines for this case study

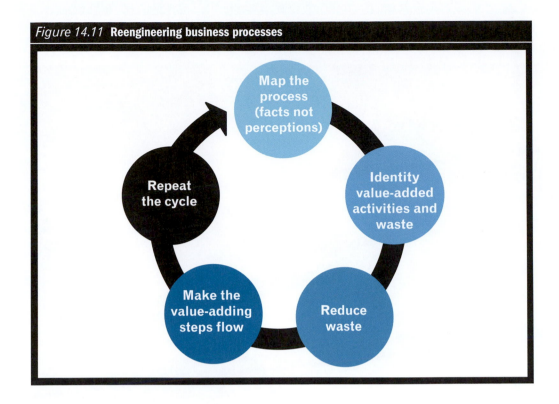

Figure 14.11 **Reengineering business processes**

Case 14.7 shows how Mutual Benefit Life, Taco Bell, JetBlue Airways and WPA have reengineered their processes and the benefits each one has achieved.

Making improvements

After deciding the appropriate improvement tools and techniques to use, businesses then need to determine who is to use them and the areas that need improving. A good starting point for doing this is to identify the different stakeholders for the business and **map** them onto the power and interest matrix shown in Figure 14.12 where:

- **Power** – is the ability of individuals or groups to persuade, induce or coerce others into following a certain course of action.

- **Interest** – is each group's level of interest in impressing its expectations on an organization's purpose and the choices it makes.

> **Stakeholder mapping** – identifies the interest and power of stakeholders and helps identify which ones can or should be used to identify and make improvements.

Figure 14.12 **Mapping stakeholder power and interest**

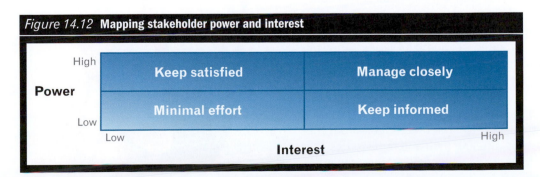

MUTUAL BENEFIT LIFE

Mutual Benefit Life handled customer applications through a series of departments: 'credit checks', 'quotations', 'rating', 'underwriting' and 'document preparation'. It typically took 5–25 days to process an application due to the delays, checks and rechecks within the process. It decided to reengineer the process and created 'case managers' who were responsible for processing a whole application from start to finish. By removing all the hand-offs, delays and backtracking, it could process an application in 2–5 days using 100 less employees who each handle twice as many applications as before.

TACO BELL

Taco Bell needed radically to improve performance. At the time, each outlet prepared food on site in its own kitchen, which took up space, reduced the seating area, increased overhead costs and lengthened service lead times. After talking to its customors, it found they didn't want extensive facilities and children's play areas. All they really wanted was good, hot food served quickly at a reasonable price. It decided to switch its outlets from making to retailing food and replaced its existing kitchens with smaller food preparation areas where staff, in response to customer orders, assembled items from ingredients (for example meat, corn tortilla shells and beans) prepared centrally and then delivered to the outlets. As a result, not only did the cost of running its outlets reduce by $87 million, but quality (both food design and delivery to this design) also improved while staff turnover reduced as employees enjoyed the new way of working.

www.tacobell.com

JETBLUE AIRWAYS

JetBlue's pilots now use sleek laptops to advise how much engine thrust they should apply for take off based on information such as outside temperature, fuel load, number of passengers, baggage weight, number of bags in each bin and length of the allocated runway. By moving away from a paper-based system with manual calculations and estimates, it has reduced the amount of fuel it uses, lightened engine wear and cut down noise. As a result, operating and maintenance costs have reduced by 5 per cent, which accumulates to millions of dollars over the life of an aircraft.

www.jetblue.com

WESTERN PROVIDENT ASSOCIATION

WPA, a UK-based health insurer, improved productivity by almost 50 per cent by re-engineering its application process. Previously, it took seven staff 28 days to process an application while now it only takes one person four days. The process includes reviewing medical histories, setting up policies and arranging collection of insurance premiums. In the old system, a file was only worked on for 45 minutes in 28 days, with most of the time spent waiting for information or for someone to work on it. After mapping the steps within the process, it identified the areas of waste, worked out how to eliminate them and then used 'image processing' and 'work flow' computer software to speed up the remaining value-added steps. The 'image processing' software captures an image of a document (including signatures) and the 'work flow' software then automatically sends this to the relevant worker for the next stage in the process.

www.wpa.org.uk

Questions

1. Identify the changes made and the benefits achieved by each of these companies.

2. Are these examples of 'breakthrough' or 'incremental' improvements?

Lecturers: visit www.palgrave.com/business/ hillom3e for teaching guidelines for this case study

Once stakeholders have been mapped, then individuals or groups who have a high interest in the activities or the organization can be used to help identify and make improvements. Typically, this involves using employees, suppliers or customers by giving them more power than they have as part of their normal role. Organizations such as Apple take a very 'closed' approach to making improvements where innovations are guarded secrets with employees being the predominant source of improvement ideas within its organization (see Case 14.8). However, Google uses a more 'open' approach by involving customers and suppliers in developing new services and ways of working (see Case 14.8). Both approaches have been highly successful, but involve completely different ways of developing and improving services, products and processes. The key issues to consider when involving employees, customers and suppliers in this way are now discussed in more detail.

Involving employees

Involving employees is essential if companies want to establish an 'improvement culture' within their business and to start driving incremental change, as discussed earlier and illustrated in Figure 14.4. Case 14.9 shows how Unipart uses its employees to identify and drive improvement within its business. For this to be effective, employees must be involved throughout from agreeing the aims of the programme to identifying and making improvements. This ensures that everyone within a business is committed, involved and empowered to make a difference. A key challenge within this is creating a working environment that helps employees develop their full potential, want to do a good job and contribute fully to improving all aspects of the business. Essential factors to making this happen include:

> **Self-managed teams** – self-organized, semi-autonomous small groups who determine, plan and manage their day-to-day activities with little or no supervision.

- **Create self-managed teams** – creating teams that are not only responsible for completing certain operations activities, but also for making decisions, implementing their ideas and being held accountable for the results they achieve. Figure 14.13 shows the four stages through which teams develop from initial 'involvement and collaboration' to 'shared responsibility' and then 'empowered ownership' before finally becoming 'self-managed teams'. Achieving this transition requires a very different organizational structure and management approach.

- **Share information** – everyone in the organization needs to be aware of how they are currently performing against competitors and other parts of the business, and the types of improvement that they are making. This helps them set the objectives for their own team and encourages them to keep looking for better ways to improve.

- **Create time for improvement** – as well as being expected to manage themselves and complete the operations activities they are responsible for, teams must also be allocated time within their working week to identify and make improvements. For example, in Google employees are encouraged to spend at least 20 per cent of their time working on new ideas, even if they are not immediately related to Google's current services or products (see Case 14.8).

CASE 14.8 CLOSED VS OPEN INNOVATION: APPLE VS GOOGLE

Computer firm Apple Inc. and internet search engine Google, both headquartered in California, USA, in a survey of 2,700 executives by Business Week have been voted the world's most innovative companies. However, they have very different approaches to developing and improving their services, products and processes.

APPLE

Apple's hardware innovation and research is a closely guarded secret. For each potential new product or product feature, it creates ten different designs, encouraging its employees to explore all different possibilities. After a few months, these are whittled down to three, and then after a few more months the company finally ends up with one strong decision. Throughout this process, teams of designers and engineers meet twice a week to discuss the product and explore alternative options, even towards the end of its development. Apple's strategy is to put all its resources into developing a few products and make them exceedingly well. Steve Jobs, Apple's CEO and co-founder, comments, 'One of the keys to Apple is that we build products that really turn us on.' Innovation of products tends to be undertaken by a small group of individuals, who identify a gap in the market. There are no hierarchies in the design team, and they work without a formal structure.

www.apple.com

©Pgiam

GOOGLE

Unlike Apple, Google uses an open approach to innovation in which it acts as a fertile ground for ideas offered by its employees, customers and suppliers. It has achieved this by developing an informal company culture that encourages employees to exchange ideas and continually make incremental improvements and add enhancements to their products. Employees are also encouraged to spend at least 20 per cent of their time working on their own ideas, even if they do not immediately relate to Google's current services or products. This approach has led to a number of developments such as the Google Directory, which provides the ability to search different topics and is offered in more than ten different languages so customers can search in their own language. As well as tapping into its employees' ideas, Google has also developed a number of partnerships with key customers to help develop new products and enter new markets, for example, its alliances with Universo Online in Latin America and China Mobile Limited in Asia. It has also partnered with major libraries such as the University of California and University of Wisconsin to digitize their holdings and make them easier to search.

www.google.com

Sources: Morris, B. 'What makes Apple golden', *Fortune Magazine*, 3 March.

Questions

1. Compare the Apple and Google approaches to innovation.

2. What are the advantages and disadvantages of each of these approaches?

Lecturers: visit www.palgrave.com/business/hillom3e for teaching guidelines for this case study

Figure 14.13 The four stages of involving employees in improvement activities

STAGE 4	**Self-managed teams**	· Teams responsible for all aspects of the process and site · Self-directed teams with integrated support from specialist groups · Site-based group for medium- to long-term decisions · An organization without rank
STAGE 3	**Empowered ownership**	· Traditional structure with overall control retained by management · Self-directed teams with some integrated support and overviewed by an operations manager · Teams responsible for all aspects of the process
STAGE 2	**Shared responsibility**	· Traditional structure with overall control retained by management · Team based – with appointed leader · Teams are responsible for output of the process and participate in problem resolution and improvement activities
STAGE 1	**Involvement and collaboration**	· Traditional structure · Teams with supervisory control · Participate in problem resolution and improvement activities · Supervisor responsible for output and behaviour · External specialist support

> **EXECUTIVE INSIGHT**
> To lead change, you have to adapt and change your leadership style, moving from being directive to becoming more supportive as your team starts to develop and lead change.

Involving suppliers

Businesses can use stakeholders such as suppliers to identify and make improvements but this requires a very different approach, as described in Figure 14.14, ultimately moving to a situation where customers and suppliers are mutually dependent on each other.

For example, Philips, the Dutch electronics company, turned its research and development facility in the Netherlands into an open campus for more than 7,000 researchers from its tier 1 and tier 2 suppliers. Suddenly, the facility changed from being a cost centre to a profit centre as the researchers paid to rent space within the facility. It also found the campus expanded its ecosystem and encouraged knowledge sharing among its suppliers. Case 14.10 shows how Apple has worked with both Fedex and the Chinese manufacturers of its iPods to produce and deliver a tailor-made iPod to a customer anywhere in the world in less than 90 hours. Case 14.11 describes how TED (Technology, Entertainment, Design) and Apple have used suppliers to develop new services and products that they distribute to customers through the www.ted.com website and Apple's iTunes 'App Store'. Involving suppliers in this way has radically changed how these businesses work and led to improvements that they would never have made on their own.

Involving customers

In the same way that businesses can get customers to serve themselves (see Chapter 5), they can also use them to improve their services, products and processes. Case 14.12

CASE 14.9 UNIPART

Unipart, the UK manufacturing and logistics company, has a training centre in each of its plants and warehouses where small groups meet to share ideas and experiences about how to improve the way they work. The training centres are also linked to each other through the company's intranet to help them collectively identify and solve the problems the company faces across the business. Over 400 internal facilitators are also used to train and coach staff and help pass on solutions and ideas between different groups.

www.unipart.com

Questions

1. What aspects of Unipart's approach illustrate the concept of continuous improvement?

2. How is employee involvement central to this initiative?

Figure 14.14 **Phases in changing attitudes to suppliers**

Threat and fear	**Traditional stance. Perceptions based upon:** · Customer dominates the relationship with suppliers · Suppliers respond to demands · Suppliers pitted against each other · Constant threat of purchases being given to other suppliers · Supplier's ongoing fear of losing contract
Reward	**First step towards cooperation and moving from a reactive to a proactive stance. Characterized by elements such as:** · Fewer suppliers · Long-term contracts · Customer is proactive in building a relationship with suppliers
Collaborate	**Progressive move towards fuller and more cooperative relationships, the pace of which is set predominantly by the customer. Evolution through a series of steps such as:** · Customer identifies improvements that a supplier can make · Customer provides support and resources (for example, technical capability) to undertake improvements within supplier's delivery systems · Customer gives actual help to improve supplier's capabilities, including training supplier's staff · Customer takes into account the processes of its suppliers when designing services and products to help them improve their support · Customer focuses attention on tier 2 suppliers as a source of improving tier 1 suppliers' support (see Figure 12.17)
Integrate and synchronize	**The final step is to integrate activities achieving benefits typically associated with ownership – the concept of virtual ownership. Based upon mutual respect and trust, these include suppliers' access to real-time information, with customers harmonising their suppliers' work and synchronizing their support. These changes range from:** · Access to design-related information and responsibility for service/product design · Suppliers' responsibility for deciding when and how much to despatch

describes how Wikipedia, Threadless and Starbucks use customers to improve their businesses. As with companies such as Facebook and eBay, this collaborative way of working gives customers the tools to develop and improve the services and products a company sells and how it delivers them to its customers. Although customers have always been interested in the activities and actions undertaken within organizations, these sorts of initiatives give them more power and, as with involving employees and suppliers, this makes them more mutually dependent on each other than before. The advantage of this sort of approach is that customer loyalty increases, research and development costs are reduced and there is almost instant demand for the services and products developed.

> **EXECUTIVE INSIGHT**
Using customers and/or suppliers to make improvements requires giving them more power than they usually have. To do this, you must first develop open, honest and trusting relationships with them.

CASE 14.10 APPLE'S IPOD: USING SUPPLIERS TO REDUCE LEAD-TIMES

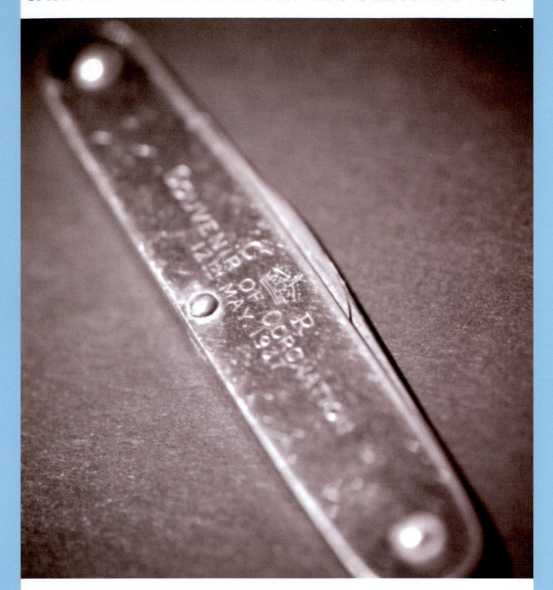

A hundred and fifty years ago, it took a cargo-laden ship 90 days to travel from Shanghai to New York, but now Apple can take an online order for a tailor-made iPod, manufacture it in China and deliver it to a home address in Pittsburgh in less than 90 hours. This is achieved by its:

- Just-in-time manufacturing agreements with its Chinese suppliers, who only make an iPod after they receive an order from a customer anywhere in the world, and a

- Priority Direct Distribution agreement with FedEx to deliver the iPods to their destinations and allow customers to track their orders by scanning them up to 12 times during their journey.

As a result, Apple is able to offer customers iPods with their names engraved on the back in less than 90 hours with significantly less inventory.

www.apple.com

Questions

1. How did Apple manage to reduce the lead-time for supplying a tailor-made iPod?

2. How can other companies learn from these developments?

Lecturers: visit www.palgrave.com/business/hillom3e for teaching guidelines for this case study

CASE 14.11 USING SUPPLIERS TO DEVELOP NEW PRODUCTS AND SERVICES: TED AND APPLE'S APP STORE

TED

TED (short for Technology, Entertainment, Design) is a US private, not-for-profit foundation devoted to 'freely spreading ideas' through the internet in the belief that these ideas can change attitudes, lives and, ultimately, the world. They see themselves as both a clearinghouse for free knowledge and inspiration from the world's most inspired thinkers, and also a community of curious souls engaging with these ideas and each other. To achieve this, they act as a portal for ideas that are developed by people who don't work for TED, but who present at their conferences and independent events. After these events, TED then publishes these talks so they can be seen and used around the world.

Initially started as a one-off event in 1984, it had become an annual event by 1990 and TED now holds conferences in the USA, Europe and Asia. The lectures held at these conferences must be less than 18 minutes and are then published on TED.com where they can be watched for free by anyone. Although initially more technology focused, the talks now cover most aspects of science and culture and have been given by a wide variety of people such as Bill Clinton, Al Gore, Gordon Brown, Richard Dawkins, Bill Gates, Bono, Jamie Oliver and various Nobel Prize winners.

There are now more than 600 talks on its website, with over 300 translated by volunteers into over 40 languages. By 2009, its talks had been viewed over 250 million times by more than 25 million people. In 2005, it also introduced 'TED Prizes' where $100,000 was awarded to three winners wishing to 'change the world'. However, it felt this was spreading its resources too thinly and in 2010 it awarded a single $300,000 prize to one winner who was Jamie Oliver wanting to 'teach every child about food'.

www.ted.com

APPLE'S APP STORE

Apple's 'App Store' is a service that allows its iPhone, iPod and iPad users to browse and download applications from its iTunes Store for free, or at a cost. These applications are developed by third-party programmers using a code that is developed and published by Apple. Developers produce software applications using the code and then submit them to Apple who then decides whether or not to accept them into its store.

In December 2009, 58 million App Store users (34 million iPhone and 24 million iPod touch) downloaded 280 million Apps generating $250 million sales of which 30 per cent goes to Apple and the rest to the developers. As of 8 April 2010, there are at least 185,000 third-party applications officially available on the App Store, with over 4 billion total downloads since it first opened in July 2008. This success has led to the launch of similar services by its competitors. However, Apple has actually trademarked the term 'App Store'.

www.apple.com

Questions

1. What do you think of these approaches to developing new services and products?

2. How is this different to Apple's traditional approach to new service and product development?

3. What are the advantages and disadvantages of such an approach?

Lecturers: visit www.palgrave.com/business/hillom3e for teaching guidelines for this case study

CASE 14.12 USING CUSTOMERS TO IMPROVE OPERATIONS: WIKIPEDIA, THREADLESS AND STARBUCKS

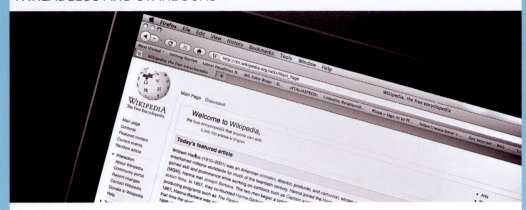

WIKIPEDIA

Wikipedia is a free, web-based, collaborative and multilingual encyclopedia supported by the non-profit Wikimedia Foundation. Its 15 million articles have been collectively created by thousands of contributors from across the world and can be edited by anyone with access to its site. It is a move away from the previous style of 'expert-driven' encyclopedia development and has also become a frequently updated news resource with articles appearing soon after an event has occurred.

www.wikipedia.org

THREADLESS

Anyone can design a T-shirt, submit it to a weekly contest and then rate their favourite designs. Threadless then selects which designs to produce from those with the highest ratings, giving prizes and royalties to the winning designers. In this way, the company uses over 500,000 people to design and select the T-shirts it produces.

www.threadless.com

STARBUCKS

Starbucks has set up a website for customers to share ideas, say what they think of other people's ideas and join the discussion. In the first six months after it was introduced, 75,000 ideas were submitted and received thousands of votes and hundreds of comments. Ideas range from healthier food options and morning coffee discussions to reusable cups.

http://mystarbucksidea.force.com

Questions

1. How have these organizations developed their products?

2. What are the advantages and disadvantages of involving customers in this way?

Lecturers: visit www.palgrave.com/business/hillom3e for teaching guidelines for this case study

Improving operations in practice

When improving operations in practice, it is important to consider the following aspects:

- **Understand market requirements** – the order-winners and qualifiers that need to be supported within your current and future markets need to be understood before current performance can be reviewed and improvements identified.

- **Develop business case for improving operations** – in particular, it is important to show the expected financial cost (time and money) and benefit of the proposed initiatives, such as:
  - *Release cash* – the expected reduction in inventories, accounts receivables, properties, buildings and equipment
  - *Reduce costs* – the expected reduction in material, labour and overhead costs
  - *Increase sales revenue* – the expected increase in sales revenue resulting from improved support for current and future markets.

- **Involve interested stakeholders** – as this will result in several business benefits. For example using:
  - *Employees* – will increase job satisfaction and motivation
  - *Suppliers* – will increase access to a broader range of capabilities and knowledge and reduce R&D costs
  - *Customers* – will increase customer loyalty, help tailor services or products to customer needs and reduce R&D costs.

- **Challenge and check opinion with data** – it is fine to use your gut feeling to identify problems that need improving. However, you then need to dig the data to really understand the type of problems that occur, how often they occur and the impact they have on the business. This data will help to really focus your resources and justify the investment required to make step-change improvements.

- **Create time and money** – to analyze the business and make improvements. A good business case will help win management support for your initiatives, but you will also need to:
  - *Dedicate time* – allocate dedicated time for employees, suppliers and/or customers to work on improvement projects
  - *Initially focus on releasing cash* – initially look for low-cost, easy ways to release cash from the business
  - *Then try to increase market support and reduce costs* – by reinvesting the cash that you have already released.

- **Use both 'proactive incremental' and 'proactive breakthrough' approaches** – as they have different advantages and disadvantages. However, it is important always to use a proactive, rather than a reactive, approach as this enables you to better control and drive change.

- **Modify your approach as the business develops** – as the business starts to improve by being:
  1. *Initially directive* – to drive the process and overcome the initial inertia to change
  2. *Then supportive* – as your team starts to drive the process themselves, you will need to change your approach by helping them focus on the right strategic objectives and sharing good practice across the business.

Driving business performance

Releasing cash

Cash can be released from an operation by:

- **Reducing inventory** – held within operations through a causal analysis asking why it is necessary, why it is there and what caused it. The systems, procedures and rules that created the inventory can then be challenged, reviewed and changed to reduce it.

- **Changing supplier payment terms** – companies can delay paying suppliers. However, this will negatively affect their suppliers' cash flow, which could have a disastrous impact on a small supplier.

- **Selling or leasing equipment** – non-essential equipment can be sold and essential equipment can be leased. Although leasing will probably increase the overall cost of the equipment, it spreads it over a longer period of time.

- **Outsourcing** – processes that require a high investment in equipment or inventory, but ensure this does not have a negative long-term strategic impact on the business.

Improving market support

The operations function of a business is critical in winning and retaining customers. Some examples of how different market order-winners and qualifiers can be better supported through improved operations are:

- **Price** – by reducing material, direct labour and overhead costs (by modifying service and product designs, finding cheaper materials, eliminating process wastes, reducing the mix of volumes and improving staff and process efficiency and productivity).

- **Quality conformance** – by reducing the quality gaps between what customers want, what a company sells and what operations delivers.

- **Delivery reliability and speed** – by reducing the gap between requested, promised and actual delivery by collecting and analyzing delivery performance data.

- **Service or product range** – by improving the capability of staff and the processes they use to deliver the current and future ranges proposed.

- **Demand fluctuations** – by improving the ability of the delivery system to respond to known or anticipated demand changes.

- **Speed of new service or product development** – reducing development lead-time by mapping the current development process and identifying areas for improvement.

Reducing costs

Significant cost reductions can be made within an operation, for example reducing:

- **Research and development costs** – by developing strategic partnerships with critical customers and suppliers.

- **Labour costs** – by getting customers to serve themselves, outsourcing, modifying designs, eliminating non-value-adding activities, reducing the range and mix of volumes delivered and improving staff and process efficiency and productivity.

- **Material costs** – by modifying service and product designs, developing long-term supplier relationships, using single sourcing policies and finding cheaper alternatives.

- **Overhead costs** – by making the operation easier to manage, getting customers to serve themselves and outsourcing management tasks to suppliers.

- **Inventory costs** – by reducing inventory levels within the operation.

Critical reflections

Businesses need to constantly look for ways to improve how they operate. If a company isn't moving forwards, it is actually moving backwards as there is always someone else looking for ways to take its customers. Improving operations can help a business progress by doing one or more of the following:

- **Releasing cash** – that can then be invested elsewhere within the business such as new equipment or research and development

- **Improving market support** – that, in turn, leads to increased sales revenue by either increasing market share, developing new markets or enabling the business to charge a higher price for its services and products

- **Reducing costs** – resulting in higher profit margins.

To achieve this and drive their businesses forward, organizations need to take a proactive approach to improvement where all stakeholders continually look for ways to do things better. Although the tools and techniques for improving operations are not revolutionary and have been around for many years, organizations are starting to use them in very different ways. Historically, businesses used their own employees to identify and make improvements, but many are now rethinking the boundaries of their organizations and starting to give more power to suppliers, customers and other individuals that are interested in the organization.

In part, the internet has helped facilitate this by improving communication between stakeholders and starting to build communities that are more powerful acting together rather than as individuals. But, it has also come from a realization that significant benefits and advantages can be gained from tapping into a broader resource of knowledge and ideas. As a result, even organizations like Apple who have traditionally taken a 'closed' approach to innovation have used an open approach with their 'App Store'. Not only is this service key to the future success of their iPhone, iPod and iPad products, but it is now generating over $75 million profit per month for Apple. Making these changes, however, requires a radically different approach and a willingness to move to a situation where customers and suppliers are mutually dependent on each other.

Summary

This chapter has looked at why organizations look to improve operations, the steps that they must go through to make improvements, the approaches they can take, the tools and techniques they can use and how they can use different stakeholders to identify and make improvements.

Why improve operations?

Operations needs to be improved to meet a variety of different corporate objectives, but the most common reasons are to release cash, improve market support (leading to increased sales) and/or reduce costs. This is done through a number of actions:

- **Release cash** – by reducing inventory, changing supplier payment terms, selling or leasing equipment and/or outsourcing

- **Improve market support** – by identifying relevant order-winners and qualifiers, translating these into strategic tasks, reviewing current performance against these tasks and identifying and implementing improvements

- **Reduce costs** – by reviewing and reducing actual material, direct labour and overhead costs, mapping activities, identifying and eliminating areas of waste, reviewing and reducing the mix of volumes within operations, reviewing and increasing the price of services or products, and choosing to no longer supply some services or products.

Process of improving operations

Improving operations involves going through four key steps:

1. **Plan** – develop an improvement plan by identifying a problem or aspect to improve, identifying areas of improvement and prioritizing which areas to look at first.

2. **Do** – implement the improvement plan.

3. **Check** – measure the impact of the actions made in step 2 to see if they have met the objectives set in step 1.

4. **Review** – review the checks made and identify further problems or aspects to improve that leads back to step 1.

Approach to improving operations

Companies need to decide if they want to take a 'passive' or 'proactive' approach to improvement where:

- **Passive** – improvements are identified and implemented through activities such as 'suggestion schemes' and 'process and technology investments' made by support functions such as IT and engineering

- **Proactive** – improvements where operations takes control and drives change by developing an 'improvement culture' and using 'kaizen blitz events'.

They must also decide if they want to make an 'incremental' or 'breakthrough' level of improvement where:

- **Incremental** – improvements come from a larger number of smaller more frequent improvements typically involving little investment through either 'suggestion schemes' or establishing an 'improvement culture'

- **Breakthrough** – improvements that result from major changes to existing practices and normally involve large investments either in assets for 'process and technology investments' or the time for the people who work within operations for 'kaizen blitz events'.

Improvement tools and techniques

A wide variety of tools and techniques are available to organizations wishing to improve their operations. The key ones include:

- **Benchmarking** – can be used to help start or maintain an improvement process by identifying, setting and measuring improvement targets against other parts of the organization, direct competitors, companies within the same sector who are not direct competitors, latent competitors, and/or companies outside of the industry.

- **Mapping the customer journey** – to help identify which services and products to deliver and how to deliver them by mapping the journey that customers take, identifying the points of interaction that they have with the business, determining in which parts of the journey they wish to interact with customers and how best to manage these interactions.

- **Mapping processes** – needs to be undertaken before they can be improved using a variety of tools such as process charts, service maps, information and material flow charts, person flow charts and/or videoing.

- **Identifying causes of problems** – once a process has been mapped, the root causes of the problems can be identified using a number of tools and techniques such as cause and effect diagrams and/or why-why reviews.

- **Generating improvement ideas** – once the root causes of the problems have been identified, then improvement ideas can be generated using techniques such as brainstorming, reverse brainstorming, listing attributes, and/or forcing relationships.

- **Reengineering business processes** – once improvement ideas have been generated, processes can be reengineered by mapping the process, identifying value-adding activities, eliminating waste, making the value-adding steps flow and then repeat the cycle by mapping the new process.

Making improvements

After deciding which improvement tools and techniques to use, businesses need to identify their 'high interest' stakeholders and start using them to help identify and make improvements. Organizations can either take a 'closed' approach to making improvements by only using their own employees and closely guarding their secrets or they can take a more 'open' approach and involve customers and suppliers in developing new services and ways of working. The key issues to consider when involving employees, customers and suppliers in this way are:

- **Involving employees** – this is essential if companies want to develop an 'improvement culture' required to drive incremental change. To make this happen, they need to establish self-managed teams, share information and create time for improvement activities.

- **Involving suppliers** – requires changing the relationship with suppliers and moving to a situation where both customers and suppliers are mutually dependent on each other for developing new services/products and improving how they are delivered.

- **Involving customers** – just as businesses can get customers to serve themselves, they can also use them to improve their services, products and processes. This can increase customer loyalty, reduce research and development costs and help tailor services/products to customer needs.

Study activities

Discussion questions

1. A retail outlet offering a range of high-specification women's clothes wishes to develop relevant performance measures. Suggest those that you consider appropriate.

2. Explain the difference between stepped and incremental change programmes. What are the advantages and disadvantages of each?

3. Draw an outline process chart for when arranging a holiday for which the hotels and flights are directly booked by you.

4. Why is the use of video gaining widespread application in the field of continuous improvement?

5. Why is there actual conflict between management and staff over productivity levels? What actions can operations managers take to resolve these differences?

Assignments

1. Develop a cause and effect diagram to explain lengthy service at a restaurant.

2. Use the Deming cycle approach to suggest and implement improvements to the library lending delivery system.

Exploring further

TED talks

Brown, T. (2008) *Creativity and play*. At the 2008 Serious Play conference, designer Tim Brown talks about the powerful relationship between creative thinking and play, with many examples you can try at home (and one that maybe you shouldn't).
www.ted.com/talks/tim_brown_on_creativity_and_play.html

Johnson, S. (2010) *Where good ideas come from*. People often credit their ideas to individual 'Eureka!' moments. But Steven Johnson shows how history tells a different story. His fascinating tour takes us from the 'liquid networks' of London's coffee houses to Charles Darwin's long, slow hunch to today's high-velocity web.
www.ted.com/talks/steven_johnson_where_good_ideas_come_from.html

Leadbeater, C. (2005) *Innovation*. In this deceptively casual talk, Charles Leadbeater weaves a tight argument that innovation isn't just for professionals anymore. Passionate amateurs, using new tools, are creating products and paradigms that companies can't.
www.ted.com/talks/charles_leadbeater_on_innovation.html

McCandless, D. (2010) *The beauty of data visualization*. David McCandless turns complex data sets (like worldwide military spending, media buzz, Facebook status updates) into beautiful, simple diagrams that tease out unseen patterns and connections. Good design, he suggests, is the best way to navigate the information glut and it may just change the way we see the world.
www.ted.com/talks/david_mccandless_the_beauty_of_data_visualization.html

Journal articles

Adler, P., Hecksher, C. and Prusak, L. (2011) 'Building a collaborative enterprise', *Harvard Business Review*, **89**(7/8): 94–101. Organizations must learn to: (1) Define a shared purpose (2) Cultivate an ethic of contribution (3) Develop scalable procedures (4) Create an infrastructure that values and rewards collaboration.

Amabile, T.M. and Kramer, S.J. (2011) 'The power of small wins', *Harvard Business Review*, **89**(5): 70–80. What is the best way to motivate employees to do creative work? Help them take a step forward every day. The key is to learn which actions support progress such as setting clear goals, providing sufficient time and resources, and offering recognition. On the flip side, small losses or setbacks can have an extremely negative effect.

Chesbrough, H.W. and Garman, A.R. (2009) 'How open innovation can help you cope in lean times', *Harvard Business Review*, **87**(12): 68–76. This article proposes that 'open innovation' can play an important role in helping companies in the current challenging business environment. Open innovation allows intellectual property, ideas and people to flow freely both into and out of an organization and includes placing some of its assets and projects outside.

Kaplan, R.S. and Norton, D.P. (2007) 'Using the balanced scorecard as a strategic management system', *Harvard Business Review*, **85**(7/8): 150–61. The balanced scorecard contains financial performance measures that report what has already happened and non-financial measures that help predict what might happen in the future. This article examines how a balanced scorecard can be used to link current actions with tomorrow's goals.

Lapre, M.A. and Van Wassenhove, L.N. (2002) 'Learning across lines: the secret to more efficient factories', *Harvard Business Review*, **80**(10): 107–11. In the quest to reduce waste on production lines, managers often find that the harder they work at improving their manufacturing processes, the more elusive the benefits become. The authors suggest the key is to make improvements that deliver both conceptual and operational learning.

Ramaswamy, V. and Gouillart, F. (2010) 'Building the co-creative enterprise', *Harvard Business Review*, **88**(100): 100–09. The article examines how companies can use their stakeholders including customers, employees and distributors to determine HR practices and design and market their services and products.

Staats, B.R. and Upton, D.M. (2011) 'Lean knowledge work', *Harvard Business Review*, **89**(10): 100–10. This article argues that knowledge work can be made lean if managers draw on six principles: (1) Continuously root out all waste (2) Strive to make tacit knowledge explicit (3) Specify how workers should communicate (4) Use the scientific method to solve problems quickly (5) Recognize that a lean system will always be a work in progress, and (6) Have leaders blaze the trail.

Thomke, S. (2001) 'Enlightened experimentation: the new imperative for innovation', *Harvard Business Review*, **79**(2): 67–75. Experimentation lies at the heart of every company's ability to innovate and at the heart of a company's ability to create and refine its services and products. To maximize the outcomes of innovation, this article puts forward a new way of looking at such approaches and explains the essentials of what it refers to as 'enlightened experimentation'.

Books
Senge, P.M. (2006) *The Fifth Discipline: The Art and Practice of the Learning Organization*. London: Random House. This book looks at how organizations expand their capacity to create results by nurturing an environment where people continually learn together.

Womack, J. and Jones, D. (2003) *Lean Thinking*. New York: Free Press. This book looks at how organizations should identify and eliminate waste within their businesses, citing examples from companies showing how their theories can be put into action.

Films
Big Chef Takes on Little Chef. TV documentary, 2009. This documentary describes how the Little Chef Restaurant management team bring in Michelin three-star award-winning chef Heston Blumenthal to help it try to recapture the commercial success it once had.
www.channel4.com/programmes/big-chef-takes-on-little-chef/4od

Dead Poet's Society. Director: Peter Weir, 1989. English professor John Keating inspires his students to sieze the day and challenge the status quo. Each, in their own way, does this, and they are changed for life.

Heston's Mission Impossible. TV documentary, 2011. This documentary describes how Heston Blumenthal uses his maverick culinary genius to dramatically reinvent food production at British Airways, the NHS, the Royal Navy and Cineworld Cinemas.
www.channel4.com/programmes/hestons-mission-impossible

Made in Britain. TV documentary, 2011. Evan Davis looks at the British economy and asks what it is good at and how it can pay its way in the world.
www.bbc.co.uk/programmes/b0125v5k

Visit www.palgrave.com/business/hillom3e for self-test questions, guideline answers to some case study questions, useful weblinks and more to help you understand the topics in this chapter

HARLEY-DAVIDSON

Like all motorcycle manufacturers, Harley-Davidson has been hit hard by the current economic crisis with sales and profits declining rapidly in the past few years. In 2009, it announced a company-wide restructuring plan closing two factories and one distribution centre, and eliminating almost 25 per cent of its total workforce (around 3,500 employees), with plans to reduce annual operating costs by $260 million. Later that year, it ended the Buell product line, and in 2010 it sold the MV Agusta business bought only the previous year, announcing further plans to cut manufacturing costs by another $54 million. Harley is no stranger to tough times. Established in 1903, William Harley and Walter, William and Arthur Davidson built their first three motorcycles in a shed in Milwaukee. Six years later, they introduced their trademark two-cylinder, V-twin engine bike able to reach speeds of 60 mph, the fastest at that time. During the First World War, overseas demand grew, and by the 1920s Harley-Davidson was the largest manufacturer in the world and considered to be a leader in innovative engineering. The US motorcycle industry was booming, but then the Great Depression hit, which the company only managed to survive through its police, military and international sales. Then came the Second World War

and production soared to record levels as a result of supplying over 90,000 military cycles while earning the Army-Navy 'E' award for wartime production excellence.

After the War, Harley-Davidson started developing recreational bikes, introducing the K-model in 1952, XL Sportster in 1957 and Duo-Glide in 1958. But again the industry was struggling, and soon it was the last remaining major US motorcycle manufacturer. It continued to do well and was sold to the American Machine and Foundry (AMF) company in 1969. Then disaster struck as Japanese manufacturers flooded the US market with high-quality, low-priced bikes. Harley-Davidson's market share fell from 78 per cent in 1973 to 23 per cent by 1981, and AMF put the company up for sale. In 1981, 13 of Harley's management team bought the company, hoping to reverse its fortunes and take on Honda, which now had 44 per cent of the market. But Harley's market share continued to fall, and it was left with a large number of unsold bikes. It decided to drastically cut production and reduced its 4,000 workforce by 45 per cent. In 1983, to help the floundering US motorcycle industry, President Ronald Reagan increased tariffs on large Japanese motorcycles from 4 to 49 per cent. While this increase was only effective for five years (declining each year), it did help to postpone the inevitable, but by 1985 Harley-Davidson was on the edge of bankruptcy.

TURNAROUND

In a last-minute bid to save the company, Richard Teerlink (Harley's CEO) convinced investors to fund a restructuring plan based on new management principles, marketing strategies and manufacturing techniques. He explained that they needed to reduce the high inventories that tied up cash and lower the high operating costs that made them vulnerable to unpredictable market fluctuations. Instead of trying to make short-term improvements through quick fixes, such as throwing in computers and state-of-the-art machinery, they needed to start listening to their employees and work with them to improve the business.

EMPLOYEE INVOLVEMENT

The first challenge was to earn the respect and trust of employees and get them to share in the vision built on the five values of 'tell the truth', 'be fair', 'keep your promises', 'respect the individual' and 'encourage intellectual curiosity'. Harley also decided to work with its unionized workforce rather than against them. Through its words and actions, the Harley management team showed that this was a new way of life, not just another 'programme'. They set up the Harley-Davidson Learning Center for employees to come with requests for specific job-training courses, and introduced a gain-sharing programme with cash incentives for maintaining and improving quality, profitability and delivery. Over the following year, everyone was trained in problem-solving and quality control techniques applicable to their area of expertise. The company also tried to insource as much work as possible, giving the union control over what was outsourced. When times are good, the company outsources, but it brings work back in-house in tough times to maintain jobs. The unions even censure their own workers for shoddy performance and have helped to introduce cross-trained, 'self-managed' teams that set their own work schedules and have responsibility for production, quality and preventive maintenance.

INVENTORY REDUCTION

The first problem to address was inventory. At the time, inventory was high and only turned over four times a year, and the company needed to work out how to reduce it to free up cash to invest elsewhere in the business. At the time, Harley-Davidson used a complex material requirements planning computer system to schedule operations, which kept inventory high to ensure the assembly line was not halted by any manufacturing problems. To solve the situation, the company moved to just-in-time (JIT) methods, making products only as they were required using visual systems to schedule production and manage stock. As inventory was reduced, problems were exposed and then solved. This resulted in a number of projects to improve material control and flow, reduce machine set-ups and improve machine reliability. The JIT system allowed quality to become the focus as inventory levels were smaller and more manageable.

Once JIT was working well, the company then started working with suppliers to improve the way they worked. As a result, inventory levels reduced by 75 per cent and inventory turnovers increased steadily

PROCESS IMPROVEMENT

Rather than buying new machinery, the company focused on improving its use of

Figure 1 Motorcycle product performance (1985–2010)										
$m	1985	1990	1995	2000	2002	2004	2006	2008	2009	2010
Sales revenue	288	624	1350	2943	4091	5015	5800	5578	4287	4177
Gross profit	74	189	411	964	1418	1899	2233	1931	1386	1427
Net profit	3	38	112	478	734	1137	1387	976	314	379
Inventory	79	60	84	191	218	227	287	379	323	326
Cash	28	13	31	420	192	275	239	569	1630	1022

$m	1985	1990	1995	2000	2002	2004	2006	2008	2009	2010
Direct	214	435	939	1979	2673	3116	3567	3647	2901	2749
Overheads	71	151	299	486	684	762	846	943	851	882
Restructuring	–	–	–	–	–	–	–	12	221	164

Figure 2 **Motorcycle product costs (1985–2010)**

existing equipment in order to increase the quality of its products. Harley-Davidson started an initiative called 'statistical operator control' that made operators responsible for the quality of the products they produced. Staff were given extensive training in tools such as control charts and histograms, and, as a result, the company saw a substantial improvement, with a 68 per cent reduction in scrap and rework and a 50 per cent increase in productivity (Figure 2). Operators could now monitor the manufacturing process to understand whether it was 'in control' (operating in a stable and predictable range) and 'capable' (consistently within specification). If a problem occurred, employees could immediately stop the process and fix it.

PRODUCTION CELLS

Harley's production was a huge, maze-like operation in which products were made in large batches on machines with long set-up times. There was no straight flow of work so operators had to use forklifts to move the materials around the factory. The improvements made through involving employees reduced inventory, improved processes and enabled them to move from a traditional batch production process to 'U-shaped' cells where one to four people worked together to produce a finished part. Each manufacturing department contained a number of cells that were easier to manage and required 25 per cent less space. Lead-times fell from over six weeks to a few hours and inventory reduced as suppliers delivered raw materials and components directly to where they were required rather than through a central stock room.

PRODUCT DEVELOPMENT

After improving its production processes, Harley then turned its attention to its products. It had always focused on heavy-weight (over 650cc) sports and touring motorcycles competing on design rather than price (see Figures 3 and 4), but only offered three basic models, all in grey. They started looking at how customers used their products and found that they often customized them to better suit their tastes and requirements. So they thought, 'Let's make their life easier and do it for them!'

The level of choice and number of options has been increased to the point where customers can now choose from over 7,000 accessories with more than 400 combinations of seats, bars, pegs and controls. Customers can now build their dream bike using their online 'customizer' and 'shop for your bike' tools and in-store 'chrome consulting' service. Also on offer is a wide range of licensed merchandise and collectibles making sure customers keep coming back to their dealerships.

TODAY

Sales and profits have grown significantly since the turnaround in the 1980s. Nevertheless, the company is constantly looking for ways to do things better. For example, when there was a capacity squeeze on its wheel production plant in Kansas City, layouts and processes were reconfigured to gain capacity. As a result, work-in-progress and handling were both reduced by 50 per cent. Equally, its Paint Group recently improved the sequencing and delivery of painted parts to assembly lines using visual management tools, while its new financial software has improved demand forecasting. Work has been undertaken to transform its York operation to make it much more flexible and efficient. The company is also looking at how it can grow international sales in order to move away from being too reliant on the US market, for example in India, where there is sufficient demand to overcome the high import duties.

Figure 3 Harley-Davidson's main product groups

Product group	Description
Touring	**Comfort and power for the long haul** – touring models have large saddlebags, large clear windshields, rear coil-over air suspensions and are the only models with radios or CBs. All models use the same frame, were introduced in 1980, extensively redesigned in 2009 and are popular with several local and state police agencies.
Softail	**Combines heritage with innovation** – these big-twin motorcycles capitalize on Harley's strong traditional image and look similar to the 'choppers' that were popular in the 1960s and 1970s.
Dyna	**Substantial in every detail** – distinguished from the Softail by the traditional coil-over suspension, and from the Sportster by their larger engines.
Sportster	**Exhilarating ride with simple style** – introduced in 1957, the Sportster is Harley's longest-running model. Initially conceived as racing motorcycles for dirt and flat-track courses in the 1960s and 1970s, they are smaller and lighter than the other Harley models and, though often modified, still look similar to their racing ancestors.
VRSC	**Where power meets speed** – introduced in 2001, these bear little resemblance to Harley's more traditional models. They compete against Japanese and American muscle bikes and use an engine developed with Porsche. They are the platform around which Harley builds drag-racing competition machines and have an enthusiastic following in the USA, Europe and Australia.
Buell	**Because sitting is not a sport** – Buell Motorcycle Company was founded by ex-Harley engineer Erik Buell to make AMA Formula 1 road racing bikes. The company partnered with Harley in 1993, and then became a wholly owned subsidiary in 2003. However, in 2009 Harley decided to discontinue this product line to focus on its own brand.
MV Agusta	**High specification sports bikes** – founded in 1945 near Milan, Italy, it began as an offshoot of the Agusta aviation company. It produces a limited number of high-specification, expensive bikes that compete with other Italian models such as Ducati. Harley acquired the company in 2008 for US$109 million, but then subsequently sold it in 2009. In 2010, MV Agusta announced sales increased by 50 per cent in the first quarter.
Financial services	**Helping customers buy our products** – Harley also provides wholesale financing and insurance programmes for their dealers, and credit cards and loans for their customers to help them buy their products.

Figure 4 Number of models and suggested retail price by product group (2000–2010)

Product group	2000				2010			
	No. of models	Price ($000s)			No. of models	Price ($000s)		
		From	To	Mean		From	To	Mean
Sportster	6	5	9	7	7	7	11	9
Dyna	5	11	15	14	5	12	15	13
Softail	7	12	17	15	7	16	19	17
Touring	6	13	19	16	9	17	30	20
VRSC	-	-	-	-	3	15	17	16
Buell	4	9	13	11	7	9	13	11
Overall	**28**	**5**	**19**	**13**	**38**	**7**	**30**	**15**

Figure 5 Annual sales and profit by product group (1985–2010)

Product group	Annual performance (US$m)									
	1985	1990	1995	2000	2002	2004	2006	2008	2009	2010
Sales revenue										
HD Motorcycle	211	485	1038	2281	3161	3928	4554	4245	3175	3137
Buell Motorcycle	–	–	14	58	67	79	102	123	47	16
Parts	34	80	192	450	629	782	862	859	767	749
Merchandise	9	30	100	151	232	224	277	314	282	259
Defense	34	29	6	3	2	2	5	38	16	15
Financial services	–	–	–	140	212	305	385	377	495	683
Total	**288**	**624**	**1350**	**3083**	**4303**	**5320**	**6185**	**5956**	**4782**	**4859**
Profit										
Motorcycles	3	38	112	478	734	1137	1387	976	314	379
Financial services	-	-	-	38	105	188	211	83	(118)	182

Figure 6 Product groups manufactured and assembled in each plant (2010)

Plant	Manufacturing	Assembly
York	• Touring • Softail • General components	• Touring • Softail
Milwaukee (Capitol Drive)	• Sportster • Buell • Parts and accessories • Engine refurbishment	• Sportster
Milwaukee (Pilgrim Road)	• Twin Cam engines	–
Tomahawk	• Fiberglass parts • Windshields • Saddlebags	–
Kansas City	• Dyna • VRSC • Sportster	• Dyna • VRSC • Sportster
East Troy	• Buell	• Buell

THE FUTURE

Harley-Davidson's past growth and success has been built on loyal customers, some of whom tattoo its logo onto their bodies. But despite its rebellious image, its average customer is now a 47-year-old white male with a $84,300 annual salary! The huge bikes that drive most of its sales don't appeal to the younger generation (15 per cent of customers are under 35) or women (only 12 per cent are female); 52 per cent of its customers owned a Harley-Davidson earlier in their life, and the company needs to think about how to enter new markets. It has always been careful that production does not exceed demand and likes to keep its customers waiting 6–18 months for a new bike. In the past, this has helped maintain prices, so a year-old Harley usually costs 25–30 per cent more than a new one. Rather than cutting prices and offering financing like its competitors, Harley believes that cutting production is a better long-term strategy.

Figure 7 Geographic market size and share (1985–2010)

Sales by region	Motorcycles sold (000s)							
	1995	2000	2002	2004	2006	2008	2009	2010
Total market								
US	163	340	442	494	543	480	304	260
Europe	233	323	333	337	361	390	314	301
Japan & Australia	40	62	61	78	100	114	105	101
Other	1	38	37	62	106	6	13	15
Total	**437**	**763**	**873**	**971**	**1110**	**990**	**736**	**677**
Harley-Davidson								
US	77	155	210	243	268	218	162	143
Europe	17	23	24	26	34	41	38	38
Japan and Australia	8	13	14	18	23	25	23	30
Total	**102**	**191**	**248**	**287**	**325**	**284**	**223**	**211**

Notes: These figures are for motorcycles with engines greater than 650cc. Not all of Harley's products have engines greater than 650cc.

Figure 8 Main competitors (2005–2010)

Manufacturer	Europe (% market share)			US (% market share)		
	2005	2007	2010	2005	2007	2010
Harley-Davidson	9	10	13	48	48	55
Honda	13	12	12	17	14	13
Suzuki	13	17	18	13	13	12
Yamaha	16	14	13	9	9	8
Kawasaki	13	11	11	7	8	8
BMW	18	15	16	2	2	2
Other	18	21	17	3	5	2
Total market (millions units)	333	388	301	518	516	260

Note: These figures are for motorcycles with engines greater than 650cc.

Some analysts have debated whether this is the right decision for Harley, particularly given that its financing arm is still haemorrhaging cash. The questions that many critics have asked include: When will demand stop falling? Will it ever regain its market share? And can it successfully penetrate new markets?

2. How did it use 'continuous improvement' tools and techniques to turn the business around before?

3. What are the lessons from that turnaround that can be applied to its current situation?

Questions

1. What are the issues that Harley-Davidson faces today?

Lecturers: visit www.palgrave.com/business/hillom3e for teaching guidelines for this case study

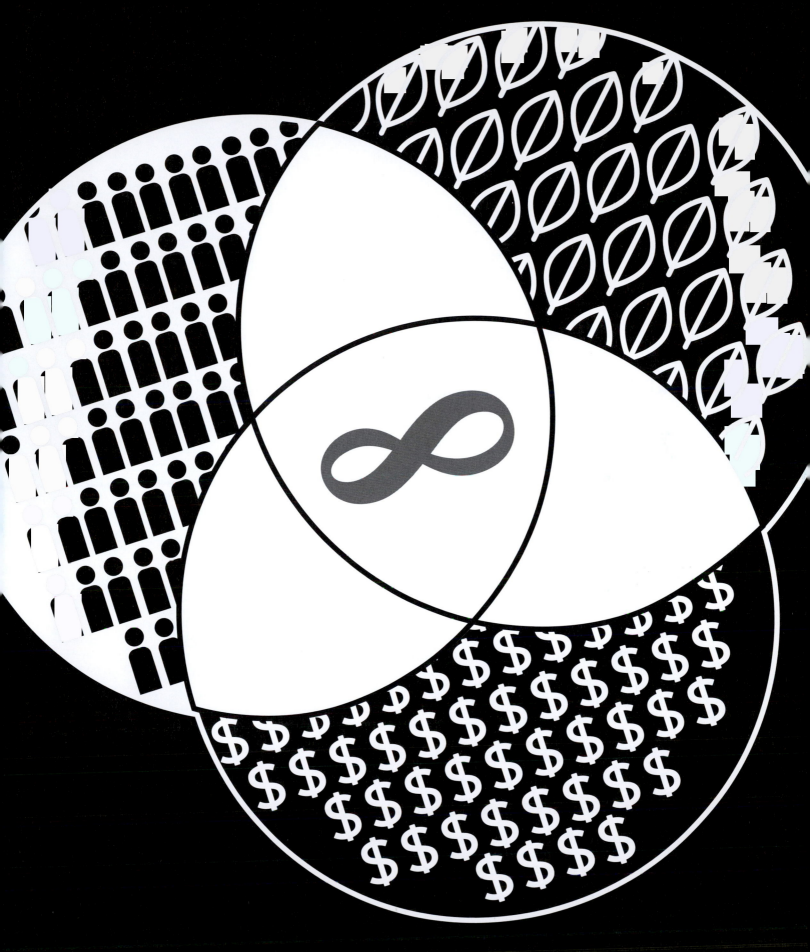

After completing this chapter, you should be able to:

- Explain what social and environmental initiatives can be undertaken within operations

- Understand the market pressure to implement social and environmental initiatives

- Critically evaluate the differing social and environmental initiatives undertaken by organizations

- Understand the benefits and criticisms of engaging in corporate social responsibility (CSR)

- Make a business case for implementing social and environmental initiatives within your organizational context

Chapter outline

What is the role of corporate social responsibility (CSR) within the business?

- It requires a firm to determine how it can meet the social, environmental and economic requirements of its various stakeholders without compromising future generations' ability to meet their own needs

- The social, environmental and economic responsibilities it needs to consider include:
  - **Social** – improving the impact on its employees and the communities in which it operates, for example by paying workers a fair salary, asking them to work reasonable hours within a safe environment, not using child labour, paying suppliers a fair price and promoting health care and education throughout the supply chain
  - **Environmental** – reducing the level of energy and non-renewable resources it consumes, the waste it produces and the environmental impact of the services and products it provides
  - **Economic** – increasing its economic value for society not only by the profit it makes, but also its contribution to the profits of the other entities with which it interacts

Why is corporate social responsibility important?

- It forces businesses not only to consider the short-term interests of their shareholders, but also to determine how to meet the long-term needs of all their stakeholders without compromising future generations' ability to meet their own needs

- Being able to meet customers' social and environmental expectations is typically an order-winner or qualifier in most markets as consumers are becomingly increasingly aware of social and environmental issues and are making choices based on ethical reasons

How does corporate social responsibility impact business performance?

- The potential benefits vary greatly depending on the nature of the organization and the initiatives being implemented. However, the business case for CSR usually rests on one or more of the following arguments:
  - **Reduced risk** – building a genuine culture of 'doing the right thing' can help prevent corporate reputations from being damaged and remove unwanted attention from regulators, courts, governments and the media
  - **Reduced costs** – by using less energy, minimizing waste and reducing materials and packaging
  - **Reduced government intervention** – undertaking substantial voluntary social and environmental initiatives can show local governments that the organization takes its responsibilities seriously and potentially reduces the level of taxation and regulation imposed on it
  - **Increased market access** – engaging a local society can open up new markets and opportunities
  - **Increased brand reputation** – by building a reputation for integrity and best practice
  - **Increased employee engagement** – adopting ethical practices can make it easier to recruit and retain good employees

What are the key issues to consider when improving corporate social responsibility?

- To understand the perceptions that exist within the markets that you serve and approach each market differently as customer perceptions of what constitutes 'ethical' business practice varies significantly between countries

- To educate consumers about the ethical practices that exist within your business as customers have different levels of awareness about ethical issues and how companies behave

- To develop social and environmental initiatives that positively impact all aspects of your operations such as:
  - Designing services and products
  - Delivering services and products
  - Managing capacity
  - Managing inventory
  - Managing quality
  - Managing the supply chain

- To ask yourself: 'Does our business have an overall positive impact on society given the environmental damage it creates in consuming precious resources to design and deliver its services and products?' If it doesn't, then work out how to change this

- Before developing and implementing CSR activities, you must:
  - **Identify the power and influence of key stakeholders** – who are they? What expectations do they have? What power or influence do they have within the organization? And, what conflicts exist between them?
  - **Determine the ethical stance** – is it driven by: only short-term shareholder interests? Longer-term shareholder interests? Its obligations to some or all of its stakeholders? Or, trying to shape society?

- Critics of CSR believe it is just a PR tool exploiting developing countries and hindering free-trade. Instead, they believe that:
  - **Governments** – should set the CSR agenda for all organizations, and
  - **Businesses** – should focus solely on increasing shareholder return

Introduction

Businesses are not only responsible for delivering services and making products, they are also responsible for the impact that those services and products have on society, the environment (both locally and as a whole) and the economy. Decisions such as where and how to source materials; how to ensure the safety of staff and consumers; how to measure and ensure appropriate ethical standards of suppliers; and how to limit the negative effects of delivery and manufacturing on the environment are some of the many corporate and social issues that companies must tackle when making products and delivering services. While policies must be decided at a corporate level, operations will inevitably be responsible for implementing and upholding them. This chapter will first define corporate social responsibility; it will then go on to look at how the needs of stakeholders, including suppliers, employees and customers, influence operations management. Next we will look at how corporate social responsibility affects each of the areas of operations that we've covered in the first 14 chapters of this book, before finally outlining some benefits and criticisms relating to corporate social responsibility policies.

A **multinational corporation** manages operations or delivers services or products in more than country.

Stakeholders are individuals or groups who depend on an organization to fulfil their own goals and on whom, in turn, the organization depends.

The **triple bottom line** framework is used by organizations to report their social, economic and environmental performance.

What is CSR?

The term corporate social responsibility (CSR) first came into use in the early 1970s with the emergence of **multinational corporations** and is often referred to in various ways such as corporate responsibility, corporate citizenship, responsible business, sustainable business and corporate social performance. The logic underpinning CSR is that companies need to meet the social, environmental and economic responsibilities of all their various **stakeholders** including their employees, consumers and the societies in which they operate. While there is no recognized standard, it is generally accepted that businesses should not only report their financial outcomes, but also their social and environmental performance using a framework such as the '**triple bottom line**' shown in Figure 15.1:

- **Social** – monitoring the impact of a business on its employee and the communities within which it operates, for example paying workers a fair salary, asking them to work reasonable hours within a safe environment, not using child labour, paying suppliers a fair price and promoting health care and education.

- **Environmental** – checking the environmental impact of a business, on both its immediate surroundings and also on a wider scale. For example, its consumption of energy and non-renewable resources, the level and toxicity of waste it produces and the 'cradle to grave' environmental impact of its products from their manufacture through to their eventual disposal after a consumer has finished with them.

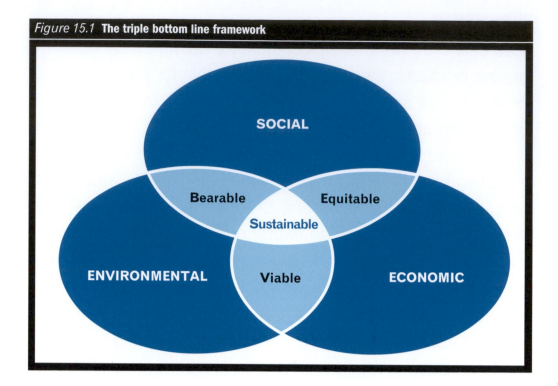

Figure 15.1 The triple bottom line framework

- **Economic** – ensuring an organization creates a positive economic value for society. This differs to the traditional accounting definition of profit as it looks at the real economic benefit to the society in which it operates by considering the profit it makes and also its contribution to the profits of the other entities with which it interacts.

If a firm integrates and meets all its social, environmental and economic responsibilities, then it can become truly **'sustainable'** and able to meet its stakeholders' needs without compromising future generations' ability to meet their own needs. A number of reporting guidelines have been developed to help companies do this such as:

- Accountability's AA1000 Standard

- Accounting for Sustainability's Connected Reporting Framework

- The Global Reporting Initiative's Sustainability Reporting Guidelines

- Social Accountability International's SA8000 Standard and

- The ISO 14000 Environmental Management Standard.

However, the level of adoption of such policies by companies varies significantly and the practice of CSR is subject to much debate and criticism. Supporters argue there is a strong business case for CSR as it provides a broader and better long-term future perspective than simply focusing on short-term profits. However, critics argue it detracts from the core economic role of a business, is nothing more than superficial window-dressing and is an attempt by governments to control powerful, multinational corporations. Although the **FTSE Group** now publishes the FTSE4Good Index (which was designed to measure the performance of companies that meet globally acknowledged standards for corporate responsibility and facilitates investment in those companies), agreement on meaningful social and environmental performance measures is difficult. Many companies now produce externally audited CSR reports, but they all have widely different formats, styles and methodologies and often do not reflect the actual social and environmental impacts of the business.

A **sustainable** business – meets the needs of its stakeholders without compromising future generations' ability to meet their own needs.

The **FTSE Group** – a private 50/50 joint venture between the Financial Times and London Stock Exchange Group. It publishes a number of indexes including the FTSE100 and FTSE4Good Index.

Meeting the needs of stakeholders

Before looking at how issues of corporate social responsibility affect the topics covered in previous chapters, let's examine how stakeholder needs are met. People are becoming more socially and environmentally aware and, as a result, businesses need to act more responsibly with all of their stakeholders from the people they employ to the customers they serve. Interest in business ethics accelerated dramatically during the 1980s and 1990s, and today most corporate websites mention their commitment to promoting social and environmental awareness under a variety of headings such as corporate and social responsibility. Some companies have even re-branded their core values in the light of ethical considerations, such as BP's 'beyond petroleum' environmental tilt. Companies need to consider the interests of all stakeholders when developing business strategy, so let's look at some key stakeholders in more detail.

> **Ethical services and products –** are designed and delivered with minimal harm or exploitation of humans, animals and the natural environment.

The ethical consumer

The market for **ethical services and products** is significant and growing. A 2009 study by the Co-op Bank found that many UK customers are becomingly increasingly aware of CSR issues and are spending their money for ethical reasons, as shown in Figure 15.2. In the past decade, consumer spending on ethical services and products grew five times as much as overall consumer spending. In particular, sales of Fairtrade goods and services grew 30 fold, energy efficient electrical appliances 12 fold, energy efficient boilers 9 fold and ethical banking and investments 3 fold. The total ethical markct is now estimated at £36 billion and the average UK household spends over three times more on ethical products and services than it did ten years ago (see Figure 15.3) with the largest amount spent on home products and services, followed by ethical food and drink (see Figure 15.4).

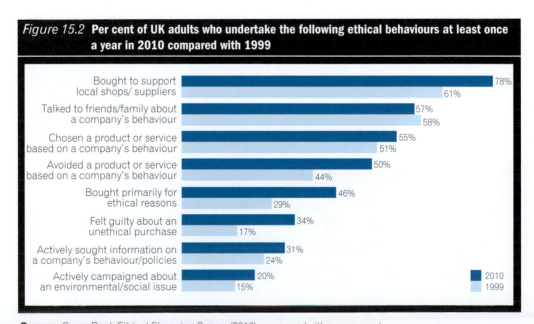

Figure 15.2 **Per cent of UK adults who undertake the following ethical behaviours at least once a year in 2010 compared with 1999**

Behaviour	2010	1999
Bought to support local shops/ suppliers	78%	61%
Talked to friends/family about a company's behaviour	57%	58%
Chosen a product or service based on a company's behaviour	55%	51%
Avoided a product or service based on a company's behaviour	50%	44%
Bought primarily for ethical reasons	46%	29%
Felt guilty about an unethical purchase	34%	17%
Actively sought information on a company's behaviour/policies	31%	24%
Actively campaigned about an environmental/social issue	20%	15%

Source: Co-op Bank Ethical Shopping Survey (2010) www.goodwithmoney.co.uk.

Source: Co-op UK Ethical Consumerism Report (2010) www.goodwithmoney.co.uk.

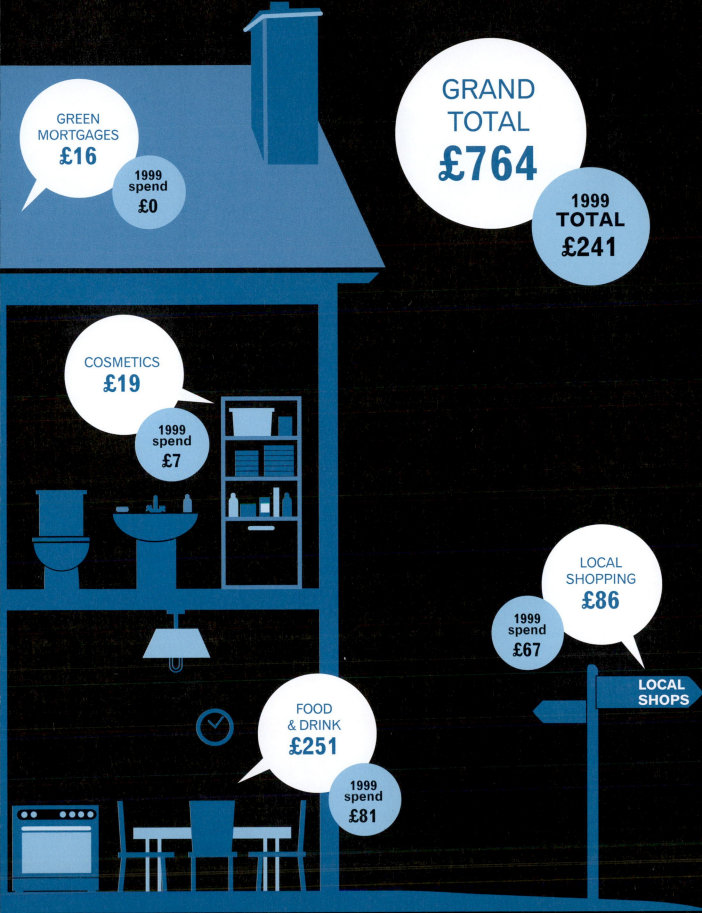

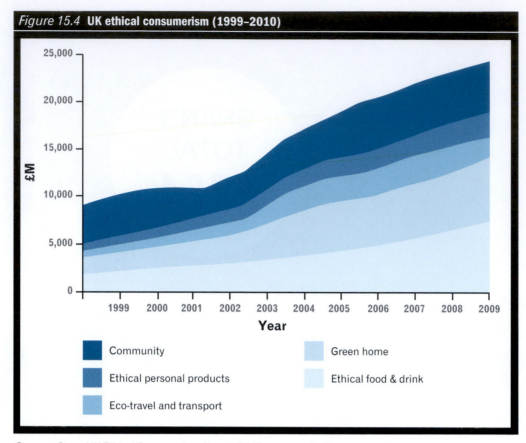

Figure 15.4 UK ethical consumerism (1999–2010)

Source: Co-op UK Ethical Consumerism Report (2010) www.goodwithmoney.co.uk.

> **EXECUTIVE INSIGHT**
> Consumers are becomingly increasingly aware of social and environmental issues and are spending money for ethical reasons. Being able to meet consumers' social and environmental expectations is, therefore, typically an order-winner or qualifier in most markets.

However, not all companies are signing up to the CSR initiative. A study conducted by GfK NOP, a market research company based in the UK, found differing consumer opinion and practice in France, Germany, Spain, the UK and the USA. Although a third of respondents were prepared to pay a 10 per cent premium for ethical products, most believed that the ethical behaviour of corporations had worsened in the past five years, a view particularly held by consumers in Germany and the USA. Although a third said they would pay a 5–10 per cent premium for ethical products, these ethical brands still only have very small market shares.

> **EXECUTIVE INSIGHT**
> Consumers are willing to pay more for ethical services and products when this is a market order-winner.

As shown in Figures 15.5 and 15.6, there are conflicting opinions about which companies are ethical and a worrying tendency to simply equate 'local' with 'ethical'. UK consumers were the most aware, critical and likely to see national brands such as the Co-op financial and retail group, or the Innocent drinks brand, as standard-bearers. Whereas, international companies such as Nike, criticized in the 1990s for its supplier relationships, or Nestlé, linked to controversies over its marketing in developing countries, were considered ethical in the other four countries despite their reported poor business practice, as described in Figure 15.7.

Consumers' perceptions of what constitutes 'ethical' business practice vary significantly across different countries. It is therefore critical to understand the perceptions that exist within the markets that you serve and approach each market differently.

The information presented in Figures 15.5, 15.6 and 15.7 shows a number of conflicting opinions and overall lack of consumer awareness of corporate behaviour in several ways:

- The top ethical brands identified by consumers differ widely across France, Germany, Spain, the UK and the USA.

- Of the 50 companies nominated (ten within each of the five countries) only eight were nominated within two or more countries and only five within three or more countries (as shown in Figure 15.6).

- The companies nominated within each country tend to originate from that country.

- Companies with well publicized poor practice (as shown in Figure 15.7) are still considered ethical in some countries.

Figure 15.5 **Top 10 most ethically perceived brands in France, Germany, Spain, the UK and the USA**

Rank	France	Germany	Spain	UK	USA
1	Danone	Adidas	Nestlé	Co-op	Coca-Cola
2	Adidas	Nike	Body Shop	Body Shop	Kraft
3	Nike	Puma	Coca-Cola	Marks & Spencer	Procter & Gamble
4	Nestlé	BMW	Danone	Traidcraft	Johnson & Johnson
5	Renault	Demeter	El Corte Inglés	Cafédirect	Kellogg's
6	Peugeot	Gepa	Adidas	Ecover	Nike
7	Philips	VW	Nike	Green & Blacks	Sony
8	Carrefour	Sony	Sony	Tesco	Ford
9	Coca-Cola	Trigema	L'Oréal	Oxfam	Toyota
10	L'Oréal	Bio Produkte	Mercedes	Sainsbury's	Levi

Source: GfK NOP, Publication date – March 2007, www.gfknop.com.

Figure 15.6 **Companies perceived as ethical in more than two countries within France, Germany, Spain, the UK and the USA**

Number of countries where perceived ethical	Company	Countries where perceived ethical				
		France	Germany	Spain	UK	USA
4	Nike	•	•	•		•
3	Adidas	•	•	•		
	Coca-Cola	•		•		•
	Sony		•	•		•
	Body Shop			•	•	
2	Danone	•		•		
	L'Oréal	•		•		
	Nestlé	•		•		

'All companies should strive for **zero footprint**'

Figure 15.7 Examples of poor social and environmental business practice

Company	Poor practice	Countries where company is considered ethical				
		France	Germany	Spain	UK	USA
Nike	Treatment of workers in foreign factories	•	•	•		•
Coca-Cola	Depletion of water supplies and pesticide residues in local Coke drinks in India	•			•	•
Walmart	Poverty wages to migrant workers in the USA					
Nestlé	Buying cocoa from Ivory Coast farms employing forced/child labour	•			•	

Note: Countries where these companies are considered ethical is based on the data in Figure 15.5.

> **EXECUTIVE INSIGHT**
> Consumers still have different levels of awareness about ethical issues and how companies behave. It is therefore important to educate consumers about the ethical practices that exist within your business.

Employee expectations

As we learned in the very first chapter, operations' key role is to manage people in order to deliver services and products successfully to its customers, but in the process it must also ensure that the welfare of those who deliver those services and products is preserved. This involves not only ensuring their physical safety from accidents in the workplace, but also making certain that they are not placed in situations that affect their mental health, and are well informed about business practices, the future of their jobs and the ethical, environmental and social outlook of the company.

Suppliers

An important part of operations management involves ensuring that the supply chain is efficient and fully integrated. However organizations also have to make important decisions about the ethical standards they will expect from their suppliers – including whether they will apply their own ethical expectations to the external supply chain. Auditing and managing the practices of suppliers falls under the responsibility of operations.

Developing social and environmental initiatives

As operations managers are typically responsible for managing the largest number of employees, designing and delivering services and products and managing the supply chain, they tend to be responsible for developing and implementing many of the social and environmental initiatives within an organization. Figure 15.8 shows some typical social and environmental developments within operations and these are then discussed in more detail.

Designing services and products

Organizations need to manage the social impact of their services and products, considering everything from the safety of the people who use them and the wider impact they have on society through to the benefits they bring versus the resources they use. For example, the environmental impact of a service or product can be reduced through initiatives such as

Herman Miller's use of recycled raw materials to reduce its **environmental footprint**, as described in Case 15.1.

> **EXECUTIVE INSIGHT**

Operations managers tend to play a key role in developing and implementing social and environmental initiatives as they:

- Usually manage the largest number of people within the business
- Design services and products that can have a lasting positive or negative impact on society and the environment
- Deliver services and products using key environmental resources
- Interact with customers and society in the delivery of services and products
- Manage the supply chain, which often has global social and environmental impact.

Figure 15.8 **Typical social and environmental developments within operations**

Operations aspect	Social developments	Environmental developments
Designing services and products	Customer safety Impact on society	Material recycled Energy used Waste generated Obsolete product disposal
Delivering services and products	Staff and customer safety Staff and customer access Hazardous materials	Resources used Energy used Waste generated Waste disposal
Managing capacity	Employment policies	Energy used Waste generated
Managing inventory	Price manipulation Warehouse safety	Material obsolescence Waste generated Product obsolescence
Managing quality	Customer and staff safety	Material scrap and waste Energy waste
Managing the supply chain	Employment policies across the chain Fair pricing Non-exploitation of developing countries Transportation congestions	Resources used Energy used Transportation emissions Packaging

Furthermore, it is necessary to consider not only the resources used and waste created in the design and delivery of services and products, but also the use and eventual disposal by consumers. Businesses are increasingly expected to provide a means for recycling the products they produce, and to make available information on the materials and energy used in delivering services, and creating and using products. For example, Apple estimates the breakdown of the total environmental impact of its products as:

- 53 per cent while it is being used by its customers

- 38 per cent during its manufacture

- 5 per cent during its transportation

- 3 per cent within its retail outlets

- 1 per cent recycling at the end of the product life.

As described in Case 15.2, Apple produces a report showing the complete environmental footprint for each of its products so that customers can see how each one affects the planet.

CASE 15.1 HERMAN MILLER: CHANGING PRODUCTION PROCESSES AND WORKING WITH SUPPLIERS TO BECOME SUSTAINABLE

Walker's belief in the increasing importance of sustainability to buyers has proven true. Herman Miller found that sustainability is not only a desirable feature, but has come to be expected by its customers and its employees are now motivated to try to make Herman Miller's products as sustainable as possible. The company uses recycled materials for interior furniture parts such as drawers, while also developing materials for exterior parts that will meet with customers' aesthetic expectations. The company has also reduced its environmental impact by restricting the types of materials, chemicals and compounds its suppliers can use. For example wood is only sourced from sustainable forests. The company is also starting to analyze how green its operations are, with aims to minimize waste and greenhouse gases produced during the manufacturing process.

**www.hermanmiller.co.uk/
Environmental-concerns.aspx**

Sources: Herman Miller, www.hermanmiller.com; Brian Walker and Josette Akresh-Gonzales (2009) 'Herman Miller CEO Brian Walker on meeting sustainability goals – with customers' help', *Harvard Business Review*, 1 December,

Herman Miller is famous for furnishing modern offices with design icons such as the Eames desk chair. However, when Brian Walker became CEO in 2004, he vowed to reduce the company's environmental footprint aiming to produce no landfill waste, hazardous waste or manufacturing emissions and to use only 'green energy' by the year 2020, as part of the company's 'Perfect Vision' programme. As he explains, 'If your ambition is lofty enough – and if you measure your progress – you eventually figure out a way to get close to it.' For Walker, strategy-making is not a formulaic process, but sometimes involves a leap of faith: 'Often you simply start with a belief, or maybe just an inkling, and if you're lucky, the evidence starts to pile up that you were right. In hindsight, people outside the company think you had a great business plan, but all you had was a belief.'

Questions

1. How is Herman Miller trying to reduce its environmental footprint? How could its approach be applied to a different business context?

2. Why does this approach take a 'leap of faith'?

3. Can you think of any potentially negative consequences of this approach?

4. Compare and contrast 'Perfect Vision' with another sustainability initiative you know about.

Lecturers: visit www.palgrave.com/business/hillom3e for teaching guidelines for this case study

CASE 15.2 APPLE ESTIMATES THE COMPLETE ENVIRONMENTAL FOOTPRINT OF ITS PRODUCTS

© instamatics

Apple estimates the total environmental impact of its products as:

Source of environmental impact		% total impact
Apple activities	Manufacture of products	38
	Transportation to stores and customers	5
	Retail outlets	3
	Total	**46**
Customer activities	Customer using products	53
	Recycling at end of product life	1
	Total	**54**

For each product that Apple sells, the company provides a 'Product Environmental Report' which documents the emissions generated during its manufacture, distribution and use. As you can see from the table above, a high percentage of emissions results from the use of the product by the customer. Because of this Apple focuses heavily on designing each product to be as energy efficient as possible and gives customers guidelines on how best to use it.

Source: www.apple.com/environment/complete-lifecycle

www.apple.com/environment

Questions

1. Where should Apple focus its efforts to reduce the environmental impact of its products?

2. What sort of measures could it take to do this?

Lecturers: visit www.palgrave.com/business/hillom3e for teaching guidelines for this case study

Delivering services and products

One of the areas where an organization makes the greatest impact on the environment is through the facilities and processes it uses in delivering its products and services. However, this impact can be minimized through initiatives such as Herman Miller's aim to produce no 'land fill waste' by 2020 (see Case 15.1) and Veja's use of green electricity in its French headquarters and ethical practices in its Brazilian factories such as not having child workers, having good working conditions and fair working hours (see Case 15.3).

> An organization disposes of **land fill waste** by burying it in the ground.

Managing capacity

Operations must be managed using fair employment practices that minimize the energy used and waste generated. For example, Veja ensures its employees have fair wage levels, while most also own their own homes (see Case 15.3).

Managing inventory

Poorly managed inventory can lead to material or product obsolescence and waste generation that has a negative environmental impact. Equally, poor warehouse management and unethical price manipulation can have a negative impact on both employees and society as a whole.

Managing quality

As with inventory, inadequate quality management wastes resources and puts the safety of both employees and customers at risk.

Managing the supply chain

Firms also have a significant impact on society and the environment through the design and management of their supply chain. Firms need to recognize this as part of their overall responsibility and take appropriate steps to help reduce the environmental impact of their suppliers' activities. For example, Herman Miller restricts the types of materials, chemicals and compounds its suppliers can use (see Case 15.1), while Apple has made its packaging smaller to reduce the environmental impact of its supply chain (see Case 15.2) and Veja use boats and barges to transport its products (see Case 15.3). Equally, companies such as Green & Blacks, Starbucks and Marks & Spencer all have fair trade practices in place with some or all of their suppliers. However, rather then just looking at tier 1 suppliers, some companies have also started looking across their supply networks. For example, Pfizer's employees work on six-month projects with **non-governmental organizations** and governments to tackle health care issues, while Ernst and Young's employees work on three-month projects with entrepreneurs to improve their strategies and business operations (see Case 15.4).

> A **non-governmental organization** pursues a social or political objective, but operates independently from any government.

> **EXECUTIVE INSIGHT**
>
> All operations management aspects have a significant impact on society and the environment. A key question to ask is:
>
> 'Does our business have an overall positive impact on society given the environmental damage it creates in consuming precious resources to design and deliver its services and products?'

Implementing social and environmental initiatives

Like many other management initiatives, successfully implementing CSR activities requires a number of key steps including:

CASE 15.3 VEJA: BUILDING A SOCIAL AND ENVIRONMENTAL SUPPLY CHAIN

Veja is not only concerned about designing and producing a stylish shoe, but also delivering it through a social and environmental supply chain using three main principles:

- Using ecological materials
- Paying a fair price
- Respecting workers' dignity.

Examples of some of the actions it has taken are described below:

PAY A FAIR PRICE

The company buys organic cotton from small producers in Northeast Brazil using fair trade rules and long-term commitments. Leather and suede are produced in South Brazil by a tannery pioneering ecological tanning processes. Its ecological leather is chromium free and tanned with natural extracts, and it uses wild rubber from the Amazonian forest that helps increase the value of the forest and preserve it. It pays twice the market price and this is not impacted by world market price fluctuations, which are strongly influenced by European and North American subsidies.

NO ADVERTISING

This saves resources and means that farmers and producers are fairly remunerated in line with their social and environmental requirements. Although Veja's fabrication costs are seven to eight times higher than other footwear brands, its 'no advertising' policy makes it possible to sell trainers at a comparable price to its competitors.

NO INVENTORY

Production is tightly controlled with orders placed six months in advance. No extra inventory is made and production has to adapt to the availability of organic cotton, which can vary and often results in the company not meeting all its retailers' orders.

ENVIRONMENTAL TRANSPORTATION

To reduce CO_2 emissions, trainers are transported by boat from Porto Alegre in Brazil to Le Havre in France. After arriving in Le Havre, they travel by barge along the canals to the Parisian suburbs. All packaging is made of recycled and recyclable cardboard, the shoe-box was made smaller in 2002 to optimize efficiency and it uses ENERCOOP (a cooperative of green electricity) in its headquarters in Paris.

ETHICAL PRODUCTION

Trainers are made in a factory located in South Brazil under the following principles: no child workers, good working conditions, fair wages, fair working hours and good living conditions for the workers. One result is that many employees are able to buy their own homes.

www.veja.fr

Questions

1. How is Veja trying to build a social and environmental supply chain?

2. What are the advantages and disadvantages of its approach?

Lecturers: visit www.palgrave.com/business/hillom3e for teaching guidelines for this case study

CASE 15.4 SOCIAL INITIATIVES: PFIZER AND ERNST & YOUNG

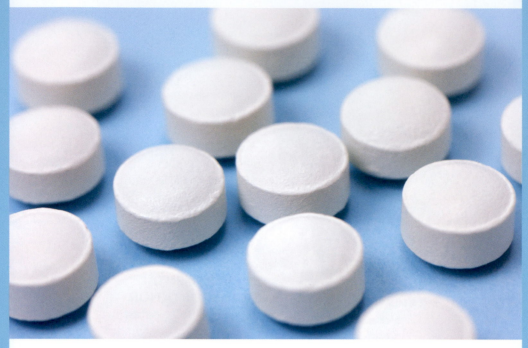

© istockphoto.com/Creativeye99

Pfizer, the US pharmaceutical firm, created the Global Health Fellowship in 2002 where its employees work as nurses, doctors, teachers, business consultants and epidemiologists with non-governmental organizations and governments to tackle health care issues and combat diseases in Asia, Latin America and Eastern Europe. Each project lasts for up to six months with all expenses paid for by Pfizer.

The company has found that these projects are not only good for the countries involved, but also provided a unique development opportunity for their Global Health Fellows, teaching them new skills and allowing them to practise these. Since 2003, 194 Global Health Fellows have worked in 38 countries with organizations such as the International AIDS Vaccine Initiative, US Agency for International Development, Transatlantic Partners Against AIDS, Family Health International, the American Cancer Society and CARE International.
www.pfizer.com/responsibility/global_health/global_health_fellows.jsp

Ernst & Young, the US management consultancy firm, created the Corporate Responsibility Fellows Program, with employees volunteering as consultants, using their skills and knowledge to help entrepreneurs in Central and South America improve their strategies and business operations. Each project lasts for three months and Ernst & Young provided funding and support, as well as partnering with Endeavor Global to match employee expertise with entrepreneurs' needs. The company found that the programmes not only benefit the entrepreneurs, but also develop their employee skills, leadership capabilities and experience.
www.ey.com

Questions

1. How do these initiatives benefit these businesses and the organizations they work with?

2. Why is it important for the initiatives to benefit both partners?

Lecturers: visit www.palgrave.com/business/hillom3e for teaching guidelines for this case study

1. **Gain senior management commitment** – to develop and implement social and environmental initiatives. Critical to this is making a clear business case showing the expected impact of the proposed CSR activities on the business and its key stakeholders.

2. **Identify the power and influence of key stakeholders** – using the stakeholder map to show who they are; what expectations they have; what power or influence they have within the organization; and what conflicts exist between different stakeholders.

3. **Determine the ethical stance** – that the business wishes to take. Should it be driven solely by short-term shareholder interests? Should it consider longer-term shareholder interests? Should it try to meet its obligations to some or all of its stakeholders? Or should it be a shaper of society?

4. **Develop a social and environmental policy** – and identify those aspects on which to focus. There needs to be benefit for both the business and its stakeholders to ensure that the initiatives have longevity.

5. **Set objectives and targets** – for each aspect within the social and environmental policy.

6. **Establish a programme** – to implement the social and environmental initiatives with clear resources and responsibilities allocated to each task.

7. **Train employees** – so as to raise awareness of the issues to be faced and develop the skills required to implement the initiatives.

8. **Implement the changes** – in line with the programme.

9. **Monitor and measure** – the improvements gained from the initiatives for all the stakeholders impacted by the programme.

> **EXECUTIVE INSIGHT**

The approach to managing the social and environmental impact of an operation depends on its ethical stance and the power/influence of its stakeholders:

- **Stakeholders** – Who are they? What expectations do they have? What power or influence do they have within the organization? And, what conflicts exist between them?
- **Ethical stance** – Is it driven by: only short-term shareholder interests? Longer-term shareholder interests? Its obligations to some or all of its stakeholders? Or, trying to shape society?

The benefits of social and environmental initiatives

The potential benefits available to an organization vary greatly depending on its nature and the initiatives being implemented. For example, some companies simply consider it sufficient to cover charitable efforts and volunteering, while others see it as key to their human resource, business development and public relations strategies, while yet others see it to be of sufficient importance to have its own department that reports directly to the CEO. Although research has shown a correlation between social and environmental performance and financial performance (Orlitzky et al., 2003)[1], the business case for CSR usually rests on one or more of the following arguments:

- **Reduces risk** – corporate reputations take decades to build and hours to ruin through incidents such as corruption scandals or environmental accidents. Building a genuine culture of 'doing the right thing' can offset these risks and remove unwanted attention from regulators, courts, governments and the media.

- **Reduces inefficiencies** – initiatives such as using less energy, minimizing waste and reducing materials and packaging all, in turn, can lead to significantly fewer inefficiencies. For example, by modifying its packaging, Walmart has cut its shipping costs by $2.4 million and its raw material consumption by the equivalent of 3,800 trees and 1 million barrels of oil (see Case 15.5). Similarly, UPS reduced its operating costs by $500 million through improving the accuracy of the customer addresses used by marketers and getting them to use recyclable materials that do not jam their mail-sorting machines (see Case 15.5).

- **Reduces government intervention** – by undertaking substantial voluntary steps, companies can persuade governments and societies that they take seriously issues such as health, safety, diversity and the environment. This, in turn, can help reduce the level of governmental interference in their business through aspects such as taxation and regulation.

- **Increases market access** – engaging a local society with your business and your services or products can open up new markets and opportunities. For example, Unilever uses women entrepreneurs to sell its products in rural Indian villages. This channel now accounts for 25 per cent of its rural sales with 100,000 entrepreneurs serving 600 million people in 500,000 villages (see Case 15.6).

- **Increases brand reputation** – several major brands such as The Co-operative Group, The Body Shop and American Apparel are built on ethical values. Service organizations can similarly benefit from building a reputation for integrity and best practice.

- **Increases employee engagement** – making a business a more ethical place in which to work and engaging employees with the local community through fundraising and volunteering activities makes it easier to recruit and retain good employees.

> **EXECUTIVE INSIGHT**
> The business case for CSR is usually based on one or more of the following:
> - **Reducing** – risk, inefficiencies and/or government intervention
> - **Increasing** – market access, brand reputation and/or employee engagement.

Criticisms of social and environmental initiatives

Despite the potential benefits of corporate social responsibility initiatives, the purpose and motivation of a business engaging in them is often criticized for the following reasons:

- **Seen as just a public relations (PR) tool** – critics suggest that companies use CSR programmes to increase their reputation while trying to distract from their products' negative impact on society and the environment.

- **Can exploit developing countries and hinder free-trade** – some believe that in developing countries these practices are a form of economic and cultural imperialism, claiming that the lower labour protection that exists in such countries allows them to be exploited by multinational corporations. However, CSR supporters such as the REALeadership Alliance and Economic Justice For All believe corporations have a responsibility to change the world for the better and should play an active role in developing these countries.

- **Governments, not businesses, should set the CSR agenda** – critics argue that government legislation and regulation should ensure businesses act responsibly rather than allowing organizations to decide what constitutes 'responsible' behaviour. However, CSR supporters argue that regulation is unable to cover all a corporation's operations and would place a large financial burden on a nation's economy.

- **Businesses should focus on shareholder return** – still others argue that although corporations should obey the laws of the countries in which they work, they have no other obligations to those societies. However, CSR supporters point out that these initiatives can improve a firm's long-term profitability by reducing risk and inefficiency while increasing **brand reputation** and **employee engagement**.

Public relations (PR) – the public relations (PR) function within a business manages its public image through methods such as the media.

Brand reputation – the public perception or evaluation of an organization.

Employee engagement – the level of commitment of employees to a company's strategy, mission or purpose.

CASE 15.5 REDUCED INEFFICIENCIES FROM ENVIRONMENTAL INITIATIVES: WALMART AND UPS

Since October 2005, Walmart has been working with its suppliers to make electronic products that use less energy and can be easily recycled. It has also launched an environmental policy with all its suppliers instructing them to use energy from renewable sources and minimize waste on packaging. Alongside this, it also intends to reduce its truck fleet's CO_2 emissions by 20 per cent, the energy used at its stores by 30 per cent and the waste from its stores by 25 per cent, by 2012.

The packaging reductions achieved in 2006 have alone cut its shipping costs by $2.4 million and its raw material consumption by the equivalent of 3,800 trees and 1 million barrels of oil. In the same year, installing auxiliary power units to its fleet of 7,200 trucks saved $26 million in fuel costs and it now uses its own electricity company to supply its own stores with an annual saving of $15million.

However, despite these improvements, it still has its critics. Walmart Watch, a campaigning organization supported by groups including the National Council of Women's Organizations, commented in a report in 2007: 'If Walmart continues to add stores at its current growth rate, its new stores alone will use significantly more energy than it has saved. Also, its out-of-town stores are responsible for over 40 per cent of the increase in vehicles miles travelled by American households for shopping purposes in the last ten years.'

It was costing the United Postal Service (UPS) a significant amount of money to deliver 'direct marketing mail' to the wrong customers (who then threw it away) or to dispose of mail that was improperly addressed. It therefore decided to look at the entire 'direct marketing mail' supply chain from the point at which marketers identified customers to target through to customers acting on the mail they received.

As a result, it developed a system for helping marketers target specific customers with accurate addresses and tested a number of materials to help mailers use recyclable materials that would not jam mail-sorting machines. This led to a $500 million saving for UPS, eliminated unnecessary printing and increased response rates.

www.walmart.com; www.ups.com

Sources: Walmart Watch, 'It's not easy being green – The truth about Walmart's Environmental makeover', September 2007, www.walmartwatch.org. Retrieved 18 August 2010.

Questions

1. How have these organizations reduced the environmental impact of their business?

2. What can other organizations learn from this approach?

3. Review the stages in the UPS 'direct marketing mail' supply chain. How is this different to other mail supply chains?

Lecturers: visit www.palgrave.com/business/hillom3e for teaching guidelines for this case study

CASE 15.6 UNILEVER: INCREASED MARKET ACCESS THROUGH SOCIAL INITIATIVES

Hindustan Unilever Limited (HUL), India's largest fast-moving consumer goods (FMCG) company, launched its rural initiative 'Project Shakti' in 2001 aimed at improving the overall standard of living of more than 100 million rural consumers by 2005. The initiative used an innovative distribution model to reach these customers by collaborating with state governments. Products were made in small businesses run by women entrepreneurs who then sold them along with their other self-made or cooperative products.

By the end of 2005, over 25,000 women entrepreneurs were earning twice the average household income as a result of this initiative. Products were also being sold in new areas that were previously inaccessible as they were too expensive to supply. By the end of 2006, 'Project Shakti' had broken even and accounted for 8 per cent of all HUL's sales, and 25 per cent of its rural sales. By 2010, it was working with 100,000 entrepreneurs serving 600 million people in 500,000 villages.

www.hul.co.in

Questions

1. How have Unilever's social initiatives helped it penetrate new markets?

2. What can other organizations learn from this approach?

Lecturers: visit www.palgrave.com/business/ hillom3e for teaching guidelines for this case study

Corporate social responsibility in practice

When developing and implementing social and environmental initiatives in practice, it is important to consider the following aspects:

- **Understand the requirements of your key stakeholders** – to understand their social, environmental and economic needs, the level of power and influence they have within the organization and what conflicts exist between them.

- **Determine your ethical strategy** – do you want to focus on:
  - *Short-term shareholder interests* – such as market share, sales revenue and profit
  - *Longer-term shareholder interests* – such as future market share, sales revenue and profit, while accepting that the business may perform less well in the short term to achieve these objectives
  - *Other stakeholder requirements* – by considering not only the short-term and long-term financial requirements of your shareholders and looking at the needs of your employees, suppliers, customers and the societies and environments in which you operate
  - *Shaping and changing society* – while the three stances above are market-driven strategies, this is a market-driving approach that involves helping to shape and change the societies and environments in which you operate. For example, do you want to design and deliver services or products that will transform how societies and environments function? Or do you want to manage employees and suppliers in ways that will challenge and change the approaches used by other organizations?

- **Develop a business case for CSR** – to win management support for investing time and money in social and environmental initiatives. Otherwise, the CSR budget will be cut as soon as there is pressure to use this time and money elsewhere in the business. In particular, it is important to show the expected financial impact of the initiatives, such as:
  - *Increase sales revenue* – by winning new ethical customers or increasing market access by engaging a local community
  - *Reduce material costs* – by using less energy, minimizing waste and reducing materials and packaging
  - *Reduce labour costs* – by having more engaged employees who are easier to recruit and retain.

- **Understand stakeholder definitions of 'ethical'** – too often, stakeholders (in particular, customers) still confuse 'ethical' with 'local'. Therefore, you need to understand the different definitions used by your stakeholders in varying situations. In particular, you need to identify the definitions of:
  - *Customers* – those you currently support and wish to support in the future
  - *Employees* – within your current and future facilities
  - *Suppliers* – within your current and future supply chains.

- **Adapt your approach for each market, facility and supply chain** – to reflect the different 'ethical' perceptions of the various stakeholders that exist. For example:
  - *Markets* – for the differing customer perceptions
  - *Facilities* – for the differing employee perceptions
  - *Supply chains* – for the differing supplier perceptions.

- **Focus on areas of maximum impact** – the business case will help you identify the expected cost (time and money) and benefit (financial and non-financial) of each of the social and environmental initiatives proposed. It is important to then use this information to focus on the areas where you have the largest impact for the minimum cost.

Driving business performance

Releasing cash

Social and environmental initiatives tend to have little or no impact on releasing cash from the business. However, they tend to help improve supplier relationships, which in turn may:

- **Reduce inventory** – improved information and material might help improve suppliers' lead-times and delivery reliability, which means that lower levels of inventory need to be held in-house.

- **Increase creditors** – as more favourable payment terms can be negotiated. However, the opposite may also be true as these more favourable payment terms for suppliers may be considered more ethical.

Improving market support

Social and environmental initiatives can help improve market support in the following ways:

- **Ethical customers** – when social and environmental issues are an order-winner, customers are prepared to spend more money for ethical services and products.

- **Non-ethical customers** – even when social and environmental issues are not an order-winner, they are increasingly a qualifier in many markets.

- **Increase market access** – engaging a local society can increase customer understanding, which can then open up new markets and opportunities.

Reducing costs

The main way CSR activities can drive business performance is to reduce costs, risks and government intervention:

- **Material costs** – by using less energy, minimizing waste and reducing materials and packaging.

- **Labour costs** – by having more engaged employees that are easier to recruit and retain.

- **Risk** – by building a genuine culture of 'doing the right thing', which can help prevent corporate reputations being damaged and remove unwanted attention from regulators, courts, governments and the media.

- **Government intervention** – by undertaking substantial voluntary social and environmental initiatives, companies can persuade governments they take their responsibilities seriously. As a result, the level of taxation and regulation imposed on them may be reduced.

Critical reflections

People are becoming more aware of social and environmental issues and, as a result, businesses need to act more responsibly with regard to their stakeholders from the people they employ to the customers they serve. However, although the market for ethical goods and services is significant and growing, consumers' perceptions of what constitutes 'ethical' business practice varies significantly across different countries as they still have different levels of awareness about 'ethical' issues and how companies behave. Part of the problem is the lack of agreement of meaningful social and environmental performance measures and the different formats of companies' CSR reports, which often don't reflect the actual social and environmental impacts of their business.

Despite this, there is no doubting the growing awareness of ethical issues and support of consumers for ethical services and products. Whether the change will be driven by consumers, governments or businesses themselves is still not clear, but we do know that CSR is becoming increasingly important. Operations managers continually need to try to recycle more materials, use less packaging and provide sustainable improvements that will ensure the future environmental, social and economic success of the communities in which they operate.

Some organizations are taking this challenge seriously and are trying to shape society rather than simply responding to the needs of their stakeholders. However, as with most business initiatives, this approach takes a leap of faith that this is the right approach for managing and developing organizations. As Brian Walker, Herman Miller's CEO, reflects, 'Pushing current boundaries starts with a belief in what needs and should be done.' To make this belief a reality governments, businesses and consumers need to work together to challenge social and environmental behaviour and set new targets to ensure the prosperity of future generations.

Summary

People are becoming more socially and environmentally aware and, as a result, businesses need to act more responsibly with all of their stakeholders from the people they employ to the customers they serve. Interest in business ethics accelerated dramatically during the 1980s and 1990s, and today most corporate websites mention their commitment to promoting social and environmental awareness under a variety of headings such as corporate social responsibility. Some companies have even re-branded their core values in the light of ethical considerations, such as BP's 'beyond petroleum' environmental tilt.

Corporate social responsibility

Since it first came into use in the early 1970s, the term corporate social responsibility (CSR) has been referred to in several different ways. It essentially requires companies to report their social, environmental and economic impact, often known as the 'triple bottom line'. The belief is that if a firm meets all three of these obligations, then it can become truly sustainable and be able to meets its stakeholders' needs without compromising future generations' ability to meet their own needs.

The ethical consumer

The market for ethical goods and services is significant and growing. However, not all companies are responding to meet these needs and, interestingly, consumers in different countries have conflicting opinions of which companies are ethical and a worrying tendency to simply equate 'local' with 'ethical'. This often makes it difficult for global businesses to be considered ethical within all of their markets.

Developing social and environmental initiatives

The operations manager is often responsible for developing many of the social and environmental initiatives within an organization because they typically manage the largest number of employees, design and deliver services and products and manage the supply chain. Throughout the chapter, a range of activities have been given to illustrate the initiatives taken by companies from the use of recycled materials and less packaging to social and business-related activities designed to provide sustainable improvements in the welfare and economic growth of communities. For example, to reduce the environmental impact of their operations:

- Herman Miller – uses recycled raw materials (Case 15.1)

- Apple – improved the efficiency of its products and reduced their size of packaging (Case 15.2)

- Veja – uses green electricity in its French headquarters to transport its products with boats and barges (Case 15.3).

Equally, companies have developed a number of social initiatives such as:

- Veja – the employees in its Brazilian factories have decent wages and most own their own home (Case 15.3)

- Pfizer – its employees work on six-month projects with non-governmental organizations and governments to tackle health care issues (Case 15.4)

- Ernst & Young – its employees work on three-month projects with entrepreneurs to improve their strategies and business operations (Case 15.5)

- Shell – has an Early Learning Centre in the Flower Valley, South Africa, to educate children and adults within the community

- Marks & Spencer – guarantees fair prices to its suppliers.

Implementing social and environmental initiatives

To implement these initiatives successfully, a company must:

- Gain senior management commitment for developing and implementing social and environmental initiatives

- Identify the power and influence of its key stakeholders

- Determine the ethical stance it wishes to take

- Develop a social and environmental policy identifying the aspects it wishes to focus on

- Set objectives and targets for each aspect outlined in the policy

- Establish a programme to implement the policy

- Train employees to raise awareness and develop the skills required to implement the policy

- Implement the policy

- Monitor and measure the improvements gained from the policy.

Benefits from social and environmental initiatives

The potential benefits vary depending on the nature of the organization and the initiatives being implemented. However, the case for CSR usually rests on one or more of the following arguments:

- Reduce risk by building a genuine culture of 'doing the right thing'
- Reduce inefficiencies by using less energy and minimizing waste, materials and packaging
- Increase market access by engaging a community with your business and your product or service
- Increase brand reputation by building a reputation for integrity and best practice
- Increase employee engagement by making it an ethical place to work
- Reduce government intervention by taking issues such as health and safety, diversity or the environment seriously.

Criticisms of social and environmental initiatives

Despite the potential benefits they bring, these initiatives are often criticized for the following reasons:

- Seen as just a PR tool to raise a company's reputation and distract from negative social and environmental impacts
- Can exploit developing countries and hinder free trade in developing countries
- Governments, not businesses, should set the CSR agenda
- Businesses should focus on shareholder return and have no other obligations to society.

Study activities

Discussion questions

1. A consumer electronics retailer wishes to reduce the social and environmental impact of one of its stores. What actions would you suggest?

2. Explain the difference between CSR and sustainable development.

3. Why do consumers have varying perceptions of what constitutes 'ethical practice'?

4. Describe the social and environmental developments that can be made using operations with which you are familiar.

5. What are the steps involved in successfully implementing CSR activities within an organization? Illustrate them with examples with which you are familiar, explaining the key issues involved at each step.

6. What are the potential benefits and criticisms of social and environmental initiatives? Compare and contrast them using companies or case studies with which you are familiar.

Assignments

1. Identify the stakeholders of an organization and map their power/influence. Review their CSR activities to date. To what extent have they been affected by the power/influence of their stakeholders?

2. Critically evaluate the CSR activities of a company of your choice. Identify the gaps that exist and propose recommendations to address these.

3. Compare the annual reports of two public companies working within the same industry. How much of the report discusses their CSR initiative? How does this vary between the two organizations? What does this tell you about these two businesses?

4. Compare the annual reports of two public companies working within different industries. How much of the report discusses their CSR initiative? How does this vary between the two organizations? What does this tell you about the different industries within which they operate?

Exploring further

TED talks

Agassi, S. (2009) *Bold plan for electric cars*. Shai Agassi discusses his radical plan to make entire countries oil-free by 2020.
www.ted.com/talks/shai_agassi_on_electric_cars.html

Gore, A. (2009) *Warns on latest climate trends*. Al Gore presents updated slides from around the globe to make the case that worrying climate trends are even worse than scientists predicted, and to make clear his stance on 'clean coal'.
www.ted.com/talks/al_gore_warns_on_latest_climate_trends.html

JR (2011) *Use art to turn the world inside out.* JR, a semi-anonymous French street artist, uses his camera to show the world its true face, by pasting photos of the human face across massive canvases. At TED2011, he makes his audacious TED Prize wish: to use art to turn the world inside out. Learn more about his work and how you can join in at insideoutproject.net.
www.ted.com/talks/lang/eng/jr_s_ted_prize_wish_use_art_to_turn_the_world_inside_out.html

Pugh, L. (2010) *Mind-shifting Everest swim*. Lewis Pugh vowed never to take another cold-water dip after he swam to the North Pole. Then he heard of Lake Pumori created by recent glacial melting at an altitude of 5,300 m on Everest, and so began a journey that would teach him a radical new way to approach swimming and think about climate change.
www.ted.com/talks/lewis_pugh_s_mind_shifting_mt_everest_swim.html

Steffen, A. (2011) *The shareable future of cities*. How can cities help save the future? Alex Steffen shows some cool neighbourhood-based green projects that expand our access to things we want and need while reducing the time we spend in cars.
www.ted.com/talks/alex_steffen.html

Journal articles

Austin, J.E. and Leonard, H.B. (2008) 'Can the virtuous mouse and the happy elephant live happily ever after?' *California Management Review*, **51**(1): 77–102. This article looks at three recent examples of giant multinational corporations acquiring relatively small companies that have iconic status as socially progressive brands. The examples analyzed are: Unilever purchasing Ben & Jerry's, Colgate acquiring Tom's of Maine and Groupe Danone buying Stonyfield Farm Yogurt.

Chouinard, Y., Ellison, J. and Ridgeway, R. (2011) 'The sustainable economy', *Harvard Business Review*, **89**(10): 52–62. This article discusses three trends: (1) Accounting for natural resources (2) Investing in socially responsible activities (3) Measuring sustainability.

Correa, M.E. (2007) 'Leading Change in Latin America', *Harvard Business Review*, **85**(10): 40–42. The study of the changes made at Masisa, a $886 million forestry and wood-manufacturing company in Chile, reveals that a key part of the company's strategy was to engage business-to-business customers in efforts to become greener and the resulting benefits are examined.

Nidumolu, R., Prahalad, C.K. and Rangaswami, M.R. (2009) 'Why Sustainability Is Now The Key Driver Of Innovation', *Harvard Business Review*, **87**(9): 56–64. The research reported here shows that sustainability is the long-term basis of organizational and technological innovation that yields both bottom-line and top-line returns. Becoming environmentally friendly lowers costs because companies end up reducing the inputs they use.

Orlitzky, M., Schmidt, F.L. and Rynes, S.L. (2003) 'Corporate social and financial performance: A meta-analysis', *Organization Studies*, **24**(3): 403–41. The research presented in this article finds a significant and positive correlation between corporate social/environmental performance (CSP) and corporate financial performance (CFP).

Porter, M.E. and Kramer, M.R. (2002) 'The competitive advantage of corporate philanthropy', *Harvard Business Review*, **80**(12): 57–68. Although corporate philanthropy is in decline, this article suggests that if this becomes 'strategic philanthropy' then it can be used to create significant competitive advantage.

Porter, M.E. and Kramer, M.R. (2006) 'Strategy and society: The link between competitive advantage and corporate social responsibility', *Harvard Business Review*, **84**(12): 78–92. This article discusses how CSR has emerged as an inescapable priority for business leaders in every country. It suggests companies need to do two things to improve the social and environmental consequences of their activities: pit business against society and think of CSR in generic ways across the organization instead of the way most appropriate to each part of their business.

Porter, M.E. and Kramer, M.R. (2011) 'Creating shared value', *Harvard Business Review*, **89**(1/2): 62–77. Companies should strive to create 'shared value' where economic value is generated in a way that also produces value for society.

Prahalad, C.K. (2010) 'The responsible manager', *Harvard Business Review,* **88**(1/2): 36. This article suggests that managers need to become more responsible as they are the custodians of society's most powerful institutions. It then suggests a number of factors that every manager should consider in an attempt to achieve this.

Smith, N.C. (2003) 'Corporate social responsibility: Whether or how?', *California Management Review*, **45**(4): 52–76. This article looks at the history of CSR within business and discusses how organizations should develop and implement the right CSR strategy.

Wilson, H.J., Guinan, P.J., Parise, S. and Weinberg, B.D. (2011) 'What's your social media strategy?', *Harvard Business Review*, **89**(7/8): 23–25. The article discusses four social-media strategies used by corporations.

Zadek, S. (2004) 'The path to corporate responsibility', *Harvard Business Review*, **82**(12): 125–32. This article reflects on Nike's metamorphosis from the poster child for irresponsibility to a leader in progressive practices. It concludes that there are five stages of organizational growth and that companies can't become model citizens overnight.

Books

Reich, R. (2009) *Supercapitalism: The battle for democracy in an age of big business*. London: Icon Books Ltd. As Secretary of Labour under Bill Clinton, Robert Reich won huge plaudits for his efforts to increase the minimum wage, close sweatshops and eliminate child labour around the world. In this book he argues that capitalism should be made to serve democracy and not the other way around.

Films

An inconvenient truth. Director: Davis Guggenheim. Documentary on Al Gore's campaign to make the issue of global warming a recognized problem worldwide.
www.climatecrisis.net

Black gold. Directors: Marc Francis and Nick Francis. Documentary looking at the world of coffee and global trade.
www.blackgoldmovie.com

Enron: The smartest guys in the room. Director: Alex Gibney. Documentary about the Enron corporation, its faulty and corrupt business practices and how they led to its fall.

The corporation. Directors: Mark Achbar and Jennifer Abbott. Documentary that looks at the concept of the corporation throughout recent history up to its present-day dominance.
www.thecorporation.com

Websites

Southwest Airlines has set up a blog to let its customers, employees and other stakeholders look inside its business and interact with it. Everyone is encouraged to join in without having to register to read, watch or comment. However, if someone wants to share photos or videos or rate a post, then they need to complete a profile. Even though the content presented on the website is moderated, it pledges to present opposing viewpoints and create discussion.
www.blogsouthwest.com

This website looks at the problems that these teams have solved within communities, what they have learnt from this process and how IBM is using this initiative to develop a new generation of global leaders.
www.ibm.com/ibm/responsibility/corporateservicecorps/

Notes and references

1. Orlitzky, M., Schmidt, F.L. and Rynes, S.L. (2003) 'Corporate social and financial performance: A meta-analysis', *Organization Studies*, **24**(3): 403–41. The research presented in this article finds a significant and positive correlation between corporate social/environmental performance (CSP) and corporate financial performance (CFP).

Visit www.palgrave.com/business/hillom3e for self-test questions, guideline answers to some case study questions, useful weblinks and more to help you understand the topics in this chapter

IBM CORPORATE SERVICE CORPS

When ten IBM management trainees set off for a weekend tour in the Philippines, they didn't expect to become local heroes. When passing a delayed water well project in the tiny village of Carmen, they decided to do something about it. They met with the key people involved and volunteered to pay $250 out of their own pockets for additional building materials. Two weeks later, the well was completed and locals no longer had to walk four miles for drinking water. They learnt a significant lesson that day: you can create a big impact by creating a shared vision, motivating people to take the extra step and putting the resources in place to get the job done.

While saving a village well wasn't one of the group's objectives, it's the kind of experience that comes from being involved in IBM's Corporate Service Corps (CSC) projects. Modelled on the US Peace Corps, the programme aims to turn its employees into global citizens. Last year, IBM selected 1,500 top management prospects out of

6,400 applicants. It then trained and dispatched them in groups of eight to ten to work for a month in emerging markets to help solve economic and social problems by working with local governments, universities and business groups doing anything from upgrading government agency technology to improving public water quality. 'The CSC programme tries to help future leaders understand how the world works and show them how to network and work collaboratively with people in other countries,' explained Trudy Gould, financial analyst. 'It's a big change from training managers in classrooms and, although other companies encourage employees to volunteer for social service, IBM's the first one to use such activities to develop managers.'

DEVELOPING THE PROGRAMME

IBM's CSC Programme assigns high-potential employees to work on short-term, skill-based community service projects in developing countries. The idea had been floating around the company for a while and had come from ongoing partnerships with US national service initiatives such as City Year and AmeriCorps. They looked at similar programmes in other organizations and felt that none of them really leveraged the strategic opportunity available. They started by thinking, 'If we set up a Peace Corps for corporations, then what would it look like? What sort of work could we do? Where could we do it? And, how long would we do it for?'

Given the possible resistance to releasing employees from their day jobs for long periods of time, they decided to consult employees who showed real enthusiasm for the programme. Once they'd got the idea down on paper, they then needed to meet up with all the key stakeholders in the company such as Human Resource, Finance, Innovation and Technology, Marketing and Communications, the global businesses and some country managers. After sitting down with each of them individually to get their input and support, they were then able to go to senior management to work out a suitable budget and plan. It was a very collaborative process getting everything together.

LAUNCHING THE PROGRAMME

Once the programme had been agreed, the real work began. The team sat down to work out which organizations they wanted to partner with, how long the programmes would last and how to select and prepare employees to work on them. They had many things to consider such as: which projects to work on? Who should work on them? How long they should last? Who would sponsor them? How would they connect to IBM's other leadership development programmes? And, what would be the impact of taking these people away from the business for several weeks?

It was decided that each programme would last six months with three months' preparation, one month working in the country and two months' post-work. Employees were allocated to programmes based on their skills and a steering committee was set up to sponsor and oversee all the initiatives with senior vice presidents from Human Resources, Marketing and Communications, the company CFO and key country general managers. In January 2008, the scheme was launched and 5,500 people applied from 54 different countries. To help whittle down the numbers, only those with two years' IBM experience together with performance within the top 15–20 per cent were considered. In addition, being part of an IBM talent development programme and previous volunteer experience were considered useful. By July, the first volunteers had started and were doing four to five hours' preparation per week on top of their day jobs looking at team development, skills development, logistics and assignment-related tasks. Some of this was delivered through formal learning modules on topics such as corporate and social responsibility, cross-cultural management and cultural awareness, and participants were also expected to share experiences and figure out how they were going to work together using telephone, video and social networks.

THE PROJECTS

Between July and October 2008, 100 employees working in 11 teams were sent to Ghana, Romania, the Philippines, Tanzania and Vietnam to work on a variety of projects. For example, in Romania they helped the Centre for Entrepreneurship and Executive Development improve their market access and customer service; in Ghana they helped improve the business processes of small and medium enterprises and in Tanzania they worked with Kickstart, a non-profit organization to develop and provide marketing, sales and supply chain training courses to African businesses. Since its launch, the programme has gone from strength to strength with 1,500 employees (136 teams) working in over 15 countries last year. Some of the achievements so far include:

- Established business incubators with leading universities in Kumasi and Takoradi, Ghana

- Modernized the financial management processes and strategic planning proposals used by the Africa Wildlife Foundation in Arusha, Tanzania

- Developed a management information system plan for Business Against Crime, a South African NGO coordinating activities within police, border guards and private security services

- Designed and delivered training workshops in Chengdu for various small and medium enterprises and government departments on talent development, strategic outsourcing imperatives and strategies to succeed in the financial crisis

As Trudy Gould explains, 'In Africa, the teams are having a profound impact by bringing highly valued skills to local projects and helping to transfer those skills to emerging business centres. They hope that this will lead to a sustainable improvement in the community and create the foundation necessary to move us into the 21st century. However, there have been significant benefits for IBM as well. As one member of a team from the Philippines reflects, 'Learning how to work effectively with the different cultures within your team was possibly more valuable than the experience of working in another country. The best part was getting to know each other, living together and sharing experiences. This all helped create a team spirit that has continued back in the business. Even though we don't still work together on a day-to-day basis, I know they're all people I could call on if I needed to.' Others also commented on how it had developed their ability to cope with adversity, and as a participant from one of the Ghana teams comments, 'Interacting with other IBM high-performers helped me identify how to become a better leader and I now realize you don't always have to know the answers to everything. You just need to know how to find the answer quickly!'

THE FUTURE

The CSC Programme is just one way IBM can meet the needs of a global world and improve the relationship between its businesses, employees and the societies they work in. 'It's trying to strengthen its brand, increase its shareholder value and market itself as a company that people and society can trust,' commented the analyst Jerry Epton. 'The CSC projects help develop employees, improve local communities and start to address global problems such as climate change, poverty and disease. It all sounds very positive, but I still have a number of outstanding questions: is one month in a country really long enough to have any significant or sustainable impact? How are projects selected to maximize business and social value? And, more fundamentally, is it right that businesses are driving such critical decisions about society and the environment? They haven't been voted in and often have different objectives to the local communities in which they work.'

www.ibm.com/ibm/responsibility/corporateservicecorps

Questions

1. Why has IBM developed its Corporate Service Corps programme?

2. What benefits has it generated?

3. What can other companies learn from this approach?

Lecturers: visit www.palgrave.com/business/hillom3e for teaching guidelines for this case study

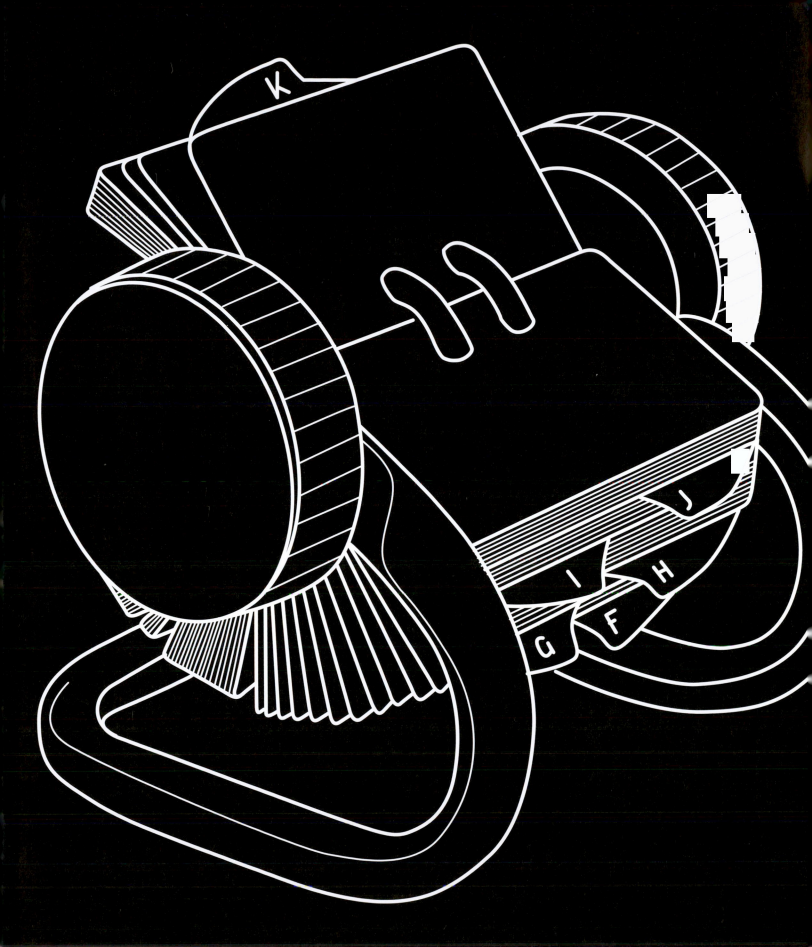

INDEX

Page numbers in **bold** indicate where key term is defined